Comparative Education

Comparative Education

The Dialectic of the Global and the Local

Third Edition

Robert F. Arnove and
Carlos Alberto Torres

ROWMAN & LITTLEFIELD PUBLISHERS, INC.
Lanham • Boulder • New York • Toronto • Plymouth, UK

ROWMAN & LITTLEFIELD PUBLISHERS, INC.

Published in the United States of America
by Rowman & Littlefield Publishers, Inc.
A wholly owned subsidary of The Rowman & Littlefield Publishing Group, Inc.
4501 Forbes Boulevard, Suite 200, Lanham, Maryland 20706
www.rowmanlittlefield.com

Estover Road
Plymouth PL6 7PY
United Kingdom

British Library Cataloguing in Publication Information Available

Library of Congress Cataloging-in-Publication Data:

Comparative education : the dialectic of the global and the local / [edited by] Robert F.
Arnove and Carlos Alberto Torres.—3rd ed.
p. cm.
Includes bibliographical references and index.
ISBN 0-7425-5985-8 (cloth : alk. paper)—ISBN 0-7425-5984-X (pbk. : alk. paper)
1. Comparative education—Philosophy.   2. Education and globalization.
I. Arnove, Robert F. II. Torres, Carlos Alberto. LB43.C68   2007
370.9—dc22

2007029844

Printed in the United States of America

♾ ™ The paper used in this publication meets the minimum requirements of American National
Standard for Information Sciences—Permanence of Paper for Printed Library Materials, ANSI/NISO
Z39.48-1992.

Contents

Introduction: Reframing Comparative Education: The Dialectic of the Global and the Local

Robert F. Arnove

This book reflects the forces shaping comparative education at the beginning of the twenty-first century. These forces are internal as well as external to the field of comparative education. Within the discipline, theories and methods for studying school-society relations undergo change in accordance with advances in knowledge, shifts in paradigms, and increases in capacity to process and analyze large data sets in more sophisticated ways. Conceptual and methodological frameworks, in turn, are constantly being reshaped by events on the world stage and corresponding changes in economic, social, and educational policies.

A central thesis of this book is that the workings of a global economy and the increasing interconnectedness of societies pose common problems for educational systems around the world. These problems relate to the governance, financing, and provision of mass education; they relate to issues of equality of educational opportunities and outcomes for differently situated social groups, especially those who historically have been most discriminated against—women, ethnic minorities, rural populations, and working-class people. Although there are common problems—and what would appear to be increasingly similar education agendas—regional, national, and local responses also vary. As the title of this book indicates, a dialectic is at work between the global and the local. Understanding this interactive process, the tensions and contradictions, is central to recasting or "reframing" the field of comparative and international education. I believe that the adoption of a focus on globalization contributes to a greater understanding of the dynamics of school-society relations as well as the potential and limitations of education systems to contribute to individual and societal advancement.

GLOBALIZATION

Globalization can be defined as "the intensification of worldwide social relations which link distant localities in such a way that local happenings are shaped by events occurring

1

many miles away and vice versa."[1] Various adjectives may be used to describe the different dimensions of this process. Certainly economic and cultural globalization are foremost among the descriptors used for the processes by which societies are increasingly linked in real and virtual time.[2] Economic globalization, the result of major transformations in the processes of producing and distributing goods and services, is integrally related to changes in the international division of labor. One of the central characteristics of this highly globalized capitalism is that the factors of production are not located in close geographic proximity. At the same time, however, national economies are increasingly integrating into regional ones. The era of "Fordist" mass-scale production within national boundaries has been replaced by "just-in-time Toyotism."[3] The fragmentation and reintegration of economies is facilitated by concurrent revolutionary improvements in telecommunications and computerization, all made possible by quantum leaps in the production of scientific and technological knowledge. The ease by which individuals can communicate via satellite, and by which products can be assembled and disseminated, has its cultural counterparts in the so-called Coca-Cola-ization and McDonaldization of the world, the spread of television programs and movies from the West and North to the rest of the world.[4] These trends are paralleled by the increasing use of English as a language of scholarly production and advanced studies, as well as the language of business and diplomacy. "Study English and Computers," found on flyers distributed at the most frequented transportation hubs and commercial centers of major cities around the world, is promoted as the surest and quickest way to find a job and enter the global economy.

In the realm of education, as the various authors in this book point out, globalization also refers to the closely intertwined economic and education agendas promoted by the major international donor and technical assistance agencies—namely, the World Bank, the International Monetary Fund, and national overseas aid agencies such as USAID (United States Agency for International Aid), CIDA (Canadian International Development Agency), and JICA (Japan International Cooperation Agency). Similar prescriptions are being offered by these powerful agencies for enhancing the equality, efficiency, and quality of education systems.[5] These reforms are being implemented by education policymakers who often have little choice but to do so in exchange for access to needed funds.

These common prescriptions and transnational forces, however, are not uniformly implemented or unquestionably received. As the title of this book suggests, there is a dialectic at work by which these global processes interact with national and local actors and contexts to be modified and, in some cases, transformed. There is a process of give-and-take, an exchange by which international trends are reshaped to local ends. Just as scholars from the developing world have challenged dominant research paradigms and conceptual frameworks of the industrialized North to propose more relevant theories related to dependency as well as education for critical consciousness and liberation,[6] so have local people appropriated and transformed the language of the former colonizers. Hickling-Hudson, for example, illustrates how the English language is received and reshaped by Creole-speaking Jamaicans into something beautifully and poetically different.[7]

The impact of globalization on education systems has significant and manifold implications that are studied in this volume. They include questions such as: Who has access to what levels of education and with what outcomes? What types of jobs will be available for whom?[8] Will decentralization and privatization of education—promoted by international donor agencies as well as by national elites—lead to greater equality, efficiency, and quality? What will be taught and in what language? These various transnational forces raise significant questions about the viability of the nation-state and the role of public education systems in creating citizens.

As the loci of economic production, political decision making, and group identity are transformed, so, too, do our understandings of the nature of public education in contributing to citizenship formation and economic development come under challenge. These changes on the world stage call for new ways of viewing education-society relations. Comparative education, which traditionally has taken as its subject matter the macro- and micro-level forces shaping education systems around the world, is a field ideally situated to study the dynamic interactions between global trends and local responses. This volume represents an attempt to "reframe," or shift the foci of, the field to this interplay between the global and the local. It seeks to provide generalizable propositions and useful insights into the forces shaping the origins, workings, and outcomes of education systems.

EVOLUTION OF THE FIELD

Although the origins of the field of international and comparative education can be traced to the pioneering work of Marc-Antoine Jullien and César August Basset in the first half of the nineteenth century, its institutionalization as a field of study and research in universities is largely a phenomenon of the post–World War II period.[9] Closely tied to major shifts in geopolitical realities and changing views of education's role in advancing personal enlightenment and social progress, the comparative study of education systems initially attempted to explain, in the words of Watson, the "beginning of a new world order in Europe" in the aftermath of the Napoleonic wars.[10] Since then, the comparative study of education has been concerned with attempting to explain the role of education in contributing to nation-state building as well as to totalitarian or democratic forms of government. Major expansion in the field occurred in the 1960s, when, according to Philip Altbach and Eng Tan, "higher education in the industrialized nations was expanding rapidly, and . . . the major powers were preoccupied not only with Cold War rivalries, but with understanding the newly emerging nations of what came to be called the Third World."[11] The emergence and widespread acceptance of notions of education's contribution to human capital formation and the economic growth of nations further fueled an interest in comparative education. More recently, the belief that there is a causal relationship between the "excellence" of a school system, as measured by national standardized examinations, and the economic success of a country in global competition, has revived the interest in the relationship between education systems and national productivity. Finally, the end of the Cold War, the breakup of the former Soviet Union with the emergence of newly independent republics, often microstates, and the outbreak of ethnic conflict in various regions of the world has, once again, led to renewed interest in the relationship of education to political stability and development.

THE DIMENSIONS OF COMPARATIVE EDUCATION

Historically, the field of comparative and international education has comprehended three principal dimensions or thrusts, which I call the scientific, pragmatic, and international/

global understanding. These dimensions are closely related and, as I shall argue, are converging to an even greater extent.[12]

The Scientific Dimension[13]

One major goal of comparative education has been to contribute to theory building: to the formulation of generalizable propositions about the workings of school systems and their interactions with their surrounding economies, polities, cultures, and social orders. As Farrell notes, all sciences are comparative. The goal of science is not only to establish that relationships between variables exist but also to determine the range over which they exist.[14] As Bray and Thomas further point out, comparison enables researchers to look at the entire world as a natural laboratory to view the multiple ways in which societal factors, educational policies, and practices may vary and interact in otherwise unpredictable and unimaginable ways.[15]

The value of a comparative perspective is illustrated in a question that education researchers pose frequently: what is more important in determining academic achievement—school-related characteristics or the socioeconomic background of the student? Research conducted in the United States by Coleman et al. and Jencks et al.—as well as by Plowden et al. in England—in the 1960s and early 1970s concluded that forces largely beyond the control of schools—namely, the characteristics of students and their families—are more significant determinants of what students learn.[16] However, studies conducted in places as far apart as Uganda and Chile reach different conclusions.[17] Schools do matter, but perhaps to a greater extent in less industrialized countries. Cross-national data over time indicate that as societies industrialize and social class formation solidifies, socioeconomic status becomes increasingly important in determining access to the highest levels of an education system and the most prestigious institutions of learning and to better jobs.[18] Given the great disparities in school resources in low-income countries, in which rural schools as well as many urban ones may not have the most basic amenities and equipment, provision of textbooks and the presence of a competent teacher who can work with well-designed learning materials can make a difference.[19] This research has played a role in convincing major international technical assistance and financial aid agencies such as the World Bank that certain key inputs (e.g., well-prepared textbooks) can contribute to substantial gains in student academic achievement. (For further discussion, see chapter 6 in this volume.)

The value of cross-national, longitudinal data is also apparent in calculating social rates of return to investments in education. George Psacharopoulos and others have argued that the best education investment for a country is at the primary school level, followed by secondary, and lastly by higher education.[20] These conclusions by prominent economists working for the World Bank have led this lender agency, as well as other bilateral aid agencies such as USAID, to propose that higher education institutions charge tuition fees representing a more substantial share of costs. The policies favored by these agencies also have led to a greater emphasis on the privatization of education. Yet the social rate of return is usually higher to primary education because the costs are minimal relative to secondary and tertiary levels of schooling. The important point is that a diminishing social rate of return to primary education occurs as access becomes nearly universal. Comparative data suggest that in some countries secondary education now has the highest rate of return. A review of the literature by Martin Carnoy indicates that social rates of return in many of the so-called NICs (newly industrializing countries) rise with higher levels of schooling.[21] Heyneman, when he was a staff member of the World Bank, found that "returns to higher education or vocational education . . . [were] greater than elementary education in Pakistan, Brazil, Botswana, China, Turkey, and Greece."[22]

James Wolfensohn, then president of the World Bank, himself admitted in March 2000 that the bank had seriously miscalculated the social rate of return to higher education, and therefore there are valid reasons for adequately funding this level of education.[23] Moreover, higher education leaders in developing countries have argued that what these societies need are not poorly funded universities but well-endowed, first-rate institutions capable of conducting the type of scientific research that helps them overcome their dependency on the metropolitan countries of the North, whose technologies often are inappropriate for them.[24]

The value of gathering comparative data guided by theory to reach reasonable propositions about the workings and outcomes of education systems in relation to their social and historical contexts is particularly pertinent to a consideration of the second dimension of the discipline.

The Pragmatic Dimension

Another reason for studying other societies' education systems is to discover what can be learned that will contribute to improved policy and practice at home. Altbach has referred to the processes involved in the study and transfer of educational practices among countries as *lending* and *borrowing*.[25] Countries may alternately or simultaneously be involved in both processes, as evidenced by the cases of Japan and the United States. One of the earliest examples of educational borrowing occurred in A.D. 607, when the Japanese court sent a mission to China to study the empire's education system. According to Kobayashi, one outcome of this visit was the establishment of Japan's first national school system.[26] At the turn of the twentieth century, Japanese education authorities looked to the West for guidance as they attempted to modernize their school system. In turn, countries such as China and Thailand found the Japanese model to be appropriate in their attempts to develop economically without abandoning their cultural traditions.

The United States, similarly, has undergone various phases of borrowing and lending. In the nineteenth century, the country was a borrower. Academics from the United States studied the higher education systems of other European countries, particularly that of Prussia, as a basis for establishing research-oriented graduate schools (Johns Hopkins University being the first such institution). Many U.S. postbaccalaureate students completed their graduate studies in Europe. Today, the flow of students and scholars has been reversed, with the United States being a principal destination for advanced scholarly studies in major research universities. Hundreds of U.S. educators now are involved in the process of lending, sometimes transplanting (whether appropriate or not) educational policies and practices to other countries. But since the 1970s, the United States has been fascinated with the so-called Japanese education miracle—the high levels of achievement of Japanese students in mathematics and sciences on the various tests administered as part of the studies of the International Association for the Evaluation of Educational Achievement.

This fascination with the Japanese school system, which has a much longer academic year, has led to increases in the number of days of schooling across the United States and

sometimes to longer school days. These modifications of the school calendar have been
based on the problematic assumption that extending the time involved in learning would
necessarily lead to improved scores on standardized achievement instruments, regardless
of the ways in which that time was used or the quality of the teaching. Moreover, to the
amazement of a past Japanese Ministry of Education official who visited Washington,
D.C., in the mid-1980s, the U.S. secretary of education noted that his office was contem-
plating the recommendation of the establishment of cram schools (*jukus*) much along the
lines of the Japanese parallel education system. The secretary's comment was made at a
time when the Japanese were seriously attempting to minimize the influence of *jukus* and
shorten the academic calendar. While the United States was attempting to instill elements
of the more rigorous and standardized Japanese curriculum and school system, reform-
minded Japanese educators were looking at the more child-centered and progressive elements of the U.S. system.[27] In other words, each system was enviously eyeing the other's
system and attempting to borrow elements of it.

However, as comparativist scholars of Japanese and U.S. education have pointed out,
the school system of each country reflects the corresponding sociocultural systems within
which they are embedded.[28] One cannot simply uproot elements of one society and
expect them to flourish in the soil of another society.[29] But, as Cogan notes, certain principles may be deduced from the study of school systems in other societies that may be
applicable to another country. These principles, however, are very general ones, such as
the greater the status accorded to a teacher, the shorter the time period or obstacles
required to obtain a teaching license; and the more opportunities for in-service professional development, the greater the likelihood that highly competent individuals will be
motivated to select a teaching career and stick with it.[30]

Moreover, the most important principle to be derived from studying the history of
educational borrowing and lending is that there is no one best system, that all systems
have strengths as well as weaknesses. Also, education systems, as I noted earlier, reflect
their societies—their many tensions and contradictions. Perhaps more can be learned
from lessons of failure—what not to do—than from stories of success. However, I do not
believe that it is necessary to experience failure in order to succeed. If understanding is to
be advanced as to what works and what does not work in a country, then such study
must be guided by knowledge of that country, by familiarity with its history and unique
qualities, as well as by recognition of what it shares in common with other societies.[31]

The role of the systematic accumulation of knowledge or guiding principles and theories (i.e., the scientific dimension) of comparative education is central to the pragmatic
and ameliorative thrust of the discipline: to improve educational policy and practice.
However, there has often been a separation or tension between these two components.
Reviews of pioneering work in the field commonly trace two different approaches to the
field—one more scientific and one more historical. In the early part of the nineteenth
century, French scholar Marc-Antoine Jullien called for the development of "detailed
research guidelines and checklists for foreign studies in education."[32] As Crossley and
Vulliamy note, Jullien's initiative is seen as the "inspiration for the twentieth century
development of international databases for education" and as the beginnings of an
attempt at establishing a scientific basis for identifying "the one best policy and practice
for all contexts." They further point out that an alternative path was marked by Sir
Michael Sadler, who drew "attention to the dangers and dilemmas of international trans-

fer, and to the importance of contextual factors in the analysis and development of education."[33] In his study of nineteenth-century Germany, Sadler noted:

> In the educational policy of a nation are focussed its spiritual aspirations, its philosophi-
> cal ideals, its economic ambitions, its military purpose, its social conflicts. For a German
> or for an Englishman to speak of his own country's educational aims is to speak of its
> ideal, of its hope and fears, of its weakness as well as of its strength. To attempt even this
> is not an easy task, but to speak of another country's education system from the stand-
> point of a foreign observer is to hazard more and to risk misunderstanding.[34]

Following in the footsteps of Sadler, Isaac Kandel, a leading figure in the field of
comparative education during the first half of the twentieth century, observes, "In order
to understand, appreciate and evaluate the real meaning of the education system of a
nation, it is essential to know something of the history and traditions, of the forces and
attitudes governing its social organizations, of the political and economic conditions that
determine its development."[35]

In later sections of this chapter, I further discuss the evolution and permutations of
these different approaches to the comparative study of education systems. At this point,
I indicate how these two paths relate to the third dimension of the field: education for
international understanding and peace.[36]

International Education: The Global Dimension

A third and significant (but previously underemphasized) dimension of the discipline
is that of contributing to international understanding and peace. This dimension will
become a more important feature of comparative education as processes of globalization
increasingly require people to recognize how forces from areas of the world previously
considered distant and remote impinge on their daily lives.[37]

The study of cross-national currents and interactions is closely linked to notions of
global education and, in many ways, to world-systems analysis. In 1980, I called for
increased emphasis on the international dimensions of our field. As I noted, studies of
the ecology of educational institutions and processes often failed to take into account an
international context of transactions. Most macrostudies of education accepted the
nation-state as the basic unit of analysis. But I argued that an examination of the international forces impinging on education systems was no less essential than an examination
of the international economic order would be to an understanding of the dynamics of
economic development or underdevelopment in any one set of countries.[38]

For those attempting to introduce international perspectives not only into scholarly
research but also into teaching at all levels of education (i.e., suffuse curricula with content and activities that enable oncoming generations as well as adults to understand the
increasingly interconnected world in which they live), a global set of lenses is absolutely
essential. Global education, as defined by Chadwick Alger and James Harf, is differentiated from international education. They contrast international education, which they
view as largely area studies or descriptive accounts of discrete countries and regions of the
world, with global education, which they distinguish as emphasizing values, transactions,
actors, mechanisms, procedures, and issues.[39]

Briefly, values education teaches that people across the globe have different ways of
viewing the world, ways that are equally valid and reflective of their life circumstances,

which they call "consciousness perspective" (based on the work of Robert Hanvey). It also recommends seeking out and building upon what interests people have in common.[40] (An example of this is Barbara Piscitelli's use of art to point out the common concerns of children all around the world—their fears and hopes—and also their differing societal contexts—why a Vietnamese eight-year-old might draw a picture of children working on a tea plantation as something very natural.)[41] In pointing out the importance of actors and transactions, Alger and Harf call attention to the multiplicity of actors (at all levels from the international to the local, governmental as well as nongovernmental) involved in diverse interactions across national boundaries in areas including telecommunications, meteorology, emergency relief, health, and education. The study of the mechanisms and procedures provides insights into what, for example, an international agency like the International Monetary Fund, an important transnational actor, does when it enters a country experiencing debt and currency crises and attempts to stabilize the economic situation. Issues are those that face all of humanity—environmental destruction, the spread of disease, the proliferation of weapons of mass destruction, as well as the increasing impoverishment of populations and the growing disparity of wealth among regions and within nations.[42]

The economic crises, commencing in 1997, in the four Asian nations of Indonesia, Korea, Malaysia, and Thailand illustrate very concretely the value of a global perspective (as outlined by Alger and Harf). The interconnected nature of the global economy has meant that as the currencies of these countries were greatly devalued, banks collapsed, and investors withdrew capital, economies all around the world were negatively affected. Headlines not only warned of the loss of jobs in export industries and tourism resulting from the Asian crisis but also how university student enrollments abroad would diminish.[43] Some university officials in countries ranging from Australia to the United States lamented the damaging budgetary effect of a decrease in fully paying students; others scrambled to see how they could assist international students who were in dire financial need and were under great economic stress. In the meantime, mechanisms and procedures for coping with the economic instability in the four nations—the conditionalities imposed by the International Monetary Fund—led to food riots and ethnic violence in Indonesia, followed by the toppling of the Suharto government.

The contributors to this volume contend that teachers, at all levels of formal as well as nonformal education, need to educate their students about the causes, dynamics, and outcomes of these transnational forces and actors and that comparative and international education can play a vital role in teacher education. Although Cole Brembeck in his 1975 Comparative and International Education Society (CIES) presidential address expressed concern about the distancing of our field from teacher education, and Stephen Heyneman in his 1993 presidential address warned of the possibility that comparative education could become a marginalized field irrelevant to the knowledge needs of policymakers, we believe that comparative education will become even more relevant to both teacher education and policymaking.[44] Gary Theisen in his 1997 CIES presidential address called on comparative educators to link the knowledge building, or scientific, dimensions of the field to better informed and effective educational policy and practice. Among the contributions he proposed was the study of how various institutions (nongovernmental as well as governmental technical assistance agencies) could better coordinate their efforts while incorporating grassroots organizations to resolve pressing education problems.[45]

These problems relate to the need to expand access to education to all groups in a society, promote effective learning, and, simultaneously, achieve greater efficiency in the running of school systems. Systems all around the world confront these problems. At the same time, the prescriptions proposed by powerful transnational actors such as the World Bank may not always be the correct medicine. The application of market mechanisms—including privatization, charging user fees for services previously offered free of charge, and decentralizing highly centralized state bureaucracies—to resolve problems of equality of educational opportunity may lead to inequitable consequences and may actually be counterproductive.

ABOUT THE BOOK

This chapter (as well as this book) is a call for efforts to unite the three strands of comparative and international education so that all work together to contribute to improved theory, policy, and practice, and the conditions for greater equity in schooling and society that contribute to global peace and justice. The initial chapters in this book address topics pertinent to (1) what theoretical and methodological frameworks promise to offer more effective ways to study education systems cross-nationally and cross-culturally (chapter 1 by Anthony Welch); (2) the importance of examining the assumptions, workings, and outcomes of major international financial and technical assistance agencies (chapter 2 by Joel Samoff); (3) the need to reconceptualize the role of the nation-state as the basic unit of collective identity and educational provision as well as the importance of studying social movements in relation to education for social change (chapter 3 by Raymond Morrow and Carlos Alberto Torres); and (4) the relevance of the study of culture and personal identity formation to continued inquiry in the field of comparative education that contributes to theory building and improved educational policy and practice (chapter 4 and chapter 5, by Vandra Lea Masemann and Christine Fox, respectively).

The various chapters in the middle section of the book examine current challenges to education systems around the world and offer new ways to study the limitations as well as emancipatory potential of different reform efforts. This section includes chapters on changing notions of equality of educational opportunity and outcomes (chapter 6 by Joseph Farrell); the significance of studying gender and social movements (chapter 7 by Nelly Stromquist); different ways of conceptualizing centralization and decentralization of education systems (chapter 8 by Mark Bray); the role of nonformal education and literacy programs in fostering social change (chapter 9 by Anne Hickling-Hudson); how neoliberal and neoconservative agendas are reshaping higher education internationally (chapter 11 by Daniel Schugurensky); and all levels of education in specific contexts, particularly in Australia, England, and the United States (chapter 10 by Edward Berman et al.).

Then follows a section examining how global economic currents and convergence in educational reform proposals play out in specific world regions—namely, Latin America (chapter 12 by Robert Arnove et al.), Asia (chapter 13 by John Hawkins), the Middle East (chapter 14 by Rachel Christina et al.), the former republics of the Soviet Union and Eastern and Central Europe (chapter 15 by Maria Bucur and Ben Eklof), and Africa (chapter 16 by Joel Samoff and Bidemi Carrol). Limited space prevents the editors from giving separate chapters to North America, Western Europe, and the South Pacific, although various chapters in the text make reference to or give special attention to specific countries within these regions.

In a concluding chapter, Carlos Alberto Torres reviews major events that have transpired internationally since the publication of the first edition of this text. He also examines the intellectual legacy left by major scholars who have passed away since 1999. In light of these global changes and legacies, Torres reflects on the way in which the field of comparative education can contribute to advances in knowledge and more informed and progressive educational policy and practice.

CURRENT TRENDS AND NEW DIRECTIONS

A review of educational change in the previously mentioned regions indicates that the field of comparative education is particularly pertinent to an understanding of the common issues and subregional, national, and local differences that education policymakers and practitioners face. Familiarity with developments in the field further suggests that higher education institutions are offering courses and instituting programs in recognition of the relevance of our field. Although some comparative programs may have been cut back or integrated into larger policy studies units of schools of education in various countries, evidence of its continued vitality and growth is found in a number of countries, especially in Asia. In a 1994 global survey of the field, Altbach and Tan identified eighty-one university programs and centers in twenty-one countries on all continents that had at least one full-time equivalent staff member and taught at least four graduate courses in comparative and international education.[46] The researchers listed 450 scholars teaching comparative courses. Although the survey was the most comprehensive one to date, it was by no means all-inclusive. Listings for European, North American, and Asian programs and centers tended to be complete, but information on Latin America, the Middle East, and Africa failed to capture the growing interest and activity in the field.

According to the Altbach and Tan survey, Europe and North America tend to dominate the field with the largest number of academic programs. However, the most significant expansion of centers and scholars over the past twenty years has taken place in Asia.[47] On a per capita basis, the Chinese Comparative Education Society–Taipei, according to Bray, is "probably the largest in the world."[48]

As of 2007, there are thirty-six constituent members of the World Council of Comparative Education Societies, with some serving a number of countries.[49] For example, the Comparative Education Society of Asia (CESA), which held its first meeting in Tokyo in 1996, serves, according to Bray, "as a mechanism through which scholars and practitioners in countries which would otherwise have no national infrastructure can meet in a regional setting."[50] These countries include the Philippines, Singapore, Malaysia, Thailand, and Vietnam as well as Brunei, Darussalam, and Pakistan. CESA further would include the newly independent states of Kazakhstan, Kyrgyzstan, Mongolia, Tajikistan, and Uzbekistan.

A central issue in the formation of the newly independent states of Eastern and Central Europe and Asia is the language of government and instruction. This issue is attracting a general interest in comparative education on the part of policymakers and scholars. The growing interest in English as an international language of communication represents a fascinating subject of study for the field of comparative and international education.

The dominance of English as the language of scholarly communication and publication is both a fact and a point of contention. Although many scholars recognize that English will continue to be the primary language for scholarly research, dissemination, and exchange, there is also a marked growth in Chinese[51] as well as in Spanish-language publications and a substantial literature in Russian. A challenge to the field will be to find ways to provide adequate outlets for articles in major scholarly journals in languages other than English or abstracts of such articles, at the very least.

The growing body of literature from different regions of the world, whether in English or not, will continue to expand the existing theoretical and conceptual framework of comparative and international education, eventually transforming the very boundaries of the field. Just as Latin American scholarship has contributed dependency theory and Freirean notions of education for critical consciousness and liberation, the literature of Asia and Africa will help offset the hegemony of European and North American scholarship.[52] What does teaching and learning mean in societies imbued with Confucian, Taoist, and Zen notions? How, for example, can North American and European art educators learn from traditional Japanese and Chinese forms of instruction in these areas? And, conversely, what can Asian educators learn from new curricular approaches to art education in the West?[53] What can North American universities attempting to achieve greater diversity in education, as well as inclusion of minority students, learn from the example of historically white higher education institutions in South Africa as they attempt to incorporate students of color, especially black South Africans, who constitute a majority population? Are the experiences of North American universities attempting to desegregate their institutions pertinent to South African higher education institutions?[54]

What is being advocated here is not only the need for different perspectives, based on different cultural traditions, to be infused into the literature but also, ultimately, a multidirectional flow of scholarship and ideas to improve not only educational policy and practice but also our ability to generalize about education-society interactions.

In his chapter, Welch asks whether comparative education is more science or more history. Similarly, the theoretical and pragmatic thrusts of education, at various times, have gone their separate ways or have been at odds with each other.[55] The answer to Welch's question is that comparative and international education, at its best, should be both science and history, contributing to theory building and to more informed and enlightened educational policy and practice. Although eclecticism may be viewed as "a disease that can be cured by taking a stand,"[56] the contributors to this volume believe in the value of a variety of epistemologies, paradigms, methods, and approaches to studying education systems across national boundaries and at various levels—from the global to the local.

Bray and Thomas provide a useful framework for attempting to link different geographic/locational levels, nonlocational demographic groups, and aspects of education and society. They note that comparative education typically has focused on countries as the locational unit of analysis, but that the units may range from that of the world/regions/continents to that of schools/classrooms/individuals. The nonlocational demographic groups may range from ethnic/age/religious/gender groups to entire populations. The aspects of education are those typically studied: curriculum, teaching methods, educational finance, management structures, as well as others. Their article recommends that comparativists can make their greatest contribution to improve theory and policy by attempting to introduce as many levels of analysis as possible to portray the complex interplay of different social forces and how individual and local units of analysis are embedded in multiple layered contexts.[57]

We believe that the vitality of our field depends on strengthening dialogue with one another and welcoming diverse approaches to gathering and analyzing data on education-society relations. These approaches are qualitative and quantitative, case oriented and variable oriented.[58] Theory building depends on attempts to generalize from case studies while also building on and contextualizing large-scale cross-national studies.

Case studies are likely to continue to be the most commonly used approach to studying education-society relations. Given the limited resources of most researchers working in the academy, the tendency of most individuals is to study areas that are familiar. More than just a convenience, Charles Ragin argues, the comparative method is essentially a case-oriented strategy of comparative research.[59] In case studies "outcomes are analyzed in terms of intersections of conditions, and it is usually assumed that any of several combinations might produce a certain outcome."[60] By contrast,

> Sometimes quantitative cross-national studies have an unreal quality to them—countries become organisms with systemic distress, for example—and the data examined have little meaningful connection to actual empirical processes. More concrete questions—relevant to the social bases and origins of specific phenomena in similarly situated countries and regions—do not receive the attention they deserve.[61]

Ragin's orientation is toward macrolevel comparative studies and causal analysis. Others, such as York Bradshaw and Michael Wallace, view the value of case studies as residing in their contribution to the refinement and modification of extant theory, and ultimately to the creation of new theory when existing explanatory frameworks are not applicable. They find much of existing social science theory, formulated in a few select countries of the North, to be inappropriate to much of the world.[62] Their concern is not so much with achieving generalizable propositions concerning causal relationships as with understanding, much in the tradition of Weber, the patterning of relationships in different types of historical and social configurations.[63]

Some recent examples of promising studies along the lines suggested by Bradshaw and Wallace are those by Sheila Slaughter and Laurence Leslie, Karen Mundy, and Christina. In these studies, different levels of government, the relationship between the state and the private sector, and the interplay of the global and the local are brought out.

One of the most sophisticated studies of what is occurring in higher education in developed industrial countries is Slaughter and Leslie's examination of the "entrepreneurial university" in Australia, Canada, the United States, and in the United Kingdom. In addition to focusing on common patterns as well as variations within the four countries with regard to strong cross-national forces promoting privatization of universities and gearing them more closely to market demands, the researchers examine two very different cases within Australia to determine how closeness to the market affects research funding, program development, and faculty rewards.[64]

Mundy's study of the nature of literacy programs and their outcomes in Tanzania, Zimbabwe, and Botswana critically examines extant theories in the light of world-systems theory. As she impressively documents, the extent of literacy provision and achievement is greatly influenced by the degree of incorporation of each country into the global economy at the time of its independence and the subsequent development paths that the governments choose.[65]

Christina, using a world-systems analysis, examines how current international notions concerning early childhood education are implemented at the national and local levels in the West Bank and Gaza, and how policies result from the interactions between nongovernmental organizations and the Palestine National Authority. She displays how these multiple forces affect the decisions of individual, institutional, and group actors in specific contexts. Studies such as Christina's demonstrate the alliance and bridge building that comparative educators can engage in to improve educational access, curriculum development, and teacher upgrading, among other things.[66]

Case studies, however, have their limitations and pitfalls. Ragin, Bradshaw and Wallace, and others, are well aware there is a danger in attempting to generalize from one case to other instances that are not appropriate and to view the world only from the lens of that which is most familiar. Major funding agencies for international research also tend to favor quicker, quantitative studies that meet the exigencies of immediate decision making and present the façade of being more scientific.[67]

Large-scale variable-oriented studies, whatever their limitations, also have great value in contributing to theory building as well as more informed and enlightened policymaking. We see great utility in studies such as those conducted as part of the International Evaluation of Educational Achievement. As Husén and others have pointed out, the great range of examples provided by such studies enables researchers and policymakers to examine the effects of introducing different subject matter (e.g., foreign languages) at certain points in the curriculum, of permitting early specialization in certain disciplines (e.g., mathematics and sciences), or of taking different pedagogical approaches to instruction (e.g., inquiry-oriented vs. more didactic science education).[68] Large-scale research can reveal, for example, what conditions favor the educational careers and life chances of females[69] or successful literacy and adult basic education programs.[70] Although such studies are useful in illuminating general patterns, we also believe the general tendencies revealed by them need to be studied in greater detail through individual cases of educational institutions and programs within their unique contexts.[71]

CONCLUSIONS

The June 1998 Western Region meeting of the CIES was called "Dance on the Edge." It was organized to "celebrate Comparative and International Education at the Cusp of the 21st Century." I quote at length the promotional brochure for the conference because it so cogently (and delightfully) captures the state of our field at the dawn of a new century:

> Comparative and international education is enjoying a renaissance. Globalization has infused the ever-present need to learn about each other with an urgency and emphasis like no other in history. At the same time, the postmodern attack on metanarratives and totalizing discourses has infused our scholarship and practice with doubt about much orthodox wisdom. Even the meaning of "comparative" and "international" is in question, accompanied by vigorous contests over who will control "education." For some,

education is an instrument of social justice and bulwark against cultural hegemony. For others it is a commodity to be bought and sold on a "free market."[72]

Yes indeed. There is vigorous debate within our field. We would also question a central point made in the conference's announcement. As the various chapters in this volume underscore, "metanarratives and totalizing discourses," although under attack, continue to be alive and well; rumors of their demise (to paraphrase the American humorist Mark Twain) are much exaggerated. Moreover, if they are to be challenged, their continued prevalence, workings, and implications need to be understood.

If there is a constant in the field of comparative education, it is its constantly changing nature. Since its institutionalization in the academy, our field has undergone marked shifts in paradigms and approaches to the field—from modernization theory and structural functionalism combined with attempts to create a science of education based on the rigorous gathering of comparative data to test theoretically based hypotheses, to neo-Marxist, world systems, and dependency theories of school-society relations, to ethno-methodological and ethnographic approaches, to a variety of isms—poststructuralism, postmodernism, and postcolonialism coupled with feminist perspectives.[73] New developments in comparative education include incorporation of theories of multiculturalism, social movements, and the state as well as critical race theory and critical modernism.[74] The field has undergone a shift from a macrofocus on the role of schooling in contributing to such outcomes as social mobility and stability, political development, economic growth, cultural continuity, and change to a microfocus on the inner workings of schools and on what is learned and taught in school. These shifts do not have clearly demarcated dates. The trends have tended to overlap. At times, advocates of these different approaches have been at odds with one another, sometimes in dialogue with one another. Now more than ever, there is a need to learn from one another, to view the strengths and limitations of different theoretical and methodological approaches to the study of education. Small-scale case studies and large-scale research demonstrate increasing sophistication in attempting to combine different levels of analysis (from the world system to the local context), quantitative, and qualitative data to reach more precise conclusions about the nature of what is being studied and what may be generalized. If a discipline is based on systematic, cumulative increases in knowledge, with studies building on previous research to refine and expand our understanding of the social world, comparative education is indeed becoming more of a discipline that can contribute to improved policy and practice.

The continued growth of a systematic, codified body of theory and knowledge, however, does not mean homogeneity or even a consensus about the boundaries of the field or the best way to go about studying education across countries and cultures. In a predecessor to this text, Gail Kelly notes that

> research in the field has been and will in the future be diverse, focusing on a range of topics which at times seem tenuously connected, like school finance, illiteracy among women, textbook publishing practices, colonial schools . . . and so forth. The field has no center—rather, it is an amalgam of multidisciplinary studies, informed by a number of theoretical frameworks. Debates in the field will likely over time shift as educational policies and practices and needs change and the trust placed in particular theories, social systems, or reforms prove themselves valid or lacking in validity. The fact that the field

has not resolved these debates about culture, method, and theory may well be a strength, rather than a weakness and point to the viability of the field and its continued growth.[75]

In the same text, Arnove, Altbach, and Kelly write that although comparative education was a loosely bounded field, it was held together by a "fundamental belief that education can be improved and can serve to bring about change for the better of all nations."[76] In this chapter and text, the various authors state the belief that our field can contribute to positive change efforts in education and society. One way in which comparative education can help effect change is by contributing to a more realistic and comprehensive understanding of the transnational forces influencing all societies and education systems—both their potentially deleterious as well as beneficial features. Also, members of our field can become more directly involved in teacher education and educational reform initiatives—infusing programs and efforts with international/global perspectives.[77] We believe that comparative education can—and should—play a significant role in contributing to the possibility that coming generations will use their talents on behalf of international peace and social justice in an increasingly interconnected world.

NOTES

The author wishes to acknowledge the editorial and substantive contributions to this chapter made by Mark Bray, Stephen Franz, Yun-Suk Oh, Toby Strout, and Carlos Alberto Torres.

1. Anthony Giddens, *The Consequences of Modernity* (Stanford, Calif: Stanford University Press, 1990), 64.

2. For further discussion, see Malcolm Waters, *Globalization* (New York: Routledge, 1995); Anthony D. King, ed., *Culture, Globalization and the World System: Contemporary Conditions for the Representation of Identity* (Minneapolis: University of Minnesota Press, 1997); and Raimo Vayruynen, *Global Transformation: Economics, Politics, and Culture* (Helsinki: Finnish National Fund for Research and Development, Sitra, 1997).

3. On "Fordism" and "Toyotism," see Wilford W. Wilms, *Restoring Prosperity: How Workers and Managers Are Forging a New Culture of Cooperation* (New York: Times Business/Random House, 1996); also Ladislau Dowbar, Octavi Ianni, and Paulo-Edgar Resende, *Desafiós da Globalização* (Petropolis, Brazil: Editora Vozes, 1998).

4. Benjamin Barber, *Jihad vs. McWorld* (New York: Times Books, 1995).

5. UNESCO (the United Nations Educational, Scientific, and Cultural Organization) and UNICEF (the United Nations Children's Fund) are important international technical assistance agencies working in the field of education, but they are not following the neoliberal economic agenda similar to that of the World Bank (WB) and the International Monetary Fund (IMF), and their educational goals often differ in a number of respects from the WB and IMF.

6. See, for example, Fernando Enrique Cardoso and Enzo Faletto, *Dependencia y desarrollo en América Latina* (Mexico City: Siglo Veintiuno, 1969); Fernando Cardoso, "The Consumption of Dependency Theory in the United States," *Latin American Research Review* 12, no. 3 (1977): 7–24; Theotonio Dos Santos, *Dependencia ecónomica y cambio revolucionario* (Caracas: Nueva Izquierda, 1970); Theotonio Dos Santos, "The Structure of Dependency," *American Economic Review* 60, no. 2 (1970): 231–36; and the seminal work by Paulo Freire, *Pedagogy of the Oppressed* (New York: Continuum, 1970).

7. Anne Hickling-Hudson, "When Marxist and Postmodern Theories Won't Do: The Potential of Postcolonial Theory for Educational Analysis" (paper presented to the annual conference of the Australian Association for Research in Education, Brisbane, December 1–4, 1998).

8. See Stanley Aronowitz and Jonathan Cutler, eds., *Post-Work: The Wages of Cybernation*

(New York: Routledge, 1998); Peter F. Drucker, *Post-Capitalist Society* (New York: Harper Business, 1993); and Robert Reich, *The Work of Nations: Preparing Ourselves for 21st-Century Capitalism* (New York: Knopf, 1991).

9. Philip G. Altbach and Eng Thye Jason Tan, *Programs and Centers in Comparative and International Education: A Global Inventory*, rev. ed., Special Studies in Comparative Education, no. 34 (Buffalo: State University of New York at Buffalo, Graduate School of Education Publications, 1995), ix. Published in cooperation with the Comparative and International Education Society.

10. Keith Watson, "Memories, Models, and Mapping: The Impact of Geopolitical Changes on Comparative Studies in Education," *Compare* 28, no. 1 (1998): 6. For the nineteenth-century origins of the field, see Erwin H. Epstein, "Comparative and International Education: Overview and Historical Development," in *The International Encyclopedia of Education*, 2nd ed., ed. T. Husén and T. N. Postlethwaite (Oxford: Pergamon, 1997).

11. Altbach and Tan, *Programs and Centers*, ix.

12. These dimensions also resonate with the three knowledge interests discussed by Jürgen Habermas in his *Knowledge and Human Interests*, ed. and trans. Jeremy J. Shapiro (Boston: Beacon, 1971). The three knowledge interests are the empirical-technical, the historical-hermeneutic, and the emancipatory. Also see Robert F. Arnove, "Comparative and International Education Society (CIES) Facing the Twenty-First Century: Challenges and Contributions, Presidential Address," *Comparative Education Review* 45, no. 4 (February 2002): 477–503.

13. The term *scientific* in relation to the field of comparative education is most frequently associated with the work of Max Eckstein and Harold Noah, particularly their *Toward a Science of Comparative Education* (New York: Macmillan, 1969).

14. Joseph P. Farrell, "The Necessity of Comparisons in the Study of Education: The Salience of Science and the Problem of Comparability (Presidential Address)," *Comparative Education Review* 23, no. 1 (February 1979): 3–16.

15. Mark Bray and R. Murray Thomas, "Levels of Comparison in Educational Studies: Different Insights from Different Literatures and the Value of Multilevel Analysis," *Harvard Educational Review* 65, no. 3 (Fall 1995): 486.

16. James S. Coleman et al., *Equality of Educational Opportunity* (Washington, D.C.: U.S. Office of Education, 1966); Christopher Jencks et al., *Inequality: A Reassessment of the Effect of Family and Schooling in America* (New York: Basic Books, 1972); Bridget Plowden et al., *Children and Their Primary Schools: A Report of the Central Advisory Council for Education, England* (London: Her Majesty's Stationery Office, 1967).

17. Stephen P. Heyneman, "Influences on Academic Achievement: A Comparison of Results from Uganda and More Industrialized Societies," *Sociology of Education* 49, no. 3 (July 1976): 200–211; and Joseph P. Farrell and Ernesto Schiefelbein, "Education and Status Attainment in Chile: A Comparative Challenge to the Wisconsin Model of Status Attainment," *Comparative Education Review* 29, no. 4 (November 1985): 490–506. For further discussion, see Claudia Buchman and Emily Hannum, "Education and Stratification in Developing Countries: A Review of Theories and Research," *Annual Review of Sociology* 7 (2000): 77–102.

18. Heyneman, "Influences"; Lois Weis, "Education and the Reproduction of Inequality: The Case of Ghana," *Comparative Education Review* 23, no. 1 (February 1979): 41–51; and Abby R. Riddell, "Assessing Designs for School Effectiveness Research and School Improvement in Developing Countries," *Comparative Education Review* 41, no. 2 (May 1997): 178–204.

19. It also is very likely that the emphasis on textbooks reflects a lack of faith in teachers as adequate sources of information as well as the power of international textbook publishing conglomerates to determine what constitutes official knowledge. See Michael Apple, *Official Knowledge: Democratic Education in a Conservative Age* (New York: Routledge, 1993); and David C. Korten, *When Corporations Rule the World* (West Hartford, Conn.: Kumarian, 1995), esp. 165–66.

20. George Psacharopoulos et al., "Comparative Education: From Theory to Practice; Or Are You A\:eo.* or B:*.ist?" *Comparative Education Review* 34, no. 3 (August 1990): 369–80.

21. Martin Carnoy, "Rates of Return to Education," in *International Encyclopedia of the Economics of Education*, 2nd ed., ed. M. Carnoy (Oxford: Pergamon, 1995), 364–69.

22. Stephen P. Heyneman, "Economics of Education: Disappointments and Potential," *Prospects* 23 (December 1995): 559–83.

23. James Wolfensohn, address given on March 1, 2000, at the World Bank, in relation to the completion of the report on "Higher Educaton in Developing Countgries: Peril and Promise," Joint World Bank/UNESCO Task Force on Higher Education and Society, Discussion Paper 14630 (Washington, D.C.: World Bank, 2000).

24. Xabier Gorostiaga, "New Times, New Role for Universities of the South," *Envío* 12, no. 144 (July 1993): 24–40.

25. Philip G. Altbach, "The University as Center and Periphery," in *Comparative Higher Education*, ed. P. G. Altbach (Norwood, N.J.: Ablex, 1998), 19–36; Gita Steiner-Khamasi, "Transferring Education, Displacing Reforms," in *Comparative Studies*, ed. Jürgen Schriewer (New York: Lang, 1998); and Gita Steiner, ed., *The Global Politics of Educational Borrowing and Lending* (New York and London: Teachers College Press, 2004). Also see David Phillips, who does not like what he calls the "simplistic notion of 'borrowing' . . . since it literally implies a temporary arrangement." Instead, he argues that "weighing of evidence from other countries in such a way as to inform and influence policy developments at home should be a very natural part of any efforts to introduce change." See his "On Comparing," in *Learning from Comparing: New Directions in Comparative Educational Research*, vol. 1, *Contexts Classrooms and Outcomes*, ed. Robin Alexander, Patricia Broadfoot, and David Phillips (Oxford: Symposium Books, 1999), 18.

26. Tesuya Kobayashi, "China, India, Japan and Korea," in *Comparative Education: Contemporary Issues and Trends*, ed. W. D. Halls (London: Jessica Kingsley; Paris: UNESCO, 1990), esp. 200; cited in Mark Bray, "Comparative Education Research in the Asian Region: Implications for the Field as a Whole," *Comparative Education Bulletin* 1 (May 1998): 6.

27. Nancy Ukai Russell, "Lessons from Japanese Cram Schools," in *Education in Eastern Asia: Implications for America*, ed. William K. Cummings and Philip G. Altbach (Albany: State University of New York Press, 1997); and Walter Feinberg, *Japan and the Pursuit of a New American Identity: Work and Education in a Multicultural Age* (New York: Routledge, 1993), 153–70.

28. John J. Cogan, "Should the U.S. Mimic Japanese Education? Let's Look before We Leap," *Phi Delta Kappan* 65, no. 7 (March 1984): 463–68; Joseph J. Tobin et al., "Class Size and Student/ Teacher Ratios in the Japanese Preschool," *Comparative Education Review* 31, no. 4 (November 1987); William K. Cummings, "From Knowledge Seeking to Knowledge Creation: The Japanese University's Challenge," *Higher Education* 27, no. 4 (June 1994): 399–415; Susan Ohanian, "Notes on Japan from an American Schoolteacher," *Phi Delta Kappan* 68, no. 5 (January 1987): 360–67; and David Willis and Satoshi Yamamura, eds., special section on "Japanese Education in Transition 2001: Radical Perspectives on Cultural and Political Transformation," *International Education Journal* 2, no. 5 (2001).

29. Harold J. Noah, "The Use and Abuse of Comparative Education," *Comparative Education Review* 28, no. 4 (November 1984): 558–60.

30. Cogan, "Should the U.S. Mimic?" 466–68.

31. Watson, "Memories, Models and Mapping," 5–31.

32. Michael Crossley and Graham Vulliamy, "Qualitative Research in Developing Countries: Issues and Experience," in *Qualitative Educational Research in Developing Countries*, ed. M. Crossley and G. Vulliamy (New York: Garland, 1997), 7; and Stewart Fraser, *Jullien's Plan for Comparative Education, 1816–1817* (New York: Columbia University, Teachers College, 1964).

33. Fraser, *Jullien's Plan*, 7–8; also see Michael Crossley and Patricia Broadfoot, "Comparative and International Research in Education: Scope, Problems, and Potential," *British Educational Research Journal* 18, no. 2 (1992): 99–112.

34. M. E. Sadler, "The History of Education," in *Germany in the Nineteenth Century: Five Lectures by J. H. Rose*, ed. C. H. Herford, E. C. K. Gooner, and M. E. Sadler (Manchester: At the University Press, 1912), 125.

35. Isaac L. Kandel, *Studies in Comparative Education* (Boston: Houghton and Mifflin, 1933), xix; cited in Crossley and Vulliamy, *Qualitative Research, Qualitative Educational Research in Developing Countries*, ed. M. Crossley and G. Vulliamy (New York: Garland, 1997), 8.

36. For a discussion of the relationship of comparative education to international education, see David N. Wilson, "Comparative and International Education: Fraternal or Siamese Twins? A Preliminary Genealogy of Our Twin Field (Presidential Address)," *Comparative Education Review* 38, no. 4 (November 1994): 449–86; also Gary Theisen, "The New ABCs of Comparative and International Education (Presidential Address)," *Comparative Education Review* 41, no. 4 (November 1997): 397–412.

37. Noah ("Use and Abuse," 553–54) has pointed out how a country's education system provides a "touchstone" for examining what values are most cherished.

38. Robert F. Arnove, "Comparative Education and World-Systems Analysis," *Comparative Education Review* 24, no. 1 (February 1980): 48–62; also see Carlos Alberto Torres, *Education, Democracy, and Multiculturalism: Dilemmas of Citizenship in a Global World* (Boulder, Colo.: Rowman & Littlefield, 1998); and the 1996 CIES presidential address of Noel F. McGinn, "Education, Democratization, and Globalization: A Challenge for Comparative Education," *Comparative Education Review* 40, no. 4 (November 1996): 341–57.

39. Chadwick F. Alger and James E. Harf, *Global Education: Why? For Whom? About What?* (Columbus: Ohio State University, 1986), ERIC Document EN 265107. Also see Erwin Epstein, "Editorial," *Comparative Education Review* 36, no. 3 (November 1992): 409–16.

40. Robert Hanvey, *An Attainable Global Perspective* (Denver: Denver University, Center for Teaching International Relations/New York Friends Group Center for War/Peace Studies, 1975).

41. Barbara Piscitelli, "Culture, Curriculum, and Young Children's Art: Directions for Further Research," *Journal of Cognitive Education* 6, no. 1 (1997): 27–39; Barbara Piscitelli, "Children's Art Exhibitions and Exchanges: Assessing the Impact," in *SEA News* 4 (1997): 1.

42. Alger and Harf, *Global Education*.

43. Randal C. Archibold, "Economic Troubles Back Home Squeeze Asian Students in U.S.," *New York Times*, February 8, 1988, 1, 10.

44. Cole S. Brembeck, "The Future of Comparative and International Education," *Comparative Education Review* 19, no. 3 (October 1975): 369–74; also see Stephen P. Heyneman, "Quantity, Quality, and Source (Presidential Address)," *Comparative Education Review* 37, no. 4 (November 1993): 372–88.

45. Theisen, "New ABCs."

46. Altbach and Tan, *Programs and Centers*, ix.

47. Bray, "Education in Asian Region," 8.

48. Bray, "Education in Asian Region"; also see Mark Bray and Chin Giu, "Comparative Education in Greater China: Contexts, Characteristics, Contrasts and Contributions," *Comparative Education* 37, no. 4 (2001): 451–73.

49. For further discussion, see Mark Bray, "Tradition, Change, and the Role of the World Council of Comparative Education Societies," *International Review of Education* 49, no. 1 (2003). The website of the World Council of Comparative Education Societies is www.hku.hk/cerc/wcces.html. Among the latest members to join the WCCES are Argentina, Egypt, and Turkey.

50. Bray, "Education in Asian Region," 7–8.

51. Bray, "Education in Asian Region," 9; and Bray and Gui, "Comparative Education in Greater China."

52. Elizabeth Sherman Swing, "From Eurocentrism to Post-colonialism: A Bibliographic Perspective" (paper presented at the annual conference of the Comparative and International Education Society, Mexico City, 1997); Vandra Masemann, "Recent Directions in Comparative

Education" (paper presented at the annual conference of the Comparative and International Education Society, Mexico City, 1997); Bray, "Education in Asian Region," 9; and Abdeljalil Akkari and Soledad Pérez, "Educational Research in Latin America: Review and Perspectives," *Educational Policy Analysis Archives* 6 (March 1998).

53. Lynn Webster Paine, "The Teacher as Virtuoso: A Chinese Model for Teaching," *Teacher College Record* 92, no. 1 (Fall 1990): 49–81; Allan Mackinnon, "Learning to Teach at the Elbows: The Tao of Teaching," *Teaching and Teacher Education* 12, no. 6 (November 1996): 633–64; Robert Tremmel, "Zen and the Art of Reflective Practice in Teacher Education," *Harvard Educational Review* 63, no. 4 (Winter 1993): 434–58; Melanie Davenport, "Asian Conceptions of the Teacher Internship: Implications for American Art Education" (unpublished paper, School of Education, Indiana University, May 1998); Ruth Hayhoe, "Reedeming Modernity, Presidential Address," *Comparative Education Review* 44, no. 4 (November 2000): 423–39; and Ruth Hayhoe and Julia Pan, eds., *Knowledge across Cultures: A Contribution to Dialogue among Civilizations* (Hong Kong: Comparative Education Research Centre, Hong Kong University, 2001).

54. Kimberly Lenease King, "From Exclusion to Inclusion: A Case Study of Black South Africans at the University of the Witwaterland" (Ph.D. diss., Indiana University, 1998); and Reitumetse Obakeng Mabokela and Kimberly Lenease King, eds., *Apartheid No More: Case Studies of Southern African Universities in the Process of Transformation* (Westport, Conn.: Bergin & Garvey, 2001).

55. See Epstein, "Comparative and International Education," in *The International Encyclopedia of Education*, 2nd ed., ed. Husén and Postlethwaite (Oxford: Pergamon, 1997); and Watson, "Memories, Models, and Mapping."

56. This is a quip of Jerome Harste of the Language Education Department of the Indiana University School of Education, Bloomington. Harste, a leading proponent of whole-language education, has difficulty with people who claim to be eclectic in their approaches to teaching reading and writing.

57. Bray and Thomas, "Levels of Comparison."

58. See, for example, Rosemary Preston, "Integrating Paradigms in Educational Research: Issues of Quantity and Quality in Poor Countries," in *Qualitative Educational Research in Developing Countries*, ed. M. Crossley and G. Vulliamy (New York: Garland, 1997); Charles C. Ragin, *The Comparative Method: Moving beyond Qualitative and Quantitative Strategies* (Berkeley: University of California Press, 1987); Robert K. Yin, "The Case Study as a Serious Research Strategy," *Knowledge: Creation, Diffusion, and Utilization* 3 (1981): 97–114; and Val Rust et al., "Research Strategies in Comparative Education," *Comparative Education Review* 43, no. 1 (February 1999): 86–109. An illustration of both large-survey data and case studies examining a common theme are these complementary volumes on civic education: Judith Torney-Purta, John Schwille, and J.-A. Amado, eds., *Civic Education across Countries: Twenty-four National Case Studies from the IEA Civic Education Project* (Amsterdam: IEA, 1999); and Gita Steiner-Khamsi, Judith Torney-Purta, and John Schwille, *Recurring Paradoxes in Education for Citizenship: An International Comparison* (Amsterdam: Elsevier Science, JAI, 2002).

59. Ragin, *Comparative Method*, 16.

60. Ragin, *Comparative Method*, x.

61. Ragin, *Comparative Method*, ix.

62. York Bradshaw and Michael Wallace, "Informing Generality and Explaining Uniqueness: The Place of Case Studies in Comparative Research," *International Journal of Comparative Sociology* 32 (January–April 1991): 154–71.

63. Max Weber, "The Fundamental Concepts of Sociology," in *Max Weber: The Theory of Social and Economic Organization*, ed. Talcott Parsons (New York: Free Press, 1964), 87–157.

64. Sheila Slaughter and Laurence Leslie, *Academic Capitalism;* also see Sheila Slaughter and Gary Rhoades, *Academic Capitalism and the New Economy: Markets, State, and Higher Education* (Baltimore: Johns Hopkins University Press, 2004).

65. Karen Mundy, "Toward a Critical Analysis of Literacy in Southern Africa," *Comparative Education Review* 37, no. 4 (November 1993): 389–411.

66. Rachel Christina, "NGOs and the Negotiation of Local Control in Development Initiatives: A Case Study of Palestinian Early Childhood Programming" (Ph.D. diss., Indiana University, School of Education, 2001); and her *Tend the Olive, Water the Vine: Negotiating Palestinian Childhood Development in the Context of Globalization* (Greenwich, Conn.: Information Age Publishing, 2006).

67. See, for example, Michael Crossley and J. Alexander Bennett, "Planning for Case-Study Evaluation in Belize, Central America," in *Qualitative Educational Research in Developing Countries*, ed. M. Crossley and G. Vulliamy (New York: Garland, 1997), 221–43.

68. Tosten Husén, "Policy Impact of IEA Research," *Comparative Education Review* 31 (February 1987): 29–46, in the special issue on the second IEA study; also see David A. Walker with C. Arnold Anderson and Richard M. Wolfe, *The IEA Six Subject Survey: An Empirical Study of Education in Twenty-One Countries* (Stockholm: Alquist & Wiksell; New York: Wiley, 1976); T. Neville Postlethwaite and David E. Wiley with the assistance of Yeoh Oon Chye, William B. Schmidt, and Richard G. Wolfe, *The IEA Study of Science II: Science Achievement in Twenty-Three Countries* (Oxford: Pergamon, 1992); and John W. Meyer and David P. Baker, "Forming Educational Policy with International Data: Lessons from the Sociology of Education," *Sociology of Education* 69 (1996): 123–30 (extra issue for 1996). Excellent data on various independent and dependent variables related to academic achievement and other school outcomes are found in the PISA (Program for International Student Assessment) website linked to the National Center for Educational Statistics (NCES), www.nces.edu.gov/surveys/pisa.

69. Abigail J. Stewart and David G. Winter, "The Nature and Causes of Female Suppression," *Signs: Journal of Women in Culture and Society* 2 (Winter 1977): 531–55.

70. Warwick B. Elley, ed., *The IEA Study of Reading Literacy: Achievement and Instruction in Thirty-two School Systems* (Oxford: Pergamon, 1997).

71. On the need to contextualize IEA data, see Gary L. Theisen, Paul P.W. Achola, and Francis Musa Boakar, "The Underachievement of Cross-National Studies of Achievement," *Comparative Education Review* 27, no. 1 (February 1983): 46–68; and for further discussion, see T. Neville Postlethwaite, *International Studies of Educational Achievement: Methodological Issues* (Hong Kong: Comparative Education Research Centre, Hong Kong University, 1999). Also see the November 2006 issue of the *Comparative Education Review* containing the 2006 CIES Presidential Address of Martin Carnoy and commentary by others, in which the value of large-scale quantitative studies for purposes of establishing verifiable propositions within the field of comparative education is contrasted with the contributions of small-scale qualitative studies to theory-building.

72. "Dance on the Edge" (brochure for the 1998 CIES Western Region Conference, Department of Educational Studies, University of British Columbia, Vancouver B.C., Canada).

73. See Gail P. Kelly, "Debates and Trends in Comparative Education," in *Emergent Issues*, ed. Robert F. Arnove, Philip G. Altbach, and Gail P. Kelly (Albany: State University of New York Press, 1992), 13–22; and Philip G. Altbach, Robert F. Arnove, and Gail P. Kelly, "Trends in Comparative Education: A Critical Analysis," in Altbach et al., eds., *Comparative Education*, 505–33.

74. For further discussion of these critical theories, see Carlos Alberto Torres and Theodore R. Mitchel, eds., *Sociology of Education: Emerging Perspectives* (Albany: State University of New York Press, 1998).

75. Kelly, "Debates and Trends," 21–22.

76. Robert F. Arnove, Philip G. Altbach, and Gail P. Kelly, introduction to *Emergent Issues* (Albany: State University of New York Press, 1992), 1.

77. See the 1992 CIES presidential address of Mark B. Ginsburg with Sangeeta Kamat, Rajeshwari Raghu, and John Weaver, "Educators/Politics," *Comparative Education Review* 36, no. 4 (November 1992): 417–45; and Arnove, "Presidential Address."

1

Technocracy, Uncertainty, and Ethics: Comparative Education in an Era of Postmodernity and Globalization

Anthony Welch

In this chapter, I argue that the theoretical trajectory of comparative education, for much of the twentieth century, paralleled that of the social sciences in general, initially describing an arc that was based upon a faith in broadly technocratic social science concepts of modernity, drawn largely from functionalism. More recently, this theoretical arc has been breaking up, revealing an increasing fragmentation of purpose, and perhaps failure of vision, which has paralleled, once again, that of the social sciences—if somewhat more slowly. The current chapter traces some principal lines of that theoretical trajectory, beginning with an outline of the technocratic elements within a broadly modernist, positivist functionalism, and then tracing the recent tendency toward theoretical fragmentation and the associated collapse of certainty. In tracing this theoretical trajectory, I trace links between the literature of comparative education and that of the social and natural sciences. Thus I argue that the more recent failure of vision, and increasing fragmentation, which is in turn a response to wider movements in industrialized nations, and perhaps the world system, is not entirely necessary. In the conclusion, I advance alternatives based on arguments as to the urgent need for reiterating ethical dimensions and responsibilities of comparative education, in an era of increasing globalization.

FROM HISTORY TO SCIENCE?

As Imre Lakatos,[1] *inter alia*, reminds us, hindsight allows a distinct, and arguably more complete, vantage point from which to evaluate competing theoretical perspectives, which the protagonists of the time may have seen rather differently. From the perspective of the beginning of the twenty-first century, then, it is easy to be somewhat skeptical as to the brash ebullience of comparative education of the 1960s, as new and more positivistic forms of comparative education were elaborated by an emerging generation of authors who variously asserted their independence from the "factors and forces" traditions of more historically oriented predecessors: *inter alia*, Nicholas Hans,[2] Isaac Kandel,[3] and Friedrich Schneider.[4] Notwithstanding substantial differences between such emerging figures of the 1960s as Brian Holmes,[5] Max Eckstein and Harold Noah,[6] and George Bereday,[7] however, the promise of scientific methodology was generally held to ensure a more certain and precise future for comparative education, in which *knowledge* and *facts* would play a major and determinate role in educational reform. Neither of these two concepts were yet much problematized, and it is in this sense that it can be argued that debates in comparative education in the 1960s were mostly conducted within the parameters of a positivistically based modernism.

What is meant by the term positivism here? Briefly, the view that the methods of the social sciences were coextensive with, indeed drawn from, those of the natural sciences, whose methodological development was generally assumed to be at a more mature stage of development than the newly developing social sciences. Although the term *positivism* is widely debated (and much abused), it is nonetheless possible to distil several broad strands that underpin positivistic forms of social science: a belief that methods of inquiry are monolithic (the so-called unity of method), a belief in lawlike generalizations in the social sciences, a technical relation between theory and practice (which thus brackets out any consideration of ethics in social theory), and the belief in a value-free science of social inquiry, in which *facts* and *knowledge* were the basis for progress and were rigidly separated from *values*, which were not the concern of the (social) scientist. This restricted form of self-understanding of science and knowledge, which informed modernism, was inherited from at least the French Enlightenment (toward the end of the eighteenth century), and arguably earlier. While it was by no means the only theory of knowledge or science, its prominence occluded the development of alternatives, in both the natural and social sciences.[8]

The *Methodenstreit* (methodological dispute) among comparativists of the 1960s, then, largely occurred *within* the bounds of that modernist faith described above, that is, in the capacity of science and technology to underpin social reform and progress, including in education, and the ability of an epistemology (theory of knowledge) entirely bounded by the philosophy of the natural sciences to root out errors in any area of knowledge. Debates thus turned largely on the question of which particular position in the philosophy of the natural sciences was superior. Holmes' more explicit attempt to base claims for a new science of comparative education upon Popperian hypothetico-deductive foundations was paralleled by the more or less explicitly inductive approaches of Bereday, and Noah and Eckstein. All ultimately fell victim to the principal tenets of the broad positivist tradition sketched above, that underpinned so much of modernist social science and was thought would herald the same golden age of progress and discovery that had been achieved in the natural sciences of the seventeenth and eighteenth centuries.[9]

It is in this sense, as Jürgen Habermas has argued, that "the concept of enlightenment functions as a bridge between the idea of scientific progress and the conviction that the sciences also serve the moral perfection of human beings,"[10] a view that stems directly from figures such as Condorcet and others in the Enlightenment: that false moral and political views are a product of false understandings of nature. Science itself was believed to be a form of enlightenment, which once perfected, would deliver the same rapid advances in knowledge to the "moral sciences" that had already been demonstrated in the natural sciences. In common with many social scientists of that era, then, major methodologists in comparative education of the 1960s were heirs to a belief, stemming from at least the Enlightenment, if not from the birth of modern science in the seventeenth century, that a base of scientific reason was a secure foundation for the epistemological, and, by extension, the social and moral, renovation and improvement of society.

The major theorists of comparative education in the 1960s made no attempt to problematize scientific reason or to subject its social effects to critical scrutiny, despite the fact that powerful critiques of the social distortions caused by the uncritical adoption of scientific reason in the human sciences by largely German social theorists such as Herbert Marcuse,[11] Alfred Schutz,[12] and Max Horkeimer and Theodor Adorno,[13] and in earlier eras, by Edmund Husserl[14] and Wilhelm Dilthey, already existed.[15] In the philosophy of science too, at least by the 1970s, scholars such as Thomas Kuhn[16] and Paul Feyerabend[17] had outlined a much more sociological profile of scientific change and development, from which none of the methods of the sciences had proved immune. Indeed, according to Feyerabend's withering critique of pretensions to a universal scientific methodology, the only rule is that there are no (final) rules: that is, "there is no 'scientific method', no single procedure, or set of rules that underlies every piece of research and guarantees that it is 'scientific' and, therefore, trustworthy."[18]

Despite these parallel attacks upon the adequacy of scientific reason, in its own sphere, and even more so in the social sciences, the "modernists" in comparative education of the 1960s viewed science and scientific reason, in its various forms, as a beneficent force, which, if it were only adopted fully and implemented rigorously, would herald the dawn of a more precise and more certain science of comparative education. It is in this sense that the major figures of the 1960s were children of Enlightenment positivism and heirs to the rationalist ideology of perfectibility—that the increasing subjection of the world to the dictates of a technology of reason would promote a more rational and more morally perfect world. Despite vigorous internecine disputes among several of the high priests of the scientific faith, such as Brian Holmes, Harold Noah and Max Eckstein, and George Bereday, the notion of the progressive rationalization of education, via the increasing methodological perfection of the science of comparative education, was common to major theorists of this era.

Perhaps one of the better-known instances of the role of scientific reason in comparative education is provided by functionalism (sometimes called structural functionalism), arguably the most prominent and persuasive form of scientism to hold sway in the postwar era, and for much of the twentieth century. Not merely was (structural) functionalism arguably the most prominent of the range of grand theories that laid claim to the mantle of "social science," but a broadly functionalist ethos underlay most of the major positions in comparative education of the 1960s, as indeed among the social sciences more generally.[19]

Stemming from the work of such founding fathers as Auguste Comte in the nineteenth century and Emile Durkheim in the early twentieth, functionalism held that *sociology*, a term invented by Comte, should be modeled closely upon the methods of the natural sciences. A functionalist social science then, like its natural science forebears, should be lawlike and socially integrative (see the quote from Francis Bacon, below). Functionalism was influenced by other movements in the natural sciences too, however, notably the nineteenth-century scientific theory of evolution, from which was incorporated the view that social change should be, just as with biological change, slow and accretive rather than swifter and/or large scale. In other words, the model of social change within functionalism was evolutionary rather than revolutionary. Lastly, functionalism asserted a supposedly value-free social science in which researchers should simply seek out and present the facts, eschewing questions of ethics or the moral dimensions of the knowledge they developed. (In practice, however, technicist values of efficiency and economy were dominant within functionalist forms of social science, if often implicitly.) Here once again, functionalism revealed its positivist heritage, drawn from the modernist presumptions of the Enlightenment and the origins of modern experimental science in the seventeenth century.

In comparative education, the functionalist tradition was arguably most clearly expressed in the substantial literature of the 1950s and 1960s devoted to the theme of modernization, particularly the elaboration of the role that education played in changing traditional societies. A common, broadly positivist agenda, based upon the technocratic values sketched above, of efficiency and economy, and a strong system concept, was often present in this literature. As well, a reified notion of social needs, evolutionary progress, social integration rather than social change, and a reliance upon supposed laws of society was evident. The basic aim was continuous with that of Comte,[20] Durkheim,[21] Talcott Parsons,[22] and others: the devising of a science of society modeled upon the natural sciences.[23] And, just as with those theoretical fountainheads, functionalism embodied the aim of control. Just as the natural sciences had already brought nature under control, so too, it was argued, would the science of society, in the guise of functionalism, bring society under control. In this sense, functionalism was a direct heir to modernist presumptions, indeed it represented a modern form of sociological positivism.

Education was of major significance within functionalist theories of modernization and was generally accorded two principal roles. First, as a prime site for the inculcation of integrative, stabilizing values, education systems were perceived to be of signal importance in this sedative process, not merely in "modern" societies but also, crucially, in modernising societies that were "developing." In this sense too, as was argued above, functionalism was direct heir to the positivist faith, in which the twin aims of the advancement of knowledge and an increase in social control were intertwined. Already in the seventeenth century, the great scientist-philosopher Francis Bacon had compared science and learning to a harp that would quiet the otherwise tumultuous and mutinous crowd, thus making them more politically malleable: "it is without all controversy that learning doth make the minds of men gentle, generous, maniable and pliant to government; whereas ignorance makes them churlish, thwart and mutinous."[24]

The second key educational role within functionalism was, of course, the provision of adequate numbers of skilled personnel to service the needs of the various branches of the workforce: both of these functions worked to ensure the ongoing stability of society.

The triumph of modernity was expressed with particular clarity in the articulation, and defense, of the unilinear teleological process whereby societies became "modern." Third world or developing countries were always assumed to be at an early stage of progress toward the same inevitable end point: a technological, industrial, advanced bureaucratic, and pluralist society, which when examined, bore an uncanny resemblance to the United States or the United Kingdom, or other societies from which the authors stemmed. Modern advanced capitalist societies were always seen as, in effect, the ultimate benchmark for the economies and politics of the former colonies of the Third World, no matter how much this disrupted traditional cultures and values. Evolutionary assumptions, common to functionalist social science, were once again adopted from biological theory, via figures such as Durkheim, and implied a specific conception of historical development that divided the world into two camps: "advanced" societies were seen as "core," whereas the former colonies of Asia, Africa, or Latin America were, in effect, viewed largely as "periphery." Clearly discernible, then, if not always stated, was "a teleological notion of history, which views the knowledge and ways of life in the colony as distorted or immature versions of what can be found in the 'normal' or Western society."[25] Modernization was, in effect, westernization. These unilinear evolutionary assumptions were of particular relevance to modernization theory and embodied, as I have already pointed out, a distaste for swift or systematic social change or political value systems that were not consonant with modern, advanced capitalism. In this sense, modern functionalism is heir to Durkheim's goal of the establishment of an integrative social science: modern society's "civil religion."[26] To repeat, however, the evolution at the center of modernization theory was always a one-way street—toward the attainment of Western capitalist structures and values—and presaged profound changes to traditional institutions and ideologies. Moreover, the process of evolution toward a state of modernity was based solidly upon a foundation of modern science, which was assumed to be able to advance the rate of human progress significantly: "Man [*sic*] in this century of science can move forward in leaps instead of steps."[27] Once again, this faith in the potential of science and technology to advance the perfectibility of humanity is a further echo of Enlightenment faith in the power of reason as *techne*, that is, embodiment of modern, technocratic society, in which instrumental reason overwhelms ethical constraints and mores.[28]

David McClelland,[29] Philip Coombs,[30] and Frederick Harbison and Charles Myers,[31] among others, saw modernization as either directly or indirectly an example of the Weberian rationalization of society, whereby traditional social mores and institutions such as kinship were replaced by a "coldly rational"[32] modernist action orientation more suited to complex, bureaucratic societies of the twentieth century. More broadly, rationalization meant "a lessening of mystical or supernatural orientation towards life, an increase in striving, orderliness, rigidity, orientation to work without reward, and other such features which Weber saw [as] characteristic of modern capitalist orientations."[33]

Indeed McClelland specifically adapted Talcott Parsons's reformulation of Weber's ideas to develop his "need achievement" index of modernization. The concept, as its name implied, comprised a composite index of modernization and argued that to achieve an increase in economic growth and to become truly modern, developing nations needed to reorient both ideologies and institutions, while individuals needed to become more achievement oriented. The suggested changes centered around the institutionalization of structural features like the increased division of labor and more contractual social relations allied to reoriented values, for example, the substitution of material for spiritual forms of satisfaction, as well as a lessening in spiritual influences generally. Here again, we see evidence of a means-ends style of rationality in which economic efficiency is, at least implicitly, accorded the status of a prime value.[34] Little or no consideration was given to alternative value systems, least of all that held by people from the "modernizing" society. The end point of this process of evolution was always that of advanced capitalist society.

THE ROLE OF WESTERN CULTURE

Positivism, often including a broadly evolutionary perspective, however, has been only one of several common assumptions underlying much modernist empirical and theoretical work in comparative education. But its influence is linked to (and helps to explain) others. The fact that modern science was an artifact associated with the rise of the West helps to explain another given within the traditions of mainstream, modernist comparative studies of education: Western culture as the apex of civilization. A common assumption of nineteenth and early twentieth-century anthropology, it remained pervasive and influential in comparative education during at least the first half of the twentieth century. Like many of their colleagues and contemporaries in political science and other social science disciplines, Coombs, McClelland, Harbison and Myers, and others in both comparative education during the period up to and including the 1950s and 1960s tended either to view "other" societies from a generally Western perspective, or in the case of modernization theorists, to situate non-Western nations at a point somewhere along the road that culminated in the attainment of "westernization." In a sense, the fact that the field of comparative education largely grew out of Western scholarly foundations, and most of its founding figures were from Europe and America, made this assumed trajectory of social development unsurprising and goes some way to explain the critique that modernization was in fact coextensive with westernization. Nonetheless the minimal value accorded the principle of difference, and the rich and long-standing traditions associated with such non-Western cultural traditions, was not a good base for a field of study that purported to analyze cultural difference.

THE NATION-STATE AS UNIT OF ANALYSIS

A further assumption of traditional comparative education was that of the nation-state as the prime unit of analysis. To some extent, this reflected the genesis of comparative education as a social science that, like others, grew to maturity during the heyday of the growth and rivalry of the nation-state in the nineteenth and early twentieth centuries, and to some extent was dependent upon major international organs such as UNESCO (United Nations Educational, Scientific, and Cultural Organization) and OECD (Organization for Economic Cooperation and Development), whose statistics were collected along national lines. Although some earlier comparativists analyzed the construction of political identity[35] or the educative role and function of mission schools,[36] even these more thematic analyses fell largely within heuristic traditions in which the dominant unit of analysis was still the nation-state. Even Holmes's well-known problem approach[37] did not realize its theoretical possibilities to undermine the convention of the nation-state as the analytic unit of choice within comparative education. Indeed, the final section of Holmes's most well-known and original work of 1965 was devoted to national case studies. Nor did Noah and Eckstein's programmatic statement that "a comparative study is essentially an attempt as far as possible to replace the names of systems (countries) by the names of concepts (variables)"[38] succeed in checking the prominence of the nation as a given within the literature of comparative education. Not all comparative education scholars of the time were trained as area specialists (Bereday was first and foremost a

Soviet specialist, but neither Holmes nor Noah and Eckstein were), yet the nation-state still figured as the analytic unit in the majority of comparative research.

TRIBUTARIES

Although the above elements characterized mainstream comparative education during the period of intense development of comparative methodologies from the 1960s, important tributaries diverged significantly. Some of these have since gone on to become significant currents. Not all comparative education of the postwar decades held that the further development of the field was dependent upon debates in postrelativity physics, nor that Western culture should be assumed as end point of all civilizations.

Two developments challenging the ubiquitous emphasis upon scientism in comparative methodology drew upon more interpretive, anthropological traditions: ethnomethodology and ethnography. The first was largely exemplified through the work of Canadian American scholar Richard Heyman, who (in a series of articles in the late 1970s and early 1980s) deliberately articulated an alternative tradition to the prevailing scientistic ethos. In common with the ethnomethodological scholars upon whom he drew, Heyman decried the influence of the natural sciences upon the methodological development of the social sciences. Following the mandate of his mentors, he proffered instead a "nonscience of comparative education."[39]

For ethnomethodologists, context was vital and thus knowledge, and the language with which it was described, was indexical, or situationally mediated. In stark contrast with most scientifically based methodologies, there was no independent reality that each individual must accept according to the dictates of a transcendental, abstract method, and irrespective of individual background or interests. Indeed, the very assumption of a scientific method of detached observation that produced objective insights into social phenomena was simply erroneous, on this account. On the contrary, every observation was itself a construction, one of many possible constructions, each of which could be further deconstructed, or subjected to further interpretation.[40] Indeed, an account of a social phenomenon was co-extensive with accounting for a phenomenon. Observation equaled interpretation, meaning that interpretation was, in principle, endless. Each account could, in principle, be subjected to yet another interpretation, and so on. Indeed, what Anthony Giddens accurately characterized as the hermeneutic vortex[41] at the core of ethnomethodology was embraced by its followers as a feature of social interpretation.

Heyman's application of such precepts to the renovation of comparative education led him to press for a focus on the microprocesses of school life via intensive study of audio- and video-taped interactions. In itself this was a worthwhile corrective to the macro, systems-based traditions of comparative education; but to go on to argue that other forms of educational investigation should be postponed pending the provision by ethnomethodologists of "a reasonable picture of the essential processes of education"[42] was both unreasonable and chimerical. Equally, although claiming to be strongly antipositivist and postulating an epistemology that celebrated the concrete and different ways in which social reality was constructed, it nonetheless claimed to produce its own facts, which were somehow prior to other interpretations. By claiming, at least implicitly, to provide a kind of epistemic bedrock upon which other researchers might then rely, it also fell victim to the self-same positivism it critiqued.[43] The other problem that dogged ethnomethodological prescriptions for comparative research in education was its field of vision. As it concentrated on the microcosm of classroom interaction, with its myriad small details, it often lost the connection to the wider world (including the often powerful ways in which this macrocosm influenced the micro world of the classroom). Indeed, one of the more insistent and powerful critiques of ethnomethodology was its failure to embrace or analyze power relations, particularly the important ways in which power structures in the larger world, including relations based on social class, pervaded the microcosm of the classroom. In a real sense, it could be argued that, in gaining one class, ethnomethodologists had lost another.

The Canadian connection was strengthened in Vandra Masemann's pregnant elaboration of critical ethnography,[44] which avoided many of the pitfalls listed above and provided an important challenge to the scientism of much contemporary comparative research:

> Is it the task of social scientists to seek ever more diligently to define objective methods of researching the social world (or education), with possibilities for change seen as simply the result of "reading out the data" and making choices on the basis of some cost-efficient or technological rationale?[45]

For Masemann, critical ethnography offered not merely a renewed emphasis on "participant observation of the small-scale . . . with an attempt to understand the culture and symbolic life of the actors involved"[46] but also "insists upon a level of agency which is persistently overlooked or denied."[47] Plumping for a form of ethnography, which sited the micro within the context of a macrotheory of social organization, Masemann argued that "it should be possible to . . . investigate the lived life in schools while not necessarily limiting the analysis to the actors' perceptions of the situation."[48] It is only in that way, she argued, that the practices by which a hegemonic rationality are imposed upon students could successfully be revealed and analyzed. By connecting the macro to the micro, she avoided the problems of ethnomethodologists, whose parenthesizing (methodological exclusion) of larger structures and ideologies rendered them unable to analyze power very successfully, if at all.

Other nonmainstream theories challenged the conventional Western-centric view of much research and/or proceeded from rather different political assumptions about the international political arena and the relationship between powerful and relatively disempowered groups in education, including the role of philanthropic agencies in fostering dependency.[49] Turning the functionalist assumption of a unilinear path to a monolithic Western modernity on its head, several of these scholars articulated a core-periphery model, often paying some allegiance to currents of the Marxist tradition, which emphasized the capacity of wealthy and powerful Western nations, as well as lending and other programs of agencies such as the International Monetary Fund (IMF) and World Bank, to deepen the dependency of Third World nations.[50] Drawing upon the theoretical work of scholars like Andre Gunder Frank,[51] Immanuel Wallerstein,[52] and others, key comparative scholars cast a critical eye on the influence of colonialism and on relations between the first and Third World. Martin Carnoy's important early book was succeeded by Philip Altbach and the late Gail Kelly's important work on colonialism,[53] which did not merely examine the educational influence of Western colonial incursions in Africa, Latin America, and the Asia Pacific region but also included an important early study of internal colonialism in the education of indigenous minorities, which applied the work of such figures as Harold Wolpe to the analysis of education among Native American peoples.

Robert Arnove's application of world-systems analysis stemmed naturally from his work on the ideological penetration of philanthropic organizations, especially in the Third World.[54] Issuing a clarion call for an international approach to understanding educational systems rather than the traditional reliance upon the nation-state as the basic unit of analysis, Arnove explored the benefits of setting educational analysis in the context of international economic, political, and social developments. The effects of colonial and neocolonial influences on areas such as Africa, Latin America, and Oceania were obvious instances of the necessity of such approaches. They underlined too the ongoing difficulties faced by these regions in overcoming an often long-standing history of dependency, fostered by the colonial relationship and often changing only in form well beyond the formal end of the colonial era. As Arnove explained, the international ideological penetration of colonial and postcolonial nations also extended within nations in the Third World:

> Dependency theory basically articulates a descending chain of exploitation from the hegemony of metropolitan countries over peripheral countries to the hegemony of the center of power in a Third World country over its own peripheral areas. Closely related to such notions of center and periphery are the concepts of Wallerstein concerning convergence and divergence in the global system.[55]

Altbach's analysis of neocolonialism and dependency also articulated the processes that developed and sustained what he termed "servitude of the mind"[56] both among and within nations, a process not merely fostered by disparities of economic wealth and power but also reflecting the fact that Third World nations

> find themselves at the periphery of the world's educational and intellectual systems. . . . The world's leading universities, research institutions, publishing houses, journals, and all the elements that constitute a modern technological society are concentrated in the industrialized nations of Europe and North America.[57]

FIN DE SIÈCLE FRACTURES

If the above theoretical development represented a divergence from mainstream modernist scientism in comparative education, the picture had altered again by the 1990s. By then, the ebullience of the postwar decades was well and truly on the wane. The oil crisis of the 1970s, as well as periods of intermittent economic recession thereafter, led to the advent of mass unemployment, especially among the young, in many parts of the world. The widening gap between rich and poor (both within and between countries) and the increasing deregulation of many economies evidenced a more general decline in government activity and intervention in social and economic affairs. In the social sciences, the confident certitudes of earlier decades were falling increasingly into disarray. Economically, politically, and epistemologically, the Zeitgeist of the 1990s was considerably less certain and confident than it had been thirty years previously; debates in the social sciences, including comparative education, reflected that changing context.[58] The rise of poststructuralist thought, with its rejection of much of the modernist platform, represented a considerable challenge, but not the only one.

GLOBALIZATION AND THE DECLINE OF THE STATE

By the 1990s, however, the assumed centrality of the nation-state as the unit of analysis in comparative education was under increasing challenge. This was reflected in the theoretical literature and politically in terms of the changing boundaries of both the nation-state, and our understanding.[59] Diffuse international economic and political changes at the end of the twentieth century pushed older conventions aside. Both centripetal and centrifugal forces substantially reshaped the boundaries of postcommunist Eastern Europe,[60] as new regional trading blocs, in part sustained by international trading and political agreements, challenged the traditional emphasis on the nation-state. The European Union, North American Free Trade Agreement (now the Free Trade Agreement of the Americas, and including Latin America), and Asia Pacific Economic Community often, interestingly, spawned educational infrastructure to support internationalization of education, at least within their region.[61]

Despite considerable divergence about the meaning of globalization, and a fair degree of hyperbole, some definite trends were discernible, notably the massive global movement of capital within a more deregulated international economic environment, and the huge growth in international communications. Each of these has had an impact on fostering more regional economic alliances, as well as on global manufacturing and financial enterprises.[62] The process of internationalizing previously more nationally based economies grew apace, while the massive growth in electronic forms of communication also represented a challenge to national borders (including in education), at least for those who had access to the technology.[63] Despite much of the rhetoric about a reorientation of understanding toward developing broader forms of understanding not bounded by the nation-state (as Roland Robertson put it, making "the world a central hermeneutic"),[64] and notwithstanding substantial differences over the real meaning of "globalization," it is possible to argue that the effects are principally economic rather than theoretical.

Analysts such as Samuel Huntington have postulated a "clash of civilizations"[65] between, for example, Islam, China, and the West, which has overtaken the preceding era of nationalist rivalries. In fact, the supposedly newer thesis of the clash of civilizations had more in common with theories of nationalist rivalries, or even earlier eras, than was usually supposed: both were predicated on an essentialism that is simply mistaken.[66] In Huntington's case, neither "the USSR" nor "Islam" is a unitary entity:

> The key weakness of Huntington's analysis is that, like the early Cold Warriors, he has fallen into the trap of depicting the enemy as a monolith. . . . At the outset of the Cold War, the Communist countries were depicted as the vanguard of a movement dedicated to the triumph of an international communist utopia. . . . In like fashion, Huntington depicts the Islamic countries as part of a wider pan-Islamic movement, united in their hostility to the West and the United States.[67]

As with globalization, it is unarguably the case that more sophisticated analysis is needed here. It is important that scholars of comparative education contribute to such clarification and analysis because, in the midst of this rapidly changing scene and despite the substantial implications of both globalization and the clash of civilizations thesis for comparative education, they are yet to figure all that largely in the literature. Approaches that integrate political economy perspectives with education and social theory are more likely to be successful here, particularly if combined with a multilevel approach,[68] which does not merely examine the effects at an international, macro level but also investigates local, small-scale effects. The story of globalization is written at the local level.

Equally, and notable exceptions notwithstanding,[69] it can fairly be said that theorizing the implications of the changing role of the state for education, as well as correlative issues such as privatization, has, in the 1980s and 1990s, remained underdeveloped in the literature of comparative education, relative to the collection of case studies that chart the effects of privatization, including (at times) access and equity in education.[70] Some scholars from within (and rather more from without) comparative education have marked the effects of the progressive erosion of the former postwar democratic settlement in advanced capitalist states such as the United Kingdom, Europe, and Australia, including its implications for education.[71] But fewer have located such accounts within the context of a systematic analysis of changes in the form of the state[72] and in international economic patterns and relations (see chapter 10 in this volume). Given the significance of the shift from what has been characterized as the welfare state (in which it was widely accepted that it was the state's responsibility to ensure that good-quality education, health, and welfare were available to all) to what has been termed the competition state (the state intervenes only to heighten national or international economic competitiveness, leaving individual success or failure as an individual or family responsibility),[73] this general omission is somewhat disturbing. Arguably, thoroughgoing analyses of this development have much to offer studies of educational change, not merely in the industrialized West but also in the former socialist nations and in various Third World contexts.

FROM POSITIVISM TO POST-ISM

Many of the changes described above, however, left major assumptions of modernism largely unchallenged. But if an adherence to many of the principles of positivism characterized mainstream modernist comparative education of the two or three decades after World War II, the gradual growth of poststructuralist thought in the West toward the end of the century gave rise to challenging postmodern critiques in the social sciences and, somewhat later, in comparative education.

What is meant by poststructuralist thought? Briefly, structuralist theories such as (structural) functionalism and the more determinist forms of Marxism emphasize the central explanatory role of structure in determining societal outcomes. The central importance that such theories accord to the social system means that individuals were powerless to struggle against a powerful, deterministic set of structures that shaped their social destinies. In a sense, it can be argued that such theories were akin to the religious doctrine of fatalism, which held that people were powerless to struggle against the fate that God had allocated them. Against such views, poststructuralist theories, including those in education, hold that social reality was shaped by people and the meanings they variously allocated to the world they inhabited. Social reality is, according to such views, contingent, localized, and a matter of negotiation. It is not monolithic but was constructed in different ways, according to how people and groups positioned themselves in the world. In principle, such views allocated more space to "agency" (people's ability to act upon the social world to change it) as compared with the more deterministic social theories described above, which emphasized "structure." Poststructuralist theories are quite mistrustful of the pretensions of large-scale "grand theory," which purport to explain how society works overall.

Work by scholars such as Rolland Paulston, David Coulby, Coulby and Crispin Jones, Peter Ninnes and Sonia Mehta, and Robert Cowen[74] has undermined many prior assumptions, such as the objectivity of knowledge or the centrality of scientific methodology, upon which much recent research in comparative education had been predicated. Postcolonialism too has begun to exert an influence, if perhaps more indirectly, and the joint insistence on heterogeneity and mistrust of grand theories informs both, and poststructuralist thought generally: "The post-colonial distrust of the liberal-humanist rhetoric of progress and universalizing master narratives has obvious affinities with poststructuralism."[75] Nonetheless, there are significant differences between postmodernism and postcolonialism, which are explored below.

Postmodern critiques are relatively recent in comparative education, effectively dating from Rust's Comparative and International Education Society presidential address of 1991.[76] This late onset of the debate within comparative education (and indeed the relative lack of engagement since) is interesting, given the potential consonance of the supposed insistence upon heterogeneity by postmodern critics and the supposed centrality of cultural diversity to comparative education.

As with Winnie the Pooh, however, all was not what it seemed.[77] On one hand, even Ninnes and Mehta's most recent work of 2004 still essentializes other theoretical traditions, refusing to acknowledge critical stances toward modernity, reason and rationalism, westernization, science (as institution and ideology), and the rise and dominance of capitalism, evident in much critical scholarship, both within comparative education and more broadly in social theory. On the other hand, just as I propose that modernism represented, *inter alia*, the triumph of science over diversity (including cultural diversity), so I will argue that postmodernism was less about the celebration of difference than was commonly supposed.

This was for two reasons, arguably. One of the original aspirations of postmodernity was to site difference at the center stage of (social) theory in an effort to overcome the universalizing, monolithic tendencies of modernist thought. In itself this was laudable and a potentially valuable corrective to the closed tendency of modernism to hew out a unilinear path and to dismiss those who diverged from it as aberrant rather than different. As part of this celebration of difference, the aim to give voice to silenced ethnic and gender minorities was enunciated. Both of these aims were reasonable, given the record of modernism, in particular its intolerance of difference. Regrettably, however, they rapidly became overwhelmed by an increasingly arcane language, in which esoteric terminology and language games/tropes rendered these original intentions largely invisible and unintelligible. In practice, difference, like other social artifacts, became textualized and hence suppressed, buried under an avalanche of recondite discursive devices. It is one thing to underline the importance of language in describing social difference, but quite another to argue that there is nothing beyond language. Postmodernism falls into the latter camp and thus operates on an abstract (quasi-systemic) model of *opposition* and *difference* where those terms are deprived of all historical and experiential content, and treated, in effect, as linguistic artifacts, or products of discursive definition.[78] "There is . . . a danger of textualising gender, denying sexual specificity, or treating difference as merely a formal category rather than having an empirical and historical existence."[79] In other words, instead of confronting and opposing social distortions and the oppression and marginalization of particular social groups, as certain forms of Marxism and feminism had tried to do, postmodernism increasingly consigned difference to a linguistic artifact, remote from the everyday world and the concerns of those marginal groups they originally claimed to be interested in. Difference became "difference."

Second, postmodernism's celebration of image(s) meant that it at times became more concerned with style rather than substance; with how things looked rather than with their importance. Having divested itself of a solid standpoint from which to analyze events, postmodernism was rendered unable to develop a position from which to make ethical judgments. Knowledge is divorced from commitment (the latter of which is reduced to the status of one value, among a potentially limitless number of others), and knowledge and meaning are made devoid of ethics.[80] Thus even if difference is encompassed (and there are considerable doubts about this), there is no longer any basis to judge this difference. As an abstract category without a moral base, the "difference" expressed by white supremacists such as the American Nazi Party is of the same inherent worth as that of the cultures they seek to oppress, such as African Americans, Jews, and Aboriginal Australians. Indeed, in some recent works, the only resort with which to complete the promise of postmodernity has been to connect it to some of the moral stances of feminism and African-American literature, as in the work of Henry Giroux.[81] Some theorists of postmodernism make much of its capacity to map the terrain.[82] By eschewing any moral compass, however, postmodern theories leave us unable to chart the course of change.

Vis-à-vis the so-called modernization of Third World states, postmodern theories (of which there are now many) appear to offer substantial critiques of functionalist modernization theories, in particular of the supposed correspondence of the modernization process with westernization and the notion that the social and economic progress of Third World states depends on advanced science and technology, as well as scientific modes of rationality. Postmodern critiques of the totalizing reason of science or other modes of universalistic reason seem to offer space for alternative views of development and for marginalized groups to position themselves more centrally in development processes. Increasingly, however, the lived reality of oppressed rural peasantry is not seen, except though several layers of arcane and obscure, densely theoretic forms of language that render the experience of those individuals unrecognizable to themselves, and invisible to other readers. Not only is the line between people's history and fictional accounts blurred, as Raymond Morrow and Carlos Albert Torres argue, but also the whole notion of domination and hegemony, by which forms of oppression have been identified and opposed, is muted, if not abandoned. Instead, according to theorists such as John O'Neill, Christopher Norris and others, people are dis-attached from their history, floating free in a semiotic world of myriad images and signs. Equity and equality, according to postmodern theories, make up just one set of values, alongside all other sets of values. They indeed may have less importance than most, given the individualizing tendencies of postmodern theories, which tend to reject acting for the collective good. Ultimately, this offers little by way of substantive critique of the concrete processes of modernity, which often destabilize long-standing cultural traditions (e.g., matriarchy) and oppress less powerful social groups (e.g., small landholders and peasants). A more progressive resolution can be achieved by allying postmodern critiques with forms of feminism and race: "Few theorists of race and gender would succumb to throwing out general theories of domination in the name of a pluralist celebration of difference."[83]

POSTMODERN, POSTCOLONIAL, AND THE "OTHER"?

As indicated above, postcolonial theories share with postmodern critiques an insistence on the centrality of difference. However, work by scholars such as Edward Said, Gayatri Spivak, Homi Bhaba, and Tejaswini Niranjana[84] forms some sort of corrective to the moral vacuum at the heart of postmodernity by incorporating the political dimension into their understanding of difference. Central to this work is both a focus on, and critique of, hegemonic processes within colonialism and postcolonial experiences, and opposition to the domination of male, white, heterosexual, and Western forms of reason and to practices associated with this form of logic. Hence Braithwaite rather than Baudrillard, Fanon rather than Foucault. Niranjana, for example offers an extended discourse on the ways in which translation is used as a medium to create an exotic and uncivilized "other" in need of the fruits of Western civilization, including the taming influence of education. In this sense she is an ally of Edward Said, whose analysis of orientalism also showed how the process of translation was deployed in colonies such as India "to gather in, to rope off, to domesticate the Orient and thereby to turn it into a province of European learning."[85]

Comparativists are familiar with the problems of translation. The experience of lawyer-novelist Louis Begley, who encountered some of his own characters in a recent translation (in a language with which he was familiar), strikes a chord:

> Not so long ago, I came across some of my personages in a translation, who were standing on the sidewalk, outside their New York City hotel, in the hope that someone would bring them a lemonade with a great deal of water in it. "How strange," I said to myself, and checked the original, to find out that in English the poor chumps were waiting for their stretch limo.[86]

The confusion of *lemo* for *limo* is one of the less serious problems of translation, which, as Niranjana indicates, can also reveal implicit or explicit strategies of portraying the other. Indeed, representations of the other often reveal as much about the interests of the translator as they do about the translated, and need to be understood in the context of strategies of intercultural communications[87] and the effects of colonialism and imperialism.[88] An illustration Niranjana provides of the work of eighteenth-century scholar and translator (Sir) William Jones is based not so much on his direct translations of key Indian classics as on his prefaces, speeches, poetry, and the like. Finally, Niranjana distills the most significant elements of Jones's work into the following:

1. The need for translation by the European, since the natives are unreliable interpreters of their own laws and culture;
2. The desire to be a lawgiver, to give the Indians their "own" laws; and
3. The desire to "purify" Indian culture and speak on its behalf.[89]

In these strategies are revealed key elements of the discourse of colonialism, in which the colonial other is characterized as a "submissive, indolent nation, unable to appreciate the fruits of freedom, desirous of being ruled by an absolute power . . . [and] incapable of civil liberty."[90] It is but a small step from here to justify the perpetuation of paternalistic forms of administration and governance that serve to speak for the colonial other and keep them in their place. By recognizing this distortion of power as a key motif of colonialism, postcolonial theories are better placed to oppose such paternalistic and oppressive practices.

A NEW COMPARATIVE EDUCATION FOR A NEW MILLENNIUM?

Given the argument above about the failures of scientism in comparative education, the absence of ethics in postmodernism, and the fissiparous social and economic effects of globalization at the end of the twentieth century, it can reasonably be argued that the time is ripe to develop new foundations for the field, as it faces a new millennium.[91] Indeed, it can be argued that it is incumbent on comparativists to not stand by, as passive observers, faced with an ever more fractured social and economic world, characterized by privatization, "user pays" ideologies in education, and increasing gaps between the "haves" and "have nots" in many societies. As social scientists we must recognize that theories are not neutral, and that a stance based on a specious pretense of objectivity is untenable. As comparativists, we either take the side of the marginalized and dispossessed, or deepen their problems.

What would such a renovated comparative education look like? Elsewhere, I have outlined the constituents of such a new vision for the field.[92] It is, first and foremost, a moral vision, in which the *telos* of the social good is still a key value, as it was for the ancient Greeks, and during the Renaissance. Reasserting a more democratic ethos for comparative education, as some in the field have begun to do,[93] should aim at developing a more mutualist, reciprocal account of intercultural relations, resisting the technicism of earlier scientistic accounts, and rejecting the moral hole at the centre of postmodernity. In so doing, such traditions offer a critical account of modernity—breaking free of some of its problematic legacy, while retaining those elements that still have something to offer a new millennium.[94]

The model sketched here draws on both hermeneutics (a form of theory originally based around textual interpretation) and critical theory. Each resists any reduction to instrumentalist accounts of understanding. According to both hermeneutics and critical theory, no set of technical steps, no given formula, will guarantee the answer. Indeed, both schools of thought have shaped themselves, at least in part, in opposition to such a naive belief.[95]

There are several methodological precepts which are broadly held in common, and that can serve as the basis for a renewed comparative education, and perhaps intercultural relations more generally. Perhaps the first of these principles is a refusal of *techne*, and its instrumental account of knowledge, reason, and being, within the positivist tradition.[96] By contrast to the emphasis on control, mastery, and manipulation, of knowledge and society, on the part of both natural and social sciences, both hermeneutics and critical theory uphold a respect for otherness, and the individual other. Unlike the positivist account of knowledge, where the other is regarded as an "object . . . of study,"[97] both critical theory and hermeneutics uphold a principle of the other as subject, with the same rights and privileges that one would expect to be granted to oneself. This openness to difference is not merely of a textual kind, as in some forms of postmodernity, but a principled openness: to cultural differences of gender, race, and class.

Scientistic pretensions to objectivity and universal validity are here seen as ill-founded. Presuppositionlessness, of the kind advanced by both Descartes, and the phenomenological tradition, is on this account, illusory. On the contrary, knowledge is informed by interest, and there is no initial understanding which escapes the need for pre-judgment:

> This is exactly the idea that Gadamer questions: could there ever be any understanding of tradition, of a text or a society, devoid of any preconception or fore-meaning. If this were true, reason would constitute the ultimate source of authority without any historical limit imposed upon it; reason would become Absolute Reason.[98]

Nor are the natural sciences immune from this critique, despite the pretensions of some scientistic epistemologies to objectivity and value-freedom: "Similarly, we can view as prejudice the way in which scientific programs and their technological implementation operate under old convictions of 'mastering' and 'exploiting' nature for the benefit of humanity."[99]

More than a century ago, the German theorist Dilthey already railed against such universalist pretensions, arguing that no universalist science could answer real pedagogical questions which were, by contrast, concrete and historical, and demanded to be answered in the same form. Indeed, Dilthey saw such universalist pretensions of objectivist science as evidence of the relative *wissenschaftliche Rückständigkeit* (scientific backwardness) of education, in comparison with other disciplines which had already recognized the historical articulation of thought.

Historicity, then, is a further key point held in common here: both critical theory and critical hermeneutics insist that the process of understanding is fundamentally historical, not abstract and idealist. Any understanding must begin with certain interests or prejudices, and is itself situated in a specific historical context, and a specific tradition: "We share the prejudices of our tradition."[100] Both theoretical strains equally proceed from the recognition of a more mutual relation between self and other in the human sciences than that which obtains in the natural sciences: "the 'subject to object' epistemological relationship firmly established in the natural sciences could not do justice to the 'subject to subject' relationship attained between the interpreter and the historical tradition in the human sciences."[101]

Another common building block for a renewed comparative education is the rejection of the binary poles that underpin mainstream Western epistemology: science versus speculation, male versus female, fact versus value, mind versus body. Both critical theory and hermeneutics espouse a more relational form of understanding, in which, for example, knowledge is related to social existence, a position far more in tune with contemporary sociology of knowledge than the fixed opposites of scientistic epistemologies.

There are some differences between hermeneutics and critical theory, however. A more critical form of hermeneutics, as defended by Habermas and others, is distinct from more conservative forms in two ways, each of which have implications for how education may be understood, for our understanding of cultural difference, and for relations between "self" and "other." Habermas importantly argues, for example, that interpretation which is not critical will tend to reproduce the very social conditions which give rise to misunderstandings, and social distortions: "A non-critical understanding simply continues, reiterates, and reproduces tradition, cultural values, ideology and power structures."[102]

The limits of language, and its role in interpretation, form a second point of difference. Critical hermeneutics holds that extralinguistic forms of domination, in particular forces such as social class and economic location, also have the capacity to significantly influence or condition interpretation and communication. Habermas "holds that language is dependent on social processes that cannot be reduced to language,"[103] therefore interpretations may be occluded by power structures and material relations in society. A key difference here is the role ascribed to critical reflection in unmasking these social distortions, and perhaps overcoming them: "Critical reflection puts the interpreter in charge of those conditions which he [*sic*] had been passively and unconsciously suffering."[104] This is indeed the role of ideology critique—for Habermas, then, it is possible to use self-reflection to break the bounds of tradition, whereas for Hans Georg Gadamer, tradition forms the limit to our understanding.

Here we see the connection to a reconstructed modernity, in that the purpose of critical reflection remains emancipation, which may mean that existing, oppressive power structures may need to be dismantled. This process of emancipation, however, presupposes mutuality and reciprocity: "in a process of enlightenment there can only be participants."[105] It is here that a critical theory of society and critical hermeneutics each display their Enlightenment heritage, and yet break free from it in important ways. It is acknowledged that in the Enlightenment, the "world was conceived as mathematicized and systematized, but the very linkage of an idea of reason as universal to an idea of reason as domination . . . gave rise to new myths and, in time, to new and ever more effective modes of domination."[106] This recognition, however, does not necessitate abandoning the Enlightenment heritage altogether; on the contrary, the need to retain the connection between human *praxis* and cognitive action is still important, and is seen in certain contemporary feminisms, and critical accounts of science, for example that of Feyerabend.

The implications both for educational processes and relationships, and for intercultural relations are now apparent. One cannot remain an impartial and uncommitted observer, "one who stands apart . . . unaffected, but rather, as one united by a specific bond with the other, (s)he thinks with the other and undergoes the situation with him (her)."[107] This means that the other, whether teacher, student, ethnic minority, or streetchild, may not have their language and needs filtered or translated by those who wish to interpret their reality for them. The preservation of the "intersubjectivity of possible action-orienting mutual understanding"[108] is central to this philosophy, which resists the domination of an instrumentalist code of reason and practice. Rather than Huntingdon's clash of civilizations, such a renewed comparative education postulates a dialogue between civilizations.

It is in this sense that a critical hermeneutics is, first and foremost, a normative theory, which proceeds dialogically, whether in the arena of education or intercultural relations. A comparative education based on such foundations will not be silenced in the face of the actively increasing social and economic differentiation and exclusion that characterize the new millennium. Insisting upon mutual and reciprocal relations, it stands opposed to the imposition of structural adjustment policies in education and society, where these violate principles of justice and freedom, and stands with the other, the dispossessed and marginalized,[109] rendered invisible by the untrammeled reign of modern science and its logic, the blasé stance of forms of postmodernity, and the ever widening influence of economic globalization.[110]

History can be a willing teacher—if we are willing to learn. The Enlightenment assisted the replacement of the older Christian religions, based on faith, with the revealed religion of Bacon, Descartes, Galileo, and Newton, based on a blend of empiricism and codified rationality. The priests of old were replaced with the new, and often equally doctrinaire, priesthood of science, thereby failing in many ways to fulfill the promise of the Enlighteners to free humanity from the constraints of a hidebound social order, and sclerotic epistemology. Despite its revolutionary potential, science, instead of heralding a new rational order of equality and human rights, was often pressed into service to sustain existing stratified societies, at times providing the basis for making the existing social hierarchy more scientific. Nonetheless, the Enlightenment was the era in which the dignity and rights of man[111] (if not yet entirely of women)[112] were clearly and passionately articulated. Although modernity did not fulfill its early promise, there was much positive potential that was available to be harnessed to the creation of a more just social order.

The contemporary rush by theorists of both left and right to jettison all the features of modernity shows little appreciation of the complexity of this history and to some extent becomes captive to a naive understanding of it. The simplistic critiques of the history of epistemology characteristic of much poststructural thought are most clearly evident in the literature of postmodernism. Here modernist thought is often mistakenly oversimplified and demonized as a field littered with grand, broken dreams, which were responsible for much of the problems and misdirections of late twentieth-century humanity. The wholesale retreat from questions of social justice (dismissed as just another such dream) therefore follows quite logically, if mistakenly, from such misconceived assumptions. As argued above, however, there is much that may be salvaged from the detritus of modernity, and much from its agenda that needs urgent and powerful rearticulation at the beginning of the new millennium, when such economically and socially fissiparous tendencies as neoliberalism, fundamentalisms, globalization, and xenophobia are widening the already existing gap between rich and poor, white and black, rural and urban, male and female, both within and among nations and regions of the world.[113]

Yet too much poststructural thought, in particular postmodernity, leaves us rudderless in a sea of blasé ironic detachment. We drift along as passive observers of the social world, observing the rising tide of imagery but unable to distinguish stark images of Third World poverty, on the one hand, from the star-studded funeral rites of Gianni Versace or Princess Diana, for example, on the other. Images all.

The methodological trajectory traced above shows that the preoccupation with making a science of comparative education of the 1960s largely fulfilled its modernist, positivist mandate, despite some oppositional crosscurrents. Although poststructuralist theories were slower to have an influence in comparative education than in other social sciences, the final decade of the twentieth century finally revealed some of their effects. I argue, however, that postmodernity is an unsatisfactory response to some of the admitted shortcomings of modernist theories and that postcolonialism is in many respects a more solid starting point for comparative methodology—not just because it sites difference at center stage but also because it rejects speaking for the other.

Postcolonial theories form one base from which such an ethical stance could be mounted. As argued above, another standpoint,[114] also based on a refusal of paternalism and an adoption of the values of mutuality and reciprocity, is found in social theorists such as Gadamer and Habermas and could equally act as an important starting point for intercultural theories such as comparative education.[115]

NOTES

1. Imre Lakatos, "The Methodology of Scientific Research Programmes," in Imre Lakatos, *Philosophical Papers*, vol. 1 (Cambridge: Cambridge University Press, 1974).

2. Nicholas Hans, *Comparative Education: A Study of Factors and Traditions* (London: Routledge and Kegan Paul, 1949).

3. Isaac Kandel, *Studies in Comparative Education* (London: George Harrap, 1933); Isaac Kandel, *The New Era in Education* (London: George Harrap, 1955).

4. Friedrich Schneider, *Triebkräfte der pädagogik der Völker* (Salzburg: Otto Muller, 1947); Schneider, *Vergleichende erziehungswissenschaft* (Heidelberg: Quelle and Meyer, 1961).

5. See Brian Holmes, *Problems in Education: A Comparative Approach* (London: Routledge, 1965); Holmes, *Comparative Education: Some Considerations of Method* (London: Allen and Unwin, 1981).

6. Harold Noah and Max Eckstein, *Towards a Science of Comparative Education* (London: Macmillan, 1969).

7. George Bereday, *Comparative Method in Education* (New York: Holt, Rinehart, and Winston, 1964); George Bereday, "Reflections on Comparative Method in Education 1964–6," in *Scientific Investigations in Comparative Education*, ed. Max Eckstein and Harold Noah (New York: Macmillan, 1969).

8. See, *inter alia*, G. H. von Wright, *Explanation and Understanding* (Ithaca, N.Y.: Cornell University Press, 1971); and Anthony Giddens, "Positivism and Its Critics," in *A History of Sociological Analysis*, ed. Tom Bottomore and Robert Nisbet (London: Heinemann, 1979); Jürgen Habermas, "Technology and Science as 'Ideology,'" in *Toward a Rational Society* (London: Heinemann, 1970). Despite corrosive criticism, such techniques still flourish, albeit less commonly. For a more egregious example, see George Psacharopoulos, "Comparative Education: From Theory to Practice, or Are You A Neo:/* or B/*ist?" *Comparative Education Review* 34, no. 3 (1990): 369–80. The World Bank's adherence to a technicist and quasi-empiricist model, currently based on rate-of-return analyses, is another example: see, *inter alia*, Phillip Jones, "On World Bank Education Financing," *Comparative Education* 33, no. 1 (1997): 117–29, and his earlier *World Bank Financing of Education* (London: Routledge, 1992); Steve Klees, "The World Bank and Educational Policy: Ideological and Inefficient" (paper presented at the *Comparative and International Education Society* annual conference, Williamsburg, Va., March 1996); and Joel Samoff, "Which Priorities and Strategies for Education?" *International Journal of Educational Development* 16 (1996): 249–71.

9. Robert Cowen, "Last Past the Post: Comparative Education, Modernity and Perhaps Post-modernity," *Comparative Education* 32, no. 2 (1997): 151–70.

10. Jürgen Habermas, *A Theory of Communicative Action* (London: Heinemann, 1984), 147.

11. Herbert Marcuse, *One-Dimensional Man* (New York: Sphere, 1968).

12. See Alfred Schutz, *The Problem of Social Reality*, vol. 1 of *Collected Papers* (The Hague: Martinus Nijhoff, 1964); Alfred Schutz, *The Phenomenology of the Social World* (Evanston, Ill.: Northwestern University Press, 1967); Alfred Schutz, "Commonsense and Scientific Interpretations of Human Action," *Philosophical and Phenomenological Research* 14, no. 3 (1953): 3–47.

13. Max Horkheimer and Theodor Adorno, *The Dialectic of Enlightenment* (New York: Continuum, 1972).

14. Edmund Husserl, *Phenomenology and the Crisis of European Philosophy* (New York: Harper, 1965); Edmund Husserl, *Cartesian Meditations*, trans. D. Cairns (The Hague: Martinus Nijhoff, 1960).

15. Wilhelm Dilthey, *Gesammelte schriften*, vol. 9, *Pädagogik* (Leipzig: Teubner Verlag, 1934); Wilhelm Dilthey, "Über die möglichkeit einer allgemeingültigen pädagogischen wissenschaft," in *Gesammelte schriften*, vol. 6 (Leipzig: Teubner Verlag, 1926).

16. Thomas Kuhn, *The Structure of Scientific Revolutions* (Chicago: University of Chicago Press, 1970); and Thomas Kuhn, "Reflections on My Critics," *Criticism and the Growth of Knowledge*, ed. Imre Lakatos and Allan Musgrave (Cambridge: Cambridge University Press, 1974).

17. Paul Feyerabend, *Against Method* (London: New Left Books, 1975); Paul Feyerabend, "On the Critique of Scientific Reason," in *Method and Appraisal in the Physical Sciences*, ed. C. Howson (Cambridge: Cambridge University Press, 1976); Paul Feyerabend, *Science in a Free Society* (London: New Left Books, 1978). For a more social scientific view, see also Habermas, "Technology and Science as Ideology," and his later *Knowledge and Human Interests*, 2nd ed. (London: Heinemann, 1978).

18. Feyerabend, *Science in a Free Society*, 98. "The validity, usefulness, adequacy of popular standards can be tested only by research that violates them" (Feyerabend, *Science in a Free Society*, 35).

19. See, for example, Roger R. Woock, "Integrated Social Theory and Comparative Education," *International Review of Education* 27, no. 4 (1981): 411–26; and Jerome Karabel and A. H. Halsey, "Educational Research: A Review and Interpretation," in *Power and Ideology in Education* (Oxford: Oxford University Press, 1977).

20. Auguste Comte, *The General Philosophy of Auguste Comte*, 2 vols., trans. Harriet Martineau (London: Trübner, 1853); Auguste Comte, *A General View of Positivism*, trans. J. Bridges (Paris: 1848, Academic Reprints, n.d.).

21. Emile Durkheim, *The Rules of Sociological Method* (London: Collier Macmillan, 1964).

22. Talcott Parsons, *The Structure of Social Action* (New York: Free Press, 1949); Talcott Parsons, *The Social System* (Glencoe, Ill.: Free Press, 1951); Talcott Parsons, *Societies: Evolutionary and Comparative Perspectives* (New Jersey: Prentice-Hall, 1966).

23. Giddens, "Positivism," in *A History of Sociological Analysis*, ed. Tom Bottomore and Robert Nisbet (London: Heinemann, 1979).

24. F. Bacon, *Of the Proficience and Advancement of Learning* (London: J. W. Parker, 1861), 14. Note that "maniable" is not used in all editions.

25. Tejaswini Niranjana, *Siting Translation: History, Poststructuralism and the Colonial Context* (Berkeley: University of California Press, 1992), 11.

26. E. Tiryakin, "Emile Durkheim," in *A History of Sociological Analysis*, ed. Bottomore and Nisbet (London: Heinemann, 1979), 188.

27. Frederick Harbison and Charles Myers, *Education, Manpower, and Economic Growth* (London: McGraw-Hill, 1964), 1.

28. Jürgen Habermas, *Knowledge and Human Interests*, 2nd ed. (London: Heinemann, 1978); Marcuse, *One-Dimensional Man*.

29. David McClelland, *The Achieving Society* (London: Van Nostrand, 1961), 174.

30. Philip Coombs, *The World Educational Crisis: A Systems Analysis* (Oxford: Oxford University Press, 1968).

31. Harbison and Myers, *Education, Manpower and Economic Growth*; and F. Harbison and C. Myers, *Education and Manpower* (London: McGraw-Hill, 1965).

32. McClelland, *Achieving Society*, 174.

33. Anthony R. Welch, "The Functionalist Tradition in Comparative Education," *Comparative Education* 21, no. 1 (1985): 11.

34. For further detail, see Welch, "The Functionalist Tradition"; and Anthony R. Welch, "La ciencia sedante: El funcionalismo como base para la investigación en educación comparada," in *Educación comparada: Teorías, investigaciones, perspectivas*, ed. J. Schriewer and F. Pedro (Barcelona: Herder, 1991).

35. Isaac Kandel, *The Making of Nazis* (New York: Teachers College Press, 1935).

36. Brian Holmes, ed., *Educational Policy and the Mission Schools* (London: Routledge, 1967).

37. Holmes, *Problems in Education*.

38. Harold Noah, "Defining Comparative Education: Conceptions," in *Relevant Methods in Comparative Education*, ed. Reginald Edwards, Brian Holmes, and John Van de Graff (Hamburg: UNESCO, 1973), 114.

39. Richard Heyman, "Towards a Non-Science of Comparative Education" (paper presented at the annual conference of the Comparative and International Education Society, Ann Arbor, Mich., March 1979), 1–17.

40. "Every procedure which seems to lock in evidence, thus to claim a level of adequacy, can itself be subjected to the same kind of analysis that will in turn produce yet another indefinite arrangement of new particulars or a rearrangement of established particulars." Aaron Cicourel, *Cognitive Sociology* (London: Penguin, 1974), 124.

41. Anthony Giddens, *New Rules of Sociological Method* (London: Hutchinson, 1976), 166.

42. Richard Heyman, "Ethnomethodology: Some Suggestions for the Sociology of Education," *Journal of Educational Thought* 14, no. 1 (1980): 46. In the same article Heyman refers to further essentialist claims to provide "knowledge about education" or "what schooling is all about."

43. Anthony Welch, "A Critique of Quotidian Reason in Comparative Education," *Journal of International and Comparative Education* 1 (1986): 37–62.

44. Vandra Masemann, "Critical Ethnography in the Study of Comparative Education," *Comparative Education Review* 26, no. 1 (1982): 1–14; Vandra Masemann, "Ways of Knowing," *Comparative Education Review* 34, no. 4 (1990): 465–73.

45. Masemann, "Critical Ethnography," 1.

46. Vandra Masemann, "Critical Ethnography in the Study of Comparative Education," in *New Approaches to Comparative Education*, ed. Philip Altbach and Gail Kelly (Chicago: University of Chicago Press, 1986), 23.

47. Paul Willis, *Learning to Labor: How Working Class Kids Get Working Class Jobs* (Westmead, U.K.: Saxon House, 1977), 194, cited in Masemann, "Critical Ethnography," 23.

48. Masemann, "Critical Ethnography," 23.

49. Robert Arnove, *Philanthropy and Cultural Imperialism: The Foundations at Home and Abroad* (Bloomington: Indiana University Press, 1980).

50. Martin Carnoy, *Education as Cultural Imperialism* (New York: Longmans, 1974); Martin Carnoy, "Education for Alternative Development," in *New Approaches to Comparative Education*, ed. Philip Altbach and Gail Kelly (Chicago: University of Chicago Press, 1986), 73–90. Little has changed, it seems: in the aftermath of the Asian financial crisis of the late 1990s, the World Bank admitted that their interventions had deepened the crisis.

51. Andre Gunder Frank, "The Development of Underdevelopment," in *Dependence and Underdevelopment: Latin America's Political Economy*, ed. James Cockcroft, Andre Gunder Franck, and Dale Johnson (New York: Doubleday/Anchor, 1972), 3–18; Andre Gunder Frank, *Capitalism and Underdevelopment in Latin America* (New York: Monthly Review Press, 1969).

52. Immanuel Wallerstein, *The Modern World System* (New York: Academic Press, 1979).

53. Philip Altbach and Gail Kelly, eds., *Education and Colonialism* (New York: Longmans, 1978); see also the second revised edition, *Education and the Colonial Experience* (New Brunswick: Transaction, 1984). Katherine Jensen wrote the chapter on internal colonialism, "Civilization and Assimilation in the Education of American Indians." The work alluded to earlier was by Harold Wolpe, "The Theory of Internal Colonialism: The South African Case," in *Beyond the Sociology of Development*, ed. Ivar Oxaal, Tony Barnett, and David Booth (London: Routledge and Kegan Paul, 1975), 229–52. Theories of internal colonialism have since been used to analyze the education of other indigenous minorities: Anthony Welch, "Aboriginal Education as Internal Colonialism: The Schooling of an Indigenous Minority in Australia," *Comparative Education* 24, no. 2

(1988): 203–17. See also the relevant chapter in Anthony Welch, *Class, Culture and the State in Australian Education: Reform or Crisis?* (New York: Peter Lang, 1997).

54. Robert Arnove, "Comparative Education and World Systems Analysis," in *Comparative Education Review* 24, no. 1 (1980): 48–62.

55. Arnove, "Comparative Education," 49.

56. Philip Altbach, "Servitude of the Mind? Education, Dependency, and Neocolonialism," in *Comparative Education,* ed. Philip Altbach, Robert Arnove, and Gail Kelly (New York: Macmillan, 1982).

57. Altbach, "Servitude of the Mind," in *Comparative Education,* ed. Altbach, et al. (New York: Macmillan, 1982), 470.

58. Robin Burns and Anthony Welch, eds., *Contemporary Perspectives in Comparative Education* (New York: Garland, 1992). Published in Italian as *Prospettive contemporanee di educazione comparata* (Catania: Nova Muse, 2002).

59. See Kenichi Ohmae, *The Borderless World: Power and Strategy in the Interlinked Economy* (London: Fontana, 1991); Kenichi Ohmae, *End of the Nation State: The Rise of Regional Economies* (London: HarperCollins, 1995); Roland Robertson, "Mapping the Global Condition: Globalization as a Central Concept," in *Global Culture,* ed. Roland Robertson (London: Sage, 1994); Anthony Giddens, *Beyond Left and Right: The Future of Radical Politics* (Oxford: Polity, 1994).

60. Anthony Welch, "Class, Culture, and the State in Comparative Education," *Comparative Education* 29, no. 1 (1993): 7–28.

61. For some examples in higher education, see, *inter alia,* Anthony Welch and Brian Denman, "The Internationalization of Higher Education: Retrospect and Prospect," *Forum of Education* 1 (1997): 14–29. For more specific analyses of regional educational schemes, see, *inter alia,* Guy Neave, "The University of the Peoples of Europe: A Feasibility Study," in *The Open Door: Pan-European Academic Co-operation* (Bucharest: UNESCO European Center for Higher Education, 1991); Ulrich Teichler, *Experiences of ERASMUS Students, ERASMUS Monographs,* no. 13 (Kassel: Wissenschaftliches Zentrum für Berufs-und Hochschulforschung der Gesamthochschule Kassel, 1992); UNESCO, *Asia-Pacific Programme of Education for All* (APPEAL) (Bangkok: UNESCO Regional Office for Education in Asia and the Pacific, 1986); International Development Programme for Australian Universities (IDP), *Curriculum Development for Internationalization,* Australian Case Studies and Stocktake (Canberra: IDP, 1995).

62. See for example, Anna Lee Saxenian, *The New Argonauts: Regional Advantage in a Global Economy* (Cambridge, Mass.: Harvard University Press, 2006), and for the implications in comparative education, see Anthony Welch, "Diaspora Re-aspora: The Place of Place in Comparative Education," *Comparative Education Review,* (in press).

63. In 2002, for example, China introduced strict regulations on the kinds of information that may legally be accessed on the Internet. For the effects on China–Hong Kong relations, see Gerard Postiglione, "The Academic Profession in Hong Kong: Maintaining Global Engagement in the Face of National Integration," *Comparative Education Review* 42, no. 1 (1998): 30–45. For a wider discussion of the phenomenon, see, *inter alia,* Pasi Rutanen, "Learning Societies and Global Information Infrastructure (GII) Global Information Society (GIS)" (keynote speech delivered at the OECD/IMHE conference, *Institutional Strategies for Internationalization of Higher Education,* David C. Lam Institute, Hong Kong, December 1996).

64. Robertson, "Mapping the Global Condition," in *Global Culture,* ed. Roland Robertson (London: Sage, 1994), 19.

65. Samuel Huntington, *The Clash of Civilizations and the Remaking of World Order* (New York: Simon and Schuster, 1996).

66. The notion of an uncivilized and monolithic "other" arguably provided the major rationale for the twelfth-century Crusades, for example.

67. Syed Maswood, "The New 'Mother of All Clashes': Samuel Huntington and the Clash of Civilizations," *Asian Studies Review* 18, no. 1 (July 1994): 19.

68. Mark Bray and R. Murray Thomas, "Levels of Comparison in Educational Studies: Different Insights from Different Literatures and the Value of Multilevel Analyses," *Harvard Educational Review* 65, no. 3 (1995): 472–90.

69. Martin Carnoy, *The State and Political Theory* (Princeton, N.J.: Princeton University Press, 1984); Carlos Alberto Torres and Adrianna Puiggros, "The State and Public Education in Latin America," *Comparative Education Review* 35, no. 1 (1995): 1–27; Robert Arnove, "Neoliberal Education Policies in Latin America: Arguments in Favour and Against," in *Latin American Education*, ed. Carlos Alberto Torres and Adriana Puiggrás (Boulder, Colo.: Westview, 1997), 79–100; Anthony Welch, "Class, Culture, and the State"; and Anthony Welch, *Australian Education: Reform or Crisis?* (Sydney: Allen and Unwin, 1996). Also published as *Class, Culture, and the State in Australian Education: Reform or Crisis?* (New York: Peter Lang, 1997).

70. Ka-Ho Mok, "Privatization or Marketization: Educational Developments in Post-Mao China," *International Review of Education*, special double issue, "Tradition, Modernity, and Postmodernity in Comparative Education," 43, no. 5–6 (1998): 547–67; Gholam Abbas Tavassoli, K. Houshyar, and Anthony Welch, "The Struggle for Quality and Equality in Iranian Education: Problems, Progress and Prospects," in *Quality and Equality in Third World Education*, ed. Anthony Welch (New York: Garland, 2000).

71. See Anna Yeatman, "Corporate Managers and the Shift from the Welfare to the Competition State," *Discourse* 13, no. 2 (1993): 3–9. Within education, see *inter alia*, Roger Dale, "Globalization. A New Word for Comparative Education," in *Discourse Formation in Comparative Education*, ed. J. Schriewer (New York: Peter Lang, 2001), and Anthony Welch, "Making Education Policy," in R. Connell et al., *Sociology Education and Change* (Oxford: Oxford University Press, 2006).

72. See P. Cerny, *The Changing Architecture of Politics: Structure, Agency, and the State* (London: Sage, 1990); Claus Offe, "Ungovernability: On the Renaissance of Conservative Theories of Crisis," in *Observations on the Spiritual Situation of the Age*, ed. Jürgen Habermas (London: MIT Press, 1984); Claus Offe, "Interdependence, Difference, and Limited State Capacity," in *New Approaches to Welfare Theory*, ed. G. Drover et al. (Aldershot: Edward Elgar, 1993); Jürgen Habermas, *Legitimation Crisis* (Boston: Beacon, 1976); Michael Pusey, *Economic Rationalism in Canberra: A Nation Building State Changes Its Mind* (Cambridge: Cambridge University Press, 1991).

73. Anna Yeatman, *Bureaucrats, Technocrats: Femocrats and Essays on the Contemporary Australian State* (Sydney: Allen and Unwin, 1990); Cerny, *Changing Architecture*.

74. See Rolland Paulston, *Social Cartography: Mapping Social and Educational Change* (New York: Garland, 1966); Rolland Paulston and Martin Liebman, "An Invitation to Postmodern Social Cartography," *Comparative Education Review* 38, no. 2 (1994): 215–52; David Coulby, "Ethnocentricity, Post Modernity, and European Curricular Systems," *European Journal of Teacher Education* 18, nos. 2–3 (1995): 143–53; David Coulby and Crispin Jones, "Post-modernity, Education and European Identities," *Comparative Education* 32, no. 2 (1996): 171–85; Robert Cowen, "Last Past the Post: Comparative Education, Modernity, and Perhaps Post-modernity," *Comparative Education* 32, no. 2 (1996): 151–70; Peter Ninnes and Sonia Mehta, eds., *Re-Imagining Comparative Education. Postfoundational Ideas and Applications for Critical Times* (London: Routledge Falmer, 2004).

75. Niranjana, *Siting Translation*, 9. But there are differences as Bhaba has indicated: "If the interest in Postmodernism is limited to a celebration of the fragmentation of the 'grand narratives' of post Enlightenment rationalism, then, for all its excitement, it remains a profoundly parochial enterprise." Homi Bhaba, *The Location of Culture* (London: Routledge, 1994), 4.

76. Val Rust, "Postmodernism and Its Comparative Education Implications," *Comparative Education Review* 35, no. 1 (1991): 610–26.

77. Winnie the Pooh, it will be recalled, lived under the name of Sanders: that is, he had the name Sanders above his door, and he lived under it.

78. Christopher Norris, *The Truth about Postmodernism* (Oxford: Basil Blackwell, 1993).

79. Peter McLaren, "Schooling the Postmodern Body: Critical Pedagogy and the Politics of Enfleshment," in *Postmodernism, Feminism, and Cultural Politics*, ed. Henry Giroux (Albany: State University of New York Press, 1991), 144–73.

80. Norris, *Truth about Postmodernism*, 16–28. See also Ben Agger, *A Critical Theory of Public Life* (London: Falmer, 1991); and Robert Young, "Comparative Education and Post-modern Relativism," *International Review of Education*, special double issue, "Tradition, Modernity, and Postmodernity in Comparative Education," 43, no. 5–6 (1998): 497–505.

81. Giroux, ed., *Postmodernism*; and Henry Giroux, *Border Crossings: Cultural Workers and the Politics of Education* (London: Routledge, 1992).

82. Paulston, "Social Cartography."

83. R. Morrow and C. A. Torres, *Social Theory and Education: A Critique of Theories of Social and Cultural Reproduction* (Albany: State University of New York Press, 1995), 421.

84. Homi Bhaba, *Nation and Narration* (London: Routledge, 1991); Niranjana, *Siting Translation*. Gayatri Spivak, *A Critique of Postcolonial Reason: Toward a History of the Vanishing Present* (Cambridge: Harvard University Press, 1999). For a useful introduction to the work of both Bhabha and Spivak, see the relevant chapters in Henry Schwarz and Sangeeta Ray, eds., *A Companion to Post-colonial Studies* (Malden, Mass.: Blackwell, 2000), and for useful treatment of differences between postmodernism and postcolonialism, see in the same volume Ato Quayson, "Postcolonialism and Postmodernism," 87–111.

85. Edward Said, *Orientalism* (New York: Penguin, 1995), 78. See also the different contexts of each, and the centrality of the fight against perceived inequalities that is seen as distinguishing postcolonialism from postmodernism, Quayson, "Postcolonialism and Postmodernism," Henry Schwarz and Sangeeta Ray, eds., *A Companion to Post-colonial Studies* (Malden, Mass.: Blackwell, 2000), 94–97.

86. Gordon Bilney, "Why Do We Got a Problem with Some Words?" *Sydney Morning Herald*, May 24, 1997, 18.

87. See the chapter by Christine Fox in this volume, and also Robert Young, *Intercultural Communication: Pragmatics, Genealogy, Deconstruction* (Clevedon, U.K.: Multilingual Matters, 1996).

88. Edward Said, *Culture and Imperialism* (London: Vantage, 1994).

89. Niranjana, *Siting Translation*, 13.

90. Niranjana, *Siting Translation*, 14.

91. Anthony Welch, "New Times, Hard Times. Re-reading Comparative Education in a Time of Discontent," in *Discourse Formation in Comparative Education*, ed. Jürgen Schriewer (New York, Berne: Peter Lang, 2000).

92. For more detailed discussion of the need for a new, ethical comparative education in the face of globalization, see Anthony Welch, "Globalization, Post-modernity and the State. Comparative Education for a New Millennium," *Comparative Education*, 37, no. 4 (Special Issue on Comparative Education facing the New Millennium): 475–982.

93. As many of the contributors in this volume have, in various ways, tried to do. See also Noel McGinn, "Education, Democratization, and Globalization: A Challenge for Comparative Education," *Comparative Education Review* 40, no. 4, (1996): 341–57.

94. It will be evident that this is very much in the spirit of Ruth Hayhoe's recent presidential address, "Redeeming Modernity," *Comparative Education Review* 44, no. 4, (2000): 423–39.

95. Within hermeneutics, as Teigas indicates, "For Gadamer, hermeneutics does not provide a methodical procedure of understanding but instead clarifies the conditions which accompany any act of understanding" (Demetrius Teigas, *Knowledge and Hermeneutic Understanding*, Lewisburg, Ohio: Bucknell University Press, 1995, 41), while within critical theory, according to one of its more systematic theorists in education, "We must remember that critique is always limited, fragmentary, and unsure" (Robert Young, *A Critical Theory of Education. Habermas and our Children's Future*. London: Harvester, 1989: 70). Habermas too, resists the simplistic self-understand-

ing of a science which reduces itself to a technical formula. For his arguments in the debate between critical rationalists and critical theorists, see T. Adorno et al., *The Positivist Dispute in German Sociology* (London: Heinemann, 1976).

96. There is a parallel here to the critiques of positivist understanding and its effects in the social sciences. See, for example, A. Giddens, "Positivism," in Tom Bottomore and Robert Nisbet, *A History of Sociological Analysis* (London: Heinemann, 1979), and the earlier *Positivism and Sociology* (London: Heinemann, 1974). To some extent Gadamer's notion of tradition, which pre-forms our understanding, parallels Kuhn's notion of paradigm, in that both refer to socially concrete communities of understanding. See Thomas Kuhn, *The Structure of Scientific Revolutions* (Chicago: University of Chicago Press, 1970).

97. Maxine Greene, "Epistemology and Educational Research: The Influence of Recent Approaches to Knowledge," *Review of Research in Education* 20 (1994): 423–64.

98. Teigas, *Knowledge*, 37.

99. Teigas, *Knowledge*, 39.

100. Teigas, *Knowledge*, 41.

101. Teigas, *Knowledge and Hermeneutic Understanding*, 32.

102. S. Gallagher, *Hermeneutics and Education* (Albany: State University of New York Press, 1992), 241.

103. Gallagher, *Hermeneutics and Education*, 242.

104. Gallagher, *Hermeneutics and Education*, 243.

105. Gallagher, *Hermeneutics and Education*, 245, citing Jürgen Habermas, *Theory and Practice* (Boston: Beacon Press, 1974), 40.

106. Greene, "Epistemology and Educational Research," 429.

107. Greene, "Epistemology and Educational Research," 438, citing H-G Gadamer, "Hermeneutics and Social Science," *Cultural Hermeneutics* 2 (1975): 306.

108. Greene, "Epistemology and Educational Research," 440, citing Habermas, *Knowledge and Human Interests*, 191.

109. For an outline of a taxonomy of possible relations between self and other, including Gadamer's notion of *fusion of horizons*, see *inter alia*, Adrian Snodgrass, "Asian Studies and the Fusion of Horizons," *Asian Studies Review* 15, no. 3 (1992): 81–94, and in education, Anthony Welch, "Class, Culture and the State in Comparative Education," *Comparative Education* 29, no. 2 (1993): 7–28.

110. For more on this see, *inter alia*, Welch, "Globalisation, Postmodernity and the State," Anthony Welch and Ka-Ho Mok, "Conclusion: Deep Development or Deep Division," Ka-Ho Mok and Anthony Welch, eds., *Globalisation, Structural Adjustment and Educational Reforms in Asia and the Pacific* (London: Palgrave, 2002), and Anthony Welch, "Globalization, Structural Adjustment and Contemporary Educational Reforms in Australia. The Politics of Reform, or the Reform of Politics?" in Mok and Welch, *Globalisation*.

111. See, for example, Thomas Paine, *The Rights of Man* (London: J. S. Jordan, 1791) and also his *Common Sense* (London: H. D. Symonds, 1793), which were influential in eighteenth and early nineteenth-century debates in the United States about independence and democracy.

112. Mary Wollstonecraft, *A Vindication of the Rights of Woman* (London: J. M. Dent, 1929).

113. Arnove, "Neoliberal Education Policies"; A. Boron and Carlos Alberto Torres, "Education, Poverty, and Citizenship in Latin America: Poverty and Democracy," *Alberta Journal of Educational Research* 42, no. 2 (1996): 102–14; Anthony Welch, "Introduction: Quality and Equality in Third World Education," in *Quality and Equality in Third World Education*, ed. Anthony Welch (New York: Garland, 2000).

114. Adrian Snodgrass, "Asian Studies and the Fusion of Horizons," *Asian Studies Review* 15 (1992): 81–94; Welch, "Class, Culture, and the State."

115. See, for example, Hugh J. Silverman, ed., *Gadamer and Hermeneutics* (New York: Routledge, Chapman Hall, 1991); and Hans Georg Gadamer, *Truth and Method*, 2nd ed. (New York: Crossroad, 1989).

2

Institutionalizing International Influence

Joel Samoff

Education for all. A global objective that must be accomplished locally. In practice, we find not the globalization of responsibility for assuring access to education for all the world's learners, but rather the localization and internalization of internationally promulgated perspectives on education, even where education for all remains frustratingly beyond reach or is not in fact a high priority objective. The story here is a tale with several threads. Understanding international influences in education requires critical attention to the faith and enthusiasm of the evangelists of global goals and standards, to the roles of foreign aid and empirical research, and to the ways in which strategies intended to promote empowerment can become vehicles for undermining education reform and entrenching poverty.

To be sure, progress has been made. In at least some settings, international support has increased the number of children in school. In many settings, education innovation and reform depend on external support, and in a few, without that support there would be no textbooks or chalk. That support does not travel unaccompanied. Even where the progress is clear, the values, expectations, approaches, and analytic constructs that have become the global standard may in practice burden education development and impede education change well into the future. Let us trace the evolution of that process, concerned especially with the experiences of the world's poorer countries and particularly those that became independent during the second half of the twentieth century. A brief overview of the international context and its principal institutions provides the foundation for an exploration of the forms and consequences of international influences and the roles of research.

CONTEXT

Exploring commonalities amid diversity is a powerful tool for examining both what is—education in different places—and how we know what is—research and the sociology of knowledge. The field of comparative education frets about its central concerns, sometimes focused on what appear to be universal patterns and sometimes oriented toward

47

the unique and exotic. Its enduring challenge is to employ each perspective to illuminate the other.

Global Convergence

Throughout human history, societal interactions have involved both borrowing and conquest. Perhaps because educational achievement has often been associated with elite status, the organization and focus of education nearly everywhere in the modern era reflects international influences, some more forceful than others.

Higher education is a clear example. Instructors regularly employ what they term the Socratic method, more or less accurately seeking to capture the intellectual master-apprentice relationship associated with classical Greece. Students of education in Asia find persisting influences of Confucian patterns and ideas. As Philip Altbach points out, universities nearly everywhere are modeled on institutions created in thirteenth-century France.[1] Academics have secured significant institutional and individual independence and self-regulation, in part by imposing their own ideological and methodological orthodoxies. Professor-centered and relatively autonomous even when state funded, that model has withstood academic, social, religious, and political challenges in diverse settings. There have, of course, been significant additions to the pattern. As institutions became advocates and enforcers of truths with universal validity, they came to be called universities. At least since the nineteenth century, notions of nation and nation building have tightened the links between universities and the state and have nurtured the expectation that contributing to national development is one of their responsibilities. Research is an increasingly important responsibility, commonly organized into a set of disciplines that are strikingly similar across the world. The institutions themselves vary, including a range of more or less vocationally oriented postsecondary institutions, many with aspirations to become fully recognized universities. The general point is clear. Notwithstanding diverse roots, different settings, and local variations, the commonalities stand out, from basic features of organization and governance to pedagogy to claims of autonomy and academic freedom. Approach and method rather than content have become the universal truth. Like their predecessors, though now generally detached from religious doctrine, more or less confidently they assert the universality of their ways of knowing—academic standards and scientific methods. Altbach concludes, "Regardless of political system, level of economic development, or educational ideology, the expansion of higher education has been the most important single postwar trend worldwide."[2] We see in this example international influence as imposition and as emulation, with both coercion and rewards.

Colonial rule provided the setting for a particular sort of international influence in education: the implantation of metropolitan education institutions in the colonized world. Emulations, models, replicas, or overseas branches, these institutions often reproduced not only the curriculum, pedagogy, and hierarchical organization of their European models but even their architecture and staff and student codes of conduct. Both the intentions of the colonizers and the aspirations of the colonized elite they socialized insisted that the new education institutions resemble as closely as possible their models. Still, they remained distinctly colonial. Charged to equip a segment of the colonized society with the skills needed to administer the colonial enterprise, in practice, they were fully integrated into neither the local society nor the metropolitan education system. Even the special schools that served expatriates and an emerging national elite were generally truncated copies of their metropolitan counterparts.

Both borrowing and imposition have occurred. In the modern era, with few exceptions, the direction of influence is from European core to southern periphery. Institutional arrangements, disciplinary definitions and hierarchies, legitimizing publications, and instructional authority reside in that core, which periodically incorporates students and professors from the periphery, of whom many never return home. There are, to be sure, challenges to this dominance. Japan is a strong claimant to core status, with a widely respected university system. Several middle-tier, rapidly industrializing countries have invested heavily in higher education, developing recognized centers of research and innovation. Occasionally an academic debate initiated in the periphery (e.g., dependency in Latin America, oral history in Tanzania) becomes a critical concern for core institutions, perhaps supporting the view that the weakest links of the global system are those at the periphery.[3] Intellectual challenges rooted in the core regularly include advocates from outside the core.[4]

Contemporary Education Reform

Contemporary education reform initiatives have roots in several different national settings. Early in the century, U.S. education reformers sought to link schools more closely with their communities and to reinforce the organic connections among learning, schooling, and work. The Bolshevik Revolution provided an opening for reconceptualizing education's role, though in practice Soviet educators drew heavily on the thinking of the U.S. reformers as they emphasized technical education and sought to link schooling even more closely to employment needs and opportunities.[5] The decolonization era following World War II saw experiment and ferment in education. For the newly decolonized countries of Africa and southern Asia, the transfer of sovereignty offered the hope and possibility of charting new directions. For parts of Latin America and China, regime transitions provided space for education innovators. The competition of capitalism and socialism, especially the efforts of the United States and the Soviet Union to extend their influence in the Southern Hemisphere, created maneuvering room for experimentation. At the same time, the widespread student and worker militancy of May 1968 highlighted a parallel upheaval in the North Atlantic. Students asserted their political role, condemning their education and the societies whose expectations and values it transmitted. Although the national mobilizations generally fell short of their political objectives, education itself became both the focus of intense reform efforts and the vehicle for broader challenges to the political order.

Similarities

Still, it is the similarities across national settings that have most intrigued scholars of comparative education. Especially striking has been the relatively rapid movement in most countries from education as the privilege of a small elite to mass education as a responsibility of the state. Many analysts have sought explanations for that transition within particular societies. In specific settings, scholars have attributed the national decision to develop mass education to the importance of schools as mechanisms of social control, the role of education as a desired good able to win public support, schooling as a common experience essential to developing social solidarity and national identity, the perceived need to prepare the labor force for industrial society, and the belief that education promotes national development. Other scholars have sought to elucidate the theories of the state embedded in national philosophies of education[6] and to understand education in terms of the national and global political economy. Refining their earlier argument about the correspondence between state and school, Samuel Bowles and Herbert Gintis argue that education necessarily reflects, and simultaneously is in tension with, the structure of the national political economy.[7]

Challenging that national orientation, John Boli and Francisco Ramirez interpret the rapid implementation of compulsory schooling in diverse societies as the global consequence of a distinctly Western set of values and cultural practices.[8] In their view, the nineteenth century produced revised understandings of the individual, the state, and social organization, which in turn required the transition from elite to mass education. Drawing on notions of modernization[9] and world system,[10] they argue that the widespread adoption of mass education reflected a global diffusion of Western cultural values, including a focus on an improved material standard of living, a sense of the individual as the fundamental social unit and the ultimate source of value and authority, and an expanded state responsible for social welfare.

Other authors focus on the agency of that diffusion in the postcolonial era. Robert Arnove and Edward Berman explore the critical roles of national commissions of inquiry and philanthropic foundations in specifying the organization of the social sciences, that is, the acceptable procedures for studying society.[11] Westernization did not mark inexorable and inevitable progress toward a universal modernity, but rather reflected a conscious process of creating and shaping institutions. Born in the changing organization of production and accompanied by the expansion of monotheistic religions and the creation of the nation-state, the development of capitalist hegemony was not a conscious design in the manner of the construction of precapitalist empires. Rather, its heterogeneity and diversity had powerful orienting and constraining currents, with key roles for particular individuals and institutions. Education was both cause and consequence.

My concern here is to build on this foundation, maintaining the notion that deeper structural relationships and pressures operate through and are thus visible in specific institutional arrangements. Within that context, I explore education and development in terms of the conjunction of international organizations, increased dependence on aid, and the development of a particular role for research.

Development Requires Foreign Aid

By the late twentieth century, development and aid had become inextricably linked. Modernization provided the theoretical underpinnings, interpreting human progress as more or less linear, characterized by a fundamental distinction between the more and the less modern.[12] Colonial rule crystallized the we/they, modern/primitive categorization and reached to notions of social obligation (colloquially, the "white man's burden") to justify the often harsh imposition of European rule and rules. Following World War II, the new United Nations system incorporated the idea of trusteeship even as it became an arena for challenging and terminating colonial rule. At the same time, the link between development and aid was formally institutionalized in the creation of the International

Bank for Reconstruction and Development. Charged with supporting the rebuilding of Europe, generally in alliance with the International Monetary Fund, the World Bank dispensed both funds and advice.

Education was to be the development dynamo. If education was associated with economic progress, then surely it had to be a prominent component of development aid. As a large number of former colonies became independent, many of them very poor and with little investment or infrastructure to support autonomous development, it became commonplace that improving education required foreign assistance. The initial promise, however, was not fulfilled. After an initial period of high expectations and apparently rapid progress, education in poorer countries became a story of decay, crisis, and dependence instead of development and independence. Indeed, increasingly that has prompted a cry for the return of colonial rule—"some states are not yet fit to govern themselves"—a proposal that might be regarded as outrageous but in fact seems sufficiently legitimate to warrant prominent attention.[13]

To take us toward the major characters in this story of the localization of global patterns in education, aid, the funding and technical assistance agencies that manage the aid relationship, and the scholars and scholarship that have become essential to its operations and legitimacy, let us consider briefly major changes in the international system.

Socialist Disarray and U.S. Triumphalism

The precipitous dissolution of communist rule is widely interpreted as the inevitable victory of the United States over the Soviet Union, capitalism over socialism, the market over planning, indeed, good over evil. Capitalism prevailed because it is inherently better. What better proof could there be than its unequivocal victory? Everything that can be linked to socialism, however tenuous the link, is presumed clearly flawed, precisely because of that link.

The arrogance of U.S. triumphalism is palpable and unceasing: "We're the only country complicated enough, sophisticated enough, big enough to lead the human race."[14]

There is a grand—and instructive—irony in a triumphalism that is politically and ideologically centered in the United States. As Przeworski puts it:

> Neoliberal ideology, emanating from the United States and various multinational agencies, claims that the choice is obvious: there is only one path to development, and it must be followed. . . . Yet if a Martian were asked to pick the most efficient and humane economic systems on earth, it would certainly not choose the countries that rely most on markets. The United States is a stagnant economy in which real wages have been constant for more than a decade and the real income of the poorer 40 percent of the population has declined. It is an inhumane society in which 11.5 percent of the population—some 28 million people, including 20 percent of the children—lives in poverty. It is the oldest democracy on earth, but has one of the lowest voter-participation rates in the democratic world, and the highest per capita prison population in the world.[15]

Where socialism can provide neither useful ideas nor instructive experiences and where only one strategy of development is worth considering, the lessons are clear. Third world poverty is a Third World phenomenon. Where poverty is the result of poor poli-

cies, policy reform—structural adjustment—is the essential remedy. The prescription follows from the diagnosis: "getting macroeconomic policies right" (especially reducing
budget deficits, increasing tax revenues, eliminating barriers to international exchange);
"taxing agriculture less"; "putting exporters first" ("rationalizing import barriers") "pri-
vatizing public enterprises"; and "financial reform" especially "reducing financial repression, restoring bank solvency, and improving financial infrastructure."[16]

This triumphalism has (at least) two powerful consequences for the relationship
between aid and policymaking. Those who have triumphed need no longer listen. Since
they know what is right and since it is their power (rather than negotiation) that secures
their interests, they can instruct rather than learn. As well, since the triumph, they believe,
proves the correctness of their perspective, they need not feel reticent or guilty about
telling others what to do.

Like its 1960s incarnation, contemporary developmentalism takes the global political
economy as given, rather like a complex weather pattern. Monsoon rains and droughts
are simply beyond human control. So, too, the world system—imposing, inexorable, and
largely out of reach. That understanding itself fosters impotence. Consciously and forcefully, contemporary developmentalism directs attention away from efforts to conceive
of the world system as a web of nation-states and corporations linked in complex but
understandable and modifiable ways. Countries and companies, after all, are organized
and managed by people and can be changed by people, sometimes even the lowest-level
laborers and poorest citizens. At issue here is not a contest between external/foreign and
internal/national explanations for the Third World's problems. Rather, it is the internalization within the Third World of the relationships and understandings of that larger
environment, the internationalization even of ways of knowing, that has largely been
excluded from the analytic and policy agendas.

Resuscitation of Modernization

Contemporary developmentalism also reflects the resuscitation of modernization
theory, which insists now, as it did more than a half century ago, that the causes of the
Third World's problems are to be found within the Third World: its people, resources,
capital, skills, psychological orientation, child-rearing practices, and more. That analytic
framework is seductive and often is assumed uncritically. Just as poverty is to be explained
by the characteristics and (in)abilities of the poor, so the problems of Third World education are to be explained in Third World schools. Institutionalized in the centers of financial, industrial, and academic authority, this fundamental misunderstanding is sheltered
from the challenge that the primary sources of contemporary problems are to be found
in the process by which most Third World countries have been incorporated into the
global economy. The international relationships are acknowledged and are at the same
time treated as fixed features of the policy environment. They are the furniture, the paint
on the walls, the air in the room—a part of the setting and thereby not a principal concern for policy attention. As normal and largely unexceptional features of the structure
of international interactions, those relationships are assigned a low priority in the search
for explanations and strategies for change. In this way, what may matter most receives
little explicit attention. Notwithstanding the fascination with globalization, the explanatory framework and research agenda that dominate the aid relationship largely exclude

from active consideration the analytic perspective that emphasizes global integration. Studies of Third World education rarely mention, and even less frequently address critically, the sources and consequences for education of the Washington development consensus. The powerful critique developed by the dependency and world-systems literature—that explaining poverty in the contemporary Third World requires attention to the role of particular countries in a world system and the institutionalization of global connections within poor countries—is widely noted and, except in its broadest sweep and most superficial form, commonly ignored. The international order is a background condition. To take as given what are potentially primary causes is to exclude them from the policy (and research) discourse. What is unseen and undiscussed cannot be the focus of policy attention or public action.

Changing Roles in the United Nations System

Especially striking has been the reorientation of roles and responsibilities among the organizations of the United Nations system. In its 1980 *Education Sector Policy Paper*, the World Bank highlights the role of UNESCO (United Nations Educational, Scientific, and Cultural Organization), crediting it for what became the World Bank's holy grail, the focus on primary education.[17] By 1995, the World Bank's major education sector overview barely mentions UNESCO and certainly does not indicate that it or anyone else will rely on UNESCO for technical assistance and expertise in education, science, and culture, a reflection of changed roles in the international system.[18] In the post–World War II mood of reconstruction, education was understood as the principal vehicle for remaking the world. Education had to be central to rebuilding and social transformation, whether in the countries shattered by war, in those recently decolonized, or in countries in which socialism was to become the ideal to be achieved and the engine of development. In many minds, there was no alternative. Education was an essential antidote to the horrors of the recent past, the Holocaust, trench warfare, and nuclear devastation. In hindsight, the optimism was nearly unbounded.

In that understanding, countries were the policymaking domains and educators were to be the critical education policymakers. The newly fashioned international system had a distinctly developmental thrust. International economic organizations were to stabilize currency flows (and thus both international trade and national growth) and to support the reconstruction and development of Europe. Special UN councils were charged with economic and social development and with overseeing the final days of the colonial system. For education, science, and culture, UNESCO was to provide technical expertise and assistance. Structured to be responsive to its member states, it was to be less constrained by the major power vetoes of the Security Council and the rich country dominance of the financial organizations. Where it had been powerful nations that sought to impose the will of the international system on former colonies, by the 1990s the international financial institutions had become the principal enforcers of global dictates.

Surprisingly rapidly, structural adjustment became both the description and the content of the imposition of that external control. Effectively, structural adjustment offered access to capital in exchange for the adoption of externally specified national policies and the surrender of some national autonomy. Although the specific mix of policies termed structural adjustment varied from one setting to another, the general strategy was similar across diverse countries. Special foreign aid not linked to specific projects and increased foreign assistance in general became available, on the condition that the recipient government adopt a series of economic policies (often termed liberalization!). Nearly everywhere the implementation of these policies meant new or increased fees for social services and increased prices for consumers. For impoverished countries and dysfunctional economies, structural adjustment was stick as well as carrot.

Although their rhetoric seemed to call for a sharply curtailed role for the state, structural adjustment programs in fact required a state sufficiently strong to implement highly unpopular measures, especially austerity and reduced price supports for basic food and other staples. Conditionalities—providing debt relief, currency support, and aid only when explicit conditions were met—meant that their own governments assumed major responsibility for the dependent integration of poor countries into the global political economy. *Effective governance* became the preferred terminology, with emphasis on administration, management, and appropriate technology.

The terminology evolves. The umbrella construct has become *poverty reduction*, an objective everyone can support. Recipient countries are required to develop an inclusive and complex poverty reduction strategy, ostensibly to guide both national and foreigners' behavior. On examination, though, we find the same thinking about the requisites for development and many of the same imposed conditions. Subtly insinuated in a rhetoric of partnership and development cooperation, these precepts for progress become difficult to discern and even more difficult to challenge. Wearing the cloak of science and resting on the staff of research, this orientation dismisses alternative perspectives as political and nonscientific, especially those that emphasize raised consciousness of inequality and exploitation, mass mobilization, and citizen participation.

In that context, international financial institutions increasingly characterized themselves as development advisory services. Human capital theory legitimized their involvement in education. The end of the Cold War was accompanied by renewed attention to the globally destabilizing consequences of persisting poverty, created maneuvering room for humanitarian and other nongovernmental organizations, and ironically made it easier for the United States and its allies to reduce UNESCO's role. By the 1990s, the World Bank had effectively eclipsed technical assistance institutions like UNESCO. Reviewing the evolution of UNESCO is beyond the scope of this discussion.[19] It is important to note, however, that the UN organization institutionally most directly responsive to the majority of its members (no major power veto, no votes weighted by affluence) has lost much of its advisory role to the World Bank.

The institutionalization of this relationship, and particularly of the World Bank's role, takes several forms, in part because there is a fundamental tension between international control and national implementation. Having analyzed the problems and prescribed the solutions, the international agencies commonly assume they must direct events. At the same time, education reform is the responsibility of national authorities. Where they perceive the agenda to be imposed and perhaps inimical to their interests, national leaders are unlikely to pursue energetically the prescribed reforms. Where they see innovations and reforms as externally initiated and managed, national education communities are unlikely to invest the energy and resources required to sustain changes. Widely proclaimed to be critical for the success of education reforms, *national ownership* often becomes the rhetorical fig leaf that avoids discussion of the barely obscured international influences that nearly everyone, foreign and local, prefers not to address.[20] For the international agencies, the challenge is to exercise influence while encouraging national commitment to and implementation of the recommended reform strategy.

A major international conference, little known outside the circle of those most directly involved in Third World education but a point of reference and legitimacy ever since, was one response to that challenge. With appropriate ceremony, a distinguished group of educators and political leaders met in Jomtien, Thailand, in March 1990 to declare their support for making education available to everyone on the planet. Initiated and guided by the World Bank, the World Conference on Education for All had several formal sponsors: United Nations Development Programme (UNDP), UNESCO, United Nations Children's Fund (UNICEF), and the World Bank. Amid formal ceremonies, official statements, and research reports, some 1,500 participants from 155 governments, 20 intergovernmental bodies, and 150 nongovernmental organizations adopted by acclamation "A World Declaration on Education for All" and "A Framework for Action." Other resolutions adopted by acclamation reflected the conference title. All people must have access to basic education, both because (basic) education should now be considered a right of citizenship and because development, however conceived, requires an educated populace.

It is far from clear, however, that the Jomtien conference and the follow-up efforts have in fact dramatically altered priorities for basic education among aid recipients. Countries already committed to basic education have continued to support it. Others have neither increased their allocations to education nor transferred funding within education from other levels to basic education. When the major participants met again in the World Education Forum in Dakar, Senegal, a decade later, none of the major targets had been met.[21] Though promised, the massive increase in global aid estimated to be necessary to achieve education for all has not been delivered.[22] What emerges most clearly is the broad adoption of a common framework for describing, categorizing, analyzing, and assessing education.

About the same time, a second strategy for exercising international influence within national responsibility for education emerged. Seeking to institutionalize its leadership position among the aid agencies active in Africa, by far the most aid-dependent continent, the World Bank supported the creation of Donors to African Education (DAE). Formally committed to promoting cooperation and coordination among the agencies and between the agencies and African education ministries, DAE became the umbrella for a series of focused working groups, with agency leadership and finance. To assure both impact and legitimacy, this initiative required the active participation of Africa's education ministers, transforming the organization. By the mid-1990s, its secretariat had moved out of the World Bank and the African education ministers had begun to play a more energetic and influential role. A name change, to the Association for the Development of Education in Africa (ADEA), reflected efforts to redefine coordination and partnership as have efforts to relocate its secretariat in Africa.

Two observations are appropriate here. First, these two initiatives employed the language of collaboration as they created an institutional apparatus for the leading role of international organizations, especially the World Bank. In practice, both reinforced particular understandings about education and development and thus institutionalized influence by making it unexceptional. Conventional wisdom on analyzing and understanding education came to reflect the perspectives of economists and bankers. That education ought to be considered an investment and that education funding should be analyzed with the tools used to assess investments in other settings become commonplace, framework assumptions that were hardly noticed. Here too, what otherwise might seem to be controversial issues that warrant extended discussion escape critical attention. Major assumptions that might be sharply contested if highlighted are embedded in ostensibly uncontroversial tools. The active debates focus on which investment yields a higher return rather than on the utility of the investment metaphor as an analytic construct for understanding education or setting education policy.

Second, both initiatives reflect education policy and practice as contested terrain. Influence is not unchallenged control. In some circumstances, institutions created for one purpose can be redirected toward another. Although the patterns of power and dominance are clear, it would be incorrect to presume that influence moves in only one direction or to ignore the ways in which the ostensible victims of the global system in fact assert initiatives and influence courses of action.

ORGANIZATIONAL DIVERSITY

The discussion thus far has been concerned primarily with the ways in which the international system interacts with national governments directly responsible for education. Since what I have termed loosely the international system has several components, all with their own interests, forms, and strategies, it is useful to note briefly the range of organizations and institutional forms.

Generally termed *multilaterals*, some organizations are juridically international, especially those that constitute the United Nations system. Commonly the members of those organizations are countries, though there are important variations. The International Labor Organization, for example, includes countries, unions, and employers' groups. Governance rules also vary: majority rule in the United Nations General Assembly, permanent members' vetoes in the Security Council, majority rule in UNESCO, votes proportional to member countries' investment in the World Bank.

Frequently and somewhat misleadingly termed *bilateral*, some organizations are distinctly national, with a primary mandate to serve national interests, for example, the U.S. Agency for International Development and the Canadian International Development Agency.

International and national agencies have initiated and supported continental, regional, national, and local organizations that assume particular education responsibilities. The World Bank, for example, has spawned the Capacity Building Foundation, the African Economic Research Consortium, the African Virtual University, and the global Development Gateway. Organizations of that sort may reflect a conflicted identity. Born with the values, orientations, and objectives of their parent or foster agencies, they also seek to establish their own independent existence and legitimacy.

The term *nongovernmental organization* has come to refer to a very wide range of groups, including some that operate within countries or even small local areas, others that are national in origin and operate international programs, and still others that have an international constitution. Some nongovernmental organizations depend so heavily on contracts with national governments and international organizations that functionally they might reasonably be regarded as quasi-governmental organizations.

Churches and other religious groups are generally also termed nongovernmental organizations. Several have a long history of involvement in education, maintain extensive education departments and programs, and support an education agenda that is sometimes more, sometimes less closely related to religious doctrine and proselytization.

Efforts of education researchers to establish enduring links with their colleagues and strengthen their voices through cooperative and collective action have resulted in the creation of several regional networks, including those that group scholars in Latin America, eastern and southern Africa, western and central Africa, and Southeast Asia, as well as education researchers in the industrialized north concerned with education, aid, and development.[23] Often still dependent on external funding and constituted by scholars themselves dependent on contracts with external agencies, those networks find it difficult to assert an effective autonomous voice and play a strong independent role.

Several philanthropic foundations, most but not all with headquarters in the United States, have also played important roles in education and development. As I have already noted, the Carnegie, Ford, and Rockefeller Foundations have all explicitly sought to influence the development of the social sciences at home and abroad. That process continues. In 2000, Carnegie Corporation, Ford Foundation, Rockefeller Foundation, and MacArthur Foundation each pledged U.S.$25 million toward institutional support for African universities. With two additional partners, that pledge was extended and doubled in 2005. Among the non-U.S. foundations with education activities in the Third World are the Gulbenkian Foundation and the Aga Khan Foundation.

Increasingly, international academic organizations have sought to influence the development of their disciplines globally. As the International Political Science Association, for example, functions to propagate the fundamental assumptions and orientations of the U.S. political science mainstream, notwithstanding periodic challenges it plays a role in promoting a global convergence of understandings and ways of knowing. Similarly, a small set of internationally recognized journals in each discipline functions to impose standards and set the terms through which Third World scholars must establish their legitimacy.[24]

AID DEPENDENCE

How do external events and forces influence what happens within particular countries? Notwithstanding the rhetoric of partnership and development cooperation, even modest aid can have a very loud voice. That is especially clear in Africa. Pulled by popular demand and pushed by the need for highly educated and skilled personnel, education quickly became an insatiable demand for resources. Especially as economic crises succeeded earlier developmental optimism and structural adjustment replaced rapid development as the realistic short-term objective in Third World countries, there was strong pressure to assign the highest priority for available funds to directly productive activities, which often did not include education. How, then, to educate the teachers, develop new textbooks, or equip the science laboratories? Or more commonly, how to fix the leaking roof? The common recourse was to external funding. For many Third World countries, aid has become the center of gravity for education and development initiatives. Over time, it has come to seem not only obvious but also unexceptional that new initiatives and reform programs require external support, and therefore responsiveness to the agenda and preferences of the funding agencies.

Although foreign aid to Third World education is substantial, in most countries it represents a small portion of total spending on education. Its influence, however, often far exceeds its volume. Until very recently, funding agencies have been unwilling to finance recurrent expenditures, of which the majority is allocated to teachers' salaries. Hence, while foreign sources have long supported development spending on education, that generally remained a very small percentage of the total education expenditures. Where nearly all national education resources are committed to paying the teachers, the foreign support becomes the key source of funds for innovation and reform, indeed nearly everything but basic system management tasks. Limited aid thus acquires substantial leverage. Aid dependence becomes endemic, even when the foreign funds pay a small portion of total costs.

Especially since the reaffirmation of the commitment to education for all in 2000, global pressure for more and more rapid aid has increased. Major funders have promised or announced significantly larger aid allocations. There has been debt relief—in some countries spending on debt service exceeded allocations to education—of several sorts, including a complex process for certifying and assisting Heavily Indebted Poor Countries (HIPC). Responding to complaints about the slow delivery of promised support, the funding agencies created the Fast Track Initiative (FTI), which shares eligibility rules and certification with HIPC. Still, the Education for All (EFA) Global Monitoring Reports regularly show that external support continues to fall short of the volume needed, jeopardizing the achievement of the EFA goals.[25]

In several countries, as funding agencies have shifted from supporting particular projects to contributing directly to the education or national budget, even recurrent expenditures have become increasingly dependent on external support. Though not directly and without saying so, the funding agencies are paying the teachers. An evaluation of external support to education in Uganda estimated that by 2003, aid provided 60 percent of total spending on basic education.[26] Support of that magnitude may well help Uganda achieve education for all. But surely it is not sustainable over the longer term. Even more important, it is difficult, perhaps impossible, for a national government and its education community to set priorities and directions for a core development activity so dependent on foreign funds.

As the reliance on foreign funds increases, so does the influence of both the finance ministry and the external agencies. Representing the government in negotiations with those agencies, the finance ministry becomes much more directly involved in policy and programmatic details across all government departments. That increased role may well suit the external agencies, which are likely to see the finance ministry as their ally in reducing and managing spending. The alliance between external agency and finance (and perhaps planning) ministry may be structured as a powerful lever for influencing national policy.

Case studies of national responses to economic crisis indicate both the forms of aid dependence and differences among countries. Heavily dependent on foreign assistance, Sénégal and Tanzania have repeatedly modified education and training policies and programs in ways that reflected the priorities and preferences of the funding agencies.[27] By the end of the 1980s, for example, the planning director in Tanzania's education ministry characterized his work as "marketing."[28] His task, he said, was to advertise and market broad ideas and specific projects in the hope of finding a sponsor—an external assistance agency—to fund them. Over time, priorities were set less by government and party leaders and more by what foreign governments and their aid organizations were willing to finance. The power brokers in education had once been those who could put together coalitions of people influential in Tanzania's public and private life. By the late 1980s, they had become those who were most successful in securing foreign funding.[29]

Marketing may be a reasonable, as well as reasonably successful, coping strategy in an adverse setting, yielding additional resources in times of economic distress and permitting national elites and their foreign partners to delay confronting major problems and undertaking serious economic, political, and social transformation. At the same time, when marketing is the prevailing orientation, innovation is limited to whatever the funders are willing to finance.

National patterns of course vary. Aid dependence does not always secure compliance with external recommendations and expectations. "A small country has no choice." Asked why his relatively affluent Third World country had accepted the conditions attached to foreign assistance, the former Costa Rican president insisted he had no alternative.[30] Already deeply in debt, economically dependent on export sales to the countries that control most of its external aid, resisting with difficulty entanglement in efforts to overthrow a neighbor government, Costa Rica acquiesced to pressures to adopt structural adjustment policies and maintained that orientation through governments led by different political parties. What else could this small country do, its leaders argued. In practice, however, Costa Rica not only secured massive external assistance but also maintained a good deal of its own agenda, protecting many of the social services, including education and training, targeted for reduction. A combination of its regional role, its history of stable democratic government and limited civil strife, its economic base and relative affluence, and the broad legitimacy of its national political system enabled Costa Rica to retain a good deal of policy autonomy even as it acceded to externally imposed conditions. Another example of local resistance and ability to retain control over local decisions were the teachers unions and militant student organizations who allied to block staff reductions and other austerity measures in Sénégal's structural adjustment program.[31] Conflicts over the imposition of higher education fees in Ghana and Kenya show that countries can reject aid conditions and continue to receive support and that effective implementation of aid conditions requires the active cooperation of the recipient country's government.[32]

Dependence on external funds leads to both explicit conditions imposed by the funding organizations and more subtle influences. Sometimes that relationship is aggressively manipulative. The funding agency may condition the provision of support on the adoption of specific policies, priorities, or programs. Conditions can be direct (aid is contingent on the adoption of a specific policy or the implementation of specified institutional changes) or indirect (support for vocational schools may be contingent on the implementation of a strategy designed to increase female enrollment in the technical curriculum). Occasionally influence flows in the other direction. To secure resources for a preferred program, the national leadership may mobilize support and bring pressure to bear on the funding agency in its home.

PATHWAYS OF INFLUENCE

Aid's indirect influences are generally far less visible, more difficult to challenge, and often far more consequential. A brief overview of other pathways of influence is instructive.

Globalization by Conference

International conferences have become increasingly important vehicles for transmitting and implanting fundamental ideas about education and shaping how education is understood, organized, and managed. As I have noted, the 1990 Jomtien conference sought to pressure governments in poor countries to highlight and fund basic education. Functionally that required an administrative apparatus, follow-up meetings, and monitoring and research. Recognizing failure to achieve the agreed objectives but reluctant to assign responsibility, the 2000 Dakar conference reaffirmed the commitment, rolled back the target dates, and rejuvenated the secretariat. The major Dakar goals were subsequently incorporated in the United Nations' Millennium Development Goals.[33] Increased pressures on governments included regional conferences and periodic progress reports to be prepared according to a specified format, itself a vehicle for imposing the constructs, categories, and terms to describe and analyze education.[34]

Here, then, is a major initiative to institutionalize international influence. Rhetoric of collaboration and partnership notwithstanding, the agenda has largely been that of the World Bank and other agencies. They sought to use this mechanism to persuade reluctant governments to reorder their priorities toward basic education. Has that been more effective than working in smaller scale, less visible settings? Thus far, probably not. The longer-term efficacy remains to be seen. The conferences and surrounding activities do provide maneuvering room and perhaps leverage for education advocates, including those critical of the funding agencies. International consensus requires the participation and legitimacy of national governments, which enables them to challenge and modify agenda, process, and resolutions. International conferences are now commonly accompanied by parallel conferences of nongovernmental organizations and alternative conferences of critics and dissidents. Still, though challenged, the guiding role of funding agencies, especially the World Bank, continues. Even more important, ways of thinking about education become even more firmly entrenched.

Some countries charged that the preference for basic education was intended to undermine support for higher education and thereby confine poor countries in their poverty. Without the development of advanced skills and research capacity, poor countries are relegated to the intellectual periphery, perpetually dependent on ideas and technologies (and, more important, ways of understanding) developed elsewhere. Acknowledging that impoverishing universities, the principal institutions for educating teachers and teacher educators, eventually undermines even the commitment to basic education, funding agencies and foundations have moved to restore support for higher education.[35]

Globalizing Standards

Calls in many countries for global education standards have spawned a series of cross-national efforts to measure and compare achievement at different levels.[36] Although they claim sensitivity to the unique characteristics of specific national and local settings, by design those assessments seek to use and thereby institutionalize internationally particular assumptions about both the content and the process of learning and teaching. The results of the assessment measures may contribute to improving the quality of education in some settings, but their more powerful role is to undermine the education philosophy that associates effective learning with education objectives and measures that are debated and decided locally.

Managing Knowledge

That information is power is so widely accepted that it has become a cliché. In the contemporary world of aid, with triumphant capitalism as the context, economics as the dominating social science, and business as the appropriate model for public institutions, that understanding of information has been transformed into the claim that knowledge is development.[37] In a knowledge economy, where information, it is claimed, becomes a more important factor of production than land, labor, or capital, eliminating poverty requires knowledge affluence. Generating, storing, managing, and disseminating knowledge thus becomes another path for institutionalizing international influence.

Funding and technical assistance agencies regularly reiterate that their advice is more important than their funds. Indeed, the World Bank goes a good deal further, proposing to develop and manage knowledge repositories and gateways.[38] "My goal is to make the World Bank the first port of call when people need knowledge about development," its former president asserted.[39]

The potential problems here are numerous and well beyond the scope of this discussion.[40] In this review of pathways of influence, it is important to note briefly some of the risks of this combination of funds and advice. What is deemed valid and legitimate information (termed *knowledge*) will become increasingly centralized in the North. Information that is collected in the South will be shaped and framed by its interpreters, that is, those who create and manage the development knowledge databases and information systems. That powerful role in determining what is and what is not knowledge will be obscured by the mystique of science and scientific method. The centralization of the determination of what is knowledge entrenches the role of the elite education and research institutions in the world, nearly all located in the most affluent countries. What is regarded as the important knowledge is likely to become more technical and less humanistic and critical. The projection of broad, nearly universal access to web-based information databases underestimates both current technical obstacles and cost and the likelihood that in the current global system, the technological gap will increase, not decrease. Overall, information databases created and maintained by authoritative institutions in the North with substantial economic leverage and ideological influence are most likely to reinforce existing power relations, both within and across countries.

Constraining Outcomes by Shaping Conceptions and Analytic Frameworks

The most powerful pathways of influence are the least visible. While the conditionalities of aid can be rigid and painful, they are clear and can be clearly challenged. Far more difficult to detect and resist are the influences embedded in the conceptions of education that seem so ordinary that they are taken for granted and in the analytic frameworks that seem so obvious that they avoid critical scrutiny. Let us consider three such frameworks: education as investment, as production, and as delivery system.

Note that the notion of external influence has to do with context and contest, not nationality. Rate-of-return analysis, for example, emerged as an analytic approach and technique in a specific setting and within a particular theoretical orientation. It reflects the interests of investors and allocators of resources, whether foreign or local, who seek to choose among alternate uses of their funds. While that approach may (or may not) prove useful to education researchers, decision makers, and managers in poor countries, it was not the creation of those responsible for education in those countries. Its proponents may be citizens of the United States, England, Hungary, Japan, Chile, or Ghana. Characterizing it as "external," therefore, highlights not the nationality of its advocates but rather the particular setting, including assumptions, ideas, interests, theory, and ideology, in which it was developed and refined.

Education as Investment

Amid alternative perspectives on education, those of economics and finance have come to dominate the discourse on education and development. For the World Bank, the starting point is human capital theory: education ought to be regarded as an investment in developing a country's human resources. In its 1995 education policy review, the assertion of its superiority is unqualified: "Human capital theory has no genuine rival of equal breadth and rigor."[41] The East Asian[42] experience proves the value of investing in education, the World Bank argues, since it is precisely that investment that differentiates the successes from the failures.

Far from universally accepted, both human capital theory and its principal tool, rate of return analysis, are intensely debated. Other funding agencies and the World Bank's own staff are among the critics: "Traditional cost-benefit studies of education have tended to indicate the advantages of investment in education at various different levels, based on analyses of the social return which each produces. Recent studies have shown this method to be both fallacious and limiting."[43]Much of the concern with education as an investment self-consciously ignores the process of education. Adopting an economic systems approach, it focuses on inputs and outputs, leaving inside the opaque black box most of what those involved in education do every day. In education, however, process is itself an output.

Schools select and socialize. For both society and individuals, schooling frequently matters more than learning. Although specific circumstances vary, the education system everywhere is central to constructing and maintaining a particular sort of social order. Often it is equally central to challenging and transforming it. To ignore the ways in which curriculum entrenches and legitimizes inequality, examinations reinforce and justify patterns of social stratification, or textbooks privilege some perspectives over others is to render meaningless findings about the number of graduates and their subject specializations. Limiting the specification to the relative values of alternative inputs and outputs permits proposing global solutions. But in practice, education is interactive, replete with discontinuities, and always locally contingent.

A second consequence of treating education primarily as a social investment is a disjunction between the issues deemed most important and the objectives articulated by Third World governments and educators, which commonly receive little attention: for example, fostering an inquiring and critical orientation, eliminating discrimination and reducing elitism, promoting national unity, preparing youth for the rights and obligations of citizenship, equipping them to work cooperatively and resolve conflicts nonviolently, and developing among learners a strong sense of individual and collective competence, self-reliance, and self-confidence. These objectives are of course more difficult to quantify and measure than, say, building classrooms or increasing the availability of instructional materials. Yet, to ignore these objectives entirely is to delete them from the education agenda.

Education as Production

A second metaphor commonly used to explain and reform schooling is education as production, which in turn leads to a focus on efficiency. But what exactly is efficiency in education?

In manufacturing, efficiency seems clear: reduce the costs of production—less expensive raw materials, less waste and breakage, more skilled workers, improved machinery, low-cost energy, simplified maintenance, and expenditures on marketing that are exceeded by income from increased sales.

Though the production metaphor is occasionally useful, education is fundamentally different from manufacturing. In an interactive process, the distinction between inputs and outputs is consciously blurred. Bottles do not contribute to their own manufacture. Students do contribute to their own education. Cars do not suggest improvements in the assembly process or reject the old way of doing things. Learners are active participants in their education, not only suggesting improvements and rejecting received wisdom but taking the initiative to chart new paths. At first glance, ever larger classes would increase an education system's efficiency by spreading teachers' salaries across more students. But of course the appropriate unit of education is not the student or the number of students per teacher but learning.

Beyond those problems, it is far from clear that efficiency, however defined, is or ought to be the primary goal to be maximized. Like those responsible for space travel, educators in poor countries may assign higher priority to redundancy. For example, economies of scale might favor centralized production of education materials. But the realities of power failures, equipment breakdowns, and the unavailability of supplies likely favor dispersed and redundant production, so that problems at one site do not disrupt all production. Whether efficiency, redundancy, or some other goal should have the highest priority cannot be assumed but must be determined in each setting.

In three important ways the constructs *internal efficiency* and *external efficiency* misdirect policy attention. Concern with reducing the unit cost per student is likely to be far less fruitful than focusing on increasing the effectiveness of each unit of expenditure. Second, since pass and graduation rates are largely the consequences of general education and national policy and therefore not of either student or school achievement, it seems particularly obfuscating to characterize the decision to promote few students as internal inefficiency. Third, recognizing that the charter of schooling is far broader than (and may not even include) vocational preparation requires discarding efforts to assess education's external efficiency from rates and types of employment. When the pressure to quantify confronts the problems in measuring learning, it is learning that is ignored. The common use of efficiency as an analytic construct in education converts major issues of policy and pedagogy into ostensibly uncontroversial issues of management and administration amenable to technical solutions, effectively excluding them from both critical review and participatory decision making.

A corollary to stress on efficiency is insistence on feasibility and practicality.[44] That apparently reasonable orientation functions in practice to constrain both education and development. Innovations are inherently risky. Attempts to change roles (e.g., teachers and students as curriculum developers), quality measures (the mix and weights of student portfolios, continuous assessment, and standardized examinations), pedagogy (mixed-ability groups, learner-centered instruction), and links with the world of work (education with production) may fail or interfere with other objectives. Since innovations are risky, funding and technical assistance agencies generally require using older, ostensibly proven and reliable approaches. If it were fully effective, that orientation would restrict creative departures to the affluent countries. Those who are poor scramble to catch up as they watch those who are more affluent discard the approaches and technologies they are told to use. In practice, poverty is deemed to preclude fundamental innovation, which in turn is likely to perpetuate the poverty.

Education as Delivery System

Aid dependence entrenches policy and programmatic change as something done *to* rather than *by* Third World education. Often, learning is understood as information acquisition. The common construct is what Paulo Freire has termed the *banking model of education*. Learners are like empty bank accounts. More or less formally, teachers and others with the relevant capital, wisdom, make deposits into those accounts. Successful students save their resources and complete their education with heads full of knowledge on which they can subsequently draw. At least for younger learners, learning is understood largely as a passive process. Teachers give or provide or offer, and students receive. But what of the extensive thinking, experimentation, and research that regard learning as far larger than information acquisition? What of the notion that what learners do is not simply acquire but generate, master, develop, and create knowledge? Educators who understand learning as an active process, who situate learners at the center of that process, and for whom learning involves the appropriation, manipulation, and integration of information have little voice in the policies and programs developed using the standard tool kit.

The terminology used is both instructive and formative. Education reforms are regularly termed *interventions*—that is, insertions from outside rather than initiatives from within. Externally funded, externally guided, and often externally managed, specific reform projects are rarely directly responsible to the settings—whether teachers, students, or the local community—in which they function. How are Third World educators to become owners of those reforms when they are the objects of the surgery, not the surgeons? Education is termed a *delivery system*, not an organic process in which learners are the doers rather than the receivers. In practice, this combination of a vantage point external to education (whether national or foreign) and very limited accountability generally proves fundamentally disempowering.

Studies, Plans, and the Specification of Constructs and Analytic Frameworks

Concerned that aid funds be used appropriately, effectively, and efficiently, the funding and technical assistance agencies have long required that proposed projects make sense in terms of overall education objectives and policies. Especially for the world's poorest countries, most in Africa, that requirement has become increasingly complex and cumbersome. To be eligible for debit relief and accelerated support, countries must now prepare a comprehensive development framework and detailed national strategy papers focused on reducing poverty, including an extensive analysis of the education sector and a statement of education policies.[45] At first glance, that seems quite reasonable. The funders seek reassurance that their support will be well used. The recipients should have a comprehensive and inclusive planning process, based on solid research, that produces objectives, policies, and indicators to measure progress.

In practice, however, the required process has become more complex than many countries can manage, diverts attention and energy from the reform and management of the education system, and notwithstanding a formal commitment to broad participation, effectively entrenches the expectations and frameworks of the funders, especially the World Bank. Overwhelmed education ministries engage consultants to prepare key documents. With a self-ascribed mandate to assure quality control and consistent planning, the funders both set the standards for acceptable plans and programs and judge which documents have met them. Open hearings that permit community groups to present their views function largely to legitimize recommended courses of action.

Most important, this process domesticates and institutionalizes key constructs and analytic perspectives. It is in this way that internal and external efficiency, rate of return analysis, and other precepts of what might be termed the Washington education consensus are rendered invisible—so ordinary and normal that they require no attention—and thereby immune to critical assessment. As the key constructs and analytic frameworks are embedded in the instructions and format for required documents, and as policy and decision makers take them for granted, institutionalizing the externally set agenda need no longer require explicit external direction.

WHEN DOES AID NOT HELP?

Among the numerous studies of foreign aid and its problems,[46] including attention to the role of the International Monetary Fund and the World Bank,[47] there has been increasing attention to aid and education,[48] though as yet little systematic attention to the links between the large-scale agenda and activities of the international and national aid agencies and the small-scale decisions and activities of education decision makers and educators.

Advocates of aid argue that the situation would have been much worse in the absence of assistance and that education in particular settings has clearly benefited from foreign support. Critics argue equally passionately that although there have been some benefits, on balance aid has been more harmful than helpful. They point to funds allocated to projects that have shown no significant benefit, to promising projects begun but not sustained long enough to bear fruit, to periodic and abrupt shifts in priorities among the aid agencies, and to a general preference for large-scale and high-tech efforts that are often situationally inappropriate. Their critique is also structural. In its very conception, foreign aid is fundamentally disempowering. Notwithstanding the widespread use of terms like cooperation, partnership, and empowerment, in practice, aid generally functions to undermine local authority and initiative. By substituting external decisions for local autonomy, it reduces rather than builds capacity. Notwithstanding periodic reform efforts, both in its conception and in its practice the aid relationship itself becomes a major obstacle to achieving its stated purposes.

Education is a sufficiently complex process that project or programmatic evaluations are unlikely to resolve this debate. Rarely is it possible to associate specific outcomes with particular reforms, whether locally generated or externally recommended. And even as they criticize particular aid programs and insist on their national autonomy, most Third

World governments are anxious to secure as much education assistance as they can get, generally accepting the accompanying conditions.

THE ROLE(S) OF RESEARCH

Though periodically castigated as too theoretical and irrelevant to education practice, researchers and research play an important role in this story. That is particularly clear in Africa. Commissioned studies abound. Externally initiated studies of education in Africa undertaken during the past three decades are most striking for their similarities, their diversity—of country, of commissioning agency, of specific subject—notwithstanding.[49] With few exceptions, these studies have a common framework, a common approach, and a common methodology. Given their shared starting points, their common findings are not surprising. Through the 1990s the conclusions were: African education is in crisis. Governments cannot cope. Quality has deteriorated. Funds are misallocated. Management is poor and administration is inefficient. More recently, more positive assessments, especially highlighting expanded enrollment and girls' participation, accompany the persisting critiques. From predominantly Islamic Mauritania in the western Sahara to the mixed cultural, colonial, and political heritage of Mauritius in the Indian Ocean, the recommendations too are similar: Reduce the central government role in providing education. Decentralize. Increase school fees. Expand private schooling. Reduce direct support to students, especially at the tertiary level. Introduce double shifts and multigrade classrooms. Assign high priority to instructional materials. Favor in-service over preservice teacher education. The shared approach of these studies reflects a medical metaphor. Expatriate-led study teams as visiting clinicians diagnose and then prescribe. The patient (i.e., the country) must be encouraged, perhaps pressured, to swallow the bitter medicine. For the most part, learning disappears from view, buried by the focus on finance.

Education is perhaps the most public of public policies. The insistence on comprehensive development frameworks and poverty reduction strategies has increased the demand for studies of the education sector. Yet most of these major studies of education, explicitly commissioned to guide policy decisions, have very limited circulation. Designated *confidential* or *restricted*, Africa's education sector studies are generally available only to the commissioning agency and a few government officials. Unpublished, they do not appear in available bibliographies and source lists.

The volume of these studies, their central role in the aid relationship, and thereby their influence on objectives and priorities in African education is a very powerful path for the institutionalization of international influence. Individually, none of these studies, or perhaps even the aid programs that spawned them, is likely to prove very consequential over the longer term. But as a group, these studies frame debate and orient policies, both international and national.

Let us return for a moment to the Jomtien conference and the apparent consensus on education for all. Few would disagree with this noble goal, even though many countries lack the resources to achieve it rapidly. But why? Why is universal mass education the highest priority? And if it is, why focus primarily on basic (primary) education in schools, rather than, say, adult and other education programs outside school settings?

There are many answers to those and related questions, but the answer that seems the most persuasive, especially to those who disburse education aid funds, is that *research shows* that investing in primary education yields the best return. Support for this focus on primary education rests on the claim that research has persuasively demonstrated that investing in primary education promises the greatest progress toward development (however defined).

It is not the specific conclusion that is most striking here. I have already noted problems with uncritical reliance on rate-of-return analysis. The history of public discourse on education suggests that every broadly accepted observation is eventually discarded as partial, misleading, incorrect, or all three. A successor truth will emerge, advocated just as ardently. Rather, what is remarkable here is the implicit consensus on research as the principal determinant, or legitimizer, of education policy. The Jomtien resolutions are but a single example of the privileged position of research (or, more accurately, claims about research and its findings) in debates on education policy. In practice, research may inform and guide policy, rationalize and justify policies adopted for other reasons, or be quite irrelevant to policy. But claims about what research shows constitute the core of the development discussion. Without the claim of research support, policy proposals lose credibility. Similarly, policy critiques that do not cite supporting research are easily ignored. Prospective participants in the policy debate must demonstrate an adequate supply of relevant research simply to have their voices heard.

The formulation "Research shows that . . ." and its synonyms are ubiquitous. The prominence and pervasiveness of the claim that "research shows" within the development arena reflect a powerful contemporary phenomenon: the emergence of a financial-intellectual complex spawned by the development business. It is important to recognize both the unique characteristics and the shorter- and longer-term consequences of that combination of research and funding. That in turn requires understanding the ways in which the increasing importance of external assistance and the privileged position of research combine to condition and constrain education's substantive content.

The Facade of Precision[50]

Where much of education research yields results that are partial, ambiguous, and contingent, policy research is expected to generate clear and confident findings that are reliable and precise. Quantification is preferred. Yet the push for precision often overstates the precision that is possible and ignores the ways in which the pursuit of precision impedes interpretation and understanding.

Consider, for example, the powerful but often little-recognized influence of prevalent computation strategies. To the present, most computing in the social sciences has been digital. High-speed combinations of bimodal choices—on/off, yes/no, either/or—permit manipulating massive volumes of information. Beyond the raw processing capabilities, digital representation of information seems to have important advantages for social scientists. For example, ambiguities in categorization are either explicitly precluded or organized into contingent connections through which individual paths are unambiguous. Events or relationships of interest can be more readily distinguished from similar phenomena and random variations. Yet the analog world is at best imperfectly captured in its digital representation. However sophisticated the sampling techniques, some information is lost. Similarly, when social scientists are constrained to construct categories that are mutually exclusive, the disadvantages of excluding inconsistency and ambiguity may outweigh the value of the apparent resulting clarity. The variations in temporal and spatial context that go unrecorded because they are smaller than the units of measure employed may prove to be critical to inference and interpretation.

Of course, even the most advanced techniques can at best provide only partial remedies for inaccuracies and inconsistencies in the original data. Many, perhaps most, reported national statistics for the Third World, for example, have a large margin of error.[51] Enumerating the multiple sources of that large margin of error is beyond the scope of this discussion. But the immediate implication of taking seriously that margin of error—that is, treating national statistics as rough approximations—is clear. Small and sometimes larger observed changes may be more apparent than real and must be treated as such. Consequently, apparent changes that fall within a reasonable margin of error are a weak foundation for broad inferences and for public policy. Although quantification may make findings more defensible, it does not automatically produce better understanding.

A second implication is that both researchers and policymakers must reject statistics whose underlying assumptions require a level of precision, linearity, or continuity that the data do not reliably support. A profusion of numbers neither makes a particular interpretation more valid nor renders a policy proposal more attractive. Indeed, the numeric shroud may well obscure far more than it reveals.

Widespread acknowledgment of the uncertainty in the available data notwithstanding, the canons of social science impel those who conduct research, those who support research, and those who rely on research to justify their actions to overstate the precision of their findings and to attach to them an unrealistically high level of confidence.

Economics as Social Science

To understand what people do and why, we need to know something about what they have done. Rarely, however, do social scientists directly observe all of the events that interest them. Hence, most often we rely on information that someone else has collected, more or less systematically, usually for some other purpose. The behavioral revolution in the social sciences, with its shrill cries of "Falsifiability!" and "Reproducibility!" has pushed us toward the sort of information that can be recorded and stored in quantitative form.

Accompanying and fueling the inclination to quantify has been the emergence of economics as the modal social science. This increasingly influential and powerful role for economics stands on two legs, one within the academy and the other outside it.

In their ideal form, the methods taught in basic economics courses correspond well to dominant currents within social science. The focus is on causal relationships, established by drawing on lawlike statements about patterned regularities and exploring the connections among precisely defined factors. Whatever is deemed extraneous may be ignored. Factors that may affect the relationship being studied are either assumed not to vary ("other things being equal") or to vary randomly (thereby having no systematic influence). Or they are directly or indirectly controlled by the researchers. Finally, the restricted set of factors to be examined (the "variables") can be studied. Ideally, those factors can be changed in some orderly way, either by careful choice of locations, times, or observations or by simulating the variation based on the information available. Expectations about causality (hypotheses) can then be rejected or supported. For many scholars, this orientation defines the social scientific method. The challenge is to approach the ideal, a controlled experiment in which the experimenter manipulates all of the factors, as closely as possible.

The current preeminence of economics also stems from its role as the social science deemed to have the most important practical consequences. The principal objective is what used to be called social engineering: how to make society function better. Especially as they seek funding, researchers resort to liberal utilitarian defenses of what they do. For that, economics serves well. Other disciplines fall short. As they do, their insights, their critiques, their voices become more faint.

Research as Currency or Perhaps Ammunition

As I have noted, research has become the currency of development planners and decision makers, used to assign value to alternative and often competing projects. Surely that is desirable. Research guides decisions. Expertise rather than politics prevails. This idealized model of the allocation and use of development assistance is deceptive in several ways.

First, the common view that competent policymakers base their decisions on a careful review of relevant research is simply inaccurate. In development, as in most other policymaking arenas, research enters the decision-making process through multiple, often indirect routes. First, decision makers draw on their academic learning as well as their practical experience to formulate questions, select proposals, specify evaluative criteria, and make decisions. That indirect influence is often both subtle and not apparent to the decision makers themselves.

Second, policymakers who are largely guided by research focused on the issue to be decided do not necessarily make better decisions. The research that is deemed relevant is generally instrumental and relatively narrowly gauged, taking as given existing economic, political, and social patterns. Yet effective and appropriate public policy cannot ignore interests, preferences, and politics. Making public policy is not an antiseptic, sheltered, apolitical process. Successfully implemented policies must confront and engage, not avoid, the conflict of interests and the tensions among the organization of production, the structure of power, and patterns of social differentiation.

Third, research enters the policy process as justification for decisions already made. Especially in a bureaucratic environment where decision makers are charged to emphasize rationality and deemphasize politics and favoritism, the claim that research supports a particular course of action is the most powerful defense against all challengers. Put crudely, in the policy shoot-out, the gunfighter quickest to draw the research pistol and best supplied with research ammunition is most likely to emerge victorious. Even a slow draw with limited ammunition may ensure survival.

Fourth, as I have argued, the conjunction of development assistance and research transforms both research and its role in the policy process, to the detriment of both. That research influences policy indirectly and that research is used to justify decisions are not necessarily problematic. In the contemporary development business, however, the same agencies are increasingly responsible for decisions, funding, and research. Just as their funds seat foreign aid organizations at the education policy table, so, too, do those funds secure powerful influence over research and the research process. Little anticipated and not yet well understood, this conjunction of external funding and education research is only beginning to be studied systematically.[52] The major outlines of this relationship have

become sufficiently clear, however, to warrant concern among both researchers and policymakers. To put the issue sharply, research and policy are both at risk.

When Research Becomes Consulting

When public funding for education is inadequate, public funding for education
research hardly exists. Just as education and training decision makers and planners look
overseas to fund innovation and development, so do scholars look abroad for support for
their research. They quickly learn that unencumbered research grants are scarce and difficult to obtain. More readily available are contracts for research commissioned by external assistance agencies. With those commissions come specifications of appropriate
approaches, methods, and analytic framework. Hence, education research too becomes
part of the aid relationship, with senior researchers regularly shuttling between cramped
offices and empty libraries on the one hand and on the other the computers, cellular
telephones, and substantial fees of client consulting.

With low basic salaries, individual researchers are highly motivated to become consultants to the external agencies. Unable to pay a living wage or to provide direct research
funding, universities are inclined to tolerate, often encourage, that practice. Obliged to
justify their programs and allocations and chastised for relying so heavily on expatriate
researchers, the funding and technical assistance agencies eagerly recruit local education
researchers. Research becomes consulting. That has several problematic consequences.

First, generally the contracting agency selects the topic to be studied and often the
methodology to be used. Only rarely do the topics studied emerge organically from interactions among educators, teachers, learners, and the community. Nor do they emerge
from debates among education decision makers and researchers. Rarely does the methodology reflect researchers' experiences, local methodological debates, or locally developed
critiques of dominant methodological orientations. Second, commissioned research generates reports with very restricted circulation.[53] Only very rarely are findings subjected to
academic and practitioners' peer review. As a result, what are taken as authoritative results
and recommendations may be partial, seriously flawed, skewed, or all three. Third, since
the reports of commissioned research rarely enter the academic literature, rather than the
cumulation and sifting and winnowing that are central to the creation of knowledge,
commissioned research produces largely disconnected lonely trees, some robust but many
quite frail, scattered across the desolate plain of bookless schools and deskless classrooms.

Fourth, research as consulting transforms the academic reward system. Africa again
provides the sharpest examples. For researchers with agency funding, promotion in university rank becomes less important and far less remunerative than securing another consulting contract. Fifth, even as commissioned studies do make research possible, their
disconnectedness functions to undermine the research institutions. Effectively unable to
set their own agenda or to control the principal reward systems for their staff, research
institutions are buffeted by the fickle winds of agency priorities and preferences. Sixth,
the current penchant for reducing government functions reinforces the privatization of
research. Beyond their individual consulting contracts, in many countries researchers
have formed local consulting firms that market their services to foreign funding and technical assistance agencies. In itself, that is desirable, not problematic. As the privatization
of research has developed, however, it leads more toward the multiplication of parasitic
organizations entirely dependent on foreign patrons than toward the development of the

institutional capacities and the autonomy that enable research centers to establish and sustain solidly grounded, high-quality research programs.

The creation of knowledge is always a complex and spasmodic process. The boundaries between the university and other knowledge-generating arenas are often productively ambiguous. And it is certainly not unique in human history to insist that knowledge creation be utilitarian or to find knowledge creators dependent on those with disposable funds. When research as consulting functions to determine how problems are specified and addressed (often with economics and its perspectives and assumptions privileged), national dependence is institutionalized well into the future.

Methodological Orthodoxy Stymies Critical Inquiry

That the external assistance agencies have influenced education policy is clear. Less discussed but equally troubling has been their influence on research. Notwithstanding the debates and disagreements among those involved in commissioned research, the conjunction of external funding and research fosters a methodological orthodoxy. Quite simply, some theories and methods are deemed acceptable—and justified by terming them *scientific*. As local researchers develop their skills within that orthodoxy, their critical edge is dulled. The presumed universalism of the accepted research canons dismisses as simply poor social science efforts to depart from the mainstream in order to tune approach and method to the local setting.

In this way, the combination of foreign assistance and commissioned research functions to disseminate globally not only particular understandings of education and development but also how those understandings are created, revised, and refined. Effectively, financial crisis and structural adjustment have reinforced and entrenched the globalization of a particular sort of social science.

The Mystification of Knowledge and Power Relations

It is striking that individual scholars may orient their work very differently in the academic and financial-intellectual spheres of operation. In the former, the relevant audience is institutional and disciplinary, academic peers and university chairs and deans, whereas in the latter the officials of the employing agency constitute the audience that matters. They are more likely than the general body of academics to have shared preferences about method, approach, and findings. Much more easily than is possible at most universities and research institutes, funding agencies can readily terminate their relationship with a particular scholar.

In the conjunction of funding and research, scholarship becomes a proprietary process. The investors have the determining voice in the selection of topics, researchers, and methods, limit access to source materials, and often control the dissemination of findings. Consequently, the process of knowledge creation is obscured, mystifying the power relations embedded in the research and thereby in the programs it supports. Perhaps not entirely aware of their own role, scholars become advocates not only for particular understandings of development and underdevelopment but also for a particular sort of global order.

Knowledge is power in this setting. Education initiatives and reforms, even maintaining the schools, require resources. Securing funds requires research findings. Those who can provide research findings gain influence, often control, over decisions and programs. Those who determine the sorts of research that are acceptable secure even broader influence and control. More troubling, that systemic ability to constrain and set agendas and priorities is barely discernible and thus generally inaccessible, since it is embedded in ostensibly apolitical and neutral rules and procedures of research. Power relations that might be regarded as profoundly problematic if they were seen clearly are so enmeshed in everyday practices that they become invisible. Research intended to clarify education functions to mystify power and authority.

EDUCATION AND DEVELOPMENT

What progress, then, over the past few decades? The World Bank regularly suggests that we know more about education and development, thanks to an improved and expanded research base. Schools, meanwhile, remain overpopulated and underequipped, and in many poor countries, education for all remains a distant dream. International organizations and national authorities are apparently unable to translate greater knowledge into useful and sustainable practices.

Cause and effect are very difficult to establish clearly in education, which is an intricate web of processes, some integrally related and others distantly connected. It is therefore not surprising that the relationships between aid-supported curricular and instructional reforms on the one hand and specific developmental outcomes on the other are complex and difficult to discern. The links between education and development more generally are still harder to establish. However daunting the challenge, though, it is essential to inquire about the consequences of education assistance programs, both positive and negative.

Note that in the debates about education aid, its actual value to recipients remains unclear. While foreign assistance is generally presented as a transfer of resources from more to less affluent countries, critics regularly charge that aid results in a net capital outflow. The actual transfer is less than the total amount of aid, since much of the aid received must be spent on products, services, and personnel from the granting country and since the uses of that aid may cause other outflows (e.g., expenditures on maintenance and fuel for aid-provided vehicles). There has been, it seems, very little analysis of education aid's claimed benefits. The apparently expanding gap between the most and least affluent countries, the rapidly increasing debt burden of many of the world's poorest countries, and the dramatic increase in aid dependence challenge those claims. Racing down the fast track to planned dependence is surely not a viable development strategy.

It seems clear that effective education reform requires agendas and initiatives with strong local roots and the broad participation of those with a stake in outcomes, including not only officials but also students, parents, teachers, and communities. Unless the beneficiaries of the reform become its bearers, it is likely to be stillborn. External agencies can support that process only when they conceive their role in terms of development cooperation rather than providing philanthropy or determining directions. Research matters here. Many studies of education and development and their recommendations function in practice not to foster and facilitate dialogue but to undermine and discourage it. Seeking to provide clear and firm findings, they announce and pronounce. They set terms. They declare. Sheltered by specialized language and the strictures of confidentiality, they remain largely inaccessible outside a very small circle. Though they talk about capacity building, far too often they are incapacitating.

NOTES

1. Philip G. Altbach, "Patterns in Higher Education Development: Toward the Year 2000," in *Emergent Issues in Education: Comparative Perspectives*, ed. Robert F. Arnove, Philip G. Altbach, and Gail P. Kelly (Albany: State University of New York Press, 1992).

2. Altbach, "Patterns in Higher Education Development," 44.

3. A perspective developed by Samir Amin, from earlier works, *Accumulation on a World Scale: A Critique of the Theory of Underdevelopment* (New York: Monthly Review Press, 1974) and *Unequal Development: An Essay on the Social Formation of Peripheral Capitalism* (New York: Monthly Review Press, 1976), through more recent publications—for example, *Empire of Chaos* (New York: Monthly Review Press, 1992) and *Obsolescent Capitalism* (London: Zed Books, 2003).

4. As, for example, the composition of the Gulbenkian Commission on the Restructuring of the Social Sciences, chaired by Immanuel Wallerstein, *Open the Social Sciences: Report of the Gulbenkian Commission on the Restructuring of the Social Sciences* (Stanford, Calif.: Stanford University Press, 1996).

5. Martin Carnoy, "Education and the Transition State," in Martin Carnoy and Joel Samoff, *Education and Social Transition in the Third World* (Princeton, N.J.: Princeton University Press, 1990), 91*ff.* and n. 12.

6. Martin Carnoy, *The State and Political Theory* (Princeton, N.J.: Princeton University Press, 1984); and Martin Carnoy, "Education and the State: From Adam Smith to Perestroika," in *Emergent Issues in Education: Comparative Perspectives*, ed. Arnove, Altbach, and Kelly (Albany: State University of New York Press, 1992).

7. Samuel Bowles and Herbert Gintis, "Education as a Site of Contradictions in the Reproduction of the Capital-Labor Relationship: Second Thoughts on the Correspondence Principle," *Economic and Industrial Democracy* 2 (1981): 223–42.

8. John Boli, Francisco O. Ramirez, and John W. Meyer, "Explaining the Origins and Expansion of Mass Education," *Comparative Education Review* 29 (1985): 145–70; Francisco O. Ramirez and John Boli, "The Political Construction of Mass Schooling: European Origins and Worldwide Institutionalization," *Sociology of Education* 60 (1987): 2–17.

9. For example, Alex Inkeles and David Smith, *Becoming Modern: Individual Change in Six Developing Countries* (Cambridge, Mass.: Harvard University Press, 1974).

10. Immanuel Wallerstein, *The Modern World-System; Capitalist Agriculture and the Origins of the European World-Economy in the Sixteenth Century* (New York: Academic Press, 1974); Immanuel Wallerstein, *The Modern World-System II: Mercantilism and the Consolidation of the European World-Economy, 1600–1750* (New York: Academic Press, 1980); Immanuel Wallerstein, *The Modern World System III: The Second Era of Great Expansion of the Capitalist World-Economy, 1730–1840s* (San Diego, Calif.: Academic Press, 1989).

11. Robert F. Arnove and Edward H. Berman, *Neocolonial Policies of North American Philanthropic Foundations* (Paris: World Congress of Comparative Education, 1984); Robert F. Arnove, "The Ford Foundation and the Transfer of Knowledge: Convergence and Divergence in the World System," *Compare* 13, no. 1 (1983): 17–18; Robert F. Arnove, ed., *Philanthropy and Cultural Imperialism: The Foundations at Home and Abroad* (Boston: Hall, 1980); Edward H. Berman, *The Ideology of Philanthropy: The Influence of the Carnegie, Ford, and Rockefeller Foundations on American Foreign Policy* (Albany: State University of New York Press, 1983). See also F. X. Sutton, "The Ford Foundation's Transatlantic Role and Purposes, 1951–81," *Review* 24, no. 1 (2001): 77–104.

12. Talcott Parson's pattern variables provided a scientific legitimacy for that differentiation; see *Structure and Process in Modern Societies* (New York: Free Press, 1963). Valentin Y. Mudimbe

explores how those who saw themselves as modern required an Other to define themselves, inventing it as necessary, in *The Invention of Africa: Gnosis, Philosophy, and the Order of Knowledge* (Bloomington: Indiana University Press, 1988), and *The Idea of Africa* (Bloomington: Indiana University Press, 1994). Achille Mbembe, *On the Postcolony* (Berkeley: University of California Press, 2001) and Jacques Depelchin, *Silences in African History: Between the Syndromes of Discovery and Abolition* (Dar es Salaam: Mkuki na Nyota Publishers, 2005), have developed that perspective.

13. For example, "Some states are not yet fit to govern themselves." Paul Johnson, "Colonialism's Back—and Not a Moment Too Soon," *New York Times Magazine*, April 13, 1993, 23.

14. Newt Gingrich, Speaker of the U.S. House of Representatives, "Gingrich Says English Must be the 'Common Language,'" June 7, 1995, quoted in the *New York Times*, June 8, 1995.

15. Adam Przeworski, "The Neoliberal Fallacy," *Journal of Democracy* 3, no. 3 (July 1992): 45–59.

16. World Bank, *Adjustment in Africa: Reforms, Results, and the Road Ahead—Summary* (Washington, D.C.: Author, 1994), 10–13, drawing on the full report, World Bank, *Adjustment in Africa: Reforms, Results, and the Road Ahead* (Washington, D.C.: Author, 1994), 184–96.

17. World Bank, *Education: Sector Policy Paper* (Washington, D.C.: Author, 1980), 79.

18. World Bank, *Priorities and Strategies for Education: A World Bank Review* (Washington, D.C.: Author, 1995) and *Education Sector Strategy* (Washington, D.C.: Author, 1999).

19. On the evolution of UNESCO's role, see Karen Mundy, "Educational Multilateralism in a Changing World Order: Unesco and the Limits of the Possible," *International Journal of Educational Development* 19, no. 1 (January 1999): 27–52.

20. Joel Samoff, "Education Sector Analysis in Africa: Limited National Control and Even Less National Ownership," *International Journal of Educational Development* 19, nos. 4–5 (July–September 1999): 249–72, and "From Funding Projects to Supporting Sectors? Observations on the Aid Relationship in Burkina Faso," *International Journal of Educational Development* 24, no. 4 (July 2004): 397–427.

21. World Education Forum, *The Dakar Framework for Action* (Paris: UNESCO, 2000), at www.unesco.org/education/efa/wef2000/index.shtml. Based at UNESCO, the EFA global monitoring unit produces annual assessments of progress and problems, beginning with UNESCO, *Education for All: Is the World on Track?* (Paris: Author, 2002). Rosa Maria Torres provides an insightful and critical perspective on the 1990 and 2000 conferences: *One Decade of Education for All: The Challenge Ahead* (Buenos Aires: IIEP/UNESCO, 2000), and *What Happened at the World Education Forum?* (Buenos Aires: 2000), at www.fronesis.org/documentos/whathappendatdakar.pdf2006.12.23.

22. The Education for All Global Monitoring Reports (n. 23) provide data on aid flows to education and on the persisting gap between projected need and actual receipts, notwithstanding the affluent countries' promise that in countries with an effective EFA strategy, lack of funds should not preclude EFA objectives. Earlier reviews of projected aid requirements for EFA include Paul Bennell and Dominic Furlong, "Has Jomtien Made Any Difference? Trends in Donor Funding for Education and Basic Education since the Late 1980s," IDS Working Paper 51, Sussex, 1997; Christopher Colclough and Samer Al-Samarrai, "Achieving Schooling for All: Budgetary Expenditures on Education in Sub-Saharan Africa and South Asia," *World Development* 28, no. 11 (2000): 1927–44.

23. Noel F. McGinn, ed., *Crossing Lines: Research and Policy Networks for Developing Country Education* (Westport, Conn.: Praeger, 1996).

24. Edmundo F. Fuenzalida, "The Reception of 'Scientific Sociology' in Chile," *Latin American Research Review* 18, no. 2 (1983): 95–112.

25. UNESCO, *Strong Foundations: Early Childhood Care and Education. EFA Global Monitoring Report 2007* (Paris: UNESCO: 2006), estimates that at least U.S.$9 billion per year will be needed to achieve universal primary education by the target year 2015 and $11 billion per year

to reach all EFA goals (p. 102), while education aid commitments (generally larger than actual disbursements) for 2004 were estimated at $8.5 billion (p. 87).

26. *Local Solutions to Global Challenges: Toward Effective Partnership in Basic Education. Uganda Case Study* (The Hague: Netherlands Ministry of Foreign Affairs for the Consultative Group of Evaluation Departments, 2003), at www.euforic.org/iob/detail_page.phtml?&username =guest@euforic.org&password=9999&groups=IOB&act_id=3330&lang=en.

27. Reported in Joel Samoff, ed., *Coping with Crisis: Austerity, Adjustment, and Human Resources* (London: Cassell/UNESCO, 1994).

28. Joel Samoff with Suleman Sumra, "From Planning to Marketing: Making Education and Training Policy in Tanzania," in *Coping with Crisis*, ed. Samoff (London: Cassell/UNESCO, 1994).

29. I review the successive strategies for formulating education policy in "Education Policy Formation in Tanzania: Self-Reliance and Dependence," in *Education Policy Formation in Africa: A Comparative Study of Five Countries*, ed. David R. Evans (Washington, D.C.: U.S. Agency for International Development, 1994). Additional case studies of education policymaking in Africa are reported in Association for the Development of African Education, *Formulating Education Policy: Lessons and Experiences from Sub-Saharan Africa* (Paris: Association for the Development of African Education, 1996).

30. Former Costa Rican president Arias, quoted in Martin Carnoy and Carlos A. Torres, "Educational Change and Structural Adjustment: A Case Study of Costa Rica," in *Coping with Crisis*, ed. Samoff (London: Cassell/UNESCO, 1994), 92.

31. Michel Carton and Pape N'Diaye Diouf, with Christian Comeliau, "Budget Cuts in Education and Training in Sénégal: An Analysis of Reactions," in *Coping with Crisis*, ed. Samoff (London: Cassell/UNESCO, 1994).

32. Joel Samoff and Bidemi Carrol, *From Manpower Planning to the Knowledge Era: World Bank Policies on Higher Education in Africa* (Paris: UNESCO Forum on Higher Education, Research and Knowledge, 2004), 20–23, also available at unesdoc.unesco.org/images/0013/001347/134782eo.pdf.

33. United Nations General Assembly, Resolution A/56/326, September 6, 2001.

34. For basic documents, country reports, monitoring procedures, meetings, and more, see the World Education Forum website: www.unesco.org/education/efa/index.shtml.

35. World Bank, *Constructing Knowledge Societies: New Challenges for Tertiary Education* (Washington, D.C.: Author, 2002). For the foundation Partnership for Higher Education in Africa, see www.foundation-partnership.org/linchpin/index.php.

36. Among the best known are: Monitoring Learning Achievement [MLA] (UNESCO/UNICEF); Program for International Student Assessment [PISA] (OECD); Programme d'Analyse des Systèmes éducatifs des pays de la CONFEMEN [PASEC] (Confemen); Southern African Consortium for Monitoring Educational Quality [SACMEQ]; Trends in International Mathematics and Science Study [TIMSS].

37. For a comprehensive and critical overview, see Manuel Castells's series on The Information Age: Economy, Society and Culture (Oxford: Blackwell): *The Rise of the Network Society* (I, 1997), *The Power of Identity* (II, 1997), and *End of Millennium* (III, 1998).

38. World Bank, *World Development Report 1998/1999: Knowledge for Development* (Washington, D.C.: Oxford University Press for the World Bank, 1999). See also the Development Gateway (www.developmentgateway.org/) and the African Virtual University (www.avu.org/). For an overview of the critiques, see Alex Wilks, *A Tower of Babel on the Internet? The World Bank's Development Gateway* (London: Bretton Woods Project, 2001). That paper and an ongoing lively debate are available at www.brettwonwoodsproject.org.

39. James D. Wolfensohn, "The Challenge of Inclusion," Address to the board of governors, Hong Kong, China, September 23, 1997, 14.

40. Joel Samoff and Nelly P. Stromquist, "Managing Knowledge and Storing Wisdom? New

Forms of Foreign Aid?" *Development and Change* 32, no. 4 (September 2001): 631–56. See also Rosa-Maria Torres, "'Knowledge-Based International Aid': Do We Want It, Do We Need It?" in *Development Knowledge, National Research and International Cooperation*, ed. Wolfgang Gmelin, Kenneth King, and Simon McGrath (Edinburgh: Centre of African Studies, University of Edinburgh, 2001), 103–24.

41. Quoting Mark Blaug, *World Bank, Priorities and Strategies for Education: A World Bank Review* (Washington, D.C.: World Bank, 1995), 21. The citation attached to this sweeping claim (Mark Blaug, "The Empirical Status of Human Capital Theory: A Slightly Jaundiced Survey," *Journal of Economic Literature* 14 [1976]) is misleading, since Blaug's writing—for example, "Where Are We Now in the Economics of Education?" *Economics of Education Review* 4, no. 1 (1985): 17–28—rejects the unqualified accolade and many of the common uses of human capital theory.

42. "East Asia" is a recurring reference in *Priorities and Strategies for Education*, presumably used to refer not to a geographic region but to the countries (and then colonies) widely regarded to have experienced rapid economic growth: Singapore, South Korea, Taiwan, and Hong Kong.

43. Overseas Development Authority, *Into the Nineties: An Education Policy for British Aid* (London: Author, 1990), 7. For the use of rate-of-return analysis to reach the opposite conclusion—in Kenya, secondary, not primary, education has the higher rate of return—see John B. Knight and Richard H. Sabot, *Education, Productivity, and Inequality: The East African Natural Experiment* (Oxford: Oxford University Press/World Bank, 1990).

44. Even as the aid agencies stress feasibility and practicality, their own studies are regularly criticized for their inattention to context and feasibility. The former functions to limit critique and innovation while the latter permits them to promote general recommendations across diverse settings.

45. The overview, eligibility rules, and related documents for HIPC are at www.worldbank.org/hipc/. Similar information for FTI is at www.fasttrackinitiative.org/education/efafti/. For Poverty Reduction Strategy Papers, including the massive instruction book, see www.imf.org/external/np/prsp/prsp.asp. Note that in practice, most aid providers require extensive documents of this sort.

46. Among them, Susan George, *A Fate Worse Than Debt: A Radical New Analysis of the Third World Debt Crisis* (London: Penguin, 1988); Joanna Macrae et al., *Aid to 'Poorly Performing' Countries: A Critical Review of Debates and Issues* (London: Overseas Development Institute, 2004), at www.odi.org.uk/publications/poorly_performing_countries/Aid_to_PPCs.pdf. Cheryl Payer, *Lent and Lost: Foreign Credit and Third World Development* (London: Zed, 1991); and Judith Randel, Tony German, and Deborah Ewing, *The Reality of Aid 2000: An Independent Review of Poverty Reduction and Development Assistance* (London: Earthscan Publications, 2000).

47. Among them, Kevin Danaher, ed., *Fifty Years Is Enough: The Case against the World Bank and the International Monetary Fund* (Boston: South End, 1994); William Russell Easterly, *The White Man's Burden: Why the West's Efforts to Aid the Rest Have Done So Much Ill and So Little Good* (New York: Penguin Press, 2006); Susan George and Fabrizio Sabelli, *Faith and Credit: The World Bank's Secular Empire* (Boulder, Colo.: Westview, 1994); Dharam Ghai, ed., *IMF and the South: The Social Impact of Crisis and Adjustment* (Atlantic Highlands, N.J.: Humanities, 1991); and Judith Randel, Tony German, and Deborah Ewing, eds., *The Reality of Aid 2004: An Independent Review of Poverty Reduction and Development Assistance. Focus on Governance and Human Rights* (London: Zed Books, 2004). Among the studies of World Bank Africa education policies have been Birgit Brock-Utne, "Education Policies for Sub-Saharan Africa as Viewed by the World Bank: A Critical Analysis of World Bank Report No. 6934," in *Education in Africa: Education for Self-Reliance or Recolonization?* (Oslo: Universitetet I Oslo, 1993); Christopher Colclough, "Who Should Learn to Pay? An Assessment of Neo-Liberal Approaches to Education Policy," in *States or Markets? Neo-Liberalism and the Development Policy Debate*, ed. Christopher Colclough and James Manor (Oxford: Clarendon, 1991); Stephen P. Heyneman, "The History and Problems in the

Making of Education Policy at the World Bank 1960–2000," *International Journal of Educational Development* 23 (2003): 315–37; Phillip W. Jones, "Taking the Credit: Financing and Policy Linkages in the Education Portfolio of the World Bank," in *The Global Politics of Educational Borrowing and Lending,* ed. Gita Steiner-Khamsi (New York: Teachers College Press, 2004); Joel Samoff, "The Reconstruction of Schooling in Africa," *Comparative Education Review* 37, no. 2 (May 1993): 181–222; and Joel Samoff, "Which Priorities and Strategies for Education?" *International Journal of Educational Development* 16, no. 3 (July 1996): 249–71.

48. Among recent contributions, see ActionAid and Patrick Watt, *Fast Track or Back Track? The Education Fast Track Initiative: Make or Break for the Monterrey Consensus* (London: ActionAid, 2003); Birgit Brock-Utne, *Whose Education for All? Recolonization of the African Mind* (New York: Falmer, 2000); David Ellerman, *Helping People Help Themselves: From the World Bank to an Alternative Philosophy of Development Assistance. Evolving Values for a Capitalist World* (Ann Arbor: University of Michigan Press, 2005); Kenneth King and Lene Buchert, eds., *Changing International Aid to Education* (Paris: UNESCO, 1999); Akanksha A. Marphatia and David Archer, *Contradicting Commitments: How the Achievement of Education For All Is Being Undermined by the International Monetary Fund* (London: ActionAid, 2005). Jeanne Moulton, Karen Mundy, Michel Welmond, and James Williams, *Education Reforms in Sub-Saharan Africa: Paradigm Lost?* (Westport, Conn.: Greenwood Press, 2002); and Oxfam, *International Aid and Education: The Squandered Opportunity* (Oxford: Oxfam International, 2000).

49. For a detailed inventory and analytic overview of studies undertaken within the context of the aid relationship, see Joel Samoff, with N'Dri Thérèse Assié-Lumumba, *Analyses, Agendas, and Priorities in African Education: A Review of Externally Initiated, Commissioned, and Supported Studies of Education in Africa, 1990–1994* (Paris: UNESCO, 1996). The Working Group on Education Sector Analysis of the Association for the Development of Education in Africa has supported several national reviews of these studies, including Burkina Faso, Ghana, Lesotho, and Zimbabwe.

50. For a fuller development of this argument and examples, see Joel Samoff, "The Facade of Precision in Education Data and Statistics: A Troubling Example from Tanzania," *Journal of Modern African Studies* 29, no. 4 (December 1991): 669–89.

51. Problems with the reported data and their major causes are well known. The basic data deficiencies are often compounded by careless use of what is available (e.g., assuming that budgeted allocations are approximately the same as actual expenditures or comparing budget data in one year with expenditure data in another).

52. For an overview, see Joel Samoff, "Chaos and Certainty in Development," *World Development* 24, no. 4 (April 1996): 611–33. Abhijit Banerjee et al., *An Evaluation of World Bank Research, 1998–2005* (Washington, D.C.: World Bank, 2006) provides a detailed assessment that highlights the institutional pressures that can undermine research quality, at siteresources.worldbank .org/DEC/Resources/84797-1109362238001/726454-1164121166494/RESEARCH-EVALUA TION-2006-Main-Report.pdf.

53. Here I conflate commissioned research (studies initiated and funded by an external agency) and consulting (individual and occasionally institutional contracts for services rendered) because that is the common usage among the practitioners. For the extent of uncirculated education research in Africa, see Richard Maclure, "No Longer Overlooked and Undervalued? The Evolving Dynamics of Endogenous Educational Research in Sub-Saharan Africa," *Harvard Educational Review* 76, no. 1 (Spring 2006): 80–109.

3

The State, Social Movements, and Educational Reform

Raymond A. Morrow and Carlos Alberto Torres

The task of this chapter is to consider the relationship between the state, social movements, and education from a comparative perspective. Though this constellation of issues
may appear to be an obvious foundation for understanding comparative education, the
relationships between social movements and education have rarely been explicitly
addressed theoretically (as opposed to individual case studies), let alone taken up in relation to theories of the state.[1] In the first section, we introduce the problematic of the
state, culminating in a conception of a critical theory of the state that we shall use as the
framework for analyzing two contrasting policy orientations for understanding the state
and education: the classic welfare state model and the neoconservative alternative to it.
Then we shall introduce the theory of social movements, giving particular attention to
the contrast between old and new social movements. In contrast to the class-based form
of the traditional working-class movements that were crucial for the institutionalization
of mass education, the new social movements, we shall argue, have rather different implications for educational policy, especially in struggles over curricular content and the organization of learning. Finally, we shall suggest that the impact of globalization provides a
challenge for understanding the changing contexts for educational policy and its relationship to the state and social movements. The discussion will draw primarily upon examples and research based on European, North American, and Latin American experiences.

Before taking up the state and social movements, we shall make a few comments
about the particular complex of problems at issue here. The unifying theme of this chapter can best be situated in terms of the question of the relationship between education
and cultural reproduction, a problematic that highlights the question of the relationships
between social movements and the state. Models of cultural reproduction begin with the
premise that society needs to be understood as a complex and contradictory whole within
which dominant institutions primarily serve to reproduce the basic form of social order.[2]
Ordinarily, this process of reproduction requires extensive changes in society and culture,
which are very selective even though they may involve major reforms. They are selective
in that normally they do not challenge the overall continuity of a given form of society.

Yet this reproduction is never completely smooth and encounters various forms of opposition and resistance, ranging from individual acts to massive mobilizations organized by social movements. Such forms of collective behavior thus become the source of conflicts that the democratic state attempts to manage and control. Though often viewed as disruptive and as a threat to the status quo, social and cultural movements are also the primary source of change and innovation in society. In the context of education, the primary sites of such conflict are schools and educational policy at all levels. Histories of education typically present the celebratory history of policymaking as a progressive process based on "reforms" culminating in the present. From the perspective of the more fundamental claims and challenges of social movements, however, such reforms can often be revealed to distort the understanding of change. In this respect such reforms may serve to conceal ongoing social conflicts and dominant interests as well as reinforce the cultural capital of the professionals charged with legitimating and organizing.[3] Accordingly, the problematic of educational reform must be situated in the context of the contested relations between the state and social movements in the overall process of cultural reproduction and change.

THEORIES OF THE STATE

The liberal conception of the state—and the commonsense basis on which most people consider themselves to be democratic citizens—is centered on the notion of separate public powers (for the government and the governed). The state is conceived as the supreme political authority within precise limits.[4] This liberal notion of political authority needs to be reconsidered from the perspective of contemporary political science and political sociology. There is a dominant tradition of liberal political analysis that primarily addresses the question of state sovereignty and citizenship, that is, the formation of the citizen and the political culture of the nation. Such accounts provide the basis for official definitions of democracy in the primary and secondary curricula of liberal democracies.

A second tradition, that of liberal democratic theory, is more critical. It questions problems of political representation and accountability, that is, how the actions of individuals, institutions, and the state itself are subject to controls and checks and balances. This is particularly relevant in regard to the actions of individuals, institutions, corporations, and state agencies in the constituting of the democratic pact and in the extent to which their actions damage or betray the democratic pact. One influential stream of thought questions the effects of excessive individualism and calls for a more communitarian conception of public philosophy.[5]

A third tradition, Marxist social theory, focuses on the power of the state, especially those aspects related to the relationship between social class structure and the forces and instruments of political coercion. This analysis supposes that obtaining consensus and implementing measures that guarantee the fair representation of interests is not outside the realm of pressured persuasion or coercion, nor outside the realm of social relations of domination and exploitation.

Finally, the perspective of political sociology, with the extraordinary contributions of Max Weber, focuses on the study of the institutional mechanisms of the operation of the state, and especially on the exercise of the authority of the state and the relationships among nation-states.[6]

Despite their differences in theories of democracy, neo-Marxism and political sociology open new dimensions in the discussion of the state. As a theoretical point of departure, the notion of the state appears as a heuristic instrument, as a concept that differs radically from the classical notions of political regime, government, or public power found in pluralist democratic theory. Its usefulness is based on how the notion of the state includes the idea of the condensation of power and force in the society, a process that renders deeper levels of power invisible. The exercise of the power of the state occurs by the exercise of actions of power and co-action over civil society (i.e., nonstate institutions and voluntary associations) by means of specialized state apparatuses. This notion of the condensation of power also refers to another central aspect of the state—the notion that the state may exercise power relatively autonomously. This power may thus be independent of the major social actors (rather than merely represent their aggregated interests), even though on occasion it is exercised according to specific interests represented in society, for example, state action on behalf of specific elites. Thus the power of the state can reflect a specific political project, a class alliance, or a coalition of specific economic, social, cultural, or moral interests. The state appears as an alliance or a pact of domination.[7]

From the perspective of the critical theory of the state linking neo-Marxian and Weberian insights—the perspective that informs the following discussion—the state is also an arena of confrontation for conflicting political projects. As an arena of confrontation, it not only reflects the vicissitudes of social struggles and the tensions inherent in agreements and disagreements between social forces, but it also reflects the contradictions and difficulties of carrying out unified and coherent actions that are within the parameters of a specific political project. Every public policy, even though it is part of a project of domination, reflects an arena of struggle and a sounding board for civil society and its inherent tensions, contradictions, political agreements, and disagreements.

Approaching the state strictly as an actor in the struggle between social classes deemphasizes other important variables related to social action. In addition to class distinctions, other aspects of race, ethnicity, gender, geographical location, or ethical-moral or religious differences among individuals produce social relations and social actions that require the state to legislate, sanction, manage, and punish. According to Claus Offe, perhaps the leading German proponent of a critical theory of the state, one of the central issues related to the state is the contradiction between the state's need for capitalist accumulation and the legitimacy of the capitalist system itself.[8] For Offe, the state is a mediator in the crisis of capitalism, and it acquires specific functions in the mediation of the basic contradictions of capitalism—the growing socialization of production and the private appropriation of surplus value. In order to measure this fundamental contradiction, the state is obliged to increase its institutional functions, a process especially evident in the field of education.[9]

For Offe, the state is a self-regulating administrative system that reflects a group of institutional rules, regulations, and conventions that have historically developed in capitalist societies. Furthermore, the capitalist state does not necessarily respond directly to those who temporarily exercise power (the government of a particular political regime or party), nor does it directly respond to the dictates of particular social sectors (economic interests) or dominant classes. Given that the state appears as a pact of domination that mediates and attempts to prevent the recurrent crises of the capitalist system from affecting the conditions of production and reproduction of that system, the class perspective of the state is not based on representing specific sectoral interests, nor does it reflect the policies of the dominant classes or of a specific political group that may control governmental institutions.[10]

In sum, the state, as a pact of domination and a self-regulated administrative system, plays a central role as mediator in the context of the crises of capitalism, especially regarding the contradictions between accumulation and democratic legitimation. The discussion of theories of the state is particularly important for education for several reasons. First, the origins and specific characteristics of mass public education can only be understood in relation to a theory of the state and its relation to social movements. Second, the definition, interpretation, and analysis of contemporary educational problems and their solutions depend to a large extent on theories of the state that justify and underlie the diagnostic and solution. Finally, the new kinds of state intervention, often defined as the neoliberal state, reflect a substantial change in the logic of public action and involvement of the state. At the same time, this change in the character of the state can also reflect new visions about the nature and limits of the democratic pact, and of the character and role of education and educational policy in the global spread of capitalism.[11] From the perspective of critical theory, the normative implications of the erosion of democratization have been discussed in terms of the notion of the decline of democratic public sphere.[12]

The following two sections discuss two antinomical visions and practices of the state—the welfare state and the neoliberal state—two visions and practices that offer distinct options in regards to educational policy. Subsequently, using a political economy of education approach, we link the discussion of the neoliberal state to the globalization of capitalism. We outline some questions about the implications of globalization to state-society relationships and the challenges to social movements in the concluding section of this chapter.

FROM THE WELFARE STATE TO THE NEOLIBERAL STATE

The welfare state represents a social pact between labor and capital. Its origins can be found in the institutional reorganization of capitalism at the beginning of the century in Europe, especially in the European social democracies, such as the Scandinavian countries.[13] More recently, the New Deal engineered during Franklin Roosevelt's administration in the United States represents a form of government in which the citizens can aspire to reach minimum levels of social welfare, including education, health, social security, employment, and housing. Such public provisions are considered a right of citizenship rather than charity.[14]

Another central aspect is that this model operates under the assumption of full employment in an industrial economy following Keynesian models. For many reasons, such as populist experiences and the extreme inequality of income distribution in Latin America, state formations with a strong element of intervention in civil society have some similarities with the model of the welfare state. However, there is also an important divergence, especially the lack of state unemployment benefits. This state, which plays an important role as the modernizer of society and culture, is also a state that undertakes protectionist activities in the economy, supports the growth of internal markets, and promotes import substitution as a central aspect of the model of articulation between the state and society.

It is important to point out that the expansion and diversification of education took place in states very similar to the welfare state—interventionist states that considered educational expenditures an investment, expanded educational institutions, including the massification of enrollments, and enormously expanded educational budgets and the hiring of teachers. The role and function of public education was expanded, following the premises of the nineteenth-century liberal state that consolidated the nation and markets. In this liberal model of the state, public education postulated the creation of a disciplined pedagogical subject, and the role, mission, ideology, teacher training models, as well as the founding notions of school curriculum and official knowledge, were all profoundly influenced by the predominant philosophy of the state, that is, a liberal philosophy that was, despite its liberal origins, state oriented.[15]

PREMISES OF THE NEOLIBERAL STATE

Neoliberalism and the neoliberal state are terms used to designate a new type of state that emerged in the region in the past three decades. Tied to the experiences of the neoconservative governments, such as those of Margaret Thatcher and John Major in England, Ronald Reagan in the United States, and Brian Mulroney in Canada, the first significant case of neoliberalism implemented in Latin America is the neoliberal economic program carried out in Chile after the fall of Allende under the dictatorship of General Pinochet. More recently, the market models implemented by the governments of Carlos Saúl Menem in Argentina and Carlos Salinas in Mexico represent, with the particularities of the Argentinian and Mexican circumstances, a neoliberal model.[16]

Neoliberal governments promote notions of open markets, free trade, reduction of the public sector, decreased state intervention in the economy, and the deregulation of markets. In the context of developing countries, neoliberalism has been philosophically and historically associated with structural adjustment programs, whether initiated locally or through international pressures.[17] Structural adjustment is defined as a set of programs, policies, and conditionalities that are recommended by the World Bank, the International Monetary Fund, and other financial organizations. Although the World Bank distinguishes among stabilization, structural adjustment, and the policies of adjustment, it also recognizes that the use of these terms is "imprecise and inconsistent."[18] These programs of stabilization and adjustment have given rise to a number of policy recommendations, including the reduction of state spending, the devaluation of currencies to promote exports, the reduction of tariffs on imports, and an increase in public and private savings. A central aspect of this model is a drastic reduction in the state sector, especially via the privatization of state enterprises, the liberalization of salaries and prices, and the reorientation of industrial and agricultural production toward exports. In the short run, the purpose of these policy packages is to reduce the size of the fiscal deficit, public debt, inflation, exchange rates, and tariffs. In the long run, structural adjustment is based on the premise that exports are the engine of development. Thus structural adjustment and stabilization policies seek to free international exchange, reduce distortions in price structures, do away with protectionism, and facilitate the influence of the market in the Latin American economies.[19]

The political rationale of the neoliberal state encompasses a mixture of theories and interest groups that are tied to supply-side economics, monetarism, neoconservative cultural sectors, groups opposed to the redistributive policies of the welfare state, and sectors worried about the fiscal deficit at all costs. In other words, it is a contradictory alliance. These state models respond to fiscal crises and the crisis of legitimacy (real or perceived) of the state. In this way, citizen crises of confidence are important crises for the exercise of democratic representation and confidence in governments. In this culturally conservative and economically liberal model, the state, state interventionism, and state enterprises are part of the problem, not part of the solution. As has been pointed out on several occasions by neoliberal ideology, the best state is the small government.

The prevailing premises of the economic restructuring of advanced capitalism and the premises of structural adjustment are highly compatible with the neoliberal models. They imply the reduction of public spending, reduction of programs considered waste and not investment, sale of state enterprises, and mechanisms of deregulation to avoid state intervention in the business world. Together with the aforementioned, it is proposed that the state should participate less in the provision of social services (including education, health, pensions and retirement, public transportation, and affordable housing) and that these services should be privatized. The notion of *private* (and *privatization*) is glorified as part of a free market. It implies total confidence in the efficiency of competition because the activities of the public or state sector are seen as inefficient, unproductive, and socially wasteful. In contrast, the private sector is considered to be efficient, effective, productive, and responsive. Because of its less bureaucratic nature, it has the flexibility needed to adapt to the transformations occurring in the modern world. Free trade agreements, such as MERCOSUR or NAFTA between the United States, Mexico, and Canada, lead to production for export and the reduction of quota barriers, which are two central elements for the global circulation of capital. This is why (in contrast to the model of the welfare state in which the state exercises a mandate to uphold the social contract between labor and capital) the neoliberal state is decidedly probusiness, that is, it supports the demands of the business world. Nevertheless, as Daniel Schugurensky rightly points out, this departure from state interventionism is differential, not total.[20] It is not possible to abandon, for symbolic as well as practical reasons, all of the state's social programs. It is necessary to diffuse conflictive and explosive areas in the realm of public policy. That is why there are programs of social solidarity in Costa Rica and Mexico, or why Brazil and other Latin American countries have passed legislation that protects street children. Thus the modification of the schema of state intervention is not indiscriminate but is a function of differential power of the clientele, which leads to policies of solidarity among the poorest of society as well as subsidies and the transfer of resources for the middle and dominant sectors, including those who are fundamentally against protectionism. Furthermore, the state does not abandon the mechanisms of discipline and coercion, nor populist strategies of distribution of wealth (or promises of such), in order to obtain electoral consensus, especially during electoral campaigns. That is, the dismantling of the public policies of the welfare state are selectively, not indiscriminately, directed at specific targets.

A central element for understanding the development of neoliberalism is the globalization of capitalism. The phenomenon of globalization is based on the transformation of capitalism, which alters the principles of the functioning of capitalism, whether petty commodity production, imperialist expansion as the ultimate phase of capitalism (in the vision of Lenin), or the notion of monopoly capitalism analyzed by theoretical currents tied to the New Left in the United States (Paul Baran and Paul Sweezy) or what Offe has denominated late or disorganized capitalism.[21] From a postmodern perspective, Fredric Jameson defines the characteristics of postmodernism as the cultural logic of late capitalism.[22] The important element to retain is the idea of globalization in a post-Fordist world. It is central to understanding the transformations of capitalism and the transformations of the neoliberal model of the state.[23]

Before turning to the question of the state and social movement, we wish to emphasize the main conflicts between the neoliberal model and the neoconservative model. These tensions are reflected in various domains. On one hand, the neoliberal model promotes individual autonomy (i.e., possessive individualism). On the other hand, it suggests that all citizens have public responsibilities, a position not reconcilable with possessive individualism. In the economic realm, a similar dilemma exists in regard to promoting individually conceived preferences and the search for an alternative selection of public policies based on "rational public social choice." If, following the paradox proposed by economist Kenneth Arrow, markets are aggregates of individual preferences totally independent of any notion of the public good, this mechanism only functions— irrespective of the form of democracy—when there is considerable convergence in the order of preferences of individuals. This model of political philosophy cannot easily reconcile individuals with autonomous individual preferences and the state as an arena of negotiation of such preferences. Furthermore, it is impossible to advance this reconciliation with presuming that there is a set of stable norms of behavior supported by a mature state structure, a formally rational public policy based on a legal-rational model, and in the context of consensual bases that are widely accepted in the political culture of society. These conditions are obviously rather different from the everyday reality of the majority of the countries in the world.[24]

THEORIES OF SOCIAL MOVEMENTS

Paradoxically, state theories have not generally been coupled with adequate conceptions of social movements: "Surprisingly little attention has been paid to the interaction between social movements and the state."[25] The reasons for this neglect vary with the type of state theory. Though classical Marxism was in key respects primarily a theory of revolutionary social movements, it tended to reduce them to class movements, identifying the working class as the only "true" one and thus dismissing other forms of movements. More recent attempts to conceptualize education in terms of a model of social reproduction linking education and economy in terms of a correspondence principle typically conclude that educational outcomes are primarily a product of structural imperatives that nullify class resistance.[26]

In contrast, other forms of liberal pluralist state theory, related functionalist conceptions of society, and elitist theories of the state tend to be concerned with problems of order and legitimation, viewing social movements primarily as disruptive forms of protest to be controlled and contained. In this context, interest groups are viewed as the legitimate form for advancing political claims, whereas social movements are implicitly branded as fanatical expressions of extremist ideologies. In the case of pluralist liberal theories, this strategy has led to a focus on social movements as a form of interest group destined to be assimilated into existing or new political parties or, in the worst case scenario, threats to be contained through strategies of "counterinsurgency."

The neglect of social movements in educational sociology reflects their more general marginality in theories of society that have tended to be preoccupied with the basis of order. Though this tendency is most obvious in functionalist theories of society, it has been paradoxically reinforced by structuralist conflict theories preoccupied with explaining hegemony and cultural reproduction. Though these theories have more recently made resistance to hegemony in education a central thematic, this concern has largely been focused on forms of expressive behavior associated with the diverse standpoints articulating identity politics, rather than a historically specific account of actual social movements.

In short, taking the topic of social movements seriously requires giving more explicit attention to collective behavior and collective action, terms referring to the range of more or less spontaneous activities (ranging from crowd outbursts to revolutionary movements) that challenge the structures of existing institutions and cultural norms.[27] By exception, the social theory of French sociologist Alain Touraine has made social movements central to a theory of society and change.[28] The stricter meaning of social movements as a challenge to existing institutions should be clearly differentiated from the more diffuse notion of resistance as well as from the quite different notion of *reform movements* in education, which for the most part have little to do with politically threatening mass mobilization outside normal political channels. The following definition of social movements captures the key issues: A social movement is a collective actor constituted by individuals who understand themselves to have common interests and, for at least some significant part of their social existence, a common identity. Social movements are distinguished from other collective actors, such as political parties and pressure groups, in that they have mass mobilization, or the threat of mobilization, as their primary source of social sanction, and hence of power. They are further distinguished from other collectivities, such as voluntary associations or clubs, in being chiefly concerned with defending or changing society, or the relative position of the group in society.[29]

Paradoxically, early social movement theory was characterized by a split between those who followed psychological theories of the "crowd," which emphasized the irrational and destructive side of collective action (here following Le Bon and Freud), as opposed to conflict and Marxist sociology, which analyzed it as a rational response to exploitation and political powerlessness.[30] Nevertheless, the problematic of social movements has long been one of the underdeveloped issues of classic Marxist theory, which was based on utilitarian assumptions about individual economic interests. On this basis it was assumed that class mobilization based on subjective class consciousness was a natural outcome of the objective conditions of class exploitation. Various explanations were first advanced in the 1930s to take into account the weak class basis of twentieth-century social movements, especially their failure to culminate in revolutionary consciousness. For the Italian Marxist Antonio Gramsci the response was to take into consideration how the cultural hegemony of the dominant classes restricted the development of working-class consciousness; similarly, the Frankfurt School tradition of Critical Theory proposed that the cultural industries of the new media along with the internalization of authoritarian personality structures in the working class had similar immobilizing effects.

The revitalization of social movement theory from the 1960s onward developed in several new directions, especially in response to the worldwide emergence of radical student movements culminating in 1968 with dramatic confrontations in Paris, Mexico City, and elsewhere. It refused to understand collective action as irrational, and various approaches radically revised the analysis of self-interest in social movement mobilization. One body of social psychological research was based on a reduction of collective action to relative deprivation theory, a thesis based on the important observation that collective outbursts are more likely to be a response to frustrated rising expectations than to absolute levels of impoverishment or deprivation.[31] But such approaches have little to say about either the structural conditions that produce deprivation or the factors that allow some movements to mobilize and others not.

Another tradition of research attempted to reformulate the implications of a utilitarian conception of mobilization based on a drastic revision of the economic argument that informed Marx's conception of social interests. According to rational choice theory, the logic of collective action is paradoxical because if human motivation is essentially based on individual self-interest, members of a collectivity have no rational interest in making sacrifices for collective gains when they can achieve the benefits without participation. The resulting "free-rider" effect has the consequence of making mobilization extremely difficult given the weakness of ideals to motivate activism for the vast majority of movement members. In this respect, rational choice theory has been more successful as a critique of classical Marxism and an account of social movement failure than as an explanation of why and when they do occur.[32]

The most influential recent sociological approach has been resource mobilization theory, which puts particular emphasis on the organizational bases of social movement success and failure. From this perspective, both psychological and social structural determinants recede into the background, and the organizational dynamic of movements takes on a life of its own as an explanatory hypothesis.[33] However useful as a corrective, such approaches also fail as a general theory of social movements, downplaying both the role of the state and ideological factors in movement mobilization.

THE STATE AND SOCIAL MOVEMENTS

Whereas the preceding social movement theories tended to focus on psychological processes and movement organization, another line of inquiry has focused on the macrosocial context through a focus on the state. Three basic positions have been influential here: classic pluralism and neopluralism; class elitist, state-centered theories; and classic Marxism and neo-Marxism.[34] Pluralist models view the state as a relatively passive and neutral umpire between competing interest groups whose motivation is often viewed in terms of rational choice theory. Elitist theories focus on the question of "state capacity" and view social movements as an expression of state weakness. Finally, classic Marxist perspectives view the state as an instrument of class power challenged by class-based oppositional movements.

The most recent developments have drastically revised Marxist approaches through a selective appropriation of insights from resource mobilization theory, as well as focusing on ideology and culture. These developments are associated with the concepts of both post-Marxist and critical social theory. From this perspective, the terrain of civil society opens up as the central arena of democratic debate and change. Social movements represent the dynamic actors in civil society in challenging the state, and they are often facilitated by various kinds of nongovernmental organizations that have become significant actors in educational and other contexts. The resulting theory of new social movements has broken with classical Marxist theory in attempting to understand the relative shift from the politics of distribution to social movements concerned as well with identity politics and the quality of life. Discussion has centered around the contested thesis of the distinctiveness of "new social movements," a conception of largely European origin that puts greater emphasis on cognitive and ideological factors, as well as the importance of civil society (as opposed to the state) as an arena for change.[35] This approach arose from the attempt (beginning in the late 1960s) to make sense of protest movements that appeared to focus on distinctive issues and drew upon new types of participants: student movements, peace and environmental movements, the women's movement, and so on. According to this perspective, the new social movements differ in key aspects with respect to ideology (quality of life, as opposed to growth and redistribution); basis of support (diverse interests and emergent networks, as opposed to social classes related to industrial labor, agriculture, or race); motivations for participation (more idealist, as opposed to objective social interests); organizational structure (decentralized, as opposed to bureaucratic); and political style (extraparliamentary, as opposed to integrated into neocorporatist processes of negotiation).[36]

OLD AND NEW SOCIAL MOVEMENTS
AND EDUCATIONAL REFORM

The neglect of the relations between states and social movements has reinforced the even greater lack of explicit attention given to the relationship between education and social movements. Though educational change and reform are central to histories of education, functionalist approaches have tended to focus on the imperatives of differentiation as an autonomous process, as opposed to the dynamics of struggle between states and collective movements.[37]

The problematic of social movements touches on the educational field in various contexts of conflict theories of educational change. First, theories of educational practice (e.g., pedagogies) have often been the basis of cultural reformist movements aligned with broader social movements. More typically, the affiliation of educational theories with social movements has remained more marginal.[38] Today, the "back to basics" movement in education is broadly affiliated with New Right political movements, much as "critical pedagogy" has ties with New Left movements.

Second, the problematic of student movements is largely associated with contexts in which the university itself (and occasionally secondary educational institutions) becomes the site of social movement activity. Such student movements have had periodic influence in advanced industrial societies (e.g., the revolutionary uprisings in Europe after World War I; confrontations in Europe involving fascists, socialists, and communists in the 1930s; and the worldwide student revolts of the late 1960s).[39] In many underdeveloped contexts, student movements have continued to be a source of agitation against more or less authoritarian states that serve to reproduce vast inequality of income and opportunity. In these settings, struggles over university autonomy have been in part triggered by the political threats posed by student movements.

Third, educational policy may be an explicit part of a general social movement, as in the case of "old" social movement theory concerned with working-class mobilization. The classic example here is the role that education played as one of the demands of European labor movements in the nineteenth and twentieth centuries.[40] The rise of public schooling in the West can be broadly described as the outcome of the struggles of class-based social movements to gain state support for inclusion as part of a universal citizenship.[41] Some of these have been associated with major social transformations. Following the Mexican Revolution, for example, educational reform was officially linked with extensive efforts to expand rural schooling and assimilate the campesino and indigenous populations.

With the decline of various single-factor theories of educational growth (e.g., human capital theory, modernization theory), more comprehensive models of educational expansion have stressed the competitive struggle between institutionalized corporate and potential primary actors, that is, those capable of collective action.[42] One general conclusion of such research is that "the cause of the initial period of educational expansion is found in the behavior of the self-consciously marginal. An essential precondition is the erosion of one's location in the traditional social order."[43] In the European case the contention between Protestants and Catholics provided the initial impetus for primary action, whereas class-based movements emerged later in response to the Industrial Revolution. For example, the English case represents a complex process in which the Chartist and Owenite movements played an important role in the development of public education.[44] Similarly, in this century, aspirations for basic educational rights have typically been part of modern urban and agrarian class-based movements (largely composed of peasants) in so-called Third World contexts.

One of the few explicit contemporary attempts to link the state, social movements, and education as part of a general theory can be found in Martin Carnoy and Henry Levin's "social-conflict" theory of the state, which "provides a framework for developing a dialectical analysis of education in capitalist society, because it views social movements as playing a vital role in affecting educational policy."[45] On this basis an effort can be made to "predict" educational reforms and assess the potential and limits of struggles over schooling. Nevertheless, this approach remains largely within the framework of the class-based assumptions of "old" social movement theory, ignoring the peculiarities of the new social movements.

Finally, new social movement theory has provided the basis for a dramatic shift in understanding the relationship between social movements and education. A distinctive characteristic of new social movements is their cognitive and ideological focus on rethinking preexisting social and cultural paradigms as part of a politics of identity. As a consequence, one of their key strategies is broadly educational as opposed to political. Although they have experienced numerous setbacks at the level of dramatic changes in policy in response to new social movement demands, they have been more successful in their educational efforts, a process reflected in significant shifts in public opinion on various issues such as gender, race, the environment, peace, and sexual orientations. In the case of the racially based civil rights movement in the United States, the dismantling of segregated schools constituted perhaps the most fundamental and far-reaching demand linking race and education.[46] Virtually every new social movement has also been characterized by the advocacy of curricular change and has generally found a few sympathetic listeners within teacher education and among education policymakers. Moreover, the pluralist mandate of public educational systems in most liberal democracies requires ongoing updates of the agenda of "legitimate" issues to be presented as part of mass education. Such effects increase dramatically at the higher levels, thus precipitating recent debates about "political correctness" on university campuses, especially in the United States.[47] To a great extent, this whole debate can be viewed in terms of the significant success of new social movements in reforming—if not fundamentally transforming—the content of higher education in the humanities, and to a lesser extent the social sciences (which have long been more attuned to inputs from social movements). For the most part these changes have proceeded along the lines of the single-issue demands often typical of identity politics. One consequence has been the need to rethink the relationships between race, class, and gender in education.[48]

Efforts to link and integrate new social movements with educational reform from the 1980s onward are most closely associated with the cultural movement most commonly identified with the term *critical pedagogy*. Known variously as *postmodern, multicultural,* and *postcolonial* education, critical pedagogies have attempted to articulate "the language of possibility" that could unite such diverse oppositional movements.[49] In this context the notion of a postmodern or postcolonial pedagogy is evoked as a diffuse reference point for an epoch in which Western universalisms and scientific certainties are called into question from diverse perspectives as a particular Eurocentric and masculinist view of the world.

The general failure of critical pedagogies to effect significant change has elicited various forms of criticism. Most fundamentally, it has been argued that such efforts to develop a general critical pedagogy and apply it to stimulating counterhegemonic resistance in schools is inconsistent with Gramsci's theory of hegemony concerned with "social and political movements, as in 1968 in France and Mexico or in 1970 in the United States."[50] More negatively, it has been argued that the failures of critical pedagogy—as a "transformative pedagogy in general"—stem precisely from the lack of a historically specific relation to social movements. The effect of critical pedagogy is to further distance new sociologists from past, contemporary, and emergent social movements; to replace with generality, the specific requirements of an educational politics; and, finally, to diminish social understanding that prohibits flight from history and politics.[51] Nevertheless, under the impetus of postmodernist and multicultural debates, critical pedagogy has consistently attempted to incorporate a multiplicity of voices from new social movements as part of the struggle against "the disconcerting proliferation of separatist forms of identity politics."[52]

Though critical pedagogies have not had a major impact on educational policy, they inform various social movements and in several developing societies have played a significant role as part of a process of political mobilization. On the one hand, there are the revolutionary experiences of Cuba, Nicaragua, and Mozambique. On the other, attempts at educational reform played a crucial part in the failure of socialist movements in Allende's Chile and, in a very different context, became the basis for innovative policies in São Paulo in Brazil.[53]

THE CHALLENGES AHEAD: THE GLOBALIZATION OF CAPITALISM, THE STATE, AND SOCIAL MOVEMENTS IN EDUCATION

From the perspective of emerging relationships between the state, social movements, and education, the theoretical problematic of globalization provides a more grounded and empirically analyzable set of questions than the slippery formulations associated with postmodernism and postcolonialism. Consequently it has been argued that "just as post-modernism was the concept of the 1980s, globalization may be the concept of the 1990s, a key idea by which we understand the transition of human society into the third millennium."[54] Though globalization in general has a long history, its specific meaning today is linked to the increasingly linear acceleration of the processes associated with it in the mid-twentieth century. In this respect globalization overlaps with processes variously described as postindustrialization, postmodernization, post-Fordism, and the information society. In sum, it can be defined as "a social process in which the constraints of geography on social and cultural arrangements recede and in which people become increasingly aware that they are receding."[55]

Economic globalization is the result of a worldwide economic restructuring that involves the globalization of economies, science, technology, and culture, as well as a profound transformation in the international division of labor.[56] Along with this transformation in the international division of labor, there has been a readjustment of economic integration among nations, states, and national and regional economies.[57] In large part, this globalization is a result of changes in communications and computer technology that increase the productivity of labor, replace labor with capital, and lead to the development of new areas of high productivity (e.g., software technology, which helped people like billionaire Bill Gates and the Microsoft Corporation have a worldwide reach). These changes are redefining relations between nations. They involve the mobility of capital via international exchanges as well as short-term, high-risk financial instruments. There is an enormous concentration and centralization of capital and production at the international level.[58]

Labor markets in contemporary capitalism are not homogeneous. The segmentation of labor markets implies that there are at least four kinds of markets: (1) a market that responds to the demands of monopoly capitalism, usually transnational; (2) a market that responds to the demands of competitive capitalism, representing the secondary labor market; (3) a market that is the public sector, one of the few labor markets relatively protected from international competition; and (4) a rapidly growing marginal labor market that includes everything from illegal transactions (such as narcotics trafficking) to self-employment, domestic work, family enterprises, small-scale subsistence production, and numerous other economic activities, which have been called marginal, underground, or informal work.

A central characteristic of this highly globalized capitalism is that the factors of production are not located in close geographic proximity. Furthermore, marginal profit rates are growing because of continuing increases in per capita productivity (which continues to increase in advanced capitalism) and a reduction of costs (via layoffs, intensification of production, replacing more expensive workers with less expensive ones, or replacing labor with capital). With the growing segmentation of labor markets in which the primary markets offer more income, stability, and perquisites, the hourly wage has been replaced by piecework. This creates a clear distinction between the nominal and real salaries and wages of workers and the social wage via indirect loans and state actions. At the same time, this set of transformations implies the decline of the working class and a reduction of the power of organized labor in negotiating economic policies and in the constitution of the social pact underscoring state domination. Over the last three or four decades, the service sectors have continued to grow, reducing the importance of the gross national product in the primary sector and manufacturing.

These changes in the global composition of labor and capital are taking place at a time when there is an abundance of labor, and conflicts between labor and capital are decreasing. The increase of supernumerary workers is also associated with an increase in international competition and the conviction on the part of the working class and labor unions that it is not possible to exclusively pressure the companies in search of more and better social services or salaries. This is impossible because of the abundance of labor, as well as the awareness of the falling profit margins of companies in the transnational and competitive environments, and the resulting loss of jobs and the accelerated migration of capital from regional markets in advanced capitalistic countries to areas in which labor is highly skilled and poorly paid. The threat of free-trade agreements such as NAFTA or the new arrangements proposed by GATT mark the limits of protectionist policies. For example, engineers and computer experts from India enter payroll information of North American companies into databases for a fraction of the cost of employing white collar workers, or low-cost mass production by Chinese workers, sometimes subject to forced labor. In order to deal with falling rates of profits, transnational capitalism is attempting to achieve more productivity per capita or the reduction of the actual costs of production, as well as transferring its production activities to tax-free zones characterized by cheap and highly skilled labor, limited organized labor, and easy, efficient, and cheap access to natural resources.

This new global economy is very different from the former national economy. National economies were previously based on standardized mass production, with a few managers controlling the production process from above and a great number of workers following orders. This economy of mass production was stable as long as it could reduce its costs of production (including the price of labor) and retool quickly enough to remain competitive at the international level. Because of advances in communications and transportation technology and the growth of service industries, production has become fragmented around the world. Production is moving to areas of the world with either cheaper or better-trained labor, favorable political conditions, access to better infrastructure and national resources, larger markets, and tax incentives.[59]

The new global economy is more fluid and flexible, with multiple lines of power and decision-making mechanisms, analogous to a spider's web, as opposed to the static pyramidal organization of power that characterized the traditional capitalist system.[60] Although the public education system in the old capitalist order was oriented toward the production of a disciplined and reliable workforce, the new global economy requires workers with the capacity to learn quickly and to work in teams in reliable and creative ways. Robert Reich defines these workers as symbolic analysts who will make up the most productive and dynamic segments of the labor force.[61]

Along with the segmentation of labor markets, full-time workers have been replaced with part-time workers (with a substantial reduction in the cost of labor due to fewer employer contributions to health, education, social security, etc.), an increase in female participation in labor markets, a systematic fall in real salaries, and a growing gap that separates salaried workers from the dominant sectors of society. A similar international phenomenon can be identified in the growing social and economic gap between developing countries and advanced capitalistic nations. The only exceptions are the newly industrializing countries of Asia.

In order to understand the changes in educational reform trends in the age of global-ization, it is necessary to consider the implications of theories of the state and theories of social movements. Cultural globalization presents important issues with respect to social movements in various ways. One expression is the increasing international links between new social movements, a process also evident in religious movements. It has been argued that globalization has contradictory effects in provoking fundamentalist religious and eth-nic movements that challenge the secularization of education and at the same time encouraging other ecumenical tendencies that force religious and ethnic movements to "relativize" their positions through the discovery of common principles.[62] But the pri-mary impact of globalization—whether political, economic, or cultural—is reflected in a broad shift toward an international standardization of educational curricula and creden-tials that goes beyond (though has not altogether escaped) earlier forms of educational colonialism.[63]

The relationship between globalization and education remains an emergent form of inquiry. One promising line of analysis builds on the concept of the creolization of cul-ture, a notion drawn from linguistics that provides a more empirically grounded basis for issues that have been taken up in the postcolonial literature under the heading of hybrid-ity.[64] Ulf Hannerz stresses that "the cultural processes of creolization are not merely a matter of constant pressure from the center toward the periphery, but a more creative interplay."[65] In short, "creolist concepts also intimate that there is hope yet for cultural variety. Globalization need not be a matter only of far-reaching or complete homogeniza-tion; the increasing interconnectedness of the world also results in some cultural gains."[66] In the context of peripheral societies, cultural flows are framed primarily by the state and markets. On the one hand, the most common focus of attention is on how states typically use education to construct citizens as well as inculcate "an almost universally replicated set of basic skills, including literacy and numeracy."[67] But there is also a very different process whereby the state serves as a transnational cultural mediator through which edu-cation becomes the filter between the metropolitan culture and the indigenous culture that remains more marginally influenced and necessarily appropriates global culture on its own terms. Though the state channels transnational influences, it cannot fully control their relation to local practices. Those with higher levels of formal education reflect the rhetoric of globalization as market-based homogenization in their consumption patterns; less visible are the opposite processes: "creolized musics, art, literature, fashion, cuisine, often religion as well, come about through such processes."[68]

NEW DEVELOPMENTS: AFTERTHOUGHT FOR THE THIRD EDITION

The potential for—and the specific types of—social movements that arise to challenge existing educational policies is closely linked to the ranking of countries in the annual UN "human development" reports, which give considerable weight to educational out-comes, as well as health and gender equity. For this reason, a country such as Cuba—with a fraction of the per capita gross national product of Mexico—is ranked at about the same level of human development. With respect to the emergence of so-called subaltern resistance movements, it is important to differentiate the rather different—if overlap-ping—effects of educational marginalization and exclusion.[69] Whereas marginalization is associated with being outside of the formal market economy and educational institutions (e.g., as expressed in high levels of illiteracy and high dropout rates for those who do have primary education), exclusion results from the inequities of status attainment produced by the inability of large, increasingly urban sectors to take advantage of educational and other resources that—according to official democratic policies—are supposed to be available to all. The higher ranked countries thus tend to have educational deficiencies linked primarily to issues of social exclusion such as regional pockets of poverty, unequal access to tertiary levels training, or ethnic conflicts related above all to refugees and migration, a problem that the European Union now shares with North America. The remaining countries with lower levels of human development vary considerably by region, with various combinations of marginalization and exclusion. Paradoxically, however, the nation-states most in need of educational reform—those ranked in the bottom half of human development with the highest levels of both marginalization and exclusion—are least likely to produce influential transformative social movements in the short run, e.g., most of sub-Saharan Africa, countries with more traditional Islamic regimes, and authoritarian states generally. Significant educational reforms—whether driven by social movements or top-down state policies—have been more likely to emerge in upper middle-level countries that have made significant—if often fragile and unconsolidated—breakthroughs with respect to democratization, such as the "Asian tigers" or South Africa, where social movements have played a very important role in postapartheid reconstruction.

The case of Latin America is distinctive, partly because of its visibility at the beginning of the twenty-first century as a test case for theories of civil society and social movements as an alternative to classical revolutionary models of class mobilization. Whereas three decades ago marginalization was the primary focus of attention in studying inequality, increasingly exclusion has become a preoccupation, especially in the urban contexts of poverty and "new" social movement formation. Traditional Marxist critics argue that more recent moderately leftist reformist regimes—symbolized by Lula's election in Brazil in 2002 and subsequent regime changes in Uruguay, Argentina, Chile, and elsewhere—have inevitably failed to produce any fundamental change.[70] In contrast, a number of other researchers have attempted to analyze the potential created by the pressures of civil society and social movements upon reformist governments attempting to expand democratic participation in the wake of democratic transitions and thus build the foundations for longer-term changes, a strategy that should in principle give educational reform a higher priority.[71] The most novel expressions of change have been regional indigenous movements (most visibly in the Zapatista movement in Chiapas, Mexico), including demands for bilingual education adapted to both indigenous traditions and the construction of new forms of cultural hybridity.[72] As well, diverse urban popular movements have emerged as a major force for challenging reformist regimes and parties.[73] In both cases the growing strength of a transnational civil society has provided occasional support for local movements, sometimes with the aid of the international media and use of the Internet.[74] Over the next decade, comparative case studies in Latin America will thus provide important evaluations of the outcomes relating to the impact of social movements, democratization, and globalization on educational policy.

A significant topic of research relates to the networks of social movements organized not only around their specific demand but also in coordination with similar efforts transnationally—what could be termed globalization from below. In the terminology of the Paulo Freire Institutes, such grassroots initiatives now constitute an international social movement, the planetarization of the world.[75] What comes to mind immediately is the developments in the last decade of the World Social Forum (WSF), sparking a multitude of regional and local Social Forums, serving as a platform challenging the premises and practices of neoliberalism. Intimately associated with the WSF are the new developments of the World Educational Forum, which has evolved into an organizationally complex and rich international development. In addition, there is a rich activism of new social movements.

There are many examples of these new realities, including the new activism in indigenous rights movements in Ecuador, Bolivia, and Peru; the interactions between the movement *Barrios de Pie* (Neighborhoods Standing Up) in Argentina, created after the 2001 economic crisis; by unemployed people to provide basic social services and run production cooperatives; and the Brazilian movement *Os Sim Terra*, questioning the basic premises of private property and seeking a comprehensive agrarian reform—even challenging the economic, social, and educational policies of President Lula's *Partido dos Trabalhadores*. These new social movements and initiatives in popular education are challenging the way we understand policymaking and educational reform, indeed a subject for theory, research, and policy.

THEORY AND RESEARCH IN SOCIAL MOVEMENTS, GLOBALIZATION, AND EDUCATIONAL REFORM: A RESEARCH AGENDA

Economic globalization has provided an impetus for efforts to reorganize education and teachers' work and curricula along lines that the New Right claims reflect the imperatives of the new world economy, a process reinforced by the pressures of international organizations such as the World Bank. As a consequence, the demands of local, movement-based struggles can often be marginalized in the name of strategies of "national" development that just happen to coincide with the longer-term interests of global, transnational capital. Though most obvious in the case of underdeveloped countries under pressure from international agencies, such processes can also be seen at work on a more voluntary basis in neoliberal, post-Fordist educational policies in advanced societies.

There are five questions that suggest future research agendas:

1. Does globalization mean that the nation-state has lost its power to control social formations and therefore to create conditions for socialization, citizenship, and the promotion of a democratic environment?
2. Did social movements decline in the 1980s and 1990s and will demobilization continue with the process of globalization, thus eroding the capacity of social movements to open up new cultural and social possibilities in the twenty-first century?
3. Can we aptly characterize the rise of right-wing social movements in education, for instance, those presented in the analysis of Michael Apple and Anita Oliver,[76] as emblematic of the crisis of the state and suggestive of the impossibility of social movements re-emerging as progressive, transformative forces?
4. Given the intersection of state crises with the apparent weakness of social move-

ments—old or new—in the age of globalization, what are the implications for socialization, education, citizenship, and democracy?

5. How will processes of global creolization affect metropolitan and peripheral societies, especially with respect to educational stratification, elite formation, and cultural change?

NOTES

This chapter was presented to the Comparative and International Education Society Conference (CIES), Mexico City, March 19–23, 1997.

1. See, for example, Robert F. Arnove, Philip G. Altbach, and Gail P. Kelly, eds., *Emergent Issues in Education: Comparative Perspectives* (Albany: State University of New York Press, 1992). The section on "contemporary reform movements" is misleading in that it focuses on reform processes driven by state bureaucracies rather than on the social movements that may have either contributed to new agendas or might oppose them. The problematic of social movements is thus largely absent from this volume.

2. Raymond A. Morrow and Carlos A. Torres, *Social Theory and Education: A Critique of Theories of Social and Cultural Reproduction* (Albany: State University of New York Press, 1995).

3. Thomas S. Popkewitz, *A Political Sociology of Educational Reform: Power/Knowledge in Teaching, Teacher Education, and Research* (New York: Columbia University, Teachers College Press, 1991).

4. David Held, *Political Theory and the Modern State* (Stanford: Stanford University Press, 1989), 12.

5. For example, Michael J. Sandel, *Democracy's Discontent* (Cambridge: Harvard University Press, 1996).

6. Held, *Political Theory and the Modern State*, in David Held, ed., *Political Theory* (Stanford: Stanford University Press, 1991); Heinz Rudolf Sonntag and Héctor Valecillos, *El Estado en el Capitalismo Contemporáneo* (México: Siglo XX Editores, 1977); David Held et al., eds., *States and Societies* (Oxford: Martin Robinson/The Open University, 1983); Andrew Vincent, *Theories of the State* (Oxford: Basil Blackwell, 1987).

7. Fernando H. Cardoso, "On the Characterization of Authoritarian Regimes in Latin America," in *The New Authoritarianism in Latin America*, ed. D. Collier (Princeton, N.J.: Princeton University Press, 1979). The term *domination* here is employed in the sense suggested by Max Weber's theory of *Herrschaft*, a German term referring to modes of relations between ruling and ruled, and variously translated as authority or domination. Hence a "pact of domination" alludes to the ways in which those ruled voluntarily accept the legitimacy of the ruler, thus producing ostensibly "legitimate" authority.

8. Claus Offe, *Contradictions of the Welfare State*, ed. John Keane (London: Hutchinson, 1984).

9. Carlos Alberto Torres, "The Capitalist State and Public Policy Formation: A Framework for a Political Sociology of Educational Policy-Making," *British Journal of Sociology of Education* 10, no. 1 (1989): 81–102; and Morrow and Torres, *Social Theory and Education*, chap. 12.

10. Martin Carnoy, *The State and Political Theory* (Princeton, N.J.: Princeton University Press, 1984), 131–40.

11. Carlos Alberto Torres, "La Universidad Latinoamericana: De la Reforma de 1918 al Ajuste Estructural de los 1990," in *Curriculum Universitario Siglo XXI*, ed. C. Torres et al. (Parana, Argentina: Facultad de Ciencias de la Educación, Universidad Nacional de Entre Rios, July 1994).

12. Craig Calhoun, ed., *Habermas and the Public Sphere* (Cambridge, Mass.: MIT Press, 1992).

13. Gøsta Esping-Andersen, *The Three Worlds of Welfare Capitalism* (Princeton, N.J.: Princeton University Press, 1990).

14. Harold R. Wilensky, *The Welfare State and Equality: Structural and Ideological Roots of Public Expenditures* (Berkeley: University of California Press, 1975); Harold R. Wilensky, *The New Corporatism: Centralization and the Welfare State* (Beverly Hills, Calif.: Sage, 1976); Popkewitz, *Political Sociology of Educational Reform*.

15. Margaret S. Archer, *The Sociology of Educational Expansion: Take-Off, Growth, and Inflation in Educational Systems* (Beverly Hills, Calif.: Sage, 1982); Adriana Puiggrós, *Democracia autoritarismo en la pedagogía Argentina y Latinoamericana* (Buenos Aires: Galerna, 1990); Adriana Puiggrós et al., *Sujetos, disciplina y curriculum en los orígenes del sistema educativo Argentino* (Buenos Aires: Galerna, 1992).

16. Without attempting to make a theoretical excursus, it is useful to point out that the notions of neoconservativism and neoliberalism have been identified by Michael Apple as two factions of the same movement of the right. See Michael Apple, *Official Knowledge: Democratic Education in a Conservative Age* (New York: Routledge, 1993). Apple's position and some of the differences between the two ideologies have been discussed in Carlos Alberto Torres, *Democracy, Education, and Multiculturalism: Dilemmas of Citizenship in a Global World* (Lanham, Md.: Rowman and Littlefield, 1998).

17. Larissa Lomnitz and Ana Melnick, *Chile's Middle Class: A Struggle for Survival in the Face of Neoliberalism* (Boulder, Colo.: Lynne Rienner, 1991), 9–47.

18. Cited in Joel Samoff, "More, Less, None? Human Resource Development: Responses to Economic Constraint" (unpublished paper, Palo Alto, Calif., June 1990), 21.

19. Sergio Bitar, "Neo-Conservativism versus Neo-Structuralism in Latin America," *CEPAL Review* 34 (1988): 45.

20. Daniel Schugurensky, "Global Economic Restructuring and University Change: The Case of Universidad de Buenos Aires" (Ph.D. diss., University of Alberta, 1994).

21. Claus Offe, *Contradictions of the Welfare State*. See also Scott Lash and John Urry, *The End of Organized Capitalism* (Madison: University of Wisconsin Press, 1987).

22. Fredric Jameson, *Postmodernism or the Cultural Logic of Late Capitalism* (Durham, N.C.: Duke University Press, 1991).

23. For a detailed discussion of the post-Fordist model of education, see Carlos Alberto Torres, *Education, Power and the State: Dilemmas of Citizenship in Multicultural Societies* (Lanham, Md.: Rowman and Littlefield, 1998), chap. 2.

24. Michael Williams and Geert Reuten, "After the Rectifying Revolution: The Contradictions of the Mixed Economy," *Capital and Class* 49 (Spring 1993): 82.

25. J. Craig Jenkins and Bert Klandermans, "The Politics of Social Protest," in *The Politics of Social Protest: Comparative Perspectives on States and Social Movements*, ed. J. Craig Jenkins and Bert Klandermans (Minneapolis: University of Minnesota Press, 1995), 5.

26. It should be noted that the correspondence theory of social reproduction developed by Samuel Bowles and Herbert Gintis in their *Schooling in Capitalist America* (New York: Basic Books, 1976) attempted to interpret the history of American education in terms of the class contexts of educational reform movements.

27. For example, Charles Tilly, *From Mobilization to Revolution* (New York: Random House, 1978).

28. Alain Touraine, *The Voice and the Eye: An Analysis of Social Movements*, ed. Alan Duff (Cambridge: Cambridge University Press, 1981).

29. Alan Scott, *Ideology and the New Social Movements* (London: Unwin Hyman, 1990), 6.

30. Clark McPhail, *The Myth of the Madding Crowd* (New York: Aldine de Gruyter, 1991).

31. Ted Gurr, *Why Men Rebel* (Princeton, N.J.: Princeton University Press, 1970).

32. Mancur Olson, *The Logic of Collective Action* (Cambridge: Harvard University Press, 1965).

33. John McCarthy and Mayer Zald, "Resource Mobilization and Social Movements," *American Journal of Sociology* 82 (1973): 1212–41; Aldon D. Morris and Carol McClung Mueller, eds., *Frontiers in Social Movement Theory* (New Haven, Conn.: Yale University Press, 1992).

34. J. Craig Jenkins, "Social Movements, Political Representation, and the State: An Agenda and Comparative Framework," in *The Politics of Social Protest*, ed. Jenkins and Klandermans (Minneapolis: University of Minnesota Press, 1995); for Latin America, see, for example, Susan Eckstein, ed., *Power and Popular Protest: Latin American Social Movements* (Berkeley: University of California Press, 1989); Willem Assies, Gerrit Burgwal, and Ton Salman, *Structures of Power, Movements of Resistance: An Introduction to the Theories of Urban Movements in Latin America* (Amsterdam: Center for Latin American Research and Documentation, 1990).

35. John Keane, ed., *Civil Society and the State* (London: Verso, 1988); Jean L. Cohen and Andrew Arato, *Civil Society and Political Theory* (Cambridge, Mass.: MIT Press, 1992); Joe Foweraker, *Theorizing Social Movements* (London: Pluto, 1995); Klaus Eder, *The New Politics of Class: Social Movements and Cultural Dynamics in Advanced Societies* (London: Sage, 1993).

36. Russell J. Dalton, Manfred Kuechler, and Wilhelm Búrklin, "The Challenge of New Movements," in *Challenging the Political Order*, ed. Russell J. Dalton and Manfred Kuechler (New York: Oxford University Press, 1990).

37. Fritz Ringer, introduction to *The Rise of the Modern Educational System*, ed. Detlef Müller, Fritz Ringer, and Brian Simon (Cambridge: Cambridge University Press, 1987); Neil Smelser, "Evaluating the Model of Structural Differentiation in Relation to Educational Change in the Nineteenth Century," in *Neofunctionalism*, ed. Jeffrey Alexander (Beverly Hills, Calif.: Sage, 1985).

38. Paul Avrich, *The Modern School Movements: Anarchism and Education in the United States* (Princeton, N.J.: Princeton University Press, 1980).

39. Alfred Willener, *The Action-Image of Society: On Cultural Politicization*, ed. A. M. Sheridan Smith (London: Tavistock, 1970); Seymour M. Lipset, *Rebellion in the University* (Boston: Little, Brown, 1972).

40. Brian Simon, *The Rise of the Modern Educational System* (Cambridge: Cambridge University Press, 1987); Brian Simon, *Education and the Labour Movement: 1870–1920* (London: Lawrence and Wishart, 1965); Julia Wrigley, *Class Politics and Public Schools* (New Brunswick, N.J.: Rutgers University Press, 1982).

41. John Boli and Francisco O. Ramirez, with John W. Meyer, "Explaining the Origins and Expansion of Mass Education," *Comparative Education Review* 29, no. 2 (1985): 145–70.

42. Margaret S. Archer, "Introduction: Theorizing about the Expansion of Educational Systems," in *The Sociology of Educational Expansion*, ed. Margaret S. Archer (Beverly Hills, Calif.: Sage, 1982); Margaret S. Archer, *Social Origins of Educational Systems* (London: Sage, 1984).

43. John E. Craig and Norman Spear, "Explaining Educational Expansion: An Agenda for Historical and Comparative Research," in *The Sociology of Educational Expansion*, ed. Archer (Beverly Hills, Calif.: Sage, 1982).

44. A. E. Dobbs, *Education and Social Movements, 1700–1850* (1919; New York: Augustus M. Kelley, 1969).

45. Martin Carnoy and Henry M. Levin, *Schooling and Work in the Democratic State* (Stanford, Calif.: Stanford University Press, 1985), 46–47.

46. Ron Eyerman and Andrew Jamison, *Social Movements: A Cognitive Approach* (Cambridge: Polity, 1991).

47. Michael Bérubé, *Public Access: Literary Theory and American Campus Politics* (London: Verso, 1994).

48. Raymond A. Morrow and Carlos Alberto Torres, "Education and the Reproduction of Class, Gender and Race: Responding to the Postmodern Challenge," *Educational Theory* 44, no. 1 (1994): 43–61.

49. Henry Giroux, *Border Crossings: Cultural Workers and the Politics of Education* (New York:

Routledge, 1992); Henry Giroux, ed., *Postmodernism, Feminism, and Cultural Politics: Redrawing Educational Boundaries* (Albany: State University of New York Press, 1991).

50. Carnoy and Levin, *Schooling and Work*, 160.

51. Philip Wexler, *Social Analysis of Education: After the New Sociology* (London: Routledge and Kegan Paul, 1987), 87–88.

52. Peter McClaren, *Critical Pedagogy and Predatory Culture: Oppositional Politics in a Postmodern Era* (London: Routledge, 1995), 187. For an excellent survey of the relationship between local struggles and educational reform in the United States, see Catherine E. Walsh, ed., *Education Reform and Social Change: Multicultural Voices, Struggles, and Visions* (Albany: State University of New York Press, 1996).

53. See Pia Linquist Wong, Pilar O'Cadiz, and Carlos Alberto Torres, *Education and Democracy: Paulo Freire, Social Movements, and Educational Reform in Sao Paulo* (Boulder, Colo.: Westview, 1998).

54. Malcolm Waters, *Globalization* (London: Routledge, 1995), 1.

55. Waters, *Globalization*, 3.

56. David Harvey, *The Condition of Postmodernity: An Enquiry into the Origins of Cultural Change* (Malden, Mass.: Blackwell, 1989); Anthony Giddens, *The Consequences of Modernity* (Stanford, Calif.: Stanford University Press, 1990).

57. Torres, *Education, Power*.

58. Martin Carnoy et al., *The New Global Economy in the Information Age: Reflections on Our Changing World* (University Park: Pennsylvania State University Press, 1993).

59. "Your New Global Workforce," *Fortune*, December 14, 1992, 52–66.

60. Several political scientists have analyzed these changes. For example, Adam Przeworski, *Democracy and the Market: Political and Economic Reforms in Eastern Europe and Latin America* (New York: Cambridge University Press, 1991); Kenichi Ohmae, *The Borderless World: Power and Strategy in the Interlinked World Economy* (New York: Harper Business, 1990); Robert B. Reich, *The Work of Nations* (New York: Vintage, 1991); Lester Thurow, *Head to Head: The Coming Economic Battle among Japan, Europe, and America* (New York: William Morrow, 1992).

61. Reich, *Work of Nations*.

62. Roland Robertson, *Globalization* (London: Sage, 1992).

63. Martin Carnoy, *Education as Cultural Imperialism* (New York: David McKay, 1974).

64. For example, Homi K. Bhabha, *The Location of Culture* (London: Routledge, 1994), 112ff.

65. Ulf Hannerz, *Transnational Connections: Culture, People, Places* (London: Routledge), 68. There are also forms of creolization in the metropolitan urban centers.

66. Hannerz, *Transnational Connections*, 66.

67. Hannerz, *Transnational Connections*, 71.

68. Hannerz, *Transnational Connections*, 74.

69. For a historical introduction to the shift from marginalization to exclusion in Latin America, see Byan R. Roberts, "From Marginality to Social Exclusion: From *Laissez Faire* to Pervasive Engagement," *Latin American Research Review* 39, no. 1 (2004): 195–97.

70. For example, James Petras, "'Centre-Left' Regimes in Latin American: History Repeating Itself as Farce?" *Journal of Peasant Studies* 33, no. 2 (2006): 278–303.

71. For a defense of a critical theory of the democratic public sphere, see Leonardo Avritzer, *Democracy and the Public Space in Latin America* (Princeton, N.J.: Princeton University Press, 2002); for a case study of education, Julio Emilio Diniz-Pereira, "Teacher Education for Social Transformation and its Links to Progressive Social Movements: The Case of the Landless Workers Movement in Brazil," *Journal for Critical Education Policy Studies* 3, no. 2 (2005), also available at www.jceps.com/?pageID=article&articleID=51.

72. A well-informed overview of indigenous movements can be found in Jean E. Jackson and

Kay B. Warren, "Indigenous Movements in Latin America, 1992–2004: Controversies, Ironies, New Directions," *The Annual Review of Anthropology* 34 (2005): 549–73.

73. For a theoretically insightful comparative study of urban movements and their relation to the state, see Bryan R. Roberts and Alejandro Portes, "Coping with the Free Market City: Collective Action in Six Latin American Cities at the End of the Twentieth Century," *Latin American Research Review* 41, no. 2 (2006): 57–83.

74. On theories and practices of a transnational civil society, see Randall D. Germain and Michael Kenny, eds., *The Idea of Global Civil Society: Politics and Ethics in a Globalizing Era* (London and New York: Routledge, 2005).

75. The work of Moacir Gadotti on this topic is one of the most insightful in the world. See his writings in Portuguese, English, and other languages in the website of the Paulo Freire Institute in São Paulo, at www.paulofreire.org/principal-i.htm.

76. Michael Apple and Anita Oliver, "Why the Right Is Winning," in *Sociology of Education: Emerging Perspectives*, ed. Carlos Alberto Torres and Ted Mitchell (Albany: State University of New York Press, 1998).

4

Culture and Education

Vandra Lea Masemann

Education can be seen through a quite different lens from the anthropological perspective than from the perspective of other disciplines. In addition, the depth of field and the focus are very different from those in large-scale comparative studies. The scope of the studies and the unit of analysis are usually much smaller, and the findings are less generalizable than in other kinds of comparative studies. The ethnographic methodology commonly used in this approach both constrains and liberates the researcher in the kinds of analysis and findings that are possible. Moreover, the voices of marginalized or peripheral populations can be heard in ways that are muted or never even listened to in large-scale comparisons.

In this chapter, the possibilities that anthropological theory and method hold for comparative education are explored. This chapter outlines the fundamental concepts of the cultural approach to the study of comparative education, shows the links between education and culture, and explores ways in which the anthropological perspective is useful in educational research. The main thesis of the chapter is that although the ethnographic approach is necessary to explore the workings of culture in the classroom, school, and administrative system, it should not constrain the researcher mainly to phenomenological approaches or ones in which the focus is only the subjective experience of the participants. I argue that a critical or neo-Marxist approach is necessary to delineate the connections between the microlevel of the local school experience and the macrolevel of structural forces at the global level that are shaping the delivery and the experience of education in every country, in even the most remote regions. In addition, a cultural approach to the study of comparative education is important to counter some increasing trends in the economistic analysis of school effectiveness that rest on productivity-oriented criteria, an analysis that is used on every level of education from early elementary school up to the tertiary level.[1]

This chapter opens with a brief summary of the central concepts used in the study of education and culture, followed by a discussion of the relationship of cultural values to education. Then the connection between culture, educational philosophy, and social class is examined. The role of evolutionism and colonialism and their relationship to the anthropological study of education is discussed and then the relationship of anthropology to functionalism and scientism is examined. The contribution of neo-Marxist approaches is considered, and, finally, the rise of school ethnography and its contribution to comparative education is presented.

THE CONCEPT OF CULTURE

The foundation stone of the anthropological approach is the concept of culture. There are many different definitions of culture, but one I find useful says that culture is "concerned with actions, ideas, and artifacts which individuals in the tradition concerned learn, share, and value."[2] Culture refers to all the aspects of life, including the mental, social, linguistic, and physical forms of culture. It refers to ideas people have, the relationships they have with others in their families and with larger social institutions, the languages they speak, and the symbolic forms they share, such as written language or art/music forms. It refers to their relationship with their physical surroundings as well as the technology that is used in any society.[3] Considerable criticism has been leveled at earlier definitions of culture in their unquestioning assumption of homogeneity and the seeming denial of plural perspectives in any one social group. There is still, however, support for the idea that although groups of people may not exhibit identical forms of behavior, they may possess similar kinds of "control mechanisms—plans, recipes, rules, instructions . . . for the governing of behavior."[4]

Other related terms are *enculturation* and *socialization*. Enculturation refers to the process of learning how to be a competent member of a specific culture or group, and socialization is considered by some anthropologists to refer to the general process of learning human culture.[5] *Acculturation* refers to the process of cultural transfer from one group to another.[6] All of these terms have relevance for the study of education, since it is important to delineate which aspect of culture is being transmitted or transferred from one group to another, whether it be a cross-generational transmission or a cross-group transfer of knowledge, skills, values, or attitudes. The terms *intercultural* and *multicultural* also carry a connotation of cross-group transfer and, in some cases, a political connotation of redrawing cultural lines to include a more pluralistic combination of what had previously been considered separate groups. All of these terms rest on the fundamental assumption that education has a cultural component and is not simply an information transfer.

Margaret Mead went so far as to define education as "the cultural process, the way in which each newborn human infant, born with a potentiality for learning greater than that of any other mammal, is transformed into a full member of a specific human society, sharing with the other members a specific human culture."[7] She thus defined all of the processes that a human undergoes as education, whereas Yehudi Cohen and many educators distinguish between the processes of socialization and formal education. (As many professors of anthropology know, it is almost impossible to dislodge the popular meaning of socialization among college students as partying.)

In Cohen's view, "socialization and education are two fundamentally different processes in the shaping of the mind—found in all societies, albeit in different proportions."[8] He defines socialization as "the activities that are devoted to the inculcation and elicitation of basic motivational and cognitive patterns through ongoing and spontaneous interaction with parents, siblings, kinsmen, and other members of the community" and education as "the inculcation of standardized and stereotyped knowledge, skills, values, and attitudes by means of standardized and stereotyped procedures" and hypothesizes that "the quantitative role played by socialization in the development of the individual is in direct proportion to the extent to which the network of kin relations coincides with the network of personal relations.''[9] Thus he argues that it is the nature of the wider social structure that provides the setting in which the socialization and education processes can be played out. This perspective is at the heart of this chapter, for it provides the anthropological and ultimately philosophical justification for seeing educational processes of any kind as inextricably linked with the social structure that gives rise to them. Thus the process of ethnographic study of education cannot be carried out without an acknowledgment of the setting in which the educational processes are taking place and the cultural content of the form of educational transmission.

CULTURAL VALUES

Another fundamental characteristic of culture is that it expresses the value system(s) of a particular society or group. In her classic work on dominant and variant value orientations, Florence Kluckhohn states that "there is a systematic variation in the realm of cultural phenomena which is both as definite and as essential as the demonstrated systematic variation in physical and biological phenomena.''[10] She links her argument to a defense of the concept of cultural relativism and explores the range of value systems that answer five basic questions common to all human groups.

First, what is the character of innate human nature? It may be (1) evil—mutable or immutable, (2) neutral—mutable, (3) mixture of good and evil—immutable, and (4) good—mutable or immutable. In other words, human beings are seen as being born evil, neutral, or good and having the possibility of changing or not. Depending on the prevailing value system in the culture, the goals of education or socialization will be aimed at trying to enforce an orientation that is considered unchangeable or at changing the child into a better person (although changing for the worse is also theoretically possible in this schema). A third possibility is not to interfere at all with what is perceived to be the essential nature of the child or the person that the child will become.

Second, what is the relation of human beings to nature (and supernature)? They may be (1) subjugated to nature, (2) in harmony with nature, or (3) dominant over nature. These values are expressed in an emphasis on learning to accept whatever nature brings, to attempt some sort of collaboration with nature, or to want to triumph over nature.

Third, what is the temporal focus of human life—past, present, or future?

Fourth, what is the valued modality of human activity—being, being-in-becoming, or doing?

Fifth, what is the valued modality of people's relationship to other people—lineality, collaterality, or individualism?[11] In other words, do people value their ties to their ancestors, to those who are living in their own generation, or basically to themselves?

The answers to these five questions form the underlying assumptions of any system of socialization or education, formal or informal, in any society. The content of what is taught through socialization or education reflects the basic value orientations of any culture, mostly with variant value orientations that allow for a range of required and permitted variation within the system. For example, the emphasis on the practical value of education as an investment for the future in modern universities is counterbalanced (but not equally) by the aesthetic values of the arts curriculum or the humanistic contribution of the liberal arts. Moreover, the valuing of athletic superiority is also counterposed to the valuing of the more intellectual aspects of the university enterprise.

Kluckhohn also argues that these dominant and variant value orientations could coexist and were complementary and that they would shift under external pressure to a varying extent. Thus values are not the individual psychological attitudes of an individual but socially structured orientations patterned in relation to the strictures of the society in which people played out their roles. She says that people could shift in their value orientations away from one set of values into another set of equally sanctioned or perhaps even preferable values, as in the case of socially mobile persons in American culture.[12]

Although this schema can be applied to the analysis of culture as it was traditionally seen by anthropologists, it can also be applied to the analysis of the cultural foundations of education, to the study of formal curriculum and policy documents, and to the analysis of classroom. In addition, it can be applied to the study of the "hidden curriculum" of the school, which resides in the unintended cultural messages of the school experience.[13] Any ethnographic study of schools can show the cultural messages that the educational experience transmits, both intentionally and unintentionally. To the educational anthropologist, all the observed behavior in the classroom and all the printed and electronic information carry their own form of cultural knowledge, whether it is overtly or covertly expressed and whether it is formally articulated or part of the informal social life of the school.[14] Thus the link between what educators call *curriculum* and culture is clearly established.

CULTURE AND EDUCATIONAL PHILOSOPHY

Kluckhohn's schema can also be applied to the analysis of changes in educational philosophy in Europe and North America (via Comenius, Rousseau, Pestalozzi, Froebel, Steiner, Montessori, and Dewey) in the last two centuries, in the shift from teacher-centered pedagogy to student-centered pedagogy as a result of changes in the conceptualization of the child from evil to good and from a creature to be dominated to one that should be nurtured, or at least allowed to develop as naturally as possible.[15] There are, of course, structural changes in the organization of society and work itself that have been concomitant with these changes in values. The perceived need for a more highly skilled workforce and the necessity for students to keep studying for a much longer number of years makes it necessary for the experience of schooling to be somewhat more endurable than in times when most people's educational biographies were relatively short.

This change of paradigm has also had a profound effect on the education of adults all over the world, and it is expressed most articulately in the work of Paulo Freire. He has proposed a "pedagogy of the oppressed" that is forged with individuals or peoples in "the incessant struggle to regain their humanity."[16] The philosophy of enabling adults to formulate their own path of learning is not, of course, a statement that they are in a situation in which there is no external authority and oppression, but that they can use their newly aroused consciousness to resist forms of external authority that they find oppressive and that they "must perceive the reality of oppression not as a closed world from which there is no exit, but as a limiting situation which they can transform. . . .

The oppressed can overcome the contradiction in which they are caught only when this perception enlists them in the struggle to free themselves."[17]

This is quite different from the situation in a middle-class school in which the students are treated as if they were not really being controlled while actually being socialized into believing that they have the freedom to control their lives and the lives of others. Basil Bernstein has commented on this seeming contradiction, that student-centered pedagogy (which he designates as *invisible*) appears to be based on the assumption that there is no external form of control to which the child must succumb, when in fact it is mainly middle-class students in progressive primary schools who are spared the most oppressive forms of teacher-centered pedagogy. He states that changing the code (underlying principle) that controls education transmission involves changing the culture and its basis in privatized class relationships. In other words, it is not possible just to teach students a new form of speech and writing in order to change society, since that results only in the social mobility of one individual or group of individuals. It is instead necessary to change the structural basis of society in which certain dialects or speech patterns are associated with certain forms of privilege or social class status, which have their basis in the economic, not the linguistic, order of society.

However, because integrated codes (those found in situations of invisible pedagogy) are integrated at the level of ideas, they do not involve integration at the level of institutions, such as school and work. Freire states that "there can be no such integration in Western societies (to mention only one group)" because the abstracting of education from work, such as in the tradition of liberal education, "masks the brutal fact that work and education cannot be integrated at the level of social principles in class societies."[18]

This is a position derived from Emile Durkheim, that the division of labor in society is the fundamental characteristic that determines the shift in the principles of social integration through schooling, as exemplified in "the movement away from the transmission of common values through a ritual order and control based upon position or status, to more personalised forms of control where teachers and taught confront each other as individuals."[19] This is the classic shift from mechanical to organic solidarity, in Durkheim's terms, in the shift from an appeal to shared values, group loyalties, and ritual to the recognition of differences among individuals as they play out individualized, specialized, independent social roles. However, it is the social class position of the students that ultimately determines how they experience any form of pedagogy. The seeming variations in values are not merely cultural but are class-based.

Thus the link is made between education, culture, and class in every society. The cultural foundations of every form of socialization or education are made explicit in all the multiplicity of admonitions and rewards that kinfolk bestow on children as they are growing up and in the content of the curriculum and the classroom practices that are experienced by students in the formal education systems worldwide. Their experience of and reactions to their education are not grounded only in culture and values that are perceived in the liberal tradition as unconnected to the material basis of their society (the world of work), but these experiences are also fundamentally shaped by the economic basis of their neighborhood, community, region, or country, and ultimately the global economy.[20] However, the relationship of education, culture, and economics is not a simple one, and the ethnographic study of education in various countries can illuminate its dimensions. I turn now to a consideration of the colonial experience as an example of this complexity.

EVOLUTIONISM AND COLONIALISM

Early conceptualizations of society by anthropologists such as Edward Tyler, Lewis Henry Morgan, and Herbert Spencer were based on a theory of evolutionism, in which societies went through a series of stages, on the basis of increasing rationality, improved technology, or a progression similar to biological organisms, from the simple to the complex.[21] Thus societies based on hunting and gathering, pastoral nomadism, agriculture, herding of domesticated animals, feudalism, and industrialism were no longer seen as static entities (labeled and classified like so many butterflies in a museum case and interesting each in its own right and unrelated to the others), but as stages through which every society had to pass in order to progress further up the evolutionary ladder.

The rise of evolutionism in the nineteenth-century context of growing belief in rationality, human perfectibility, progress, and the promotion of technological advancement laid the foundations of the belief in development that reached its apogee in the twentieth century. The promulgation of Darwin's theory of biological evolution reinforced this theory of social evolution, with its attendant notions of "survival of the fittest" and an underlying assumption that all societies had to progress through the stages in the same order. No longer were the armchair anthropologists sitting in Europe simply applying labels to other cultures and groups; they were now proposing that all other peoples were evolving to more complex levels of society. Eventually, education was seen as the major means of forcing this evolutionary process to speed up.

Even though anthropological theorizing has become far more eclectic since those early days, and probably is characterized now by a willingness to study societies from a much more pluralistic perspective, education as a field has clung to this implicit evolutionary schema for a much longer period of time. As anthropologists were developing their "stages of society" schemata, educators were developing the beginnings of comparative education. These early comparativists were not searching for any kind of relativism, however, but for "borrowing from abroad useful educational devices for the improvement of education at home."[22]

This implicit evolutionary schema has not persisted merely as a heuristic device or some lingering trace of a firmly entrenched tenet of teacher ideology, however. The foundations for the growth of the development idea were firmly laid during the last several hundred years of colonial education. It has been held in place by the history of the colonial relationships between the major European countries and the rest of the world, the newer neocolonial relationships that emerged after the "granting" of independence to the former colonies, and the creation of new forms of fiscal dependency of poor countries on the major international lending agencies. Gail Kelly and Philip Altbach note that forms of internal colonialism still exist in the case of "populations still dominated by foreign nations existing within the same national boundaries"[23] (such as the case of native peoples of the Americas and South Africa at the time the book was written). There is also the case of populations still dominated by elites within their own national borders (such as women, African Americans, and the working class in America).

In colonial situations, education took on various forms. It was not just a simple matter of the colonial powers establishing schools so that the colonies produced citizens who resembled their colonial masters. Kelly notes that colonial schools were sometimes quite removed from the metropolitan experience and were meant to produce subjugated people who could not function in the metropole. In other cases, they produced a distorted version of education in the metropole, particularly in relation to gender roles. Kelly describes vividly, for example, the classes for the teaching of English to Vietnamese refugees in the United States, in which women who were previously independent, income-earning fisherwomen were taught gender-stereotyped phrases (in American terms) for performing domestic duties and passing their time in leisure pursuits.[24]

This imposition of gender-stereotyped expectations is also reflected in curriculum materials in colonial (or formal colonial) countries. I give examples of a home economics curriculum in a West African girls' boarding school, in which the exercises were entirely based on the operation of a European-style household, with cooking and laundry activities being performed by a wife in a nuclear family. In fact, the presence of domestic servants and various relatives as well as a hired laundryman from the home village usually meant that well-educated women were not expected to perform these duties. Thus even the everyday life of the students outside of school was distorted in its curriculum representation in school.[25]

Johann Galtung's work on center-periphery theory deals with colonial education as part of the process of penetration of the dominant country into the countries to be dominated in such a way that "structural power really becomes operational when one nation gets under the skin of the other so that it is able to form and shape the inside of the nation."[26] Galtung distinguishes between the processes of *subversion* (from the bottom or periphery) and *supervision* (from the top). In the latter process, the education system is a key institution in the production of elites. Through being educated either in elite schools in the colonized country or in the metropole itself, colonial elites have more in common with their colonizers than they do with the peripheral populations in their own country. This process also fragments the peripheral populations, as Galtung believes that the relative affluence of the peripheral elites of the major colonial countries results in their having a greater political loyalty to their own national interest, and to the international bourgeoisie, than to the world proletariat of which they are a part.

He sees structural domination as made up of three processes—exploitation, fragmentation, and penetration—and notes that it is still in place wherever the Western model of technical-economic development is accepted and the periphery depends on the center to supply something that the periphery thinks is indispensable and unavailable elsewhere. Moreover, "the Periphery thinks these things are indispensable because it has been taught to think so, because it has adopted and adapted to the culture of the Center."[27]

Although the direct colonial relationship has been altered since the political independence of many countries, this form of domination continues. However, the metaphor of evolution has changed, and the metaphors of educational development have become increasingly technicized, as if a new rationality had been invented that could make the old evolutionary processes speed up. Absent is any politicized discourse that might include notions of social justice or equity. Moreover, it is not only the process itself that is accelerated but the definition of time itself is linear and industrial. Christine Fox describes the dimensions of the new metaphors as being based on

> economic, structural images of building models, drawing analogies to the formulation of ground plans, making a blueprint for program implementation, delivery of materials, the sending "in" of a "team," the tight time line, inputs, and outputs, product flow, monitoring and so on. . . . The language used by consultants "in the field" is often particularly distorting, since they move within the "packaged" time frame, speaking of strategic plan-

ning and delivery, while their counterparts move within the more fluid and broader cultural framework of their ongoing educational context, speaking of people's lives.[28]

A similar point is made by Shen-Keng Yang in his analysis of the cultural assumptions underlying the passage of time in educational research and policy planning studies, and the way ordinary people experience or plan their lives. He refers to the concept of *time institutionalized* and points out that the railroad and now latterly the development of information technology are the means by which ordinary people experience the speeding up of institutionalized time.[29] In the preindustrial concept of time, the length of the task at hand and the repetitive cycle of the days, the week, the months, and the seasons of the year formed the basis of a nonlinear sense of time that was incorporated into the rituals of the culture and the sense of the worth of an individual human life span. In the industrial concept of time, human actions are arranged and connected in a linear sequence that is conceived of as having a purpose and a goal. The imposition of one concept on the other leads to the frustration of planners at the seeming lack of impact of their ideas, as well as bafflement on the part of the planned-for about the seeming impatience of such highly educated but apparently impractical people.

Arturo Escobar refers to development as

> a powerful and encompassing discourse which has ruled most social designs and actions of those [underdeveloped] countries since the early post–World War II period . . . [that has] shaped in significant ways the modes of existence of Third World societies, mediating in a profound sense the knowledge they seek about themselves and their peoples, mapping their social landscape, sculpting their economies, transforming their cultures.[30]

Writing from the perspective of an anthropologist, he states that "there is an acute need to assert the difference of cultures, the relativity of history, and the plurality of perceptions"[31] in order to negate the view that more Development (his capitalization) is needed.

He presents an analysis of the debacle of the development idea, in which grassroots and other social movements "are opening the way for the creation of a politics for an alternative Development anchored in the grassroots and . . . providing new possibilities for satisfying human needs (including foods, nutrition, and health)."[32] He points to the importance of local knowledge in this process and notes that "a new dialectic of micro-practice and macro-thinking seems to be emerging, one which is advanced by intellectuals and activists engaged in processes of social transformation."[33]

Galtung explicates this relationship still further in his analysis of the education of the elites of the countries of the center and the periphery. He notes that the interests of the elite in the center were well served by having the elite of the periphery educated either in elite colonial schools that were able to reproduce the social relations of the center in the peripheral country or in the elite schools of the center itself. Kelly's analysis fits in with Galtung's more in relation to the education of the peripheral populations of the periphery. She is mostly dealing with peripheral populations that have been colonized by representatives of the center, either by external colonizers (as in the case of classical colonialism) or by internal colonizers (as in the case of internal colonization).

Freire's analysis of mental colonialism takes the analysis still further. He postulates that the main effect of colonial education was to produce a mindset in which the colonized took on the mentality of the colonizer and judged himself or herself and others from the viewpoint of the colonizer.[34] This perception was the essence of the neocolonial mentality. African leaders such as Kwame Nkrumah used to fulminate against it in their public speeches, warning their countrymen not to continue to think like their former colonial masters. Even West African schoolchildren in the 1960s were well aware of the danger of having a neocolonial mentality (Masemann, personal recollection).

However, as Archie Mafeje has pointed out, the dangers of the neocolonial mindset went far deeper than comparing one's appearance, one's art, or one's politics to those of Europeans. Instead, the epistemology of European functionalist, positivist thought became embedded in the pursuit of knowledge, which was a far more insidious mechanism for depriving Africans of their birthright.[35] (Also see chapter 1 in this volume.) Mafeje saw the major epistemological links as being between the bourgeois colonial mind, on the one hand, and functionalism and scientism, on the other.

FUNCTIONALISM AND SCIENTISM

Functionalism was a major strand in the development of anthropological and sociological thought. The two anthropologists most commonly associated with functionalism in anthropology were Bronislaw Malinowski and A. R. Radcliffe-Brown. Malinowski's version of functionalism focused more on the cultural needs approach—societies had to have institutions that functioned to meet the various needs of human beings. He saw ethnographies as showing how any society was able to meet the needs of its members. Radcliffe-Brown's version of functionalism was more of an analogy that compared the social system with a functioning human body, the various social institutions playing their respective roles in the healthy functioning of the whole. There was an underlying sense of harmoniousness in both models; conflict and social change did not fit well in these models of societal function.[36]

Functionalism formed the foundation of quantitative social science in the twentieth century and became very popular as the foundation of research in the "applied" areas of social science such as education. It was also the foundational research paradigm for educational research and statistics. Therefore, it has had an impact on educational research, which has been even stronger, perhaps, than on its own original disciplines.

It is not possible in this chapter to outline all the criticisms that have been leveled at the functionalist school in anthropology. Mafeje does an excellent job of this in his article on the subject. He states primarily that anthropology, functionalism, and positivism were the handmaidens of colonialism and bourgeois social science in that they were an essential part of the imperialist enterprise:

> Their decision to leave their desks and disappear into the jungles of Africa, South America and Asia were not determined by love of unknown natives, but rather by the imperatives of European development, including intellectual curiosity and growing impatience with speculative theories of the nineteenth century evolutionists.[37]

He continues his argument with a discussion of the contradiction in many liberal anthropologists' position on subject-object relations and of their conception of knowledge itself:

The harder the positivists insist on their conception of science as a guarantee for a closer and closer relation between knowledge and the real, the more they exacerbate the anomaly. In their belief that knowledge grows by secretion and that it is a result of specialized subjects (the scientists) who are able to extract knowledge from an object-world, they have overlooked the important principle of the reversibility of the subject-object relation in knowledge-formation.

If at first it seemed that "positivist science" was making the world, it is now the same world that is forcing a crisis in positive science by throwing up contradictions and anomalies in real life. . . . As a consensus model, it is inherently incapable of dealing with contradiction and revolution except in negative terms. These terms are not a problem of syntax but of ideology which precedes and predetermines possible forms of knowledge.[38]

He thus concludes that anthropology is

generically a child of imperialism [which] has been a systematic extension of bourgeois economic, political, intellectual, and cultural forms. From the twenties onwards anthropologists became embroiled in colonial affairs with the best intentions but with identical results as those of their soldier-administrator brethren.[39]

The implications of these arguments for the field of comparative education lie in the relationship between the forms of knowledge developed throughout the colonial and imperial experience and the spread of formal schooling in many countries, particularly after the end of the Second World War. The comparison was implicitly between the kinds of school systems developed in the European context and all other forms of schooling. Moreover, the rise of a scientist culture allied with evolutionary notions of development coincided with the independence of a number of countries in the post–World War I period. Not surprisingly, their newly established education systems became linked with a world educational research enterprise firmly embedded in a functionalist framework. This research endeavor was primarily linked to European and North American publishing houses and later to the development of the computer. The implicit positivistic bias of the computer in its facilitation of the analysis of "more data" meant that the emphasis shifted from anthropological interest in indigenous cultures to a more sociological preoccupation with collecting statistics on the new or expanding social institutions in newly developed states.

The result has been the increasing homogenization of the culture of education on a worldwide scale, with the accompanying assumption by educators that there is only one valid epistemology. From a functionalist perspective, there is an assumption that the most scientifically reputable view has prevailed.

SCHOOL ETHNOGRAPHY

Following the logical implications of Mafeje's conclusions concerning the culture of positivism, the "new" sociologists of education such as Michael Young[40] and others during the 1970s rejected that culture and based their accounts of schooling on the experiences of those who were the participants in the daily life of the schools. This approach opened the way for the development of ethnographic approaches to educational research that harked back in a methodological sense to the heyday of anthropological fieldwork. It was an approach that could be carried out effectively in schools anywhere, whether at home or abroad. The work of George and Louise Spindler in the United States was also a pioneering effort in making the workings of schools in many different cultural contexts the focus of anthropologists' interests.[41]

Madan Sarup, in a review of anthropological studies in education from a neo-Marxist perspective, notes that these educational ethnographers could not ground their accounts of education in an objectively available social world because that world itself would be a feature of their method. Sarup asks, "What, then, is the justification of their own theorizing and how do they ground their accounts? What are the 'auspices' of their theorizing and on what grounds is their own enquiry better or more adequate?"[42] He suggests that their orientation to political egalitarianism is the particular interest in which their accounts are grounded. These are questions that deserve further consideration.

In my earlier work on the utility of anthropological approaches to the study of comparative education, I outlined the various ways in which ethnographic studies could be useful. First, the cross-cultural study of socialization can provide information on the kinds of values and cognitive categories that children in various cultures learn before they even enter school. It can illuminate the study of learning in natural settings from a natural history participant-observer approach, and it can provide detailed accounts of the cross-cultural study of cognition.

Second, the comparative study of schooling, as well as the interface between socialization and the formal demands of the school system, is enhanced by the holistic ethnographic study of schools in their communities. Third, the ethnographic study of the workings of schools themselves as formal institutions can yield valuable comparative insights into current issues, such as underachievement, of concern to educators, and can provide the grounded theoretical perspectives from which more large-scale survey-type studies can be developed.[43]

In terms of the theme of the chapter, immanent functionalism, all the suggestions above about the use of ethnography in comparative education seem to be tied to an implicitly functionalist paradigm. Subsequently, I examined constraints on the development of a neo-Marxist school ethnography. I argue that "school ethnography today is limited . . . in the same way early colonial anthropology was limited. It is essentially microcosmic, and can be carried out by researchers who see education as an essentially autonomous and isolated phenomenon."[44] (Thus the dialectic of the global and the local comes back to haunt us again. If ethnography is based on the liberal distinction that education and work are separate, then there is no need to postulate that education is related to the outside world.)

I asked if the trend to ethnographic studies could be likened to a metaphoric shift from "hard" to "soft" educational research in which, from a Bernsteinian perspective, educational researchers themselves had been socialized into an "elaborated code" of research, "with its shades of meaning, the ambiguities, the ambivalences, the unwillingness to judge, the interest in social relations, the emphasis on context."[45] In other words, just as Bernstein postulates that the middle class is more likely to be socialized into a code of language production that includes elaborate distinctions and complex syntax and lexicon, so also the ethnographers have become socialized into a more complex form of educational research in which their findings cannot be easily synthesized into results. Similarly, whereas members of the middle class are thus less likely to make judgments based on ideology because they are so overwhelmed by the complexity of all the knowledge they can discuss, members of the working class have a certainty about ideology that is made possible by the form of discourse they command, in which answers are somewhat more sharply defined as positive or negative choices. I conclude that the success of education itself leads to the inability of middle-class persons to think in ideological terms because they are involved in a form of knowledge production in which issues of ideology become subverted by issues of technique or, in this case, methodology. Thus school ethnography has become a technique widely used in colleges of education, but it has become deracinated from its place in the history of anthropological theory.

I conclude that school ethnography with a neo-Marxist perspective would be unlikely to proliferate because the power of statistical research itself will increase with the spread of formal education, which is associated with the concept of *modernization.* However, I also conclude that the value of neo-Marxist approaches to ethnography lies in the researcher's eschewing the assumptions of neutrality and objectivity of functionalist positivistic approaches and assuming the autonomy and isolation of the school and classroom. Neo-Marxist approaches, instead, call for researchers to seize the opportunity of doing a political analysis in which their role, as well as that of the teacher, the student, and educational equality itself, is defined in new ways.[46]

In a further examination of the role of critical ethnography (studies that use a basically anthropological methodology but rely on a body of theory deriving from critical sociology and philosophy) in the study of comparative education, I raise the following issues:

> Is it the task of social scientists to seek ever more diligently to define objective methods of researching the social world (or education), with possibilities for change simply seen as the result of "reading out the data" and making choices on the basis of some cost-efficient or technological rationale? Or is it their task to attempt to understand as accurately as possible the subjective understandings that actors have of their own version of "social reality"? Or, third, is there some way of seeing social science in Marx's terms that would forever blur the objective/subjective distinction and thus make necessary the redefinition of social research itself?[47]

After a discussion of sociological and interpretive approaches to educational research, I examine the value of critical approaches in their treatment of social conflict and structuralism: "Neo-Marxist interpretations of school life have questioned the established categories of education and have raised fundamental questions about the social control functions of schools and the social contradictions they create or participate in."[48] Douglas Foley's work has been particularly noteworthy in this respect, in his studies of student alienation in Texas. He notes that critical ethnology offers the only way to study the techniques that schools and teachers use to organize, model, practice, and reward the behaviors that socialize students into technological rationality.[49]

I conclude by suggesting various uses to which critical ethnography could be put in comparative education: the study of socialization of students into preferred language dialects or national languages, national political cultures, or elite values; the study of the penetration of dominant ideology or imported "innovative" rationality; comparative studies of systems of student credentialing, and the penetration of computer technologies. Finally I suggest the study of rationality itself could be an interesting new focus of comparative education.

Since these papers were written, a great deal of ethnographic research has been done in educational settings, most prolifically in the United States and Great Britain. It is doubtful if the majority of these studies have been done from a critical perspective. Ethnographic method has been adopted as a tool of educational research, but in many cases its theoretical basis has been eschewed. Bradley Levinson, Douglas Foley, and Dorothy Holland have summarized the major work in critical educational research in the last two decades, and their book also provides a very complete bibliography of the most recent works in this field.[50] In their introduction, they review the more recent developments in critical educational studies: social reproduction, cultural reproduction, the cultural difference approach, ethnography and cultural reproduction, and cultural studies and the cultural production of the educated person. They also examine the Western schooling paradigm in global context and explore "how concepts of the 'educated person' are produced and negotiated between state discourses and local practice."[51] Their work provides a very comprehensive and forward-looking assessment of the state of the art of critical educational studies. Another volume that addresses studies of education in a globalised context is that edited by Kathryn Anderson-Levitt.[52] It consists of set of studies that address the question of whether education or schooling is becoming an increasingly homogenous institution or whether cultural differences create a diverse set of educational experiences, depending upon their context.

CONCLUSION

In conclusion, I return to the major themes of this chapter, particularly the relationship between culture and comparative education. Kelly raised the question in 1986: "Vandra Masemann and Douglas Foley urged the field to engage in qualitative research that seeks to understand educational processes. No debate followed, nor for that matter did much research of a qualitative nature on school processes. The field neither accepted nor rejected the challenge; it simply acted as if it were never made."[53] I am not so lugubrious as Kelly. She measured the acceptance of research by its appearance in the major journals in comparative education. As Levinson, Foley, and Holland's book documents, a great deal of ethnographic research was done in the 1980s and 1990s. It is generally published in journals such as *Anthropology and Education Quarterly*.

Other questions, however, arise about the context in which critical perspectives thrive. From a Marxist perspective, there is a curious absence of focus on the dialectical struggle in comparative education, as if somehow the only struggle had been between East and West, when the epistemological struggle is being waged at a deeper cultural level between the North and the South and between industrial forms of culture and the more local, rooted forms of culture. Since schools are inherently sites of local cultural formation, this phenomenon should come as no surprise.[54] Moreover, the struggle of cultural groups that have not accepted the major epistemological assumptions of scientism has been widely ignored in the field of comparative education. The first Commission on Indigenous Education, for example, was held at the Ninth World Congress of Comparative Education in Sydney, Australia, in 1996.[55]

Although the cultural differences in education in industrial countries are perceived to be diminishing and the forces of standardization are growing ever stronger, even if only in the interests of sharing data on education, the struggle is still being waged between those who do not share the scientist epistemology of the world and those who assume their view has triumphed. Some protests can be heard, for example, from the growing numbers of home schoolers who resist state domination of educational systems, from religious and linguistic minorities, from feminists, from philosophical alternative schools, and from aboriginal and indigenous minorities worldwide. The growth of this plurality of voices is addressed in other chapters in this book that address the impact of critical theory and postmodernism on education.

With their emphasis on studying other cultures as complete wholes, as well as on cultural relativism, anthropologists attempted to ignore the impact of the colonial endeavor itself on cultural change. Moreover, the colonial enterprise was so laden with racist assumptions about the "other" people in the world that it became part of a convenient fiction to philosophize about human progress and perfectibility in order to implement cost-efficient forms of government such as Indirect Rule in West Africa and other areas, while at the same time providing forms of education that kept colonial subjects from competing academically on the same terms as their metropolitan masters.

On the other hand, attempts to equalize educational opportunity on a global scale have led to the ignoring of local cultural values and traditional forms of knowledge and ways of thinking, which are in danger of becoming extinct. Anthropological studies of education in every country and setting can help bear witness to the rich diversity of modes of cultural transmission and the great variety of experiences that can be called educational.

NOTES

1. Jan Currie and Lesley Vidovich, "The Ascent toward Corporate Managerialism in American and Australian Universities," (paper presented at the Ninth World Congress of Comparative Education, Sydney, Australia, 1996).

2. Felix M. Keesing, *Cultural Anthropology: The Science of Custom* (New York: Rinehart, 1960), 25.

3. Thomas Rhys Williams, *Introduction to Socialization: Human Culture Transmitted* (St. Louis, Mo.: Mosby, 1972), 125.

4. Clifford Geertz, quoted in Stanley Barrett, *Anthropology: A Student's Guide to Theory and Method* (Toronto, Ont.: University of Toronto Press, 1996), 239.

5. Williams, *Introduction to Socialization*, 1.

6. Keesing, *Cultural Anthropology*, 28.

7. Margaret Mead, "Our Educational Emphases in Primitive Perspective," in *From Child to Adult: Studies in the Anthropology of Education*, ed. John Middleton (Garden City, N.Y.: Natural History Press, 1970), 1.

8. Yehudi Cohen, "The Shaping of Men's Minds: Adaptations to Imperatives of Culture," in *Anthropological Perspectives on Education*, ed. Murray Wax, Stanley Diamond, and Fred Gearing (New York: Basic Books, 1971), 21.

9. Cohen, "Shaping of Men's Minds," in *Anthropological Perspectives*, ed. Wax, Diamond, and Gearing (New York: Basic Books, 1971), 22.

10. Florence Kluckhohn, "Dominant and Variant Value Orientations," in *Variations in Value Orientations*, ed. Florence Kluckhohn and Fred L. Strodtbeck (Westport, Conn.: Greenwood, 1961), 3.

11. Kluckhohn, *Variations in Value Orientations*, 12.

12. Kluckhohn, *Variations in Value Orientations*, 39.

13. Young Pai and Susan Adler, *Cultural Foundations of Education* (Upper Saddle River, N.J.: Prentice-Hall, 1997).

14. George Spindler, *Doing the Ethnography of Schooling: Educational Anthropology in Action* (New York: Holt, Rinehart, and Winston, 1982).

15. Robert Ulich, *Education in Western Culture* (New York: Harcourt, Brace, and World, 1965), chaps. 5–7.

16. Paulo Freire, *Pedagogy of the Oppressed* (New York: Seabury, 1974), 33.

17. Freire, *Pedagogy of the Oppressed*, 34.

18. Basil Bernstein, *Class, Codes, and Control*, vol. 3, *Towards a Theory of Educational Transmissions* (London: Routledge and Kegan Paul, 1977), 145–46.

19. Bernstein, *Class, Codes, and Control*, 69.

20. Lynn Ilon, "Structural Adjustment and Education: Adapting to a Growing Global Market," *International Journal of Educational Development* 14, no. 2 (1994): 95–108.

21. Barrett, *Anthropology*, 51.

22. Harold J. Noah and Max A. Eckstein, *Toward a Science of Comparative Education* (New York: Macmillan, 1969), 112.

23. Gail Kelly and Philip Altbach, *Introduction to Education and Colonialism*, ed. Philip Altbach and Gail Kelly (New York: Longman, 1978), 1.

24. Gail Kelly, "Vietnam," in *International Feminist Perspectives on Educational Reform*, ed. David Kelly (New York: Garland, 1996), 146.

25. Vandra Masemann, "The 'Hidden Curriculum' of a West African Girls' Secondary School," *Canadian Journal of African Studies* 8, no. 3 (1974): 479–94.

26. Johann Galtung, *The European Community: A Superpower in the Making* (Oslo: Universitetsforlaget; London: George Allen and Unwin, 1973), 43.

27. Galtung, *European Community*, 46.

28. Christine Fox, "Metaphors of Educational Development," in *Social Justice and Third World Education*, ed. Timothy J. Scrase (New York: Garland, 1997), 60.

29. Shen-Keng Yang, "Shih and Kairos: Time Category in the Study of Educational Reform." Reprinted from *Proceedings of the National Science Council, Part C: Humanities and Social Sciences* 1, no. 2 (1991): 253–59.

30. Arturo Escobar, "Reflections on Development: Grassroots Approaches and Alternative Politics in the Third World," *Futures* 24, no. 2 (June 1992): 411–12.

31. Escobar, "Reflections," 412.

32. Escobar, "Reflections."

33. Escobar, "Reflections."

34. Freire, *Pedagogy of the Oppressed*, 29–30.

35. Archie Mafeje, "The Problem of Anthropology in Historical Perspective: An Inquiry into the Growth of the Social Sciences," *Canadian Journal of African Studies* 10, no. 2 (1976): 307–33.

36. Barrett, *Anthropology*.

37. Mafeje, "Problem of Anthropology," 317–18.

38. Mafeje, "Problem of Anthropology," 325.

39. Mafeje, "Problem of Anthropology," 326–27.

40. Michael Young, *Knowledge and Control* (London: Collier Macmillan, 1971).

41. George Spindler and Louise Spindler, eds., *Interpretive Ethnography and Education: At Home and Abroad* (Hillsdale, N.Y.: Erlbaum, 1987); also see Spindler, *Doing the Ethnography*.

42. Madan Sarup, *Marxism and Education* (London: Henley; Boston: Routledge and Kegan Paul, 1978), 33.

43. Vandra Masemann, "Anthropological Approaches to Comparative Education," *Comparative Education Review* 20, no. 3 (October 1976): 368–80.

44. Vandra Masemann, "School Ethnography: Plus ça Change?" in *Anthropologists Approach-*

ing Education, ed. Adri Kater (The Hague: Centre for the Study of Education in Developing Countries, 1981): 85–99.

45. Bernstein, *Class, Codes, and Control.*

46. Masemann, "School Ethnography," 94.

47. Vandra Masemann, "Critical Ethnography in the Study of Comparative Education," *Comparative Education Review* 26, no. 1 (February 1982): 1.

48. Masemann, "Critical Ethnography," 11.

49. Douglas E. Foley, "Labor and Legitimation in Schools: Notes on Doing Ethnography" (paper presented at a meeting of the Comparative and International Education Society, Ann Arbor, Mich., 1979). Also see Douglas E. Foley, *Learning Capitalist Culture: Deep in the Heart of Tejas* (Philadelphia: University of Pennsylvania Press, 1990).

50. Bradley Levinson, Douglas E. Foley, and Dorothy C. Holland, *The Cultural Production of the Educated Person: Critical Ethnographies of Schooling and Local Practice* (Albany: State University of New York Press, 1997).

51. Levinson, Foley, and Holland, *Cultural Production*, p. 18.

52. Kathryn Anderson-Levitt, *Local Meanings, Global Schooling: Anthropology and World Culture Theory* (New York: Palgrave Macmillan, 2003).

53. Gail Kelly, "Comparative Education: Challenge and Response," in *International Feminist Perspectives on Educational Reform: The Work of Gail Paradise Kelly*, ed. David H. Kelly (New York: Garland, 1996), 99.

54. Michael Apple, *Cultural Politics and Education* (New York: Teachers College Press, 1996).

55. Vandra Masemann and Anthony Welch, eds., *Tradition, Modernity and Post-Modernity in Education* (Amsterdam: Kluwer, 1997).

5

The Question of Identity from a Comparative Education Perspective

Christine Fox

"THE LOGIC OF BINARY OPPOSITIONS IS ALSO A LOGIC OF SUBORDINATION AND DOMINATION"[1]

This chapter explores a perspective of comparative education that focuses on the intersection of cultural identity and education as it affects our understandings of different educational systems. These concerns particularly affect that curious breed of educators—international educational consultants—who are confronted and immersed in contexts other than their own but claim some kind of universal authority to speak about educational change and development. I am an educational consultant as well as a teacher-educator in my native Australia, and so this exploration is partly autobiographical. Nevertheless, I claim that it is possible, as well as desirable, to reach uncoerced understandings interculturally that do not fall into Seyla Benhabib's logic of subordination and domination. The coming together of difference signals a potential to construct binary opposites; and where there are perceived opposites there are power games. The coming together of common ideas signals a potential to construct meaning; and where this occurs, there is transformation in education.

COLONIZERS AND COLONIZED: A BRIEF FORAY INTO THE LITERATURE OF INTERCULTURAL INTERACTION

Comparative education has traditionally been a search for similarities and differences in educational systems or activities, ideas, and ideologies. Early attempts to compare are reminiscent of early narratives, or travelers' tales, which presented vivid descriptions of groups of peoples, recognizing that they, like us, had intriguing differences in lifestyles. However, the tales of distant places soon became a mechanism for legitimating conquest and the stories expunged the humanness of colonized people.[2] In the nineteenth and early twentieth centuries, anthropological research came into its own, epitomizing Eurocentric

117

interpretations of the Other, making much of the contrasts between two supposed opposites. Metaphors of *primitive* or *savage* placed the Other firmly in another world from the *civilized*.[3] Educational research, as well as educational planning in "developing" world settings, tended to be dictated by European perceptions of what was good for the Other.

In more recent times, the subtleties of linguistic and philosophical dilemmas of translation are often confused with a binary process of substituting one set of meanings for another. In education, the complex process of intercultural interaction has been analyzed by Western educators as a one-way adaptation and integration of the Other into the dominant educational norm, rather like Young Yun Kim's theory of adaptation of strangers into a host society.[4]

With the challenge of postmodernism, the notion of fundamental norms and values, or generalizable interests, has lost its appeal. It is increasingly being recognized that there are multiple voices and that diversity can be celebrated. The danger, of course, lies in a belief that diversity is an indicator that no common agreements on values or ethics are realizable, that all is culturally relative. The upshot of that argument is to claim that no authentic communication is possible across cultures. Now if this is the case, it may be argued that comparative education and international education are dead disciplines, particularly when educators come from diametrically different cultural backgrounds. This chapter posits the opposite argument, that the visibly embodied difference of the Other is a boundary that can and must be crossed and that in regard to education, such boundaries are artificial, founded for the most part on historical racism.[5]

The theoretical background of this chapter draws on some key issues arising from Jürgen Habermas's communicative action theory. Habermas posits a hypothetical "as if" ideal speech situation, coercion-free, in which interlocutors can develop a mutual understanding through a rational dialogic process.[6] Laudable as it is, Habermas's theory assumes that there must be a common cultural background between communicators for this to happen. He thus dismisses most forms of communication in a postmodern, intercultural world.[7] Is this a paradox, then, and is this another case for dismissing comparative educational approaches? No, it is not. Procedures of communicative interaction can indeed be created that are sensitive to multiple modes of reasoning and to multiple differences of identity.[8]

Authenticity in cross-cultural professional communication about education is not only desirable but also possible. An authentic communicative situation is an honorable kind of conversation based on mutual trust and a respectful sharing of intended meanings. It requires a sense of resonance between those who seek to reach agreement and understanding—intuitively, poetically, or experientially—by identifying shared moral values or through rational discourse, or a bit of each. The idea that cultural incompatibility is more or less inevitable is a logocentric view that stereotypes the Other and marginalizes those who identify with nondominant cultures. The ideas explored in this chapter show how people from contrastive worldviews can indeed bridge deep chasms of discursive difference if they work together to create authentic intercultural communicative situations—that is, if they create their own intercultural space.

What a pessimistic, and dangerous, view it is to dismiss the possibility of creating situations in which two people (or groups of people) from very different cultures can get together and achieve real understanding. It is almost like saying that incompatibility is inevitable and communication is therefore impossible and that a peaceful solution to any conflict cannot be brokered. The disastrous consequences of failing to find compatibility between values and goals of groups of people has seen whole nations and ethnic groups oppose each other with violence and hatred. Atrocities committed in the name of a group or an ideology are a violation of any human value system, as has been experienced to terrible effect in the first decade of the twenty-first century.

Anthropologists and sociolinguists have raised similar doubts for a long time now, possibly for different reasons. Westerners used to feel that cultures from less industrialized countries were less complex and that Western concepts could not be adequately translated into languages used by so-called traditional societies. And yet, as Edward Said, Giyatri Spivak, and others have noted,[9] this marginalizing of the Other stems from erroneous assumptions based on stereotyping of culture and language less known to a European, as well as racially motivated feelings of superiority over others. Just as feminist critiques of a supposed dichotomy between the public sphere and the private sphere show up gender blindness, so do I critique any supposed dichotomy between the West and the Third World as culture blindness. Surely, if two cultural groups were perceived as equally powerful, and their values and beliefs able to be equally expressed without coercion, there would be scant reason why an "authentic" discussion about those differences could not take place—with sincerity, truthfulness within one's own position, and a willingness to accept and engage in different expressive discourse practices.

The idea of incompatibility tends to come mainly from an ideological construction of unequal relationships of power between two cultures. As Homi Bhabha says:

> An important feature of colonial discourse is its dependence on the concept of "fixity" in the ideological construction of otherness. Fixity, as the sign of cultural/historical/racial difference in the discourse of colonialism, is a paradoxical mode of representation: it connotes rigidity and an unchanging order as well as disorder, degeneracy and daemonic repetition. . . . The stereotype . . . is its major discursive strategy.[10]

Authentic communication implies, as Hans-Georg Gadamer states, the opening of oneself to the full power of what the Other is saying. He shows that such an opening does not entail agreement but rather the to-and-fro play of dialogue.[11] It is this potential that comparative educators and international educational consultants must pursue in response to the increasingly polarized context of global politics and its impact on education and intercultural research and, by implication, on the threat to authentic communication. These issues have been eloquently discussed by Bradley Levinson and by Pauline Lipman in a special thirty-fifth anniversary issue of *Anthropology and Education Quarterly* in 2005.[12]

INTERCULTURAL COMMUNICATION, EDUCATION, AND THE NOTION OF IDENTITY

Over many years, and in particular over the past five years, I have been involved in a number of educational projects that have raised important issues about the influence that formal education has on the development of individual identity—compared with, say, developing the nation, developing human resources, or developing participation rates in schooling. These projects have included research into the development of education in Western Samoa;[13] the degree to which students from language backgrounds other than English are expected to participate in society;[14] the participation of girls and women in education in Papua New Guinea;[15] the experiences of girls and minority groups in schools in Laos;[16] the experiences of Spanish-speaking students in some Australian schools; the issues of undergraduate students in Sri Lankan universities;[17] and most recently, the reforms of governance in a decentralized education system in Indonesia.[18] What this work has indicated, and what my daily teaching at the university also indicates, is that the interplay of culture, education, and the state economy tends to create or support structural inequalities that mediate against the transformation of society into a just and peaceful place. Yet within these structures, there are enormous possibilities for cultural change through the agency of those who refuse to be relegated to the margins.

In this chapter, I discuss some of the issues that arise for those who feel they are marginalized individuals and/or belong to subordinated groups. At stake here is how education has influenced the ways people construct their cultural identity and how others construct that identity for them. I posit that schooling is not necessarily unchangeable and is not merely a site for social and cultural reproduction. Rather, it presents possibilities for transformation, even if those possibilities are today being attacked more than ever before by economic rationalism and globalization. If such a transformation does take place, then it takes place largely through a reconceptualization of the identity of those who see themselves as agents of their own destiny, as resisters in a struggle to redefine who they are. The process itself transforms individuals, yet it takes place in a context of cultural identification of Other. The process challenges the conventional wisdom of the inevitable reproduction of inequality.

EDUCATION, IDENTITY, AND TRANSFORMATION

The explanations of cultural reproduction have changed as researchers focus more on documenting the transformative experiences of the heretofore invisible or silenced minorities. Well-known writings by Paulo Freire and others on development and literacy point to ways in which education can be transformative—as a process of conscientization. In a similar vein, the case study by Anne Hickling-Hudson in this volume points to new theories of how such a transformation takes place. Other comparativists have been influenced by a body of ethnographic literature, such as the work of Clifford Geertz and other anthropologists. A significant collection of ethnographic examples of the interplay of culture, identity, and schooling has been compiled and edited by Bradley A. Levinson, Douglas E. Foley, and Dorothy C. Holland,[19] illustrating how subordinated groups seek to use schools as sites for cultural politics and challenges. Their argument is that through the production of cultural forms created within the structural constraints of sites such as schools, subjectivities form and agency develops.

Some of the empirical examples that I discuss raise further issues about the formation of identity and identities. Identity is not fixed, nor is identity a single definable condition. Yet the construction of identity can be the construction of inequalities, as well as a powerful force in transforming the structures that seek to reduce the identity of Otherness to a single, stereotyped dimension. J. B. Thompson could have been speaking about the events of September 11, 2001, when he stated, back in 1990: "While it is certainly true that modern societies are interconnected in many ways and at many levels both nationally and internationally, it is also the case that a great deal of diversity, disorganization, dissensus and resistance exists, and is likely to continue to exist, within modern societies."[20]

The "Silent Indian"

An illustrative case discussed by Foley[21] is that of the "silent Indian" stereotype that emerged in earlier literature on the experiences of Native Americans in schools set up by, and usually taught by, the dominant white majority in the United States. Foley revisits the myths and stereotypes of Native American schoolchildren by providing a close and personal inside view of how, and why, some Native Americans might choose silence as a resistant discourse, "a political retreat into a separate cultural space and identity far from the white world." He interviewed a number of leading members of the Mesquaki community with whom he had gone to school several years before. He found that a number of the interviewees had successfully used silence as resistance so that they could avoid conflict and gain space—in other words, to create possibilities for their own development of an identity separate from domination. Earlier assumptions that this silence was a cultural trait were simplistic explanations for a multifaceted cultural *performance* in the Bakhtinian sense. Even so, such a widespread myth tends to be reinforced by the potential for the resisters to lose opportunities for future educational participation. Foley's analysis indicates how wrong it is to portray silence as a cultural stereotype instead of listening to how local actors articulate their own history.

The "Ethnic" Australian

Despite nearly twenty years of multicultural policy in the schools of most states of Australia, a notion persists of students from overseas, or students from language backgrounds other than English (LBOTE), somehow failing to match up to the standards and culture of the dominant culture. The "ethnic" Australian has been stereotyped as nonparticipative, possibly dull-witted, and unimaginative. LBOTE students who have left school and reflect on their schooling say that their participation was limited when English as a Second Language programs tended to peter out after a couple of years of tuition, whereas curricula continued to draw much of their knowledge base from a fairly narrow band of cultural understandings that were confusing at best for someone unfamiliar with them, as well as disempowering and isolating.[22]

In a study of the experiences of Spanish-speaking students from Uruguayan, Chilean, and Spanish families in three high schools in New South Wales, David Plaza[23] shows how the students try to resist the image they present in their schools of lacking ability through an approach similar to that of the "silent Indian"—that is, projecting a concept of themselves as bored and withdrawn. Yet, when interviewed, students proffered a number of differing explanations. One girl in a year ten class commented that she did not like to read aloud in her English class because she was never encouraged and was afraid she might make a mistake and be ridiculed. The teacher's explanation was that the girl was not interested in the subject and seemed unmotivated to try to move up to a higher level.

Another girl in the Plaza study maintained that it was not much use to participate in class because of a general sense of negativity by teachers toward her and her friends, most of whom the girl classified as "wogs" or "ethnics": "In the class there are no Australian girls; it is a group of ethnic people and many times he treats you as if you were nothing; many times he says you don't get good marks because you are this kind of person or that."

On the other hand, many of the students celebrated their multiple identities, being

Uruguayan, Chilean, or Spanish at home, "wog" at school, and "gringo" (white for-
eigner) when visiting their parents' country of origin. They lived in two worlds in Australia, isolated by their minority culture but participating in a variety of ways at school,
particularly if they were born in Australia and were bilingual. Plaza found that many of
the differentiating characteristics of their minority group depended not just on how dark
their skin was but on the accent detected in their English by the dominant group and in
the extent to which the family remained in what Plaza calls their "cultural bubble." The
children could go beyond the bubble and could go on to fulfill at least some of their
dreams through various forms of both resistance and compliance.

The "Gendered" Papua New Guinea Woman

In 1995, a team of consultants (including myself) undertook an exploratory study
of the levels of participation of females in Papua New Guinea in education and training.[24]
In the course of this visit, we interviewed a number of women to discuss their perceptions
of the ways in which girls and women were able to participate in schools and in further
education and university. The structural inequalities were obvious—girls' participation
was far lower than boys', their job opportunities were fewer, and their status in society
on the whole was far lower than for boys and men. It appeared that the greatest negative
influence on female participation was an overwhelming and systemic subordination of
women in much of Papua New Guinea society.

Some of the men interviewed during this same visit claimed that the subordination
of women is a time-honored cultural factor in Papua New Guinea society. These interviewees claimed that any transformation of the role and status of women in society was
a Western imposition of their concept of equity and equality, which went against traditional culture. When pressed, even those in high-status positions who were responsible
for implementing gender equity in the education system and agreed in principle with the
policy maintained that yes, cultural traditions were stronger than school-based ideas.
Thus, the perpetuation or reification of the image of a gendered Other tended to institutionalize the unequal state of affairs to the public "as if it were permanent, natural and
outside of time."[25] The illusion was reinforced by images of women depicted by the local
media, in the community, in schools and other educational institutions, and in the workplace.

However, this claim was disputed by the women who were interviewed and by other
men interviewed who supported equity. The women maintained that it was merely convenient for the men to lock women into a subordinated position in order to maintain
their power and that it could hardly be culturally determined if only the male half of the
population were in agreement. They saw the dangers of being determined by cultural or
gendered relativity. Labeling and fixing the Other is a form of colonial discourse that
perpetuates unequal relationships of power, and it is perhaps nowhere more overt than
in Papua New Guinea between the male as powerful and the female as Other.[26]

In spite of the powerful structural inequalities, several of the women interviewed in
Papua New Guinea described how they had redefined their identity by establishing their
voice through increased economic and educational participation and thereby creating
spaces for a more powerful voice to transform their subordinated image in the community.

One way in which women had been able to use the school site to transform female experiences was in a particular girls-only secondary school managed by a Catholic nun, who explained in the interview that she was deliberately teaching the girls at the school to be independent thinkers, conscious of the need to combat discrimination and violence against them when they went on to further education. This approach to the construction of a gendered identity can be compared to that described by Skinner and Holland in their study of Nepalese females who challenged the so-called traditional compliant identity of girls in society.[27] In this account, the authors describe how the Nepalese school was a forum for the development of critical discourses on the legacies of caste and gender privilege. The students had their own ways of constructing their new identities and self-understandings, in this case by writing their own end-of-year revue of skits and songs focusing on their anger and resistance.

The "Educated" Sri Lankan

Over twenty years ago, Ronald Dore published his well-known study of educational credentialing in four countries, *The Diploma Disease*. Among the case studies was one on Sri Lanka and its education system, in which Dore showed that per capita levels of education were among the highest in the world, and yet employment and development were not as high as would have been expected at that time. At the start of the twenty-first century, the proportion of graduates from education systems is still extremely high, although there are continuing concerns in industry and in government that the "educated" person is not necessarily employable. The identity of the educated person remains fixed on the white-collar worker, whereas the needs of the economy point to the desirability of greater emphasis on technological skills and competencies for the workplace, a need emphasized as long ago as 1943 by the Sri Lankan educational reformer C. W. W. Kannangara.[28] The government of Sri Lanka was concerned in 2002 that the unemployment rates of new graduates was as high as 60 percent, particularly among graduates from faculties of humanities, and particularly among women.[29]

Sri Lanka is fortunate in having successive governments that placed a high priority on education, even though there are inequalities in the supply of resources and access to higher education. The participation of females and males in the formal sector is fairly even; participation between rural and urban is far less even, with fewer opportunities for employment in rural areas and fewer resources supplied to schools. The government applies a quota system for admission to higher education in the thirteen public universities, whereby a certain percentage of students must come from each of the country's provinces; nevertheless, fewer than 3 percent of the total of school leavers are admitted to these public universities. In spite of these barriers, many rural students who otherwise would not have been able to study at this level have become well-known scholars within these universities.

There is often a discrepancy between the concept of the *educated person* as one who has knowledge and the *educated person* as one who can deal with change, manage resources, and learn how to learn, as stated in the new education reform program in Sri Lanka. This complex and seemingly contradictory positioning is multifaceted and is by no means an either/or situation. It rests on the definition of an educated person, and what characteristics pertain to such a label, and on examinations, which are seen as the gateway through which the educated person must walk.

TACKLING THE ISSUE OF IDENTITY
AS A SOCIAL JUSTICE ISSUE

The various studies briefly mentioned in the previous section are meant to illustrate how the notion of identity construction is closely connected to the construction of a socially just society. They call to mind other studies of education and equity in multicultural societies, and they are reminiscent of more recent studies of citizenship and identity,[30] in which the discourse considers who is included and who is excluded from being a citizen.

For members of ethnic minorities, culture plays a key role as a source of identity and as a way of organizing resistance to exclusion and discrimination. Reference to the culture of origin helps people maintain self-esteem and personal identity in a situation in which their capabilities and experience are undermined.[31]

Plaza's analysis of identity is pertinent to this discussion. Plaza places the construction of identity in its social context, showing how it is both a self-reflexive and an interactional process, one that is never determined and fixed but is bound in time, culture, and location. He agrees with Homi Bhabha,[32] who puts forward the notion that separating the public from the private identity or the psyche from the social is a false dichotomy. Plaza's account tallies well with the thesis put forward by Levinson et al., who see the construction of the educated person as culturally and contextually defined and by no means a common process in Western or Western-influenced societies.[33]

Hall et al.'s notion of identity tends to draw on the idea of cultural relativity, developing beyond the ideas of the subject as an individual unfolding from inside and beyond the concept of subjects forming their identities through the interaction of self with society.[34] Identity becomes a moveable feast formed and transformed continuously in relation to the ways individuals are represented or addressed in the cultural systems that surround them. It is historically, not biologically, defined. The subject assumes different identities at different times, identities that are not unified around a coherent self.

Many writers describe the present as a new era of diaspora, a period in which the identity of the millions of migrants, refugees, and asylum seekers has been "marginalised, fragmented, disadvantaged and dispersed"—in other words, Bhabha's notion of the *unhomely* (denizens of the contemporary world). This is a process of migranthood: "A sense of moving from a certain predictable world into one of unpredictability and change"[35]—what many, for example, Leon Tikly, refer to as the postcolonial condition.[36]

Migration is considered the most important experience of this century. Bammer uses the term *displacement* to refer to the phenomenon of people being separated from their native culture either through physical dislocation (as refugees, immigrants, exiles, or expatriates) or through the colonizing imposition of a foreign culture.[37]

Identity construction works in both directions. In the case of immigrants living in English-speaking countries, local people sometimes see them as intruders. In response, the immigrants cluster themselves in groups, creating a kind of vicious circle in which interactions reinforce preconceived ideas. Thus, when the local and the migrant interact, the former positions the latter as disadvantaged and marginalized and in a situation that is peripheral to the main activities. The local sees the migrant as the Other and vice versa. In that way the metaphor of Otherness perpetuates the effects of cultural difference.

An important element that contributes to the construction of immigrants' cultural identity is their home culture. Validation of their culture would eliminate sentiments of inferiority, which sometimes make immigrants feel so different. For some adolescent students in Plaza's study, this was certainly the case. They found themselves caught between two cultures. A year twelve Spanish Australian girl said: "It is very difficult because I don't know what you should be called: Spanish, Australian or what? It is like being in the middle of both. At home I always speak in Spanish, and so I call myself Spanish, but as I live in Australia and I was born in Australia, then I'm Australian; it is very difficult."[38] Of course, some of the construction of identity forms around the language people use. The relationship between language and diversity, and between language and equity in schooling, is clear but complex. This observation brings me back to the first part of the chapter and completes the connection among identity, power, and communication. Intercultural communication is heavily influenced by relative positions of perceived power of the speakers, whether in their individual positioning or by dint of their positioning in the context. Several comparative educators are involved in comparative studies of language policy in various countries, including the ways in which language policy can be used to create inequities of power.[39]

The postcolonial contextual position of the twenty-first-century diaspora encompasses those who have emigrated to an English-speaking country but whose lack of competence in English makes them feel jeopardized and insecure. They are negatively stereotyped by the host because of their perceived linguistic deficiency and often take low-skilled jobs because these are the only positions left open for them. Australia, with a population of immigrants coming from practically every corner of the world, faces the great challenge of helping these linguistic minorities to overcome the linguistic isolation and the emotional consequences that their marginalization produces in their everyday lives: "There is no language change without emotional consequences. Principally: loss. That language equals home, that language is a home, as surely as a roof over one's head is a home, and that to be without a language, or to be between languages, is as miserable in its way as to be without bread."[40]

The relationship among language, identity, education, and social justice is thus closely intertwined. The twenty-first century has seen national reforms that were transformational being challenged by the forces of globalization, but which have tried to utilize the technological advantages of recent reforms—for example, South Africa, Sri Lanka, Papua New Guinea, Mexico, and Venezuela. In the current era of uncertainty in intercultural relationships, so starkly evident for example in the context of Middle Eastern countries, educational change and transformation must encompass the issue of social and cultural identity in specific contexts; the social justice issue must address the needs of particular groups of people as well as tackle the inequalities in the system in general.

NOTES

1. Seyla Benhabib, *Situating the Self* (Cambridge: Polity, 1992), 15.
2. M. Pratt, *Imperial Eyes: Travel Writing and Transculturation* (London: Routledge, 1992).
3. Clifford Geertz, *The Interpretation of Cultures* (New York: Basic Books, 1973).
4. See W. Gudykunst, "Towards a Typology of Stranger-Host Relationships," *International Journal of Intercultural Relations* 7 (1983): 410–13; and Young Yun Kim, *Communication and Cross-Cultural Adaptation: An Integrative Theory* (Clevedon: Multilingual Matters, 1988). The debate on adaptation has been carried through several issues of the *International Journal of Intercultural Relations*, including an article I wrote in 1997 titled "The Authenticity of Intercultural Communication," *International Journal of Intercultural Relations* 21, no. 1: 85–104; and that by C. R.

Hillett and K. Witte, "Predicting Intercultural Adaptation and Isolation: Using the Extended Parallel Process Model to Test Anxiety/Uncertainty Management Theory," *International Journal of Intercultural Relations* 25, no 2. (2001): 125–40.

5. M. Crossley and K. Watson, eds. *Comparative and International Research in Education: Globalisation, Context and Difference* (London: RoutledgeFalmer, 2003).

6. Jürgen Habermas, *The Theory of Communicative Action*, vol. 1, trans. T. McCarthy (Boston: Beacon, 1984).

7. Christine Fox, "A Critical Examination of Intercultural Communication: Towards a New Theory," (Ph.D. diss., University of Sydney, 1992). For a more recent discussion of the issues, see Christine Fox, "Stories within Stories: Dissolving the Boundaries in Narrative Research and Analysis," in *Narrative Research on Learning: Comparative and International Perspectives,* ed. S. Trahar (Oxford: Symposium, 2006).

8. Christine Fox, "Listening to the Other: Social Cartography in Intercultural Communication," in *Social Cartography*, ed. R. Paulston (New York: Garland, 1996).

9. Edward Said's influential *Orientalism: Western Conceptions of the Orient* (Harmondsworth, U.K.: Penguin) was published in 1978 and has become a classic. His much acclaimed *Culture and Imperialism* (London: Chatto & Windus) appeared in 1993. A later collection of his works appeared in 2000: *Reflections on Exile and Other Essays* (Cambridge, Mass.: Harvard University Press). Important work on identity includes Gayatri Spivak, *The Post-colonial Critic: Interviews, Strategies, Dialogues*, ed. S. Harasym (New York: Chatto & Windus, 1990) and more recently Sara DeTurk's "Intercultural Empathy: Myth, Competency, or Possibility for Alliance Building?" *Communication Education* 50, no. 4 (2001): 374–84.

10. Homi Bhabha, "Frontlines/Borderposts," in *Displacements: Cultural Identities in Question*, ed. A. Bammer (Bloomington: Indiana University Press, 1994), 66.

11. Hans-Georg Gadamer, *Truth and Method*, 2nd rev. ed., trans. revised by J. Weinsheimer and D. Marshall (New York: Crossroad, 1989; originally published as *Wahrheit und Methode* [Tübingen: Mohr, 1960]).

12. See B. Levinson, "Reflections on the Field: Citizenship, Identity, Democracy: Engaging the Political in the Anthropology of Education," *Anthropology and Education Quarterly* 36, no. 4: 329–40. See also P. Lipman, "Educational Ethnography and the Politics of Globalization, War, and Resistance," *Anthropology and Education Quarterly* 36, no. 4: 315–28.

13. Fox, "A Critical Examination of Intercultural Communication."

14. See Robyn Iredale and Christine Fox, with T. Shermaimoff, *Immigration, Education, and Training in New South Wales* (Canberra: Bureau of Immigration and Population Research/Australian Government Publishing Service, 1994); Robyn Iredale and C. Fox, "The Impact of Immigration on School Education in New South Wales, Australia," *International Migration Review* 23, no. 3 (1997): 655–69.

15. Christine Fox, "Girls, Education and Development in Papua New Guinea," in *Education and Development for Girls in Less Industrialised Countries*, ed. C. Heward and S. Bunwaree (London: Zed, 1999).

16. Christine Fox, "Tensions in the Decolonisation Process: Disrupting Preconceptions of Postcolonial Education in the Lao People's Democratic Republic," in *Disrupting Preconceptions: Postcolonialism and Education* (Flaxton, Queensland: Post Pressed, 2004).

17. Christine Fox, "Higher Education Competencies Required for Sri Lankan Undergraduates to Promote Social Harmony" (paper presented at UNESCO Conference on Intercultural Communication, Jyväskylä, Finland, June 2003).

18. R. Allaburton and C. Fox, "Mid-Term Review" (unpublished report on two Basic Education Projects for the Indonesian Government, Canberra: Australian Agency for International Development, 2006).

19. See Bradley Levinson, Douglas Foley, and Dorothy C. Holland, eds., *The Cultural Pro-*

duction of the Educated Person: Critical Ethnographies of Schooling and Local Practices (Albany: State University of New York Press, 1996).

20. J. B. Thompson, *Ideology and Modern Culture* (Cambridge: Polity, 1990), 107.

21. Douglas Foley, "The Silent Indian as Cultural Production," in *The Cultural Production of the Educated Person*, ed. Levinson, Foley, and Holland (Albany: State University of New York Press, 1996).

22. See Iredale and Fox, "The Impact of Immigration."

23. David Plaza Coral, "Experiences of Spanish Speaking Students in Australia: A Case Study" (Ph.D. diss., University of Wollongong, 1998). Acknowledgment is given to David Plaza, one of my doctoral students at the University of Wollongong, who has supplied some of the discussion on identity, and to Janice Wright, his cosupervisor.

24. Fox, "Gender and Development in Papua New Guinea."

25. Thompson, *Ideology and Modern Culture*, 65.

26. The status of women has changed little in the intervening decade, as reported (2006) by Australian doctoral researcher and former resident of Papua New Guinea, Suzanne Lipu, who has presented a number of unpublished papers on women's empowerment in Papua New Guinea.

27. D. Skinner and D. Holland, "Public Education in Nepal," in *The Cultural Production of the Educated Person*, ed. Levinson, Foley, and Holland (Albany: State University of New York Press, 1996).

28. Information provided by the Sri Lankan Minister for Tertiary Education and Training, September 12, 2002.

29. "Strengthening Undergraduate Education" (2002), a project managed by Melbourne University Private in Sri Lanka to provide recommendations to the government of Sri Lanka for a future five-year internationally funded higher education quality improvement project.

30. Levinson, "Reflections on the Field."

31. See S. Castles and M. Miller, *The Age of Migration: International Population Movements in the Modern World* (Basingstoke, U.K.: Macmillan, 1993), and Carlos Alberto Torres, *Democracy, Education and Multiculturalism: Dilemmas of Citizenship in a Global World* (Lanham, Md.: Rowman & Littlefield, 1998); see also S. Batia's analysis of the construction of self as both homeland and hostland influenced, "Acculturation, Dialogical Voices and the Construction of the Diasporic Self," *Theory & Psychology* 12, no. 1 (2002): 55–77.

32. Bhabha, "Frontlines/Borderposts," in *Displacements*, ed. A. Bammer (Bloomington: Indiana University Press, 1994), 66; Plaza Coral, "Experiences of Spanish Speaking Students."

33. Levinson, Foley, and Holland, eds., *The Cultural Production of the Educated Person*, 18.

34. S. Hall, D. Held, and T. McGrew, eds., *Modernity and Its Futures* (Cambridge: Polity, 1994).

35. Hall, Held, and McGrew, eds., *Modernity and Its Futures*, 275–77.

36. When exploring the construction of the diasporic self as part of the *postcolonial condition*, readers should refer first to Leon Tikly's excellent article on "Globalisation and Education in the Postcolonial World: Towards a Conceptual Framework," *Comparative Education* 37, no. 2 (2001): 151–71.

37. See A. Bammer, *Displacements: Cultural Identities in Question* (Bloomington: Indiana University Press, 1994).

38. Plaza Coral, "Experiences of Spanish Speaking Students."

39. Birgit Brock-Utne has written extensively on this area—for instance, "Education for All—In Whose Language?" *Oxford Review of Education* 27, no. 1 (2001): 115–34; and "Globalisation, Language and Education," in *International Handbook on Globalisation, Education and Policy Research: Global Pedagogies and Policies*, ed. J. Zajda (Dordrecht: Kluwer, 2005): 549–65. See also J. Arthur, "Perspectives on Educational Language Policy and Its Implementation in African Classrooms: A Comparative Study of Botswana and Tanzania," *Compare* 31, no. 3 (2001): 347–62; David Corson, *Language, Minority Education, and Gender: Linking Social Justice and Power* (Phila-

delphia: Multilingual Matters, 1993); Pak-Sang Lai and Michael Byram, "The Politics of Bilingualism: A Reproduction Analysis of the Policy of Mother Tongue Education in Hong Kong after 1997," *Compare* 33, no. 3 (2003): 315–34; Rebecca Clothey, "China's Policies for Minority Nationalities in Higher Education: Negotiating National Values and Ethnic Identities," *Comparative Education Review* 49, no. 3 (2005): 389–410.

40. A. Y. Kaplan, "On Language Memoir," in *Displacements: Cultural Identities in Question,* ed. C. Heward and S. Bunwaree (Bloomington: Indiana University Press, 1994).

6

Equality of Education: A Half-Century of Comparative Evidence Seen From a New Millennium

Joseph P. Farrell

Debates about (and occasional action on) educational reforms, which are common currency in the early years of this century (e.g., decentralization, privatization, education for "global competitiveness," use of "new technologies" such as the Internet, standards and "accountability") have a considerable history. They are in many fundamental respects current manifestations of debates and reform efforts that have spanned, in one form or another, the past five decades, and in some cases longer. To think seriously about the possible import of currently fashionable reform movements for equality of education, particularly for the most marginalized members of various societies, requires that we review and try to make some sense of that history. That is the intent of this chapter. Comparative education, as a field of scholarly inquiry and as an applied discipline, has been central to what has been learned.

BACKGROUND: THE OPTIMISTIC REFORMS OF THE SIXTIES

The twenty-five years following the end of the Second World War was an epoch of great and widespread optimism regarding questions of educational and socioeconomic equality. It was assumed generally that the evident gaps in wealth and power among nations could be rather quickly eliminated; that those already industrialized and "developed" nations that had been devastated by the war could be quickly put "back on their feet"; and that those nonindustrialized or generally poor nations (whether newly independent from European colonialism or long independent) could rather quickly and easily be placed on the "road to development," and that obvious gaps in access to income and power among individuals and collectivities within nations could be equally quickly reduced. It was also assumed that more general acquisition of education (understood mainly as the provision of formal schooling) was essential to the lessening of inequalities among and within nations. Increasing provision of education was seen as a major (in some views the most important) engine that would drive the world to a more equal provision of access to wealth, power, and opportunity. Poverty and inequality (absolute or relative; individual, collective, national, or international) came to be seen widely as relatively easily solved policy problems rather than necessary, unavoidable, and/or unresolvable human conditions.

The advent of human capital theory in the late 1950s and early 1960s put education even more squarely in the center of this optimistic vision. Education was no longer seen as simply one among many competing consumer goods to be acquired individually (for personal gain) or collectively (through taxes for perceived collective gain) to the extent that it could be afforded. Rather, education was constructed as an investment opportunity. Public expenditures on increasing the availability of education would produce net social benefits, increasing the total amount of wealth in a society and improving its distribution.[1] The confluence of these events and ways of understanding them led to enormously increased expenditures on education around the world, a major increase in access to education (in poor nations, access to primary education and adult basic education; in richer nations, which had already achieved nearly universal primary education, in access to secondary and tertiary education), and major educational reform efforts attempting to make it more accessible and effective for marginalized or disadvantaged individuals or groups.

In rich nations, primary education was already effectively compulsory and universal, and secondary and tertiary education was relatively widely available. There educational reforms focused on increasing the proportion of age-eligible youth who completed secondary schooling and went on to some form of postsecondary education, and on improving the educational "chances" of specifically targeted "educationally disadvantaged" groups, whether the disadvantage was based on race, ethnicity, socioeconomic status, gender, geographical location, or some combination of these. In many such nations there was a massive expansion of secondary education facilities, with the policy target often being universal access and usually universal completion. Existing universities expanded rapidly, large numbers of wholly new universities were created, and in many nations, entire new systems of nonuniversity, technically oriented postsecondary institutions were established.[2] In the United States, massive resources and political energy were devoted to attempting to end racial segregation of schooling and to develop and implement changes that might increase the educational success of disadvantaged groups. In much of Western Europe, academic secondary schooling led to university (e.g., the English grammar school, the French lycée, the German gymnasium) and served a small proportion of the eligible age-group—predominantly the children of already privileged families. Major attempts at comprehensivization of secondary schooling took different forms in different nations, but the general goals were to increase the proportion of youngsters who had access to a form of secondary schooling that could lead to university and to equalize the opportunities to access to such education across social groups.[3]

In developing nations, many children had no access to primary schooling and most adults were illiterate (although this varied dramatically from nation to nation). The main educational-change focus was on simple quantitative expansion, and many nations mounted national literacy campaigns. In the early 1960s, UNESCO convened a series of regional meetings of ministers of education that set broad targets for quantitative growth designed as a framework for national educational planning. The general aim was to move as quickly as possible (and it was assumed that this would be quickly indeed) to universal primary education and universal literacy, both seen as necessary components of national development. During this epoch, scholars fiercely debated the precise nature of national development, but a fairly general consensus developed that it entailed at least three main components: (1) the generation of more wealth within a nation (economic development), (2) the more equitable distribution of such wealth or at least more equitable distribution of opportunities for access to that wealth (social development), and (3) the organization of political decision-making structures and development of values supporting them, that would be close approximations of those prevalent in developed nations (political development). More widespread and equitable provision of formal schooling was seen as essential to all three. Massive enrollment increases resulted from the application of this general view to educational policy in developing nations. Between 1960 and 1975, the number of children in school in developing countries increased by 122 percent; the proportion of age-eligible children in primary schooling increased from 57 to 75 percent during the same fifteen-year period, with corresponding increases at the secondary level (14 percent to 26 percent) and postsecondary level (1.5 percent to 4.4 percent).[4]

RESULTS: MUCH LESS THAN ANTICIPATED

However, by the early 1970s it was already apparent to many observers that this massive worldwide effort at educational reform in the name of growth and equality was not producing the expected results. As early as 1968, Coombs wrote the aptly titled book *The World Educational Crisis: A Systems Analysis.*[5] The structural reforms in Western Europe were seldom fully implemented, if at all, and were not, in most cases, significantly changing the social composition of academic secondary schooling. In the United States, desegregation programs and other attempted reforms were not significantly improving the educational success of African Americans and other marginalized groups. In both instances some individuals benefited, but the overall pattern of structural inequality remained intact. In developing nations, because population was growing rapidly relative to the rate of educational expansion, the absolute numbers of primary-aged children out of school grew from 109.2 million in 1960 to 120.5 million in 1975.[6] The same pattern held for adult literacy. Overall literacy rates were increasing (in some cases quite rapidly), but the absolute number of illiterate adults was increasing as well. Moreover, it was becoming clear that the rates of educational expenditure increase that had occurred during the 1960s and drove the expansion of school places could not be sustained over a longer period. Beyond this, although many developing nations had been experiencing economic growth, the already wealthy nations were for the most part growing even faster, creating an ever widening gap between rich and poor countries. Furthermore, the gap between richer and poorer groups within many nations was also increasing, although this was a very mixed pattern.[7]

Within schooling systems themselves, in nations rich and poor, distributional inequalities were generally persisting, in some cases getting better and in some, worse. In many societies, urban children benefited more than rural children from increased educational provision. In other societies, particular ethnic, tribal, or religious groups benefited more. In many societies, boys received more of the newly available schooling than did girls. In most societies, newly available school places, whether at the primary, secondary, or tertiary level, were occupied mainly, or almost exclusively, by children of the already well-to-do.

This led to a significant modification—for many a complete rejection—of the earlier optimistic view that had guided the actions of policymakers and advisers in rich and poor nations. Claims about the power of schooling to equalize the life chances of children who are born into very different social and economic circumstances generally became much more cautious. Don Adams once characterized this mood shift as the change from the "optimistic sixties" to the "cynical seventies."[8]

As the comparative evidence continued to accumulate through the 1980s and into the 1990s, it strengthened and reinforced the cynical view established in the 1970s. It became increasingly clear that educational reforms aimed at increasing equality were very difficult to enact and implement successfully, and even when implemented reasonably well, seldom had the intended effects on comparative life chances of the children of various social groups within and among nations. There were some success stories but far more examples of partial or complete failure. In many developing nations, the situation was made even more difficult by the fiscal crises produced by the oil shock of the 1970s and the debt crisis of the 1980s. In most rich nations the difficulty was aggravated by economic restructuring, which produced significant reductions in public educational expenditures and severe reductions in the numbers of middle-class jobs that had been the traditional target occupations for youngsters from marginalized groups who had managed to use education as a vehicle for social mobility (it is hard to be mobile if there are few jobs into which to be mobile!). In 1997, I summarized the experience of the past three decades as follows:

> One general lesson is that planning educational change is a far more difficult and risk-prone venture than had been imagined in the 1950s or 1960s. There are far more examples of failure, or of minimal success, than of relatively complete success. Far more is known about what doesn't work, or doesn't usually work, than about what does work. . . . Moreover, when planned educational reform attempts have been successful, the process has usually taken a very long time, frequently far longer than originally anticipated. There are in the experience of the past decades a few examples where an unusual combination of favorable conditions and politically skilled planners has permitted a great deal of educational change to occur in a relatively brief period, but these have been rare and ideosyncratic.[9]

THEORETICAL ACCOUNTS OF REFORM FAILURE

Partly as a result of this experience, a very complex and confusing theoretical debate has developed. Although the details of the debate are discussed elsewhere in this book, some of the main features that pertain directly to the theme of this chapter are discussed below. Core aspects of the debate for present purposes can be framed by the title of George Counts's famous book from the 1930s, *Dare the School Build a New Social Order?*[10] To pose the question at all assumes a positive answer to a previous question: Can the school build a new social order? The optimism of the 1960s was founded on a positive answer to that question. The schools could do it and we collectively should dare to do it, by marshaling nationally and internationally the appropriate mixture of knowledge, resources, and political will. One major set of theoretical explanations of and proposed remedies for the subsequent widespread failure continue to assume a positive answer. Schools can build a new social order. The problem is that we haven't yet "gotten it right." First, we have been operating from an incomplete and/or imperfect and/or badly interpreted knowledge base and, second, a wrong or incomplete set of political actors and stakeholder groups have been involved in the policy development and implementation process. The "problem" is a matter of technique and knowledge base. The "solution" is to continually improve the knowledge base (through basic and applied research and the dissemination of the results) and refine our interpretations of it, as well as to improve our micro- and macro-political techniques. This understanding, in one variant or another, continues to be the dominant view.[11]

A wholly opposed view of the nature of the problem began to emerge strongly in the mid-1970s, arguing that schools could not build a new social order. The causal process works the other way round. Changing the socioeconomic order is a necessary pre- or co-condition for changing education in an egalitarian direction. Many scholars, particularly those arguing from a Marxist, neo-Marxist, or dependency theory approach, claimed that formal schooling could necessarily do little more than reproduce structural inequalities in existing societies, at least capitalist ones; this is its basic sociopolitical and economic function; this is inevitably part of the normal development of capitalist societies and of developing countries linked to such nations through dependent economic, political, and social connections.[12] This view gained considerable popularity among some sectors of the scholarly community and among some policymakers in developing countries and international aid agencies. However, it never became the predominant view. By the mid-1980s some of the academic proponents of this view began to significantly modify their earlier position, arguing that formal schooling could function both to reproduce existing structural inequalities and to produce structural change, at least in democratic societies.[13] Following the collapse of the former Soviet Union and its associated state socialist nations, new evidence has become available suggesting that structural inequalities in those societies have been very nearly as resistant to the meliorating influence of education as in capitalist nations.[14] This may suggest that the problem of resistant structural inequality is endemic across political-economic regime types and is created by some deeper pattern that we have not yet identified—it simply takes different forms and manifestations in different societies.

An intermediate view has also developed. It suggests that educational change can affect the social order but only under particular circumstances and only if the educational change program is carefully tailored to the particular circumstances. This can be seen as a profoundly pessimistic position in that the conditions for success are rare and idiosyncratic, and thus cannot be widely duplicated. A more optimistic take on this view has recently developed, arguing that the widespread failure has been due to a common tendency to try to design and implement (from whatever theoretical/ideological point of view) universalistic "one size fits all" educational reform approaches and strategies. Thus success in using educational change to promote social equality is widely possible but is contingent on carefully tailoring the reform to the particular local conditions. Some scholars have begun trying to work out possible relationships between particular sets of conditions and potentially successful educational reform approaches. I argue elsewhere that taking this point of view fundamentally challenges almost the entire corpus of modernist theory that has informed comparative education over the past several decades.[15]

CHANGING MEANINGS OF EDUCATIONAL EQUALITY

Running through this broad theoretical debate has been a constant modification, amplification, and nuancing of what is meant by the term *educational equality*. Next I shall briefly review these changes in meaning and introduce a model meant to bring together many of these changes in meaning in a way useful for thinking about the mass of accumulated evidence.

Categories of Differentiation

Thirty to forty years ago, discussions of social equality tended to focus on a limited set of categories of differentiation then considered to be most important in determining or influencing (depending on how deterministic or contingent and loosely coupled a view of large-scale social interactions one held) how large numbers of people were able to live their lives in rich, industrialized nations (especially social class and race/ethnicity) and to apply these Western categories to developing nations. The understanding of such potential categories of differentiation is now much more complex. All extant societies have some form of internal social differentiation, with some members being valued or rewarded more than others. However, the degree of such differentiation and its significance for the way individuals and social groups lead their lives varies dramatically across societies. Moreover, there are many different bases or criteria for such differentiation. Among the most common are race, occupation, ethnicity, gender, regional origin, lineage, income, political power, and religion. Both across and within societies there is considerable variation in which one of these, or which set of them, is most powerful as a determinant of how different people can and do live their lives. Those of us who are creatures of the historical experience and intellectual traditions of the industrial nations of the West, whether we embrace some form of structural-functional or Marxist social theory, tend to collapse a common set of these—particularly occupation, income, and political power—into the notion of social class or social status. It is not at all clear now that these theoretical constructs are the most salient for understanding social differentiation in rich nations (feminist scholars, for example, would generally argue that gender is at least as important, if not more important, a category of differentiation) nor that they are directly applicable to all, or even most, less developed societies, either as accurate descriptors or as meaningful categories of social thought and behavior among individuals in those societies.

As the list of potential categories of social differentiation has expanded, some categories have come to be seen as more mutable or "disguisable" than others, which has an effect on the degree to which they may constrain children's life chances and what education can "do" about them. An instantly identifiable basis of social categorization is, in general, much harder to overcome by educational (or, more generally, social) policy. Race and gender, for example, are generally immutable and immediately identifiable characteristics. In contrast, the social class of origin of someone who has used education (or some other means) to become upwardly mobile is frequently nonidentifiable unless he or she chooses to advertise it. It is a characteristic that is mutable and often easily disguisable. It is thus more easily altered by education than characteristics that are immutable and nondisguisable. It has recently become apparent that consideration of the full implications of this set of issues is complexly related to the question of identity—the identity that people assign to themselves and the one that others assign to them. There is not space here to work out the full implications of this. However, it can be noted that some scholars, particularly those working from a postmodern feminist stance, argue that we must move from an idea of identity (as personally understood or socially assigned) as something essential and fundamentally unchangeable to a conception of identity, in both its senses, as something that is multiple and malleable. That is, we must move from thinking of identity to thinking of identities.[16] These new ways of thinking about educational equality represent a challenge to traditional modernist and grand theory approaches to comparative education, which are about as fundamental as the challenge represented by the contingency approach noted above. The implications of these ways of thinking for our understanding of educational equality are only beginning to be worked out, but it is becoming quite obvious that the meaning of the phrase is far more slippery and difficult to understand than we thought even a few years ago.

From Opportunity to Results[17]

The notion of educational equality, which grew originally with the development of systems of tax-supported public schooling, focused on opportunity. The general assumption was that the job of the state was to ensure that all children (with the exception in some areas of groups that were consciously excluded, on the basis, for example, of race or gender) had access to schools that were free of direct cost, with generally similar facilities and curricula, at least through the stage of compulsory attendance. It was assumed that it was the child's responsibility to use the opportunity thus provided. Responsibility for a child who did not do well in school, through lack of intelligence, diligence, motivation, and so on, rested with the individuals involved, not the state. Over the past several decades it has become increasingly apparent that large numbers of children are unable to use the educational opportunity provided because of their social origins. The concept of educational equality has gradually been extended to include some notion of equal educational results. The task of the state has been extended to include ensuring that all children, whatever their social origin, have an equal ability to benefit from the educational opportunity provided, in terms of what they learn and how they can use that learning in later life, particularly in the labor market.

Equality as Similarity or Equality as Valuation of Difference

Embedded within the standard discussions of equality of results is an even more complex set of questions: Do we really expect (indeed, do we want) the results to be similar, if not identical, for everyone? What do we actually mean by "results"? What do we mean by "an equal opportunity to benefit from" educational provision? Many discussions and arguments in both the scholarly and the popular literature imply quite directly that equal results means, for example, equal achievement test scores across social groups, schools, or nations (the "league table" approach), or equal access to particular highly valued occupational categories or salary levels. But it is increasingly argued that this view is too narrow and restrictive and that it is legitimate, indeed desirable, for different individuals and groups to want/need to learn different sorts of things and to use them for different life purposes. This alternative claim is expressed very strongly, for example, in many arguments for "relevant" education for particular subgroups within larger social/

national groups (say, rural children in poor areas of developing nations).[18] This "valuation of difference rather than similarity" approach asserts that different types of learning, and ways of learning, as well as different uses of it throughout life, are equally (but differently) valuable socially and individually. If one accepts this concept of educational equality, it is not clear what "equality of results" might mean, let alone how we might assess it within or across societies.

A Review

The past several decades have been characterized by increasing conceptual confusion. This conceptual confusion has to a considerable degree resulted from the circulation of a bewildering quantity of comparative information regarding how different individuals and widely differing social groups utilize education and the effect it exerts on their destinies. Untangling some of that data and deriving meaning from it with respect to equality as a goal for education is the task of the remainder of this chapter. In the following pages, I present a model for thinking about educational equality that summarizes much of what we now understand by that concept, and I use that model to organize and summarize what much of the now available comparative data tells us about education's role in equalizing the life chances of children born into very different social circumstances as they grow into adults.

A MODEL OF EDUCATIONAL INEQUALITY

When considering problems of educational inequality in recent years, we have come increasingly to view schooling as a long-term process in which children may be sorted at many different points and in several different ways. We recognize that schooling, whatever else it may do, operates as a selective social screening mechanism. It enhances the status of some children, providing them with an opportunity for upward social or economic mobility. It ratifies the status of others, reinforcing the propensity for children born poor to remain poor as adults, and for children born into well-off families to become well-off adults. Recognizing this, we need to address the following questions: At what points in the process, to what degree, and how are children of which social groups screened out or kept in? From this point of view, several facets of equality can be usefully distinguished:

1. Equality of access—the probability of children from different social groupings getting into the school system, or some particular level or portion of it.
2. Equality of survival—the probability of children from various social groupings staying in the school system to some defined level, usually the end of a complete cycle (primary, secondary, higher).
3. Equality of output—the probability that children from various social groupings will learn the same things to the same levels at a defined point in the schooling system.
4. Equality of outcome—the probability that children from various social groupings will live relatively similar lives subsequent to and as a result of schooling (have

equal incomes, have jobs of roughly the same status, have equal access to sites of political power, etc.).

The first three types of inequality refer to the workings of the school system itself. Equality of outcome refers to the junction between the school system and adult life, especially (but not exclusively) the labor market. With reference to the first three, each represents a mechanism by which children are sorted and screened by the school, and all three occur at each level or cycle of the system (i.e., a child may or may not enter primary schooling, may or may not survive to the end of the primary cycle, may or may not learn as much, or the same things, as other students by the end of the primary cycle; having completed primary, a child may or may not enter secondary schooling, may or may not survive to the end of secondary, etc.). Thus in a three-level system (e.g., primary, secondary, higher) there are at least nine sorting points of children; in a four-level system (e.g., primary, junior secondary, higher secondary, higher) there are at least twelve sorting points. It should be noted that this classification of types of inequality is itself an oversimplification. For example, in systems that have different types of schools or "streams" at the same level (e.g., university-preparatory vs. technical secondary schools or streams, or universities vs. two-year technical colleges at the third level) the access question is not simply whether a student enters the cycle but the type of institution or stream to which the student is given access. We should also bear in mind that the same factors will not necessarily affect the destiny of children at all of the sorting points. Since children confronting a later sorting point are themselves "survivors" of earlier sortings, we can assume that factors which are critical at the earliest points may lose their significance at later points (having already had their effect), with new factors coming into play as the lengthy process moves along.[19]

WHAT DO WE KNOW?

Our task here is to try to make some sense of the welter of comparative data regarding educational inequality that have been developed during the past several decades. With respect to some aspects of the model just presented, the evidence is sufficient to permit a reasonably coherent summary; with respect to other aspects, the evidence is spotty or inconsistent.

Equality of Access

For the vast majority of children in developing nations, access is a problem at the primary level. As I noted above, a major objective of educational policy at the start of the 1960s was to provide school places sufficient to permit every child to have access to at least a few years of primary schooling. Although primary enrollment ratios have increased during the past thirty years in all regions of the developing world, these general figures mask what is in some nations, often very populous ones, a much grimmer reality. Consider, for example, the three nations of the Indian subcontinent, whose combined population is almost equal to that of China. Their net primary enrollment ratios in 2005 were 77 percent, India; 79 percent, Bangladesh; 56 percent, Pakistan.[20] Moreover, during the decade of the 1980s, primary enrollment ratios actually declined in forty-five countries, leading many observers to refer to that period as a "disastrous decade for education."[21] A recent UNESCO publication notes the not-surprising principal causes for lack of access to primary education: "Where are the 'missing children'? Most live in remote rural areas or in urban slums. Most are girls. Most belong to population groups outside the mainstream of society: they pass their days in overcrowded refugee camps, displaced by manmade or natural disasters, or wander with their herds. Often [they are] marginalized by language, life-style and culture."[22] Faced with estimates that if the pattern of the 1980s continued, there would be 162 million children without access to primary education, the World Conference on Education for All, held in Thailand in 1990, set a goal of universal access to basic education by the year 2000, and set in place elaborate international mechanisms to encourage and monitor progress. It seemed to many an unlikely quest. Resources would have had to be found, from shrinking national and international agency budgets, to create within a decade about as many new school places as were created in the twenty years between 1965 and 1985.[23] Nonetheless, some progress was made, as noted at a follow-up meeting held in Dakar, Senegal, in 2000. Between 1990 and 1998, the number of children with no access to primary schooling dropped from 128 million to 113 million. By the end of the century the number of nations still experiencing post-1980 net primary enrollment ratio declines had dropped to eleven; in the same period twenty-one nations had increased those enrollment ratios by 15 percent or more; and thirty-two developing nations had achieved near-universal access (net primary enrollment ratios above 90 percent), including such very populous nations as China, Indonesia, and Brazil. The Dakar meeting referred to these as "tangible but modest gains" and set a new target date of 2015 for universal primary access, while noting that the challenge was greatest in sub-Saharan Africa and South Asia. In the developing nations that have achieved nearly universal primary education and in rich nations generally, the main access problem occurs at a later point in the schooling process. In the former nations it is generally at the entrance to secondary schooling (among those thirty-two developing nations the secondary enrollment ratios range from 36 percent [Honduras] to 95 percent [South Africa], but generally run between 50 percent and 70 percent).[28] In the latter, the key access question is the type or stream of secondary schooling into which youngsters are admitted. In very rich nations that have achieved nearly universal secondary education, the access question arises most seriously at the entrance to postsecondary education. Not even the richest nations have seriously contemplated the universal provision of that level of education. In all nations, rich or poor, there is some point (or points) in the educational system at which schooling (or some favored types of it) is a scarce good that not all can acquire. The ideal equality model then becomes one of random access, with the paradigm case being a fair lottery. The available comparative data (as outlined immediately above and earlier) indicate that the ideal random access situation is rarely even approximated. The same general set of factors that discriminate at the door of the primary school in poor nations simply operate in richer nations at a later point in children's lives.

It is commonly assumed that, particularly at the primary level, the problem of inequality of access is almost entirely a question of inadequate supply of schools and teachers; that an effective demand for primary schooling exists almost everywhere and that if the resources and political will can be found to provide an adequate number of primary schools, all children will attend. As I have shown, the obstacles on the supply side are indeed formidable. However, there are obstacles on the demand side as well. In most middle-income nations (and in some favored regions of low-income nations) there are more than enough school places, in the appropriate locations, for all age-eligible children. In such circumstances, when children do not attend school, and they often do not, it is because their parents will not send them. Parents may regard the education provided there as inappropriate (e.g., on religious or cultural grounds), irrelevant or of little use, or not worth the opportunity cost of the child's labor.[25] This is a particularly serious obstacle to the enrollment of girls in many nations.

Equality of Survival

Among middle-income developing nations between 80 and 100 percent of an entering grade one cohort will complete the primary cycle. In low-income nations the completion proportions are lower, generally ranging between 50 and 80 percent.[26] These high rates of nonsurvival are a result of the combined effect of (1) high repetition rates and (2) high proportions of children dropping out of school—frequently after having repeated an early grade one or more times.[27] Although the time-series data are spotty, there was a general trend for repetition rates to decrease and survival rates to increase between 1980 and 2000.[28] In many developing nations, the survival rates at the secondary or postsecondary levels, for the very small proportion of the population who reach those levels, are also very low. However, the patterns at this level are highly variable. In some nations, access to secondary schooling is very restricted and is based on scores on primary leaving examinations and/or socioeconomic privilege. The few who gain access to secondary or higher levels of schooling tend in large proportions to complete the cycle.[29]

In richer nations, survival becomes a serious policy issue at the point in the schooling cycle at which effective compulsory education ends, usually at some midpoint in the secondary cycle. Survival rates and patterns at this level vary greatly across such nations, in ways that are not easily accounted for. Policy expectations clearly have some effect. For example, in some nations all students are expected to complete secondary schooling. High dropout rates are considered a major problem, and various policies are put in place to keep kids in school. These are sometimes quite successful. For example, in Canada the official dropout rate in secondary schooling is around 30 percent, and a variety of avenues have been developed to allow such young people to "drop back in" in ways that fit with their life needs. Following these various alternative tracks, roughly 85 percent of an age cohort have attained a secondary diploma or equivalent by age twenty-five. That is, about half of the officially identified dropouts eventually completed the cycle.[30] A roughly similar situation obtains in the United States.[31] On the other hand, in societies that do not expect all secondary-level students to complete the full cycle, dropping out is not seen as a policy problem but as a natural and normal circumstance.

A survey of all available comparative evidence shows generally that in any given level of the educational system, poor children are less likely to survive educationally than are well-to-do children; that children born in rural areas are less likely to survive educationally than urban children; that repetition and dropout rates are higher among girls than among boys. However, the evidence regarding the relationship between any particular aspect of a child's personal or family circumstances and the probability of completing a given level of education is so scanty and contradictory that general conclusions cannot be drawn easily. The patterns vary dramatically from country to country in ways that cannot be explained simply. Variations in the influence of gender on survival potential are particularly striking. Among middle-income nations, primary-level survival rates for boys and girls are essentially identical. In the few cases where there is a noticeable gender difference, all three favor girls by 6 percent. Among low-income nations there is much variation, which is difficult to interpret. The gender differences are somewhat larger (most in the 5 percent to 10 percent range) but they favor boys or girls in almost equal measure. Among the few cases of more extreme differences (greater than 10 percent) all are in sub-Saharan Africa, five favor boys and two favor girls, but in the region overall there are about as many cases favoring girls as favoring boys. Secondary level survival patterns are roughly similar. As the statistical assessment for the Dakar conference notes: "gender disparities at the national or regional level are minimal with regard to the international efficiency of [i.e., survival within] the education system, and slightly favor girls in the majority of cases."[32] Overall there has been considerable progress toward gender equality on this dimension, and the remaining pockets of severe female disadvantage do not appear related in any obvious way to national income, geo-cultural area, religious tradition, or colonial heritage. It is a puzzle!

It is important to bear in mind that survival rates, for entire populations or for subgroups thereof, can only be understood correctly with respect to educational policy by referring as well to access figures for the same societies. For example, in both Syria and Mali approximately 90 to 95 percent of children entering grade one will reach the end of primary schooling. In Syria almost all eligible children enter grade one, whereas in Mali only about 40 percent do so. In contrast, Ethiopia has about the same grade one access rate as does Mali, but only about 50 percent of its entrants complete primary schooling.[33] In spite of their similarity on either equality of access or equality of survival, the interaction between the two types of inequality produces three very different educational situations by the end of primary schooling. It is especially important to note the interaction between access and survival for particular subgroups of a nation's population in trying to assess the overall educational equality situation. For example, if a particular group is heavily discriminated against in terms of access to schooling, those few of its members who do get into schooling (any particular level or type thereof), being themselves the winners in a very rigorous previous screening process, may (and often do) have a very high subsequent survival potential.

Equality of Output

A system's output is whatever the system produces directly—in the case of an educational system, learning. Children with the same numbers of years of schooling (thus with equal access and equal survival) may have learned quite different things, or the same subjects to quite different levels. There is a substantial amount of cross-national evidence indicating that differences in levels of achievement are systematically associated with differing social origins of children in a particular society. Generally, among those who have reached a given level of a nation's school system, children who are poor, rural, female, or from any other socially marginalized group, learn less. However, here too the differences among nations and cultures in the effect of such social characteristics on learning are impressive.

Given this comparative evidence, the following question has bedeviled educators: considering the powerful influence of home background on relative levels of school learning, is there much, if any, room at all for changes in schooling policy and practice to improve the learning levels of socially marginalized children which will allow them, particularly as groups, to live better lives thereafter? Based on an increasingly large array of nation-specific studies, using many different methodological approaches and a smaller set of cross-national studies (many of which have turned out to be methodologically flawed),[34] scholars identified what appeared to be a quite clear pattern emerging in the 1970s and 1980s. The less developed the society, the less the effect of social origin on learning achievement, and the greater the effect of school-related (and thus social-policy-directed) variables.[35] However, the methodological critiques (particularly of those studies based on an "educational production function" approach) suggest that the overall pattern is not as clear as it once seemed.[36] Nonetheless, assessing all of the evidence from several distinct methodological traditions, shows that the general pattern still seems to hold. Why should this be so?

Several different, and still quite tentative, explanations have been advanced. Quite early on, as the pattern was just beginning to become evident, Foster advanced the following:

> In broadest terms, as less developed nations "modernize" the pattern of "objective" differentiation of populations becomes more complex with the growth of a monetized economy and a greater division of labour. Not only this, possession of a "modern type" occupation becomes an increasingly important factor in determining the generalized social status of an individual. In other words, social strata defined in objective terms of occupations and income begin to emerge. Initially, however, this pattern of objective differentiation may not be accompanied by an equivalent degree of cultural differentiation as represented by increasing divergence of values, attitudes and life-styles among various subgroups. In time, however, this may occur and we move, in effect, toward a pattern of stratification that more closely resembles that obtaining in developed societies.[37]

For example, child-rearing patterns, attitudes toward schooling, aspirations, and other family traits that may affect a child's school success in a newly rich African family may differ little from those of families not yet participating in the cash economy, or participating at a much more marginal level, at least during the early stages of the social change process. What we may be observing here is the educational effect of the process of class formation (in the Western sense), as poor nations become more like Western societies. This explanation actually fits rather well within Marxist, neo-Marxist, and traditional structural-functional understandings of social change (which may be rather annoying to singular minded and ideologically driven adherents of any of those theoretical stances). Of course, it is also observably the case that in societies in which standard Western indexes of social status are not (or are not yet) relevant to a child's educational destiny, other traditional stratification patterns may be very important, for example, caste, tribe, or lineage.

A different but related explanation is that there is much greater variation in the availability of school resources in developing nations than in developed nations. For example, in rich nations almost all students have complete sets of textbooks, and the differences in the formal educational levels of teachers are relatively small. In developing nations, however, there are great variations in such indicators. In a poor nation, even modest increments in the provision of textbooks can thus have a major effect on student learning. In rich nations, students are already abundantly supplied with books, and increases in learning require difficult and costly improvements in the quality of books—assuming knowledge of the aspects of book quality that actually influence student learning. In a poor nation, many primary teachers have low levels of formal schooling and little if any pedagogical training. Thus a very modest change in preservice or in-service training could significantly improve teacher performance and hence student learning. In a rich nation, almost all teachers have university degrees, high-level pedagogical training, and many opportunities for in-service education, and thus even small improvements in teacher performance are difficult to achieve and hard to identify.

I have combined both of these explanations in a previous publication. In rich nations, which are close to the limits of perfectibility of the "standard model of schooling" as we know it, "even modest additional gains in achievement require very difficult and costly educational effort." In developing nations "even the very modest improvements in school quality which a poor nation can realistically contemplate have the potential for providing important increases in student learning," particularly among the most marginalized students.[38] The possibility of improving equality of output in developing nations, within the very modest resources available to them, is particularly important because the evidence indicates that levels of learning among students in developing nations are systematically lower than among students in rich nations. Cross-national comparisons of student achievement levels that have been carried out over these past decades, principally under the auspices of the International Association for the Evaluation of Educational Achievement (IEA), UNESCO, and the Organization for Economic Cooperation and Development (OECD) have consistently demonstrated that the achievement test scores of children from low- and middle-income nations are lower than those of children of comparable age or grade levels in industrialized nations. The differences are large in some subject areas and small in others, but they are consistent. Until quite recently these cross-national studies have compared young people at the secondary level, or in some cases the senior primary level. In most developing nations, as I noted above, children who are neither socioeconomically advantaged nor academically gifted do not typically survive to this level of schooling. Thus the differences in learning output could be expected to be even greater at the early primary level, which is as far as most youngsters in developing nations progress in their formal education.[39] Evidence from an IEA study of reading levels among nine-year-olds in twenty-nine nations, reported in 1992, plus a 1997 UNESCO study of grade four reading and mathematics achievement in eleven Latin American nations, suggest that this may be the case. Unfortunately the number of developing nations in these samples is too small to firmly ground the conclusion.[40]

Much recently published evidence indicates that the fiscal crisis in most developing nations, combined with expanding enrollments, is dramatically decreasing the instructional resources available per student, which is in turn increasing the learning gap between students in rich and poor nations.[41] Regional assessments near the turn of the century indicate that the problem remains. Even where additional resources for education have been found, they have typically increased access and/or survival without improving learning levels.[42] A question which arises is whether individuals or societies benefit from increasingly equal access to and survival through a schooling system in which student learning remains low, or even declines.[43]

Equality of Outcome

Relatively equal distributions of access to, survival through, or learning within the formal schooling system is considered socially beneficial by many only if it pays off for the recipients in relatively equal access to life chances (particularly but not exclusively jobs) as adults. To what extent can, or does, education have an intervening effect on intergenerational status transmission? To what extent, and under what conditions, can it produce upward social mobility rather than simply ratify or reproduce existing patterns of structural inequality? Consideration of this question brings us back to the basic questions noted earlier in this essay. Can—and under what conditions—the school build a new social order? Can it provide opportunities for individual social mobility for at least some children of marginalized groups within a society? A huge amount of evidence has been generated over the past decades regarding these questions, mostly within nations but occasionally comparatively across nations. The results are, at least in a comparative sense, systematic, but theoretically they are confusing. In 1975, Lin and Yauger reported data from a quite limited data set, from Haiti, from three Costa Rican communities at three levels of development, from Britain, and from the United States, and concluded that "the direct influence of educational attainment on occupational status is curvilinearily (concave) related to degree of industrialization."[44] Schiefelbein and Farrell noted that data from Uganda at three points in time and from four Brazilian communities fitted the same pattern.[45] More recent results from Chile have reinforced the same pattern.[46] The general pattern seems to be as follows: in very poor societies almost everyone is engaged in subsistence agriculture, except for a few (typically young) occupants of newly created civil service posts and some commercial entrepeneurs. Education can have very little effect on occupational mobility because there are very few occupational destinations into which one could be mobile (partially explaining the lack of effective demand for education among such populations, as noted above). As the local economy grows and becomes more differentiated, it creates a variety of new job openings. In the absence of a traditionally dominant class or group that can exploit all of the new opportunities, formal education becomes a predominant influence on the level of job acquired. Significant numbers of even very disadvantaged children can use education to obtain positions in the "modern" economy. (In many developing societies the growth of the educational system has much surpassed the growth of the economy, producing a problem of educated unemployment. Even in such societies, youngsters often continue in school as long as possible because the potential payoff is high if, or when, they can obtain any job at all.) As societies become very developed, their economies become so complex and rapidly changing, and the possible avenues to economic success are so varied, that the independent effect of formal education begins to diminish.[47]

Evidence from the advanced state-socialist societies of Eastern Europe, which collapsed in the early 1990s, suggests that there too this general pattern has been evident.[48] Some economists have argued that in very advanced postindustrial economies, the phenomenon of the *declining middle*—the elimination of well-paying industrial and middle-class jobs in favor of lower-paying service sector jobs—is reducing even further the mobility-generating potential of formal schooling.[49] Pushing this argument a step further, Farrell and Schiefelbein claim that all of the major studies that have provided data regarding the effect of education on intergenerational status transmission—which form the empirical foundation for the theoretical arguments on this question—are flawed and fundamentally uninterpretable because they fail to take into account long-term structural changes in the economy and how these necessarily constrain what education can do.[50] However, in spite of this growing empirical and theoretical confusion, it is still clear that even in societies in which education has the weakest effect upon intergenerational status transmission, and the weakest effect upon social structural change, some individuals and social groups benefit from both its more widespread provision as well as increases in its quality. Rarely, if ever, does the provision of more formal education, or the improvement of its quality, have no mobility-generating or life-enhancing consequences for at least a few children of marginalized groups. Analyses by Paquette and by Levin in the 1990s,[51] however, can be interpreted as suggesting that even that minimal effect of formal schooling on individual and collective life chances may be disappearing (or has already disappeared) in North American societies, and perhaps, by extension, in other societies as well.

CONCLUSION

In this final section I wish to apply the massive amount of comparative data analyzed above to the central theme of this book: the effect of recent educational reform movements, proposals, and occasionally enacted policies (e.g., privatization, decentralization, educational change for global competitiveness, the testing driven standards movement, etc.) on equality of educational opportunity and outcome among the most marginalized members of the many societies of our world. This is necessarily a highly speculative enterprise. As we have seen, major educational change is generally a failure-prone, slow, and long-term process. It takes even longer to begin to really see and understand its eventual effects upon how today's students actually can and do live their lives. It has taken almost four decades for us to begin to really understand the results of the massive educational change efforts of the optimistic sixties, and even now we are still arguing about the quality and completeness of the available comparative information and about how to interpret and understand it. We could hardly expect less with respect to the most recent waves of educational reforms. Moreover, local, regional, or worldwide events can significantly change the context of long-term reform efforts such that results can move in totally unpredictable directions. For example, if we had been creating this book in the late 1980s, none of the authors could have predicted the sudden demise of the former Soviet Union and its associated states, nor the consequences for our understanding of educational change and educational equality, which are still very unclear and will likely remain so for a long time. An ancient (probably apocryphal) proverb has it, "Prediction is always difficult, especially with respect to the future." A central lesson for the theme of this book from the comparative data assembled over the past several decades is this: don't take seriously anyone who speaks with certainty about the probable effects of the current wave of educational reform proposals. We have, however, learned a few things since the end of the Second World War. These lessons can provide us with some guidance regarding how to think about outcomes, if not how to predict them. A central lesson learned is the necessity of a high degree of intellectual and moral humility, as well as tolerance for a high degree of ambiguity.

Another lesson learned is that the common trend over the past decades toward centrally directed and command-driven forms of educational change, most commonly following national and international faddism and a "one size fits all" view of educational change, have poorly served the interests of those who might benefit from increases in educational equality. This applies equally as well to the current wave of educational reform fads. The possible or probable effects of the current reform fashions on educational inequality depend on specific local conditions and history. For example, university education in many nations of Latin America has long been highly privatized. The effects on educational inequality vary dramatically from nation to nation, depending on specific national conditions.[52] The effects of further privatization in any of these nations, however, would be almost certainly very different from privatization of higher education in the completely state-controlled higher education systems of many other nations. Similarly, as Mark Bray notes in chapter 8 of this volume, decentralization has different meanings and different possible long-term consequences, depending on where a particular nation starts on some sort of centralized-decentralized continuum.[53] Just as there are no universally applicable solutions to educational inequality, there are no universally applicable predictions of reform consequences. There is, however, one general claim that can be made. If the experience of the past sixty years is any guide (the experience base in the United States goes back more than a century, but the lesson is the same[54]), it seems that the broad reform proposals now being widely discussed will often not be enacted; if enacted, they will seldom be well or fully implemented; if implemented well, they generally will not have significant effect on equality of access, survival, or output (as discussed in the model presented above), at least for large numbers of youngsters; and if they do manage to improve these within-school aspects of equality, they are highly unlikely to have significant impact on equality of outcome by altering the life chances of large proportions of poor or marginalized children.

Overall, then, the picture appears rather bleak. There have been significant gains in educational equality over the past fifty years, but they have been for the most part not the result of broad-scale, centrally driven, international agency-supported reform programs. Rather, they have been the result of economic growth or social structural change outside the realm of the school, or of an option that is now generally unavailable or that political leaders are unwilling to choose: massive increases in educational expenditure.[55]

However, I end this chapter on a hopeful note. Throughout the world, particularly the developing world, there are small and large attempts to fundamentally alter the traditional teacher-directed model of schooling. They typically use some or all of the following modalities: combinations of fully trained teachers, partially trained teachers, para-teachers, and community resource people; radio, correspondence lessons, television, and in a few cases computers; peer tutoring; self-guided learning materials; student and teacher constructed learning materials; multigrade classrooms; child-centered rather than teacher-driven pedagogy; free flows of children and adults between the school and the community; locally adapted changes in the cycle of the school day or school year. They typically spread not by a centrally planned and commanded reform plan but through an innovation diffusion process. They depend for their success not on the ability and willingness of teachers to follow orders from on high, but rather on stimulating and unleashing the creative energy, enthusiasm, and personal practical knowledge of teachers. Such change programs do not simply alter one feature of the standard school (e.g., change one part of the curriculum), strengthen one or several parts of the standard schooling model (e.g., add more textbooks or improve teacher training), or add one or two new features. Rather, they represent a thorough reorganization and a fundamental re-visioning of the standard schooling model such that the learning program, although often occurring in or based in a building called a school, is far different from what we have come to expect to be happening in a school. They tend to break down the boundaries between formal and nonformal education and to focus less on teaching and more on learning. Where they have been evaluated, the results have generally been very positive. New groups of learners are reached successfully, and the learning results are at least as good as, if not better than, those obtained in standard schools. And the costs are typically no more than, if not less than, those of the standard model. Moreover, because they serve the most marginalized, hardest to reach and teach (in the standard mode) students, the learning results from a value added perspective are quite spectacular.[56]

Some major examples of these model-breaking educational change programs include the *Escuela Nueva* program in Colombia, which has now reached close to 30,000 rural schools and has been adapted on a large- or small-scale basis in at least ten other Latin American nations; the multi-grade program in Guinea, now operating in over 1,300 schools; the MECE Rural Program (*Programa de Mejoramiento de la Calidad de la Educación para las Escuelas Multigrados Rurales*) in Chile, which is now present in over 3,000 schools; the Nonformal Primary Education program of the Bangladesh Rural Advancement Committee, which operates in 35,000 villages in that nation and is spreading into urban areas and other nations; a wide network of community schools supported by the Aga Khan Foundation in Pakistan and other developing nations; and the Community Schools Program in rural Egypt, which is now operating in thousands of schools. What is important about such programs is that they focus on learning rather than teaching and provide a pedagogically superior experience for highly marginalized young people. In addition, they generally operate either outside of or on the margins of the national school system (indeed, one of the major design issues with such systems, particularly at the early stages, is protecting or insulating them from the heavy bureaucratic hand of the state schooling system). They thus provide us with examples of successfully delivering opportunities for high-quality learning to the most disadvantaged children that do not depend on the eroding fiscal and managerial capacity of increasingly "fragile"[57] states. They present us with an operationally successful vision of a more hopeful future.

Even in these cases, however, it is far too early to tell whether these major increases in the availability and quality of schooling for poor and marginalized children will ultimately have any major effect on the socioeconomic and political structures that have created and maintained that poverty and marginalization in the first place. Indeed, ultimately we cannot know and predict that in advance. As I have argued elsewhere recently, human learning is, by its very nature, not subject to coercion and control nor to prediction of its consequences. In the final analysis all we can really do is enable it and hope for the best.[58] In that context, whatever the ultimate effects of these new schooling programs on the broad social structural level, significantly improving the availability and quality of schooling is in and of itself a notable achievement and a very worthy social goal.

NOTES

1. A vast literature was generated during the 1950s and 1960s regarding the nature of development, its causes, and education's presumed role in the process. Space here does not permit a detailed analysis of the differing theoretical views that have been advanced, although it should be noted that almost all scholars at the time operated from a consensus or equilibrium rather than a conflict model of social change. For a useful review of the general development literature through the mid-1960s, see C. E. Black, *The Dynamics of Modernization* (New York: Harper and Row, 1966), esp. 175–99. For a detailed review of what was then understood to be education's role in economic and social development, see, respectively, Arnold Anderson and Mary Jean Bowman,

eds., *Education and Economic Development* (Chicago: Aldine, 1965); and Don Adams and Joseph P. Farrell, *Education and Social Development* (Syracuse: Syracuse University Center for Development Education, 1967).

2. For example, during the decade of the 1960s, the province of Ontario, Canada, implemented a secondary education reform (the Robarts Plan) that aimed at (among other things) allowing all young people to complete that level of schooling. It built enough new universities and expanded the capacity of existing universities to more than double the capacity at that level, and established an entirely new system of more than twenty postsecondary colleges of applied arts and technology.

3. Jean-Pierre Jallade, "The Evolution of Educational Systems in Industrialized Countries: A Summary," *Western European Education* 4, no. 4 (Winter 1972–1973): 330–36; Henry Levin, "The Dilemma of Comprehensive Secondary School Reforms in Western Europe," *Comparative Education Review* 22, no. 3 (October 1978): 434–51; G. Neave, "New Influences on Educational Policies in Western Europe during the Seventies," in *Politics and Educational Change*, ed. Patricia Broadfoot et al. (London: Croom Helm, 1982), 71–85.

4. Data from the statistical division of UNESCO, as compiled at the World Bank. See *Education Sector Policy Paper*, 3rd ed. (Washington, D.C.: World Bank, 1980), 103–6.

5. Philip H. Coombs, *The World Educational Crisis: A Systems Analysis* (New York: Oxford University Press, 1968).

6. World Bank, *Education Sector Policy Paper*.

7. Mitchell A. Seligson and John T. Passe-Smith, *Development and Underdevelopment: The Political Economy of Inequality* (London: Lynne Rienner, 1993).

8. Don Adams, "Development Education," *Comparative Education Review* 21, nos. 2–3 (June–October 1977): 299–300.

9. Joseph P. Farrell, "A Retrospective on Educational Planning in Comparative Education," *Comparative Education Review* 41, no. 3 (August 1997): 277–313.

10. George S. Counts, *Dare the School Build a New Social Order?* (New York: John Day, 1932).

11. The literature here is vast. For some recent and representative examples, see Marlaine Lockheed and Adrienne Verspoor, *Improving Primary Education in Developing Countries: A Review of Policy Options* (Washington, D.C.: World Bank, 1990); K. N. Ross and L. Mahlick, *Planning the Quality of Education* (Paris: International Institute for Educational Planning, 1990); K. N. Ross and L. Mahlick, *Education and Knowledge: Basic Pillars of Changing Production Patterns with Social Equity* (Santiago, Chile: UNESCO-CEPAL, 1993); J. M. Puryear, *Education in Latin America: Problems and Challenges*, Prealc Occasional Paper no. 7 (New York: Inter-American Dialogue, 1997). Inter-American Development Bank, *Reforming Primary and Secondary Education in Latin America: An IDB Strategy* (Washington, D.C.: Inter-American Development Bank, 2000).

12. For classic statements of this view, see Martin Carnoy, *Education as Cultural Imperialism* (New York: McKay, 1974); and Samuel Bowles and Herbert Gintis, *Schooling in Capitalist America* (New York: Basic Books, 1976).

13. See, for example, Martin Carnoy and Henry Levin, *Schooling and Work in the Democratic State* (Stanford, Calif.: Stanford University Press, 1985). See also Daniel P. Liston, *Capitalist Schools: Explanation and Ethics in Radical Studies of Schooling* (New York: Routledge, 1990). It is salutary to remind ourselves that while we have learned much from comparative information over the past forty or more years, the fundamental debates about the possibility and desirability of using schooling as a form of social engineering go back a very long time. See P. S. Hlebowitsch and W. Wraga, "Social Class Analysis in the Early Progressive Tradition," *Curriculum Inquiry* 25, no. 1 (Spring 1995): 7–22.

14. Cesar Birzea, "Education in a World in Transition: Between Post-Communism and Post-Modernism," *Prospects* 26, no. 4 (1996): 673–81.

15. See D. Rondinelli, J. Middleton, and A. Verspoor, *Planning Educational Reforms in Devel-*

oping Countries: The Contingency Approach (Durham, N.C.: Duke University Press, 1990); and Farrell, "Retrospective on Educational Planning."

16. Joseph P. Farrell, "Narratives of Identity: The Voices of Youth," *Curriculum Inquiry* 26, no. 3 (Fall 1996): 1–12, plus the articles that follow this editorial essay. See also Elizabeth Ellsworth, "Claiming the Tenured Body," in *The Center of the Web: Women and Solitude*, ed. D. Wear (Albany: State University of New York Press, 1993), 63–74; S. K. Walker, "Canonical Gestures," *Curriculum Inquiry* 24, no. 2 (Summer 1994): 171–80; and Patti Lather, *Getting Smart: Feminist Research and Pedagogy within the Post-Modern* (New York: Routledge, 1994). Ming Fang He, "Professional Knowledge Landscapes: Three Chinese Women Teachers' Enculturation and Acculturation Processes in China and Canada" (Ph.D. diss, Ontario Institute for Studies in Education/University of Toronto, 1999).

17. A particularly useful historical analysis of early changes in conceptions of educational equality is found in James S. Coleman, "The Concept of Equality of Educational Opportunity," *Harvard Educational Review* 38, no. 4 (Winter 1968): 7–22.

18. V. J. Baker, "Education for its Own Sake," *Comparative Education Review* 33, no. 4 (November 1989): 507–26.

19. For an expansion of this discussion and an application of the model to the problem of educational equality over time in a particular developing nation, see Joseph P. Farrell and Ernesto Schiefelbein, *Eight Years of Their Lives: Through Schooling to the Labour Market in Chile* (Ottawa: International Development Research Centre, 1982).

20. UNICEF, *The State of the World's Children 2006* (Paris: UNICEF, 2006), table 5, pp. 114–17. The data pertain to the years 2000–2004.

21. UNESCO, *Education for All: Status and Trends* (Paris: UNESCO, 1993): 17.

22. UNESCO, *Education for All*, 10.

23. Lockheed and Verspoor, *Improving Primary Education*, 31.

24. The World Bank, *World Development Report 2000/2001: Attacking Poverty* (Oxford: Oxford University Press, 2001) and UNESCO, *The Dakar Framework for Action. Education for All: Meeting Our Collective Commitments* (Paris: UNESCO, 2000): 9–13.

25. For an extended analysis of these demand-side obstacles, see Mary Jean Bowman, "An Integrated Framework for Analysis of the Spread of Schooling in Less Developed Countries," *Comparative Education Review* 21, no. 4 (November 1988): 563–83.

26. The World Bank, *World Development Report 2000/2001*, 284–85.

27. The World Bank, *World Development Report 2000/2001*, 284–85, and UNESCO, *The Dakar Framework*, 9–13.

28. Compare Lockheed and Verspoor, *Improving Primary Education* with UNESCO, *Education for All Year 2000 Assessment: Statistical Document* (UNESCO: Paris, 2000).

29. Joseph P. Farrell, "Improving Learning: Perspectives for Primary Education in Rural Africa" (paper presented at the World Bank/UNESCO Seminar on Primary Education in Rural Africa, Lusaka, Zambia, 1998).

30. Jerome Paquette, "Universal Education: Meanings, Challenges and Options into the Third Millennium," *Curriculum Inquiry* 25, no. 1 (Spring 1995): 23–56; Benjamin Levin, "Dealing with Dropouts in Canadian Education," *Curriculum Inquiry* 22, no. 3 (Fall 1992): 257–70; Joseph P. Farrell, "Educational Problems and Learning Solutions," *Curriculum Inquiry* 22, no. 3 (Fall 1992): 231–34; Stephen P. Heyneman, "The Use of Cross-National Comparisons for Local Educational Policy," *Curriculum Inquiry* (in press).

31. T. Bailey, "Jobs of the Future and the Education They Will Require: Evidence from Occupational Forecasts," *Educational Researcher* 20, no. 2 (February 1991): 11–20. See also Heyneman, "Cross-National Comparisons."

32. UNESCO, *Education for All Year 2000 Assessment*, 36, and The World Bank, *World Development Report 2000/2001*, 284–85.

33. The World Bank, *World Development Report 2000/2001*, 284–85.

34. Riddell provides a particularly useful summary of the methodological critique and its implications for analysis. Abby R. Riddell, "Assessing Designs for School Effectiveness Research and School Improvement in Developing Countries," *Comparative Education Review* 41, no. 2 (May 1997): 178–204.

35. A classic study is Stephen P. Heyneman and William Loxley, "The Effects of Primary School Quality on Academic Achievement across Twenty-nine High and Low-Income Countries," *American Journal of Sociology* 88, no. 3 (May 1983): 1162–94.

36. Riddell, "Assessing Designs."

37. Philip Foster, "Education and Social Differentiation in Less Developed Countries," *Comparative Education Review* 22, nos. 2–3 (June–October 1977): 224–25.

38. Joseph P. Farrell, "International Lessons for School Effectiveness: The View from the Developing World," in *Educational Policy for Effective Schools*, ed. Mark Holmes et al. (New York: Teachers College Press, 1989), 14.

39. Joseph P. Farrell and Stephen P. Heyneman, eds., *Textbooks in the Developing World: Economic and Educational Choices* (Washington, D.C.: World Bank, 1989), 3–5. See also Farrell, "International Lessons," and Lockheed and Verspoor, *Improving Primary Education*.

40. W. B. Elley, *How in the World Do Students Read?* (The Hague: International Association for the Evaluation of Educational Achievement, 1992); Laurence Wolff, Ernesto Schiefelbein, and Paulina Schiefelbein, *Primary Education in Latin America: The Unfinished Agenda* (Washington, D.C.: The Inter-American Development Bank, 2002), 11–15; UNESCO, *Informe Sub-regional de America Latina de EFA* (Santiago, Chile: UNESCO Regional Office for Education in Latin America and the Caribbean, 2000).

41. Farrell and Heyneman, *Textbooks in the Developing World*, 3–4; Farrell, "International Lessons."

42. Wolff, Schiefelbein, and Schiefelbein, *Primary Education in Latin America*; and Association for the Development of Education in Africa (ADEA) Newsletter, 14, no. 2 (July–September 2002); UNESCO. Also, see *The Dakar Framework*.

43. This question was debated vigorously in "Symposium: World Bank Report on Education in Sub-Saharan Africa," *Comparative Education Review* 33, no. 1 (February 1989): 93–133. A possibly necessary trade-off between access/survival and equality was debated further at the World Conference on Education for All. See Kenneth King, "Donor Support to Literacy, Adult Basic and Primary Education," *NORRAG News*, no. 7 (March 1990): 52.

44. Nan Lin and D. Yauger, "The Process of Occupational Status Achievement: A Preliminary Cross-National Comparison," *American Journal of Sociology* 81, no. 6 (November 1975): 543–62.

45. Ernesto Schiefelbein and Joseph P. Farrell, "Selectivity and Survival in the Schools of Chile," *Comparative Education Review* 22, no. 2 (June 1978): 326–41.

46. Farrell and Schiefelbein, "Education and Status Attainment in Chile," 490–506.

47. For classic studies among the richest nations, see Christopher Jencks et al., *Inequality* (New York: Basic Books, 1972); R. Boudon, *Education, Opportunity, and Social Inequality* (New York: Wiley, 1973); and OECD, *Education, Inequality and Life Chances* (Paris: Author, 1975).

48. Joseph Zajda, "Education and Social Stratification in the Soviet Union," *Comparative Education Review* 16, no. 1 (March 1980): 3–11; Alison Price-Rom, *The Pedagogy of Democracy in Seven Post-Soviet States* (paper presented at the Annual Meeting of the Comparative and International Education Society, Orlando, Florida, March 2002); and Birzea, "Education in a World in Transition."

49. For an early statement of this position, see Bob Kuttner, "The Declining Middle," *Atlantic Monthly*, July 1983, 60–72; Bob Kuttner, *Economic Growth/Economic Justice* (New York: Houghton-Mifflin, 1984). For a more recent argument, see Paquette, "Universal Education."

50. Farrell and Schiefelbein, "Education and Status Attainment."

51. Paquette, "Universal Education," and Levin, "Dealing with Dropouts."

52. Daniel C. Levy, *Higher Education and the State in Latin America: Private Challenges to Public Dominance* (Chicago: University of Chicago Press, 1986); Joseph P. Farrell, "Higher Education in Chile," in *International Encyclopedia of Higher Education*, ed. Philip Altbach (London: Pergamon, 1991), 325–42; Laurence Wolff and Claudio de Moura Castro, *Public or Private Education for Latin America: That Is the (False) Question* (Washington, D.C.: The Inter-American Development Bank, 2001).

53. Jennifer Adams, "Teacher Attitudes toward De-Centralization in a Decentralized and Centralized System: Ontario and France" (Ph.D. diss., Ontario Institute for Studies in Education, 1996).

54. Joseph P. Farrell, "Why is Educational Reform So Difficult? Similar Descriptions, Different Prescriptions, Failed Explanations," *Curriculum Inquiry* 30, no. 1 (Spring 2000): 83–103.

55. There are of course exceptions, nations that have found the political will to significantly increase educational expenditures and effectively implement reforms that appear to be having a positive impact on educational inequality. Egypt is one such case. See UNESCO, *Review and Assessment of Reform of Basic Education in Egypt* (Paris: Author, 1996); Joseph P. Farrell and Michael Connelly, *From a Massive Reform Model to an Innovation Diffusion Model of Change, Report for UNICEF-Egypt* (Cairo: UNICEF, 1994). Chile is another such case. During the decade of the 1990s, a succession of democratically elected governments doubled spending on education, producing a significant improvement in all three within-school aspects of equality discussed here. See Noel F. McGinn, "Commentary," in *Unequal Schools, Unequal Chances: The Challenges to Equal Opportunity in the Americas*, ed. Fernando Reimers (Cambridge, Mass.: Harvard University Press, 2000): 179–81.

56. For a summary and analysis of the available evidence regarding these alternative programs see Joseph P. Farrell, "Community Education in Developing Countries: The Quiet Revolution in Schooling," in *Sage International Handbook of Curriculum and Instruction* (Sage Publications: forthcoming, 2006), chap. 21.

57. Bruce Fuller, *Growing Up Modern: The Western State Builds Third World Schools* (New York: Routledge and Kegan Paul, 1991).

58. Farrell, "Retrospective on Educational Planning."

7

Women's Education in the Twenty-First Century: Balance and Prospects

Nelly P. Stromquist

Almost thirty years have elapsed since the international women's movement called attention to the social and economic inequalities confronting women. During this time, substantial progress has occurred in problem definition and theorization of gender, including the role of education and schooling in the advancement of women. Less progress has taken place in the type and degree of change within formal school systems. Industrialized countries, with greater resources, more organized women's groups, and institutions more sensitive to public pressure have attained greater changes than the developing countries, but even in the former much work remains to be accomplished.

When discussing the connection between gender and education, it is necessary to make a distinction between education and schooling. *Education* is used herein to refer to the transmission of broad and specific knowledge that includes but also goes beyond that imparted by national school systems. Education may occur in formal situations, nonformal situations (e.g., programs and classes provided for adults by community groups), and informal situations (notably the knowledge conveyed within the home and through the mass media). *Schooling* relates specifically to the structured and institutionalized type of knowledge transmitted through formal educational institutions, mainly schools and universities. This distinction is essential because, given the conservative nature of most schooling, it is within nonformal education settings that most gender-transforming processes have occurred and will likely occur.

This chapter discusses schooling and education in developing countries, focusing on their implications for and linkage to gender issues. It emphasizes developments in the 1990s and seeks to present an overview of the most recent developments along the lines of theory, policy, and practice.

Discussions of conceptual and practical changes must identify certain key groups involved in education, for their positions are not the same. Among governments and development agencies (both bilateral and multilateral), the question of women's education has moved from invisibility to explicit recognition of the need to consider it a priority. Official recognition tends to be more rhetorical than real and is so far based mostly on an understanding of women as important mediators in the modernization process—not yet on an understanding of women as autonomous citizens. International development agencies have continued their policy of dealing primarily with governments and in their actions tend to side with those governments. Their education efforts to promote women have generally focused on access to schooling and skills for production. Among groups within or closely associated with the women's movement, education is considered an important avenue toward empowerment, and valuable knowledge has been gained from experiences in this direction. Gail Kelly, one of the pioneer thinkers on the question of gender and education in the context of developing countries, admonished us to understand not only how education of women can improve society but also how education can improve the lives of the women themselves.[1] This point has not been fully captured by either governments or international agencies.

Educational studies on gender in the 1970s concentrated on documenting sex inequalities in educational opportunity (primarily access to schooling). In the 1980s, the studies expanded this focus to examine such issues as the determinants of these opportunities, the relationship between education and work/remuneration, and the benefits of women's education for society.[2] Later studies in the 1990s under the support of the World Bank continued the line of exploration of barriers to girls' education and, particularly, the personal and social benefits derived from their education.[3] Such studies have been useful in highlighting the importance of education as a resource for women and the fact that it is neutral neither in its offerings nor in its consequences. A consistent finding has been that schooling increases women's earnings but does not remove their economic dependence on men. Women's years of schooling affect decisions on marriage, but there is no linear relationship between the two. These two critical shapers of women's lives indicate that although schooling is important for economic and social advancement, it is not sufficient to alter women's subordinate position. Even after higher levels of schooling, women have retained marginal positions in the political arena. Studies focusing on Latin America, a region in which gender parity is very close at all levels of education, have looked at issues beyond access and quality, such as the effects of coeducational settings on social outcomes, the participation and power of women in teachers' unions, student women in politics at the university level, and experiences in popular education for adult women.[4] A third generation of studies on gender and education has probed educational phenomena not often seen from a gender perspective, such as the role of women teachers in the process of educational change, the treatment of gender and ethnicity in history textbooks, tensions between the professional and personal identity of women teachers, and the contested experience of the incorporation of controversial subjects such as sex education in the curriculum.[5]

THE CONTRIBUTIONS OF FEMINIST THEORY TO THE UNDERSTANDING OF EDUCATIONAL INSTITUTIONS

Society is based on complementary but hardly symmetric levels of reciprocity in social interaction. Several codes are used to create stable hierarchical social systems. Gender is not the only one but is pervasive as the main type of differentiation in all societies. Feminist theory seeks to place women and their lives in a central place to understand social relations as a whole. Feminism is best conceptualized as a form of critical theory and a movement that enables its member-users to see behind appearance and to understand the structure underlying it and giving meaning, albeit distorted, to their lives.[6] Through a gender lens, we can understand mechanisms of oppression and identify forces that shape the apparent "free choices" that women and men make through various phases of their lives.

Feminist theory has highlighted the need to link analytically the micro and the macro: the personal/intimate and the institutional, the family and the community, the individual and her society, the school and the state. These settings are related in real life, and their connection should be recognized in examinations of institutions such as schools and universities.

Schooling presents a paradoxical situation in the process of gender transformation. Schooling is undoubtedly a major source of cultural capital, employment, and social mobility. Its importance is so widespread that most countries have moved into mandating compulsory public education for all. At the same time, however, educational institutions are conservative settings that reflect the values and rules of patriarchal society.[7]

Among gender scholars today, there is an increased understanding of the necessity to undertake a comprehensive analysis of educational institutions so that the various aspects that constitute the totality of the schooling experience—curriculum, instructional methodologies, peer relations, extracurricular activities—are investigated. Schooling is organized in gendered ways and has differential impacts on girls and boys, often creating polarized forms of masculinity and femininity. Studies in developed countries—which tend to have more open social systems than countries in the Third World—reveal school authority structures, teacher expectations and classroom practices, and peer exchanges that are organized along gender lines.[8] Knowledge about the gendered nature of schooling certainly existed in the 1980s, but in recent years more evidence has been accumulated to demonstrate the pervasive nature of these conditions and their existence despite variations in social class and ethnicity. The tools of qualitative research have been instrumental in documenting the everyday experience of students in educational institutions, noting the sometimes mild but cumulative nature of many events that gradually yet inexorably shape individuals' perception of self and their roles in society.[9] Also in recent years there has been greater conceptual attention given to the intersection between gender, social class, and ethnicity. These concerns, however, have not always materialized in actual studies because this type of research requires substantial financial resources, due either to more complex research designs or to the need to gain access to more heterogeneous school settings, which are not easy to find. The question of the intersection of social markers, although conceptually important, runs the risk of introducing innumerable differences that, although correcting the conception of the "grand narrative" so criticized by postmodernism, also threaten to depoliticize social issues through the introduction of multiple variability of situations and elusive complexity. This tension—acknowledging complex and fluid gender identities versus working with broad categories such as *women*—has not been satisfactorily resolved (see chapter 1 in this volume). It does appear that for purposes of strategic action and political mobilization, it is essential to work with group definitions; we cannot operate politically on the basis of diffused identities. Although there are diverse experiences through which women live, they are simultaneously lived because of the social and cultural interpretation of their sex.[10]

Gender theories today are more sensitive to power and the role of the state in shaping society. The extension of this understanding to schooling has highlighted the role that schools play in the creation of the binary categories of femininity and masculinity and how the state, through its quasi-monopoly of schooling, is implicated in this process. Thinkers such as Robert Connell[11] have been instrumental in explicating the centrality of organized state power and highlighting the function of schools in the development of gendered subjectivities.

According to the analytic framework proposed by Louis Althusser, schooling functions as an ideological apparatus of state. Yet it is also a space into which students bring their own preconceptions and make them a reality through the power of peer pressure. Schooling does not act by itself. Students and teachers bring into the classroom an array of values, attitudes, and beliefs they have learned in their homes and community. These become reenacted in the school, through the treatment of women and men in textbooks, teacher-student interactions, peer group transactions, and the school culture and organization in general.

A key feature of feminist theory is its emphasis on linking knowledge and action. Schools must be not only understood but also seen as potentially transformative social spaces in which useful knowledge can be inculcated, reflection on existing knowledge and culture can take place, and alternative ways of being and living can be imagined and striven for. The dominant global public debate regarding education and women has accepted the importance of women's participation in schooling, at least in terms of access to basic education. This defense of women's right to education is certainly to be welcomed. At the same time, it has emphasized the aspect of access and has been rather unquestioning of other aspects of schooling—curriculum content, teacher-student interactions, and peer culture—that tend to reproduce a patriarchal social order. This definition of the situation creates a significant challenge for the women's movement. Without access, the question of the knowledge to be acquired is a moot point; without questioning existing educational institutions, the knowledge gained will tend to affirm the unequal and inequitable status quo.

In common with critical theory, feminist approaches are sensitive to the notion of individual and collective agency—the possibility of resistance by those oppressed, a phenomenon derived from the Foucauldian principle that power exists not only in official institutions and hierarchies but also through the multiple and lower-level interactions in our everyday lives. There is an increased emphasis on analyzing schooling as a contested terrain in which teachers and students try to create new definitions and personal identities and students do not passively accept dominant gender representations but argue about values and meanings. The potential of teacher subjectivities and negotiations of the everyday life of schools is increasingly visualized as an avenue to attain the transformation of schooling.

In recent years, therefore, feminist work in schools and universities has moved toward more proactive strategies. At lower education levels, these include bringing patriarchy, sexism, and racism into the context of the lives of young girls, creating spaces within schools and classrooms in which young girls can explore their experience and create situations of equal exchange. It also includes recognition and protection of the students' sexual orientation. At the university level, these practices include participation in the various women's studies courses and in the creation of mentoring mechanisms by which younger scholars (doctoral students and junior faculty) are helped by senior academic professors in ways that range from fostering research production to "learning the ropes" for promotion into tenured status.[12]

Models of the impact of the expansion of schooling on life chances are becoming more complete than they have been in the past. If before they included variables such as forgone earnings, current and future benefits, direct costs, supply of school facilities, and mass communication,[13] today they are more open to questions of patriarchal ideology reflected in such variables as early marriage and son preference. These variables do not directly address a society's belief in drastically distinct roles for women and men, but they do acknowledge that there are differential logics at work, rationales that are not necessarily economically based but reflect long-standing cultural norms. Researchers are also becoming more precise in their economic arguments. One example is Christopher Colclough, who remarks that rates-of-return analyses compare the cost of schooling to parents with the economic returns to the child, but in practice what determines schooling is the cost and benefits to *parents* of sending a child to school.[14] This observation illuminates why certain parents harm the educational opportunities for their children by depriving them of schooling in early years. Given the centrality of domestic work and, more specifically, the time invested in fuel and water fetching in rural households, it is becoming increasingly clear that opportunities for greater access of girls to school will have to pass through greater investment in physical infrastructure by the government.

Lynn Ilon's study of macroeconomic and social variables[15] reinforces this point. She finds that countries that become export intensive and improve their per capita GNP tend to increase the rate of females attending secondary school. This finding is compatible with the feminist argument and the empirical fact (observed in both the United States and Latin America) that women need more education to be as competitive as men in the labor force (reflected in women's need for about four more years of education than men to qualify for similar salaries). Also, as household incomes improve there is a diminished need for girls' domestic work.

In short, contributions from feminist perspectives to education underscore the need for holistic probing of the educational system, for a multidisciplinary analysis that considers influences at various level of social organization, and for policies or advocacy positions that exploit the opportunities for transformation within the narrow and somewhat temporary fractures that are possible.

THE CONDITIONS OF WOMEN'S SCHOOLING

Access to schooling has increased over time; comparisons of groups aged twenty to twenty-four with older cohorts invariably show higher levels of education among the younger generations. Some observers[16] note that the expansion of educational systems occurs independently of economic, political, and social factors within national borders, thereby suggesting that influential "transnational forces" are at work. Additional reasons for the expansion of schooling include international economic dynamics (i.e., countries becoming more export intensive or improving their per capita income, as shown by Ilon), social imitation, and, in the case of women's schooling, the increasing pressure of the women's movement. Supporting the latter assertion is the observation that over the past fifteen years, the participation of women in education has been generally increasing faster than that of men, even though gender gaps remain and the pace of growth is exceedingly slow, at most 1.1 percent in favor of women during the 1988–1993 period.[17]

Official data regarding educational statistics are notoriously inaccurate; nonetheless, they are the only figures to which we have access for regional and cross-national comparisons. Recent statistics indicate that women have closed the gender gap at all levels of schooling in the developed countries, representing 49 percent of the enrollment in primary education, 50 percent of the enrollment in secondary education, and 53 percent of the enrollment in tertiary education. In the developing countries, the situation shows marked disparities as women represent 46 percent of the enrollment in primary education, but only 43 percent and 40 percent of the enrollment in secondary and tertiary education, respectively.[18] These statistics, based on gross enrollment rates, include repeaters and overage children; they also mask the large number of failures in terms of students who drop out of school and do not complete their respective educational cycle, many of whom are women. According to UNESCO data for 2005, two-thirds of those of primary school age who are not in school—about sixty million—are girls. And most of these girls—71 percent—suffer compound disadvantage by ethnicity, rural residence, and language. Groups especially excluded are indigenous and Afro-Latino populations in Latin America, hill tribes in East Asia, and scheduled castes and tribes in India.[19] With a primary schooling completion rate of about 76 percent, it can be predicted that the illiteracy rates of women will continue to exceed those of men.

Table 7.1 presents enrollment data by specific developing region. It also uses an equity index (EI) to show the enrollment of women compared to that of men; under

Table 7.1   Gross enrollment by region, level, and sex (in thousands), latest available data (1997)

		Primary			Secondary			Tertiary		
		Male	*Female*	*EI*	*Male*	*Female*	*EI*	*Male*	*Female*	*EI*
Sub-Saharan Africa	1970	14,421	9,983	69	1,644	806	49	143	36	25
	1980	29,228	22,969	79	5,934	3,438	58	438	125	29
	1990	35,365	29,213	83	8,536	6,327	74	950	438	46
	1997	44,524	36,511	82	11,688	9,327	80	1,408	769	55
Latin America and	1970	22,543	21,440	95	5,508	5,161	93	1,059	581	55
Caribbean	1980	33,459	31,860	95	8,509	8,458	99	2,791	2,139	77
	1990	38,795	36,684	95	10,684	11,395	1.07	3,966	3,450	87
	1997	44,587	40,590	91	14,057	15,096	1.07	4,923	4,525	92
Eastern Asia and	1970*									
Oceania	1980	115,175	95,701	83	46,592	32,513	70	2,982	1,680	56
	1990	103,298	91,533	89	45,192	35,424	78	5,311	3,520	66
	1997	111,861	102,821	92	61,156	52,248	85	9,963	6,827	68
Southern Asia	1970*									
	1980	59,391	36,447	61	28,916	13,491	47	3,022	1,041	34
	1990	78,215	55,569	71	45,297	25,336	56	7,026	2,278	32
	1997	91,053	66,642	73	58,477	36,130	62	6,111	3,192	52
Arab States	1970	8,011	4,570	57	2,488	1,059	43	339	105	31
	1980	12,567	8,743	70	4,855	3,341	69	1,025	462	45
	1990	17,106	13,244	77	8,637	6,299	73	1,606	908	57
	1997	20,292	16,333	80	10,275	8,435	82	2,316	1,590	69

Source: UNESCO, 1982, 1995, 2002.
*Statistics for 1970 provide only a single "Asian" category and thus do not permit the distinction used in this table.
EI = equity index, or the proportion of girls to boys, assuming boys represent 100 percent.

ideal circumstances the index, representing the number of women for every hundred men, should be 1.0. In most cases, women are still at a disadvantage compared to men. However, significant changes have occurred in the past three decades. Steady improvement has occurred in all developing regions in primary and secondary education; and significant increases have occurred in the representation of women in higher education. Within the Arab states, rather dramatic changes have occurred at all levels of education. In Latin America and the Caribbean, women, on the aggregate, are slightly more represented than men at the secondary education level and are close to parity in tertiary education (see chapter 12 in this volume).

Household survey data for forty-seven developing countries, which, unlike common educational statistics, permit the collection of family income information, show that in all regions and across social class and age groups, girls attend schools less than boys (except for Latin America for the age twenty to twenty-four group). As youths reach adolescence, the relative disadvantage of poor girls increases substantially, reflecting the interaction between gender and social class.[20]

In several countries (e.g., Mauritius, Lesotho, Botswana, and Namibia in Africa; Mongolia and Korea in Asia; Jordan in the Middle East; and Honduras, Jamaica, Colombia, and Argentina in Latin America) there are more girls than boys attending primary school. This greater participation does not reflect simply an absence of gender asymmetries but rather the particular gender dynamics in those societies. For instance, in the case of Lesotho and Namibia, where men have more physical mobility than women, male labor is exported to South Africa, leaving more women behind for schooling. Some small islands such as Jamaica suffered the destruction of the family under slavery, with the consequence that women assumed more economic responsibilities and thus had a greater need for schooling. Mongolia is a cattle-herding country in which boys, because of the sexual division of labor and sexual norms, are considered more suitable for unsupervised work. Colombia and Argentina reflect a higher propensity for young men to be incorporated early into the urban labor force despite lower levels of education than women. These explanations are not based on detailed studies exploring such phenomena—those investigations have not been conducted.

It can be affirmed that women's greater access to the various levels of schooling does not automatically reflect the disappearance of gender as a discriminating marker in their respective society. If such were the case, there would be a much more even distribution in the salaries, professions, and political positions of men and women. One of the most accepted measures of equality between women and men in society, the Gender Empowerment Measure (GEM) developed by the Human Development Report,[21] reveals that the country closest to such parity is Sweden, with an index of 0.76 (showing that Swedish women have two-thirds the access to economic and political power that men have). The highest GEM score among developing countries is 0.54, held by Barbados. Another important statistic concerns the number of adult illiterates who are women: of the some 900 million illiterate youths and adults, about two-thirds are women.[22] Table 7.2 represents a projected distribution of literacy rates by region. It shows a substantial gender gap in Asia and Africa. It should be observed that some of these projections reflect very optimistic outcomes, which might not be warranted given the degree of investment in literacy programs in many of the developing countries.

Specific data for Brazil and India echo the global pattern. In general, 15 percent of the boys who enter first grade in India finish secondary school in India, but only 10

Table 7.2   Estimated adult illiteracy in developing countries by sex, 2005 projection

		Percentage of Illiterates	
	Total	Women	Men
Africa	35.2	43.3	26.9
Asia	21.8	28.7	15.1
Latin America and the Caribbean	5.0	6.5	5.6

Source: UNESCO, EFA Global Monitoring Report 2002. *Education for All: Is the World on Track?* (Paris: UNESCO, 2002).

percent of the girls are similarly successful.[23] Further, most of those excluded from school belong to scheduled caste and scheduled tribe populations.[24] Brazil is a country in which some research on the intersection of race and gender has taken place. Fulvia Rosemberg[25] finds that the average years of schooling of a black woman from the northeast (the most rural area of Brazil, where African slave labor predominated until the late nineteenth century) is 2.1 years in contrast with 5.7 for a woman in the southeast (the most industrial and Europeanized area of the country) and 5.9 for a man of the same area. In a subsequent study focusing on preschool education in seven Brazilian states, Rosemberg notes that black children represented by far the largest group of preschool children over seven years of age. In her view, many black children are placed for several years in preschool with little possibility of access to primary school. All the preschool teachers were women, but Rosemberg finds that 85 percent of them had not received training as preschool teachers and that 79 percent had not finished primary school. In other words, black children in Brazil, the slight majority of whom are boys, seem to be trapped in dead-end schooling, being taught mostly by unprepared teachers. If one were to look merely at aggregate access indicators, without disaggregating by geographic region, age, and ethnicity, the complex manifestations of multiple forms of discrimination would not be visible.

Enrollment statistics may miss important additional aspects. Indian scholars report that a preappraisal mission by the World Bank (a prerequisite to granting loans) found that the state of Kerala was quite close to attaining universal primary enrollment. On the basis of this finding, the bank declared that no gender interventions were required. Contrary to this declaration, fieldwork found a prevalence of dowry and women suffering the double burden of paid and unpaid work with no share in family or political decision making.[26]

PRIMARY AND SECONDARY EDUCATION

As the tables in this chapter indicate, access to schooling at primary education levels is moving toward gender parity, even though the pace is very slow and substantial differences between boys and girls exist in many developing regions. The ratio of girls to boys enrolled in primary school throughout the world (i.e., aggregating figures for developed and developing countries) has been increasing, from 65 girls per 100 boys in 1960 to 85 girls per 100 boys in 1990. In the developing countries, the average six-year-old girl in 1980 could expect to attend school for 7.3 years; by 1990 the figure had increased to 8.4 years. Gender differentials had not disappeared, however. In 1990 the average six-year-old boy could expect to attend school for 9.7 years.[27]

Equally important indicators of access to schooling are cycle completion, academic achievement, and transfer to a higher level of education (e.g., from primary to secondary school). These statistics are very scarce and, when available, seldom disaggregated by sex. Moreover, few countries have engaged in policies and activities specifically designed to enable girls and women to overcome social obstacles. A few exceptions do exist. The most notable example is *Oportunidades* (previously PROGRESA) in Mexico, a nationwide integrated approach that comprises education, nutrition, and health and which provides education subsidies to poor families, with stipends slightly larger for girls than for boys in secondary school. In Guatemala, scholarships for primary-school girls are being offered in the poorest regions of the country. In Bangladesh and Malawi, stipends (to compensate in part for family forgone income) for secondary school girls are being provided. Evaluations of these programs indicate that girls' enrollment increases when stipends are provided, which suggests that parental support for girls' education can be stimulated. On the other hand, some of the evaluation findings also indicate that rarely is the sexual domestic of labor at home modified.

Another important policy focused on girls is being implemented in India, as the government has initiated the District Primary Education Program (DPEP) to pursue two objectives: access to quality education for all children and equality and empowerment for women. Gender studies in eight states to provide additional inputs for DPEP to address the issue of women's equality and empowerment more effectively found that in only two states (Maharashtra and Haryana) were the textbooks relatively free of gender bias.[28] Through structured interviews of a variety of school actors in more than four hundred villages and urban slums, researchers found that girls' domestic work, sibling care, and helping parents in remunerative employment were the main reason for dropping out among girls. The same study found that the girls perceived their own illnesses as an important reason for dropping out in four of the eight surveyed states. Household poverty was strongly linked to girls' participation in schooling, but poverty in itself did not create cultural practices in favor of sons and boys. It simply made more acute the necessity of using girls and women in the biased division of labor. The study found that parents wanted girls to be educated, the most common reason given being that parents recognized that education prepares girls for economic contribution and that it develops a positive self-image and confidence among girls.[29] This finding corroborates another study in Balochistan, one of the least advanced provinces of Pakistan. Contrary to popular belief, including that of ministry of education officials, a large proportion of parents—especially mothers—recognized the importance of educating their daughters and were even willing to participate in the provision of school facilities.[30]

Another important insight regarding access to schooling comes from a study by Donald Warwick and Haroona Jatoi,[31] based on a large survey of schools and teachers in Pakistan. The authors set out to trace the causes of low performance by girls in math. Using hierarchical linear modeling, they were able to decompose effects and locate as the main cause the training of girls in multigrade schools in rural areas staffed preponderantly by poorly trained women teachers. This finding verifies the complex relations among gender, patriarchal ideologies, and educational policies. Given patriarchal cultural norms, trained women teachers tend to avoid the rural areas for reasons of distance from their families and safety. Although more women are being trained as teachers, educational administrators' leniency in assigning these women to urban areas reproduces a pattern of poorly trained women teachers in rural areas, which makes better-trained women teachers avoid the rural areas for reasons of safety and proximity to their families and leads educational administrators to allow this placement pattern.

THE CONTENT AND EXPERIENCE OF SCHOOLING

The discursive and material representation of women and men contributes to the definition of self and others. The role of schooling in differential gender socialization can be captured through content analysis of textbooks and through observations and in-depth interviews with teachers, administrators, and students. Studies of classroom dynamics and school climate, unfortunately, are very scarce in developing countries, although steps have been taken to expand this probe. Most of the educational investigations of this type have been conducted through M.A. theses and Ph.D. dissertations. Since these products are not normally readily available in libraries, their contributions cannot be fully exploited.

Studies conducted in the 1980s found that textbooks presented negative representations about women. As Audrey Smock observed then,[32] textbooks do not make explicit statements on women's inferiority, but they present them in limited roles and as reduced personalities. In a few countries receiving development assistance, efforts are under way to "eliminate sexual stereotypes" from the textbooks and curricula (e.g., Pakistan, Malawi, Bangladesh, Mexico, and Sri Lanka). The changes are operating at rudimentary levels of alteration.

Three levels of textbook modification can be conceptualized. First, the gender-neutral approach, the mildest effort, centers on the removal of biased language—excessive use of masculine pronouns and examples depicting mostly men. Second, the nonsexist approach eliminates stereotypical references to women and men in the work they do, the roles they play in society, and the traits that supposedly characterize them. Third, the antisexist approach presents alternative images of women and men, and it discusses ways to reach a different social organization.[33] As can be surmised, the antisexist approach is the most transformative. Typically, the role of governments in revising textbooks is limited to the first level of content change, making the textbooks gender neutral. In a few cases, the efforts involve the nonsexist mode. Introducing changes in language and in the representation of women is not an easy matter, since it calls for modifying how we think and requires a deep understanding of how language and images shape our thinking.

To assure the success of girls in schooling, careful monitoring of their everyday experience and their interactions with boy peers is needed. This type of research would not only produce rich insights into the creation of gender differences but would also enable us to understand what is required to achieve transformative action. Some research along these lines is being funded, albeit in modest scale, by the Forum of African Women Educationalists (FAWE) in sub-Saharan Africa (discussed later).

In developed countries, research on girls' education has moved from documenting inequalities—which still exist—to (1) researching how these inequalities develop by looking at classroom situations, specifically the relations between students and teachers and among students, and (2) experimenting with how these inequitable situations can be transformed. In several school settings in the United States, new spaces are being created within schools so that lopsided patterns may be questioned and avoided and replaced with more equal relations. A number of feminist pedagogical efforts are seeking to incorporate the experiences and voices of students, promoting self and social empowerment, and making the classrooms less teacher centered. Recent efforts in U.S. schools have tried, for instance, to explore problems such as patriarchy, sexism, and racism in the context of the girls' contemporary lives. In contrast, in developing countries, engagement in this type of effort has been minuscule. There is increased understanding, however, that a curriculum content that acknowledges the body and sexuality and addresses citizenship in its widest meaning should receive early attention.

Some qualitative work is beginning to unveil gender practices in schools in developing countries. An ethnographic study of a Mexican high school focusing on how femininities and masculinities are created presents evidence that forceful groups of girls were called *marimachas* (tomboys) and that those who "excelled academically and aggressively pursued leadership roles took the risk of censure . . . from male and female classmates alike,"[34] even though these girls tended to defend their leadership on the ground of greater discipline and moral superiority. Bradley Levinson finds a prevailing belief that girls were unfit to serve as student body president, to carry the flag during parades, or to fulfill leadership roles, areas for which masculine force was seen as essential. But he also finds that the climate in the school was open to change. Levinson notes that the new high school leadership was causing transformations such as including girls in the flag escort and increasing participation of girls in classes and in activities traditionally associated with boys, leading him to be optimistic about the possibility of changing gender beliefs in schools.

In several countries, efforts to modify the existing curriculum to include sex education or a discussion of the social relations of gender have encountered significant opposition. Two pieces of evidence come from Latin America, a region relatively open to modernizing forces. In Argentina, the National Program for the Promotion of Women's Equal Opportunities in Education (PRIOM), operating within the Ministry of Education, was able to deliver a number of nonsexist and antisexist teacher training workshops on the question of gender and education for several years.[35] PRIOM also worked during an extended period on the production of a comprehensive women's studies curriculum that was to be incorporated into the overall curriculum at the primary school level. PRIOM's curriculum also addressed linguistic sensibility and the unwarranted use of the masculine gender in words such as "citizen" (*ciudadano*), recommending instead collective nouns such as the "reading public" (*el público lector*) as opposed to "readers" (*lectores*) to make it easier to avoid the use of the masculine gender. Conservative parents and members of the Catholic Church accused PRIOM's staff of being antifamily and trying to introduce homosexuality in the schools, a complaint promptly heeded by the government. The document was reviewed to such an extent that PRIOM's technical team resigned. Persons closely involved in the development of the gender curriculum noted that the new document was not even concerned with nonsexist language.[36]

In Mexico, in a twist that divided parents and government officials, parents denounced and succeeded in removing a textbook coedited by a state branch of the Ministry of Education that would have addressed adolescent sexuality with a discussion of the positive and negative consequences of engaging in sexual behavior during adolescence. Conservative parents and high officials of the Catholic Church invoked instead the principle of abstinence and insisted that sexuality should be practiced "at the right time" and "within marriage," a discourse amply indifferent to the reality of the country.[37]

Interventions to increase girls' access to the secondary school level are very infrequent. Those to modify content are even less frequent. In terms of access, a notable exception is a scholarship program for secondary school girls in Bangladesh. When it was evaluated in its pilot version, it was able to double the participation of girls.[38]

NONFORMAL EDUCATION PROGRAMS
FOR PRIMARY SCHOOL CHILDREN

A development of considerable importance in recent years is the use of nonformal education (NFE) settings to expand the education of girls. This approach is being tried primarily in populous Asian countries that have very low rates of school participation and sizable gender gaps in enrollment, notably Bangladesh, Pakistan, and India. The largest and perhaps most innovative NFE education program for girls in the world functions in Bangladesh, where it is run by the Bangladesh Rural Advancement Committee (BRAC). This program covers about a million children (or about 8 percent of the total primary school enrollment in the country) through NFE "centers," each of which serves a group of thirty to thirty-three students who become a cohort that moves together from first to third grade. The BRAC program has been designed so that at least 70 percent of the students served in each center are girls. The curriculum is highly innovative and includes many activities aimed to promote the development of confidence and assertiveness in girls. The fact that, unlike the formal schools, most teachers are women provides the students with positive role models. The BRAC centers have been highly successful in cycle completion, but problems have emerged in transferring the students to regular schools to complete their primary education (fourth and fifth grades). According to a recent study, about 30 percent of BRAC girls do not advance to the next educational cycle, possibly due to early marriage or the distance of the regular public school.[39] In addition, BRAC girls drop out in the regular school at higher rates than BRAC boys (it is unclear whether this occurs because the students find the new environment hostile or because school distance or domestic work prevents them from further attendance).

The NFE programs in India—*Shiksha Karmi* and *Lok Jumbish*—present some of the features of the BRAC program, except that many of the rural teachers are men. On the other hand, the Indian programs cover the entire primary school cycle, and the work is not done separately by nongovernmental organizations (NGOs) but in conjunction with government officials. This joint participation assures a coordinated and mutually supportive plan of action. In Baluchistan the program is conducted by an NGO, also working in cooperation with the provincial government. By design, this program serves a large number of girls and uses locally hired women teachers. It offers a gender-sensitive curriculum and has succeeded in attracting the cooperation of parents in the running of the school. According to program statistics, girls have not only enrolled in large numbers but also have shown good attendance rates. The participation of women as teachers and mothers in the running of Village Education Committees has provided new and alternative roles for women in their traditional communities.[40] Most of these projects operate with external support. Although governmental funds have been increasingly assigned to cover part of the costs, it remains to be seen whether the programs will continue without donor funds.

HIGHER EDUCATION

It might serve as a good point of contrast to remember that in May 1897, slightly over one hundred years ago, Cambridge University roundly defeated a resolution that would have given women the right to the bachelor of arts degree.[41] Such a position would seem bizarre in many countries today. Should people therefore conclude that the educational situation of women in higher education has dramatically improved?

In terms of numerical access to university, it is beyond doubt—as is the case for the other two levels—that tertiary enrollment of women has been expanding. What remains difficult to change is the concentration of women in typically feminine fields and, conversely, the overrepresentation of men in fields perceived as masculine, such as those dealing with science and technology. Despite the potential contribution of women's perspectives to such fields as agriculture and engineering, their representation in them remains insignificant. Women's choice of fields considered socially appropriate for their gender reflects the influence of multiple societal and cultural forces, but it also suggests that the academic experience of women reinforces this influence. There are very few instances of efforts to change the experience of women at the university level. One such exception comes from an incipient effort in Chile to begin exploration of gender bias and ways to make the curriculum more gender sensitive in the fields of education and journalism.

The most positive development in recent years within higher education in developing countries is the rapid expansion of women's studies programs and units. These can be quite extensive, as they are in India and Brazil, countries in which ties between feminist scholars and women in popular women's movements are strong. Women students in these universities are encouraged to produce master's theses and doctoral dissertations on gender issues, and they find intellectual spaces to discuss ways to analyze and combat gender discrimination. With time, women in the feminist movement are realizing that for change on gender ideologies and practices, women need to develop a deeper understanding of economics and finances. These are areas that under present neoliberal policies are playing substantial roles in decision making, affecting thereby the enactment of public policies and often determining the slight allocation of state funds to social programs, of which education is one of the most affected.

EDUCATION FOR ADULT WOMEN

Since most formal education settings present endemic institutional barriers to gender-sensitive changes, it is essential to consider the transformative role of adult education, which lies outside the formal system. The increased gender awareness of such education not only affects the students but is also transmitted to their children. Women, as key organizers of the household environment, can influence what their children do and learn at home.

Transformative work in women's education—in the form of both oppositional discourse and practical actions against inequities—has been undertaken mostly by women-based or feminist nongovernmental organizations.[42] The areas they have addressed have included such issues as empowerment, legal literacy, domestic violence, and income generation. A current theme within women-based NGOs in Latin America concerns citizenship training, lobbying and advocacy skills, health education practice, and the training of trainers. NGOs in Latin America are also moving from denunciation of women's unequal and exploitative situations to making proposals based on statistics and information, creating spaces for training, and making concrete demands on government.[43]

It is not easy to provide adult women with educational opportunities. Various studies focusing on the participation of low-income women in adult education programs have determined that women's domestic work, frequency of domestic violence, and the need for serving children and families leaves them with very little time and inclination for education, even though NFE programs often offer schedules and locations that make them accessible to the women.[44]

Important lessons have derived from these experiences. After many years of effort with literacy classes and condensed programs for which there were no takers, Indian scholars and practitioners have learned that skills and education cannot be forced on women.[45] With the involvement of the Indian government and substantial funds coming from external sources, the *Mahila Samakhya* program has been implemented in India for several years. Women in this program were not offered literacy training but were given the opportunity to discuss in a social space their experiences and desires. Village-level forums were created exclusively for women, the assumption being that these women "in due time could emerge as strong pressure groups for raising genuine demands, fighting injustice and creating an environment for 'equal' treatment of women," and that these forums would enable them to "discover and re-discover their identities and problems as women, and mobilize around issues that were of priority to them."[46] By most accounts, the women in the Mahila Samakhya have succeeded in changing their self-concept and have made successful demands on their local government. These women have acquired the skills and insights to analyze their situation of subordination and, as one observer summarized it, they have been able to turn fear into understanding.[47]

Adult education offers much potential for gender transformation. It tends to unite women from different social classes, with low-income women as beneficiaries and middle-income (but increasingly low-income) women as leaders and staff members of the NGOs. These groups are usually confronted with two demands: to address immediate problems, mostly linked with basic needs (what has been called women's practical needs) and to address macrolevel issues such as gender-fair legislation affecting the family, wages, access to credit, and so on (what is usually termed women's strategic needs).[48] The resolution of these tensions is not easy, yet there are encouraging examples of women being able to shift toward more encompassing and long-term objectives that will call for transforming institutions and enacting new policies. It is becoming increasingly clear to these women-based NGOs that formulating large-scale change within society will require influencing the state, which will require these NGOs to acquire mobilization and organization skills and engage in social action.[49] It is also becoming increasingly evident that major transformative educational efforts cannot bypass the engagement of women-led NGOs and, as such, these groups will need to receive much more funding than in the past, both from the state and from international sources. In Latin America, the unprecedented mobilization of women in the 1980s due to the economic crisis and the existence of dictatorial regimes provided unexpected skills for many of the low-income women, skills and practices they have retained—speaking in order to express an opinion, making demands, representing. They have also been able to produce more accurate evaluations of the social functions of interpersonal relations and of their own personal development.[50]

At present, NGOs in general and women-based NGOs in particular are making efforts to redefine such taken-for-granted concepts as *citizenship* and *social life*, and introducing new ones such as *empowerment*. The mutual recognition of women's great burdens and logistical problems in becoming NFE students and simultaneously their preference to learn through imitation and informal apprenticeships has prompted feminist adult educators to recognize the importance of mediators in the process of social learning. These mediators can play an effective role in the provision of training. Walters explains: "This approach refocuses the problem away from the masses of poorly schooled people to the mediators. It is up to the mediators to learn to serve people across class, language, culture, etc., so that learning can occur more effectively through everyday experiences."[51]

There are two instances in which NGOs are engaged in major efforts to improve schooling. The Forum of African Women Educationalists (FAWE) is a group consisting of some forty-four women who hold key official educational roles in their country, such as ministers of education, vice chancellors, and other senior policymakers. This group is engaged in projects that include, among others, examining girls' and boys' performance in math and science, providing gender sensitization to educational personnel, exploring the extent of sexual harassment in secondary schools, and addressing women's issues in teaching and education management. Because of its prominent membership, FAWE's work is expected to find a direct and relatively unblocked application in the school system. In Latin America, the Popular Education Network of Women (REPEM) is affiliated with the Adult Education Council of Latin America and the Caribbean. Composed of 150 women-based NGOs and committed to strengthening popular education with a gender perspective, REPEM is working very intensively on the development of nonsexist and antisexist educational materials.

THE STATE AND WOMEN'S EDUCATION

The state shapes education through policies governing tuition fees, books, uniforms, and other expenses that families must fulfill. State policy can also influence schooling by providing incentives such as scholarships or stipends for girls to counterbalance the opportunity cost to parents.

I noted earlier that despite the disadvantaged situation of girls in most educational systems, few official policies address this situation. Most projects focusing on girls begin and end as pilot projects supported by donor agencies and are rarely incorporated into national policies.[52] On the other hand, since 1985 states have committed themselves in a series of public and official meetings to work for the advancement of girls' education. This was explicitly acknowledged in the Forward-Looking Strategies signed in Nairobi at the end of the Third World Conference on Women (1985). The commitment was reiterated and expanded in the Platform for Action signed at the Fourth World Conference on Women in Beijing (1995). The proliferation of related documents is perhaps nowhere more visible than in sub-Saharan Africa. Since the Education for All Declaration in Jomtien (1990)—a document that is widely agreed to represent a breakthrough in terms of national and international support for basic education and girls—African governments have signed documents drafted at the International Conference on Assistance to the African Child (1992), the Pan-African Conference on the Education of Girls (also known as the Ouagadougou Declaration, 1993), the International Conference on Population and Development (1994), the African Common Position on Human and Social Development (1994), and the Fifth African Regional Conference on Women (Dakar, 1994). All of the documents approved at these conferences identify the education of girls as a top national priority. Some even call for affirmative action as a method of reducing the educational disparity that exists between boys and girls. There is a wide disjunction between rhetoric and actual action; it is to be hoped that as many of these documents are known and circulated, women and men who seek equality and equity in education will use these promises to force governments into compliance.

DONOR AGENCIES AND THEIR SUPPORT FOR EDUCATION

It must be noted that there is a strong disjuncture between discourses of equality, enunciated in many global agreements and even conventions (which carry the force of international law), and a position in favor of government austerity implemented through structural adjustment programs (SAPs, increasingly replaced by Poverty Reduction Strategy Papers) and new loans approved by the World Bank and sanctioned by the International Monetary Fund that avoids discussing the reality of power asymmetries and inequalities in the North. Following such major women's conferences as those in Nairobi and more recently Beijing, gender has become a more explicit policy objective of both bilateral and multilateral development agencies. In 1996, for instance, the Swedish International Development Agency (SIDA) adopted gender as one of its six development objectives. The advocacy in favor of girls' education and the financial support of donor agencies have been instrumental in fostering attention to this issue, since, as noted earlier, governments are reluctant to invest their own funds on issues concerning gender, especially when such issues may incur strong opposition from certain segments of their constituencies. There is increasing support for girls' education among development agencies, although this support tends to be limited to basic education. Nonetheless, the strong leadership of agencies in favor of girls' schooling, such as UNICEF and the United Nations Development Programme (UNDP) and the Dutch and Scandinavian agencies in support of women's education, has made gender an unavoidable issue in national development politics. The influential Human Development Report for 1995[53] coined the slogan "If human development is not engendered, it is endangered," a phrase that seems to have lodged itself in the subconscious of many governments.

The actual performance of development agencies is contradictory. A substantial number of staff members within these agencies believe (erroneously, given the high number of national and international declarations of commitment to the education of girls and women) that to press for attention to gender issues constitutes a form of cultural imperialism. Several agencies are now working with new principles of international assistance, such as "recipient responsibility" and "program support," which might end up discriminating against women. These two principles call for much greater dialogue with governments and for greater discretionary powers by the recipient state. For many issues regarding national development, government autonomy is a desirable situation. But in the case of gender, this autonomy could easily result in the avoidance of gender issues. A very strong indicator that governments are not interested in the pursuit of gender issues is that almost all projects focusing on women's (or girls') education are funded through grants from international agencies, not loans. A further weakness in dealing exclusively with governments in the area of gender and education is that they tend to operate mostly on questions of access and, if curriculum and textbook revisions are involved, changes operate at the gender-neutral (first) level.

Often development agencies present limited definitions of a situation even though their new principle appears on target. For instance, in recent years the World Bank has become very interested in the question of "good governance," a code phrase for countries eager to compete in the global economy. A 1995 World Bank publication on policies for gender equality identifies four areas affecting the welfare of women to be addressed through legal action: land and property rights, labor market policies and employment law, family law, and financial laws and regulations. But since the prescriptions to make reforms in these areas are not based on a profound and complete understanding of the causes of women's inequality, the recipient state is assigned—quite unproblematically—the implementation of these reforms. Even though NGOs are identified as important "players from civil society," there is no specific recognition of the role that women-based NGOs, and other elements in civil society clearly identified with the women's movement, can play in these socioeconomic transformations.

Today, however, women are much more aware of the institutions that conduct key work in social and economic policies. The World Bank is currently the object of strong feminist pressure. This emphasis started in 1995 at the Fourth World Women's Conference in Beijing when a letter signed by nine hundred women's organizations from around the globe was given to James Wolfensohn, the first president of the World Bank to attend a world women's conference. The letter requested that the bank act toward increasing participation of grassroots women in the design of macroeconomic policies, institutionalizing the perspective of gender as a standard practice in its policies and programs, increasing the bank's investments in the sectors of education, health, agriculture, land ownership, employment, and financial services for women.[54] Since Beijing, the women have organized an umbrella group called Women's Eyes on the World Bank, with chapters in different parts of the world. In early 1997, this group wrote a second letter—widely circulated on the Internet—to President Wolfensohn stating that it had reviewed the World Bank's initiatives during 1996 and found that "the admirable commitment from the top has yet to be translated into concrete action in the majority of Bank programs and operations, where there remains a lack of understanding among many Bank staff of gender inequities and their implications for development." A review of a specific project designed to improve the quality and efficiency of primary education, to address gender in training teachers and principals, and to provide education for girls, especially indigenous girls, found that the indicators on which performance would be based were not even disaggregated by sex.[55] Several observers of the World Bank's position in education criticize its instrumental conception of gender, in which women are useful because the more educated the women, the fewer children they will have and the more they will participate in the labor force; infant mortality will be lower, and possibilities for work will increase, as will income. Instead, these observers call for more human and anthropological conceptualizing in which women are seen not as mere economic agents but as citizens with individual rights.[56]

Commitments made in the 1990 Education for All (EFA) Declaration signed in Jomtien identified among EFA's major objectives not only universal basic education but also the reduction of the gender gap within countries. This was to be attained by 2000, but the UNESCO assessment conducted at the end of the EFA decade in Dakar, Senegal, concluded that progress toward the goals had been uneven and very slow. Today, the attempt to reduce gender disparities at the primary education level—which is really too low to make a difference in the economic realm—has been postponed to 2015, without any explicit analysis explaining how the new deadline will be reached. Many development agencies and countries are today following the Millennium Development Goals, a plan of action on education, health, ecology, and national development, promoted by the United Nations and agreed to by 189 countries. Education figures prominently among the eight objectives of the millennium goals. Objective 2 proposes universal access to education for both boys and girls, but it continues to be limited to basic education. Objective 3 seeks "gender empowerment," yet the key action considered under this rubric refers exclusively to the elimination of gender disparity at all levels of education. This definition of empowerment is very narrow and represents in many ways a step backward since much of the feminist thought and research findings to date have a much broader understanding of empowerment—one that does not equate access to education with the development of an analytical and socially active mind, but rather defines empowerment as a process that enables the development of critical thought and agency at individual and collective levels.

A recent review of actual resources indicated that the assistance to basic education from bilateral donors in the mid-1990s in real terms was lower than it had been before the Jomtien conference. This study, based on a survey of twenty bilateral aid agencies, found that such assistance had increased in six of these agencies but remained static or fell in the other fourteen. The World Bank, which had been a major contributor in 1994 (U.S.$2.l6 billion), decreased considerably by 1996 (U.S.$1.7 billion), according to Paul Bennell.[57] Both governments and donor agencies have endorsed helping women, but primarily through skills training for the purpose of increased productivity. The overwhelming emphasis on productivity is rejected by feminist scholars. As Sara Longwe states, "On the contrary, gender training must be largely concerned with providing the analytical tools for participants to become dissatisfied with the current unequal gender division of society, which they (may have) previously accepted and taken for granted."[58]

Training, from a gender transformative perspective, should also enable women to generate mobilization around the analysis of gender issues and public action to address these issues.

A quantitative study based on 157 country behaviors between 1975 and 1998 found that the strongest predictors of state adoption of national machineries for women included (in addition to contact with transnational networks) the proportion of women in ministerial positions, the degree of democracy in the country, and the extent to which women had similar access to men for secondary education. (Interestingly, the study did not show an impact due to the proportion of women enrolled, but rather on the degree of parity between women's and men's enrollment in secondary education.)[59] These findings capture in telling ways what has become increasingly understood in the women's movement: that political mobilization at transnational levels is effective, that women in political positions do bring political agendas that men might not, and that access to higher levels of education (beyond primary) in equal numbers to those of men create strong empowering conditions among women. In other words, an educational agenda must be accompanied by a political agenda.

CHALLENGES IN DEVELOPING COUNTRIES

In the past twenty years, women have been gaining increased access to education. In several parts of the world there is a clear tendency toward gender parity, at least at the elementary level. The positive content, experience, and outcomes of schooling are not so much taken for granted now, and efforts are taking place, albeit very modest vis-à-vis the nature of the problem, to advance the condition of women's education. Against this background, four major challenges remain.

The first is globalization, a process that is gearing all countries, and their school systems in particular, for economic competition and not for critical understanding. Globalization forces are promoting an increase in scientific and technological courses, yet it is not certain what efforts will be made to include women in this expansion. Competitiveness has created a demand for *quality* of education, an issue several observers see as involving three dimensions: efficacy, process, and relevance. The positive side of efficacy resides in its focus on learning as opposed to merely attending school. The process dimension highlights the quality of inputs, such as good physical facilities, trained teachers, good textbooks, and adequate instructional methodologies, necessary for a successful learning process. Relevance, however, introduces some conservative thinking in that it tends to emphasize the economic usefulness of education rather than the social and affective development of individuals. For instance, efforts to renovate the educational system in Latin America recognize the poor quality of the educational system in such areas as reading, math, and science; the neglect of the teaching profession; and the existence of inequities. Yet this last recognition tends to focus almost exclusively on social class, downplaying both gender and ethnic differences.[60]

Ironically, globalization, as it relates to women, seems to be based on an assumption similar to that first introduced by Marxist thought. The "woman question" in Marxism argued that women's oppression was rooted in their exclusion from productive participation in economic activity so that their incorporation in the labor force would make their subordination disappear. Globalization implies that if women were to join the labor market, multiple benefits would accrue to them and to society. In both cases, it is the labor market that creates transformation for women. Yet the unpaid work of women in reproduction, the gender division of labor and resources within the household and in society, and the role of patriarchal ideology are ignored in both perspectives.

The second challenge derives from the serious economic crisis that many developing countries still face and the simultaneous retrenchment of the state through the imposition by the World Bank and the International Monetary Fund of SAPs. There is wide consensus that these programs have generated more poverty than in the past as increases in the price of basic goods and cuts in social services such as health care, family planning, child care, and education have affected poor and middle-class households. Women and girls have absorbed the heaviest burden of SAPs through their increased household work and participation in formal and informal labor markets.[61] Sub-Saharan African countries are particularly affected as they have entered a cycle of unpayable external debt characterized by more funds going abroad to pay the debt than financial resources moving into the region. Since 1987, the International Monetary Fund has received U.S.$4 billion more from sub-Saharan Africa than it has provided in new finance.[62] The retrenchment of the state, which characterizes countries undergoing SAP policies, has negative consequences for women because the state is clearly a major institution capable of both applying pressure and creating large-scale change.

Comparisons between developing countries undergoing SAPs and those that are not have clearly shown that education budgets have suffered with SAP programs and that primary education levels (including teacher salaries) have suffered considerably.[63] Obviously, less public money for education investments also means a reduced ability and willingness to consider specific populations. Since the countries with the heaviest per capita burden linked to economic indebtedness are also those with the largest disparities between men and women, this forecasts a period of disregard for girls' and women's education.

The third challenge emerges from the paucity of educational research in developing countries. Very limited national funds are available for research and development; most of the existing gender research has been conducted under the auspices of international assistance. Frequent calls by the World Bank and other institutions for developing nations to remove subsidies at the tertiary level of education and offer student loans instead suggests that funds thereby released may be used by educational systems to invest in other areas, research presumably being one of them. But several scholars doubt this. Colclough,[64] for example, contends that loans and scholarships involve higher administrative costs and are more expensive than the typical structure of subsidies. In his view, alternative measures would be to create better and more progressive tax structures and to use private firms for the provision of education. In the case of women, a progressive tax structure would reduce the burden of social class, but the dynamics of privatization may be much less supportive. Since the education of girls and women tends to be seen as consumption (not an investment) by many families, particularly low-income families, privatization might end up having harmful effects on their participation, particularly their participation in higher education. Research, especially of a qualitative kind, is needed to identify spaces of rupture of dominant gender norms and representations, and to document the instances in which agency is beginning to take place.

The fourth challenge is perhaps the most significantly promising of the set. It concerns teachers. In critical theory literature, teachers are perceived as major change agents, with a tremendous potential for "border crossing"—their ability to bring themselves and their students to appreciate the position of other social and ethnic groups.[65] At the same time, since teachers, like everyone else, are products of their time and environment, many of them subscribe to traditional gender views. In several developing regions, Latin America in particular, women constitute the larger proportion of primary teachers. Teachers could be made to play a role in promoting reflection on society and gender roles; they could also be made to work on the transformation of gender representations and norms. To be successful, the teachers themselves would need to undergo a transformation; this would entail providing them with appropriate in-service and preservice teacher training and gender-sensitive curricula. Work on teachers is occurring in industrialized countries, but in developing countries this area has been considered only in exceptional circumstances (the Argentine case discussed above being one of them).

Women and men alike should consider three key questions from this review of women's education: (1) How do we change a patriarchal education system that has been in existence for so long, (2) how can we further promote gender transformation through women-led NGO educational programs, and (3) how do we create spaces for change today amid social and economic situations that tend to be competitive and instrumental rather than solidaristic and socially reflective?

It might be suitable to end this chapter with a quote from the late Bella Abzug, a former member of the U.S. Congress and an extremely active feminist:

> In answer to those who think that women just want power for power's sake, it's not about that at all. It's not about simply main-streaming women. It's not about women

joining the polluted stream. It's about cleaning the stream, changing stagnant pools into fresh, flowing waters. Our struggle is about resisting the slide into a morass of anarchy, violence, intolerance, inequality, and injustice. Our struggle is about reversing the trends of social, economic, and ecological crisis.[66]

NOTES

1. Gail Kelly, "Research on the Education of Women in the Third World: Problems and Perspectives," *Women's Studies International Quarterly* 1, no. 4 (1978): 365–73.

2. See, for instance, Audrey Smock, *Women's Education in Developing Countries: Opportunities and Outcomes* (New York: Praeger, 1981).

3. One of the best examples is Elizabeth King and Anne Hill, eds., *Women's Education in Developing Countries: Barriers, Benefits, and Policies* (Baltimore, Md.: Johns Hopkins University Press, 1993).

4. Nelly Stromquist, ed., *Women and Education in Latin America: Knowledge, Power, and Change* (Boulder, Colo.: Rienner, 1992).

5. Nelly Stromquist, ed., *Gender Dimensions in Education in Latin America* (Washington, D.C.: Organization of American States, 1996).

6. John Wilson, "The Subject Women," in *Theory on Gender/Feminism on Theory*, ed. Paula England (New York: Aldine de Gruyter, 1993).

7. Gail Kelly and Ann Nihlen, "Schooling and the Reproduction of Patriarchy: Unequal Workloads, Unequal Rewards," in *Cultural and Economic Reproduction in Education*, ed. Michael Apple (London: Routledge, 1982); Sara Longwe, "Education for Women's Empowerment—or Schooling for Women's Subordination?" (paper presented at the international seminar-workshop Promoting the Empowerment of Women through Adult Learning, Chiang Mai, Thailand, February 24–28, 1997).

8. See the series of studies on the United States sponsored by the American Association of University Women (AAUW): AAUW, *How Schools Shortchange Girls* (Washington, D.C.: Author, 1992); AAUW, *Hostile Hallways: The AAUW Survey on Sexual Harassment in America's Schools* (Washington, D.C.: Author, 1993); Judy Cohen, *Girls in the Middle: Working to Succeed in School* (Washington, D.C.: AAUW, 1996); Peggy Orenstein, *School Girls: Young Women, Self-Esteem, and the Confidence Gap* (New York: Doubleday, 1994); Sunny Hansen, Joyce Walker, and Barbara Flom, *Growing Smart: What's Working for Girls in Schools* (Washington, D.C.: AAUW, 1996).

9. For an ethnographic account of socialization at the college level, see Margaret Eisenhart and Dorothy Holland, *Educated in Romance* (Chicago: University of Chicago Press, 1990).

10. Kate Soper, "Postmodernism and Its Discontents," *Feminist Review* 39 (1991): 97–108.

11. Robert Connell, *Gender and Power: Society, the Person, and Sexual Politics* (Stanford, Calif.: Stanford University Press, 1987); Robert Connell, "Poverty and Education," *Harvard Educational Review* 64, no. 2 (1994): 125–49; Louis Althusser, *Essays on Ideology* (London: Verso, 1984).

12. See, for instance, J. Aaron and Sidney Walby, eds., *Out of the Margins: Women's Studies in the Nineties* (London: Falmer, 1991).

13. Mary Jean Bowman, "An Integrated Framework for Analysis of the Spread of Schooling in Less Developed Countries," in *New Approaches to Comparative Education*, ed. Philip Altbach and Gail Kelly (Chicago: University of Chicago Press, 1986).

14. Christopher Colclough, "Education and the Market: Which Parts of the Neoliberal Solution are Correct?" *World Development* 24, no. 4 (1996): 589–610.

15. Lynn Ilon, "The Effects of International Economic Dynamics on Gender Equity of Schooling," *International Review of Education* 44, no. 4 (1998): 335–56.

16. Francisco Ramirez and John Boli-Bennett, "Global Patterns of Educational Institutional-

ization," in *Comparative Education*, ed. Philip Altbach, Robert Arnove, and Gail Kelly (New York: Macmillan, 1982).

17. UNESCO, *1995 Statistical Yearbook* (Paris: Author, 1995).

18. UNESCO, *1995 Statistical Yearbook*, 2–15 and 2–16.

19. UIS, *Children Out of School: Measuring Exclusion from Primary School* (Montreal: UNESCO Institute for Statistics, 2005).

20. Cynthia Lloyd, ed., *Growing Up Global. The Changing Transitions to Adulthood in Developing Countries* (Washington, D.C.: The National Academies Press, 2005).

21. UNDP, *1995 Human Development Report* (New York: Author, 1995).

22. UNDP, UNESCO, UNICEF, and World Bank, *Education for All: Achieving the Goal: Final Report of the Mid-Decade Meeting of the International Consultative Forum on Education for All* (New York: UNDP, 1996).

23. National Council of Educational Research and Training, *Education of the Girl Child in India: A Fact Sheet* (Delhi: Author, 1995).

24. Scheduled tribes and scheduled castes represent ethnic minorities traditionally disadvantaged in Indian society and therefore constitutionally recognized to receive special compensatory measures in employment, education, and other areas (UIS, 2005).

25. Fulvia Rosemberg, "Education, Democratization, and Inequality in Brazil," in *Women and Education in Latin America*, ed. Nelly Stromquist (Boulder, Colo.: Rienner, 1992); Fulvia Rosemberg, "Educación, género y raza," (paper presented at the twentieth congress of the Latin American Studies Association, Guadalajara, April 17–19, 1997).

26. Usha Nayar, "Planning for UPE of Girls' and Women's Empowerment: Gender Studies in DPEP," in *School Effectiveness and Learning Achievement at Primary Stage*, ed. National Council of Educational Research and Training (New Delhi: National Council of Education Research and Training, 1995).

27. World Bank, *Toward Gender Equality*.

28. Nayar, "Planning for UPE."

29. Nayar, "Planning for UPE."

30. Nelly Stromquist and Paud Murphy, *Leveling the Playing Field: Giving Girls an Equal Chance for Basic Education—Three Countries' Efforts* (Washington, D.C.: World Bank, 1995).

31. Donald Warwick and Haroona Jatoi, "Teacher Gender and Student Achievement in Pakistan," *Comparative Education Review* 38, no. 3 (1994): 377–99.

32. Smock, *Women's Education*.

33. Janice Streitmatter, *Toward Gender Equity in the Classroom* (Albany: State University of New York Press, 1995).

34. Bradley Levinson, "Masculinities and Feminities in the Mexican Secundaria: Notes Toward an Institutional Practice of Gender Equity" (paper presented at the twentieth congress of the Latin American Studies Association, Guadalajara, April 17–19, 1997).

35. Gloria Bonder, "From Theory to Action: Reflections on a Women's Equal Opportunities Educational Policy" (paper prepared for the expert group meeting on gender, education, and training, Division for the Advancement of Women, United Nations, New York, October 10–14, 1994).

36. Lea Fletcher, "No Hemos Hecho Demasiado Bien Nuestra Tarea," *Perspectivas* 5 (1997): 7–10.

37. Barbara Bayardo, "Sex and the Curriculum in Mexico and the United States," in *Gender Dimensions in Education in Latin America*, ed. Nelly Stromquist (Washington, D.C.: Organization of American States, 1996).

38. Anne Hill and Elizabeth King, "Women's Education and Economic Well-Being," *Feminist Economics* 1, no. 2 (1995): 21–46.

39. Gajendra Verma and Tom Christie, "The Main-Streaming of BRAC/NFPE Students"

(paper prepared for the Manchester faculty of education, University of Manchester, December 1996).

40. Stromquist and Murphy, *Leveling the Playing Field.*

41. "1897: Degrees Denied," *International Herald Tribune*, May 22, 1997.

42. Many NGOs also provide maternal health and childhood clinics that serve as informal vehicles for the education of women. This type of education, though useful, is not gender relations-transformative. Women receive little education from agricultural extension workers. This type of education would enable women to increase their productivity, but, again, it usually is not transformative.

43. Celita Eccher, "The Women's Movement in Latin America and the Caribbean: Exercising Global Citizenship" (paper presented at the International Seminar-Workshop Promoting the Empowerment of Women through Adult Learning, Chiang Mai, Thailand, February 24–28, 1997).

44. Nelly Stromquist, *Literacy for Citizenship: Gender and Grassroots Dynamics in Brazil* (Albany: State University of New York Press, 1997); Shirley Walters, "Democracy, Development and Adult Education in South Africa" (paper presented at the international seminar-workshop Promoting the Empowerment of Women through Adult Learning, Chiang Mai, Thailand, February 24–28, 1997).

45. Sharda Jain and Lakshmi Krishnamurty, *Empowerment through Mahila Sanghas: The Mahila Samakhya Experience* (Tilak Nagar, India: Sandhan Shodh Kendra, 1996).

46. Jain and Krishnamurty, *Empowerment through Mahila Sanghas*, 13, 16.

47. Jain and Krishnamurty, *Empowerment through Mahila Sanghas*, 63.

48. Maxine Molyneux, "Mobilization without Emancipation? Women's Interests, State, and Revolution in Nicaragua," *Feminist Studies* 11, no. 2 (1985): 227–54; Marcy Fink and Robert Arnove, "Issues and Tensions in Nonformal and Popular Education," *International Journal of Educational Development* 11, no. 3 (1991): 221–30. See also Nelly P. Stromquist, *Feminist Organizations and Social Transformation* (Boulder, Colo.: Paradigm Publishers, 2006).

49. Renuka Mishra, "Promoting the Empowerment of Women through Adult Learning" (paper presented at the international seminar-workshop Promoting the Empowerment of Women through Adult Learning, Chiang Mai, Thailand, February 24–28, 1997).

50. Virginia Guzmán, *Las organizaciones de mujeres populares: Tres perspectivas de análisis* (Lima: Centro de la Mujer Peruana Flora Tristan, 1990); see also Fink and Arnove, "Issues and Tensions."

51. Walters, "Democracy."

52. Hill and King, "Women's Education."

53. UNDP, *1995 Human Development Report.*

54. Laura Frade, "Women's Eyes on the World Bank," *Social Watch* 1 (Montevideo: Instituto del Tercer Mundo, 1997): 67–70.

55. Frade, "Women's Eyes."

56. Frade, "Women's Eyes."

57. Paul Bennell with Dominic Furlong, "Has Jomtien Made Any Difference? Trends in Donor Funding for Education and Basic Education since the Late 1980s," *IDS Working Paper no. 51* (Sussex, U.K.: Institute of Development Studies, 1997).

58. Longwe, "Education for Women's Empowerment."

59. Jacqui True and Michael Mintrom, "Transnational Networks and Policy Diffusion: The Case of Gender Mainstreaming," *International Studies Quarterly* 45, no. 1 (2001).

60. Jeffrey Puryear and Jose Joaquin Brunner, "An Agenda for Educational Reform in Latin America and the Caribbean," in *Partners for Progress: Education and the Private Sector in Latin America and the Caribbean*, ed. Jeffrey Puryear (Washington, D.C.: Inter-American Dialogue, 1997), 9–13.

61. Lourdes Beneria and Savitri Bisnath, *Poverty and Gender: An Analysis for Action* (New York: UNDP, 1996).

62. "Borrowed Burden," *Development and Cooperation* 2 (1997): 33.

63. Fernando Reimers and Luis Tiburcio, *Education, ajustement, et reconstruction: Options pour un changement* (Paris: UNESCO, 1993).

64. Colclough, "Education and the Market."

65. See, for example, Michael Apple, "Work, Gender, and Teaching," *Teachers College Record* 84, no. 3 (1983): 611–28; and Henry Giroux, *Border Crossings: Cultural Workers and the Politics of Education* (New York: Routledge, 1992).

66. Bella Abzug, "Women Will Change the Nature of Power," in *Women's Leadership and the Ethics of Development*, ed. Bella Abzug and Devaki Jain, *Gender in Development Monograph Series*, no. 4 (New York: UNDP, 1996).

8

Control of Education: Issues and Tensions in Centralization and Decentralization

Mark Bray

Debates about the appropriate locus of control in education systems are often heated and are usually difficult to resolve. The reasons for this are political as well as technical, for the nature and degree of centralization or decentralization influence not only the scale and shape of education systems but also the access to education by different groups.

Much can be learned from comparative study concerning the advantages and disadvantages of different arrangements. Comparative analysis can also enhance understanding of the reasons why some societies and systems have particular shapes and are moving in certain directions; and for politicians or administrators embarking on reforms, comparative study can demonstrate the need for certain preconditions and support systems.

This chapter commences by presenting some definitions, noting some of the motives for centralization and decentralization, identifying some models of governance, and outlining discussion on ways to measure centralization and decentralization. Then I turn to some specific domains to show variations in administrative systems in different places: school-leaving qualifications, textbooks, and universities. The next two sections are a comment on the implications of different types of arrangements for efficiency and for social inequalities. The penultimate section notes some specific factors that must be taken into account during the design of administrative reforms, and the last section concludes the discussion.

MEANINGS, MOTIVES, MODELS, AND MEASUREMENTS

Meanings

The words *centralization* and *decentralization* can mean different things to different people. I must therefore begin by noting some possible meanings of the terms.

A starting point is to note that centralization and decentralization are processes—they are "-izations"—rather than static situations. This chapter is therefore concerned with a variety of starting points. I discuss centralization in systems that were previously

175

decentralized; but I also discuss further centralization in systems that were already central-ized. Similar points apply to systems in which control was centralized but is then made less centralized, and to systems which were already decentralized but become even more decentralized.

A second observation is that the terms *centralization* and *decentralization* usually refer to deliberate processes initiated at the apex of hierarchies. However, sometimes patterns change by default rather than by deliberate action. Also, power may be removed from the center either with the acquiescence of or in the face of resistance by the center.

Next it is necessary to distinguish between various types of centralization and decen-tralization. The literature on this topic is not entirely consistent, but there is general agreement on some major points.[1] Among them is the distinction between functional and territorial dimensions. *Functional* centralization/decentralization refers to a shift in the distribution of powers between various authorities that operate in parallel. For example:

- In some countries, a single ministry of education is responsible for all aspects of the public system of education. A move to split such a body into a ministry of basic education and a separate ministry of higher education could be called func-tional decentralization.
- In some systems, all public examinations are operated by the ministry of educa-tion. Creation of a separate examinations authority to take over this role could be called functional decentralization, even if that examinations authority remained directly controlled by the government.
- In many countries, schools are operated by voluntary agencies as well as by govern-ments. A loosening of government control on voluntary-agency schools could be called functional decentralization. Conversely, a tightening of control could be a form of functional centralization. Nationalization of voluntary agency schools, to place them under direct government control, would be an even more obvious form of functional centralization.

Territorial centralization/decentralization, by contrast, refers to a redistribution of control among the different geographic tiers of government, such as nation, states/provinces, dis-tricts, and schools. A transfer of power from higher to lower levels would be called territo-rial decentralization. This is a spatial conception of the term.

The category of territorial decentralization includes three major subcategories.

- *Deconcentration* is the process through which a central authority establishes field units or branch offices, staffing them with its own officers. Thus, personnel of the ministry of education may all work in the same central building, or some of them may be posted out to provinces and districts.
- *Delegation* implies a stronger degree of decision-making power at the local level. Nevertheless, powers in a delegated system still basically rest with the central authority, which has chosen to "lend" them to the local one. The powers can be withdrawn without resort to legislation.
- *Devolution* is the most extreme of these three forms of territorial decentralization. Powers are formally held at subnational levels, the officers of which do not need to seek higher-level approval for their actions. The subnational officers may choose

to inform the center of their decisions, but the role of the center is chiefly confined to collection and exchange of information.

Some writers describe privatization as another form of decentralization.[2] Certainly privatization may be a form of decentralization in which state authority over schools is reduced. However, it is not necessarily decentralizing. Some forms of privatization concentrate power in the hands of churches or large private corporations. In these cases, privatization may centralize control, albeit in nongovernmental bodies.

Motives

The motives for centralization/decentralization of the control of education are commonly political but may also be administrative, or a combination of both. Politically motivated reforms aim to strengthen the power of the dominant group (in the case of centralization) or to spread power to other groups (in the case of decentralization). Administratively motivated reforms aim to facilitate the operation of bureaucracies. Often the origin of education reforms lies in wider political or administrative changes rather than in the specifics of the education sector.

Among the most dramatic examples of politically motivated reforms have been territorial decentralization schemes in Ethiopia, the Philippines, Spain, and Sudan. Regionally based separatist movements in these countries were sufficiently powerful to threaten secession if not granted stronger autonomy. The central authorities conceded power in order to persuade the secessionist groups to remain within the national framework.

However, secessionist threats can lead to different reactions. For example, in 1961 the Ghanaian government reacted to separatist stirrings in the Ashanti Confederacy by creating a strongly centralized unitary state. The Indonesian government reacted similarly during the 1960s to secessionist tendencies in the province of Irian Jaya. Alternatively, central governments may respond to secessionist threats with a strategy of "divide and rule." For example, when Nigeria's federal government was threatened by Biafran secession in 1967, it decided to split the country's four regions into twelve states. To respond to further political demands, the number of states in Nigeria was increased to nineteen in 1976, twenty-one in 1987, thirty in 1991, and thirty-six in 1996.

Other examples of political motivations include the desire through reforms to include or exclude certain groups from decision making. A 1972 decentralization reform in Peru attempted to strengthen the social participation of indigenous Indians and other disadvantaged groups,[3] and a 1989 Colombian initiative sought to promote unity by involving dissident groups and by incorporating all major segments of the population.[4] In contrast, decentralization in Mexico reduced the power of the teachers' union by transferring salary negotiations from the central to the state government level.[5]

On a more bureaucratic plane, both centralization and decentralization may be advocated in order to improve efficiency. The main centralizing argument is that operations can be directed more efficiently by a small group of central planners without cumbersome duplication of functions in parallel or subnational bodies. This has been a major factor underlying reduction in the number of municipalities in Denmark, Netherlands, and Sweden, for example.[6] The main decentralizing argument is that specialist parallel bodies are better able to focus on the needs of clients and that territorially decentralized subnational units are closer to the clients and are better able to cater for local diversity. The latter point has been elaborated upon by Donald Winkler, who pointed out that efficiency arguments for territorial decentralization typically focus on the high unit costs of primary and secondary education provided by the central government. One explanation for such costs, he continued,

> is inadequate national government capacity to administer a centralized educational system. Another explanation is the costs of decision making in a system where even the most minor local education matters must be decided by a geographically and culturally distant bureaucracy in the capital city. Yet another explanation is the frequent application by education ministries of national standards for curriculum, construction, teacher quality, etc., thereby preventing cost savings through adjustments of educational inputs to local or regional price differences.[7]

Allied to this set of justifications are others based on cultural differences. Hans Weiler points out that decentralization may be advocated in order to provide greater sensitivity to local variations in educational needs:

> Except in very small or culturally very homogeneous societies, most countries vary considerably across regions, communities, and language groups in terms of cultural and social frameworks of learning. The frames of reference for the study of history, botany, social studies, and other fields vary obviously and significantly between southern and northern Italy, Alabama and California, or Bavaria and Berlin. Differences such as these, in countries such as the Federal Republic of Germany and the United States, historically have sustained the argument for a federal or local structure of educational governance and for varying degrees of cross-regional differentiation, as far as the content of education is concerned.[8]

In contrast, centralization may be advocated on the grounds that intranational diversity in the cultures of learning is excessive and that there is a need for standardization of at least the core elements in curriculum and instruction. This was among the justifications for partial centralization in the United States during the 1930s[9] and more recently has been a motive in England, the government of which introduced a centralizing national curriculum in 1988.[10] In the same vein, in many African countries the curriculum remains centralized since their governments consider the curriculum to be an important tool for nation-building.

Finally, one negative motive for decentralization is a desire by the center to reduce its responsibilities for education because of financial stringency. Central governments which realize that they do not have sufficient resources for adequate provision of services may choose to evade the problem by decentralizing responsibility to lower tiers or to nongovernmental bodies. This has been an underlying consideration of reforms giving subnational bodies greater responsibility for education in Argentina, China, Kyrgyzstan, and several West African countries.[11] It has also been a major motive in various privatization initiatives.[12]

Models

As already implied, the range of models for the governance of education is very wide. Decisions on the choice of models must be made in the context of political ideologies, historical legacies, and such factors as linguistic plurality, geographic size, and ease of communications.

An obvious starting point is with the overall structure of government. Australia, Canada, India, Nigeria, and the United States all have federal systems in which substantial powers are vested in state or provincial governments. The degree of provincial decision making in Canada, for example, is so great that the structure and content of education is substantially different in such provinces as Alberta and Quebec. Most obviously, in the former the education system is mainly conducted in English, whereas in the latter it is mainly conducted in French. Differences are not quite so marked between the different states of the United States, but they are still substantial in that country. These systems therefore appear to be highly decentralized.

Many unitary systems also appear to have high degrees of decentralization. For example, in 1976 Papua New Guinea adopted a quasi-federal system with nineteen provincial governments, each of which had considerable autonomy including in matters of education.[13] The United Kingdom, although not a federal system, has a strong degree of decentralization to its constituent parts—England, Northern Ireland, Wales, and Scotland. The education systems of England and Wales are closely linked, but those of Scotland and Northern Ireland operate separately.[14]

Some confederal systems have even greater degrees of decentralization. Switzerland, for example, has twenty-six cantons, each of which has its own school laws and education system.[15] Cantonal authorities are empowered to decide on the structure of the system, the curriculum, the language of instruction, and the time spent on each subject in each grade. The national government plays hardly any role in the decision-making process.

Linguistic pluralism plays a major role in several of the countries already mentioned, particularly Nigeria, Canada, and Switzerland. Belgium has parallel education systems serving French speakers and Flemish speakers, and linguistic pluralism was among the factors behind the territorial decentralization initiatives in Papua New Guinea. In Vanuatu, by contrast, efforts have been made to coordinate the separate English-medium and French-medium systems under a single ministry—an initiative which is a form of functional centralization.[16]

Concerning geographic size, one might be tempted to look at countries with large areas, such as Canada, India, Russia, and the United States, all of which have federal systems, and assume that all large countries have decentralized administrations. However, the fact that this is not the case is demonstrated by consideration of Indonesia and China, which until recently have had highly centralized administrations. Conversely, it cannot be assumed that small states necessarily have centralized systems. This is certainly true in some small states, such as Malta and Brunei Darussalam; but it is not true of St. Lucia and The Gambia. The latter two countries have district administrations and also permit some decision making at the school level.

The importance of the school as a level of consideration deserves emphasis. Since the mid-1980s, school-based management has received considerable emphasis in a wide range of countries.[17] In New Zealand, for example, a far-reaching initiative was launched in 1988 under the heading Tomorrow's Schools.[18] The government's Department of Education was abolished, and school-level boards of trustees were formed. The boards were required to enter contractual agreements with their communities, and were empowered to manage school budgets and hire and fire teachers. Similar initiatives were launched at about the same time in Australia, Canada, the United States, and the United Kingdom.[19]

A reform in Spain took democratization to the extent of requiring school councils to elect the principals of schools.[20]

Finally, models of administration are influenced by the ease or otherwise of communication. In the Democratic Republic of the Congo, for example, administration is decentralized by default simply because communications are poor. The center does not know what the periphery is doing, and the periphery would be unable to secure regular and detailed instructions from the center even if it wanted to. In other parts of the world, the advent of the fax machine and the Internet has greatly reduced remoteness and has permitted stronger central supervision.

Measurements

The complexities of centralization or decentralization become even more apparent when efforts are made at measurement. Many people suppose that countries can be ranked on a scale, with some having strongly centralized systems at the top and others having strongly decentralized systems at the bottom. However, attempts to create such rankings usually produce findings that are questionable and potentially misleading.

An initial problem arises from the custom of taking the nation-state as the unit for analysis. National boundaries are in most cases arbitrary, and they form countries of greatly differing sizes. Thus, to describe Japan (population 122,600,000) as having a centralized administration would mean something very different from describing Tonga (population 97,000) as having a centralized administration. Likewise, although at one time the government of India devoted much publicity to its decentralized District Primary Education Project,[21] the fact that some of these districts have populations above five million, which is considerably greater than the total populations of many countries, might make some observers feel that the unit of government is still very large.

Enlarging on this point, when the Soviet Union was a single country, the autonomy held by individual republics such as Azerbaijan, Georgia, and Latvia made the administrative system appear decentralized. Now that those republics are independent countries, the administration of their education systems, from the perspective of the nation-state, is commonly described as centralized. Conversely, when Hong Kong was a separate self-governing territory, its administration was widely described as centralized.[22] However, after the 1997 reincorporation of Hong Kong into the People's Republic of China, Hong Kong remained a Special Administrative Region with considerable autonomy which, at least from the perspective of Beijing, seemed a highly decentralized arrangement.[23]

A different difficulty in measurement arises from value judgments on the importance or otherwise of different powers. Thus the power to determine the structure of school systems, or the language of instruction, might be considered very important. In contrast, the power to hire school cleaners might be considered rather less important. This would require weighting within any model for measurement.

A further complexity is that reforms might move systems simultaneously in opposite directions. During the 1980s, the government in England greatly changed the nature of educational decision making.[24] As already noted, one component of reforms was the introduction of a national curriculum, which centralized power in the hands of the national government. Another component, however, was the requirement for all schools to have boards of governors that had considerable powers at the school level over such matters as budgets, recruitment of teachers, and facilities. The coexistence of trends that are both centralizing and decentralizing creates major difficulties for classification.

Also creating major difficulties is the fact that in some systems, the main balance of power is between the national and the school levels, with rather little power at intermediate provincial or district levels. One might ask whether such systems should be described as centralized or decentralized because they could seem to be both at the same time. Jamaica, for example, has elements of strong control in the Ministry of Education, combined with other elements at the school level and a generally weak intermediate regional level.[25] Related to this point is that the extent to which a system of government is centralized or decentralized cannot be prejudged from the existence or absence of subnational institutions. Many constitutions give federal governments powers of veto which act as a considerable constraint on state or provincial governments, and which mean that the systems are not as decentralized as they appear at first sight. Also, the power of federal and quasi-federal governments is commonly strengthened by control of major sources of finance.[26] By contrast, even in countries with no state or provincial governments, national authorities may be willing to decentralize substantial powers to the school level.

Finally, while deconcentration is usually described as a form of decentralization, it can be a mechanism for tightening central control of the periphery instead of for allowing greater local decision making. When central government staff posted to the periphery are permitted to take local decisions to reflect local needs and priorities, then deconcentration may reasonably be described as a form of decentralization. But when staff in the periphery are responsible for tightening implementation of policies determined by the central government, deconcentration is more reasonably described as a form of centralization.

Yet despite all these complexities, and the questions they raise, some observers have persisted with efforts at measurement. One such attempt is presented in table 8.1. The figures led the authors to describe Zimbabwe as the most centralized of the ten countries covered, followed by Senegal and Malaysia. At the other end, the United States was described as the most decentralized, followed by the United Kingdom, India, and Nigeria.

Although these figures shed some light on the topic, they should be viewed with extreme caution. To establish the distributions, the authors counted functions, assigned

Table 8.1 Balance between levels of decision making for education in ten countries

	Central		Regional		District		Local		Total	
	#	%	#	%	#	%	#	%	#	%
France	24	59	4	10	9	22	4	10	41	100
India	16	38	16	38	4	10	6	14	42	100
Malaysia	26	63	4	10	4	10	7	17	41	100
Mexico	24	45	13	25	7	13	9	17	53	100
Namibia	25	57	2	5	6	14	11	25	44	100
Nigeria	21	42	20	40	0	0	9	18	50	100
Senegal	26	76	1	3	0	0	7	21	34	100
UK	16	36	3	7	11	25	14	32	44	100
U.S.	4	6	24	36	22	33	16	24	66	100
Zimbabwe	25	81	0	0	1	3	5	16	31	100

Source: William M. Rideout and Ipek Ural, *Centralised and Decentralised Models of Education: Comparative Studies* (Halfway House, South Africa: Development Bank of Southern Africa, 1993), 108.

each of them a score of one, and calculated percentage distributions at each level. Different total numbers for each country arose because in some cases functions were undertaken at more than one level. The authors made no allowance for the fact that some functions are arguably more important than others. Moreover, "local" may mean something very different in India and in Namibia. As such, the example shows the dangers as well as the benefits of efforts to place countries on a single continuum for comparison.

THEMES AND VARIATIONS

The factors behind different models, and the implications of different arrangements, may be further illustrated with a few examples. Three specific foci of decision making are presented here. They are school-leaving qualifications, school textbooks, and the operation of universities.

Control of School-Leaving Qualifications

Considerable diversity may be found in the control of secondary-school leaving qualifications. Table 8.2 highlights this diversity in the European context. In most countries the qualifications were dependent upon results in examinations, though in some cases they resulted from continuous assessment of various kinds. Among the twenty-six countries shown, the ministry of education set the examinations in seven cases, separate examination boards operated in four countries, and qualifications were determined through school-based assessment in fifteen cases. In two cases, other arrangements existed. Assessment was controlled by a curriculum and examination center in Latvia, and by a university board in Malta.

As with other aspects of administration, the factors underlying different arrangements reflected a combination of historical legacies and deliberate policies. The United Kingdom has a long tradition of independent examination boards, some associated with tertiary institutions such as the Universities of London, Oxford, and Cambridge, but others, such as the Associated Examining Board, operating with a different framework. This has fitted an educational culture that has permitted schools to determine their own curricula and approaches to education. Other countries, such as Poland, Romania, and Russia, have more centralized traditions with examination units under direct government control in the Ministry of Education. Yet other countries, such as Iceland, Sweden, and Turkey, have no formal final examinations. Students in these countries are instead subject to school-based assessment throughout their secondary school careers. Institutions of higher education may set entrance examinations of various kinds, but that process can be a separate activity from certification of completion of secondary education.

Focus on examinations helps to show that the locus of real control over educational processes may be hidden. Examinations are a major determinant of actual (as opposed to officially intended) school curricula, and where there is a divergence between what is taught and what is tested, students generally pay greater heed to the latter. In England, where, up to 1988, schools had considerable freedom to determine their own curricula, the public examinations ensured some commonality, albeit with multiple centers of gravity.

Viewing the matter from a different angle, however, when the government of

Table 8.2   Bodies responsible for secondary-school leaving qualifications in twenty-six European countries

Country	Ministry of Education	Examination board	School	Other
Austria		*		
Belarus			*	
Bulgaria			*	
Croatia			*	
Cyprus			*	
Denmark			*	
Estonia			*	
Finland		*		
Germany			*	
Iceland			*	
Italy	*			
Latvia				*
Liechtenstein		*		
Lithuania	*			
Luxembourg	*			
Malta				*
Netherlands			*	
Norway			*	
Poland	*		*	
Portugal	*			
Romania	*			
Russia	*		*	
Slovakia			*	
Sweden			*	
Turkey			*	
United Kingdom		*		

Source: Sergij Gabrcek, *Guide to Secretary School-Leaving Certificates in European Countries* (Cheltenham, UK: Universities and Colleges Admissions Service, 1996), 103.

Note: Data apply to 1994.

England wished to introduce a common national curriculum with a single center of gravity, it saw the existence of diverse examination boards as an obstacle rather than an asset. A mechanism had to be negotiated through which the various independent boards would come together to operate a new examination called the General Certificate of Secondary Education and operate "under the direction of the Minister" through a School Examinations and Assessment Council.[27]

For a rather different example of the dynamics of change, the Maltese case is interesting. Even for two decades after Malta's achievement of independence from the United Kingdom in 1964, most Maltese secondary school students sat for the school-leaving examinations of the University of Oxford or the University of London. Among the benefits of this arrangement for Maltese candidates were access to professional expertise in examination design and administration, and international recognition of the qualifications.[28] However, a desire to localize processes and increase in-country control led to the creation in 1989 of an examinations board at the University of Malta. This change could not easily be called decentralization since, as noted above, that word usually implies a process of decision making at the top to transfer power to a lower level, and in this case the decision was made at the locality rather than at center. The effect was the same, however, for Maltese leaders asserted their autonomy and took charge of their own affairs. The fact that the Maltese initiative was based at the university rather than the Ministry of Education is also instructive. The decision was no doubt partly influenced by the fact that many examination boards in the United Kingdom were university based; but the arrangement encountered resistance from officers in the Maltese Ministry of Education, many of whom felt that they should have more direct control over this important aspect of the educational process. Ronald Sultana has indicated that ministry officials whom he interviewed "generally presented the University as 'an empire' dominating most aspects of the new examinations, and resented what was ultimately felt to be an impositional rather than a collaborative structure."[29] From the government viewpoint, therefore, the new situation seemed to have some continuity with the old one. Ministry personnel probably felt that they had more influence over the assessment system than before, but not as much as they would have liked.

Control of Textbooks

Commonality and diversity of textbook policies may be illustrated by comparing patterns in four parts of East Asia which themselves have much in common but also display major differences. The following account focuses on mainland China, Taiwan, Hong Kong, and Macao. All four are mainly inhabited by people of Chinese ethnicity, and their dominant cultures have Confucian roots. One has a communist government, whereas the other three have capitalist governments. Hong Kong and Macao share histories of colonization by European powers, but despite this commonality they have significant differences in the nature of educational provision.

The government of China, chiefly in order to spread the official ideology of communism, has held tight control over curricula and textbooks. Shortly after the foundation of the People's Republic in 1949, the government decided that only one basic set of textbooks, published in Beijing by the People's Education Press, would be permitted for use in schools. Since 1985, however, the central government has permitted increasing diversification in the production and contents of textbooks. The change has reflected the introduction of a market economy and increased tolerance of pluralism in both economic and social sectors. The relaxation of control began with Shanghai, which was followed by other economically advanced coastal areas and then by other regions.[30]

Taiwan contrasts with mainland China in many aspects of political ideology. Most obviously, whereas China became a communist society after the 1949 revolution, Taiwan remained a capitalist society which was strongly antagonistic to the political changes on the mainland. Yet despite this ideological difference, the Taiwanese authorities have been just as keen as their counterparts in mainland China to control the content of the curriculum. Textbooks are standardized and published by the National Institute for Compilation and Translation. Official goals for primary education include inculcation of patriotism and anticommunism, and textbooks are seen as a major vehicle for achieving these goals.[31]

Hong Kong, another society with long capitalist traditions, was a British colony between 1842 and 1997. As one might expect, the colonial authorities were also concerned about the content of textbooks, and particularly about the extent to which such books could disseminate ideas that conflicted with those promoted by the government. However, the policies of the Hong Kong colonial government were not as rigid as those in China or Taiwan. The authorities only permitted schools to use books that had been placed on an official list, but the schools could choose books produced by independent publishers and sold on the open market.[32]

Macao provides yet another model. Like Hong Kong, Macao has been a colony of a European power; but the administration within Macao has been much more laissez-faire than that in Hong Kong. Macao became a Portuguese colony in 1557 and remained under Portuguese administration for over four centuries. In 1987, the governments of Portugal and China agreed that sovereignty over Macao would revert to China in 1999, two years after the transition in Hong Kong. That political initiative did cause some changes in the education system, but the schools remained completely free to decide which textbooks on the market they wished to use. The government of Macao did not itself produce any textbooks for schools, and the lack of controls resulted in considerable diversity in what was taught in different institutions.[33]

This set of examples shows on the one hand that similar administrative systems may be found in different political environments, and on the other hand that different administrative systems may be found in similar political environments. The governments of both mainland China and Taiwan exerted tight control over textbooks, even though one was communist and the other, capitalist. Mainland China's move to a market economy was accompanied by some relaxation of control, and at that point contrasted with Taiwan which had always had a market economy but in which schools had never been permitted freedom of choice in textbooks. Hong Kong and Macao were both colonies of European powers, but the colonial government in Hong Kong only permitted schools to use books that had been vetted, whereas the colonial government in Macao adopted a complete laissez-faire policy. The difference in this case partly reflected the colonies' importance to the metropolitan authorities. Hong Kong was a sizeable colony in which the British government was anxious to maintain stability; Macao was a very small colony that had been important to the Portuguese empire up to the nineteenth century but subsequently declined in significance. The resulting neglect was evident in all sectors, including education.

CONTROL OF UNIVERSITIES

Concerning relationships between governments and universities, two main models may be identified.[34] The first is the state-control model, which is exemplified by higher education systems of continental Europe and particularly by that of France. These systems were created by the state and are almost completely financed by it. At least formally, the state controls nearly all aspects of the dynamics of these higher education systems. The national ministries of education regulate the access conditions, curriculum, degree requirements, examinations, and appointment and remuneration of academic staff. One objective of this detailed government regulation is the standardization of national degrees, which in several countries are awarded by the state rather than by the universities themselves.

In this model, the power of the state is combined with strong authority at the level of senior professors. The latter hold considerable collegial power within the faculties and the institutions. This model is therefore characterized by a strong top (the state), a weak middle (the institutional administration), and a strong bottom (the senior professors).

In contrast is the state-supervising model, which was found in the United States and the United Kingdom up to recent times, as well as many former British colonies. In this model, senior professors have strong powers, while the institutional administrators have modest powers and the state also accepts a modest role. Each institution recruits its own students, hires its own staff, and determines its own curricula. Many systems influenced by the U.K. model have buffer bodies modeled on the University Grants Committee, which operated in the United Kingdom from 1919 to 1988. Table 8.3 summarizes information on buffer bodies in eight countries. Although the table shows variation in their roles, the bodies typically liaise between the institutions and the government, seeking on the one hand to respect institutional autonomy but on the other hand to secure accountability in the use of public resources. Also in the state-supervised model are systems such as that in the Philippines, which have large numbers of institutions which are private but which are to some extent regulated by the state.

Guy Neave and Frans van Vught highlight the merits of the state-supervising model in contrast to the state-control model.[35] They suggest that the former is more likely to permit and to stimulate the types of innovation within institutions that may be necessary to cope with rapidly changing circumstances. Because of this advantage, several higher education systems, including those in Chile, Argentina, and China, have moved in the direction of this model. However, Neave and van Vught recognize that the state-control model may also have advantages and that other higher education systems, for example in Kenya, Uganda, and Ghana, have moved in that direction. The reasons for this countermovement include a government desire to control high-level human resources output and to restrict political threats from universities, a legacy of centralized direction derived from theories of a planned economy and pressure on resources that requires a relatively elitist system. In this connection, movements in the United Kingdom are also instructive. In that country, the University Grants Committee (UGC) was replaced in 1988 by a University Funding Council (UFC) through which the government can take much more direct control.[36] This was a form of functional centralization. It permitted the government to require institutions to conform to demands to measure their research output and the quality of their teaching. Just as the United Kingdom led parts of the world with its

Table 8.3   Functions of university buffer funding bodies in eight countries

Country	Name of body	Core budget allocations	Preserving autonomy	Quality control	Enrollment determination
United Kingdom	University Grants Committee	x	x	x	
Nigeria	National Universities Commission	x		x	
Israel	Planning & Budgeting Committee	x		x	
New Zealand	University Grants Committee	x	x	x	
India	University Grants Committee			x	
Pakistan	University Grants Committee			x	x
Kenya	Committee on Higher Education			x	
Sudan	University Grants Committee				x

Source: Adrian Ziderman and Albrecht, *Financing Universities in Developing Countries* (London: Falmer Press, 1995), 117.

original model of the UGC, it has also led parts of the world with its new model of research assessment exercises and quality audits.[37]

IMPLICATIONS FOR EFFICIENCY

As noted above, in various circumstances arguments for efficiency may be used to support both centralization and decentralization. These points deserve elaboration to identify the types of factors involved.

Experiences in Papua New Guinea provide a good starting point for discussion.[38] In 1977, the government of Papua New Guinea launched a major scheme for territorial devolution to nineteen newly created provincial governments. The reform was not without critics. For example, in 1978 the Leader of the Opposition highlighted the costs of an increase in the number of provincial-level politicians:

> Papua New Guinea is to have more than 600 paid politicians. We have three million people. Australia has about 600 paid politicians, and it has 14 million people. It took Australia almost 100 years to develop to the stage where it now has 600 politicians. It has taken us three years. Britain, which has a population of 40 million, has about as many politicians as Papua New Guinea. Does anyone seriously believe that a developing country like Papua New Guinea can afford that much government?[39]

Nevertheless, the reform went ahead. Provincial governments were formed with substantial responsibilities in most sectors including education—and including for each a provincial minister of education.

One result of the reform was a massive expansion of the bureaucracy. This was especially visible at the provincial level but was also evident at the national level, since more staff were required for coordination and training. In one province between 1977 and 1983 primary school enrollments expanded by 15 percent and secondary school enrollments expanded by 7 percent, but the number of senior administrative officers expanded by 208 percent. The smallest province had just twenty-five thousand people (which elsewhere would have been equivalent in size to a small town) but nevertheless acquired a bureaucracy with the same major components as all other provinces. Moreover, at that stage in its development Papua New Guinea was severely short of skilled personnel. Given these circumstances, it is perhaps unsurprising that the whole reform encountered major problems and in the 1990s was reversed.[40]

However, other types of decentralization can increase efficiency. Among them are school-based management projects of the types launched in Australia, England, and New Zealand during the 1980s and early 1990s. Typical features of these projects include competition between institutions for pupils and teachers, and allocation of block grants to the school level so that principals and other administrators can switch between budget categories according to needs and priorities. Most schemes also allow some funds to be retained from one year to the next, which gives an incentive to school-level administrators to save money rather than simply disburse all surpluses towards the end of the financial year. Evaluations have shown increased personal stress at the school level, and critics have asserted that some of the pedagogic goals of school principals have been subsumed by the demands of managerialism.[41] Nevertheless, it generally appears that the reforms have led to much greater consciousness of costs and of ways to improve efficiency.[42]

The government of Jamaica has similarly encouraged school-based management, though it has also attempted to improve efficiency through deconcentration of the Ministry of Education. Between 1990 and 1994, six regional offices were created with the goal of improving the delivery of services and supervising more effectively the educational process. In Jamaica, this was the second attempt at such structural reform, for the ministry operated branch offices from the mid-1970s to 1984. That initiative was abandoned because the regional offices

> did not have the information to make decisions or the authority to do so and were viewed as "post office boxes" for the central ministry. Financial constraints in combination with the concern that the operation of the Regional Offices increased administrative costs without increasing the efficiency of the system resulted in the closure of the Regional Offices.[43]

At least in its early years, the initiative of the 1990s also seemed problematic. Factors included reluctance of headquarters staff to relinquish authority, and general inertia within the system. This experience therefore highlights problems in implementation, and the fact that improved efficiency is certainly not an automatic outcome even of decentralization reforms that specifically aim at that goal.

Also related to issues of efficiency is the need for coordination in decentralized systems. This may consume considerable time as well as labor. With reference to Switzerland, Arnold Gretler suggests that the decentralized structure creates close links between the people and their education systems. However, he adds, "since all important decisions are voted on by the population, the changes in the system of education are normally very slow."[44] The response from advocates of decentralization might be that the changes, although slow, are more likely to be solid because they would be grounded in general acceptance. This viewpoint implies that speed of change is only one indicator of efficiency and that effectiveness of change must be included as another. The example once again indicates the complexity of the subject and of the implications of administrative reform.

Taking another type of centralization/decentralization, it is useful to consider the functional as well as the territorial distribution of responsibilities. As noted above, one type of functional decentralization is the splitting of ministries to perform specialized tasks; and, conversely, combining separate ministries would be a form of functional centralization. The attraction of such splitting lies in the specialization that each body can achieve. However, separate bodies may find that their functions overlap, and that they cannot achieve economies of scale. It was partly for the latter reason that in 1990 the Ministry of Basic Education in Benin was merged with the Ministry of Secondary and Higher Education.[45] Likewise in Vietnam, four ministries were merged in 1987 to become two ministries, which in 1990 were themselves merged to form a single ministry.[46]

Implications for Social Inequalities

In general, decentralization is likely to permit and perhaps encourage social inequalities. Conversely, centralization provides a mechanism for reducing inequalities; but whether that mechanism is actually used depends on goals and willpower at the apex of the system. Commentary here will focus on geographically distributed inequalities and on socioeconomic inequalities within particular populations.

Concerning geographic disparities, discussion can usefully begin with territorial devolution to the provincial or state level. Such devolution permits subnational bodies to determine the nature and direction of development. Some bodies are likely to be more active than others, in which case regional disparities in the quantity and/or quality of education will increase. Further down the spatial hierarchy, the same point would apply to districts and to individual schools. Devolution is not usually just a matter of decision making, it is also a matter of resource allocation. Highly decentralized systems commonly permit subnational bodies to retain most or all of the resources which they generate. Since prosperous communities can afford better quality and/or greater quantities of education, disparities remain or even widen.

To expand on the earlier example, one major part of the devolution package in Papua New Guinea was the provision for provincial governments to retain much larger proportions of locally generated revenue than had previously been permitted. The national government controlled external aid and various other revenues, and it was able through this mechanism to ameliorate some disparities. However, the national government was not able to make full compensation for the structural imbalances created by the devolution framework.[47]

Administrative structures have also created major imbalances in the United States, both within and between states.[48] The U.S. Constitution does not give a direct educational role to the federal government, though increasing federal funds have in fact been allocated to the education of disadvantaged groups. Within states, the problem is that some school districts are able much more easily than others to mobilize resources for education from property taxes and other sources. Taking a historical perspective, table 8.4 shows the changing balance between federal, state, and local financing for elementary and secondary schooling during the twentieth century. Whereas in 1919–1920 the bulk of revenue was raised at the local level, by 1999–2000 both federal and state government revenues were more prominent. This showed the existence of a mechanism to reduce some imbalances, though disparities remained to the extent that in 1999–2000, districts in New Jersey had average per pupil expenditures of U.S.$11,500, compared with just U.S.$5,300 for their counterparts in Utah.

Table 8.4 Revenue sources for public elementary and secondary schools, United States

School year	Federal (%)	State (%)	Local (%)
1919–1920	0.3	16.5	83.2
1929–1930	0.4	16.9	82.7
1939–1940	1.8	30.3	68.0
1949–1950	2.9	39.8	57.3
1959–1960	4.4	39.1	56.5
1969–1970	8.0	39.9	52.1
1979–1980	9.8	46.8	43.4
1989–1990	6.1	47.1	46.8
1999–2000	7.3	49.5	40.9

Source: U.S. Department of Education, *Digest of Educational Statistics* (Washington, D.C.: Author, various years).
Note: The figures for 1999–2000 do not add up to 100 percent because a fourth category had been added, for private sources of revenue (2.3 percent).

Inequalities may also be exacerbated within socioeconomic groups. For example, the literature on community financing of education points out that richer communities are more likely and better able to embark on self-help projects than are poor communities.[49] In Zimbabwe, for example, the policy of decentralization to the community level permitted the advantaged segments to retain their lead. As noted by O. E. Maravanyika:

> Schools in former white areas established Management Agreements with government. These enabled Management Committees to levy parents so that the schools could buy additional school equipment and other teaching resources or recruit additional staff to reduce the government stipulated teacher/pupil ratio which some white parents considered too high for effective teaching, or introduced specialist subjects not covered by government such as music and computing.[50]

The large amounts charged by the management committees of these schools were generally out of the reach of ordinary black parents, and the system therefore perpetuated racial as well as socioeconomic inequalities.

In a very different context, a similar point has been made about New York City. In this case, reforms aimed to decentralize decision making to the community level, with the idea that community boards would be more responsive to the immediate needs of parents and students. However, the politics of many communities proved at least as factionalized as citywide politics; and when factions assumed control, they were at least as exclusionary in their policies and practices toward minorities. As observed by Richard Elmore: "To be an African-American in East Harlem, where community politics is effectively dominated by Puerto Rican Hispanics, is to be an even smaller minority than an African-American would be in the city at large."[51]

He adds:

> To say, then, that creating smaller institutions that are closer to "the people" is as often as not to substitute democratic sentiment for analysis. . . . There is no absolute presumption that "the people" at one level are any wiser, more informed, or better equipped to make decisions than "the people" at any other level; the only presumption is that factional interests will exert different influences at different levels of aggregation.[52]

Taking reforms of the opposite type, there is of course more scope for centralized authorities to oversee situations and to redistribute resources to those in need. This may happen, and it has been among the arguments used to support centralization in countries as different as Malta and China. However, much depends on the intentions of those in power, for of course centralized regimes are not necessarily more sensitive to the needs of disadvantaged groups.

Preconditions and Support Systems for Administrative Reform

The literature on administrative reform pays much greater attention to ways to achieve effective decentralization than to ways to achieve effective centralization. This probably reflects the value judgments of the individuals and organizations producing that literature, though it may also reflect a perception that decentralization is more difficult to achieve than centralization. As the examples in this chapter have pointed out, in some cases centralization is more desirable than decentralization, and it should not be assumed that centralization can be achieved simply by issuing decrees.

Juan Prawda focuses on lessons learned from decentralization efforts in the education sector in Latin America.[53] He presents seven lessons, some of which would presumably also apply to attempts at centralization. Successful decentralization, he suggests, requires the following:

1. Full political commitment from national, regional, provincial, municipal, and local leaders;
2. A model addressing the issue of which educational functions and responsibilities could be more efficiently and effectively delivered at the central level, smaller decentralized government units, and/or the private sector, and explicitly defining the degree of accountability of the different participants;
3. An implementation strategy and timetable;
4. Clear operational manuals and procedures;
5. Continuous training for the skill levels to be performed at the central and decentralized units of government;
6. Relevant performance indicators to be continuously monitored through a management information system by policymakers and senior government officials; and
7. Adequate financial, human, and physical resources to sustain the process.

Turning to reforms of the opposite type, most analysts would consider the most important requirements for centralization to be full commitment from the central leadership, and acquiescence at lower levels. Questions about capacity may be just as relevant to centralization as to decentralization initiatives, since both may collapse if they fail to deliver promised benefits.

Missing from Prawda's list is a public relations campaign to explain the need for reform, which would be equally valuable for centralization and for decentralization reforms. Allied to such a campaign would be the need to secure cooperation from teachers' unions and similar groups.

Also important in all reforms is the time element. The exigencies of political forces sometimes require results before reforms have had time to become fully effective. This is one reason for the swings evident in some countries from centralization to decentralization and back again. Prawda points out that the first accomplishments from decentralization in Mexico and Chile surfaced only five years after the reforms had been launched.[54] However, such a period may be too long for many political regimes. During the 1970s and 1980s, the average stay of a minister of education in Colombia and Argentina was around sixteen months. In Papua New Guinea, the pace of change was even more rapid. In the decade up to 1985, the country witnessed eleven changes in the national minister of education—quite apart from the multiple changes occurring at the provincial level. This instability was also a factor in the policy swing in that country.

CONCLUSION

The political context of reforms is among the points most deserving emphasis. Although centralization and decentralization are often officially justified by technical criteria, political factors are usually the most important.[55] Centralization and decentralization are about matters of control, about the distribution of resources, and, in the education sector, about access to opportunities which can fundamentally influence the quality of life for both individuals and social groups.

For scholars who are more concerned with dispassionate analysis than with manipulation of variables, the first task in any review of centralization or decentralization is to identify precisely what is meant by the terms as used in each case. This chapter has shown that the words *centralization* and *decentralization* can have many different meanings. Not only are the terms vague, they may even have contradictory meanings depending on the circumstances and perspectives of the persons making the judgments. Deconcentration, for example, may seem like a form of decentralization when viewed from the central ministry but may be a mechanism to exert tighter control on the periphery and may thus be seen as a form of centralization from those who are distant from the ministry. Likewise, splitting of a single ministry into two parts may seem like decentralization from the perspective of those who are closely involved but may appear to make little difference to those who are more distant. Although attempts to empower local communities may appear to be laudable attempts at decentralization, the fact that such communities may be dominated by factional elites may leave other groups feeling at least as marginalized as before.

Also important to note are rather sober assessments about the impact of structural reforms on teaching and learning in classrooms. David Tyack's review of debates and shifting patterns of control in the United States led him to conclude that "governance reforms have been mostly disconnected from what students learn."[56] A similar view has been presented by Elmore:

> Whatever the politics of centralization and decentralization is "about" in American education . . . it is not fundamentally or directly about teaching and learning. This disconnection between structural reform and the core technology of schooling means that major reforms can wash over the educational system, consuming large amounts of scarce resources—money; time; the energy of parents, teachers, and administrators; the political capital of elected officials—without having any discernible effect on what students actually learn in school.[57]

Although analysts in other parts of the world would recognize the thrust of these points, it would be an overstatement to suggest that shifts in the locus of control do not affect life in classrooms. Certainly the reforms may not be tied fundamentally or directly to teaching and learning, but many reforms have had marked impact on school curricula and on the access to education by different groups. Indeed it is mainly for this reason that the battles over control of education are so intense.

As was noted at the beginning of this chapter, comparative analysis can certainly highlight the advantages and disadvantages of different models of governance. It can also enhance understanding of the reasons why some societies and systems have particular shapes and are moving in certain directions; and for politicians and administrators embarking on reforms, comparative study can highlight the need for certain preconditions and support systems. However, it is impossible to reach a single recipe that will be appropriate for all countries. It does seem that societies with strongly entrenched democratic values and well-educated populations are more likely than others to demand decentralized systems and to make them work. But even this is a broad generalization which does not hold in all cases. The future, like the past, is likely to bring continued shifts in forms of governance in all parts of the world. Some of these shifts will be centralizing, others will be decentralizing, and yet others will be both centralizing and decentralizing at the same time. This need not be cause for bemusement or despair. Rather, it can be taken as part of the ever-present dynamic of human endeavor.

NOTES

1. See, for example, Christopher Bjork, ed., *Educational Decentralization: Asian Experiences and Conceptual Contributions* (Dordrecht: Springer, 2006); Jon Lauglo, "Forms of Decentralisation and Their Implications for Education," *Comparative Education* 31, no. 1 (1995), 5–29; Jerry M. Silverman, *Public Sector Decentralization: Economic Policy and Sector Investment Programs*, Technical Paper no. 188 (Washington, D.C.: World Bank, 1992); B. C. Smith, *Decentralization: The Territorial Dimension of the State* (London: George Allen and Unwin, 1985).

2. See, for example, William K. Cummings and Abby Riddell, "Alternative Policies for the Finance, Control, and Delivery of Basic Education," *International Journal of Educational Research* 21, no. 8 (1994); Ka-ho Mok, "Centralization and Decentralization: Changing Governance in Education," in *Centralization and Decentralization: Educational Reforms and Changing Governance in Chinese Societies*, ed. Ka-ho Mok (Hong Kong: Comparative Education Research Centre, The University of Hong Kong, and Dordrecht: Kluwer Academic Publishers, 2003), 8.

3. Nelly Stromquist, "Decentralizing Educational Decision-Making in Peru: Intentions and Realities," *International Journal of Educational Development* 6, no. 1 (1986), 47–60; Erwin H. Epstein, "Peasant Consciousness under Peruvian Military Rule," in *Comparative Perspectives on the Role of Education in Democratization. Part II: Socialization, Identity, and the Politics of Control*, ed. Erwin H. Epstein and Noel F. McGinn (Frankfurt am Main: Peter Lang, 2000).

4. E. Mark Hanson, "Democratization and Decentralization in Colombian Education," in *Comparative Perspectives on the Role of Education in Democratization. Part I: Transitional States and States of Transition*, ed. Noel F. McGinn and Erwin H. Epstein (Frankfurt am Main: Peter Lang, 1999).

5. Noel McGinn and Susan Street, "Educational Decentralization: Weak State or Strong State?" in *Comparative Perspectives on the Role of Education. Part I*, ed. McGinn and Epstein (Frankfurt am Main: Peter Lang, 1999); Carlos Ornelas, "The Politics of Privatisation, Decentralisation and Education Reform in Mexico," *International Review of Education* 50, nos. 3–4 (2004), 397–418.

6. Smith, *Decentralization*, 69.

7. Donald R. Winkler, *Decentralization in Education: An Economic Perspective*, Working Paper no. 143 (Washington, D.C.: World Bank, 1989), 2.

8. Hans N. Weiler, "Control versus Legitimation: The Politics of Ambivalence," in *Decentralization and School Improvement: Can We Fulfill the Promise?* ed. Jane Hannaway and Martin Carnoy (San Francisco: Jossey-Bass, 1993), 65.

9. David Tyack, "School Governance in the United States: Historical Puzzles and Anomalies," in *Decentralization and School Improvement*, ed. Hannaway and Carnoy (San Francisco: Jossey-Bass, 1993), 3.

10. Nick Adnett and Peter Davies, "Schooling Reforms in England: From Quasi-markets to Co-opetition?" *Journal of Education Policy* 18, no. 4 (2003), 393–406.

11. UNESCO, *Decentralization in Education: National Policies and Practices* (Paris: UNESCO, 2005), 17–20; Cheng Kai-Ming, "The Changing Legitimacy in a Decentralising System: The State and Education Development in China," *International Journal of Educational Devel-*

opment 14, no. 3 (1994), 265–69; Igor Kitaev, "Challenges of Realities: An Overview of Trends and Developments in Educational Finance in Central Asia and Mongolia," in *Educational Finance in Central Asia and Mongolia*, ed. Igor Kitaev (Paris: UNESCO International Institute for Educational Planning, 1996), 74; Candy Lugaz and Anton de Grauwe, *Ecole et décentralisation: Résultats d'une recherche en Afrique de l'Ouest* (Paris: UNESCO International Institute for Educational Planning, 2006).

12. Mark Bray, "Privatization of Secondary Education: Issues and Policy Implications," in *Education for the Twenty-first Century: Issues and Prospects* (Paris: UNESCO, 1998); Clive R. Belfield and Henry M. Levin, *Educational Privatization: Causes, Consequences and Planning Implications* (Paris: UNESCO International Institute for Educational Planning, 2002).

13. Mark Bray, *Educational Planning in a Decentralised System: The Papua New Guinean Experience* (Waigani: University of Papua New Guinea Press; Sydney: Sydney University Press, 1984); Charles Hawksley, "Papua New Guinea at Thirty: Late Decolonisation and the Political Economy of Nation-building," *Third World Quarterly* 27, no. 1 (2006), 161–73.

14. David Phillips, ed., *The Education Systems of the United Kingdom* (Oxford: Symposium Books, 2000).

15. G. M. Hega, "Regional Identity, Language and Education Policy in Switzerland," *Compare: A Journal of Comparative Education* 31, no. 2 (2001), 205–23.

16. Colin E. Hindson, "Educational Planning in Vanuatu—An Alternative Analysis," *Comparative Education* 31, no. 3 (1995), 327–37.

17. Ibtisam Abu-Duhou, *School-Based Management* (Paris: UNESCO International Institute for Educational Planning, 1999); Anton de Grauwe, "Improving the Quality of Education through School-based Management: Learning from International Experiences," *International Review of Education* 51, no. 4 (2005), 269–87.

18. Government of New Zealand, *Tomorrow's Schools: The Reform of Education Administration in New Zealand* (Wellington: Government Printer, 1988).

19. Brian Caldwell, "Decentralisation and the Self-Managing School," in *International Handbook of Educational Research in the Asia-Pacific Region*, eds. John P. Keeves and Ryo Watanabe (Dordrecht: Kluwer Academic Publishers, 2003); B. Lingard, J. Knight, and P. Porter, eds., *Schooling Reform in Hard Times* (London: Falmer, 1993).

20. E. Mark Hanson and Carolyn Ulrich, "Democracy, Decentralization, and School-Based Management in Spain," *La educación: Revista Interamericana de desarrollo educativo* 38, no. 2 (1994), 324. See also Julián Luengo, Diego Sevilla, and Monica Torres, "From Centralism to Decentralization: The Recent Transformation of the Spanish Education System," *European Education* 37, no. 1 (2005), 46–61.

21. N. V. Varghese, "Decentralisation of Educational Planning in India," *International Journal of Educational Development* 16, no. 4 (1996), 355–65; M. V. Mukundan and Mark Bray, "The Decentralisation of Education in Kerala State, India: Rhetoric and Reality," *International Review of Education* 50, nos. 3–4 (2004): 223–43.

22. See, for example, Paul Morris, "Identifying the Strategies of Curriculum Development within a Highly Centralized Education System," *International Journal of Educational Development* 6, no. 3 (1986), 171–82; Paul Morris, *The Hong Kong School Curriculum: Development, Issues, and Policies* (Hong Kong: Hong Kong University Press, 1996), 91–95.

23. See Mark Bray and Ramsey Koo, eds., *Education and Society in Hong Kong and Macao: Comparative Perspectives on Continuity and Change* (Hong Kong: Comparative Education Research Centre, The University of Hong Kong, 2004; and Dordrecht: Springer, 2005).

24. David Turner, "Privatisation, Decentralisation and Education in the United Kingdom: The Role of the State," *International Review of Education* 50, nos. 3–4 (2004), 347–57.

25. Lorraine Blank, *Education Decentralization in Jamaica* (Washington, D.C.: World Bank, 1994).

26. Keith Hinchliffe, *Federal Finance, Fiscal Imbalance, and Educational Inequality*, Report no.

EDT 72 (Washington, D.C.: World Bank, 1987); Donald R. Winkler, "Fiscal Decentralization and Accountability in Education: Experiences in Four Countries," in *Decentralization and School Improvement*, ed. Hannaway and Carnoy (San Francisco: Jossey-Bass, 1993).

27. Max A. Eckstein and Harold J. Noah, *Secondary School Examinations: International Perspectives on Policy and Practice* (New Haven: Yale University Press, 1993), 82.

28. Ronald Sultana, "Malta," in *Examination Systems in Small States: Comparative Perspectives on Models and Operations*, ed. Mark Bray and Lucy Steward (London: Commonwealth Secretariat, 1998).

29. Sultana, "Malta," 133.

30. Keith M. Lewin, Xu Hui, Angela W. Little, and Zheng Jiwei, *Educational Innovation in China: Tracing the Impact of the 1985 Reforms* (Harlow, U.K.: Longman, 1994), 147–62; Zhang Xiangyang, "New Curriculum Reform and Basic Education Experiment," in *China's Education Bluebook*, ed. Yang Dongping (Beijing: Higher Education Press, 2004).

31. Yi-Rong Young, "Taiwan," in *Education and Development in East Asia*, ed. Paul Morris and Anthony Sweeting (New York: Garland, 1995), 120; Wing-Wah Law, "Translating Globalization and Democratization into Local Policy: Educational Reform in Hong Kong and Taiwan," *International Review of Education* 50, nos. 5–6 (2004), 497–524.

32. J. Y. C. Lo, "Curriculum Reform," in *Education and Society in Hong Kong and Macao: Comparative Perspectives on Continuity and Change*, ed. Mark Bray and Ramsey Koo (Hong Kong: Comparative Education Research Centre, The University of Hong Kong, 2004; and Dordrecht: Springer, 2005).

33. Mark Bray and Kwok-chun Tang, "Building and Diversifying Education Systems: Evolving Patterns and Contrasting Trends in Hong Kong and Macau," in *Educational Decentralization: Asian Experiences and Conceptual Contributions*, ed. Christopher Bjork (Dordrecht: Springer, 2006).

34. Guy Neave and Frans van Vught, "Government and Higher Education in Developing Nations: A Conceptual Framework," in *Government and Higher Education Relationships across Three Continents: The Winds of Change*, ed. Guy Neave and Frans van Vught (Oxford: Pergamon Press, 1994), 9–11. See also Burton R. Clark, *The Higher Education System: Academic Organization in Cross-national Perspectives* (Berkeley: University of California Press, 1983).

35. Guy Neave and Frans van Vught, conclusion to *Government and Higher Education Relationships*, ed. Neave and van Vught (Oxford: Pergamon Press, 1994), 309.

36. Geoffrey Walford, "The Changing Relationship between Government and Higher Education in Britain," in *Prometheus Bound: The Changing Relationship between Government and Higher Education in Western Europe*, ed. Guy Neave and Frans van Vught (Oxford: Pergamon Press, 1991).

37. See, for example, Joshua Ka-ho Mok and Hiu-hong Lee, "Reflection on Quality Assurance in Hong Kong's Higher Education," in *Globalization in Education: The Quest for Quality Education in Hong Kong*, ed. Joshua Ka-ho Mok and David Kin-keung Chan (Hong Kong: Hong Kong University Press, 2002), 223.

38. Bray, *Educational Planning in a Decentralised System*, 99–114.

39. Iambakey Okuk, "Decentralisation: A Critique and an Alternative," in *Decentralisation: The Papua New Guinean Experience*, ed. R. Premdas and S. Pokawin (Waigani: University of Papua New Guinea, 1978), 21.

40. Constitutional Commission, Papua New Guinea, *NEC [National Executive Council] Endorse Changes to Provincial Governments System* (Waigani: Constitutional Commission, 1994).

41. See, for example, Neil Dempster, "Guilty or Not: The Impact and Effects of Site-based Management on Schools," *Journal of Educational Administration* 38, no. 1 (2000): 47–65; T. Fitzgerald, H. Youngs, and P. Grootenboer, "Bureaucratic Control or Professional Autonomy? Performance Management in New Zealand Schools," *School Leadership and Management* 23, no. 1 (2003): 91–105.

42. Kenneth N. Ross and Rosalind Levacic, eds., *Needs-Based Resource Allocation in Education via Formula Funding of Schools* (Paris: UNESCO International Institute for Educational Planning, 1999).

43. Blank, "Education Decentralisation," 13.

44. A. Gretler, "Switzerland," in *International Encyclopedia of National Systems of Education*, ed. T. Neville Postlethwaite (Oxford: Pergamon Press, 1995), 952.

45. R. Sack, "Benin," in *International Encyclopedia of National Systems of Education*, ed. T. Neville Postlethwaite (Oxford: Pergamon Press, 1995), 101.

46. D. C. Bernard and Le Thac Can, "Vietnam," in *International Encyclopedia of National Systems of Education*, ed. T. Neville Postlethwaite (Oxford: Pergamon Press, 1995), 1063.

47. Bray, *Educational Planning in a Decentralised System*, 72–87; Y. P. Ghai and A. J. Regan, *The Law, Politics, and Administration of Decentralisation in Papua New Guinea*, Monograph no. 30 (Waigani: National Research Institute, 1992), 233–83.

48. William T. Hartman, "District Spending Disparities Revisited," *Journal of Education Finance* 20, no. 1 (1994): 88–106; Linda Hertert, Carolyn Busch, and Allan Odden, "School Financing Inequities among the States: The Problem from a National Perspective," *Journal of Education Finance* 19, no. 3 (1994), 231–55.

49. Mark Bray, *Decentralization of Education: Community Financing* (Washington, D.C.: World Bank, 1996); Mark Bray, "Community Initiatives in Education: Goals, Dimensions and Linkages with Governments," *Compare: A Journal of Comparative Education* 33, no. 1 (2003), 31–45.

50. O. E. Maravanyika, "Community Financing Strategies and Resources within the Context of Educational Democratization" (paper presented at the conference on Partnerships in Education and Development: Tensions between Economics and Culture, University of London Institute of Education, London, 1995), 12.

51. Richard F. Elmore, "School Decentralization: Who Gains? Who Loses?" in *Decentralization and School Improvement: Can We Fulfill the Promise?* ed. Jane Hannaway and Martin Carnoy (San Francisco: Jossey-Bass, 1993), 45.

52. Elmore, "School Decentralization," 46.

53. Juan Prawda, "Educational Decentralization in Latin America: Lessons Learned," *International Journal of Educational Development* 13, no. 3 (1993), 262.

54. Prawda, "Educational Decentralization," 262.

55. Ernesto Schiefelbein, "The Politics of Decentralisation in Latin America," *International Review of Education* 50, nos. 3–4 (2004): 359–78; Susara J. Berkhout, "The Decentralisation Debate: Thinking about Power," *International Review of Education* 51, no. 4 (2005), 313–27.

56. Tyack, "School Governance," 1.

57. Elmore, "School Decentralization," 35.

9

Beyond Schooling: The Role of Adult and Community Education in Postcolonial Change

Anne Hickling-Hudson

This chapter considers experiments in adult education in order to explore its role in national development, particularly in postcolonial societies that were until relatively recently part of the former European empires, attaining their independence only with the ending of World War II. Using a case study approach, I discuss lessons that postcolonial societies can learn from comparing the Caribbean experience of two approaches to adult basic and popular education. The main question is that of the potential—or lack thereof—of adult education to contribute to sociopolitical change, not in the sense of providing catch-up schooling on the cheap but in the sense of helping participants play a political role in challenging the structures of injustice, inefficiency, and dysfunctionality that are still entrenched in most societies. The case of Grenada, a microstate of about ninety thousand people, helps to explore this because of the comparative analysis made possible by its socialist-oriented revolution (1979–1983), the overthrow of this process of change, and the return to a traditional path of market-led development between 1984 and the present.[1] The discussion in this chapter compares two models of adult education: one designed within the context of postcolonial socialist orientation, and the other tending to characterize postcolonial capitalism. I argue that in spite of some strengths, both models have flaws and that we need to go beyond them to meet today's imperatives.

In comparing the two models of adult education, I put forward a theoretical framework for comparison. First, I use a postcolonial perspective to explain the context of the case. Next, I combine three concepts of *literacies* into a theory of literacies that is powerful for analyzing education in class-stratified societies. I then apply this theoretical frame to understanding the case study, an approach which has significance for case study analysis of education in any society.

THE POSTCOLONIAL CONTEXT

A postcolonial perspective starts by analyzing context, since this influences the cases being investigated. It pays particular attention to understanding the ideological power of the colonial historical context, how this power continues to influence material conditions across the globe, and how it is challenged. It explores the extent to which the colonial is embedded in the postcolonial, in economies, societies, institutions and ideologies, and analyzes contradictions and ambiguities in the process of change.[2] Grenada is an example of a developing society caught in the contradictions of the postcolonial condition: on the one hand shaped by the poverty, underdevelopment, dependence on the North, and class stratification inherited from colonialism, and on the other struggling to challenge these distortions and move to more equitable and viable ways of living. Many of the social institutions of the Caribbean, including education, reflect and reproduce the region's economic underdevelopment.[3] Yet the beliefs of modernism, which characterized colonialism, are still entrenched—faith in Western "reason," the Western metanarrative, or all-encompassing story, that "progress" is brought about by the adoption of a consumerist economic model in spite of its problematic record in labor relations and environmental destruction. Postcolonial ideas are challenging these modernist assumptions and are analyzing and modifying the colonial-derived institutions, but at this point only partially, and often ineffectively. To the extent that education, and particularly adult education, falls into the category of an inappropriately modified institution, it is all the more urgent to recognize the limits and weaknesses of reform in order to move forward.

Grenada's revolution, although brought to an end by fratricidal conflict that paved the way for invasion and overthrow by the United States in October 1983, left a social legacy of deep significance. The path of socialist transition tried there was an example of an alternative development model that made a start, and looked likely to succeed, in restructuring and revitalizing the stagnant economy, establishing better social services in health and housing, implementing legislation that sought new rights for disadvantaged groups, especially women and workers' unions, massively expanding education for adults, and forging communities and groups into alliances for improving community life and articulating a more culturally confident national vision. However, the weaknesses of the party structure, with its highly restricted membership and inadequate structures of public accountability, proved a poor foundation for supporting such changes and ultimately contributed to the collapse of the revolution.[4] After this experiment, the society returned to the regional model of dependent capitalism, which is aggressively advocated and endorsed by the United States and other governments of the North for developing countries. This model, while expanding global business opportunities for impoverished economies, at the same time opens these economies even further to "free" trade and foreign capital seeking cheap and minimally protected labor, maintains traditional export agriculture and tourism, and cuts back public sector employment and state services, including education. So far it has widened the gap between already impoverished majorities and wealthy minorities.[5]

Like most Caribbean people at the current juncture, Grenadians vote for the various parties that sustain the neoliberal model in a context in which there appears to be no other viable option but globalizing capitalism. This swing back to tradition is inevitable, given the disastrous circumstances in which the revolution collapsed as well as the general failure of socialist revolutionary leadership globally to have established a consistently participatory and viable change process or economic model. However, in Grenada, in spite of the overthrow of the revolution, the reversal of most of its programs, and the swing to conservative capitalism, the memory of its social achievements has not been erased, and this kind of memory may also be important in informing future political development in other impoverished countries.[6] Adult basic and popular education is an important element of this social memory, seen as a particularly creative achievement of the revolution. The next sections discuss a theory of literacies, the revolution's experiments in adult basic and popular education, and the strengths and limitations of these experiments compared to those in the neoliberal model.

LITERACY, LITERACIES, AND THE ANALYSIS OF EDUCATIONAL CHANGE

A theory of literacy and literacies embedded in a sociopolitical framework is necessary for analyzing issues in the practice and improvement of adult education. This section briefly outlines a literacy theory that facilitates comparison of the conservative, system-maintenance role of adult education with the role that it would play were it to make a significant difference in contributing to change in the society. The term *adult education* is used in this chapter as a comprehensive reference to compensatory or second-chance schooling and vocational training (basic education), and community education organized in voluntary structures accessible to all citizens (popular education). The term *nonformal* is not used, since not all components of adult education are nonformal in the sense of being informally structured, or outside of the formal education sector. A politically aware theory of literacies enables the analyst to explore questions that are often neglected in reports and analyses of adult education which have a technicist focus on narrowly interpreted notions of efficiency and effectiveness. Do adult basic and popular education structures reflect and reinforce the deep-seated inequities in decolonizing societies? Or do they challenge inequity with a view to establishing greater democracy? Or perhaps some combination of these? Why is it so difficult to achieve democratic change in and through adult education? How might such change be pushed forward?

Scholars of literacy see it not as a unitary skill of reading and writing but as a set of discourses and competencies applied to tasks in a given culture. They demonstrate that people are initiated into these discourses in different ways according to their socioeconomic and cultural status and that literacies are practiced along a continuum that ranges from basic to critical and powerful.[7] It is inadequate to assume that literacy is, by its very nature, empowering. As Colin Lankshear argues, for claims of empowerment to be clear they should spell out at least four variables: the subject of empowerment (person or group), the power structures in relation to which, or in opposition to which, that subject is being empowered, the processes through which empowerment occurs, and the sorts of outcomes that can or do result from being thus empowered. The outcomes of acquiring literacy competencies are not necessarily empowering—people can acquire disempowering or subordinate literacies rather than powerful or dominant ones.[8]

The model put forward by Rob McCormack is useful in conceptualizing literacy as comprising at least four domains, each of which embodies a type of knowledge and a set of competencies.[9] The domain of epistemic literacy refers to the uses of written text associated with formal knowledge conceptualized along the lines of traditional academic disciplines. Technical literacy is interpreted as procedural knowledge in areas of practical action. A high degree of technical literacy in the modern workplace would demand competence in technology-based forms of creating, storing, and conveying information, although in developing societies, technical and mechanical skills are still as economically important as the skills of information technology. Humanist literacy refers to the ability to construct narratives that enable individuals to conceptualize, explain, and draw strength from their cultural, social, and gender identities. Public literacy is seen as the ability to participate in the public sphere, understanding and being able to contribute to opinion, debate, political judgment, and the shaping of collective identity.

These separately developed concepts—literacy domains, the literacy continuum from basic to powerful, and dominant/subordinate literacies—become more useful when they are combined. My argument is that when, in combination, they are applied to social analysis, it becomes much clearer that in socially stratified education systems such as those in the Caribbean and other postcolonial societies across the globe, literacy domains are inculcated into citizens along lines of social class/status. Through schooling, people are placed on a certain track or channel in the educational hierarchy. Some are initiated by their education and upbringing into the content and techniques of dominant literacy in each domain, which is then used to justify their continuance in the elite educational channel (lined by the best schools and colleges) and their socioeconomic dominance and political power. Others are denied this initiation. Instead, they are shunted into the less adequate, often grossly under-resourced and neglected educational channels that provide subordinate literacies, which are then penalized as being of inferior worth and status in the society.[10] The "literacies" of these economically poorer people may be functional for survival in the disadvantaged layers of society,[11] but do not gain them any systematic access to the corridors of power or the levers of political change. This stratified model of literacies exists in any class-divided society, but the divisions are deepest, and the barriers to mobility highest, in postcolonial societies whose recent colonial history left them with maldeveloped and distorted economies subordinated in the world capitalist system. Across the Caribbean region, although functional literacy is widespread, it is at a minimal and subordinate level for the majority (with the possible exception of Cuba). Adult education, with its catch-up schooling to a primary level and its vocational training for subsistence jobs, is too underdeveloped to provide adequate opportunity for adults either to gain the education necessary for well-paid employment and social mobility, or to gain the political skills necessary to put consistent pressure for democratic change on the system. Instead, it entrenches them in their position in the lowest levels of the socioeconomic pyramid. Thus the social role of adult education is, arguably, largely a system-maintenance one.[12]

When a political process is serious about putting in place change with equity, it has to learn how to change the stratified nature of these literacies. In postcolonial experience it tends to have been socialist-oriented regimes that have taken this task seriously, since it has been in their interest to provide conditions, including more and better education, that will encourage people to support and defend revolutionary change.[13] The option of socialism in its twentieth-century form has been largely superseded, but seeking radical change remains vital for people marginalized by social injustice. Change that challenges inequity must include acquiring literacies that are powerful enough to enable them to critique negative social patterns and help to change them. From the perspective of striving for social justice, education should be contributing toward improving the entire society's material conditions by helping people to establish viable self and group employment economic structure projects and to demand from the state a commitment to development policies that are fair, sustainable, and accountable. It should be changing the contextual pattern of stratified channels of education and occupation so as to help reduce the barriers that sustain an obscene level of inequality between social classes, strata, and gender groups. Politically, education should prepare people to assess the quality and performance of their political systems, to analyze international patterns of injustice and trends for change, to hold politicians accountable, to discuss and experiment with problem-solving, both nationally and in alliance with international movements, to run for local and national political office on the basis of informed and creative platforms. To consider the potential of adult and community education for playing such roles, experiments need to be examined for their strengths and limitations, and new ones designed on this basis. The focus of this analysis is not on how many adult education programs there are or how many adult students pass the tests they offer. It is on the social role of these programs, and therefore needs the tools of literacy theory within the postcolonial political economy framework suggested above.

ADULT BASIC EDUCATION: STRUCTURAL AND CURRICULUM ISSUES

Educators in the Grenadian revolution designed a completely new structure to provide adult basic education for impoverished people, mostly subsistence farmers and seasonal agricultural laborers. The new structure became known as the Center for Popular Education (CPE) and initially attracted four thousand learners to enroll—about 24 percent of the approximately seventeen thousand adults assessed as ranging from nonliterate to minimally literate. Many postcolonial societies, including several Caribbean ones, have designed and implemented structures and programs of compensatory and vocational adult education, but there were unusual features in how Grenada's CPE tackled the problems of articulation of levels, access, and program design. First, a new and completely government-funded program was created, with one educational level leading to another (literacy, primary, secondary, postsecondary, and tertiary). Second, the program was intended to be equivalent to but not the same as schooling. It had a specially designed curriculum geared to workplace needs and adult interests and maturity. Third, each level from primary onward included compulsory vocational education and certification that prepared adults for jobs. Fourth, successful completion of the secondary level of the program could lead into scholarships for vocational or university education either at home, where the tertiary education level was being expanded, or abroad, most likely in Cuba, which was assisting the Grenadian government through tertiary education scholarships. And fifth, the political ethos of the program, illustrated in its newly designed textbooks, reflected the government's desire to contribute to the confident and creative reconceptualization of cultural and national identity. The impetus of the revolution led to a high degree of community participation by adult education students in organizing CPE programs and extracurricular activities in their neighborhoods.[14] Each of these features promoted epistemic, technical, and to a certain extent, humanist literacies.

This new adult education model disappeared with the demise of the CPE and the discarding of its textbooks after the collapse of the revolution and the U.S. invasion. Adult education was then taken over by a department within the newly amalgamated Grenada National College, and it was redesigned along the lines of the old model common to the rest of the anglophone Caribbean. The focus shifted to the preparation of fee-paying adults for retaking the annual secondary-school-leaving exams set by the

Caribbean Examinations Council or the British General Certificate of Education. In 1992–1993, there were about eight hundred students in these programs, mostly people who had attended high school but failed or dropped out of their final exams. Since then, these numbers have continued to increase. Relatively minor attention is given to the most disadvantaged adults, those who seek literacy and the primary level of education—the people who had received the most attention during the revolution. Adult literacy is still government-funded, but now as a minimal beginners' program involving fewer than a hundred learners, and with no provision of specially designed literacy materials. Adult primary education is no longer conceptualized as a program specially designed for maturity and workplace needs, but is the same as the "senior primary" (all age) program for adolescents who were denied entry to secondary schools. The senior primary exam is taken by up to a hundred adults each year, which is likely to be far less than the number needing that level of education.[15] The features of this model, then, include a drastic reduction of government funding, a promotion of "user pays" in both government and nongovernment programs, the slotting in of adults to the school curriculum and selective examinations as soon as they become sufficiently literate, and a reduction of vocational training. The model provides for improving schooled epistemic literacy for adults who already have basic schooling, but is likely to reduce opportunities for developing technical, humanist, and public literacies, and neglects the provision of a systematic, specifically designed education for nonliterate adults—those who are least able to pay.

The CPE, for all its innovative programs and its enrollment of more than four thousand adult learners, had serious weaknesses that should be examined if an effort is to be made to understand the lessons of the model in order to develop a more appropriate one in the future. There was a dropout rate of about two-thirds, a common feature of adult education programs throughout the world.[16] This was partly because the CPE structure was larger and more complex than available government resources could handle efficiently, which puts immense strain on both volunteer teachers and economically impoverished learners. It may be that the revolutionary government should have considered making the CPE a statutory body with the independence to invite philanthropic assistance from nongovernmental organizations (NGOs) and other bodies, and to seek funding from more countries than Cuba (which had helped with the production of materials). The complete dependence of the CPE on the revolutionary state made it vulnerable to being erased with a change of government.

The CPE's failure to have more than average success might also have something to do with another, more qualitative factor—the new adult education structure did not challenge many of the entrenched, elitist assumptions of the colonial model of education because it did not even recognize them. Stratification is so entrenched that often even the most radical of educators do not know exactly how to change things. After all, they were socialized within the old, constrained metanarratives of Western education. Among these are traditions of prescriptive rather than critical texts, didactic pedagogy based mainly on written text, and the necessity of "schooled literacy" in the sequential stages similar to those of the formal education system. This was as characteristic of the CPE as it was of the adult continuing education programs in Grenada after it. The CPE was like pouring new wine into old bottles. New were the elements of radical content and participatory structures; old was the continuation of the restrictive educational philosophy particularly unjust for the majorities brought up in a folk tradition rather than a middle-class one. The philosophy assumes the necessity of institutionalized education peddling the kind of formalist literacy offered to school students. The approach is didactic rather than interactive, ignores or demotes vernacular languages, and tends to promote politically prescriptive content, whether on the left or the right. It may be that this explains the low attractiveness, relative to need, and high dropout rates common in adult education programs. Even if adults gain a degree of epistemic and technical/vocational literacy through them, it is not the dominant literacy that enables them to surmount the barriers to social, political, and economic mobility, far less the powerful literacy that can empower them to make structural changes that would remove these barriers. The approach of failing to respect or build on vernacular literacies stultifies the politically radicalizing and humanist potential of new content and structures.

It is for this reason that I argue that adult basic education providing individual catch-up schooling and job training has limited potential to carry out some of the radicalizing aims of change that challenges inequity as outlined above. Popular education based on the development of political and cultural capacities in local communities has greater potential for carrying out such aims. This is not to say that adult basic education is not necessary; it is to say that it needs to be redesigned within the nourishing context of a popular education structure. In the next section I lay the basis for discussing this by considering the strengths and limits of popular education as it was experienced in Grenada.

POPULAR EDUCATION IN GRENADA: STRENGTHS AND LIMITATIONS

To what extent can the experiences of popular education contribute to transforming the power relations within civil society? Can participants take the opportunities for growth offered to them by leaders who are usually middle class and "run with them" in creative ways that are not necessarily directed? If they could learn this role, and help others to learn it, it would indeed have the potential to become part of a cultural revolution or the kind of "cultural action for freedom" that Paulo Freire describes.[17] Light is thrown on these questions by the attempt during the Grenadian revolution to mobilize a level of popular involvement in community education and social reform that had never been experienced in Grenada, indeed, in the Caribbean, before. This popular education movement was led by the New Jewel Movement (NJM), the revolutionary political party from which most of the members of the government were drawn. The goal was to create a tradition of educated activism in community-based and workplace-based groups outside of educational structures that promoted formal and vocational knowledge, that is, outside of the CPE and vocational training programs of a quasi-school nature. Since the new groups involved a broad cross-section of the population and combined political and educational aims, I shall refer to them as community associations and to their educational aspect as the popular education process. There were two categories of community association representing two types of activity. First, communities of citizens gathered to discuss and contribute ideas to local and national goals and policies of transformation. In this category were nationwide peoples' councils (comprising associations called Workers' Parish Councils and Zonal Councils) and the people's budget process in which local communities all over the country met politicians and technocrats to help plan the national budget. Second, interest groups worked for improvements in their particular group, on a national rather than a local scale. These were called mass organizations and were grouped around women, youth, farmers, and trade union members.[18]

The political role of the community associations was inextricably linked to their role in developing public and humanist literacy. They were the chief means of giving Grenadians a new voice in national affairs traditionally handled by the government. Through the associations, the broad population got increasingly pulled into an ongoing cultural revolution in an experiential way that involved affect as well as intellect.

"HUMANIST" LITERACY AND CULTURAL IDENTITY

The role of the community associations in developing humanist literacy was to contribute to challenging traditional images related to social class roles, gender, and national identity and reshaping them in new ways. For example, the preconceptions about stratified economic roles started to be reshaped. Through the activities of the community associations, all became "workers." Middle-class professionals were seen as intellectual workers, and they frequently met and interacted with manual workers in the same discussion groups. Political and social roles started to be reshaped in that people from different social class groupings had to learn how to interact—cooperating in identifying, prioritizing, and carrying out tasks, listening to and communicating with each other. Most of the members of the community associations would not have attended elite schools and would therefore have been deprived of the chance to acquire skills in the public and humanist literacy domains that are provided for in the curriculum and extracurricular activities in elite schools. The community associations helped give them public and humanist knowledge, supplementing the education provided through the CPE, which had its main focus on the epistemic and technical domains of literacy.

The community associations were the main locations in which people could engage with what it meant to develop a self-confident national identity in a global context. Through them, people experienced visits and speeches from famous international figures associated with political transformation, such as Jamaica's Michael Manley, Mozambique's Samora Machel, African-American activists Harry Belafonte and Angela Davis, and those associated with cultural transformation such as Barbadian novelist George Lamming and Guyanese poets Martin Carter and Robin Dobreau. They listened also to their leaders' explanations of international events, and they became associated with campaigns such as fund-raising to assist countries that had experienced natural disasters. In the collectives, Grenadians worked closely with and became friendly with many internationalist workers from other countries in the Caribbean and beyond, who had also joined these groups. National identity was increasingly expressed through the cultural activities of the community associations, especially the mass organizations, which were the chief vehicles in the communities for organizing cultural events that publicized the unprecedented outpouring of artistic expression in vernacular Creole poetry, drama, and music that was taking place.[19]

In the sphere of gender identity, it proved necessary to persuade some women as well as many men that women were entitled to equal rights with men. New images of women's social and political roles took shape through the community associations, especially the National Women's Organization (NWO), which at one time had some eight thousand members.[20] There was a long way to go before some men yielded to this challenge, but it started. The NWO played a key part in mobilizing women, regardless of traditional political divisions, to articulate and represent to the government the legal and social changes for women that they wanted. The uneven process of development showed in the fact that on the one hand, the government passed laws such as those institutionalizing paid maternity leave without loss of job, a minimum wage, and equal pay for women, and those that imposed sanctions on the sexual exploitation of women workers in an attempt to bring this to an end. On the other hand, sexism continued to exist in the NJM itself. Male double standards in sexual behavior were rife, and NJM men refused on several occasions to make any concessions to the women in consideration of their extra burden of domestic responsibilities. Further problems of sexism that had to be overcome were male reluctance to take on equivalent responsibilities for the financial support of all of their children, and their overwhelming predominance in employment and leadership positions.[21] The women's confrontation of many spheres of gender inequality was initial and tentative. Little attention was given to reconceptualizing masculinities and femininities. Yet these flaws, together with the problem of the middle-class, didactic conception of leadership education, could not blunt the real achievements and the powerful potential of the women's organization as one that could substantially increase the strategic power of Grenada's women to make changes benefiting the whole society.

"PUBLIC" LITERACY AND POLITICAL PARTICIPATION

Community associations played an enormous role in developing public literacy. Reflection on their work facilitates a deeper and more complex conceptualization of this literacy region than that put forward by McCormack. Public literacy can be understood to have at least three major aspects. One aspect relates to the image of what political parties do and how they operate. Another is the development of participation, responsibility, and leadership. Another has to do with power relationships between social classes. The development of critical competencies in all of these aspects is what would lead to a high level of public literacy. In turn, it was envisaged that this would lead to a theoretical understanding of "the nature and structure of opinion, political judgement and political argument, the dynamics of political action, the forms of political consciousness, and the way a political community appropriates its past, projects its future, and conceptualises its historical continuity."[22]

In the anglophone Caribbean, the traditional political parties, shaped by the British model of parties as electoral vehicles, tend to be hostile to each other—in Jamaica, sometimes to the point of hundreds of murders being committed in the tense run-up to elections. In contrast to this neocolonial tradition of political socialization within competing and hostile party organizations, the mass organizations, citizens' councils, and worker education classes developed in Grenada sought to involve and unite broad cross sections of Grenadians in educational, social, and political activity regardless of their past or current political allegiance. Some mass organizations, such as the National Women's Organization, were more successful than others in achieving this goal. Other mass organizations were less successful in uniting a political cross-section. The National Youth Organization and the Productive Farmer's Union, for example, had a reputation of consisting mainly of members and supporters of the NJM.

The community associations were the vehicles which achieved people's engagement in shaping change structures, speaking at meetings, becoming leaders. This affected both privileged and less privileged social groups. For working-class and agricultural workers, the associations provided an opportunity for participation open to everyone, not just those who had registered as adult learners in the CPE. As far as middle-class people were concerned, the community associations pulled more of them into political activity than is usual in Caribbean multiparty systems. Workers' parish councils were regular meetings between NJM politicians, government officers, and local communities to discuss their needs, as well as to shape policy ideas in the context of social and economic developments in the nation. At one meeting, for example, the manager of Grenlec, the newly established state electric company, explained the problems of the old electric equipment and the policies of repair and development. At another, the government town planner explained some of the present regulations and future plans for land use. These representatives would then have to answer the people's questions, write down their concerns, and respond to any challenges. At each meeting, the NJM leader who was present would have to explain to the people what progress had been made on attending to matters brought up at a previous meeting. A workers' parish council meeting had the right to request in advance the presence of any government official it wished to question. Within a year, attendance at these meetings had grown so large that there was no hall big enough to hold the hundreds who wanted to get in. The workers' parish councils were then subdivided into zonal councils, the zone being a cluster of villages in a parish. At the high point of development, there were about thirty-six zonal councils.[23]

Although the government was willing to listen to and assist with local suggestions for change, funds were scarce, and it became clear that little could be achieved without a national volunteer effort. The importance of volunteer donations of time and effort was highlighted. Taken together, the CPE, the parish and zonal councils, and the mass organizations involved thousands of Grenadians in voluntary work and activities that not only started to raise their levels of education but also mobilized their hope and power to confront poverty and begin the long and complex process of working to eradicate it.

The political activity that took place in the parish and zonal councils and the mass organizations ensured the success of the PRG (People's Revolutionary Government) "People's Budget," unique and unprecedented in the Caribbean. This transformed the annual, traditionally secretive and technocratic exercise of making a national budget, controlled by the Ministry of Finance, into a planning operation that directly involved the participation of the masses of the people. Launched in 1982 and repeated in 1983, the People's Budget exercise was an extended procedure lasting about three months, during which the national economic plan was presented to communities all over the country for their study, criticisms, and recommendations. Then it was modified in the light of this interaction between politicians, technical advisers, and people:

> First, expenditure requests from all government departments were studied by the Ministry of Finance, headed by Bernard Coard. A preliminary draft was then submitted to the PRG Cabinet for discussion. This was followed by a period during which officials from the ministry went before the trade unions, mass organisations, zonal and parish councils to discuss the draft with them. The high point . . . was the national conference on the economy, which was attended by delegates from all the mass organisations. Breaking up into workshops devoted to specific areas of the economy, the delegates made detailed comments and criticisms on the draft proposals. The budget then went back to the Min-

istry of Finance for final revisions and then to the cabinet for approval. Finally, a detailed report was made to the people by the ministry and an explanation was given as to which recommendations had been rejected and why.[24]

Personal involvement in these activities is at the basis of my understanding of them as being a deeply educative process. Like most of my colleagues in teacher education, I attended all of the large workers' parish council meetings in the parish of St. George's as well as many of the smaller zonal council meetings in our area to discuss local community matters and the budget draft. It was possible to merge anonymously with the crowded audience at the workers' parish council meetings and simply listen with interest to the proceedings in which government officials explained national programs, answered questions, responded to criticism, and noted suggestions from members of the crowd. But mere listening was not possible at the smaller zonal council meetings. These involved our neighbors and the people in our local district, and discussion was lively. In our small groups studying the budget proposals we had to help each other come to terms with economic concepts like gross domestic product, inflation rate, real growth, balance of trade, the social wage, and many others. We sent our suggestions to the government, and attended the final budget conference. The climax was the realization that what was eventually adopted as the national budget was the product of a unique three-month process of consultation involving a broad spectrum of social interests and strata. Public technocrats had been required to describe the economic situation in accessible language; and the people in turn were challenged to grapple with national development issues.[25]

The third major aspect of public literacy relates to power relationships between privileged and less privileged social strata. Community associations went beyond the CPE's circumscribed sphere of teaching and learning, in which middle-class teachers had, compared to the learners, demonstrably more power derived from their high-status cultural capital and their dominant role in shaping the CPE materials and controlling the pedagogy. A contribution of the community associations to public literacy, then, was their role in gradually reshaping this traditional, stratified relationship. The associations were a forum in which people who had been marginalized learned to recognize and value their contribution to shaping change and middle-class people started learning how to share power. The mutual interaction involved in community and political work was a process in which teachers and other educated volunteers learned immensely from the people they were teaching. A teacher involved in the process of community consultations on the preparation of the national budget remarked that it was "an eye-opener" to realize that "these people who did not go to a secondary school and did not have a degree had such good ideas."[26] Angus Smith, a young Grenadian who at the age of twenty-three was appointed accountant general in the Ministry of Finance, described how his own development was enhanced by the process of interacting with community groups in discussing the People's Budget:

> Like many others, I was surprised at the high level of consciousness of the people throughout the budget process, at their knowledge of general affairs and their eagerness for involvement. Numerous practical and useful ideas were constantly coming out, things that technicians like ourselves would never have thought about, things which gave us a much wider perspective of the issues and ideas in the minds of the people around the country. . . . The experience brought home to us the need for our technicians to have a much wider view of things, to look at the country from the widest possible angle,

and not just from behind a desk. Everybody in our society has a viewpoint and we must pool all these together. For us it was genuinely exciting to be able to translate these budget figures that pass across our desks every day into the living reality of people's lives, and doing so learn more and more about how our people live.[27]

The community associations showed the importance of the language question. A wider range of middle-class people than literacy teachers were involved in them, and had to start to grope for an appropriate form of communication—perhaps not in the vernacular Creole, as some critics[28] felt should be the case, but at least in the sense of struggling to get away from jargon and elitist language. This was particularly evident in the People's Budget process. Ministry of Finance technocrats were given the responsibility of compiling a book that set out information about the economy and the budget issues for the community meetings at which they were to discuss the issues. They sought help from educators at the Teachers College in doing this, and the budget books were compiled only after these educators had helped them make the language more direct and clear. Using the books assisted the discussion groups, and the discussion groups forced Ministry of Finance facilitators to clarify concepts even further.

The community associations had immense democratic potential, but they also had problems associated with being at the beginning of a change process. They were to a large extent dependent on the leadership of the NJM, although local, non-party leadership was starting to emerge. There was a tendency for many group leaders to expect members to listen to sessions based on prepared texts that sought to promote the messages of the revolution. A didactic communication process usually characterized occasions when the leaders sought to implement classes of "political education" based on their often inflexible images of socialist vision. This sometimes occurred in spite of the fact that the teachers gained a lot of knowledge from listening to the people with whom they were interacting in community work. In a paper analyzing some of the weaknesses of the NJM leaders, Charles Mills[29] argues that many of them seemed to regard their political analysis of the Grenadian situation as the only correct interpretation, based as it was on the "scientific thought" of Marxism. This argument holds that NJM philosophy, in spite of some strengths, did not take enough into account the contribution of local Caribbean thought and popular traditions. It failed to heed Antonio Gramsci's observation that a philosophy of praxis must, dialectically, both criticize and incorporate common sense and must base itself on common sense in order to demonstrate that everyone is a philosopher. "It is not a question of introducing from scratch a scientific form of thought into everyone's individual life, but of renovating and making critical an already existing activity."[30] If the NJM, as Mills suggests, failed in some important areas of activity to achieve this pedagogical dialectic, "this would inevitably have contributed to that distancing from the population, that partial estrangement from popular discourse and ways of seeing things, that is both the strength and potential danger of Marxism."[31] This narrow social vision is one of the serious weaknesses of the modernist tradition, which assumes that a single prescriptive voice can (and has the right to) shape the answers to social problems. It afflicts both the left and the right side of politics, with the result that people have not been able to achieve grounded critique or strive for the powerful synergies of blending several visions of change. This insight throws light on areas of failure in many revolutions, including the one in Grenada. The Grenadian revolutionary party's internal conflicts over strategy, leadership structure, and pace of reform were not resolved because each faction, convinced it had the correct view, took this to the point of armed struggle against each other. Too late, Bernard Coard, one of the imprisoned survivors of the struggle, reflected on how the potential power of the community associations could have been further tapped:

> I have thought, often, over the past five years what would have happened if either the minority or the majority faction had taken the matter in a principled manner to the masses. And what better fora for doing it than the Zonal Parish and Workers, Women, Youth . . . Assemblies . . . ? With copies of all relevant minutes printed and distributed to the people; with representatives of both trends in the leadership putting their view forward to the people in the Assemblies . . . and being questioned and grilled by the people in return and hearing their views . . . what better way could there have been for resolving our differences?[32]

Comparing the revolution's popular community education process with the traditional approach reverted to after the revolution throws light on the significant issues that need to be considered in striving for the improvement of popular education. The new community structures in the revolution sought what should be the basic thrust of popular education—to produce a reorganization of the social basis of power in the communities, and on this foundation, in the overall society. Marginalized people were educated into adopting more powerful ways of behaving politically—articulating demands, building organizations to carry out specified purposes, exchanging views with educated government officials and party politicians, holding these people accountable for the carrying out of their promises, uniting across the partisan divisions of the past. The associations reflected both the strengths of genuinely participatory learning and leadership and the weaknesses of didactic authoritarianism that were contradictory facets of the process. Their potential for change was weakened by flaws that contradicted the rhetoric of people's power, for example, by the fact that the accountability of national leaders was limited by a lack of electoral processes and by the secrecy of a Marxist-Leninist style centralist political organization.[33]

In traditional politics, electoral processes maintain a much more open, competitive government-versus-opposition structure that allows for a multitude of rival political parties (in Grenada there have been nine political parties jostling for power since the 1983 U.S. invasion)[34] but provides little potential for cooperation between adherents of these groups. Popular education is on a minimal scale rather than a national one. Instead of being multiclass, it is directed at the economically disadvantaged. It takes the form of consciousness-raising about specific, narrowly defined social problems and carries out some pressure-group advocacy through religious groups, drama groups, and a few fragmented women's groups. Limited political information-giving, such as talks about current events, occurs in some groups, for example, in Grenadian groups funded by the Agency for Rural Transformation, an NGO that was one of the few institutions established during the revolution that survived. In general, there is minimal development of education that develops political and humanist literacy, encourages public and community voice, or facilitates collective political activism for change within the prevailing structure. The challenge for the future is to find a way of balancing an open electoral process with the kind of popular education that promotes participatory democracy—collective activism for meaningful community development on a national scale—and through this, the production of powerful, transformational knowledge.

ADULT EDUCATION: WAYS FORWARD

A comparative view of Caribbean experiments in adult basic and popular education in the Grenada revolution and in traditional polities provides postcolonial societies with clues about how adult education can seek ways forward out of the model that consigns it to being the minimalist educational channel at the bottom of the social hierarchy. First, the context. What pushed forward educational change in the Grenada revolution was a combination of the political goals of a socialist-influenced vision and the correlating economic changes that increasingly required skilled and educated workers. Such workers are even more urgently required in today's context, as postindustrial changes and new trade blocs are making the neocolonial, dependent economic model redundant. A socialist-oriented path based on the classical model of revolution is not viable in most of the postcolonial world, but the answer does not lie in neoliberal capitalist structures such as the ones that continue in the Caribbean. Only a minority is highly developed for the new opportunities in the high-tech and global markets, and the majority remains in an exploited or marginalized position. Change is needed that draws on two strands of thought. One strand is based on social justice ideas searching for a mode of economic organization and work conditions that facilitate more widespread and sustainable employment, and greater political power, for those unjustly marginalized. Another strand foregrounds the ideas of economists stressing the urgent need for a creative and educated response from entrepreneurs and workers ready to seize new global, postindustrial opportunities in new enterprises and niche markets. Transforming a weak postcolonial economy depends on better articulation among the productive sectors, the governmental system, and the society's educational and research-and-development institutions.[35] It also needs a continuing and united pressure on the international economic system for changes in structures that maintain injustice for impoverished countries.[36] No section of the population can be omitted from the educational change that would be an integral part of this vision of interrelated political, economic, and cultural activism. Governments can be pushed into supporting the kinds of changes needed if articulate social groups among the population are informed and motivated enough to push them. Social alliances in civil society could more effectively engage in local action for change if they joined forces with global transformative movements such as those for ecologically sustainable development, feminism, literacy, and media reform. It is these kinds of activities that would be supported by a combination of adult basic and popular education, each informing the other.

Second, rethinking is needed about the structure and goals of adult education. What varieties of institutions and groups, in what arrangement relative to each other and relative to employment, would best form this combination of basic and popular education? Although details cannot be prescribed, the principles of an empowering adult education structure—basic education and popular education nourishing each other—will address the importance of developing all of the literacy regions toward the "powerful literacy" that facilitates critique and activism. This structure will not simply provide instrumentalist education for practical subsistence needs or train semiskilled workers, which appears to be the main function of much contemporary basic adult education. It will provide a host of opportunities for combining an academic and a practical education with a sophisticated and activist general and political knowledge.

A Brazilian example of the kind of structure that could promote such education challenges the familiar shadow-schooling-for-subordinate-literacies approach of adult education in the contemporary Caribbean. The Cajamar Institute was founded by workers in a region of northeastern Brazil dominated by plantation agriculture. Paulo Freire was elected president of the council of this institute in 1986. He describes how workers managed to acquire a 120-room building that used to be a motel and created there the Cajamar Institute as an organization for the "training of the working class, peasants and the urban workers under their responsibility." Seminars and courses were offered to workers, some on a weekend basis. The staff included teachers from the working class and teachers from the university—intellectuals, says Freire, whose political choice coincided with their (the workers') choice, also, "who don't think that they possess the truths to give to the workers. Intellectuals who respect the workers' process of knowing and who want to grow up with the workers." The programs were oriented toward developing a critical understanding of Brazilian history and society, and particularly of the struggles of the Brazilian working class. Freire saw the institute as a kind of seed for a popular university that would be able to depart from the formalism of the traditional model and play the important role of being "a theoretical context inside of which the workers can make a critical reflection about what they do outside of the theoretical context." Worker institutes such as Cajamar could play the role of allowing men and women to achieve the distance from their daily work that facilitates studying society theoretically, "in order to understand the reason for the struggle and to make better methods for this struggle, and how to choose."[37]

Adult education organizers, to achieve such goals, usually cannot rely on the cash-strapped, timid, conservative governments of the current political context. The best hopes of development sometimes lie outside of government control or interference, and beyond the limited horizons of narrow, instrumentalist adult education institutions, whether state controlled or private. Several excellent independent NGOs with an adult education component already exist in the Caribbean, for example, the Social Action Center in Jamaica and SERVOL in Trinidad.[38] They could form the basis of a potentially powerful alternative adult education movement. Existing and new groups could be strengthened by interacting with each other regionally for systematic knowledge exchange and development and by drawing on the support of international institutions and networks. This networking would be a source of empowerment and independence outside of the parameters of state control. Yet state-led initiatives can sometimes be a catalyst for development through dynamic structures for lifelong learning. The potential for this seems strong, for example, with the adult education structure in St. Lucia, which is being re-engineered to prepare adults with educational, practical, civic, and cultural skills and with capacities for self-directed learning. Courses are being systematically articulated in a new accreditation system that links to school and tertiary education. Course materials are designed by individuals, groups, and agencies on the island, thus enhancing flexibility and responsiveness of content. Literacy in folk culture and Kweyol (Creole) as well as global culture and English are being promoted.[39] Trinidad and Tobago is another Caribbean nation with a state-run adult education division which caters well for adult learners, both by collaborating with nongovernment agencies, and by operating nationwide centers offering a large range of classes from basic to workplace education, from civic affairs to leisure and family-life education.[40]

Adult educators, whether in state or independent agencies, need to develop their fund-raising skills in order to draw on the goodwill of wealthy strata, both nationally and internationally. Funds would be urgently needed to acquire or construct buildings for worker-peasant education, to pay for the development of libraries, staff, and resources, and to support the economic and cultural projects necessary for grounding adult learning in a material basis so as to meet the practical needs of people who have been marginalized. These needs include training in modern communications technology (especially the Internet) that can enhance local and international activist links. Training adult learners in the skills of radio production and community radio is, arguably, particularly important for impoverished communities that depend largely on the radio for information and entertainment.[41] Sometimes funds from unlikely sources can be used for genuinely popular education. U.S. Agency for International Development funds have been used in Central America to establish a community education program regionally organized across three Central American countries: Costa Rica, Honduras, and Guatemala. This program of education for participation aimed to develop among participants in local communities the knowledge and skills that would enable them collectively to use popular processes effectively in improving their life circumstances, for example, by (1) making claims on public resources and services and (2) engaging in local and national political life. A detailed evaluation led by Robert Arnove reports on the ways in which the program achieved and sometimes surpassed its major objectives. It did this by working within the progressive Latin American tradition of popular education which, although not necessarily involving formal skills of reading and writing, nevertheless created a participatory education approach that enabled community organizations in impoverished and marginalized communities to define their problems and design and implement action strategies for tackling them.[42]

A third essential element of the way forward for adult education is that there needs to be a reconceptualizing of the literacy-and-education nexus. A fundamental task for adult educators is that of "rewriting literacy," that is, critiquing, restructuring, and redeveloping the learning activities offered by educational institutions, whether basic or popular. The foundation is to understand the domains, the philosophical qualities and discourses, the social practices, and the dynamic potential of literacies. At the stage of development that characterized the CPE educators during the Grenadian revolution, educational transformation was seen as combining socialist ideals of highlighting worker/peasant roles and middle-class conceptions of epistemic literacy. The stage of development necessary now would have to expand equity goals to include educational respect for orality, folk discourse, and the border crossing flexibility that empower learners to experiment with a range of perspectives and learning experiences. Popular education of the type experimented with in the Grenadian community associations has strong potential for building humanist literacy as the foundation of a self-confident cultural identity, without which few challenges to negative aspects of tradition can be mounted. This is the first step toward rewriting epistemic literacy for most postcolonial countries in which the literacy of the folk roots has been subordinated. Fashioning epistemic literacy anew requires blending a people's literacy with postcolonial epistemological advances such as those contained in the work of C. L. R. James, Walter Rodney, and Paulo Freire. Validation of vernacular or Creole literacy for serious study rather than informal communication and entertainment is essential for this.[43]

Another necessity is the pedagogy of participatory education characterized by the Freirean approach of the learner as subject rather than as the object into which predetermined content is "banked." Education as communication praxis, which combines the voices of learners and teachers into a cycle of social analysis, social activism, and reflection, must became part of the philosophical base of teachers and learners.[44] Yet another essential for rewriting literacy is the incorporation of a feminist perspective that challenges the older concept of integrating women in development (given the socially and ecologically disastrous impact of the present development model of international capitalism) and replaces this with a search for gender-sensitive and sustainable development.[45] Finally, reconceptualized literacies and pedagogy need not depend on the kind of text-based, school-imitative adult education model taken for granted in most postcolonial countries. Adult education can be creatively located as one component of economic, cultural, or political projects. It does not have to take the form of a unitary national system that shadows the centrally designed curriculum levels, texts, and examinations of schooling. Each project could have an education team that designs learning experiences related to the project, to participants' levels of education, their aspirations, and other needs that they may express. Methods and ideas do need to be coordinated between projects, but in such a way that there is an enriching relationship between local and central concerns in a search for effective socioeconomic development.

CONCLUSION

Adult and popular or community education, particularly in impoverished countries, has to facilitate the development of approaches for tackling material and cultural problems simultaneously. There is the need, for example, to balance culturally the growing power of global mass media with confidence in the best of local culture, design small-scale enterprises that suit both local and global niche markets, seize work opportunities with international concerns while protecting worker rights and the environment, and utilize governments and international agencies while not relying on them. Such goals require crossing boundaries of class, gender, and location in sharing and extending knowledge. They can be better sought by collective networks of like-minded people operating globally and locally. It is more necessary than ever to draw on and rework the best of the revolutionary changes implemented by Grenada's Center for Popular Education and the community associations in order to challenge the Caribbean tradition of providing a ruling minority with dominant, exclusionary literacies and a majority with subordinate literacies. Structures of adult education need to be based on the shaping of material change, as well as on involvement in pressure-group politics and other types of political activism. They can promote an alternative, politicized curriculum, a deep exploration and appreciation of culture, alternative forms of assessment and recognition, and the integrated rather than marginal use of vernacular languages as well as English. Changes such as these can give people the confidence to demand the end of the stratification of education channels so firmly entrenched in societies of the South. Considering the adult education experiments in Grenada helps us to learn from their weaknesses and draw from their strengths, but also to see beyond them in the search for education strategies to overcome disadvantage.

NOTES

1. Two in-depth studies of adult education in the Caribbean are those by Didacus Jules, "Education and Social Transformation in Grenada" (Ph.D. diss., University of Wisconsin, 1992);

and Anne Hickling-Hudson, "Literacy and Literacies in Grenada: A Study of Adult Education in the Revolution and After" (Ph.D. diss., University of Queensland, 1995). Both writers are Caribbean educators who worked in Grenada during the revolution and have had extensive experience in education in other Caribbean countries.

2. Anne Hickling-Hudson, Julie Matthews, and Annette Woods, "Education, Postcolonialism and Disruptions," in *Disrupting Preconceptions: Postcolonialism and Education*, ed. A. Hickling-Hudson, J. Matthews & A. Woods (Flaxton: Post Pressed, 2004). See also Leon Tikly, "Postcolonialism and Comparative Education Research," in *Doing Comparative Education Research*, ed. Keith Watson (Oxford: Symposium Books, 2001).

3. The crises of development underlying Caribbean economies and institutions are discussed in Kenneth Hall and Dennis Benn, eds., *Contending With Destiny: The Caribbean in the 21st Century* (Kingston, Jamaica: Ian Randle, 2000); Carmen Deere et al., *In the Shadows of the Sun: Caribbean Development Alternatives and U.S. Policy* (San Francisco: Westview, 1990); and Stanley Lalta and Marie Freckleton, eds., *Caribbean Economic Development: The First Generation* (Kingston, Jamaica: Ian Randle, 1993), especially part 4, "The Path Forward." Problems and possibilities of Caribbean education within a development context are discussed in Anne Hickling-Hudson, "Caribbean 'Knowledge Societies': Dismantling Neo-colonial Barriers in the Age of Globalisation," *Compare* 34, no. 3 (2004): 293–300.

4. See Anne Hickling-Hudson, "Literacy and Literacies in Grenada," 254–56; Fitzroy Ambursley and James Dunkerley, *Grenada: Whose Freedom?* (London: Latin American Bureau, 1984); Gordon K. Lewis, *Grenada: The Jewel Despoiled* (Baltimore, Md.: Johns Hopkins University Press, 1987), chap. 7; Tony Thorndike, "People's Power in Theory and Practice," and Paget Henry, "Socialism and Cultural Transformation in Grenada," in *A Revolution Aborted: The Lessons of Grenada*, ed. Jorge Heine (Pittsburgh: University of Pittsburgh Press, 1991). Jamaica in the 1970s and Guyana from 1979 to 1990 were the other English-speaking Caribbean countries that experimented with variants of a socialist orientation. Economic and ideological weaknesses meant that the approaches could not be sustained. See "National Experiments: The Radical Options," in Clive Thomas, *The Poor and the Powerless: Economic Policy and Change in the Caribbean* (New York: Monthly Review Press, 1988), 210–37, 251–64.

5. The impact of neoliberal globalization in the Caribbean is discussed by Tyrone Ferguson, "Social Disintegration in the Context of Adjustment and Globalisation: The Caribbean Experience," in *Contending With Destiny: The Caribbean in the 21st Century*, ed. Kenneth Hall and Dennis Benn (Kingston, Jamaica: Ian Randle, 2000). In Grenada, GDP per capita in 1988 was U.S.$1,346. The average for the Commonwealth Caribbean, excluding the Bahamas, was about $2,254. See Deere et al., *In the Shadows of the Sun*, 6.

6. Joel Samoff, ed., "Education and Socialist (R)Evolution," special issue of *Comparative Education Review* 35, no. 1 (1991).

7. James Gee, "What Is Literacy?" and "Discourse Systems and Aspirin Bottles: On Literacy," in *Rewriting Literacy: Culture and the Discourse of the Other*, ed. Candace Mitchell and Kathleen Weiler (New York: Bergin and Garvey, 1991); Peter Freebody, *Research in Literacy Education: The Changing Interfaces of Research, Policy and Practice* (Brisbane: Griffith University, 1994); Daniel Wagner, "Literacy Assessment in the Third World: An Overview and Proposed Schema for Use," *Comparative Education Review* 34, no. 3 (1990): 112–38; Ian Winchester, "The Standard Picture of Literacy and Its Critics," *Comparative Education Review* 34, no. 1 (1990): 21–40.

8. Colin Lankshear with James Gee, Michele Knobel, and Chris Searle, *Changing Literacies* (Buckingham, Milton Keynes, U.K.: Open University Press, 1997), 63–79.

9. Rob McCormack, "Framing the Field: Adult Literacies and the Future," in *Teaching English Literacy in the Pre-Service Preparation of Teachers*, ed. Frances Christie et al. (Darwin: Northern Territory University, 1991).

10. This argument is developed in detail in Anne Hickling-Hudson, "Literacy and Literacies in Grenada," 117–33. Figures showing the immense disparity in levels of formal educational

attainment between the highly educated minority (about 3 percent) and the less schooled majority are set out in *Time for Action: Report of the West India Commission,* ed. S. Ramphal (Jamaica: The Press, University of the West Indies, 1993), 237.

11. A study that emphasizes the concept of the functional practice of literacies in local contexts is Mastin Prinsloo and Mignonne Breier, eds., *The Social Uses of Literacy: Theory and Practice in Contemporary South Africa* (Cape Town: Sached Books/John Benjamins, 1996).

12. The system-maintenance role of adult education is explored in John Bock and George Papagiannis, eds., *Nonformal Education and National Development* (New York: Praeger), 3–20; Thomas LaBelle and R. E. Verhine, "Nonformal Education and Occupational Stratification: Implications for Latin America," *Harvard Educational Review* 45 (1975): 161–90; Robert Arnove and Harvey Graff, "National Literacy Campaigns in Historical and Comparative Perspective: Legacies, Lessons, Issues," in *Emergent Issues in Education: Comparative Perspectives*, ed. R. Arnove, P. Altbach, and G. Kelly (Albany: State University of New York Press, 1992).

13. Joel Samoff, "Education and Socialist (R)Evolution."

14. Hickling-Hudson, "Literacy and Literacies in Grenada," chap. 6.

15. Hickling-Hudson, "Literacy and Literacies in Grenada," chaps. 8–9.

16. See Robert Arnove and Harvey Graff, "National Literacy Campaigns in Historical and Comparative Perspective: Legacies, Lessons, and Issues," in *Emergent Issues in Education: Comparative Perspectives,* ed. R. Arnove, P. Altbach, and G. Kelly (Albany: State University of New York Press, 1992), 287.

17. Paulo Freire, *Pedagogy of the Oppressed* (Harmondsworth, U.K.: Penguin 1972), 81–82. See also Carlos Alberto Torres, "Education and Social Change in Latin America," *New Education* 12, no. 2 (1990): 2–6.

18. These adult education associations are described and analyzed by Didacus Jules, "The Challenge of Popular Education in the Grenada Revolution," in *Critical Literacy: Policy, Praxis and the Postmodern,* ed. Colin Lankshear and Peter McLaren (Albany: State University of New York Press, 1993); Thorndike, "People's Power in Theory and Practice"; and Hickling-Hudson, "Literacy and Literacies in Grenada," chap. 7.

19. See Chris Searle, *Words Unchained: Language and Revolution in Grenada* (London: Zed, 1984).

20. David Franklin, "The Role of Women in the Struggle for Social and Political Change in Grenada, 1979–1983" (B.A. diss., University of the West Indies, Mona Campus), 73.

21. NJM Women, "Proposals for Women with Children within the NJM" (report for the New Jewel Movement, Grenada, 1983); Charles Mills, "Getting Out of the Cave: Tensions between Democracy and Elitism in Marx's Theory of Cognitive Liberation" (paper presented at thirteenth annual conference of the Caribbean Studies Association, Guadeloupe, May 25–27, 1988).

22. Rob McCormack, "Framing the Field," 32.

23. Tony Thorndike, "People's Power in Theory and Practice," 41.

24. Ambursley and Dunkerley, *Grenada: Whose Freedom*, 38.

25. Didacus Jules, *Education and Social Transformation in Grenada* (Madison: University of Wisconsin Press, 1992), 183, 327.

26. Jules, *Education and Social Transformation*, 327.

27. Angus Smith, quoted by Chris Searle and Don Rojas in *To Construct from Morning: Making the People's Budget in Grenada* (St. Georges, Grenada: Fedon, 1982), 56–58.

28. Hubert Devonish, the major critic of the language policy of Grenada's revolutionary government, argues that although educators encouraged the vernacular Creole more than before, they continued to relegate it to the inferior status of oral expression (or, at the most, as being a bridge to learning high-status English) instead of promoting it as a serious medium of communication. Hubert Devonish, *Language and Liberation: Creole Language Politics in the Caribbean* (London: Karia, 1986).

29. Mills, "Getting Out of the Cave."

30. Antonio Gramsci, *Selections from the Prison Notebooks* (New York: International Publishers, 1971), 120.

31. Mills, "Getting Out of the Cave."

32. Bernard Coard, *Village and Workers, Women, Farmers and Youth Assemblies during the Grenada Revolution: Their Genesis, Evolution, and Significance* (London: Caribbean Labour Solidarity and the New Jewel Movement/Karia Press, 1989), 10–11.

33. Brian Meeks, *Caribbean Revolutions and Revolutionary Theory* (London: Macmillan, 1993), 153, 160–65.

34. See James Ferguson, *Revolution in Reverse* (London: Latin American Bureau, n.d.), 41–65.

35. Clive Y. Thomas, "Alternative Development Models for the Caribbean," in *Caribbean Economic Development: The First Generation,* ed. Stanley Lalta and Marie Freckleton (Kingston, Jamaica: Ian Randle, 1993), 326. See also Anne Hickling-Hudson, "Caribbean 'Knowledge Societies': Dismantling Neo-colonial Barriers in the Age of Globalisation," *Compare* 34, no. 3 (2004): 293–300.

36. Trevor Farrell, "Some Notes towards a Strategy for Economic Transformation," in *Caribbean Economic Development*, ed. Lalta and Freckleton (Kingston, Jamaica: Ian Randle, 1993); and A. Sivanandan, "New Circuits of Imperialism," *Race and Class* 30, no. 4 (1989): 1–19.

37. Myles Horton and Paulo Freire, *We Make the Road by Walking: Conversations on Education and Social Change* (Philadelphia: Temple University Press, 1990), 213–14.

38. Hickling-Hudson, "Literacy and Literacies in Grenada," 360; Patricia Ellis and Angela Ramsay, *Adult Education in the Caribbean at the Turn of the Century* (Kingston, Jamaica: Office of the UNESCO Representative in the Caribbean, 2000), 139–40.

39. Didacus Jules, *Adult and Continuing Education in St. Lucia: Addressing Global Transformation and the New Millennium* (Castries, St. Lucia: Ministry of Education, Human Resource Development, Youth and Sports, 1999, Unpublished paper). See also Hubisi Nwenmely, "Language Policy and Planning in St. Lucia: Stagnation or Change?" *Language and Education* 13, no. 4 (1999): 269–79.

40. Patricia Ellis and Angela Ramsay, *Adult Education in the Caribbean at the Turn of the Century* (Kingston, Jamaica: Office of the UNESCO Representative in the Caribbean, 2000), 136–54.

41. The importance of radio education and development in the Nicaraguan revolution is discussed by Penny O'Donnell in *Death, Dreams, and Dancing in Nicaragua* (Sydney: Australian Broadcasting Corporation, 1991), 110–41.

42. Robert Arnove, *An Evaluation of the Program of Education for Participation (PEP)* (Washington, D.C.: United States Development Agency, Bureau of Latin America and the Caribbean, 1989).

43. See Hubert Devonish, *Language and Liberation*; and Nan Elasser and Patricia Irvine, "English and Creole: The Dialectics of Choice in a College Writing Program," *Harvard Educational Review* 55, no. 4 (1985): 399–415.

44. Anne Hickling-Hudson, "Towards Communication Praxis: Reflections on the Pedagogy of Paulo Freire and Educational Change in Grenada," *Journal of Education* 170, no. 2 (1988): 9–38.

45. Peggy Antrobus, "Gender Issues in Caribbean Development," in *Caribbean Economic Development: The First Generation*, ed. Stanley Lalta and Marie Freckleton (Kingston, Jamaica: Ian Randle, 1993).

10

The Political Economy of Educational Reform in Australia, England, and the United States

Edward H. Berman, Simon Marginson, Rosemary Preston, and Robert F. Arnove

The ideological underpinnings of the educational reform efforts in Australia, England and Wales, and the United States over the last twenty-five years are strikingly similar despite these nations' differing political structures and the varied organizational patterns of their respective school systems. The common element linking reform efforts in all three locales is the attempt to weaken public control over education while simultaneously encouraging privatization of the educational service and greater reliance on market forces. Proponents contend that these reforms will enhance efficiency within individual schools while providing students with the requisite skills to make them more productive when they move into the workforce.

Undergirding these beliefs is the acceptance of the principle of economic rationalism, whereby decisions concerning national economic growth become the determining factor in all public policy decisions, including those affecting education. Issues of political democracy increasingly are defined as economic equations to be calculated and evaluated. Economic rationalism, in turn, draws on an updated version of human capital theory, which holds that contemporary economies can only be viable if based on the foundation of an educated, skilled, and technically competent labor force. There is a major difference between today's infatuation with this theory and its initial appearance in the 1960s, however. As Simon Marginson notes, "In the free market climate now prevailing, the emphasis is on private rather than public investment."[1]

This emphasis is hardly surprising, given the degree to which politicians of various persuasions in all three countries denigrate the public sector's role while ascribing almost mystical and liberating powers to the invisible hand of the market. This neoliberal commitment to market forces and minimalist governments has led to a reduction of state ownership of major resources and a concomitant increase in the privatization of services that once fell within the public domain, for example, railroads, utilities, and health care, to name the most obvious. The success of the Thatcher/Reagan agenda in shifting the balance between the public and private sectors decidedly in favor of the latter, and its durability even some time after its authors left office, helps to explain the concerted attack on continuing public control of the school, which after all is the epitome of the state sector.

The assault on the public sector has been accompanied by efforts to reduce government bureaucracies, which are accused of being both bloated and inefficient. Critics insist that centralized decision making has been too far removed from local communities, which need greater voice in matters concerning their well-being. Within educational systems, this rationale has led to a managerial revolution that has reduced the authority of central bureaucracies while devolving responsibility (but not necessarily authority) for school activities down to the local level. This in turn has led to an increase in local control over school finances, more school-based decision making, and more active efforts to involve community groups in school affairs. A cursory examination of these new arrangements might lead to the belief that these efforts represent movement toward a more participatory and thus democratic form of school governance in the public sector. This would be an incorrect reading of the situation, however. While fiscal and policy responsibilities have been partly transferred downwards from central government offices to the institutions themselves, the model is that of a consumer market rather than the Athenian *polis*: in markets, the power of the consumer is constituted not by equal rights of citizenship, but by the buying power in the hands of individuals, which varies according to individual wealth and social standing. At the same time, budgetary supervision, performance requirements, standardized management, and accountability based on measured outcomes have been deployed so as to secure closer ideological and political control over institutions in the public sector. The movements of the 1960s and 1970s toward a more democratically controlled public sector, based on an alliance of teachers and other educational professionals with politically active parents and local communities, have been reined in. Local autonomy continues but it has become managed and corporatized. School and university administrations have become focused on making their institutions appear more competitive in the marketplace rather than on reflecting, articulating, and meeting community needs.

Paradoxically, those private educational institutions that are funded by governments—private schools in the UK and Australia, private universities in the United States—have been treated very differently. In a policy framework which even erases market competition and private ownership, private educational institutions have an ever-increasing legitimacy. They are seen as *intrinsically* superior to public institutions, somehow avoiding the problems of bureaucracy, "producer capture," low productivity, and questionable standards that are seen as inevitable to the public sector. The remarkable result is that while public institutions have seen unit funding per student fall and political controls increase, private institutions have received increasing levels of government funding without a concurrent increase in centralized political control.

For example, in the public schools sector in all three countries, individual schools have gained greater autonomy in budgetary and local administrative matters—and more freedom to sell services and sponsorship and thus raise additional funds—but they have no voice over the size of the government funding outlay they will receive, and a reduced control over the educational uses to which it is put. Budgetary allocations continue to be determined centrally, and schools are required to provide additional student performance data to central offices. Increased student testing at various levels is seen as a way to accomplish this. There is greater movement toward centrally derived national curricula. But perhaps the most important issue that continues to be determined centrally is educational restructuring itself, which has become more or less continuous. The justification driving school reform efforts in Australia, England, and the United States is unambiguously instrumental, although this is now increasingly obscured by the current emphasis on the reform process. Educational reform proponents argue its necessity to ensure economic competitiveness in the global economy. Nothing more.

This shift in public policy discourse in a decidedly rightward and instrumental direction is not as seamless as its advocates hope, nor can it mask numerous contradictions. As mentioned above, the neoliberal commitment to market forces and minimalist government has been accompanied by an increase rather than a reduction in the power of central governments over educational decisions. In Australia, the commonwealth (federal) government in Canberra has assumed an unprecedented control over educational policy while the various state administrations have tightened their hold on school curricula. The Thatcherite reforms in Britain have concentrated more power in central government ministries in London while considerably weakening the influence of the democratically elected Local Education Authorities. At the same time, central government fiat a decade ago seriously undermined the universities' traditional autonomy while simultaneously strengthening the oversight powers of a government-dominated regulatory body. Reforms in the United States have resulted from the advocacy of a coalition of corporate executives and state functionaries who maintain that America's continuing global hegemony rests on massive school restructuring. This has been accompanied by calls for a standardized national curriculum and the implementation of mandatory testing measures to ascertain the efficacy of the far-reaching reforms; both changes would seriously undermine the long tradition of local control of school affairs.

The effort to "downsize" the public sector while simultaneously lessening government oversight of market activity represents an effort to reinvent a nineteenth-century laissez-faire political economy characterized by a class of robust capitalist entrepreneurs assured of a supportive investment climate and a plentiful and pliable labor force. It is significant that in the nineteenth century few people had access to publicly funded social welfare services. By the 1950s, the majority of citizens had access to medical care and education. With the neoliberal reforms introduced in the 1970s, the quality of such provision is being seriously undermined. The reforms have weakened the long secular trend to the expansion and universalization of educational participation—in certain instances actually leading to reduced enrollments, despite the ever-increasing role of education as gateway to employment. In nearly all cases they have weakened the value of participation at the bottom of the hierarchy of educational institutions; as the schools and universities attended by the wealthy become richer, those populated by the poor tend to become poorer. The economic rationalist argument concerning the primacy of material interests (economic growth, consumer self-interest) leaves little room for such issues as self-development or collective development, participation, equity, social justice, or even democracy. Educational reforms in Australia, England, and the United States shed considerable light on the degree to which, and the manner whereby, concerns over property rights have come to challenge, if not to supplant, concerns over citizenship rights. The abbreviated case studies that follow demonstrate how the latter have been subordinated to the former in current educational policy formulation, and they demonstrate as well how an overarching ideological proclivity has played itself out so similarly despite the considerable cultural and political differences that characterize these countries.

CENTRALIZATION AND MARKETIZATION IN
AUSTRALIAN EDUCATIONAL REFORM

In Australia, the states have constitutional responsibility for education; but since World War II generated a national interest in human resource management, the commonwealth government in Canberra has played a growing role, sustained by its control over four taxation dollars in every five. The functions of the respective levels of government vary by education sector. The commonwealth provides nearly all the public funding of universities, thirty-six of thirty-nine of which are in the public sector, though public funding is now just 40 percent of university income. Schooling in Australia is 70 percent in the public sector and 30 percent private. Unlike the situation in the United States, there is no constitutional barrier to state aid to private schools. The commonwealth provides the great bulk of public funding to the private schools—in fact it covers almost half of all the dollars, public and private, that these schools receive—but provides just one dollar in ten in the public schools administered and funded by the states. The two levels of government share the public funding of public and private vocational training.

The commonwealth government's role in educational reform has far exceeded its direct financial contribution. Most funds allocated by the individual states for educational provision are encumbered, for example, for teacher and staff salaries, transportation expenses, supplies, and the like. In contrast, moneys earmarked for educational purposes from commonwealth funds are more discretionary and can be directed toward strategic and innovative programs and concerns, sometimes playing a significant role in shaping educational priorities and decisions at state and local levels. The role of national government increased both from the 1940s to the mid-1970s, when the first modern mass educational systems were created, led by public institutions; and again from the late 1970s onwards, when policy was guided by very different neoliberal assumptions that modeled education as a market. Since the mid-1990s, this has been associated with a fall in the commonwealth share of total education funding, with some increase in state funding, a more noticeable rise in private contributions through fees, donations, and corporate investment, and the tightening of the commonwealth's ideological hold. The ultimate ideological wellsprings are located in the federal treasury and corporate-funded think tanks such as the Centre for Independent Studies and the Institute for Public Affairs. Correspondingly, there has been a major shift in the dominant education policy issues.

Until the early 1970s the primary policy problems were the expansion and modernization of education, the creation of greater equality of opportunity and support for individual merit, the perceived inadequacy of the human resources and physical infrastructure, the introduction of scientific curricula led by educational psychology, the professionalization of teaching, funding (where the fiscal weakness of the states opened the way to the commonwealth role), and the problem of state aid to private (particularly confessional) schools. The last was a contentious issue that became a regular feature in electoral campaigns as both sides of politics struggled to secure the Catholic vote. By the late 1960s, the Labor Party had joined the other major parties in agreeing to state aid for nongovernment schools, though there were differences on the extent to which state aid should be provided to the wealthier private schools of the largely Protestant social elite.

The election of a federal Labor government in 1972 triggered a major increase in public funding at all levels, the assumption of full commonwealth responsibility for the funding of universities with the abolition of both student tuition charges and state government funding, and the creation of a new policy machinery for central intervention, through the (commonwealth) Australian Schools Commission, the Tertiary Education Commission, and a Curriculum Development Centre with a never-clearly-defined potential to create national curriculum materials. Policymakers set out to expand participation, increase equality of outcomes by social group and lift material (and thus, it was assumed, intellectual) standards at the same time. It was believed that, left to itself, private investment would be insufficient to fund the desired levels of participation, and would be associated with both material gaps in provision and greater social inequalities in access.

The 1975 defeat of the Labor Party government and its replacement by a conservative Liberal-Country Party coalition coincided with the economic policy shift from Keynesian demand management to monetarism and opened the way to neoliberalism. The first economic rationalist policies began. Public spending on education was defined as a cost rather than an investment and its growth was halted, except for the funding of private schools. There was a new concern with outputs, productivity, and efficiency in educational administration, though less clarity on how to implement it. The old assumption that more public spending would more or less automatically deliver better outcomes was discarded.

The focus on outcomes was fueled by the rise in youth unemployment after 1975 and widespread claims from conservative ideologues and educators that this was driven by poor academic standards, teacher militancy, and an alleged progressivist "capture" of public school curricula. Concerns about increasing participation were temporarily discarded and the commonwealth focused on ensuring that school leavers had better skills and appropriate workplace attitudes, establishing the School-to-Work Transition Programme in conjunction with the states. The 1979 report *Education, Training, and Employment* recommended more vocationally oriented secondary schooling and a rationalization of the postsecondary system. University enrollments were to stop growing and vocationally oriented institutions were to manage any continuing expansion.[2] In 1981, after little consultation with the higher education sector, the government closed or merged many small colleges of advanced education, while reducing the emphasis on teacher education and liberal studies. Institutions were told that scientific, technical, and applied fields would be favored in future funding cycles. It was also announced that tuition fees would be reintroduced for some tertiary students, though the government backed down after student protests; and at this stage, tuition was introduced only for foreign students.[3]

In 1983, the Labor Party again formed the national government in Canberra under the former leader of the Australian Council of Trade Unions, Bob Hawke, followed by Paul Keating from 1991. It remained in office until early 1996, by which time Australian education had been structurally transformed. The transition to the Australian Labor Party did not signal an abrupt change in policy. What is striking about the changes in Australian education in the 1980s and 1990s is the shared view by politicians of both major parties concerning educational policy. Although the two main sides of politics did not always agree on particular policies (e.g., the Labor Party was more focused on access, and less generous to elite private schools), it was agreed that the Australian educational system should be closely aligned with the needs of industry and the global capitalist market;[4] and Labor came to adopt the dominant neoliberal reform agenda, albeit in more modest form. When Hawke took office, inflation was high, unemployment was rising, the price of the mineral exports that Australia depended on was falling, and manufacturing, especially elaborately transformed (technology-intensive) manufacturing for export, was weak. Rather than moving to boost the economy with a major increase in government spending, as in the previous era, Labor adopted neoliberal supply-side deregulation strategies underpinned by industrial relations peace and a social consensus in which an expanded, modernized, and cheapened education and training system played a central role.[5]

The currency was deregulated in 1983, opening the economy more directly to global markets. Support for deregulation and privatization in other sectors began to gather pace—telecommunications, transport, later health and education. Australia was to build itself through advanced manufactures, service capitalism, and higher quality human capital, all while lightening the fiscal burden on companies and high-income earners. This meant shifting an increasing proportion of educational costs from public to private sectors, and developing more market competitive educational institutions, seen as crucial to greater labor productivity. The principal reform strategies were all drawn from the neoliberal textbook: market competition between institutions, corporations, and employees in place of bureaucracies and professionals; increased tuition charges and consumer choice; together with a new dose of political centralization to ensure compliance and control. At the same time, it was believed that a strong linkage between national economic well-being and education necessitated increased educational participation so that more students could gain the skills enabling them to contribute to economic growth, at lower unit cost than before. Educational institutions had to produce better results with fewer resources. Policymakers believed that this was possible because educational professionals had secured too much autonomy and educational management was too lax, or was leaden and bureaucratic.

In 1986, the Business Council of Australia published a report criticizing education. Students' basic skill levels had declined, it was claimed, and the schools needed to give greater attention to workplace issues and less to nonproductive academic subjects and custodial care; similar arguments were advanced by the network of conservative think tanks. These claims were not substantiated by empirical data but this in no way lessened their impact on public perceptions; and public officials everywhere moved to tighten the focus on basic skills and other outcomes by testing students and teachers. Decision makers became increasingly sympathetic to economic arguments that better material resources (e.g., smaller class sizes) were not necessarily linked to better outcomes and policy should focus on "quality." The new orientation was symbolized in the 1985 report of the Quality of Education Review Committee, chaired by Peter Karmel. Generally the Labor Party supported these arguments, while joining them to an egalitarian rhetoric about equal opportunity. From 1984, the Participation and Equity Programme sought to encourage students to stay in school while equipping them with marketable skills,[6] supporting this initiative with an expanded student allowances scheme. The allowances were later withdrawn when the participation targets were reached.

After winning a second term in 1987, Hawke moved swiftly to bring education to the top of the reform agenda and into line with economic policy. A new Department of Employment, Education, and Training was created, headed by former finance minister John Dawkins. Absorbing part of the former industry department, it essentially became an economic ministry. Many of the senior staff were trained economists, including the head.[7] The autonomous Commonwealth Schools Commission and Tertiary Education Commission—now seen as "captured" by education institutions and interest groups—

were abolished, and its functions absorbed into the department. A new Australian Research Council established greater national government control over research funding and policy.

The most striking changes were at the tertiary level. The government's schema for higher education was summarized in the 1988 white paper *Higher Education: A Policy Statement*. This document elevated all higher education institutions to university status while raising funded institutional size and forcing the merger of smaller institutions with larger ones. A single Unified National System regulated by the ministry was established, in which universities were explicitly positioned as competing with each other for an increasing proportion of public funding, particularly for research and innovation. The white paper also supported funding for teaching on the basis of performance indicators including institutional efficiency, student completion rates, and a loosely defined series of evaluations and reviews of individual sites.[8] This proved too difficult to implement and performance funding was implemented only for research infrastructures. Institutions, however, were encouraged to develop internal competitive performance measures based on product formats and many did. Dawkins also successfully encouraged a more executive-professional and less collegial approach to leadership and management. Individual faculty and executive leaders alike were expected to raise an increasing proportion of incomes from industry funding for consultancy, research, and short courses, and the new tuition-based student markets opened up by Labor in international and postgraduate education. Although mainstream undergraduate education continued to be regulated by government subsidies and planned enrollments, rather than a tuition market, programs that failed to build market share were increasingly in question. They were now vulnerable to serious cuts in funding or termination. By this stage the principal growth was in business studies, which together with computing was to be the boom discipline of the 1990s. Science enrollments leveled off and education department enrollment fell.[9]

Dawkins provided increased government grants to support a major expansion in higher education enrollments, almost 50 percent in five years, but funding did not keep pace, in part because the government was not funding the newly designated universities for research at the same rate as those universities founded prior to 1986. From 1987, public resources per student fell, a trend that sharpened after Labor's exit in 1996. Meanwhile the government reinstated tuition charges through the Higher Education Contribution Scheme (HECS). The HECS functioned like a loan: it was a deferred income contingent charge repaid only when income reached a threshold level, set originally at average weekly earnings. At first HECS was set at an average 20 percent of course costs but later it rose sharply. The proportion of university income derived from all forms of student charges and fees began to rise, from 1 percent in 1986 to 20 percent in 1989 and 25 percent in 1996.[10] Institutions were free to enroll as many full fee-paying foreign students as they wanted and the number jumped from 24,998 in 1990 to 53,188 in 1996.[11] They were mostly from Chinese families from East and Southeast Asia, especially Singapore, Malaysia, Hong Kong, and Indonesia, and in business or computing. Dawkins was less successful in securing more industry funding, but through the Council for Business/ Higher Education Cooperation, the private sector stepped up its influence in Australian higher education.

Later, from 1993 to 1995, the commonwealth government conducted three successive quality audits of all higher education institutions, and published the results of these audits in the form of institutional rankings. This strengthened the culture of competition, formalizing a market-sensitive hierarchy of universities, and reinforced the neoliberal message that teaching and research were ultimately the responsibility of the individual corporate universities rather than the government or public policy. It also installed quality assurance mechanisms as a permanent part of institutional life. In 1995, Labor decided not to proceed with the full inflation-linked adjustment of university grants, a measure which was to remain in place under the coalition from 1996, and to force a continuing incremental substitution of market incomes in place of public funding. This initiative placed sharp downward pressures on resources for research and undergraduate teaching, which continued to be dependent on the government's proportion of the cost of HECS places.

In vocational education and training, Dawkins presided over a major restructuring along similar lines to the introduction of competency standards in the U.K. (In Australia, vocational education and training colleges are not defined as *higher education*. That designation is confined to institutions granting at least three-year degrees.) The outcomes of training were defined in solely instrumental terms and training standards set by industry-dominated committees in each occupational sector. It was hoped that more transparent and standardized outcomes would hasten the development of a market in training. User charges were introduced into public institutions, and private training institutions were brought into a common framework with increased subsidies. The reforms were pushed through from Canberra with the support of the Australian Council of Trade Unions. They were facilitated by Labor's special relationship with education unions as well as with other unions and employers in each industry. This was typically Australian Labor, whereby a social contract was used to implement a neoliberal modernization agenda.

In schooling, Labor established more instrumental national norms across the state-based systems. It secured agreement on a national curriculum framework in eight "areas of knowledge" that students must master, though the consensus was later fractured by party politics. State education ministers moved to secure greater accountability from individual schools and supported system-wide standardized testing of students despite the opposition of the teaching profession, which was concerned that testing would drive the curriculum and that the publication of school-by-school results would undermine the standing, capacity, and resources of those schools serving less advantaged students.[12] By the middle of the 1990s, a dual system of policy-regulated schooling markets had emerged, bifurcated between the private and public sectors. The two markets were very different. In the private sector, government funding continued to increase—despite the fiscal blanket on the rest of education—while the schools remained independent of direct policy controls. In the public sector, funding was constrained by commonwealth cutbacks and by the poor capacity of the states to pay, while official control over the curriculum was stepped up and institutions were ranged against each other in a competitive framework. Local enrollments were deregulated and in some states, public schools were encouraged to raise some of their own monies. In the state of Victoria, the government favored self-governing public schools, akin to private schools, though without the latter's independence in educational matters. The state further appeared sympathetic to the full privatization of those public schools deemed successful in the market. Critics of the public sector argued that government provision of schooling had failed to halt a decline in academic standards, thus hindering economic growth and individual social mobility; and, in any case, it had removed the locus of control from where it belonged, with local communities, parents, and employers. According to this line of argument, the solution was to introduce a market-based system with voucher funding enabling parents to choose their children's school. The work of John Chubb and Terry Moe was often cited in support.[13]

In March 1996 the Labor government was replaced by the Liberal-National Party coalition (the former Country Party had become the National Party) led by John Howard. The new government quickly signaled its desire for a more rapid transfer of funding from public to private sources. The 1996 budget cut direct public funding of universities; between 1996 and 1999, public-sourced funds per student dropped by 20.1 percent. There was a 12 percent staff reduction at the federal Education Department. The level of tuition payments under the HECS was increased sharply: revenues from both the HECS and from direct fee-charging doubled in the five years after 1996. By 1999, less than half the funding of public universities was from government sources; by the middle of the next decade, the level was 40 percent from the commonwealth and 2 percent from the states. The number of fee-paying postgraduate students expanded to $125 million in 2004. But with the level of student payments under HECS increasing, total domestic student numbers plateaued. Enrollments fell three times in the early 2000s, at a time when most Organization for Economic Co-operation and Development (OECD) countries were experiencing a marked expansion in tertiary participation. Meanwhile, the number of foreign students rose even more dramatically under the coalition than under Labor, from 53,188 in 1996 to 96,607 in 2000, and to 239,495 in 2005 (with China now the largest single source country, enrollments from India growing rapidly, and some decline in numbers from Indonesia and Singapore). By 2005, one-third of all foreign students were enrolled off-shore in distance education and Australian branch campuses mostly in East and Southeast Asia. An extraordinary 25 percent of all students were foreign students, much the highest level of any large national education system in the world, with foreign students generating 15 percent of all university revenues. In 2004, foreign students generated U.S.$1.3 billion in university tuition payments; and in 2006, the Australian Bureau of Statistics estimated that the total value of exports in all sectors of education, taking into account both tuition and other expenditures by students, was $7 billion. Education had become the third largest Australian export industry behind coal and iron ore, and just ahead of tourism and transport.

The remarkable growth of international education was forcibly generated by the financial incentives provided by the 1996 cutbacks in public funds, plus the refusal to fully index grants. It was associated with a further corporatization of internal university culture, feeding into the expansion of functions in marketing, recruitment, financial management, and quality assurance. At the national level, the establishment of the Australian Universities Quality Agency, which audited institutions' quality assurance mechanisms, was designed to assure the foreign student market that Australia was maintaining standards amid the off-shore recruitment drives being vigorously pursued by all institutions. Nevertheless, in the worldwide rankings of research universities issued by the Shanghai Jiao Tong University each year from 2003 onwards, Australia had only two universities in the top one hundred; and one of these, the Australian National University, was a modest player in fee-based markets. Australia's research standing was weaker than the other English-speaking nations apart from New Zealand. This suggested that a price had been paid for the force-fed business orientation and the shift from public to private funding. Regardless of neoliberal dogmas, basic research is public funding dependent.

Other trends inherited from the Dawkins eras were continued and enhanced. Student numbers in business and computing majors continued to grow rapidly until the early 2000s, when a downturn in the information technology job market was followed by declining enrollments in computing. Business studies numbers kept increasing, however, and by 2005 had reached 28.6 percent of all higher education enrollments.[14] Although there was continuing concern that numbers enrolled in science and engineering might be inadequate to meet future national needs, the problem was less one of total student numbers—relatively poor labor market returns to science graduates indicated little unmet demand for them—than one of declining numbers of high-scoring school students entering science amid the growing numbers heading for medicine, law, and commerce.

In 2003, a more advanced neoliberal reform was implemented in higher education. Under Minister Brendan Nelson, the commonwealth introduced FEE-HELP, a system of income contingent tuition loans parallel to the HECS that could be applied to either full fee undergraduate places in the public universities or places in those private higher education institutions approved by the Howard government. Though the expansion of full fee numbers in the public universities was slow at first—the relative affordability of HECS places undermined market development—there was a spectacular growth of private institutions, most of which received public subsidies for the first time. The government also announced its intention to adopt a Research Quality Framework, similar to the UK Research Assessment Exercise, in that it would be based on periodic assessments of research performance, with funds distributed accordingly. It was expected that research assessment and the greater emphasis on domestic fee-based incomes would strengthen the relative position of the leading institutions, enhancing stratification. It was apparent that in an increasingly competitive higher education system, institutions that started with superior status and resources tended to attract and manifest a growing share of those qualities.

In vocational education, the agreement between the commonwealth and the states on shared funding in Technical and Further Education (TAFE) broke down at the end of the 1990s and was not renewed. The commonwealth share of TAFE funding fell. The cross-governmental coordinating authority, the Australian National Training Authority, was abolished and not replaced. These changes left TAFE very substantially underfunded and undersupported. Vocational training institutions were able to enroll fee-paying foreign students, but those institutions did not have the same private income–earning potential as universities. By the mid-2000s, TAFE's resource position was substantially worse than schools and universities with little obvious prospect of change. The commonwealth government provided selected funding for private providers, but was unsuccessful in fostering a full-scale market because in most industries, employers were unwilling to meet the full costs of training. Institutions became increasingly absorbed in the tasks of selling themselves, competing with each other and sustaining their resource base by casualizing their staff. In some TAFE colleges, more than 80 percent of teaching was provided by part-time employees, compared to 50 percent in the universities.

In the schools sector, the changes were less spectacular. In a return to the policy tendency of the 1975–1983 coalition government, the Howard government further liberalized the funding of new private schools, thereby underwriting a more rapid expansion of that sector. By the 2000s, private schools were enrolling 30 percent of all school students and closer to half of all students in the final year of secondary school. The advantages of the private schools continued to be underwritten by commonwealth investment. The funding levels applied to individual private schools were adjusted upwards. In terms of improving their position, the main beneficiaries were the wealthiest independent private schools, whose resources already exceeded those of all other schools. In the 2005–2006 financial year, 65.1 percent of all commonwealth school funding was allocated to private schools. The private schools sector received U.S.$3.7 billion from the commonwealth, slightly more than the universities at just $3.6 billion.[15] In all three sectors, the Howard government was moving beyond the mixed public/private education system created in the Dawkins era to a system grounded in a more pristine brand of neoliberalism, in which the common good functions of education tended to fall away; private was good; education was a consumption market; and institutions were quasi-firms focused on their own economic bottom line. It was a long way from the 1970s, when achieving equality of opportunity was often *the* burning issue in Australian education.

THE NEOLIBERAL TRANSITION IN ENGLAND

After World War II (WWII), Britain's welfare state reduced the opportunity gaps between rich and poor, with education a pillar of the reforms. If they failed to touch the elite systems of private preparatory and public schooling,[16] the majority (from 1944 to 1975) had fairer access from primary into secondary levels, with a growing minority continuing to postcompulsory technical training, upper secondary, and tertiary levels.[17] Long foreseen that a future Conservative government would redress Labour achievements and restore the ascriptive powers of the rich,[18] it was thirty years before adverse economic and educational conditions combined to permit promarket rationalization and the reshaping of Britain's postwar systems of health, education, and social services.

Following the oil and employment crises of the 1970s, radical reform was mooted by the then Labour government[19] and aggressively planned by the Conservatives.[20] They whooshed into power in 1979, under Margaret Thatcher, promoting productivity and efficiency, entrepreneurialism, consumer choice, and reduced fiscal dependency, along with a return to "traditional" values of the family and individual.

Worldwide, national policies are shaped by external and internal forces. Embedded social arrangements shape adjustments to reforms to make them workable. Pragmatism sees the retention of earlier policy reforms by administrations inheriting them and previously opposed to them. With hindsight, an apparently radical change in government may do no more than consolidate policy processes long since begun. In the U.K., U.S. inspiration has informed policy since WWII, its underlying thinking and the ways in which it is implemented.[21] Central government pressures to harmonize public services across the country, monitor performance, and relate costs to projected outcomes are well-documented, not least in education, over the postwar decades preceding 1979.[22]

The Conservative project of the 1980s was to bring Britain from a declining mixed economy to a rising free market, guided by principles of U.S. monetarism.[23] The governments of Margaret Thatcher (1979, 1983, 1987–90) and John Major (1990, 1992–1997) withdrew support from failing industry and accompanied the collapse of manufacturing and mass unemployment with narratives promoting flexibility in production and employment.[24] Nationalized industry, utilities, and transport were privatized. Fixed budgetary support was diverted from public services and replaced by systems of competitive tendering. Tax adjustments favored the rich, discriminating against the poor and middle classes.[25] Thatcher became the heroine of the protagonist right and a devil incarnate to the reactionary left. She was in constant battle with the European Parliament. In waging the short Falklands war against Argentina, she was able to reconstruct the greatness of Britain in the eyes of (at least some of) the people.

Turning to education, this middle section of chapter 10 examines what the public sector reforms of successive British governments from 1979 to the present period have implied in England[26] for educational opportunity and outcomes.

Shaping the Early Conservative Years

Labour introduced nonselective, comprehensive secondary schooling in the late 1940s.[27] Successive Conservative governments (committed to selection) allowed the comprehensive system to grow through the 1950s and 1960s, by when it was the majority postprimary option provider. In the 1960s there was Labour government pressure to centralize educational programs, assessment, finance, and management, but this did not occur.[28] By the mid-1970s there was evidence that Britain's performance was trailing that of Germany and France[29] and that mass secondary schooling was reproducing patterns of inequality, with improved opportunities for only small numbers of children, mostly from professional and white-collar families.[30] The majority still left school without qualifications and basic skills below the minimum levels required by employers. An international report from the OECD[31] highlighted the failure of the U.K.'s Department of Education and Science (DES)[32] to link education to wider socioeconomic development or consult with teachers and local authorities on policy innovations.[33] By 1979, these problems had triggered persuasive right wing publications, attacking the comprehensive system, its socialist mission, and its inability to achieve either intellectual excellence or the entrepreneurship required for national well-being.[34]

Diminished trust in education to promote growth or counter inequality legitimated the Thatcher government reforms of 1979–1988. The DES, scapegoating teachers, unions, and Local Education Authorities (LEAs), commissioned a flood of policy papers and legislation, across subsectors, all in accord with earlier centrist inclinations and the new economic thinking. They threatened the longstanding tripartite management of public sector education (between central government, local government, and teachers) and syllabi devised by individual teachers. As in the 1950s, the government gave parents the right to choose which state schools their children attended and funded private school places for state school children.[35] LEAs were to include parents on school governing bodies and to publish curricula for schools in their areas.[36] There was encouragement for schools to opt out of LEA control and set themselves up as private trusts and LEAs were to justify requests for school funding allocations.[37] In 1987, LEA responsibility for tertiary polytechnics and colleges was passed to a central government *quango* (Quasi Autonomous Non Government Organisation),[38] the Polytechnic and College Funding Council.[39] Separately, there were threats to university tenure, severe cuts to funding, and the transfer of financial management to central government, under another quango, the Universities Funding Council.[40] Finally, having dismantled the large metropolitan city authorities (including that for Greater London, in 1986), the government moved to close the innovative, Labour-controlled, Inner London Education Authority, effective from 1990.[41]

Beyond the attack on LEAs, Conservative distrust of middle class professionals led to an assault on teachers' pay and conditions, specifying duties, hours of work, and in-service training requirements, with the DES setting salaries and rescinding consultative pay-bargaining rights.[42] Ensuing industrial action (working-to-rule and strikes) was used to turn popular anger against the teachers and unions, deflecting attention from professional concerns, associated with overload in all areas of work.[43] Prerequisites to a centralized curriculum for schools saw the end of the independent Schools Council (1984) and authority for curriculum development passed to two new quangos, a policy-oriented, state-appointed School Examination Council and a practice-focused School Curriculum Development Council,[44] later subsumed under a Qualifications and Curriculum Authority.[45]

There were dozens of studies of curriculum in schools, colleges, and teacher education institutions (DES, 1979–1988),[46] with those reflecting the humanist philosophies of the pre-Thatcher era available to justify more instrumental and efficient approaches. New school-based vocationalization included the Technical and Vocational Education Initiative (TVEI) for fourteen- to eighteen-year-olds. Bypassing the DES,[47] TVEI was a European Union program, with U.K. implementation overseen by the Manpower Services Commission, a quango answerable to the Department of Employment.[48] Twenty independent inner City Technology Colleges (CTCs) were to be created for postprimary eleven- to eighteen-year-olds, with capital investment from business and recurrent funding from the state.[49] To become a model in future quasi-privatization, the CTCs were to ensure technical skills for those in areas of low educational aspiration and assist their placement in work.

At postcompulsory levels, the general studies component of vocational education and training (VET) programs were nationalized.[50] An on-the-job Youth Training Scheme for sixteen- to seventeen-year-olds was initiated, with industrial placements, payments, and government funding (DES 1982–1986).[51] Policy was for VET to meet employer needs.[52] A new industrial quango was to create a competency-based, vocational qualifications framework,[53] delineating skills for previously undifferentiated occupations.

Through the Thatcher years, debate raged between those promoting the reforms to enable individual fulfillment and those who saw them eroding equality of opportunity, through a return to laissez-faire and privilege. In 1987, the new measures were endorsed by forceful conservative intellectuals. They urged independent education for all and the conversion of schools into markets unfettered by LEAs and charging parents for services consumed by their children.[54] The timing of these New Right papers, before the massive general election victory of 1987, heralded in 1988 a doubtful policy coincidence: the infamous "section 28" of the Local Government Act,[55] prohibiting "the promotion of teaching the acceptability of homosexuality as a pretended family relationship" and the pivotal educational moment of the Conservative years: the Education Reform Act (ERA).

Among many commentaries, Stuart Maclure sees the ERA as embedding two strategies:[56] top-down government direction of change with legislation to realize it and mechanisms to raise standards through enhanced consumer choice and management innovations. The measures were to foment quality-improving competition, within and between sections and subsections, at all levels of the state system, and between it and others in the private and voluntary sectors.

Many note the hasty drafting of the Act and the plans to implement it.[57] It failed to justify links between identified problems (LEA inefficiency, inadequate learning from classroom-based curricula, catchment area school allocations) and the measures proposed to resolve them,[58] with pervasive inconsistencies in the policy rhetoric. The case for democratically desirable devolution of decision-making power to parents and individual schools is ill-matched with the building of a state bureaucracy to control curricula, testing, and accountability.[59] The least-cost imperative of market-driven choice and competitiveness between schools seeking students may not accord well with assuring effective learning for work or life in the community. Choice favors the already advantaged (individuals, schools, territories), reducing opportunities for those less fortunate, in school and in the labor market, making it a matter of time before deprivation and exclusion lead to organized revolt, market failure, and social disorder.

The Later Conservative Years

Such contradictions were to affect the implementation of measures put in place before the 1988 Act and the new ones it initiated (the centralized curriculum, testing systems, local management and finance of schools, LMS).[60] They were also to influence post-ERA policy and legislation required for the implementation of the Act (e.g., changing the inspectorate),[61] revising its terms to make implementation feasible (reducing the breadth of the new curriculum, provision for noncompliant and failing schools),[62] extending outstanding reform to school funding,[63] higher education,[64] early learning,[65] and selected subgroups with particular needs (deviant children, minorities).[66]

The centralize/decentralize axis of the ERA was being replicated across public and corporate sectors at a time when new management styles and frequent internal mobility were transforming the U.K. work place. Head-hunted CEOs received huge pay packets and bright young managers worked hard for six-figure salaries, driven by outcomes-based-management. At the same time, the demise of manufacturing, retrenchment, and redundancies created mass unemployment, a drop in the real value of wages (and social security payments), a reduction in public sector housing, and endemic poverty.[67] Downsizing and new accountability procedures increased the workloads of residual public and private staff, while outsourcing of hitherto in-house services introduced temporary staff needing induction and support, raising organizational stress and weakening institutional memory.

In education, changes in government (John Major replaced Margaret Thatcher in 1990) and elected ministers, some of whom served for very short periods,[68] led to adjustments in policy intentions and realization. A major step was the privatization of the respected schools inspectorate. It was replaced by the new Office for Standards in Education (OFSTED),[69] with responsibility for standards in early learning, primary, secondary, and postcompulsory further educational institutions, including teacher education. OFSTED was immediately notorious for its brazen naming and shaming of schools (and teachers) not meeting its range of prescribed standards. New legislation in 1994 created a national curriculum for teacher education, under another quango, the Teacher Training Authority, with responsibility for initial and in-service instruction.[70]

In schools, the mandatory devolution of responsibility for the financial management to governors and parents was generally unwelcome, in spite of formula funding to confer supplements on schools achieving high enrollments.[71] Few schools were willing to accept the additional burdens to be incurred by withdrawal from LEAs and the adoption of grant-maintained status. With strong resistance to responsibility for teaching appointments,[72] only a small number were attracted by even improved incentives to change their status.[73] The ERA implications for senior teacher workloads were immense. Under LMS, school heads negotiated financial arrangements with governors and parents seeking private sponsorship to compensate for cuts in government funding allocations. Heads oversaw the introduction of the national curriculum and assessment, including SATs, and met detailed new requirements for the constant monitoring of individual teacher and child performance, along with gargantuan preparation for OFSTED visits.[74]

Classroom teachers, reeling under the early Conservative changes, faced ERA implementation with trepidation, planning how to introduce (often through formal training) the costly and changing new measures,[75] while protecting the quality of commitments in the existing system. The calm acceptance of curriculum centralization became dismay at its principles, its scale, and the work to implement it. One minister proposed extending the school day to accommodate the curriculum, but, loyal to its prescriptions, his successor negotiated a significant reduction of content.[76] This calmed the teachers and was approved by Parliament.[77] Teacher and parent resistance to the testing regime proposals was equally strong.[78] With considerable modifications, officially to reduce its workload impact, Parliament accepted the proposals. They included the publishing of school performance indicators and league tables, as key elements in raising standards.[79] Punitive measures were put in place to upgrade failing schools and those taking insufficient measures to increase their competitiveness.[80] Committed to school vocationalization, the DFE[81] extended technology teaching in primary and secondary schools. Specialist schools, introduced in 1994, would supplement the national curriculum in any two of ten skill areas, nine of which were vocational,[82] but difficulties continued in finding commercial sponsorship for the City Technology Colleges, even with recurrent expenditure met by government:[83] only fifteen of the twenty proposed in 1986 were operating in 1990 and results were variable.

In the postschool vocational sector, Training and Enterprise Councils were formed in 1989 to broker training for the unemployed and professional development for staff in small firms.[84] Responsibility for the funding of further education and the more academic upper secondary (sixth form) colleges was removed from LEAs (1992) and handed to a Further Education Funding Council, under the DES.[85] Work-based Modern Apprenticeships were introduced (1994/1995), along with renewed social security support for out-of-work youth in training.[86] The schools career service was privately contracted, through the Training and Enterprise Councils (1994).[87] In 1995, an indelible vocational stamp was put on the whole school and further education system, when the DFE and the Department for Employment merged into the Department for Education and Employment, located within the Department of Trade and Industry.

In higher education, new legislation targeted students, staff, and administration. From 1991, student numbers were driven up to maximize the use of resources, increase outreach to those hitherto excluded, and raise fee revenue. Student maintenance grants, which had enabled mass higher education in the postwar decades, waned. A U.S.-style loan scheme, gradually introduced in 1988 and extended in 1996, leaves students with debts, payable after graduation, at rates relating to future income levels.[88] By the mid-1990s, per capita student allocations to universities fell to between a half and a third of what they had been, while the number of institutions increased when polytechnics were given university charters (1991).[89] A year later, the new Higher Education Funding Council for England introduced interinstitutional competitive funding.[90] By then, most had extended existing business mechanisms to attract research and development work (from foundations, business, and consultancy), in the UK and overseas. They were also devolving central administration to departments. Tenure was abolished and the number of short-term teaching and research contracts increased.[91] Self-assessment, appraisals, and performance-related pay informed contract renewals and promotions, with varying implications for self-esteem and workload. The research process became tightly regulated, under project management rules, with pragmatic as much as conceptual outcomes prioritized. As with schools, competition between universities and departments within them was heightened by published league tables, purporting to reveal service quality, effectiveness, efficiency, and social impact, on growing numbers of indicators.[92]

Universities lost control over teacher education, as departments became government agents contracted to deliver the prescribed curriculum. Liable to sometimes punishing OFSTED inspections, a number of distinguished departments withdrew from training teachers.[93] From the mid-1990s, there were periodic subject reviews of university teaching quality, emphasizing not content, but the organizational environment in which learning occurred.[94] The reviews required months of preparation for the two-day visit of external assessors, colleagues from other institutions, themselves undergoing the same inquisitorial process. Without financial implications, universities publicized those departments awarded maximum points. Unsatisfactory scores resulted in further investigation of the department and institution, with eventual closure a possibility. The equally demanding Research Assessment Exercise, introduced in 1996, has had major funding implications for institutions and departments.[95] High-scoring departments and centers are deemed to be making significant contributions to international knowledge. They are awarded substantial research funding, leaving those with low scores to find resources as best they may. The process discriminates against new and interdisciplinary specializations and newly established institutions (former polytechnics) with little tradition of research, designating them as inferior teaching establishments.

The Major years, 1990–1997, saw the continuity of the Thatcher reforms, but after the 1993 election there were distractions: the Kuwait war, media accusations of corruptive sleaze,[96] and interminable wrangling for position within the Conservative party. The educational priority was the implementation of the ERA and the system-wide movement away from secure state funding. There was tinkering with the executive councils put in place under Thatcher and since (the amalgamation of the National Curriculum Council and School Examinations and Assessment Council) and the creation of more, often higher tier quangos (e.g., the Qualifications and Curriculum Authority). A few of the measures bore a particular Major stamp. The Parents Charter of 1991 (revised in 1994)[97] was a statement of what parents should expect of primary and secondary schooling. The Back to Basics campaign of 1993 reversed progressive student-centered education, restoring didactic teaching and factual rote learning to impart traditional values into the classroom.[98] A nursery school voucher scheme proved impossible to implement (1996). Intended to give infants a few hours in local preschools, the policy required parents to pay the majority fee for full-time participation, which few could afford.[99] Finally, there were efforts to restore prereform collegiality, but many feared continuing confrontation—framing ways of working between teachers, LEAs, and government agencies.

The New Labour Role

Reelection to government in 1997 was New Labour's priority. Pragmatically, from the mid-1990s, its plan was not to change the neoliberal political and economic foundations of the Conservative reforms, but to align the policies already in place with New Labour values and continue the reform process.[100]

With a massive majority in 1997, a slew of new policies were set to affect schools. Opposed to selection, there was the knee-jerk abolition of the assisted places scheme in 1997 and the cosmetic redesignation of grant-maintained status as "independent" trusts in 1998.[101] In 2005, however, New Labour launched an energetic campaign to persuade schools to opt out from LEA control, but the proposal was received as a failed Conservative initiative to convert schools into charitable companies. To increase support, the word *trust* was replaced in 2006 by the term *foundation* for schools choosing to opt out.[102] Although this mollified some of the Parliamentary Labour Party, approval of the amendment was dependent on significant numbers of Conservative votes. Persistent nationwide doubt that private school trusts/foundations will guarantee open selection, financial security, or stable learning was fuelled by recent City Technology College reports to the effect that they may not.[103] Schools are now asked to observe a code of nondifferential selection.

New targets were set for literacy, with mandatory reading and numeracy hours in every school (1999).[104] There was also an acerbic debate on policy requiring phonics versus contextualized "look and say" methods, threatening teacher authority to decide what is needed when for each child.[105] The innovative Beacon Schools Programme created partnerships between high-performing schools to disseminate effective practice to raise standards and attainment in neighboring schools.[106] Piloted in 1998, there were 1,150 partnerships by 2005. At the secondary level, the scheme was replaced with the Leading Edge Partnership Programme, with fund-holding lead schools (205 by 2007) supporting initiatives to raise standards in partner schools. Primary Strategy Learning Networks, with DfES[107] funding and LEA supervision, enable clusters of schools to enrich curriculum and raise attainment in literacy and mathematics. Announced in 2004, all schools should be involved by 2008.

The eleven- to eighteen-year-old specialist schools initiated under John Major continue to increase from 196 in 1997 to 1,000 in 2002, and to 2,000 in 2005. Replicating the 1980s Conservative illusion with eleven- to eighteen-year-old City Technology Colleges, twenty independent City Academies are to be created by 2008, rising to 200 by 2010. They will be autonomously owned and managed by private sponsors who have contributed £2 million to physical plant and infrastructure, with government meeting recurrent expenditure.[108] LEAs are coerced to create Academies, as a precondition of other new institutional funding, still without solid evidence of how public or private management affects achievement. There is strong parent resistance.[109] This follows OFSTED reports indicating doubtful Academy performance,[110] concern that corporations investing in a number of Academies will create private bureaucracies, and the familiar fear that selection bias will re-create by stealth the inegalitarian grammar/technical/modern school divide of the post-WWII years. To counter objections, a new set of specialist Diplomas (fourteen of them) combining vocational and core skills will be offered to sixteen-year-olds completing basic schooling, with an A-level equivalent two years later.[111] From 2008, the first diplomas will be in construction and the built environment, creative arts and media, engineering, IT, health, and social care. It is far from clear how schools will react, given limited capacity in the range of vocational subjects being proposed and decades of successful resistance to change in the academically elite A-level examination.

Training programs introduce new management skills to heads and governors in their roles as business executives.[112] Teachers on enhanced pay oversee erstwhile peers with regard to reform implementation,[113] while classroom assistants, without qualifications, on hourly pay, assume increasing responsibilities, including teaching.[114] With LMS and competitive tendering for variable core funding, some heads note that the ring-fencing proportions of allocations for Department for Education and Skills-specified purposes (e.g., Beacon Schools) restrict the fulfillment of agreed local priorities (e.g., teacher appointments).[115]

Responding to ethnic minority unrest, community demand, and backwash from the promotion of a war on terror,[116] there will be an increase in the number and range of faith schools,[117] along with a complex new internationalization strategy.[118] As in the United States, the development of Education Action Zones to improve failing schools is privately contracted.[119] Family support, parent training, discipline, and truancy targets are in place to address social issues, among them nutrition, childhood obesity, and exercise; disruptive, deviant, and violent children; and aggressive parents. Legal penalties are an option, including imprisonment for parents of truants, where other measures fail to achieve compliance.[120]

At postcompulsory levels, the Training and Enterprise Councils were to be revitalized from 1998, to increase access to better quality vocational training. By 2001, they were subsumed under a second tier nondepartmental public body,[121] the Learning and Skills Council (LSC), with regional offices across the country.[122] The LSC has consolidated a massive postbasic education sector with a remit to tailor workforce skills to employer needs. It includes: over sixteen academic, vocational, community, and adult learning, work-based training for young people, and continuing professional development for adults. There was change to the further education curriculum (2000): vocational qualifications were renamed and a new allowance was made to keep those over sixteen in education or training.[123] Specialist postsixteen colleges are being introduced, with curricula in computing and math, science, engineering, business and enterprise, leading to new diplomas in core and practical skills. Sponsored and managed by industries employing half a million people and facing recruitment deficiencies, the colleges will offer work-based training and distance learning to those wanting to enter the sector. Plans were advanced in 2006 for technical training in the nuclear, chemical, hospitality, and creative and cultural industries. Others will be announced in 2007, probably in construction, finance, and manufacturing.[124]

At the university level, contrary to what was happening in further education, student grants were abolished (1998). Loans were privatized and tuition fees for European community residents (including British residents) were introduced, initially up to £1,000 a year, rising to £3,000 in 2006.[125] The prospect of graduate debt in tens of thousands of pounds has seen a socially biased drop in English applications for 2006 and 2007 entry.[126] Most universities now offer required graduate-level, on-the-job training for new academic entrants, but arrangements are far from clear for increasing numbers of academic staff on fixed-term contracts. There are multiple other modes of professional development. Frequently provided by management consultants delivering standard packages, they are insensitive to the work, culture, and abilities of academic communities. The government presses for high-quality scientists, while recruitment difficulties mean the closure of sometimes long-established departments.[127] The removal of second language requirements for university entrance is reducing demand for foreign language courses.[128] Closures here have unknown long-term implications for international economic relations. Importing of international graduate students paying full-cost tuition fees for courses in the U.K. remains crucial, to the extent that some institutions restrict U.K./European Union enrollment to a small proportion of a cohort (e.g., no more than 25 percent). Supported by the Department of Trade and Industry initiative "Education for Export" there has been extensive overseas delivery of U.K. courses, and the international franchising of knowledge services continues to develop.[129]

Where Are We Going?

The Blair government has had it easy, with economic stability the platform for its nine-year rule. This has cushioned the effects of popular discontent at being drawn into the war with Iraq on false pretences, extended fighting in Afghanistan, and accusations of corruption among parliamentarians and party stalwarts at home.

Some claim that support to the poor has been a priority, but most feel achievement is very limited.[130] Following the Conservative line, those marginalized are blamed for failing to better themselves; and single mothers and rebellious boys, from whatever ethnic group, are media pariahs. Finance continues to be withdrawn from community health, social welfare, and housing, while commercial interests that encourage alcoholism, gambling, and other costly addictions are nurtured. In education, espousing conservative values makes endorsement of women's right to pregnancy terminal equivocal.[131] The surprising repeal of Clause 28 (the law prohibiting the promotion of homosexuality) received so little publicity that, outside the gay community, the majority of teachers and the general public believe that the restrictions still apply.[132] As the educational performance of girls and women has increased, the priority is given to restore the performance of boys.[133]

With multiculturalism celebrating diversity, the professional and educational success of selected minorities is undisputed, but little account is taken in schools of how specific home background traits, including nationality and religion, influence integration and achievement.[134] Since 1979, poorly educated minorities have been forced into worsening conditions of work and housing, with high proportion minority schools the only option for their children. Ghettoization is exacerbated by white parent preference for schools without a significant minority presence.[135] Public services for refugees, asylum seekers, and their children are restricted, including access to education, and totally denied to growing numbers of undocumented families.[136] School-related racial attacks are frequent and sometimes lethal, on and off school premises. They reflect patterns of unrest in the wider community, where race, gender, and poverty, interacting with education, are key parameters of unrest.

New Labour has continued the public sector transformation begun two decades ago, with dizzying amounts of legislation. In spite of the upheaval, the life cycle and the need for initial basic learning leave the educational system appearing much as it did in the 1970s. Central government plays a crucial and expanded role, with leaner departments devolving responsibilities to expanded tiers of executive councils responsible for the different subsectors, along with complex measures to monitor performance.[137] LEAs have experienced reduced, but now increasingly significant, roles in the support and management of schools, not least when things go wrong[138] and teachers' unions are rediscovering their voice. Most children still attend internally streamed comprehensive secondary schools and the elite independent system thrives; while parental involvement in resourcing schools is increasing, it remains small when compared to levels of state investment. After compulsory education, academic education maintains its preuniversity status. Post-sixteen (diversified and enormously increased), work and college-based vocational, professional, and community learning through adult life, are the norm. An expanded university sector delivers familiar research, teaching, and related services to an increasing range of clients in the U.K. and beyond.

Such continuities lead to the question of what is being achieved. The moves in the 1960s to introduce instrumental business planning and management by results[139] have been realized across the education sector, with huge doubts about their efficiency. Internal funding and external sponsorship are determined to an extent by the quality of competing budgetary proposals from client institutions, posing selectivity problems, but a controlling (rather than enabling) state is more than ever before the key player. The "independence" of established and more recent private institutions has long since been questioned, with subsidized places, charitable tax relief, and free ideological support.[140] Numerous market limitations explain parent and teacher unwillingness to opt out of LEA administration.[141] Consumers (especially young ones) cannot make informed buying decisions and one-time purchases do not allow sampling to find the best. Neither school entry nor exit markets are open, with geography and achievement preventing choice. New privatization is promoted through public-private partnerships, in which commercial and nonprofit companies (often together) facilitate access to basic levels of state-funded teaching and learning.[142] Under restrictions preventing profit from education, there is difficulty finding sponsors, possibly linked to fears of high transaction costs, for the three state school privatization models now operating (foundation trusts, special schools, and city academies). For the present, participating commercial companies are facilitating state-driven education on a nonprofit basis.[143]

Inseparable from business involvement in educational management, pervasive vocationalism justifies all education. From an early age, children compete in a world of targets and routines, valuing the practical, distrusting the conceptual, as manifested in a-contextual multisyllabic spelling lists and selection tests for those over eleven, disinterred and unchanged since the 1950s. Technology infuses learning from age five to sixteen. New incentives for postsixteen work-oriented training keep the majority off the streets, maybe affording narrowly defined, labor market entry certificates. Middle class demands to prepare children for professional careers are accommodated in academic streams and institutions offering broadly liberal secondary and tertiary education. To prepare more rounded humans, parents with money pay for private training in the creative arts and sports, formerly within the curriculum for all. As university graduates fail to find work commensurate with expectations, they use their superior social capital to find positions they want. Taking unpaid posts for increasingly protracted periods (even as apprentices in high status companies), they displace less qualified competitors, often for newly certificated work. Making education obligatory to eighteen, as currently proposed, will be a new elevation of the educational barriers to work and do nothing to redress the widening social bias in occupational allocation,[144] with personal capital an increasingly important converter of educational assets to income. For Brown, this ascription is displacing merit in the competition for status, with the rejection of prolonged education turning on its head the belief that increasing investment in education generates increasing lifetime returns.[145]

Labour's 1976 admission that things were wrong in education[146] invited the political and economic spin in which twenty-five years of reform was swathed. Indistinguishable between governments promoting opposing social visions, we should have resisted the common narrative, as the twists of repeated policy change revealed a strategy to mask vanishing opportunity and reward.[147] Devolving competitive financial management to differentially competent constituencies (parents, teachers, institutions, and communities) has stratified the quality of service offered, with the difference exacerbated by government awards for high scores on quantitative indicators of performance. In education, from preschool to postretirement courses on managing old age, a stifling bureaucracy prescribes provider and client roles at every stage and how they are assessed. With equivalent reforms in other social sectors, the British now accept that state surveillance penetrates every aspect of people's lives and adapt to it. Few perceive the underlying imperative of its complementarity with equivalent European[148] and global monitoring systems, what it represents or portends.

STATE AND PRIVATE INTERESTS PUSH EDUCATIONAL CHANGES IN THE UNITED STATES

Contemporary school reform efforts in the United States date from the issuance in 1983 of a spate of reports highly critical of the nation's educational system. The reports appearing then and over the following years were sponsored by a variety of organizations— federal government agencies, consortia of corporate and financial institutions, major foundations. Their overriding message was similar despite the varied sponsorship: the security of the United States was threatened by a deeply entrenched economic crisis, and the nation's educational system was central to reversing this situation and restoring the nation's economic prosperity. Some commentaries even suggested that the schools had caused the downturn, but past errors could be overlooked if the schools would now reform themselves by recognizing the realities of the new global marketplace and the productivity needs of American capitalism. Translated, this meant that school reform should proceed in a manner that would provide youngsters with those skills and traits required to make them more productive upon graduation into the labor market.[149] The Reagan administration strongly supported such sentiments, and it joined as well in the rising chorus of criticism that located the nation's economic malaise in the schools rather than in corporate sector practices.

American education is the responsibility of individual states; the federal government's contribution totals less than 10 percent of annual school appropriations. Accordingly, the influence both of Washington, D.C., agencies and of such external agencies as corporations and foundations is limited to advice and exhortation, while state legislatures retain statutory authority over educational matters. (There are several obvious exceptions to this generalization, however—one being the significant role played by the federal government in extending educational opportunities for children with disabilities.) Having said that, however, we need to note that this diffused educational decision-making process has never been immune from external pressure groups seeking to organize schools in one manner or another. In the present context, the series of reports issued by federal government agencies, corporations, and major foundations helped to establish the parameters of debate within state legislatures regarding the direction that school reform should take. One brief example serves to illustrate how this process operates in the United States.

Tennessee governor Lamar Alexander had been importuning his legislature to overhaul the state public education system even before the appearance of the 1983 education reports. His argument was that the perilous state of the Tennessee economy necessitated foreign investment, but what sensible investor, foreign or domestic, would locate a manufacturing or assembly plant in a state with such a lamentably poor educational system and consequently low level of worker literacy? Members of the state legislature initially ignored the governor's admonitions—that is, until the first education reports appeared in 1983. Alexander then brandished them at balking legislators, arguing that the reports of these prestigious corporate bodies, foundations, and federal agencies reinforced his contention that the state educational system needed overhauling to stimulate the economy. The Tennessee legislature soon passed a bill mandating a thorough restructuring of the state's public education system.

The perspective of the organized corporate community was unequivocal concerning what was required of American schools. A representative report, *Investing in Our Children: Business and the Public Schools*, was issued in 1985 by the Committee on Economic Development, a consortium of the nation's largest corporate and financial institutions. This document notes, among other things, that "economic productivity and the quality of education cannot be separated" and that "human resources [education] are more important than physical ones." Data collected by committee staffers confirmed suspicions about the inadequacy of America's human resources, especially compared to the nation's main European and Asian competitors. The solution to this problem was clear. What was required was "nothing less than a revolution in the role of the teacher and the management of the school."[150]

A key figure in the corporate offensive to overhaul the nation's schools was David Kearns, one-time head of the Xerox Corporation and an influential member of the Committee on Economic Development. In 1991, he became assistant secretary of education in the first Bush administration. In 1988 he had coauthored a book titled *Winning the Brain Race: A Bold Plan to Make Our Schools Competitive*. Many of the Bush administration ideas concerning education were drawn from this volume and from John Chubb and Terry Moe's *Politics, Markets, and America's Schools*, which appeared in 1990. Kearns's perspective on the role of American schools, together with his reasons for encouraging reform, were succinctly summarized in a 1987 newspaper interview in which he denounced the public schools as "a failed monopoly" guilty of producing workers "with a 50 percent defect rate."[151] In September 1989, President George H. W. Bush (1989–1993) summoned the fifty state governors to discuss the problems besetting the educational system. The outcomes from that meeting formed the basis for the first Bush administration's proposals for school reform, which appeared in April 1991 under the title "America 2000: An Education Strategy." Pulling together the conferees' generalities into a coherent strategy was one of the initial responsibilities of President Bush's new secretary of education, former Tennessee governor Lamar Alexander.

Some of the proposals in "America 2000" were as widely accepted as they were innocuous; for example, the suggestion that all children come to school ready to learn. Opposition began to mount around other aspects of the Bush administration's proposals, however, particularly those that would encourage privatization of large parts of the school system, and related choice and voucher provisions. Proposals for a national curriculum and mandatory standardized testing of schoolchildren also engendered opposition.

The Bush education department included among its staff a group of neoconservative intellectuals who increasingly despaired of effecting meaningful reform within the public system. The most vocal of these, Chester Finn and Diane Ravitch, occupied influential policy positions within the bureaucracy. Ideas and proposals regularly filtered into the department from a handful of like-minded associates, many affiliated with one of the Washington, D.C., conservative think tanks (e.g., the American Enterprise Institute, the Heritage Foundation, the Hudson Institute). John Chubb and Terry Moe were among this group, as was Denis Doyle, who had coauthored *Winning the Brain Race* with Kearns. Doyle's perspective on the role of schooling in America is both straightforward and representative of the advice influencing educational policy during the Reagan and Bush administrations. In a 1994 article, he wrote that "public schools must learn to take a page from other organizations' books and squarely address the question of productivity." Competition, private initiative, reduced government involvement, market forces: these were the factors required to get America's schools back on the right track.[152]

The first Bush administration made several attempts to effect school reform directly, despite the traditional limits on federal educational initiatives. In mid-1992, the New American Schools Development Corporation announced its first grants for innovative educational projects. The corporation had been organized as a private foundation by business leaders at President Bush's behest, and its funds solicited from private sources. The corporation's chief executive was a former secretary of labor in the Reagan administration. The Bush team had less success with another effort, however, the so-called 435 + Bill, which would have given U.S.$1 million to any of the nation's 435 congressional districts supporting innovative school programs.

The Clinton administration's approach to schooling issues did not repudiate all its predecessor's educational initiatives. This is understandable since, as governor of Arkansas in the late 1980s, Bill Clinton played a key role in drafting documents that subsequently formed the basis for President Bush's "America 2000" plan. Clinton's staff merely refashioned the Bush program, adding something here while removing a particular emphasis there; the Goals 2000: Educate America Act was signed into law by President Clinton in 1994. Taken together, this act, the pronouncements of influential policy advisers such as Secretary of Labor Robert Reich, and the president's emphasis in his second inaugural address in January 1997 left no doubt concerning the rationale for school reform as seen from the White House. The nation's schools needed to be aligned with the realities of the new global economy. Or, as succinctly summarized by Clinton's assistant secretary of education in 1995, "The primary rationale . . . for the concern about human capital [within the administration] was based on the ever-present challenges of international economic competition and a changing workplace."[153]

This official emphasis on aligning education more closely with the nation's human resource needs enjoyed, unsurprisingly, strong support within the American corporate and financial community. Representatives of these sectors have long attempted to influence the direction of American public education. It is only recently, however, that its concerns have been so coincident with official educational policy statements as articulated both at the federal and state levels. The past twenty-five years have also seen a notable increase in the amount of direct private involvement, as well as investment, in the public school system. Contemporary efforts are marked by both a quantitative increase in program proliferation and a heightened degree of receptivity by local school districts that either welcome private sector initiatives into the educational process or simply take them for granted, as if they are just the "normal" way to operate a school system. Examples abound, but mention of several will illustrate the magnitude of the issue.

A clear example of the degree to which the private sector has penetrated public education is offered by the checkered story of Whittle Communications, a unit of the Time-Warner media conglomerate. In the late 1980s, entrepreneur Chris Whittle began to distribute posters to public schools, gratis. They featured barely disguised advertisements for various products in addition to uplifting slogans. Several years later Whittle started a national news program anchored by student announcers. His corporation agreed to provide participating districts with some U.S.$50,000 worth of telecommunications equipment in exchange for agreement from individual schools that they would make the program mandatory for all students. This highly controversial Channel One venture features a daily ten-minute news program, several minutes of which are given over to advertising products especially appealing to youngsters. Revenues to finance this expensive project come from fees paid by corporate sponsors who wanted their products beamed to student audiences.

Yet another manifestation of corporate efforts to penetrate the public school system is represented by the appearance during the last decade of a host of management companies seeking to administer entire school districts. The number of these "contracting-out" arrangements, whereby the administration of public districts become the responsibility of for-profit corporations, has increased considerably. Among the best-known companies are the Nashville-based Alternative Public Schools and the Minneapolis-based company Educational Alternatives Inc.

Since 2000, another major player in the redesign of American public schools has been the Bill & Melinda Gates Foundation, by far the largest educational philanthropic player, eclipsing previous major foundations like Ford, Rockefeller, and Carnegie. In 2006, just five grants, among dozens of others, totalled over U.S.$80 million to (1) Chicago public school students, (2) Envision Schools in the San Francisco Bay Area, (3) Communities in Schools (expanding a network of nontraditional schools from Georgia to North Carolina, Pennsylvania, Virginia, and Washington, D.C.), (4) the College Entrance Examination Board, and (5) NewSchools Venture Fund. These grants were aimed at reaching at-risk students and dropouts with academically demanding, innovative programs that prepare them for higher education or challenging jobs in the information age economy.[154]

Efforts to provide public aid to private schools and to offer students a wider choice of educational environments continued during the Clinton years and the administration of George W. Bush. A hodgepodge of programs including vouchers, charter schools, and corporate schools have won at least scattered support across the country. Market models informed most of these experiments, with proponents arguing that competition among schools will inevitably increase educational quality and provide a welcome relief from stifling bureaucratic control. Support for these efforts has come not just from corporate interests or political conservatives, however, but also from liberals who seek alternative styles in education, from supporters of parochial schools who prefer a stronger religious and moral education for their children, and most recently from some African Americans, who believe that choice may offer the only effective antidote to the wretched condition of inner-city schools.

Federal support for educational choice has been ambiguous. President Clinton favored choice within public schools but did little to bring it about. The first Bush administration offered rhetorical support for some version of private school choice; the second Bush administration (2001–2009) has done the same but, like the first, has not been able to win congressional approval of any effective legislation. Instead, where experiments in choice have emerged, states and localities have been the innovators. Perhaps the most radical attempts to provide public money to students attending private schools have come in Milwaukee, Wisconsin, and Cleveland, Ohio, where states have provided vouchers for lower income students to attend private schools. The constitutionality of these experiments, although still in dispute, received support from a June 2002 decision of the United States Supreme Court that ruled in favor of the legality of the contested Cleveland voucher plan. With regard to academic outcomes of such experiments, early results were decidedly mixed, with the preponderance of evidence suggesting higher levels of parental satisfaction but relatively insignificant gains in academic achievement.[155] Faced with legal uncertainty and strong opposition from teachers' unions and other supporters of public education, most localities have been reluctant to offer full-blown voucher programs.

Charter schools (publicly funded institutions granted a large amount of autonomy) and other forms of public school choice have been much more widespread, with both state legislatures and local school districts showing growing support for at least a limited number of schools offering alternative educational programs.[156] Supporters of these ventures have come from across the political spectrum, but a majority seems motivated by a distrust of bureaucracy and by a conviction that competition holds the key to educational improvement.

Although there are cases of individual charter schools that show dramatic improvements in student academic achievement—as well as in students' behaviors and attitudes—recent studies fail to show statistically significant gains, overall, for students enrolled in charter schools.[157] In fact, a 2006 report of the U.S. Department of Education revealed that fourth grade students in traditional public schools outperformed comparable students in charter schools on reading tests administered as part of the National Assessment of Educational Progress. Furthermore, charter schools more closely affiliated with local school districts achieved better results than those relatively more independent from local control.[158]

An ongoing and uneven movement, public school choice has been both more popular and less controversial than vouchers, and charter schools, despite a number of failures, appear to have a greater chance of success than alternatives that would provide public aid to private schools. Moreover, the most recent data provided by the National Center for Education Statistics show that public school students (once raw data are controlled for race, gender, and parents' education and income) outperformed, in 2003, private school students in fourth grade reading and math as well as on eighth grade math, on standardized achievement tests. Private schools fared better than public schools only in eighth grade reading, and conservative Christian schools scored significantly lower than public schools in eighth grade math.[159] Despite the results showing that public school students generally did as well as, if not better than, comparable private school students, Education Secretary Margaret Spellings responded to this study by urging Congressional Republicans in July of 2006 to allocate U.S.$100 million in vouchers for low-income students in failing public schools to attend private and religious schools.[160]

While privatization in its various forms remains a goal of many, the primary interest of both federal and state policymakers shifted during the 1990s from choice to the establishment of academic standards and programs of testing. With the support of Clinton and both Bushes and with the endorsement of state governors, many legislatures have begun to set academic standards and to require that public schools participate in state-wide testing. Building on a momentum already established in some localities, the U.S. Congress passed legislation in December 2001 that would effectively require states to create standards in English and mathematics and to test the proficiency of all students in grades three through eight. Known as the No Child Left Behind Act (NCLBA), the legislation mandates that both positive incentives and negative sanctions be applied to schools according to results on standardized tests. Parents of children in failing schools are given the option of sending their children to other schools, assuming, of course, that they are available and can accommodate additional students. This, patently, has not been the case: in 2004, in New York State, for example, a third of a million students were entitled to transfer to better schools, in which there were only eight thousand places.[161]

Although parental choice and involvement are supposed to be key features of reform legislation, a recent study ironically noted that "parents were left behind" under No Child Left Behind. A 2002 report from the Association of Community Organizations for Reform Now (ACORN) found that parents in Chicago, Denver, and the Bronx had not received enough information to participate in changes under the law; similarly, a survey of parents conducted by the Annenberg Institute for School Reform at Brown University found that nearly half (47 percent) of parents in poor urban areas had never even heard of the NCLBA.[162]

Many states also remain in the dark as to how they are to implement a number of mandated reforms under current recession conditions with significant cutbacks in school funding. Mandates are inadequately funded, if at all, for such priority items as developing quality achievement tests, busing children from schools that fail to make progress on standardized tests for two years in a row, and having a "highly qualified" teacher in every classroom by 2006. No state had achieved this goal as of 2006, the same year in which fifteen states were suing the federal government for its failure to fund adequately imposed testing requirements amounting to U.S.$3.9 billion—approximately the same amount authorized for refunding NCLBA.[163]

Reasons for concern about the various unfunded requirements of NCLBA stem from the serious fiscal constraints facing many states In 2002, for example, poorly funded rural school districts in seven states shortened their work week to four days in order to save money.[164] Across the country, school districts, in order to raise needed funds, have resorted to signing contracts with junk food vendors, fast-food franchises, and other merchandisers to promote their goods at the expense of the health and well-being of their students.[165]

Local school districts also are in a quandary as to how to cope with unrealistic expectations, such as a 100 percent pass rate by 2014 on what many consider to be extremely rigorous achievement tests, particularly given that, in the short-term, the higher the standards, the more likely it is that schools already in trouble will find it increasingly difficult to meet rising requirements.[166] In some cases, school districts have scaled back what they consider to be passing rates on achievement tests so as to lower the number of failing schools.[167] In other words, the reverse is happening: standards are being lowered in reaction to federal mandates.

Moreover, individual teachers and their unions as well as many school district administrators object to the straightjacket, "one size fits all" approach to measuring the work of their schools and the abilities of students. De-skilling of teachers and dumbing down of curricula, as indicated earlier, are more likely outcomes of federal and state education initiatives rather than the purported upgrading of teaching as a profession and improvement in student knowledge.

While there is widespread dissatisfaction with these initiatives, support for standards and testing has come from a variety of constituencies, including some liberals concerned about the low state of education for minorities and the poor. The primary impetus, however, has come from those who believe that schools are not equipping the youth of the nation to compete in an increasingly sophisticated global economy. Anxiety was particularly high in the 1980s when American test scores lagged behind those of many other countries and when the Japanese were challenging American economic supremacy. Yet even when the American economy was booming in the late 1990s, market theorists continued to worry about educational rigor in the United States. Suspicious of public school teachers and administrators, teacher-training institutions, and progressive pedagogical practices, they have sought to use standards and testing as a way of reforming education along lines set out in *A Nation at Risk* and other alarmist reports of the early 1980s. Although state standards and testing do not challenge the central position of the public school in American life, critics charge that they bring to the system a hard-edged market mentality, measuring schools less by what they provide in the way of civic or moral education than by how well they prepare students for economic efficiency and global competitiveness.

This market mentality is further evident in higher education policies and practices. Increasingly, private as well as public universities use the discourse of the business world to promote their programs and products. Buzzwords like *niche markets, friendly mergers* and *hostile takeovers*, and *students as consumers* abound. Online courses and programs, and virtual institutions like the private University of Phoenix, represent the fastest-growing elements and sectors of higher education in the United States and are aggressively marketed overseas as well. Although the use of new instructional technologies represents opportunities for many nontraditional students to pursue further studies with the promise of social mobility, distance education programs, without adequate support services and opportunities for on-campus face-to-face interaction with faculty and fellow students, are likely to fall short of their promised benefits. Such programs tend to have high dropout rates and generally do not provide the residential socialization experiences that are associated with the social and cultural capital essential to entering the most modern and prestigious segments of the workforce.

Higher education access for low-income and minority students is increasingly problematic as tuition costs rise significantly relative to family incomes and public financial support falls relative to demand. Student loans (which low-income and minority students are reluctant to take) have steadily replaced student grants with major beneficiaries being the banking industry.[168] Adding to the difficulties faced by low-income students is the trend of leading public higher education institutions to compete for high-income, high-achieving students. As noted in a *New York Times* editorial, "In recent years, aid to students who earn over $100,000 has more than quadrupled at the public flagship and research universities. Incredibly, the average institutional grant to high-income families is actually larger than the average grant to low- or middle-income families."[169]

Minority student access to higher education institutions also is threatened by challenges to affirmative action programs that take race into account in admissions policies. In mid-January 2003, the Bush administration joined litigants in a case before the United States Supreme Court that challenged undergraduate and law school policies of the University of Michigan that gave preferential points to minority students, among other factors. The Supreme Court in June of 2003, however, "upheld the right of universities to consider race in admissions procedures in order to achieve a diverse student body."[170] At the same time that the Court ruled in favor of the law school admissions policies, it overturned the University of Michigan's undergraduate policy which involved a point value being added to minority student applications, thereby conflicting with the past decision of the Court in the case *Regents of the University of California v. Bakke.*[171]

The Bush administration, declaring itself in favor of diversity, maintained that a preferable and more legal policy would be to accept students according to their high school academic standing. Such approaches in California, Texas, and Florida require state higher education institutions to accept a certain percentage of a graduating class—in the above cases, ranging from 4 to 20 percent—regardless of the quality of the school and the students' scores on nationally standardized tests. While such policies have contributed to increasing minority student enrollments in some institutions, this has not been the situation in the more prestigious institutions and in the most selective professional school programs. Critics, furthermore, point out that these policies do not directly address issues related to the great disparity in the quality of schools and the continuing existence of racially segregated schools. In fact, gains made in school integration during the 1960s and 1970s are being undone by lax enforcement of previous court-mandated desegregation and by federal policies that accept the status quo.[172] Equally troubling with regard to integration and equality of educational opportunity are the flight of white teachers from black schools and the phenomenon of low income and minority neighborhood schools having less qualified teachers.[173] Also problematic is who will be considered "highly qualified" under current Bush administration regulations. Because of the disdain of former Department of Education Secretary Rod Paige and other members of the Bush administration for university schools of education and what they teach, alternative training programs are favored.[174] A novice in training in an alternative program, as of January 2003, was considered "highly qualified," whereas licensed teachers imparting instruction outside their specific areas of qualification are not so considered.[175] Moreover, teachers in charter schools and other private schools favored by the Bush administration appear to be largely exempt from the standards applied to public school teachers. What the Bush administration has failed to grasp is that effective teaching requires more than just subject matter expertise; pedagogical knowledge—how to effectively communicate curricular content and engage all students as active learners—is as important as the ability to create inclusive environments in which everyone feels validated as a person.

Achieving this noble goal is even more difficult in the post–September 11 environment in the United States, characterized by alarming moves toward a national security state with its concomitant hostile climate toward critical inquiry. The role of an education system in preparing participatory and reflective citizens is undermined by moves to quash dissent or classify people who oppose warmongering as unpatriotic. Civil liberties, such as freedom of speech and assembly, are increasingly under attack.

For those concerned with universities as a forum for free debate and critical inquiry, as well as centers of learning open to the whole world, legislation related to national security poses a threatening environment for international students as well as Americans, particularly those of Middle Eastern or Arab descent. Punitive regulations related to the 2001 Patriot Act involve fines, jail sentences, and deportation for international students who violate their academic standing by failing to register full-time or notify the National

Immigration Service within ten days of an address change. These are only some of the egregious restrictions, which also prevent spouses of international students from enrolling in degree-granting programs.

Countering these negative trends are examples of resistance at all levels of society from impoverished urban and rural communities to elite universities. As a case in point, the Massachusetts Institute of Technology, in 2003, rejected nearly $500,000 in federal research funds because the government wanted to restrict participation by foreign students. Other universities, according to the *New York Times*, are resisting government demands to scrutinize research "in the name of national security before scientists can publish or even talk about it."[176] At the other end of the institutional spectrum, grassroots organizations, such as ACORN, actively involve low-income communities in examining how federal and state education policies are affecting the education their children receive and equip individuals to become more effectively engaged in change processes.[177] The 2002 national and state elections, despite largely conservative victories, also were the occasion for various education referenda. In twelve out of fifteen state initiatives, voters favored additional funds or protecting existing funding levels for public schools. According to People for the American Way, "voters gave their leaders a 'homework assignment'—support reduced class size, after-school programs, and other proven reforms, and provide the resources public schools need to makes these reforms happen."[178]

The 2006 elections, in which the Democratic Party regained control of both houses of the U.S. Congress, also bode possible significant changes in major education policy, especially with regard to the funding of NCBLA and its various requirements. Various state elections also provided a setback to conservative religious forces aligned with the conservative political agenda of the Bush ("W") administration. In Kansas, for example, the election of moderate members to the state board of education bode well for a reversal of standards (the most far-sweeping nationally) that required the questioning of evolution as established theory.[179] Various local and state initiatives to teach "intelligent design" as a plausible theory to be taught in science classes also received a setback in a federal court in December of 2005, when the court ruled that it was unconstitutional for a Pennsylvania school district to offer intelligent design as an alternative to teaching evolution in biology classes. According to Judge John E. Jones, intelligent design is a "religious viewpoint that advanced a particular version of Christianity" that should not be taught in public school science classes. The judge went so far as to say that the school board in endorsing this policy had made a decision of "breathtaking inanity."[180]

This ruling and controversial policies in other school districts across the country involving the teaching of the Bible and various forms of creationism (as opposed to evolution) are likely to come before the U.S. Supreme Court. In 2006, with the retirement of Chief Justice William Rehnquist and Judge Sandra Day O'Conner and their replacement with conservative judges Samuel A. Alito Jr. and John G. Roberts Jr. (the new Chief Justice), the outcomes of lower court decisions placing a strict wall of separation between state and church may be in question, as well as previous decisions concerning desegregation of major urban areas. In December of 2006, the Supreme Court heard two challenges concerning the Louisville, Kentucky, and Seattle, Washington, school districts and plans that involved taking race into account, among factors, in assigning students to various schools.[181]

The configuration of opposing liberal and conservative forces at the beginning of 2007 may disrupt dominant trends in education policy over the previous twenty-five years. The neoliberal economic policies involving the application of market forces to the running of schools districts, combined with a conservative agenda in matters curricular, emphasizing standards and testing and traditional (read religious) values, is under serious attack. The centerpiece of the George W. Bush administration's efforts to expand educational opportunities and improve the quality of instruction for all children, NCLBA, has largely failed to demonstrate significant overall gains for low-income and minority students. The most recent data available on student achievement, as of 2006, indicate that the gap between upper- and low-income students and majority white and minority students has not been closed. To cite just a few examples: between 2002 and 2005, the percentage of black sixth grade students proficient in reading dropped from 13 percent to 12 percent, while the percentage for white students dropped from 41 percent to 39 percent. Not only were there not gains, but, notwithstanding the racial gap, the overall level of proficiency of both groups was dismal and for African Americans dismaying. In fourth grade mathematics, while the percentage of proficient low-income and black students increased respectively from 8 to 19 percent and from 5 to 13 percent, 47 percent of white students on average were proficient.[182] According to the NAEP, considered the nation's report card, "at least half of students failed to demonstrate even a basic understanding of . . . [science] in ten major cities."[183] An analysis of test outcomes suggested that background factors (race and income) were more influential than school location, which itself is highly correlated with degree of concentration of low-income and minority students.

These disappointing results are not surprising, for during the same period that historically disadvantaged students were not showing significant gains on standardized tests, the gap between social classes and between white and minority families (with the exception of Asians) itself was either increasing or remaining largely the same. In 2005, the median income for white households was $56,622; for blacks, $30,039; and for Hispanics, $36,278. While the difference in high school completion rate has narrowed between whites and blacks, the gap in bachelor's degrees has widened with 30 percent of white students as compared with 17 percent of black adults and 12 percent of Hispanic adults completing a college education.[184] Dramatic increases between the wealth of the richest top 1 percent and the rest of the population, including the "merely rich" and middle class, are characteristic outcomes of the economic policies of the George W. Bush administration.[185] At the same time, the number of people living in extreme poverty has been increasing.[186]

Furthermore, the average pay of college graduates has been decreasing and the prospects of guaranteed stable employment have been diminishing for all, except those who attain the very highest levels of education or graduate from the most elite institutions and have the most desirable social capital. While globalization and technology have widened the gap between those in the most lucrative jobs and the rest, these forces also have led to outsourcing of professional and white-collar jobs and a less secure future.[187]

CONCLUSION

In all three countries, attention focuses on such issues as a national curriculum and regular testing to measure reform's efficacy. The language of reform is regularly couched in metaphors drawn directly from the workplace. This was also the case early in the twentieth century, at least in the United States, when F. W. Taylor's principles of scientific management, which were designed for the factory floor, were widely heralded as the panacea for the nation's educational ills.[188] In today's reform climate, schools are told to develop performance indicators, that detailed plans should be as efficient and effective as they are quantifiable, and rewards should be reserved for those who successfully enhance productivity (i.e., student learning). Alliances between school districts and business interests are encouraged in all three locales, as is school privatization, which is frequently conflated with efforts to introduce choice and/or voucher programs. Higher educational institutions are also strongly encouraged by public agencies to seek additional corporate sponsorship. Policy advice regarding the appropriate direction for educational reform is provided by a network of right-wing think tanks, which emphasize a reduction in government services and ownership and the enforcement of market discipline in school matters. In Australia, these sentiments are regularly articulated at the Centre for Policy Studies, the Institute of Public Affairs, and the Centre for Independent Studies; in England, such advice emanates from the Centre for Policy Studies, the Institute of Economic Affairs, and the Hillgate Group; while in the United States these pronouncements are the common mantra at the Heritage Institute, the American Enterprise Institute, the Hudson Institute, and, most recently, the Brookings Institution.

Reductions in social welfare expenditures in all three societies have coincided with robust economic expansion at the national level and a correspondingly inequitable distribution of wealth. A result of this, in the United States and in England, is a notable increase in the number of children living in poverty, now generally agreed to be one in four and one in three respectively. Schools and universities are asked to perform the same (or additional) services with reduced budgets. From Australia to America, the outcomes have been predictably similar: cuts in needed remedial and support services for those in greatest need. Examples include the dismantling of the Inner London Education Authority in 1989, which involved a reduction in English as a Second Language programs for newly arrived immigrants whose mother tongue was, say, Chinese or Bengali; in President Bush's home state of Texas in 2002, funds were eliminated for education programs for eight thousand homeless children, for fifty thousand children in after-school programs, and for thirty-three thousand in child care.[189] Such issues appear to be of little concern to growing numbers of parents who can afford private education for their children or lobby to have public subsidies, in the form of vouchers, subsidize their children's private schooling.

Educational reform efforts in Australia, England and Wales, and the United States can only be understood in the context of concerted efforts by neoconservatives to return their nations to more halcyon days before a newly emergent middle class of women and people of color began to demand their citizenship rights. These retrograde efforts coincide with attempts to roll back the influence of the state and replace it with a form of "free market" competition that neoconservatives imagine existed at an earlier, less complicated time. Here conservatism and neoliberalism coincide. "Back to the basics" with its focus on functional outcomes, typified by standardized testing, signifies at the same time a return to conservative culture and its social order, a clarion call for efficiencies, dumbing down education in a language that parents, students, and industry can all understand, and the identification of commodity forms of education, learning that can be bought and sold. Greater competition among educational purveyors is meant to enhance consumer "sovereignty," increase choice in school placement, minimize government influence in educational provision, force-feed efficiencies, and maximize market principles. Evidence to support the superiority of such arrangements is readily available in the form of reputedly "objective" social science research data as collected in, say, Chubb and Moe's *Politics, Markets, and America's Schools.*

Jim Carl has summarized the issue succinctly: "Central to New Right school reform is the construction of an ideology that equate[s] public education with bureaucracy and inferior schools and associated private education with the marketplace and superior schools."[190] This does not augur well for those groups who, especially since 1945, have relied on the public sector, including its schools, to gain a voice in their nation's affairs. The right wing's continuing assault on and downsizing of the public sector can only impede the advance of those traditionally marginalized, for whom public education can be so vital.

NOTES

The authors wish to acknowledge the invaluable assistance of Stephen Franz in preparing this chapter.

1. Simon Marginson, *Education and Public Policy in Australia* (Cambridge: Cambridge University Press, 1993), 40.

2. Committee of Inquiry into Education, Training, and Employment, *Education, Training and Employment* (Canberra: Australian Government Printing Service, 1979).

3. For specifics, see Marginson, *Education and Public Policy in Australia*, chap. 6; and Susan Lee Robertson, "The Corporatist Settlement in Australia and Educational Reform" (Ph.D. diss., University of Calgary, 1990), passim, but especially chap. 5.

4. This modus vivendi between management and labor is generally known in Australia as the Accord. Its consolidation is seen by many as an unambiguous effort to more closely integrate Australia into the rapidly expanding global economy. See Robertson, "Corporatist Settlement in Australia," passim.

5. Marginson, *Education and Public Policy in Australia*, 85, notes that commonwealth spending on education fell from 9.6 percent of the total budget in 1974–1975 to 6.8 percent in 1986–1987, both periods when Labor was in power in Canberra. Similar decreases are noted in state spending as well. In 1975–1976 the proportion of states' budgets committed to education was 28.8 percent; in the 1986–1987 budget year, the figure was 19.8 percent.

6. For specifics on the Participation and Equity Programme, see Robertson, "Corporatist Settlement in Australia," 175–80.

7. Don Smart, "Reagan Conservatism and Hawke Socialism: Whither the Differences in Education Policies of the US and Australian Federal Governments?" in *Education Policy in Australia and America*, ed. William L. Boyd and Don Smart (London: Falmer, 1987); and Marginson, *Education and Public Policy in Australia*, 26.

8. Grant Harman, "Institutional Amalgamations and Abolition of the Binary System in Australia under John Dawkins," *Higher Education Quarterly* 45 (Spring 1991): 176–98; David Mahoney, "The Demise of the University in a Nation of Universities: Effects of Current Changes in Higher Education in Australia," *Higher Education* 19 (1990): 455–72; Neil Marshall, "End of an Era: The Collapse of the 'Buffer' Approach to the Governance of Australian Tertiary Education," *Higher Education* 19 (1990): 147–67.

9. Between 1979 and 1990, course completions in business/administrative studies in Australian higher education increased by 130 percent while those in arts/humanities/social sciences increased some 46 percent. During the same period, enrollments in education studies declined by 4 percent. Marginson, *Education and Public Policy in Australia*, 131.

10. Lesley Vidovich et al., "Australian Higher Education Policy and Practice: Effects of Economic Rationalism and Corporate Managerialism" (paper presented to the Canadian Society for

the Study of Higher Education, Calgary, June 1994); Jan Currie, "The Emergence of Higher Education as an Industry: The Second Tier Awards and Award Restructuring," *Australian Universities Review* 35, no. 2 (1992): 17–20.

11. Commonwealth Department of Education, Science and Training data. Education Statistics, at www.dest.gov.au/sectors/higher_education/publications_resources/statistics/publications _higher_education_statistics_collections.htm.

12. On the curriculum debate: Cherry Collins, "Curriculum and Pseudo-Science: Is the Australian National Curriculum Project Built on Credible Foundations?" (unpublished manuscript, Murdoch University, January 1994). The quote over the testing debate: Sheena MacLean, "Teachers' Unease Grows over GAT and Testing," *The Age*, April 19, 1994, 15.

13. Cf. Sheena MacLean, "A Private Obsession with Class," *The Age* (Melbourne), May 24, 1994, 14; John Chubb and Terry Moe, *Politics, Markets, and America's Schools* (Washington, D.C.: Brookings Institution, 1990).

14. Data from the Commonwealth Department of Education, Science and Training. Higher Education Statistics, at www.dest.gov.au/sectors/higher_education/publications_resources/statis tics/publications_higher_education_statistics_collections.htm.

15. Australian Education Union analysis of the 2006 federal budget, at www.aeufederal .org.au/Publications/2006Budget.pdf.

16. Now often known as "independent," Britain's fee-paying "public" schools should not be confused with those of the state sector.

17. Melissa Benn and Fiona Millar, *A Comprehensive Future: Quality and Equality for All Our Children* (London: Compass, 2006).

18. Reginald Crosland in Phillip Brown, "The Third Wave: Education and the Ideology of Parentocracy," *British Journal of Educational Sociology* 11, no. 1 (1990): 65–85.

19. James Callaghan, "Towards a National Debate" (speech given at Ruskin College, Oxford, October 18, 1976).

20. Conservative Party, *The Right Approach* (London: The Margaret Thatcher Foundation/ Conservative Central Office, 1976).

21. Chris Pierson, *Beyond the Welfare State?* (Cambridge: Polity, 1991).

22. John Fletcher, "Policy-making in DES/DfE, via Consensus and Contention," *Oxford Review of Education* 21, no. 2 (1995): 133–48.

23. For a brief summary, see Will Hutton, *The State We're In* (London: Jonathan Cape, 1995).

24. Richard Edwards, Katherine Nicholl, Nicky Solomon, and Robin Usher, *Rhetoric and Educational Discourse: Persuasive Texts* (London: Routledge and Falmer, 2004), chap. 9.

25. John Scott, *Poverty and Wealth: Citizenship, Deprivation and Privilege* (Harlow: Longman, 1994).

26. Parliament in Westminster administers education in England and Wales. The new Welsh Assembly Government, created in 1999, plays an increasing role with respect to the curriculum in Welsh, Welsh history and culture, inspections, and in the abolition of school league tables, reintroduction of free school milk for children under seven, and the piloting of a Welsh baccalaureate. Space no longer allows the separate treatment of Wales. See R. Daugherty, R. Phillips, G. Rees, eds., *Education Policy-making in Wales: Explorations in Devolved Governance* (Cardiff: The University of Wales Press, 2000). Gareth Elwyn Jones, "Policy and Power: One Hundred Years of Local Education Authorities in Wales," *Oxford Review of Education* 28, nos. 2–3 (2002): 343–58; R. Daugherty and P. Elfed-Owens, "A National Curriculum for Wales: A Case Study of Education Policy-making in the Era of Administrative Devolution," *British Journal of Educational Studies* 51, no. 3 (2003): 233–53.

27. Benn and Millar, *A Comprehensive Future*.

28. Fletcher, "Policy-making in DES/DfE."

29. Stuart Maclure, "Through the Revolution and out the Other Side," *Oxford Review of Education* 24, no. 1 (1998): 5–24.

30. Phillip Brown, "The Third Wave."

31. Kogan, 1975, cited in Fletcher, "Policy-making in DES/DfE."

32. The name and position of the government department administering education have changed over the years. [1944–1965: Ministry of Education; 1965–1992: Department for Education and Science (DES); 1992–1996: Department for Education (DFE); 1996–2001: Department for Education and Employment (DfEE); 2001– : Department for Education and Skills (DfES)].

33. Fletcher, "Policy-making in DES/DfE."

34. See C. B. Cox and R. Boyson, eds., *Black Paper* (London: Temple Smith, 1977).

35. DES, *Education Act* (London: HMSO, 1980); John Fitz, Tony Edwards, Geoff Whitty, "The Assisted Places Scheme: An Ambiguous Case of Privatization," *British Journal of Educational Studies* 37, no. 3 (August 1989): 222–34.

36. Stephen Ball, *Politics and Policy-Making in Education: Explorations in Policy Sociology* (London: Routledge, 1990).

37. DES, *Better Schools* (London: HMSO, 1986).

38. The Thatcher government in London replaced existing networks of independent consultative committees with new executive agencies. Said to be independent, they were rarely separate legal entities and their accounts were presented within those of their parent department. Their number and power grew, as their remit was first to manage formerly devolved local authority responsibilities and then develop national policy and oversight systems. They were known disparagingly as QANGOs or QUANGOs (Quasi Autonomous Non Government Organisations), and collectively as a quangocracy. To avoid pejorative connotations, they are now more often described as non-departmental public bodies (NDPBs) and/or executive councils (ECs).

39. DES, *The Education Reform Bill* (London: HMSO, 1987).

40. DES, *Higher Education: Meeting the Challenge* (London: HMSO, 1987).

41. Ian Gordon, "Family Structure, Educational Achievement and the Inner City," *Urban Studies* 33, no. 3 (1996): 407–24.

42. DES, *School Teachers Pay and Conditions of Employment* (London: HMSO, 1987).

43. Chris Pierson, "The New Governance of Education: The Conservatives and Education, 1988–1997," *Oxford Review of Education* 24, no. 1 (1998): 131–42.

44. Hutton, *The State We're In.*

45. DfEE, *Education Act 1997* (London: HMSO, 1997).

46. DES, *National Curriculum: From Policy to Practice* (London: HMSO, 1989).

47. See Note 32 for an explanation of DES.

48. Paul Sharp and J. R. Dunford, *The Education System in England and Wales* (London: Longman, 1990); Martin Merson, "Exploring the Reform of In-Service: TRIST in Three Authorities," *Oxford Review of Education* 15, no. 1 (1989): 73–83.

49. Geoffrey Walford, "The Privatisation of British Higher Education," *European Journal of Education* 23, nos. 1/2 (1988): 47–64; Fitz et al., "The Assisted Places Scheme."

50. P. Branwood and R. Boffy, "Full Circle? The Further Development of General Studies in Further Education," *Journal of Further & Higher Education* 5 (1981): 10–16.

51. DES, *A New Training Initiative: A Programme for Action* (London: HMSO, 1980), brought into operation in 1983.

52. J. R. Shackleton and S. Walsh, "The UK's National Vocational Qualifications: The Story So Far," *Journal of European Industrial Training* 19, no. 11 (1995): 14–27; S. Williams, "Policy Failure in Vocational Education and Training: The Introduction of National Vocational Qualifications (1986–1990)," *Education and Training* 41, no. 5 (1999): 21–22.

53. DES, *Working Together: Education and Training* (London: HMSO, 1986).

54. Hillgate Group, *Whose Schools? A Radical Manifesto* (London: The Hillgate Group, 1986); Hillgate Group, *The Reform of British Education—From Principles To Practice* (London: The Claridge Press, 1987), 55; Local Government Act, Section 28 (2A) (1988) at www.opsi.gov.uk/acts/acts1988/Ukpga_19880009_en_5.htm.

55. Clause 28 reads: (1) The following section shall be inserted after section 2 of the [1986 c. 10.] Local Government Act 1986 (prohibition of political publicity):

2A. — (1) A local authority shall not—
    (a) intentionally promote homosexuality or publish material with the intention of promoting homosexuality;
    (b) promote the teaching in any maintained school of the acceptability of homosexuality as a pretended family relationship.

56. Maclure, "Through the Revolution."
57. Maclure, "Through the Revolution"; Fletcher, "Policy-making in DES."
58. Chris Pierson, "The New Governance of Education."
59. Chris Pierson, "The New Governance of Education."
60. DES, *Education Reform Act* (London: HMSO, 1988).
61. John Lee and John Fitz, "HMI and OFSTED: Evolution or Revolution in School Inspection," *British Journal of Educational Studies* 45, no. 1 (1997): 39–52; E. Bolton, "HMI: The Thatcher Years," *Oxford Review of Education* 24, no. 1 (1998): 45–55.
62. DFE, *Education Act* (London: HMSO, 1993); Sally Tomlinson, "Sociological Perspectives on Failing Schools," *International Studies in Sociology of Education* 7, no. 1 (1997): 81–98.
63. DFE, *Education Act* (1993).
64. M. Tasker and D. Packham, "Changing Cultures? Government Intervention in Higher Education 1987–1993," *British Journal of Educational Studies* 42, no. 2 (1994): 150–62.
65. DFE, *Nursery and Grant Maintained Schools Act* (London: HMSO, 1993).
66. DES, *The Elton Report: Discipline in Schools* (London: HMSO, 1989).
67. Scott, *Poverty and Wealth.*
68. Thatcher Ministers: Carlisle (1979–1981); Joseph (1981–1986); Baker (1986–1989); McGregor (1989–1990). Major Ministers: Clarke (1990–1992); Patten (1992–1994); Shepherd (1994–1997). Blair Ministers: Blunkett (1997–2001); Morris (2001–2002); Clarke (2002–2004); Kelly (2004–2006); Johnson (2006).
69. DES, *Education (Schools) Act* (London: HMSO, 1992).
70. DFE, *Education Act* (London: HMSO, 1994).
71. DES, *Education Reform Act* (1988).
72. The four categories are community, trust, voluntary aided, and voluntary controlled. Each is in a different management relation with the LEAs, in terms of resources, admissions, appointments, standards, governance, and ownership of capital assets. Under New Labour, trusts were to be renamed foundation schools; see Melissa Benn and Fiona Millar, "Private reservations," *The Guardian*, May 14, 2006.
73. DFE, "Education Act" (1993).
74. Norah Jones, "The Real World Management Preoccupations of Primary School Heads," *School Leadership & Management* 19, no. 4 (1999): 483–95.
75. Maclure, "Through the Revolution."
76. Ron Dearing, *The National Curriculum and its Assessment* (London: Schools Examinations and Assessment Council, 1993).
77. Chris Pierson "The New Governance of Education."
78. Dearing, *The National Curriculum*; J. Williams and J. Ryan, "National Testing and the Improvement of Classroom Teaching: Can They Co-Exist?" *British Educational Research Journal* 26, no. 1 (2000): 49–73.
79. Benn and Millar, *A Comprehensive Future*, suggest that British children are tested more heavily than any in the world.
80. Tomlinson, "Sociological Perspectives."
81. DFE, *Education Act* (1993).
82. DfES, "What are Specialist Schools?" at www.standards.dfes.gov.uk/specialistschools/

what_are/?version = 1; Tony Edwards and Geoff Whitty, "Specialisation and Selection in Secondary Education," *Oxford Review of Education* 23, no. 1, special issue on Choice, Diversity and Equity in Secondary Schooling (1997): 5–15.

83. Richard Hatcher, "Privatisation and Sponsorship: The Re-Agenting of the School System in England," *Journal of Education Policy* 21, no. 5 (2006): 599–619.

84. Robert Huggins, "Local Business Co-operation and Training and Enterprise Councils: The Development of Inter-firm Networks," *Regional Studies* 32, no. 9 (1998): 813–26.

85. DES, *Further and Higher Education Act 1992* (London: HMSO, 1992); Alan Felstead and Lorna Unwin, "Funding Post Compulsory Education and Training: A Retrospective Analysis of the TEC and FEFC and Their Impact on Skills," *Journal of Education and Work* 14, no. 1 (2001): 91–111.

86. Alison Fuller and Lorna Unwin, "Creating a 'Modern Apprenticeship': A Critique of the UK's Multi-sector Social Inclusion Approach," *Journal of Education and Work* 16, no. 1 (2003): 5–25.

87. Susan Harris, "Partnership, Community and the Market in Careers Education and Guidance: Conflicting Discourses," *International Studies in the Sociology of Education* 7, no. 1 (1997): 101–19.

88. DfES, "Higher Education Student Support," at www.dfes.gov.uk/studentsupport.

89. See www.scit.wlv.ac.uk/ukinfo/alpha.html for a full list.

90. DFE, *Further and Higher Education Act 1992* (London: HMSO, 1992).

91. Colin Bryson, *Hiring Lecturers by the Hour: The Case for Change in Higher Education* (London: NAFTHE/AUT, 2005), 40.

92. DFE, *Higher Education: A New Framework* (London: HMSO, 1993) made provision for a new Higher Education Statistics Agency (HESA); M. Tight, "Do League Tables Contribute to the Development of a Quality Culture? Football and Higher Education?" *Higher Education Quarterly* 54, no. 1 (2000): 22–42.

93. Jim Campbell and Chris Husbands, "On the Reliability of OFSTED Inspection of Initial Teacher Training: A Case Study," *British Educational Research Journal* 26, no. 1 (2000): 39–48.

94. Tight, "Do League Tables Contribute."

95. Kelly Coate, Ronald Barnett, and Gareth Williams, "Relationships between Teaching and Research in Higher Education in England," *Higher Education Quarterly* 55, no. 2 (2001): 158–74.

96. D. Leigh and E. Vulliamy, *Sleaze: The Corruption of Parliament* (London: Fourth Estate, 1997).

97. DFE, *Our Children's Education: Updated Parents' Charter* (London: HMSO, 1994).

98. DFE, *Choice and Diversity* (London: HMSO, 1992).

99. Jo Sparkes and Anne West, "An Evaluation of the English Nursery Voucher Scheme 1996–1997," *Education Economics* 6, no. 2 (1998): 171–84.

100. Martin Powell, "New Labour and the Third Way in the British Welfare State: A New and Distinctive Approach?" *Critical Social Policy* 20, no. 1 (2000): 39–60; Lindsay Paterson, "The Three Educational Ideologies of the British Labour Party, 1997–2001," *Oxford Review of Education* 29, no. 2 (2003): 165–85.

101. This represents a continuing Tory/Labour battle. The Conservative first moves had been to reintroduce assisted places and grant-maintained schools after their earlier abolition by Labour in the 1970s.

102. DfES, *Higher Standards, Better Schools for All: More Choice for Parents and Pupils* (London: The Stationery Office, 2005); Fiona Millar, "Johnson's Junk Mail," *The Guardian*, May 22, 2006.

103. Melissa Benn and Fiona Millar, "Private Reservations," *The Guardian*, May 14, 2006.

104. DfEE, *Excellence in Schools* (London: HMSO, 1997).

105. Alexandra Smith and agencies, "Schools to use phonics to teach reading," *Education Guardian* (March 20, 2006)

106. See DfES, "The Beacon Schools Programme," at www.standards.dfes.gov.uk/beacon schools/.

107. See note 32 above for an explanation of DfES.

108. Hatcher, "Privatisation and Sponsorship."

109. Fiona Millar, "Whose Schools Are They?" *The Guardian*, July 6, 2006.

110. Matthew Taylor, "Ofsted Condemns Failing Academy," *The Guardian*, January 21, 2006.

111. Richard Garner, "Diplomas to Take Place of GCSEs and A-levels within a Decade," *The Independent*, November 4, 2006.

112. Sonia Blandford and Linda Squire, "An Evaluation of the Teacher Training Agency Head-teacher Leadership and Management Programme (HEADLAMP)," *Educational Management and Administration* 28, no. 1 (2000): 21–32.

113. BBC News, "'Super-teachers' to Receive Super Salaries," March 2, 1998, at news.bbc .co.uk/1/hi/uk/61246.stm.

114. Barbara Lee and Clare Mawson, *Survey of Classroom Assistants* (Slough, UK: National Foundation for Educational Research, 1998), 65; Staff and agencies, "Classroom Assistants to Get Recognition," *The Guardian*, January 16, 2002, at education.guardian.co.uk/schools/story/ 0,5500,634478,00.html.

115. In use since the 1980s, ring-fencing guarantees the protection of funds-specified projects.

116. The War on Terror has strong faith associations. It is being waged by the United States and its allies in response to the September 11, 2001, attacks on the United States, for which al-Qaeda claimed responsibility.

117. DfES, "Race Equality Impact Assessment prepared in response to the White Paper and Education Bill 2006," February 2006, 45; DfES, *Achieving Success* (London: The Stationery Office, 2001).

118. DfES, *Putting the World into World-Class Education—An International Strategy for Education, Skills and Children's Services* (London: The Stationery Office, 2004).

119. Hatcher, "Privatisation and Sponsorship."

120. *The Guardian*, "No Place for a Mother. Truancy is Bad: Prison Won't Solve It," May 15, 2002.

121. See note 38 above for an explanation of NDPB.

122. With £8,700m in its first year, equivalent to one-third of the DfES budget, it is the largest EC in Britain, responsible for administering six million learners, half a million staff, and four thousand vocational qualifications, with services delivered through countless institutional and partnership arrangements. Frank Coffield et al., "A New Learning and Skills Landscape? The Central Role of the Learning and Skills Council," *Journal of Education Policy* 20, no. 5 (2005): 631–56.

123. DfES, *14–19 Education and Skill* (London: Stationery Office, 2005); Ewart Keep, "Reflections on the Curious Absence of Employers, Labour Market Incentives and Labor Market Regulation in English 14–19 Policy: First Signs of a Change in Direction?" *Journal of Education Policy* 20, no. 5 (2005): 533–53.

124. Richard Garner, "Specialist Colleges to Teach Rock Music and Nuclear Physics," *The Independent*, November 1, 2006.

125. John Mace, "Top-Up Fees: Theoretical and Policy Issues," *Higher Education Review* 34, no. 1 (2001): 3–17.

126. BBC News, "Q&A: Student Fees," May 26, 2006, at news.bbc.co.uk/go/pr/fr/-/1/hi/ education/3013272.stm.

127. Stephen Court, "Subject to Closure," *Public Finance Magazine*, December 8, 2006, at www.publicfinance.co.uk.

128. Court, "Subject to Closure."

129. For a summary, see Stephen Adam, Carolyn Campbell and Marie-Odile Ottenwaelter, "Transnational Education Project Report and Recommendations" (paper presented to the Confederation of European Union Rectors' Conferences, Paris, France, March 2001), 34–36.

130. For a balanced to positive review see John Hills and Kitty Stewart, eds., *A More Equal Society? New Labour, Poverty, Inequality and Exclusion* (London: The Policy Press, 2004).

131. Ruth Gledhill and Tony Halpin, "Scientists are Alarmed by Ruth Kelly's Strict Beliefs," *The Times*, December 22, 2004.

132. Unison, "UNISON welcomes repeal of Section 28," press release September 19, 2003, at www.unison.org.uk/asppresspack/pressrelease_view.asp?id=359; Pink UK (seen May 2007), www.pinkuk.com/community/law/.

133. Carolyn Jackson, "Can Single-sex Classes in Co-educational Schools Enhance the Learning Experiences of Girls and/or Boys? An Exploration of Pupils' Perceptions," *British Educational Research Journal* 28, no. 1 (2002): 37–48.

134. J. A. Glossop, D. Warwick, and R. A. Preston, *The Measurement of Home Background and School Effects, Final Report to the DES* (Department of Sociology/School of Education, University of Leeds, 1984), 358.

135. Sally Tomlinson, "Diversity, Choice and Ethnicity: The Effects of Educational Markets on Ethnic Minorities," *Oxford Review of Education* 23, no. 1, special issue on Choice, Diversity and Equity in Secondary Schooling (1997): 63–76.

136. Rosemary Sales, "The Deserving and the Undeserving? Refugees, Asylum Seekers and Welfare in Britain," *Critical Social Policy* 22, no. 3 (2002): 456–78.

137. The prototype of these councils is the boards of governors, executive directors, and trustees (paid and unpaid) of commercial and nonprofit organizations.

138. Paul Sharp, "Surviving Not Thriving: LEAs Since the Education Reforms Act of 1988," *Oxford Review of Education* 28, nos. 2 and 3 (2002): 197–215. Maclure, "Through the Revolution."

139. DES, *Output Budgeting for the Department of Education and Science. Report of a Feasibility Study. Educational Planning Paper No. 1* (London: HMSO, 1970).

140. Geoffrey Walford, "How Dependent Is the Independent Sector?" *Oxford Review of Education* 13, no. 3 (1987): 275–96.

141. Chris Pierson "The New Governance of Education."

142. Hatcher, "Privatisation and Sponsorship."

143. Hatcher, "Privatisation and Sponsorship."

144. Mike Ion, "We Must Support Staying On," *The Guardian*, November 16, 2006.

145. Phillip Brown, "The Opportunity Trap: Education and Employment in a Global Economy," *European Educational Research Journal* 2, no. 1 (2003): 142–80.

146. Sharon Gewirtz, Marny Dickson, and Sally Power, "Unravelling a 'Spun' Policy: A Case Study of the Constitutive Role of 'Spin' in the Education Policy Process," *Journal of Education Policy* 19, no. 3 (2004): 321–42.

147. Callaghan, "Towards a National Debate."

148. See Richard Edwards et al., *Rhetoric and Educational Discourse*.

149. The first report issued was probably the most influential: National Commission on Excellence in Education, *A Nation at Risk: The Imperative for Educational Reform* (Washington, D.C.: Government Printing Office, 1983). See also Carnegie Corporation of New York, *Education and Economic Progress* (New York: Carnegie Corporation, 1983).

150. The quotes appear on pp. ix–xx, 10.

151. Pat Ordovensky, "Failed Monopoly: 'Defect Rate' 50 Percent from Public Schools," *USA Today*, October 27, 1987, 1A.

152. Denis P. Doyle, "The Role of Private Sector Management in Public Education," *Phi Delta Kappan* 76 (October 1994): 132.

153. Marshall S. Smith and Brent W. Scoll, "The Clinton Human Capital Agenda," *Teachers College Record* 96 (Spring 1995): 390. For a commentary on the direction of Clinton's educational initiatives as sketched out in his inaugural address, see "Mr. Clinton's Challenge on Schools," editorial, *New York Times*, February 18, 1997, A14.

154. Data contained on the website of the Bill & Melinda Gates Foundation, at www.gates foundation.org/unitedstates/education. According to a recent study of the Editorial Projects in Education (EPE) Research Center, Bill Gates is considered to be the most influential person in American education. See www.edweek.org/ew/section/tb/2006/12/12/1138.html?qs = influential + person + Bill_Gates, last accessed on May 9, 2007.

155. See Dan O. Goldhaber and Eric R. Eide, "What Do We Know (and Need to Know) about the Impact of School Choice Reforms on Disadvantaged Students?" *Harvard Educational Review* 71, no. 2 (Summer 2002): 157–76; and Diana Jean Schemo, "U.S. Report Makes No Call on For-Profit Schools," *New York Times*, November 30, 2002, A19.

156. For further discussion of charter schools, see Amy Stuart Wells, *Where Charter School Policy Fails: The Problems of Accountability and Equity* (New York: Teachers College Press, 2002); and Peter W. Cookson, *Expect Miracles: Charter Schools and the Politics of Hope and Despair* (Cambridge, Mass.: Westview, 2002).

157. Paul Tough, "What It Takes to Make a Student," *New York Times Magazine*, November 16, 2006: 44–51, 69–77 passim. Tough argues that charter schools have the flexibility to pioneer exciting new approaches to reaching and enhancing the academic careers and life chances of students frequently left behind by poor public schooling.

158. Diana Jean Schemo, "Study of Tests Scores Finds Charter Schools Lagging," *New York Times*, August 23, 2006, A12.

159. Diana Jean Schemo, "Public Schools Close to Private in U.S. Study," *New York Times*, July 15, 2006, A1.

160. Diana Jean Schemo, "Republicans Propose National School Voucher Program," *New York Times*, July 19, 2006, A7.

161. Greg Palast, "No Child's Behind Left: The Test," at www.gregpalast.com/no-childs-behind-left.

162. See ACORN website: www.acorn.org/index.php?id = 2660; and Diana Jean Schemo, "New Law Is News to Many," *New York Times*, October 5, 2001, A21; the catchy title "Parents Left Behind," comes from the PEN *Newsblast* for November 22, 2002, available by contacting Public Education Network, at www.publiceducation.org.

163. Greg Palast, "99.9 Percent Bunk: Why NCLB Is Far from Perfect," at www.teachermagazine.org/tm/articles/2006/10/01/02pers.h18.html.

164. Bob Herbert, "States of Alarm," *New York Times*, December 29, 2002, Week in Review, 9.

165. Eric Schlosser, *Fast Food Nation: The Dark Side of the All-American Meal* (New York: Houghton Mifflin, 2001, 2002), especially 51–57 in the latest edition; and Elizabeth Becker and Marian Burros, "Eat Your Vegetables? Only at a Few Schools," *New York Times*, January 13, 2003, A1, 12.

166. For further discussion, see Robert L. Linn, Eva L. Banker, and Damien W. Betebenner, "Accountability Systems: Implications of Requirement of the No Child Left Behind Act of 2001," *Educational Research* 31, no. 6 (August/September 2002): 3–16. Also, Public Education Network, "NCLB is 'Like Ivory Soap,'" Public Education Network *Newsblast* August 31, 2006, concerning criticism of The National Conference of State Legislators and more than eighty organizations about assessment goals, instruments, and processes.

167. Richard Rothstein, "How U.S. Punishes States with Higher Standards," *New York Times*, September 18, 2002, A21.

168. For further discussion, see Margaret Clements, "An International Comparison of Student Loan Programs" (paper presented at the forty-fourth annual meeting of the Comparative and International Education Society, San Antonio, Texas, March 8–11, 2000); and "Planning for Affirmative Student Loans for Higher Education: A Transformative Possibility?" (paper presented at the forty-fifth annual meeting of the Comparative and International Education Society in Washington, D.C., March 14–18, 2001). Contact information: mcappell@indiana.edu.

169. "Public Colleges as 'Engines of Inequality,'" editorial, *New York Times*, November 12, 2006, A30.

170. "U.S. Supreme Court Rules on University of Michigan Cases," *UM News*, June 23, 2003, at www.umich.edu/news/Releases/2003/June03/supremecourt.html.

171. *Regents of the University of California v. Bakke*, 438 U.S. 265 (1978).

172. "White Teachers Fleeing Black Schools," summarized in the Public Education Network *NewsBlast* of 17 January 2003; study found at www.cnn.com/2003/EDUCATION/01/13/reseg regation.teachers.ap/index.html; and for more extended discussion of resegregation in U.S. schools, see Gary Orfield and John T. Yun, Resegregation in American Schools [computer file] (Cambridge, Mass.: Civil Rights Project, Harvard University, 1999). The website for the project is www.civilrightsproject.harvard.edu/. The project issued a press release on Martin Luther King Jr. Day, January 20, 2003, deploring the current status of minority education and racial desegregation in the United States.

173. Orfield and Yun, "Resegregation."

174. See U.S. Department of Education, Office of Post-Secondary Education, Office of Policy, Planning, and Innovation, *Meeting the Highly Qualified Teachers Challenge: The Secretary's Annual Report on Teacher Quality* (Washington, D.C.: Author, 2002); and Linda Darling Hammond and Peter Young, "Defining 'Highly Qualified' Teachers: What Does 'Scientifically-Based' Research Actually Tell Us?" *Educational Researcher* 31, no. 9 (December 2002): 13–25.

175. Diana Jean Schemo, "Law Overhauling School Standards Is Seen as Skirted," *New York Times*, October 15, 2002, A1, A21.

176. Associated Press News Release, cited in the *Herald Times* (Bloomington, Indiana), January 3, 2003, B6.

177. Further information on community organizing available on the ACORN website, www.acorn.org.

178. With regard to the November 5, 2002, state referenda, see "The Voters Speak in 2002: Fully Fund and Strengthen Public Education," summarized in the Public Education Network *NewsBlast* for January 17, 2003; the full story is found on the website of People for the American Way, www.pfaw.org/pfaw/general/default.aspx?oid=7051.

179. Monica Davey and Ralph Blumental, "Evolution Fight Shifts Direction in Kansas Vote," *New York Times*, August 3, 2006, A1; and "The Evolution of Kansas," *New York Times* editorial, August 30, 2006, A22.

180. See Laurie Goldstein, "Issuing Rebuke, Judge Rejects Teaching of Intelligent Design," *New York Times*, December 21, 2006, A1; and Laurie Goldstein, "Schools Nationwide Study Impact of Evolution Ruling," *New York Times*, December 22, 2005, A1.

181. Linda Greenhouse, "Court Reviews Race as Factor in School Plans," *New York Times*, December 5, 2006, A1, 20.

182. Tough, "What It Takes," 47.

183. Diana Jean Schemo, "Most Students in Big Cities Lag Badly in Basic Sciences: Tests Find a Lack of Even Rudiments," *New York Times*, November 15, 2006, A20.

184. "Racial Disparities," *New York Times* editorial, November 14, 2006, A22.

185. Louis Uchitelle, "Very Rich Are Leaving the Merely Rich Behind," *New York Times*, November 27, 2006, A1, 18.

186. Rick Lyman, "Census Reports Slight Increase in '05 Incomes: More Work Is Seen, Not Bigger Paychecks," *New York Times*, August 30, 2006, A12.

187. "New Inequality," *New York Times Magazine*, December 10, 2006, 63.

188. The particulars are the subject of Raymond Callahan, *Education and the Cult of Efficiency* (Chicago: University of Chicago Press, 1962).

189. Molly Ivins, "Bush Discovers Hunger and Looks the Other Way," op-ed, *Chicago Tribune*, December 16, 2002.

190. Jim Carl, "Parental Choice as National Policy in England and the United States," *Comparative Education Review* 38, no. 3 (August 1994): 304.

11

Higher Education Restructuring in the Era of Globalization: Toward a Heteronomous Model?

Daniel Schugurensky

Any attempt to examine international trends in higher education in a few pages inevitably risks some degree of generalization and simplification. A global analysis of this type cannot account for the significant differences in models of national development, in the history and organization of national higher education systems, and among and within individual institutions. It can, however, describe some tendencies and discuss them in terms of the context of the world system.

In the first decade of the twenty-first century, higher education systems continue the trend toward institutional diversification, regionalization, and vocationalization. In many countries, the typical student of several decades ago (male, upper class, and young) is no longer the norm, as women, minority groups, and mature students have entered the system in increasing numbers. Technological advances are nurturing unprecedented innovations in the transmission of information, greatly affecting the quantity, speed, and nature of knowledge production and distribution.

From a broader perspective, during the last two decades we have witnessed the intensification of a variety of social, cultural, economic, and political developments that affect higher education. Prominent among them are the globalization of the economy, the retrenchment of the welfare state, and the commodification of knowledge. This has been complemented with an ideological shift in policy circles from Keynesianism to neoliberalism, and with it a wave of privatization and an increasing presence of market dynamics in social exchanges.

The impact of these developments on the university is reflected in a new discourse that emphasizes value for money, accountability, planning, cost-efficiency, good management, resource allocation, unit costs, performance indicators, and selectivity. Tenure is under attack, and disciplines must prove their worth by their contribution to the economy. The fiscal crisis of the state, resulting in budget cutbacks, generates an increased reliance on private sources of revenue (through links with the business sector and user fees), restrictions on enrollments, proliferation of private institutions, deregulation of working conditions, and faculty entrepreneuralism. Like a chain reaction, these developments impact many others. Changes in the origin of university revenues (e.g., higher fees and more service to industry) may have serious implications for accessibility and autonomy, respectively. Limited accessibility, in turn, can lead to the reduction of student diversity and to the proliferation of second-class institutions, creating two, three, or more tiers in the system. Likewise, a reduction in autonomy may have an impact on areas like governance, curriculum, and research priorities. In general, most of these changes are expressions of a greater influence of the market and the government over university affairs. Overall, due to its long-term implications, probably the most significant trend worldwide is the drastic restructuring of higher education systems. At the core of this process is a redefinition of the relationship between the university, the state, and the market, with a net result of a reduction in institutional autonomy. Although advocates and detractors of the current higher education restructuring may disagree on a number of issues, most of them would agree that such restructuring can alter not only the modus operandi of the university but also its social purpose.

A striking feature of the current restructuring process is the unprecedented scope and depth of changes taking place as well as the similarity of changes occurring in a wide variety of nations having different social, political, historical, and economic characteristics. Although the pace and the dynamics of this change vary according to the specific historical conditions and social formation of each country, any review of recent policy initiatives implemented by governments throughout the world shows that the direction of reforms follows an unmistakably similar path. In all continents, a myriad of government plans, constitutional reforms, legislative acts, regulations, and recommendations are moving universities closer to the demands of the state and the marketplace. This has serious consequences for the financing, governance, and mission of higher education, and ultimately for the degree of autonomy enjoyed by individual institutions to define proactively their agenda.

This restructuring (also referred to as repositioning, reengineering, streamlining, downsizing, adjustment, etc.) is not so much a genuine reform as it is a response. Although both involve change, reform is active and by choice, whereas response is reactive and of necessity.[1] In most cases, university restructuring is not emerging from democratic deliberation among internal actors but from external pressures linked to economic globalization, the dismantling of the welfare state, and the increasing commodification of knowledge. Restructuring is often implemented in spite of considerable opposition from the academic community, reflecting the increasing power of international and domestic political and economic forces in influencing higher education policy.[2]

THE CONTEXT OF UNIVERSITY CHANGE: THE ERA OF GLOBALIZATION

The changing role of the university today cannot be isolated from the emergence of a postindustrial economy, in which productivity relies predominantly on science, technology, knowledge, and management, rather than on the amount of capital or labor. This is particularly clear in advanced countries, in which the new economy is increasingly based on information-processing activities. The new economy is also abandoning the Fordist principles found in standardized mass production and moving into a customized, flexible, "just in time" model known as Toyotism. Most important, the new economy is global.

Production processes, markets, capital, management, telecommunications, and technology bypass national boundaries. Although nation-states are still important centers of power, national economies are now subsumed in real time with (and increasingly dependent on) the global economy.

Globalization, a dynamic that has economic, political, social, and cultural ramifications, implies the intensification of transnational flows of information, commodities, and capital around the globe (eroding technical, political, or legal barriers), the development of new trading blocs, and the strengthening of supranational governing bodies and military powers.[3] This increasingly globalized economy is largely controlled by a transnational elite composed of the G-8 countries, international financial institutions, and multinational corporations.

Parallel with globalization is the retrenchment of the welfare state, which is being replaced by a neoliberal state geared at promoting economic international competitiveness through cutbacks in social expenditure, economic deregulation, decreased capital taxes, privatization, and labor flexibilization.[4] This new state abandons its role as direct economic agent (producer of goods and services) and as regulator of economic life (minimum wages, maximum prices, protectionism, subsidies, etc.), becoming instead a subsidiary agent whose main function is to guarantee a social and economic environment propitious for capital accumulation. For the average person, the dismantling of the welfare state results in higher unemployment rates, lower wages, and less job security. It also implies the withdrawal of the state's commitment to universal provision of public services such as education, health, housing, and social security, which are now becoming increasingly regulated by market dynamics. This withdrawal, coupled with increasing incentives to capital via lower taxes and labor flexibilization, is referred to as a shift from social welfare to corporate welfare.

The transition from the welfare state to the neoliberal state implies not only structural changes but also ideological ones. Growing public deficits and declining economic growth provide fertile soil for the cultivation of conservative ideology. Fostered mainly by the business community, this ideology attributes economic problems to excessive state expenditure and to an oversized state bureaucracy and calls for drastic cutbacks in university funding. The progressive, optimistic view that links investment in education with economic growth and democratization of society is being replaced by a much tougher view based on the assumption that the private sector creates wealth, whereas public expenditure based on high taxation fuels inflation and discourages entrepreneurs.[5]

Amid globalization pressures and welfare state retrenchment, inequalities between and within nations are increasing. At the global level, there is a growing concentration of capital and power in multinational corporations (MNCs), international agencies, and supranational organizations over sovereign nation-states and labor organizations.[6] Currently, six hundred major multinational corporations control 25 percent of the world economy and 80 percent of world trade. Most MNCs have their home base in core countries, which fuels the ever growing financial and technological gap between North and South. In an increasingly knowledge-based society, the average proportion of researchers per million people in developed countries reaches 850, whereas in developing countries it is 127, and the percentage of the GNP allocated to research and development is 1.78 and 0.45 respectively.[7] Some analysts are talking about the emergence of a fourth world, a category including those pauperized economies that, as they become marginalized from the world system, shift from a structural position of exploitation to one of irrelevance.[8]

At the national level, many countries, rich and poor alike, are experiencing higher levels of social and economic polarization.[9]

In developing countries, governments are pressured by lending agencies to implement austerity programs in order to be eligible for emergency loans. These programs, known as structural adjustment programs (SAPs), aim at a reduction in the redistributive role of the state and an increasing role of the market in regulating societal exchanges. Among the policies recommended by lending agencies are liberalization of imports, elimination of subsidies, privatization of public enterprises, user fees in public services, and drastic cuts in government expenditures in areas such as health, education, housing, sanitation, transportation, and environment. Privatization proposals, generally defended on the grounds that they promote efficiency, equity, and decentralization of decision making, usually result in the disentitlement of large sectors of the population to services that once were considered an inalienable right.

At the same time, both production and dissemination of knowledge are increasingly commodified. As cultural and scientific endeavors must become profitable activities, cultural goods become commercial products, the public is redefined as customers, the university becomes a provider, and the learner, a purchaser of a service. Technological advances go hand in hand with the ascendance of "home delivery" electronic cultural goods (cable TV, Internet, videos, instruction, etc.), the predominance of megaindustries in the production and distribution of cultural goods, and a time-space compression of human interaction.

Public universities are not immune to this new climate. During the Fordist period, universities were perceived as the most vital of public investments, whereas in the post-Fordist era they are seen as a major part of the economic problem. The aims of accessibility, social criticism, cultural development, and institutional autonomy are being subordinated to the three Rs of the economic crisis (recession, rationalization, and restraint), further aggravated in many developing countries by the R of repayment of the external debt. Since the decline of state funding for public universities has been in many cases very noticeable, many students and faculty tend to equate the current university crisis to a financial crisis. But budget cuts, although they constitute a serious problem, represent just one element of the ongoing restructuring process. In other words, it is not that universities must do the same with fewer resources but must do different things and in different ways. The scope and depth of university restructuring throughout the world, with the adoption of similar ideologies and policies in so many different settings, cannot simply be attributed to a spontaneous upsurge of mass disaffection with higher education. It is neither an inevitable nor an impersonal process but the product of a double process of consensus and coercion carried out by concrete social actors.

On the one hand, simultaneous developments in a variety of countries reflect a common response to common problems. To some extent, higher education restructuring results from technical analysis and its ensuing recommendations, which flow from country to country (usually from developed to developing ones) in a process of cultural diffusion through networks of experts who borrow what they perceive as the most sensible alternatives. This process is usually piecemeal and works through arenas such as demonstration effects, conferences, debates, literature, and study abroad programs. On the other hand, restructuring is part and parcel of a conscious effort on the part of powerful interest groups to adapt the university (and education in general) to the new economic paradigm. This effort is organized through institutional arrangements that put together business and government representatives who pressure academic institutions to redefine their priorities and adopt new operational principles. Those institutional arrangements have different expressions in core and peripheral countries. In the former, the interests of the corporate sector are advanced through a bevy of business-higher education fora, joint research groups, government-industry conferences, and the like. In the latter, they are advanced by what Joel Samoff calls the "intellectual/financial complex of foreign aid."[10] Prominent among this network are international financial institutions like the World Bank, which have the means to concentrate research, funding, and policy formulation under one roof.

In spite of the fact that these donors and lenders have become hegemonic powers in influencing educational policy in the developing world, this does not mean that restructuring measures are applied consistently in every country. Although most higher education systems are moving in a similar direction, the transition is full of adaptations, partial rejections, and conflicts. In each national formation, which has its own history and educational traditions, local actors actively struggle over policy recommendations emanating from the world system. Furthermore, even in the same country, restructuring processes vary according to the unique features of each individual institution.

CONVERGENCE

The trend toward convergence pointed out fifteen years ago by Philip Altbach, one of the pioneers in the field of comparative higher education, is intensifying.[11] This convergence does not mean that all higher education systems are one and the same, but that they are increasingly governed by similar pressures, procedures, and organizational patterns. As the fiscal crisis of the state continues, universities all over the world are still affected by deep financial constraints. The budget cutbacks of recent years have forced public universities to reduce costs through a variety of means and to seek private sources of revenue. This has enhanced university-business linkages in teaching and research and has prompted institutions to rely more on fund-raising activities and increased (or imposed, if they did not exist) tuition and fees.

However, privatization is not only expressed in the introduction of private elements in public institutions but also in the rapid growth of the private sector. Moreover, with the increased direct and indirect state financial support of private institutions, what is emerging in many countries is a hybrid system that combines public and private features in all institutions, to the point that, if the tendency continues, in a few years it will be difficult to distinguish, at least in terms of funding, a private university from a public one. The shift from a dual public-private system toward a hybrid model is one among several elements of a general trend toward the Americanization of higher education systems. This trend is not necessarily new. For different reasons, the U.S. system has constituted the dominant higher education paradigm for the past several decades. Even back in the 1970s, Altbach asserted that "there is no question that higher education planners and others often look to the United States as the most relevant model for academic development in their countries."[12] What is new is the widening and intensification of this convergence process.

The convergence of higher education systems at the global level is related to at least three related phenomena: the influence of international and national organizations on higher education policy, the consolidation of regional blocs, and a broader consolidation of international epistemic communities. First, the role of international agencies and financial institutions in higher education policy is an important element to consider in understanding the direction of university systems, particularly in developing countries. These organizations have great coercive power over nations in need of funding, and this power is exercised not only through conditionalities to access credit (structural adjustment policies based on budget cuts and promarket reforms) but also through agenda setting, collection and interpretation of data, workshops and conferences, recommendations and consulting, and so on. In developed countries, the role of these international organizations is fulfilled by a variety of think tanks, state-industry committees, and business-higher education fora that typically advance a procorporate agenda.[13]

The process of world convergence among higher education systems has been assisted by processes of regional convergences, which occur as nation-states integrate into trading blocs such as the North American Free Trade Agreement (NAFTA), the Mercado Común Sudamericano (Mercosur), the European Union (EU), the Association of South East Asian Nations (ASEAN), or the African Economic Community (AEC). These common markets, with their political, legal, economic, and cultural requirements and their need for regional harmonization, create new demands on universities. For instance, agreements on labor mobility lead to stricter recognition of credentials and transfer of equivalencies, which in turn influences the homogenization of curricula and the standardization of educational experiences, particularly regarding professional programs. At the same time, the consolidation of these regional communities has prompted a wave of institutional cooperation, joint projects, and student and academic exchange programs. The most recent expression of this process at the world level is the effort carried out by the World Trade Organization (WTO) through the General Agreement on Trade and Services (GATS) to make higher education an internationally traded commodity. Indeed, GATS/WTO recognizes four kinds of cross-border trade in services: (1) studying abroad (now considered an export of educational services); (2) cross-border supply (e.g., sale of courses on the Internet or in the form of CD-ROMS or DVDs); (3) commercial presence (e.g., opening private institutions run by foreign firms); and (4) presence of natural persons means (e.g., employing foreign teachers).

The convergence of higher education systems is also related to a broader consolidation of international epistemic communities (networks that generate more or less consensual definitions of problems and solutions across a variety of fields) that rapidly accelerates the convergence of scientific discourses. Although academic elites continue circulating their ideas through the traditional avenues (conferences, seminars, journals, study abroad programs, etc.), the proliferation of online communications and the universalization of English as the academic lingua franca in academic discourse and among symbolic analysts have considerably speeded up the process.

However (and paradoxically), at the same time that a relatively small number of symbolic analysts are able to interact more fluidly in closed networks, a large contingent of academics and students in poor countries who have restricted access to up-to-date computer technologies are likely to be marginalized by this interaction. If they live in non-English-speaking developing countries, the process of marginalization is compounded, as translations have difficulty keeping pace with the increasing number of scientific papers published every year. Arguably, this situation is more relevant for some disciplines than for others.

LANGUAGE, SCIENCE, AND DEPENDENCY

Dependence on English as the primary language of scientific communication not only raises concerns about exclusion and translation delays but also about forced inclusion. In addition to longstanding issues of neocolonialism and cultural imperialism, in some national settings (such as the Arab countries or the Philippines), specific concerns have arisen regarding the most appropriate language of instruction at the university level. These concerns are not only about pedagogy, textbooks, and proficiency of students and faculty, but also about a potential detrimental impact of these practices on the preservation of domestic languages. This preoccupation is not exclusive of poor nations. In France, for instance, reservations against the Internet were advanced on the grounds of the preservation of local language and culture. In Holland, the issue of the potential disappearance of Dutch as a national language and its possible replacement by English has led the Dutch Ministry of Education and Science to express in the national press its strong commitment to "a flourishing Dutch culture and, consequently, to the survival of Dutch as the language of instruction in schools, the government and the courts," while recognizing that this will not be an easy task, since "the internationalization of higher education and research make the use of other languages beside Dutch indispensable."[14] For universities in developing countries, the language situation is a symptom of a deeper issue. With a few exceptions, the production and distribution of research and development (R&D) is still concentrated in core countries.

Indeed, peripheral countries are basically consumers of knowledge, especially in the areas of science and technology. The knowledge produced in Latin America, for example, represents less than 3 percent of the world's scientific production, which is not surprising in light of its low investment in research and development. The public expenditures in R&D of all Latin American countries together are equivalent to the expenses in R&D of a couple of multinational corporations.[15] In the two leading countries of the region in terms of scientific production (Brazil and Mexico), R&D expenditures as percentage of GNP are 0.4 and 0.3 respectively, a low proportion when compared to the 3.0 allocated by Japan and the 3.5 by Sweden. These differences in resource allocation are reflected in the critical mass of researchers. In Mexico and Brazil there are only 95 and 165 scientists and engineers per million people, respectively, whereas in Sweden there are 3,714 and in Japan, 5,677. The Latin American situation is no different from that in other developing regions. To take two examples from Africa, Nigeria allocates to R&D only 0.1 percent of the GNP and the Central African Republic, 0.2 percent, with 15 and 55 scientists per million, respectively. In Asia, Thailand assigns to R&D 0.2 percent of the GNP, China, 0.6 percent, and India, 0.8 percent, with 73, 537, and 151 scientists per million, respectively.[16] Likewise, Sweden and Japan are not atypical examples of advanced countries, in which the figures for resource allocation are usually above 2.5 percent of the GNP, and the number of scientists and engineers per million is close to 3,000.

The current model of development implemented in most developing countries, highly dependent on foreign capital and technology, does not provide the most propitious conditions for the production and application of indigenous knowledge. In many of these countries, scientific dependence is indirectly assisted by higher education systems that do not pay enough attention to research and development. In many developing countries, for instance, in spite of current efforts to increase the proportion of full-time academic staff, most professors still work part time or by the hour, which in many cases limits the possibilities of developing a critical mass of researchers. Likewise, the emphasis of academic activities rests largely with the professional training of undergraduate students. Although graduate programs have recently expanded and multidisciplinary programs are growing, the experience of most students is confined within the narrow limits of their disciplines. This professional orientation provides little room for a flexible curriculum. Students specialize in their discipline from the first year and in general terms are not prepared with the research tools and interdisciplinary skills that are required in graduate programs. In this context, it is not entirely surprising that in the 2006 world university ranking of the Times Higher Education Supplement, there is only one university from Latin America and not even one university from Africa among the top 200 universities in the world. Even if one may disagree with some of the indicators used in this ranking, it is difficult to dispute that world inequalities in the distribution of wealth are associated with international inequalities in the production and distribution of knowledge.

The technological dependence of developing countries and the relatively low incomes of scientists, among other factors, contribute to the continuation of human capital transfers to more developed countries. Continuous impoverishment and deterioration of living conditions in developing countries, coupled with the scarcity of relevant employment opportunities for university graduates, result in an escalation of the brain drain, which in turn aggravates the cycle of technological and scientific dependency.[17] As long as the gap in scientific development and working conditions in both settings persists, the exodus is likely to continue.

TECHNOLOGY AND INSTRUCTION

Higher education instruction is being affected by the rapid development of new interactive technologies, which are impelling quantitative and qualitative changes in distance education programs. These programs are not only growing but also are being reconceptualized, from correspondence, telephone, or one-way televised courses to a much more sophisticated model of immediate interaction between instructors and students, particularly through the use of the Internet and weblogs. The technological advances have allowed the emergence of many virtual universities (both public and private), in which students can complete a degree online without setting foot on campus. In a related development, some traditional private universities (like the Massachusetts Institute of Technology) are making all their web materials available to the public at no cost. The area of distance education that is expected to have the most growth in the upcoming years is the one of asynchronous (anytime/anywhere) courses, offered not only by interactive video but also by software that can be used by students at their preferred time and place. This emerging model of "flexible learning" is receiving special attention from governments because it promises three goals that usually are not found together: cutting costs, improving quality, and broadening access to instruction. Moreover, emerging open source and open access initiatives reduce costs to retrieve information and provide opportunities for the creation of collective intellectual works that build on previous contributions and contribute to societal wealth of knowledge.

THE IMPACT OF BUDGET CUTBACKS

The unprecedented expansion of the 1960s, 1970s, and early 1980s raised concerns among a variety of actors, particularly when enrollments were not matched by appropriate budgetary increases. Although several university systems have moved successfully from elitism to massive access during the postwar period, the expected transition to universal access has been interrupted by stricter admission policies and higher tuition and fees.[18] The two main arguments advanced by governments to justify the interruption of mass expansion were that the rapid growth in enrollments of the second half of the twentieth century led to a quality decline, and that financial resources could not increase indefinitely. As the welfare state retrenched, government financial cutbacks became a reality, and higher education institutions were forced to reduce enrollments, increase revenues, and/or save costs. Many universities, then, began to selectively cut certain programs and services as well as diversify their revenue sources, including contracts with the business sector, client fees, alumni contributions, and donations. Self-recovery programs were encouraged, and fund-raising activities came to the forefront. Cost savings were achieved through a variety of strategies, including the replacement of high-paid faculty by less expensive staff, early retirement packages, attrition, larger classrooms, outsourcing, interruption of library subscriptions, cancellation of major renovations of facilities, and reductions in equipment acquisition. Administrators are also reducing labor costs and labor conflicts by contracting out a variety of services previously performed by staff directly employed by the university.

The new rules of the game are not being accepted without conflict. Budget cuts, restrictive entrance requirements, and new or higher fees, for instance, have prompted a new wave of faculty and student militancy in different parts of the world, particularly in developing countries. In spite of occasional student resistance, user fees are becoming part of the reality in many countries with a long tradition of free higher education. This constitutes a considerable departure from just a decade ago, when the possibility of charging students for attending public universities was unthinkable. Tuition and fees, then taboo issues, are now openly debated and implemented.

To cope with social demands for accessibility, many governments are encouraging the expansion of nonuniversity postsecondary institutions. This institutional diversification allows governments to cope with the new cohorts of high school graduates, shifting resources from universities to lower-cost institutions such as technical institutes, regional universities, community colleges, and professional training programs. The effects of institutional diversification are still to be seen. On the one hand, the proliferation of nonuniversity postsecondary institutions provides greater choice and increased accessibility to the system. On the other hand, it could lead to a further stratification of higher education, in which the mechanisms of closure are redefined and masked under a facade of democracy and meritocracy.

To further reduce pressures for accessibility without incurring budgetary increases, many governments (particularly in Latin America, Asia, and the former socialist bloc) have allowed (and in many cases encouraged) the growth of private higher education. A case in point is Chile, where, as a result of the growth of private institutions, public expenditures on higher education decreased from $171 million in 1981 to $115 million in 1988.[19] The private sector not only absorbs the social demand for higher education when it exceeds the public supply, but it also reduces political conflict due to limited student activism and increases the availability of choice by providing different content and (theoretically) better quality. Although the introduction of market dynamics in higher education promotes competition and could raise efficiency and quality, it could also lead in some cases to a dual structure, with an expensive and high-quality education for the elites and a deteriorating and impoverished education for the masses.[20]

In many developing countries, both elite and nonelite private universities continue their steady growth. The demand for these institutions comes from those who believe that the quality of public universities has declined, those who are dissatisfied with its excessive politicization, those who believe that private credentials are more marketable, and those who are rejected by public universities on academic grounds.[21] Although in most developing countries the contribution of private universities to national development is acknowledged, the public sentiment toward some of these institutions is not always positive, particularly when they are perceived as profit-seeking businesses in which financial considerations are more valued than academic ones. This perception is reinforced by the fact that in some countries a significant proportion of private universities tend to invest almost exclusively in programs that are marketable, require low infrastructure, and have fast rates of return. In addition, research activities are scarce and quality standards are usually unregulated, partly because strict accreditation mechanisms are seldom in place.

VOCATIONALIZATION

In many countries, rich and poor, the relationship between higher education and labor markets shows less-than-perfect correlations. Enrollment expansion and economic slowdown have led to significant numbers of educated unemployed and underemployed (performing tasks below their qualifications or, as a sort of internal brain drain, in fields different than those from which they graduated), and to an escalation of credentialism (by which higher degrees are required to perform essentially the same jobs). This situation has provided a fertile soil for the vocationalization of higher education. Pressures for vocationalization come from students who become more pragmatic and focus on material rewards and remunerative job prospects, from business and industrial groups demanding a curriculum that is responsive to the needs of the workplace, from governments demanding a closer connection between education and economic development, and from opinion leaders (mainly politicians and the media) accusing universities of irrelevance and esoterism.[22]

The growth of vocational and professional programs undermines the tradition of liberal education (the idea that knowledge is a worthwhile end in itself) and the image of the community of independent scholars pursuing truth. A strong emphasis on a restrictive version of vocational education may be counterproductive, given the difficulties of forecasting labor needs in a constantly changing labor market. It may also backfire against employers and limit the employment prospects of students, as graduates of these programs will lack the problem-solving skills and the flexibility to adapt to changing situations and new technologies typical of a post-Fordist work environment.

DIVERSIFICATION AND RESTRATIFICATION
OF THE STUDENT BODY

In terms of demographics, the traditional higher education student population has changed, with increasing participation by female, minority, and mature students. In many countries, women now represent approximately 50 percent of enrollments. However, although expansion has improved accessibility, a full democratization of higher education has not occurred. The system is stratified, with female and minority students underrepresented in high-status, high-paid fields, and overrepresented in low-status careers and institutions.

In higher education institutions that have implemented positive discrimination policies, an increase in the representation of disadvantaged groups has taken place. These progressive policies, established during the 1960s and 1970s under the "principle of redress," aimed to equalize opportunity and increase access and successful participation of underrepresented groups, and gave rise to a variety of programs such as affirmative action, need-based grants and scholarships, subsidized student loans, and so on. Today, in an environment dominated by conservative thought, these policies are being challenged ideologically and legally. Their critics contend that affirmative action has been abused, that unfair quotas have been established, and that it has contributed to an alleged quality decline. In some cases, the attack on affirmative action has been successful through political and legal actions, with a negative impact on equity and accessibility.

THE ACADEMIC WORKFORCE AND
ACCOUNTABILITY PRESSURES

The increasing flexibilization of labor is also present in universities, as a recomposition of the academic workforce is taking place. This is particularly noticeable in countries in which academic staff have traditionally enjoyed stability and good working conditions. During the last decades, the proportion of full-time faculty has shrunk considerably, whereas the number of staff holding part-time or non-permanent non-tenure track appointments (known formally as sessionals, readers, adjuncts, lecturers, contingent, or extramurals, and informally as "roads scholars" or "McProfs," etc.) has increased at unprecedented rates. As in other areas of the labor market, academic workers are being restratified and segmented into a small group of core workers (with high stability and good working conditions) and a large army of low-paid flexible workers perpetually haunted by the ghost of labor insecurity. In the emerging division of labor, the core workers are likely to be tenured professors who concentrate on the coordination of research projects and graduate teaching. The contingent workers are more likely to teach undergraduates and collaborate in research projects on a temporary basis. Part and parcel of labor flexibilization are attacks launched on tenure, on the grounds that its original purpose (protection of academic freedom) has been distorted into job security for faculty members. Pressures for the elimination of tenure have been occasionally successful, but so far, the academic community has been able to preserve it or at least negotiate it. However, in spite of the preservation of tenure codes, university administrators are enjoying increasing managerial flexibility in firing employees based on new clauses such as financial exigency or program redundancy, and on increasing the proportion of faculty who are not tenure-track.

The calls for the elimination of tenure, together with the intensification of the academic workforce, are part of a larger pressure from governments to make universities more efficient and accountable. In times of budget constraints, there is a widespread assumption among state officials that universities are not cost-effective institutions and that they are unresponsive to societal needs. As a result, there is an increasing importance attributed to the evaluation of university activities. In general terms, the evaluation of the quality of higher education institutions is shifting from an approach exclusively based on inputs (academic credentials of faculty members, library resources, laboratories and research facilities, teacher/student ratios, academic/nonacademic staff ratios, per-student expenditures, etc.) to one that also includes processes and outcomes. However, outcomes are generally measured in terms of performance indicators (program completion rates, levels of satisfaction of graduates and employers, etc.) that tend to disregard qualitative data and ignore the particular "historic missions" of individual institutions.

Although performance indicators are broadly accepted in the political and administrative discourse as the most adequate tools to evaluate universities (in teaching, research, and service), in practice they mainly provide statistical measures of efficiency, speed, and productivity. Although there is a general agreement that university activities should be accounted for and evaluated, controversies have arisen about the differences between evaluation and assessment, the definition of quality and the best indicators to evaluate it, and the criteria to measure efficiency. Debates consider not only the technical dimension of evaluation but also the political one, usually addressed in terms of who carries out the evaluation, and for what reasons. For instance, disputes have taken place on the most appropriate evaluating entity (whether the evaluation should be best carried out by the government, an internal body of the university, a team acceptable to both parties, etc.) and on the purpose of the evaluation (to assist universities in improving their performance or to provide governments with supposedly objective information to reward and punish with the power of the purse).

HIGHER EDUCATION RESTRUCTURING: TOWARD A HETERONOMOUS MODEL?

The common denominator of current higher education changes worldwide is the gradual loss of institutional autonomy. Autonomy allows institutions to set, collegially and free from external interference, their own objectives and missions, content and methods of instruction, evaluation criteria, admission and graduation requirements, research agendas, promotion and demotion procedures, and the like. Since its medieval origins, and in spite of considerable tensions with the church and the state, the university has enjoyed a large degree of autonomy. It was recognized early on by its ecclesiastical masters that the university, as a self-governing community of scholars, warranted independence from external powers. The assumption was that scientific knowledge is most effectively produced, maintained, and disseminated in relatively autonomous institutions whose members enjoy a high degree of academic freedom. In addition to institutional autonomy and academic freedom, the medieval university was characterized by a participatory approach to learning and inquiry, a collaborative internal government, open admissions, and a belief in knowledge for its own sake.[23]

Today, however, in the midst of globalization pressures, market-friendly economic reforms, state adjustment, and calls for accountability, the principle of autonomy is being challenged and drastically redefined. While most public institutions have been affected by neoliberal policies, privatization processes, and budget cutbacks, the university's situation is aggravated by a generalized distrust of its contribution to economic development. Such distrust, sometimes induced by governments, business, and some sectors of the media, is often related to the growth of educated unemployment and underemployment, the widespread belief that universities are "ivory towers" disconnected from the "real world," complaints about alleged waste and mismanagement, suspicions about the productivity of tenured academics, and problems related to student unrest.

In this context, universities are experiencing a transition (sometimes voluntary, usually forced) toward a heteronomous model.[24] Following Weber, an institution can be considered heteronomous when its mission, its agenda, and its outcomes are defined more by external controls and impositions than by its internal governing bodies. Thus, a heteronomous university is one increasingly unable to proactively design its itinerary, and whose success derives from its effective and rapid response to external demands. Whereas autonomy implies self-government and refers to the quality or state of being independent, free, and self-directed, heteronomy, by contrast, implies a subordination to the law or domination of another. The available evidence indicates that a significant number of universities throughout the world are increasingly forced to reduce their degree of autonomy by reacting both to market demands and state imperatives.[25]

The heteronomous university stems from the combined effect of two apparently contradictory dynamics: laissez-faire policies and state interventionism.[26] Indeed, the emerging model encompasses two university models usually addressed independently in the literature on the topic: the "commercial" model and the "state-controlled" model. The commercial dimension includes a variety of policy instruments promoting the spread of private institutions, corporate-like management, faculty entrepreneurialism, client fees, consumer-oriented programs, contracts with industry, and a multiplicity of fund-raising, cost-recovery, and cost-saving mechanisms. At the same time, the state is able to influence the university's behavior through budget cuts and new funding mechanisms based less on enrollments and more on performance evaluations and institutional competition. In the commercial university, the institution becomes an enterprise, faculty become entrepreneurs, and students and research products become outcomes for industry—the ultimate customer of the service.[27] As traditional values and organizational patterns are replaced by those of the marketplace, the university enters full-fledged into the phase of academic capitalism.[28] This includes an unprecedented growth of administrative structures separated from the academy; consequently, managerial professionalism becomes the ultimate model in decision making.

The corporate rationality is also expressed in mergers among departments, faculties, and institutions, in departmental structures that promote autonomous units, in reward mechanisms, and in hiring, promotion, and firing criteria. As mentioned above, the logic of the market is also expressed in contracting out, in a general emphasis on efficiency and cost-reduction strategies, and in an increasing institutional diversification of the system, encouraging differentiation and choice. It is also noticeable in an increasing vocationalization of the system, with the introduction of short cycles closely connected with labor market requirements that sometimes lead to an excessive utilitarianism. As well, more restrictive admission policies, with a rhetoric of excellence and an explicit rejection of models based on open access or compensatory justice for disadvantaged groups (i.e., affirmative action), are creating a swing back in the long quality versus equality debate.

At the same time, individual professors, departments, and schools of public and private universities must engage in competitive behavior similar to that prevailing in the marketplace for funding, grants, contracts, and students. Among academics, entrepreneurship is greatly promoted, tenure is endangered, and the proportion of part-time faculty increases. Education is considered more as a private consumption or investment than an inalienable right or a search for disinterested knowledge. As a language that centers on user fees, rational choices, job prospects, and private rates of return becomes increasingly hegemonic and the commercial model becomes paradigmatic, attacks on competing models escalate. The academic haven model (scholars seeking truth in an uncontaminated environment) is perceived as an irrelevant ivory tower, the human capital model that led to the educational expansion of previous decades is discredited after the recurrent failures of labor forecasting, and the social transformation model that had so many sympathizers during the 1960s and 1970s is now portrayed as cheap populism that leads to an extreme politicization of academic activities.[29]

The commercial model is complemented by an increasing number of control mechanisms designed and implemented by the state. Indeed, it is important to note that the consolidation of academic capitalism does not mean a total withdrawal of the state. The withdrawal is more financial than anything else, and decreasing state appropriations—contrary to the expectations of some observers—do not necessarily grant universities greater autonomy. One of the paradoxes of the heteronomous model is that governments tighten controls and regulations of higher education outcomes even as they demand higher education institutions to rely more and more on private sources of revenue (fees, donations, research contracts, etc.). The leverage exercised by the state in defining the direction of the system as a whole, including each individual institution, is largely augmented by linking a shrinking budget to performance evaluations based on debatable criteria.

Under a new model known as distance evaluation, universities maintain autonomy to decide on internal matters and the means to achieve stated goals (process control) while the state retains the power to decide those goals (product control).[30] This conditional funding (which is defended by state officials on accountability grounds) increases the university's procedural autonomy but reduces its substantive autonomy;[31] it also allows the state to play a key role in determining enrollments in different areas, the type of skills delivered, the kind of postsecondary institutions to be strengthened, the resources for research across disciplines, the number of staff per students, and so forth. As part of state funding conditions, universities must make tough choices, such as cutting programs with low enrollments or in vulnerable (low marketable) fields such as the humanities and creative arts, or cutting library acquisitions and research and instructional equipment.

CONCLUSION

During the postwar period, the most important trend worldwide in higher education was the expansion of the system. At the dawn of the twenty-first century, however, the most significant trend is probably the shift from autonomy to heteronomy. The context of this shift is a rearrangement of economic, ideological, and political forces. Among them are the globalization of the economy, the implementation of neoconservative and neoliberal policies, the consolidation and expansion of international corporate powers, and a redefinition of the role of the state. Whereas these forces are not homogeneous but characterized by complex and contradictory dynamics, and are expressed in different ways at the local level, a comparative analysis of contemporary developments suggests that the shift toward heteronomy goes beyond particular changes in a given university or in a particular country, becoming structural in nature and global in scope.

Although academic institutions are subject to the influence of these international and national forces, the dynamic between university actors who support and who resist specific changes mediates these outside pressures and the final outcomes in each institutional setting. However, because the very nature of many of these undergoing changes makes universities less autonomous and produces deep shifts in the academic culture, the university community is increasingly less resistant—and sometimes even more receptive—to further changes in the same direction, and less able to formulate an alternative policy. For these reasons, the heteronomous model often tends to be imposed upon the university community rather than designed purposely through the exercise of free choice. The emerging model not only changes the university's relationship with the state and the market, but also its goals, its agenda, and the way it manages its internal affairs.

The full impact of the ongoing transition toward the heteronomous university is still to be seen. On the positive side, more stringent government regulations can help to avoid duplications, improve efficiency, monitor standards, ensure social responsibility, link public funding to priority development goals, enhance equity and quality, and, in general, increase the accountability of universities. Likewise, the adoption of market values and practices can promote the adoption of better managerial procedures, improve efficiencies, encourage healthy competition among institutions, bring additional funding to cash-strapped universities, and nurture a closer relationship with business in which both partners benefit equally.

However, it is pertinent to point out the potential risks inherent in this transition. So far, the greater influence of the market and the government over university affairs during the last decades has been expressed in budget cutbacks, an increased reliance on private sources of revenue (including higher tuition and fees), a growth of private institutions, and the deregulation of working conditions. If this trend continues, the heteronomous model can lead to the erosion of important values and traditions in higher education such as the social mission of the university, its institutional autonomy and academic freedom, its pursuit of equity and accessibility, its disinterested search for the truth, and the free flow of information. In the same vein, the notion that the university should be the critical consciousness of a society, the engine of new knowledge, and the long-term guardian of the public good is likely to be displaced by visions more aligned with the economic and political masters of the day. We may also see displaced the idea that universities should play a role in promoting equality of educational opportunity, environmental sustainability, human rights, peace, and equitable models of development as proclaimed in Article 26 of the 1948 Universal Declaration of Human Rights and a variety of international covenants. Likewise, the idea that evaluation should be used mainly to diagnose problems and to provide feedback to improve an institution's work can be overshadowed by disputable rewards and punishments, accountability measures and performance indicators.

If the heteronomous model becomes hegemonic, it is possible to expect that linkages with the market will intensify, entrance requirements to high-quality institutions will be higher, quotas will be imposed on programs with limited employment opportunities, students will pay higher fees, more faculty will be seconded to government and business, and research activity will be linked more directly to market applications and to joint ventures between industry and university. Furthermore, public universities will probably accrue more revenue from private sources, while private institutions receive more subsidies from government as well as expand in size and number. In terms of hiring policies, we can expect a reduction in the proportion of career academics with full-time contracts and an increase in the proportion of part-timers hired only to teach specific courses or to assist with research projects with limited contracts. In many countries, low salaries will continue to discourage professors from remaining in public universities, prolonging both internal and external brain drains.

There are still other red flags to consider in this transition. If the heteronomous model consolidates, changes in curriculum may take place, with a stress on instrumentalism and the marginalization of courses related to social critique. Lower ranked universities may have to live with overcrowded classrooms and laboratories, although this may be compensated by distance education and the intensive use of media. Collegial models of governance may be reduced significantly, and replaced by managerial and hierarchical decision-making processes based on a corporate rationality. In research-intensive universities, changes in the organization of academic work may continue to reformulate the balance between the main university missions, with a reward structure placing even more emphasis on research than today.

If the university agenda is increasingly shaped by market dynamics and by state controls, its activities and products are more likely to benefit powerful economic, social, and political groups. In other words, a heteronomous university is more likely to cater to the particular interests of industry, the political agenda of the government in place, and the social and economic aspirations of the upper classes than serve the public interest, the authentic quest for knowledge, or the needs of the most marginalized sectors of society. Moreover, external pressures may limit the range of choice that academics have over priorities and methods of work, changing many historical traditions of public universities. For instance, the work process of university environments, characterized by self-paced work, discretion over organization and management of research, freedom of communication and publication and the like, could be replaced by the logic of business, which emphasizes profit and commercialization, deadlines, secrecy, proprietary rights, and a competitive edge in the marketplace, and by the logic of governments, which often emphasizes budget reductions, bureaucratic control, and short-term political opportunism.

In short, these drastic changes in the production and distribution of knowledge may force universities to establish a new modus operandi that can erode their commitment to accessibility, their reliance on open debate, and their critical voice in society. Heteronomy—that is, greater dependency on external powers—could lead to a factory-like model in which the bottom line is acquiescence and cost-effectiveness, learners are considered either customers or outputs, and intellectuals are guided more by market imperatives than by the search for truth. This, in turn, can lead to the deterioration of the academic environment, with more cases of censorship and conflict of interests, an emphasis on vocational and professional disciplines, lower support for basic research and nonmarketable disciplines, further exclusion of disadvantaged groups, and a curtailment of academic freedom. Moreover, a reactive approach to market demands could also have deleterious implications for long-term development. Examples of this situation are the elimination of unpopular courses in enrollment terms (but important in terms of strategic needs) or the reduction of nonapplied research, which in turn will decrease the capacity of the state to develop sustainable plans in terms of both professional training and research and development. Pushing this argument even further, if in the next decades university resources shift significantly to more lucrative research and teaching programs through matched funding, sponsorships connected to public relations agendas, and commercialization arrangements, who will address the increasingly cozy connections between university research and the war industry, and who will raise ecological concerns, arguably the main issue that humanity will face in the twenty-first century?

Interestingly enough, while the two logics of market pressures and state controls often complement each other, they can also create contradictory dynamics. On the one hand, the university must satisfy the demands of clients, who act as consumers and demand value for money. On the other, it must fulfill the performance indicators developed by the government in order to receive funding. This situation can open the door to new problems. For instance, if students act as customers, they may demand lower teacher-student ratios and higher contact time with professors. As a university adjusts to these two pressures, the logical consequence is an increase in per-student costs and a decrease in the number of faculty publications in academic journals. This, in turn, leads to government punishment expressed in funding cuts, thereby reducing the university's capacity to provide a quality service to the students, which was the original problem generating this cycle.

The concerns outlined above should not be read as predictions, but as possible scenarios that may occur if the heteronomous model has few or no counterbalances. To be sure, closer connections of universities to the needs of the economy and to the priorities set by elected governments, and the implementation of better accountability mechanisms, are certainly laudable goals. However, in the context of present political economies that more resemble plutocracies than democracies, it is important to develop guidelines to protect the common good. Hence, the main challenges for universities are how to contribute to economic development while preserving integrity, openness, autonomy, and societal interests, how to balance an efficient management with a collegial democratic governance, how to expand while protecting quality, and how to engage in scientific and technological ventures that are guided by social, ethical, and ecological values.

In many countries, the heteronomous agenda has achieved incontestable hegemony. It seems that the university as an institution has become too weak to contest outside forces, and most faculty and administrators feel that they are unable to mount a credible defense. However, although universities may be less capable than ever of defining the ways in which they are distinct from other institutions, of articulating how the principles on which they operate differ from those of business and government, and of explaining to society why they should enjoy special privileges, it is important to remember that nothing in history is a final script. The depth and pace of the restructuring is contingent upon the correlation of forces and the historical traditions of each nation-state and each individual institution. In many countries, there are university actors who denounce and resist—albeit with different degrees of success—the pervasive effects of excessive market and state influences. Eventually, these and other societal actors may be able to advance viable alternative projects that find a balance between autonomy and heteronomy that is appropriate for academic institutions and for the protection of the common good.

NOTES

1. Following Cerych and Sabatier, a *reform* is a planned and intentional process consistent with a set of values shared by a given community, whereas a *response* is something that must be done in reaction to a situation. See L. Cerych and P. Sabatier, *Great Expectations and Mixed Performances: The Implementation of Higher Education Reforms in Europe* (Paris: Trenharn, 1986).

2. For a detailed discussion of the direction of universities in the new global context, see Robert Rhoads and Carlos Alberto Torres, eds., *The University, State, and Market: The Political Economy of Globalization in the Americas* (Stanford, Calif.: Stanford University Press, 2006).

3. David Held, "Democracy, the Nation-state, and the Global System," *Economy and Society* 20, no. 2 (May 1992): 38–72.

4. The *welfare state* refers to the intervention of the capitalist state in the form of social policies, programs, standards, and regulations in order to reduce class conflict and provide the conditions for the long-term reproduction of the capitalist mode of production. The welfare state intervenes in five main areas of social reproduction: (1) physical reproduction of the working class (universal health care, subsidized housing, and social benefits for mothers and children such as subsidized child care, child or family allowance, food stamps, etc.); (2) preparation of the new generations for the labor market through the provision of certain skills and attitudes (universal and cost-free basic education, technological and vocational institutes, etc.); (3) provision of adequate labor supply and working conditions (subsidized public transportation, regulations on minimum wage, work hours, child labor, retirement age, training, injury insurance, immigration, etc.); (4) provision of an institutional framework for class conflict (collective bargaining rights, recognition of unions, employment and health and safety standards, etc.); and (5) provision of income for the "unproductive" and retired (unemployment insurance, old-age pensions, etc.). See Gary Teeple, *Globalization and the Decline of Social Reform* (Toronto: Garamond, 1995); and Claus Offe, "The German Welfare State: Principles, Performances and Prospects after Unification" (paper presented at the annual colloquium series "The End of the Nation-state?" at the University of California at Los Angeles, 1997).

5. Offe, "The German Welfare State."

6. According to World Bank data, the sales of foreign affiliates of these corporations currently exceed the world's total exports. Multinational corporations are also creating their own education and training systems, including costly and well-equipped postsecondary institutions.

7. José J. Brunner, *Educacion superior en América Latina: Cambios y desafíos* (Santiago, Chile: Fondo de Cultura Económica, 1990).

8. Manuel Castells, "The Informational Economy and the New International Division of Labor," in *The New Global Economy in the Information Age*, ed. Martin Carnoy et al. (University Park: Pennsylvania State University Press, 1993).

9. During the last three decades, the ratio of the income share of the richest 20 percent to that of the poorest 20 percent has more than doubled from thirty to one to sixty-one to one. The poorest 20 percent saw their share of global income decline from 2.3 percent to 1.4 percent over the last thirty years. World poverty is increasing at about the same rate as world population. The World Bank recently estimated that 1.3 billion people survive on less than a dollar a day, and the number of people with incomes of less than U.S.$750 per year, hardly more than $2 per day, is about 3.3 billion people, or 60 percent of humanity. Between 1960 and 1993, total global income

increased sixfold to U.S.$23 trillion, and the average world per capita income tripled, but three-fifths of humanity still lives in poverty. Today, the assets of the world's 358 billionaires exceed the combined annual incomes of countries accounting for nearly half, 45 percent, of the world's people. See *United Nations Development Project Report* (New York: UNDP, 1996).

10. Joel Samoff, "The Intellectual/Financial Complex Of Foreign Aid," *Review of African Political Economy* 53 (March 1992).

11. Philip Altbach, "Patterns in Higher Education Development: Toward the Year 2000," in *Emergent Issues in Education: Comparative Perspectives*, ed. Robert Arnove, Philip Altbach, and Gail Kelly (Albany: State University of New York Press, 1992).

12. Philip Altbach, *Comparative Higher Education: Research Trends and Bibliography* (London: Mansell, 1979), 28.

13. For an expansion of this argument, see D. Schugurensky, "Global Economic Restructuring and University Change: The Case of Universidad de Buenos Aires" (Ph.D. diss., University of Alberta, 1994).

14. Ministry of Education and Sciences of the Netherlands, *Information on Education*, no. 0–02-F, February 1992. Cited by Zaghloul Morsy in the introduction to *Higher Education in International Perspective*, ed. Zaghloul Morsy and Philip Altbach (Paris: UNESCO, 1993).

15. Mario Albornoz, "Editorial," *Redes: Revista de estudios sociales de la ciencia* 2, no. 3 (April 1995), 5–9.

16. See UNESCO, *Statistical Yearbook* (Paris: UNESCO, 1996).

17. Philip Altbach, ed. *The Decline of the Guru: The Academic Profession in Developing and Middle-Income Countries* (New York: Palgrave MacMillan, 2003).

18. See Martin Trow, *Problems in the Transition from Elite to Mass Higher Education* (Berkeley, Calif.: Carnegie Commission on Higher Education, 1973). In Trow's classification, higher education systems are considered elite when they enroll less than 10 percent of the age group, mass when enrollments are above 15 percent of the age group, and universal when more than 50 percent of the age group enters higher education.

19. E. Schiefelbein, "Chile: Economic Incentives in Higher Education," *Higher Education Policy* 3, no. 3 (1990): 21–26. See also E. Schiefelbein, "The Chilean Academic Profession: Six Policy Issues," in *The International Academic Profession: Portraits of Fourteen Countries*, ed. Philip Altbach (Boston: Boston College Center for International Higher Education, 1996).

20. J. Tilak, "Privatization of Higher Education," in *Higher Education in International Perspective: Toward the Twenty-first Century*, ed. A. Morsy and Philip Altbach (Paris: UNESCO, 1993).

21. This situation is particularly clear in Latin America. See Daniel Levy, "Recent Trends in the Privatization of Latin American Higher Education: Solidification, Breadth, and Vigor," *Higher Education Policy* no. 4 (1993).

22. Philip Altbach, "Patterns in Higher Education Development: Toward the Year 2000," in *Emergent Issues in Education: Comparative Perspectives*, ed. Robert Arnove, Philip Altbach, and Gail Kelly (New York: State University of New York, 1992).

23. Ronald Barnett, *The Idea of Higher Education* (Buckingham: Society for Research into Higher Education/Open University Press, 1990).

24. The features of the heteronomous university can by summarized in ten Cs. Seven of them correspond to the commercial university: (1) cultivation of private and foreign universities, (2) customer fees, (3) client-oriented programs, (4) corporate rationality, (5) cooperation with business, (6) casualization of labor, and (7) contracting out. The other three Cs refer to the controlled university: (8) cutbacks, (9) conditional funding, and (10) coordination, which in turn combines the dynamics of collaboration and competition in the system. For an elaboration of these features, see "The Political Economy of Higher Education in the Time of Global Markets: Whither the Social Responsibility of the University?" in *The University, State and Market: The Political Economy*

of Globalization in the Americas, ed. Robert A. Rhoads and Carlos Alberto Torres (Stanford, Calif.: Stanford University Press, 2006).

25. Some clarifications regarding the term *heteronomy* are pertinent at this point. First, it is true that universities have been conditioned by state and private interests before; however, the emerging pattern constitutes a new structural and globalized model of dependency to the market and subjection to the state that goes beyond the classic control of a specific institution by a business person through endowments or donations, and beyond conjunctural infringements on institutional autonomy by the government in a particular university or nation-state. Second, the term heteronomy as used in this context does not imply that universities are being (or are going to be in the near future) stripped of any vestige of institutional autonomy. It rather indicates that this space is being reduced, and gradually taken over, by external powers that are increasingly capable of imposing their own logic and interests. It is not so much that the university is operated by nonacademic actors as that its daily practices (its functions, internal organization, activities, structure of rewards, etc.) are subsumed into the logic imposed by the state and the market. Third, heteronomy is used here as an abstract concept, and hence its application to the analysis of a specific reality should be appropriately contextualized. Finally, the transition to the heteronomous university is not a smooth, linear, and consensual process, welcomed by all members of the academic community; this process is usually obstructed by resistance from advocates of alternative visions of the university.

26. In this unusual combination of market liberalization and state interventionism, the state pulls out of education funding and market takes its place, but at the same time that economic controls are relaxed, ideological controls are strengthened. See Adriana Puiggrós, "World Bank Education Policy: Market Liberalism Meets Ideological Conservatism," *NACLA Report on the Americas* 29, no. 6 (May–June 1996).

27. Donald G. Stein, ed., *Buying In or Selling Out* (New Brunswick, N.J.: Rutgers University, 2004).

28. Sheila Slaughter and Larry Leslie, *Academic Capitalism: Politics, Policies, and the Entrepreneurial University* (Baltimore, Md.: Johns Hopkins University Press, 1997).

29. For a detailed description of these models, see J. Newson and H. Buchbinder, *The University Means Business: Universities, Corporations, and Academic Work* (Toronto: Garamond, 1988).

30. G. Neave and F. Van Vught, eds., *Prometheus Bound: The Changing Relationship between Government and Higher Education in Western Europe* (New York: Pergamon, 1991).

31. Berdhal distinguishes between substantive and procedural autonomy. *Substantive autonomy* refers to the power of the university to determine its own goals and programs, whereas *procedural autonomy* is the power to determine the means by which its goals and programs are pursued.

12

Education in Latin America: Dependency, Underdevelopment, and Inequality

Robert F. Arnove, Stephen Franz, and Carlos Alberto Torres

To understand education in Latin America at the beginning of the twenty-first century, it is necessary to view the nature of the state and how international economic and political forces influence the governance, financing, workings, and outcomes of school systems. After defining the state and its relationship to education, we make the case that the state in Latin America is further conditioned by the neoliberal economic and social policies being followed by countries in the region in order to gain access to international capital and markets. After discussing enrollment patterns, we examine how the structural adjustment policies recommended by the World Bank, the International Monetary Fund, and national technical assistance agencies like the U.S. Agency for International Development have affected educational provision and practice. We argue that gains made in extending education to previously neglected populations during the period from the late 1960s to the mid-1980s have been substantially eroded by the introduction of market-based policies designed to decentralize and privatize education. At the same time, examples are provided of grassroots movements that counter education policies that serve elite interests. Such programs provide an alternative to externally imposed and top-down reforms, while equipping individuals and their collectivities with the means to articulate their interests and gain access to needed resources and services.

DEFINING THE STATE AND ITS RELATIONSHIP TO EDUCATION

Generally, the state may be conceptualized as a pact of domination, as an arena of conflict, and as a purposeful actor that must select among competing political projects. According to F. H. Cardoso, the state should be considered to be the "basic pact of domination that exists among social classes or factions of dominant classes and the norms which guarantee their dominance over subordinate strata."[1] As an arena of confrontation, the state displays the tensions and contradictions of competing political projects as well as the political agreements of civil society. Moreover, social class, racial, ethnic, gender, geographical, ethical-moral, and religious factors influence the actions of the state in legislating and executing social policies.

Although the state in a capitalist society, by its very nature, favors policies that are directed toward the constitution and reproduction of the capitalist system,[2] it also is the representative of the nation as a whole and, in liberal democratic societies, is a proponent of the extension of personal rights and greater mass participation in the determination of public policy.[3] Hence, as noted above, the state has a dual character: it is both a pact of domination and a contested terrain. Various groups intervene to shape public policy to serve their interests. Although education can be used to legitimate a political system, it also can serve to interrogate it; although an education system may function to perpetuate the social division of labor, it also can equip individuals with the skills and knowledge to humanize the workplace and change the class structure of a society.

THE "CONDITIONED" STATE

Education policies and programs are significantly limited in their ability to bring about fundamental social change or improvements in the lives of the majority by the fact that Latin American countries, with the notable exception of Cuba, and more recently Venezuela, are dependent or "conditioned" capitalist states.[4] According to Cardoso, an "associate-dependent development" has characterized Latin America.[5] As he notes, the economic systems of Latin America are built upon an alliance among the state bureaucracy and state managers, the multinational corporations, and the highest strata of the national bourgeoisie. Not only multinational corporations but also U.S. hegemony exercised in the region for the past one hundred years—a hegemony that has involved frequent military interventions, particularly in the Caribbean region and Central America—has thwarted alternative and more independent models of economic development.[6] The typical political economy of Latin America strengthens a more concentrated economic system that is inherently less redistributive and increasingly excludes the subordinate classes.

According to Martin Carnoy, the educational implications of dependent capitalism in Latin America are that "(l) the state is often unwilling or unable to mobilize enough resources to make public education (state-defined knowledge) generally available; and (2) even if education is made generally available, the private production sector and the state are often unable to provide sufficient wage employment to absorb those with average education."[7]

INCOME INEQUALITY AND EDUCATIONAL EQUITY

Not only the "conditioned state" and "dependent development" but also the attendant disparities in wealth greatly determine who will complete the highest levels and most prestigious types of education and thereby have access to the most lucrative and desirable jobs in the modern sector of the economy. Latin America is characterized by greater income inequality than other developing regions. And, as George Psacharopoulos et al. note: "Education is the variable with the strongest impact on income inequality."[8]

According to the Inter-American Development Bank report "*Education: The Gordian Knot*": if you want to find a root cause for Latin America's income inequality, you don't have to look much further than its skewed educational system.[9] This report, issued on the eve of the April 1998 Summit of the Americas in Santiago, Chile, found that the region's public schools are mired in crisis. Rather than contributing to progress, the report states, schooling is "reinforcing poverty, perpetuating inequality and holding back economic growth." The problem is not access but completion rates. By the fifth year, nearly 40 percent of the poor have dropped out, while 93 percent of the richest students are still in the system. By the ninth year, only 15 percent of poor students remained in school, compared to 58 percent of the richest.[10]

We would argue, however, that the root cause of economic stagnation resides not in the education system, but in the social and economic inequality generated by the economic policies that have been implemented by governments in the region since the mid-1980s. According to a report in the January–March 2005 Newsletter of UNESCO's International Institute for Educational Planning on "Education and Equity in Latin America," ten years after undertaking various economic growth and social recovery policies, "the social situation in the region has not improved and the impact of educational reform in terms of equity is minimal."[11] The report continues:

> On the one hand, poverty no longer stems from an economic scenario of crisis and inflation, but is the result of new growth strategies adopted by most countries in the region. . . . The divide between rich and poor in the region has considerably widened and wealth distribution has become central to an analysis of the social situation.[12]

The report describes "wealth distribution patterns which benefit the better off, allowing some to enjoy one of the highest standards of living in the world"—very similar, we would add, to the privileged position enjoyed by whites in apartheid South Africa—a situation of internal colonialism which also may serve as an apt description of the condition of rural indigenous populations in Bolivia, Ecuador, Peru, and Guatemala, and African Americans in the northeast region of Brazil. Not only these countries, but also Nicaragua, El Salvador, Honduras, and Haiti (all of which have suffered civil war and natural disasters in recent years as well as a history of foreign interventions and neocolonialism), not surprisingly, show the highest illiteracy and dropout rates in the region. In the cases listed above, the majority of their populations live in poverty and, according to the Economic Commission for Latin America, the average poverty rate throughout the entire region in 2004 was 42 percent (37 percent urban and 58 percent rural); and with regard to extreme poverty, the average rate was 17 percent (12 percent urban and 34 percent rural).[13]

Although Latin America, historically, has had a greater percentage of children and youth enrolled in schools than in other developing areas of the world, enrollment patterns reflect the particular history of the region. In a number of countries, there is a bimodal distribution of enrollment. Large numbers of students from the least privileged sectors of society (ethnic minorities, rural populations, and women) do not attend or complete primary schooling while a substantial number of students attend universities, often at rates, in the past, exceeding those of European countries.[14] At the same time, Latin American workers have fewer years of schooling than their counterparts in Asia and the Middle

East.[15] The average amount of schooling of the adult population (fifteen to sixty-four years of age) is less than six years.

EDUCATION AND ENROLLMENT PATTERNS

Despite increases in primary school enrollment since 1990, in 2004 all but six countries were below 90 percent enrollment for ages six to eighteen. In Colombia, Ecuador, El Salvador, Guatemala, Honduras, and Nicaragua, 25 percent to over 40 percent of children between six and eighteen years of age are not in school.[16] In the Dominican Republic, Ecuador, El Salvador, and Nicaragua, one-fourth of the students do not reach the sixth grade.[17] At the same time, despite slower expansion of higher education since 1990 relative to that of Europe, enrollment rates for 2003 in Argentina (64 percent), Chile (43 percent), and Bolivia (41 percent) compare favorably with those of Italy (59 percent), Portugal (56 percent), Hungary (52 percent), Romania (36 percent).[18] Higher education enrollment rates are 51 percent for the region of Central and Eastern Europe.

Table 12.1 illustrates age range enrollment rates in urban and rural areas. Four countries—El Salvador, Guatemala, Honduras, and Nicaragua—have rural enrollment rates which are 80 percent or less than urban enrollment rates. The countries which have taken the most outstanding strides to decrease the urban-rural gap in enrollment rates are Brazil, Chile, Peru, and Venezuela. Rural enrollment rates are climbing and are now 90 percent of those found in urban areas for these countries.[19]

Although the figures from table 12.2 show significant gains regarding decreasing the

Table 12.1   Specific age range enrollment rates in urban and rural areas

Country	Ages 6–18 Urban	Rural	Ages 6–7 Urban	Rural	Ages 8–13 Urban	Rural	Ages 14–18 Urban	Rural
Argentina	93.2	NA	98.8	NA	99.0	NA	84.0	NA
Belize	88.0	75.8	99.0	91.8	98.3	97.4	71.3	43.6
Bolivia	92.0	75.1	92.1	81.3	97.0	92.0	87.0	52.3
Brazil	92.0	82.4	90.2	80.9	97.2	95.0	79.7	67.8
Chile	94.3	85.9	94.0	89.1	99.0	97.8	88.7	70.2
Colombia	85.7	73.5	93.5	82.5	94.2	88.0	72.4	52.4
Costa Rica	86.9	75.0	96.6	91.4	96.8	92.9	71.2	47.1
Dom. Rep.	92.5	88.7	94.6	88.8	98.3	96.7	84.6	79.1
Ecuador	85.7	69.9	94.4	88.8	93.0	86.8	73.5	42.1
El Salvador	84.4	67.9	83.5	67.3	94.4	84.8	72.8	47.8
Guatemala	77.2	57.7	82.7	65.6	90.0	79.0	60.9	30.6
Honduras	75.8	58.0	76.3	65.5	91.4	81.4	56.8	27.0
Mexico	86.1	75.0	97.5	92.2	96.0	94.0	69.7	45.5
Nicaragua	82.9	63.1	81.5	63.5	93.9	81.5	70.2	40.9
Panama	92.4	82.4	97.2	92.5	98.5	96.2	82.0	61.9
Paraguay	88.6	75.3	94.0	83.9	98.1	92.3	75.2	51.3
Peru	89.0	80.9	97.3	93.6	98.1	94.9	74.7	59.1
Uruguay	87.8	NA	97.6	NA	97.9	NA	71.6	NA
Venezuela	87.8	84.2	97.2	93.9	97.6	96.3	72.2	66.0

Source: Miguel Urquiola and Valentina Calderón, "Apples and Oranges: Educational Enrollment and Attainment across Countries in Latin America and the Caribbean," *International Journal of Educational Development* 26 (2006): 572–90, table 3 (urban), table 5 (rural).
Note: NA = not available

Table 12.2 Percentage of population between fifteen and twenty-four, by years of schooling, urban vs. rural areas, 1979–2004

Country	Year	Urban areas Years of schooling				Rural areas Years of schooling			
		0–5	*6–9*	*10–12*	*≥13*	*0–5*	*6–9*	*10–12*	*≥13*
Bolivia	1997	11.9	31.1	44.4	12.6	48.3	34.9	15.3	1.5
	2002	8.8	29.5	45.8	15.9	44.3	34.1	20.5	1.2
Brazil	1979	48.2	34.6	14.1	3.1	86.8	9.7	1.9	1.6
	2003	18.2	40.8	35.9	5.1	48.2	37.9	13.2	0.7
Chile	1990	5.7	33.2	45.4	15.8	16.6	57.1	22.4	3.9
	2003	1.6	28.3	51.8	18.4	5.4	45.4	44.2	5.1
Colombia	1991	21.8	37.9	29.7	10.6	60.1	25.7	13.6	0.5
	1999	14.6	32.4	43.2	9.8	46.2	30.7	21.8	1.3
Costa Rica	1981	7.3	50.5	33.9	8.2	19.8	64.7	13.8	1.7
	2002	7.3	49.4	30.4	12.8	19.1	61.4	15.5	4.0
Dominican Republic	2000	13.1	35.5	37.1	14.3	37.4	38.7	20.4	3.5
	2003	10.7	35.9	38.1	15.3	26.4	38.0	28.9	6.7
El Salvador	1995	20.6	41.4	28.8	9.2	60.4	31.2	7.3	1.1
	2003	14.2	40.5	32.8	12.6	42.9	42.7	12.7	1.7
Guatemala	1989	33.9	42.6	19.2	4.3	75.9	21.8	2.1	0.2
	2002	19.1	42.4	30.2	8.3	56.5	35.4	7.2	0.8
Honduras	1990	24.1	55.7	15.3	5.0	57.6	39.8	2.3	0.3
	2003	16.1	52.4	23.8	7.7	45.4	49.9	4.1	0.6
Mexico	1989	8.3	60.5	22.1	9.1	31.4	59.2	7.7	1.7
	2004	4.5	46.6	32.2	16.7	14.1	56.8	23.1	6.0
Nicaragua	1993	24.6	53.8	19.5	2.1	68.9	26.5	4.3	0.3
	2001	19.8	46.4	26.1	7.7	60.5	33.2	5.5	0.7
Panama	1979	6.3	49.1	35.5	9.1	20.5	61.3	16.2	1.9
	2002	3.5	38.6	41.8	16.1	20.2	56.3	21.2	5.1
Paraguay	1997	6.2	48.1	37.1	8.6	33.2	54.2	11.4	1.3
	2001	7.3	39.0	40.7	12.9	32.0	48.8	17.2	1.9
Peru	1999	3.4	32.9	49.6	14.1	25.1	49.0	22.7	3.2
	2003	3.9	25.8	47.8	22.5	19.9	47.5	26.5	6.1
Venezuela	1981	13.5	58.5	20.4	7.7	46.1	46.4	6.8	0.7
	1994	10.2	48.2	28.8	12.8	38.2	48.4	10.9	2.5

Source: CEPAL, *Social Panorama of Latin America, 2005* (Santiago, Chile: Author, 2005), table 30.

rural-urban gap in total years of schooling, there still remains much to be done. For example, as of 2002, the majority of the rural population in Guatemala had between zero and five years of schooling, whereas nearly three-quarters of the urban population had between six and twelve years of schooling. On the other hand, countries such as Brazil are decreasing the urban-rural gap. In 1990, about 20 percent of the rural population had between six and twelve years of schooling while the majority of the urban population had the same amount of schooling. By 2003, although figures for the urban population continued to increase for six to twelve years of schooling, the rural population showed significant gains in that the majority now has between six and twelve years of schooling.[20]

Gender

There are gender differences in literacy levels and educational attainments, but over the years women have been making substantial gains, especially when compared with women in other regions of the world. For example, in 2000, estimated illiteracy figures for developing countries were 26.4 percent overall and 33.9 percent for females, whereas the corresponding figures for Latin America were 11.1 percent overall and 12.1 percent for females.[21] From 1980 on, the rate of increase in female enrollments at all three levels of education decelerated in developing regions; in the 1990s, there was almost no increase in enrollment rates: 46 percent at the primary level, 43 percent at the secondary level, and 40 percent at the tertiary level. By contrast (and rather surprisingly), female enrollment rates for Latin America are on par with those of "developed" countries: 48 percent at the primary level, 52 percent at the secondary level, and 51 percent at the tertiary level. In Argentina, Brazil, Colombia, Cuba, El Salvador, Nicaragua, Panama, Uruguay, and Venezuela, women comprise 50 percent or more of higher education students.[22] In Latin America, despite increasing access to education and the narrowing of the percentage difference in illiteracy by gender, there were still approximately twenty-two million illiterate women in the region in 2000.[23] When the combined effects of social class, region, and gender are taken into account, the highest illiteracy rates are found among poor women living in rural areas.[24] Gender differences in literacy attainment become even sharper when ethnicity is taken into account. It is not uncommon to find illiteracy rates greater than two-thirds to three-quarters of indigenous women living in rural areas.

Ethnicity

Indigenous populations or "first peoples" and ethnic minorities (especially Afro-Brazilians) are the most discriminated against populations with regard to access to educational services for two reasons. First, they are commonly located in the most impoverished and underdeveloped regions of their countries and second, the language of instruction is invariably Spanish (Portuguese in Brazil). Even when efforts are made to begin instruction in maternal languages during the first year or two of schooling, Spanish (or Portuguese) becomes the language of instruction as one progresses through the education system. The countries with the largest indigenous populations—Bolivia, Peru, and Guatemala—tend to have the highest illiteracy rates and lowest school attendance rates. This is also true of Brazil, with a large number of descendents of former African slaves who inhabit the destitute northeast region. Disadvantage manifests itself with regard to ethnicity, where primary education noncompletion rates for 2002 were 40 percent, 70 percent, and 87 percent higher than those of nonindigenous groups for Guatemala, Bolivia, and Panama, respectively. In Brazil, completion rates for Afro-Latin children are 86 percent of those for their peers. However, recent initiatives of the Workers' Party of President Luiz Inácio Lula Da Silva have been increasing the college-going rates of Afro-Latins. The ethnic gap also is decreasing for countries such as Ecuador and Peru, where indigenous primary school noncompletion rates are 18.0 percent and 11.6 percent, compared to 7.6 percent and 9.5 percent for nonindigenous groups.[25]

EDUCATION, THE DEBT CRISIS, AND THE NEOLIBERAL AGENDA

The distorted economic policies being pursued by countries throughout the region reflect the hangover from the debt crisis of the 1980s, often referred to as the "lost decade" of development. Economic expansion, experienced at high rates from the 1950s through the 1970s, slowed considerably in the 1980s and 1990s. In the 1960s, the average annual GNP growth rate for Latin American economies was 5.7 percent. In the 1970s, the growth rate was 5.6 percent, despite difficulties caused by the oil crisis. By the 1980s, the average annual GNP growth rate for Latin American countries dropped to 1.3 percent.[26] The falling gross national product translated into decreasing per capita income for the majority of Latin Americans. On average, Latin American per capita incomes fell 9 percent.

In response to the ever deepening economic crisis, most Latin American governments adopted the neoliberal fiscal stabilization and economic adjustment policies promoted by international donor agencies like the International Monetary Fund (IMF) and the World Bank. The term *neoliberal* derives from the neoclassical economic theories expounded by these agencies and their consultants. The theories are based on the work of the classical economists Adam Smith and David Ricardo, who believed that the role of the state consisted in establishing the conditions by which the free play of the marketplace, the laws of supply and demand, and free trade based on competitive advantage would inevitably rebound to the benefit of all. Government policies based on these notions have led to a drastic reduction in the state's role in social spending, deregulation of the economy, and liberalization of import policies. The educational counterparts of these policies have included moves to decentralize and privatize public school systems.

Although neoliberal policies are designed to reduce a country's fiscal deficits and external debt while bringing inflation under control, they also have contributed to deepening poverty in the region. In many countries, the social safety net provided by government subsidized services in health, education, and other basic services has been removed. Consequently, social class differences have intensified. Income losses didn't only severely affect the poorest of the poor: 50 percent of the households located in the middle of the scale lost between 3 percent and 10 percent of their income.[27] As a result, class structures in Latin America have become more polarized, with rich and poor sectors separated by an increasingly wider gap. This is also true in Mexico, Chile, and Argentina which have served as models of structural adjustment for other countries in the region.

With the economic downturn, all Latin American nations experienced decreases in educational expenditures in terms of gross national product and total governmental expenditure. Under neoliberalism, significant improvements in education spending made during the 1960s and 1970s were effectively negated by drastic spending cuts in education. On average, (unweighted) per capita expenditures in education in Latin America increased by 4.29 percent per year between 1975 and 1980, while they decreased by 6.14 percent between 1980 and 1985. According to Fernando Reimers, "The progress in educational finance made in the seventies was undone in the eighties."[28]

The spending cuts in education in Latin America substantially affected recurrent expenditures like the purchase of teaching materials and the maintenance of school buildings. Moreover, cuts in educational spending directly affected teacher salaries, which declined dramatically in a number of countries, such as El Salvador, which experienced a 68 percentage drop in wages.[29] Decreased expenditures, outdated pedagogies and curricula, and restricted access all contributed to the general decline in the quality of education.

As the debt crisis worsened and it became clear to education ministries that future funding would be limited, many ministries began to pursue other means of financial support. Primary among these options were privatization and decentralization. These two policies are favored methods of improving educational efficiency commonly sponsored by international donor agencies such as the World Bank and the IMF. International donor agencies provided essential financial support to many Latin American nations in the 1980s and 1990s.

Consequently, education ministries were, to an extent, obligated to subscribe to donor agency policy. As a result, "[donor agencies] have advocated a decrease in the amount of government involvement in the education process, an increase in the private sector's role, and greater application of market principles to the organization of Third World educational systems."[30]

It should be noted that since the late 1990s, educational expenditures once again are on the rise. The overall funding picture for Latin America, however, is more complicated. According to a report of the International Commission on Education, Equity and Economic Competitiveness, by the end of the 1990s, Latin American governments, were, on average, investing 4.6 percent of GNP on education each year, a figure superior to 3.9 percent for developing countries and only slightly inferior to the 5.1 percent invested by developed countries. These figures, according to the report, are deceptive because they do not take into account the age distribution of Latin American populations. Given the disproportionately large number of school-age children, the countries of the region would need to invest a greater percentage of GNP to achieve adequate levels of education expenditures per child. Furthermore, achieving a workforce with a level of education appropriate for countries with comparable incomes would require an additional investment of 0.5 percent per year over twenty-five years.[31] Accomplishing these goals is very problematic in light of economic policies that have cut social spending and have unevenly distributed the benefits of economic growth to the wealthiest segments of Latin American societies.

A key question here is who is benefiting from neoliberal and education policies promoted, if not imposed, by international financial and technical assistance agencies. In briefly reviewing major initiatives to privatize and decentralize education systems in Latin America, as well as elsewhere, we argue that these reforms have benefited primarily the rich and powerful.

PRIVATIZATION

Privatization has taken a variety of forms, including charging user fees in public schools that were previously free of charge. As the educational sector turned toward private interests to fund educational endeavors, policy planning changed to accommodate private investors. Parallel to education ministries' desire to conform to private interests was their need to create self-supporting school systems. This does not mean that education ministries abandoned the finance and support of public education. Rather, education ministries allowed for accelerated development and accreditation of private institutions (primary, secondary, and higher education). A number of states, for example Brazil until recently, also have subsidized private schools and provided tax credits to parents who opted out of the public school system. Private institutions are attractive to middle- and upper-class students because high-quality ones offer smaller classes, improved facilities, and an overall atmosphere that is more conducive to learning.

Such policies and practices have negative effects on the public schools.[32] When middle-class parents leave the public school system, the most vocal advocates for quality in the schools disappear. The lower classes, although constituting the majority of the population, lack the political and economic clout necessary to promote quality in the public school system. Without middle-class support, and facing decreased funding, many public school systems have fallen into decline. Both educational quality and facilities have deteriorated significantly. These problems are exacerbated by decentralization of national education systems.

DECENTRALIZATION

Another option pursued by educational ministries in response to financial crisis was decentralization. Decentralization is essentially the practice in which subnational levels are given responsibility for governing the educational sector. Unlike the highly decentralized U.S. school system, education in most Latin American nations has been dominated by a strong central education ministry controlling all budgetary and curricular issues. In the past twenty years, there has been considerable debate surrounding the issue of decentralization. Many nations have taken steps to decentralize their educational systems, shifting many financial and curricular planning responsibilities as well as personnel decisions to the provincial, departmental, municipal, and even local (as in Nicaragua since 1993) school levels. Prominent examples of countries that have implemented a national decentralization policy are Colombia (1968 and 1986), Argentina (1976), Mexico (1978), and Chile (1981).[33] Lower territorial/political units have been given significant funding responsibilities for local schools. The idea is that schools considered superior in quality and services can attract more students and thereby increase their funding capacity. The state partially subsidizes education, but the local territorial/political units are responsible for paying the balance. For example, the Chilean government subsidizes approximately 50 percent of education costs at the preprimary and primary levels (grades one and two); and at the general secondary education and the upper levels of technical secondary education, roughly 60 percent.[34]

Decentralized systems may be successful in resource rich urban and suburban areas, but present serious problems for lower-class municipalities and rural areas. These areas do not have the resources necessary to make up for educational costs not covered by government subsidies. Nor do they have the same resources to make informed decisions regarding market mechanisms and cost-containment incentives introduced by the government as new educational practices.[35] Both privatization and decentralization exacerbate preexisting socioeconomic inequalities in the education system. Although the elite continue to benefit from quality education, the marginalized sectors of the population are disproportionately the victims of the growing educational crisis. Results of national standardized tests in countries like Chile are considered by knowledgeable observers to be a direct proxy for social class with students in urban private schools tending to score highest and students in rural public schools lowest.

POPULAR EDUCATION AND OTHER INNOVATIONS

In contrast to state-sponsored education programs, there are a number of grassroots education programs in Latin America that form part of a "popular education" movement. Although limited in resources and small in scope, these programs nonetheless are significant in that they offer an alternative model of education that empowers individuals and communities to place demands on national governments for social services and resources that should be the right of all citizens of a country.

Since the 1960s, nonformal and popular education programs, inspired by the critical consciousness raising philosophy and pedagogy of the late Brazilian educator Paulo Freire, have been important alternatives to the formal education sector. *Nonformal education* implies an educational experience that occurs outside the standard education sphere. *Popular education*, a subset of nonformal education, is distinguished by its pedagogical and political characteristics.[36]

Pedagogically, popular education programs emphasize nonhierarchical learning situations in which teachers and students engage in dialogue, and learners' knowledge is incorporated into the content of instruction. According to Carlos Alberto Torres, "education appears as the act of knowing rather than a simple transmission of knowledge or the cultural baggage of society."[37] Politically, popular education programs tend to be directed at meeting the special needs of marginalized sectors of society (women, unemployed, peasants, and indigenous groups). They have played a significant role in facilitating the development of collective survival strategies to confront the economic crises of the past two decades in the region. Furthermore, the ultimate aim of many popular education programs is not just adaptation or survival for hard-pressed populations but sweeping social change that leads to more just societies.[38] One example of a popular education program is *Asociación Peru Mujer* (Peru Woman) which organizes and educates women in the fields of discriminatory labor codes and practices, inheritance and family law, and domestic violence issues. Another nongovernmental organization REPEM (*Red de Educación Popular Entre Mujeres de América Latina y el Caribe*), located in Montevideo, links over 150 organizations at the global, regional, and national levels. It serves as a focal point for research, information dissemination, and advocacy on behalf of low-income women with little formal education. A major goal of both *Peru Mujer* and REPEM is to meet women's demands for greater equality and opportunity and the chance to participate actively in the formulation of alternative social change strategies.

Although popular education programs are generally effective on the community level, they often fail to bring about change at the level of governmental policy. Moreover, innovative grassroots popular education programs often are viewed by governments implementing neoliberal policies as substitutes for national effort. Of concern to those working in literacy, adult basic education, and various forms of popular education is that state funding for such programs has begun to dry up in recent years. National school systems are increasingly focusing their literacy efforts on school-aged children or adults under thirty-five years of age. Governments such as Nicaragua (between 1990 and 2006) have largely relegated the state's role in meeting the educational needs of out-of-school youths and adults to the civil sector. However, if universal literacy and comprehensive lifelong learning systems are to be achieved, the state and civil society will have to work in tandem rather than in opposition.[39]

State-Civil Society Collaboration

There are, nonetheless, examples of ambitious state-sponsored educational innovations that do benefit traditionally underserved populations. One example is *Fe y Alegría*. This Venezuelan nongovernmental organization began in 1955 educating one hundred children in a single room. By 2001, the program had expanded to fourteen countries with more than a million students in formal and nonformal education programs, with over thirty-three thousand teachers and staff. According to Reimers, the mission of Fe y Alegría is to "provide quality education to the poor as expressed in their motto 'Where the asphalt road ends, where there is no water, electricity or services, there begins Fe y Alegría.'"[40] Reimers states that innovative programs such as Fe y Alegría are usually not embraced by Latin American ministries of education until they have proven themselves.[41] Fe y Alegría was initially privately funded but went on to secure substantial government funding in most cases, especially in Venezuela.

State-Sponsored Innovations

An impressive example of a state-sponsored innovation is *La Escuela Nueva* (the New School) in Colombia, which is designed to meet the special needs of rural schools and communities by creating a curriculum that emphasizes communal needs and values. The New School reform actively encourages a strong relation between schools and communities, and a flexible school calendar and promotion policy that is adapted to local agricultural production cycles. One of the goals of the New School is to teach civic values by encouraging student and parent participation in important decisions concerning local educational policy. The emphasis the New School places on participation and decision making accords with the overarching child-centered, constructivist philosophy framing the program.

The effectiveness of this education reform may explain why Colombia is the only country in the 1997 UNESCO study of academic achievement in which rural third grade schoolchildren outperformed their urban counterparts on standardized language tests and, with the exception of students in Colombian mega cities, their urban counterparts on standardized mathematics tests. New School students also demonstrate strong democratic values on various measures related to civic knowledge, skills, and attitudinal dispositions.

As Alfredo Sarmiento Gómez notes, "the New School was consolidated as a framework for resolving . . . [the problems of rural schooling] in an economically sustainable and pedagogically skilled manner."[42] Between its creation in 1989 and the mid-1990s, the program expanded from eight thousand to over twenty thousand schools reaching approximately 40 percent of rural school children.

Although widely admired and emulated, attempts to replicate the New School, without significant adaptation to local circumstances, have proven problematic, even within Colombia itself. A key to the success of this reform, and others, is the preparation of teachers and, as Henry Levin has pointed out, constant monitoring, problem solving, and adjustment.[43] Vicky Colbert, one of the founders of the New School Movement and a past vice-minister of education, became somewhat disenchanted with how (over time) it had become overly bureaucratized under centralized Ministry control.[44] She left the project some five years ago to form her own private foundation (*Volvamos a la Gente*) in order to disseminate the guiding principles of the reform to grassroots groups who would be the initiators of improvements in their schools.

Whatever the limitations of the New School Program may be, its positive features resonate with those of an ideal model of what Latin American countries need to do in order to achieve more equitable education for all. A review of relevant research from Latin American and other regions suggests that there are some general policy initiatives that would contribute to greater equality of educational opportunities and more equitable outcomes for the most marginalized and disadvantaged populations.

The recommended reforms include quality preschool; early childhood programs with supplementary nutrition and health care services; more adequate school infrastructure so that poor, rural, and indigenous children have the same amenities (schools, desks and chairs, electricity, running water, and toilets) enjoyed by their more advantaged peers in urban and private schools; a flexible academic calendar responsive to the socioeconomic context of schools in different regions of a country; sufficient supplies of textbooks and culturally sensitive as well as socially relevant curricular materials in the appropriate languages; teaching guides matched to transformed curricula; student-centered, more active pedagogies that involve collaborative work as well as personalized attention to each child; significantly improved preservice and in-service teacher education and professional development programs and opportunities; incentive pay for teachers working under difficult conditions and, generally, more adequate remuneration and social recognition of the importance of teaching; and, importantly, greater participation of teachers, parents, and communities in the design of education programs to meet their self-defined needs. A final set of policy initiatives pertain to family income support, payments for school attendance and completion.

The last initiative is particularly important in the light of the extensive poverty in the region, where there is often a trade-off between the income derived from child labor and school attendance with a problematic promise of future greater earnings for a family. The largest programs involving cash transfer to needy families are in Brazil, where there are plans to reach 11.4 million families by 2006 (more than 45 million people) with incentive funds for their children to complete basic education. In Mexico, a similar program now reaches twenty million people. A rigorous evaluation of the program found that children in schools receiving transfer funds that include money for staples (such as rice and beans) and school supplies were healthier and stayed in school longer than children in a control group.[45] According to Laurence Wolff and Claudia De Moura Castro, the *Progresa Programa* in Mexico has increased entry rates into lower secondary schools in rural areas by almost 20 percent.[46]

Targeting funds for disadvantaged populations, known as *focalización* in Spanish, is not without controversy. A number of eminent scholars of Latin American education have indicated that such policies often fail to discriminate among different levels of poverty and therefore do not provide enough support to help the most desperate families. They have criticized these fund transfers as largely ameliorative and not attacking the root causes of poverty; and they argue for more comprehensive policies that meet the needs of the vast majority of students in a country.[47]

ROLE OF UNIVERSITIES

Finally, it is necessary to point out the important role that universities can play, through their research, development, and dissemination activities, in contributing to income and job generation to overcome the devastating effects of the debt crisis and the current neoliberal agenda. Higher education leaders like the late Xabier Gorostiaga of the Central American University (UCA) of Nicaragua have proposed a vision of a new role for "universities of the South." His vision calls for utilizing existing university departmental extension programs and research and development institutes affiliated with the UCA as nuclei for experimentation, training, and popular education. Building a university education around the knowledge generated by rural-based centers would contribute to the formation of professionals who, because they had a more realistic understanding of their society, would be better prepared to address its most pressing problems. Moreover, the work of such centers would contribute to empowering the "producing majority" to become major historical actors involved in the transformation of an unsatisfactory status quo that has marginalized and exploited them. These engagements are critical to the development and dissemination of appropriate and self-sustainable technologies; and, according to Gorostiaga, they offer prospects of collaboration between universities of the North and the South.[48]

CONCLUSION

The implementation of structural adjustment policies to liberalize the economies of Latin America and integrate them more tightly into the world capitalist system has provoked a number of crises throughout the region. In diminishing the role of the state in the provision of basic social services—part of the cost-cutting policies recommended by the World Bank and the IMF—the social safety net provided the most marginalized populations has been significantly dismantled. The disparity between the wealthy and the poor is increasing. This situation has limited educational access and opportunities for the most vulnerable populations to gain access to a quality education and equitable life chances. Moreover, moves to decentralize and privatize economies are paralleled by initiatives to reduce the role of the state in the financing of education. Another intended outcome of such initiatives has been the erosion of the bargaining power of national teacher unions, in many cases the single most important voice for a universal, free education system preparing individuals not only for productive economic roles but the exercise of democratic citizenship rights.

These fiscal austerity and structural adjustment policies have resulted in growing social unrest and mass demonstrations that have threatened and toppled governments, most recently in Bolivia and Ecuador. In the education field, the introduction of these neoliberal economic policies and a conservative ideological agenda into the education system has led to numerous protests—teacher strikes and student and parent occupations of schools and Ministry of Education offices in countries ranging from Argentina to Mexico. As was documented in Arnove's case study of Nicaragua, these initiatives have polarized education, despite the ostensible goals of government to use education as a means of achieving social consensus.[49]

It is possible, but unlikely, that consensus concerning education can be achieved without a national agreement being reached around a model of economic development. This model must be based on protecting the autonomy and sovereignty of individual countries to devise economic and social policies that are reflective of their individual histories and social and cultural dynamics, rather than economic agendas determined in the major metropolitan centers of the North. It would be a model that recognizes and supports autonomous, sustainable development at the grassroots level and in the informal sectors of the economy, the so-called industries of the poor, providing employment for as much as one-half of the workforce of many Latin American countries.[50] It would be a model that draws upon features of a free-market economy to generate goods and services but also upon those of social democracies that provide a social safety net—the basic conditions for all to live decently.

A struggle is now taking place in Latin America, as elsewhere, as to who will determine the goals, processes, and outcomes of national economic and social policies. The achievement of more equitable development is integrally related to the ability of countries to affirm their national sovereignty as well as their collective interests. To do so requires the joining of like-minded countries to challenge the external constraints imposed upon them not only by the one current superpower, the United States, but also by transnational actors ranging from the international financial, technical assistance, and trade agencies—most recently the World Trade Organization. The growing number of more progressive governments that have come to power in recent years (i.e., in Argentina, Bolivia, Brazil, Chile, Ecuador, Uruguay, and Venezuela) is a sign that populations are fed up with the existing status quo. Leaders from these countries are now attempting to form alternative economic blocs to the Free Trade Area of the Americas (FTAA) and the Central American Free Trade Area (CAFTA) while reaching out to counterparts in Africa and the Middle East to shift the terms of trade and unequal relationships between North and South. From the more rapid economic growth of Argentina, which rejected IMF conditionalities and renegotiated its external debt on more favorable terms,[51] to the leading role played by progressive Latin American governments and other Third World countries in challenging harmful free trade agreements of the World Trade Organization in Cancun in September of 2003, there is evidence that things can be changed.

The technologies that are now in place to facilitate the international flow of capital and the global assembly line also can be used to connect progressive social movements across national borders. Such has been the case with labor unions, peasant federations, and indigenist, feminist, environmental and other movements that now mobilize transnationally to protect their habitats, affirm and preserve their cultural identities and communities, receive a living wage in safe places, and achieve more equitable societies.[52] Such social movements have been the driving force for the election of more populist and nationalist governments as well as the overthrow of corrupt governments that have sold out national rights. In the field of education, networks exist to connect scholars, policymakers, and practitioners concerned with issues of globalization and "Education for All."[53] In the spring of 2005, Mary Compton, the president of the National Union of Teachers in England, called for "solidarity among teachers around the world to combat forces of globalization and privatization."[54] As she noted "We Are the World."

If a more satisfactory consensus is to be achieved between the various protagonists and antagonists over how economic and social development is to occur and the nature and role of education systems in contributing to a more desirable future for the countries of Latin America and the Caribbean, it will not be the result of the beneficence of the multinational corporations and international organizations, nor even of popularly elected governments. It will be the outcome of the sustained, collective efforts of these grassroots movements inspired by alternative visions of the future. As researchers, educators, and activists concerned with issues of social justice around the world, we can contribute to those struggles through our multiple engagements with the production and dissemination of knowledge. Rather than despair over the magnitude of major transnational problems facing humanity, we should be grateful for the challenges and opportunities to contribute what we can to public understanding of the nature of globalization, its negative as well as positive features, and more promising courses of action leading to a better future for all.

NOTES

1. F. H. Cardoso, "On the Characterization of Authoritarian Regimes in Latin America," in *The New Authoritarianism in Latin America*, ed. David Collier (Princeton, N.J.: Princeton University Press, 1979).

2. Claus Offe, *Contradictions of the Welfare State* (Cambridge, Mass.: MIT Press, 1984); Claus Offe and V. Ronge, "Theses on the Theory of the State," *New German Critique* 6 (Fall 1975): 137–47.

3. Martin Carnoy and Henry Levin, *Schooling and Work in the Democratic State* (Stanford, Calif.: Stanford University Press, 1985); Samuel Bowles and Herbert Gintis, *Democracy and Capitalism* (New York: Basic Books, 1986).

4. Sheryl L. Lutjens, *The State, Bureaucracy, and the Cuban Schools: Power and Participation* (Boulder, Colo.: Westview, 1996); and Richard Gott, *Hugo Chávez and the Bolivarian Revolution* (London and New York: Verso, 2000).

5. F. H. Cardoso, "Las contradicciones del desarrollo asociado," *Desarrollo económico* 14, no. 53 (1974), 3–32; F. H. Cardoso, *Political Regime and Social Change: Some Reflections Concerning the Brazilian Case* (Stanford, Calif.: Stanford University/University of California, Berkeley, Stanford-Berkeley Joint Center for Latin American Studies, 1981), 28–29.

6. See, for example, Walter LaFeber, *Inevitable Revolutions: The United States in Central America* (New York: Norton, 1993); Noam Chomsky, *Hegemony or Survival: America's Quest for Global Dominance* (New York: Metropolitan Books, 2002).

7. Martin Carnoy, cited in Carlos Alberto Torres, *The Politics of Nonformal Education in Latin America* (New York: Praeger, 1990), x.

8. George Psacharopoulos et al., *Poverty and Income Distribution in Latin America: The Story of the 1980s* (Washington, D.C.: World Bank, 1992); cited in Jere R. Behrman, "Investing in Human Resources," in *Economic and Social Progress in Latin America: Annual Report* (Washington, D.C.: Inter-American Development Bank, 1993), 196.

9. Inter-American Development Bank (IDB), *Education: The Gordian Knot: Shortfalls in Schooling Are at the Root of Inequality* (Washington, D.C.: Author, 1998); also available at www.iadb.org/idbamerica/Archive/stories/1998/eng/e1198e4.htm.

10. IDB, *The Gordian Knot.*

11. International Institute of Educational Planning (IIEP)/UNESCO, "Education and Equity in Latin America," *Newsletter*, vol XXIII, no. 1 (2005).

12. IIEP, "Education and Equity," 1.

13. Comisión Económica para América Latina (CEPAL), *Anuario estadístico de América Latina y el Caribe* (Santiago de Chile: Author, 2005): 74.

14. Robert Arnove, Stephen Franz, and Kimberly Morse Cordova, "Education and Develop-

ment in Latin America," in *Understanding Contemporary Latin America*, 3rd ed., ed. Richard S. Hillman (New York: Rienner, 2005).

15. Programa de Promoción de la Reforma Educative en América Latina y el Caribe (PREAL), *Quedándonos atrás: Un informe del progreso educativo en América Latina* (Santiago, Chile: Author, 2001), 13, 42–46, also available at www.preal.org; and Behrman, "Investing in Human Resources," in *Economic and Social Progress in Latin America: Annual Report* (Washington, D.C.: Inter-American Development Bank, 1993), 205–6.

16. Miguel Urquiola and Valentina Calderón, "Apples and Oranges: Educational Enroll-ment and Attainment across Countries in Latin America and the Caribbean," *International Journal of Educational Development* 26 (2006): 572–90.

17. UNESCO Institute for Statistics, "Table 12: Measures of Progression and Completion in Primary Education," at stats.uis.unesco.org/TableViewer/tableView.aspx?ReportId = 213.

18. UNESCO Institute for Statistics, "Table 14, Tertiary Indicators," available stats.uis.unes co.org/TableViewer/tableView.aspx?ReportId = 214.

19. Urquiola and Calderón, "Apples and Oranges."

20. CEPAL, *Panorama social de America Latina* (Santiago, Chile: Author, 2005), table 30.

21. UNESCO Institute for Statistics, "Table on Literacy and Nonformal Education Sector, Regional Adult Illiteracy Rate and Population by Gender," at www.uis.unesco.org/en/stats/ statistics/UIS_Literacy_Regional2002.xls.

22. UNESCO Institute for Statistics, "Table on Literacy."

23. UNESCO Institute for Statistics, "Table on Literacy."

24. See, for example, James W. Wilkie, ed., *Statistical Abstract of Latin America,* vol. 31 (Los Angeles: UCLA American Center Publications, 1995), 1, table 900; and UNESCO Institute for Statistics, "Gender Breakdown of Illiteracy Rates of Selected Countries in Latin America and the Caribbean," at www.uis.unesco.org/ev.php?URL_ID = 4928&URL_DO = DO_TOPIC& URL_SECTION;eq201&reload = 1043161154.

25. ECLAC, *The Millennium Development Goals: A Latin American and Caribbean Perspec-tive* (Santiago, Chile, 2005), 91, figure III.7, at www.eclac.org/publicaciones/xml/0/21540/ chapter3.pdf.

26. CEPAL, *Transformación productiva con equidad* (Santiago, Chile: Author, 1990); CEPAL, *Panorama social de América Latina* (Santiago, Chile: Author, 1991); World Bank, *Brazil: Public Spending on Social Programs: Issues and Options*, World Bank Report 7086-BR (Washington, D.C.: Author, 1988).

27. CEPAL, *Panorama Social.*

28. Fernando Reimers, "The Impact of Economic Stabilization and Adjustment on Educa-tion in Latin America," *Comparative Education Review* 35, no. 2 (1991): 322, 339.

29. Ernesto Schiefelbein Wolff and Jorge Valenzuela, *Improving the Quality of Primary Edu-cation in Latin America and the Caribbean* (Washington, D.C.: World Bank, 1994), 154; also see PREAL, *Quedándonos atrás*; and Organization for Economic Cooperation and Development (OECD), "Education at a Glance" (Washington, D.C.: Author, 2002).

30. Edward Berman, "Donor Agencies and Third World Educational Development, 1945–1985," in *Emergent Issues in Education: Comparative Perspectives,* ed. Robert Arnove, Philip Alt-bach, and Gail Kelly (Albany: State University of New York Press, 1992), 69.

31. PREAL, *Quedándonos atrás*; CEPAL, *Panorama social de América Latina* (Santiago de Chile: Author, 2002).

32. David Plank, Jose Amaral Sobrinho, and Antonio Carlos ca Resurreiçao Xavier, "Obsta-cles to Educational Reform in Brazil," *La Educación* 1, no. 177 (1994): 81–82.

33. Mark Hanson, "Education Decentralization: Issues and Challenges" (paper delivered at the Annual Meeting of the Comparative and International Education Society, Orlando, Florida, March 6–10, 2002); and Inaiá Maria Moreira de Carvalho and Robert Evan Verhine, "A Descentralizaçao da Educaçao," *Revista sociedade e estado* 16, no. 2 (1999): 299–321. Furthermore,

Cuba, as part of its 1986 "rectification" overhaul of centralized government, also initiated a process of decentralization in education. Unlike municipalization plans in other Latin American countries, it tended to shift more power to local school councils and various forms of "popular power" (see Lutjens, *State, Bureaucracy*).

34. Patricia Matte and Antonio Sancho, "Primary and Secondary Education," in *The Chilean Experience: Private Solutions to Public Problems*, ed. Christian Larroulet (Santiago, Chile: Editorial Trineo S.A., 1993): 106.

35. Juan Prawda, "Educational Decentralization in Latin America: Lessons Learned," *International Journal of Educational Development* 13, no. 3 (1993): 262.

36. Marcy Fink and Robert Arnove, "Issues and Tensions in Popular Education in Latin America," *International Journal of Educational Development* 11, no. 3 (1991): 221–30.

37. Carlos Alberto Torres, "Paulo Freire as Secretary of Education in the Municipality of Sao Paulo," *Comparative Education Review* 38, no. 2 (1994): 198–99.

38. Carlos Alberto Torres and Adriana Puiggrós, "The State and Public Education in Latin America," *Comparative Education Review* 39, no. 1 (1995): 26.

39. Moagir Gadotti, "Latin America: Popular Education and the State," in *Community Education in the Third World*, ed. Cyril Poster and Jurgen Zimmer (New York: Routledge, 1992); Rosa Maria Torres, *Para revencer la educación de adultos* (New York: UNICEF, 1995).

40. Fernando Reimers, "Role of NGOs in Promoting Educational Innovation: A Case Study in Latin America," in *Education and Development: Tradition and Innovation, vol. 4, Non-Formal and Non-Governmental Approaches*, ed. James Lynch, Celia Modgil, and Sohan Modgil (London: Cassell, 1997), 35.

41. Reimers, "Role of NGOs," 38.

42. Alfredo Sarmiento Gómez, "Equity and Education in Colombia," in *Unequal Schools, Unequal Chances: The Challenges to Equality Opportunity in the Americas*, ed. Fernando Reimers (Cambridge, Mass.: Harvard University Press, 2000): 233.

43. Henry Levin, "Effective Schools and Comparative Focus," in *Emergent Issues in Education*, ed. Arnove, Altbach, and Kelly (Albany: State University of New York Press, 1992), 240.

44. Conversation with Vicky Colbert, president of the *Fundación Volvamos a la Gente* and co-founder of *La Escuela Nueva*, August 19, 2002, Bogotá, Colombia; summary information available in the pamphlet *Improving the Quality of Basic Primary Education: The Case of Escuela Nueva from Colombia* (Bogotá, Colombia: Ministry of Education, Back to the People Foundation, and National Federation of Coffee Growers Association, n.d.).

45. Celia W. Duggan, "To Help Poor Be Pupils, Not Wage Earners, Brazil Pays Parents," *New York Times*, January 3, 2004, 3.

46. Laurence Wolff and Claudio De Moura Castro, *Education and Training: The Task Ahead* (Washington, D.C.: Institute for International Economics, 2003): 196.

47. For further discussion, see Xavier Bonal and Aina Taberini, "Focalización y lucha contra la pobreza: Una discusión acerca de los limites y posibilidades del programa bolsa escola," *Globalización, educación y pobreza en América Latina: Hacia una nueva agenda política*, ed. Xavier Bonal (Barcelona: Editorial Bellaterra, 2006), as well other essays in this volume.

48. Xabier Gorostiaga, "New Times, New Role for Universities of the South," *Envío* 12, no. 144 (July 1993): 24–40.

49. Robert Arnove, *Education as Contested Terrain: Nicaragua, 1979–1993* (Boulder, Colo.: Westview, 1994).

50. Gorostiaga, "New Times."

51. Larry Rohter, "Economic Rally for Argentines Defies Forecasts," *New York Times*, December 26, 2004, A1, 8.

52. Typical of these efforts was a coming together of indigenous, labor, environmental, feminist, and antiglobalization movements in Cochabamba, Bolivia, December 8–9, 2006, to discuss an alternative to the neoliberal agenda, at the same time that the heads of state of twelve South

American countries met to discuss regional integration. The meeting represented a joining of transnational forces initiated by the Comunidad Sudamericana de Naciones (CSN) with the inter-state initiatives of President Evo Morales of Bolivia. See "Evo Morales propone CSN para 'vivir bien.'" "Red de redes en defensa de la humanidad," at www.defensahumanidad.cu/artic.php?item=1029. Last accessed May 7, 2007.

53. See, for example, the initiatives of Rosa María Torres (fronesis.org/prolat.htm) as a follow-up to the Jomtien 1990 and Dakar 2000 international conferences.

54. Mary Compton, "We are the World," *Rethinking Schools* (Spring 2005): 8–9.

13

Education in Asia: Globalization and its Effects

John N. Hawkins

ASIAN EDUCATION*

The impact of the Asian region on the world economy has increased enormously during the past two decades. This region, with a long tradition and history, is home to the largest population of any region in the world and, increasingly, is taking a leadership role in economic development and educational competitiveness. For the purposes of this chapter the focus will be on the subregions of East Asia, Southeast Asia, and South Asia.[1] The contemporary political economic systems of Asia vary significantly from one country to another. Some are market economy democracies, some have socialist/communist governments with centrally planned economic systems, some former command economies are now market/socialist hybrids, some are still ruled by kings, and some come from a mixed system of hereditary kings and democratically elected rulers. All appear to be influenced and driven to some degree by neoliberal policies and the effects of worldwide globalization.[2]

While great advances have been made in overall economic and educational development goals for Asia, the region still has some of the poorest countries in world (two-thirds of the world's poor live in Asia), most of them in South Asia. Other parts of Asia, notably East Asia, have achieved parity with many nations in the West and fall into the general category of middle-income countries.[3] Japan was the first Asian nation to compete successfully with the West, followed by the "Four Tigers" (Taiwan, South Korea, Hong Kong, and Singapore) and now by China.[4] Indonesia, Malaysia, and India are all experiencing high growth rates and educational achievement levels. Most nations have achieved universal primary and secondary education levels and many have started to invest heavily in research and development and the expansion of higher education.[5] As we shall see, much remains to be done, as the region goes through a major transformation in light of globalization and neoliberal forces that have led to privatization and decentralization. Before focusing on the subregions in Asia, it is useful to briefly identify some critical issues that cut across the region as a way of informing the discussion of specific issues in the subregions.

Most of the nations in modern Asia, with the possible exception of Japan, continue to be concerned with the overall issues of development and what it means. Some scholars have suggested that there is a special form of development that applies specifically to Asia, one involving the judicious intermixing of the state and private sectors.[6] Most writers on the topic, however, are focused on the economic aspects of development, especially in the face of great pressure for educational expansion.[7] Other issues have to do with the role of human resources in science and technology, the effect of decolonization and neocolonization on educational development, and the relationship between the different tiers of the educational system.[8] The principal concern, however, in the discussion of development and education, is that it is primarily seen as country specific; that is, nations are much concerned about their own development issues but not necessarily so concerned about the region as a whole.

This is where a second major issue emerges, that of globalization. Here policymakers see that the actions of one country have an impact on those of its neighbors and this creates a tension between local and global needs.[9] For example, in Hong Kong, a setting that has been historically supremely globally connected, educators now face a challenge to maintain that global connectiveness while reintegrating with China. A number of other Asian nations face similar challenges in balancing the global with the local.[10]

Related to both of these issues is one focused on educational access and equity. The increasing demand for education, driven by the forces of development and globalization, has meant that educational planners and policymakers have had to make difficult decisions about who gets educated at what levels. For some this has meant developing controversial tracking systems.[11] For others there have been implications for expanding education to neglected areas, a policy that has severe cost implications.[12] China, with the largest population in the region, has long struggled with the issue of educational access and equity ranging from dramatic political movements to demographic realities of rural-urban change.[13] Who gets educated will remain one of the central issues of education in Asia for the foreseeable future.

A somewhat more controversial issue has to do with values and moral education. Given the pace of social change in Asia in the last quarter of a century and the rapid economic advances, it is not surprising that the new affluence has unleashed a quest for ever greater material success, seemingly eroding traditional conceptions of moderation and virtue, or what some have called "Asian values."[14] There are many reasons why this is an important issue. The region is becoming increasingly important strategically and it is necessary to understand the value systems that underlie it. Second, the region is extremely diverse in its history and traditions, offering many approaches to moral education. Finally, values education is a prominent part of education in most of the Asian nations and there are lessons to learn. For example, it has been pointed out that there are important implications of Confucian values for education, not just in Asia but in the West as well.[15] There is also a debate that Asian values have suffered as a result of modernization and that this has created social disorder in some societies.[16] Is there something that can be called Asian values and how do they differ from Western values?

Equally sensitive are the issues of intergroup relations and women's education in Asia. Asia is an incredibly varied region, in terms of linguistic and ethnic groups, religious affiliations, and indigenous populations. Issues of power and control, access and equity, and nationalism all are magnified when juxtaposed with Asia's many groups. Most recently, more attention has been paid to how majorities treat minorities, especially with respect to religion. For example, in China, a nation with relatively few non–Han Chinese (perhaps 6 percent of the population), the topic of Islamicization and the role of schools in this process has increasingly been of interest to Chinese policymakers (as well as others in the West).[17] Language and schooling have also posed a challenge to policymakers throughout the region and in societies like Hong Kong, where educators felt it had been settled. However, it has appeared again with Hong Kong's changed status as it has in the Philippines as nationalist sentiments have reemerged.[18] The education of women remains a priority for many Asian nations with much work to be done. Women have increasingly become aware of the value of education and its ability to empower them, and a variety of feminist movements have emerged as a result.[19] Yet in many societies the education of girls falls far below that of boys. The gender gap continues to be a major obstacle to a more balanced educational development strategy.

The following discussion of the similarities and the differences in educational development in Asian nations in the context of some of the issues identified above is divided into three sections: East, Southeast, and South Asia. The discussion in each section includes illustrations of selected critical issues in education from selected nations. We emphasize the effect that recent reform efforts in education have had on equality of opportunity and outcomes for the most disadvantaged groups in different Asian nations.

EAST ASIA

The subregion of East Asia can be considered either geographically or culturally and typically includes the settings of China, Tibet, Hong Kong, Macau, Japan, Korea (North and South), Taiwan, and Mongolia. Sometimes Singapore is included but we will discuss it in the section on Southeast Asia. It covers about 15 percent of the Asian continent. It is sometimes referred to as Sinified Asia, as China has had an important cultural and historical influence on the region. China, with over 1 billion people, and Japan, with its early modernization and powerful economy, dominate the region. This is the region that has been referred to as the East Asian Miracle because of the generally high levels of economic development. The Asian economic crisis in 1997–1998 raised serious questions about the sustainability of this model of development but the region recovered and even with Japan's slow recovery the region remains a powerful economic and strategic force not just in Asia but also throughout the world. Strong, state-led development has characterized this region in general and even with the current (2006) decentralization movement, the state continues to exert a high level of "guidance."

Major educational progress has been made in East Asia since the end of WWII. It is safe to say that the entire region (with some exceptions) has achieved universal literacy

Table 13.1 East Asia: Primary and secondary attendance, and literacy, 2004

	Primary %	*Secondary %*	*Literacy %*
China	100	73	90
Republic of Korea	100	91	98
Japan	100	100	100
Hong Kong	100	85	NA

Source: UNESCO Institute for Statistics, at www.uis.unesco.org/profiles/selectCountry_en.aspx.
Note: NA = not available.

and primary attendance, as well as high levels of secondary education (China lags in secondary education, at about 73 percent in 2004). Although the transition from primary to secondary school is high,[20] wastage remains a problem for several nations in the region. China and Korea spend about 4 percent of their GNP on education and Japan's expenditures remain low (about 1 percent) even as reforms call for an increase.[21]

Ka Ho Mok[22] notes there are several key challenges common to the East Asia region:

- Rapid economic growth and social progress;
- The rise of the knowledge economy and the transformation of higher education;
- The key role that information technology is playing in education delivery;
- Massification of higher education and the need for quality control;
- The lingering effects of the East Asian financial crisis; and
- Major social and political changes (i.e., decentralization) and implications for higher education.

The World Bank has also identified several critical issues for the future of educational development in the East Asian region. Despite the advances made in enrollments and access, there is still a need to reach the last 10 percent in basic education. These challenges exist in the more remote areas of the region, typically among minority populations, and require finding a balance between local belief systems and those of the broader national and global communities.[23]

A second issue focuses on educational quality and how to assess it. Although educational systems are well developed and have expanded enormously, there remain a variety of issues related to learning and teaching. Improvements in the learning environment and the instruction process will be important for the region to continue to maintain high achievement levels. And this is closely connected to a third area of concern, which has to do with teacher development and teacher education. Most nations in the region recognize the need for better preservice education as well as ongoing professional development.

At the secondary level of schooling, there is still progress to be made in achieving a more appropriate gender balance, as well as access to and understanding of information technology. There remain large rural-urban access and equity issues as well as the well-known digital divide. A more determined effort to bridge these gaps will be important for the next decade.

As has been mentioned above, there is a region-wide decentralization movement affecting all areas of education from management and governance to educational finance. How this movement develops in the future will determine whether educational achievement, access, and equity issues will continue to positively develop in the region. This movement is also related to the increasing role that private resources are playing in overall educational development, but especially at the higher education level. While this movement has contributed to the continued expansion of educational opportunity, there is evidence that it is also creating educational inequities as low-income parents find it difficult to afford the increased costs of schooling.[24]

The overall issue of mass higher education is important in its own right. As one analysis says:

> The crucial policy decisions about higher education development and lifelong learning [in East Asia] that are made by each country along the way have enormous import in

relation to achieving ideal societal outcomes. Will there be open access for young people of disadvantaged family, ethnic, and geographical backgrounds? Will there be appropriate balance between forms of higher education that meet labor market needs at the middle level and those that nurture leadership at the political, cultural, intellectual and corporate level? Will there be an appropriate balance between public support for higher education and various forms of private investment?[25]

In the case of East Asia, Japan, Taiwan, and Korea have already reached the stage of mass higher education and China is on its way. Now they are struggling with the problem of quality as well as those above.

Finally, the link between education and the labor market in the new knowledge economy is another major issue facing the East Asian region. As central planning has given way to decentralization and shorter-range planning, societies in the region have to find new ways to provide a more appropriate fit between the output of the formal and nonformal educational systems and the labor needs of the knowledge economy.

The two major nations in the region, Japan and China, have both been going through rapid and significant educational transformations in the last five years. Japan, the first Asian nation to modernize and compete with the West both economically and militarily, has always been a model of educational achievement and success. However, in recent years a number of factors have contributed to a set of circumstances that have led to what many call the third major educational reform (the first being the Meiji Restoration of 1868 and second the U.S. occupation following World War II).

The fundamental reform that characterizes the new century focuses on the privatization and incorporation of Japan's highly regarded national universities. By 2003, the basic outlines of incorporation began to emerge and consisted of the following features:

- Institutionalized management under the university president (supplanting the faculty committees and chair systems);
- The National Institution for Academic Degrees, formed in 2000 and later renamed the National Institution for Academic Degrees and University Evaluation (NIADUE), charged with evaluating the quality of all National University education and research;
- Faculty and administrators' status changed from government employees to nongovernmental employees;
- Top-down, centralized strategic management (based on private sector models);
- Higher Education Institutions (HEIs) given greater autonomy and flexibility (within limits) in planning and management of budget, personnel, and organization;
- Strong emphasis on HEI collaboration with the private sector and industry;
- Presidents of National Universities to be appointed by the Ministry, which set the term, approve mid-term plans, and oversee the evaluation of their performance by NIADUE.[26]

If the goal of all of this was to increase autonomy of the National Universities, this, at least remained a topic of debate. Some argued that all of the assessment and monitoring procedures and especially the role played by NIADUE meant in fact that the National Universities were under even more government control than before.[27] Others noted that the new incorporation left out key elements that would make them work, first and fore-most of which was a Board of Trustees or of Governors to whom the newly empowered president would report. The new body, called a Board of Directors (*yakuinkai*), is com-posed of appointees who are all internal to the university and mimicked private sector management practices. The Management Councils (*keiei kyogikai*) resemble a Board of Trustees but play only an advisory role. The whole structure appears to be a compromise between politicians who wanted to introduce private sector methods and academics that resisted this. Lacking is any form of coordination between policy, administrative, and academic levels. The presidency was strengthened, which would work as long as the presi-dent is capable but even then there is no protection by a Board of Trustees from meddling by the Ministry or other political bodies. Management Councils, which could play a coordinating role between the presidents and the Ministry, are staffed by old Ministry of Education bureaucrats, and are not significantly engaged.[28] Incorporation represented a significant move in the direction of commodifying the national university system in Japan while at the same time retaining significant features of state-led change and bureaucratic interference. It did, however, form the basis for other more detailed changes in the fabric of higher education in Japan.

The reforms initiated for Japan's National Universities will have a significant impact not only on Japan's collegiate level but also on the precollegiate, as curriculum and assess-ment at the primary and secondary level will also adjust to meet the new demands of higher education. Particularly impacted will be Japan's private higher education sector, which has already suffered a dramatic decline in enrollment and now will have to com-pete with a more privatized public sector.[29]

China (and Taiwan and Korea) is also going through a major higher education reform process that will have profound implications for their educational system as a whole as well as the human resource training capacity of the East Asia region in general. Higher education decentralization is the key element of this reform. China has clearly set itself on a path to become not only a regional but also a world leader. But in order to do so, its leaders are convinced that China's power is linked to producing and retaining the best and brightest students and to reforming its educational system.[30] A major feature of the current educational reform movement to achieve these goals is the focus on decentral-ization. China's educational leadership has been struggling with the issue of centralization and decentralization almost since the founding of the People's Republic in 1949. Terms such as *walking on two legs* (combining both centralized and decentralized approaches to education) and *minban* schools (community run schools), once again in vogue, date back several decades.[31] In the latter years of the commune system, communes and production brigades were being urged by provincial authorities to run rural primary and junior mid-dle schools independently, raising funds through their own efforts, and hiring teachers in a competitive manner.[32] These early efforts to shift authority from central to local levels did not represent, however, a national decentralization policy of the scope we are witness-ing today.

China's educational authorities, in reaching the decision to decentralize the system, lodged several critiques at the previous, centralized model. More specifically, it was stated that

- Government control of schools was too rigid and management inefficient;
- Authority should be devolved to lower levels;

- Multiple methods of financing should be sought;
- Devolution of authority for the nine year compulsory system should be gradual, based on a regional approach in the order of: coastal cities, developed interior regions and cities, and less developed interior;
- "The power for administration of elementary education belongs to local authorities"[33];
- Secondary schools will establish tracking, either toward higher education or vocational-technical education combined with some devolution of authority and financing; and
- The central level (State Education Commission, SEC, later replaced by the Ministry of Education) will continue to monitor the process and provide basic guidelines, but "subordinate units" will have more power and bear financial costs.[34]

It took about twenty years for the system to begin to exhibit the features noted above. By 2003, university leaders had increased authority to make most academic decisions while still being required to report their results to the Ministry of Education. They were especially independent when it came to financing their universities, now being required to raise a good share of their total expenses from nongovernmental sources such as tuition, sales and services, research grants, private giving, and university-run enterprises. Through such initiatives as Project 211, China's leaders are seeking to promote one hundred key universities to be internationally competitive during the twenty-first century. Decentralized financial reforms have also raised the criticism that traditional academic values have been compromised. And, while academic reforms have been carried out (largely imitative of the U.S. system of higher education), the predominance of the national and local examination system continues to stifle the more creative efforts to restructure the curriculum, for example, along more multidisciplinary lines. General education programs are being created on many campuses but have yet to make the impact that is hoped for, largely due to the rigidity of the central and local entrance examinations. The development of a credit system, more independent and autonomous academic departments, and more transparency in the higher educational system are all hallmarks of the current reforms but while they all speak to greater autonomy, a parallel increase in assessment and accountability measures on the part of the Ministry of Education calls into question the degree of real decentralization that has taken place. The system is clearly in flux and it will be instructive to monitor Chinese higher education reforms, as they will undoubtedly influence the East Asian region as a whole in the years to come.[35] As has already been noted, similar reforms are underway in both Taiwan and Korea.

Thus, the decentralization and privatization movement that characterizes educational reform in East Asia leaves many questions unanswered. Chief among them is the degree to which the central authorities continue to cling to power and the possible deleterious effects that privatization may have on issues of educational equity and diversity.

SOUTHEAST ASIA

Southeast Asia is a sprawling region consisting of two parts: mainland and insular. The total area covers 3,209,506 sq km of land and the rest, 1,665,562 sq km, is water. There are ten countries that are members of the principal regional organization, the Association of Southeast Asian Nations (ASEAN): Brunei, Cambodia, Indonesia, Lao People's Democratic Republic (PDR), Malaysia, Myanmar, Philippines, Singapore, Thailand, and Vietnam, with a combined population of around 540 million. Education, growth, and development vary widely in the region and all of the nations, with the exception of Thailand, were under colonial rule prior to World War II.

The goal for ASEAN nations remains focused on human resource development for national development, and each nation in the region struggles in various ways with the broad issue of globalization. It is safe to say that for most nations in the region, universal primary education has been achieved; however, Myanmar, Cambodia, and Laos continue to struggle when it comes to making the transition from primary to secondary education.[36] The same nations lag behind when considering female transitions from primary to secondary. Secondary net enrollment ratios also are generally high for the region but fall off in Cambodia, Myanmar, and Laos (averaging around 30 percent). And gross enrollment ratios in tertiary education, while expanding throughout the region, remain relatively low (from a low of 3 percent in Cambodia to around 30 percent in Thailand, Malaysia, and Singapore).[37] Near universal primary education and successful literacy campaigns have meant that literacy is high throughout the region.

Specific goals for the nations in the region differ in focus from "education for all" in the Philippines, to an emphasis on quality in Myanmar. In Malaysia, the focus is on technological and scientific development and the growth of world class education.[38] However, in tiny Brunei, the concern is providing a minimum of twelve years of schooling for all children.[39] Singapore and Thailand both are concentrating on education for the knowledge society and lifelong learning.[40] Yet, for all of the nations in the region, two major issues seem to be at the forefront of educational reform: equity in education and quality of education.

While much progress has been made in the region with respect to general basic education and even in the area of further expansion of higher education, a number of equity issues continue to loom over the region, preoccupying educational policymakers. The inequalities in the region are many, ranging from the rural-urban divide to differences between public and private institutions, as well as gender inequalities, and finally, the continuance of stubborn socioeconomic status (SES) differences. The digital divide is a relatively new inequality that is increasing in importance. One must remember that despite the substantial economic progress shown by Thailand, Malaysia, Singapore, and now Vietnam, Southeast Asia still has about one-third of its population living below the poverty line as defined by international agencies.[41] The Lao PDR, Philippines, Vietnam,

Table 13.2   Southeast Asia: Primary and secondary attendance, and literacy, 2004

	Primary %	Secondary %	Literacy %
Indonesia	100	64	90
Malaysia	93	70	88
Philippines	100	86	92
Vietnam	98	73	90
Myanmar	96	40	90
Thailand	99	77	92

Source: UNESCO Institute for Statistics, at www.uis.unesco.org/profiles/selectCountry_en.aspx.
Note: NA = not available.

and Cambodia all are in the 35–40 percent range below the poverty line, and Indonesia comes in around 27 percent. The others come in around 8–10 percent.[42]

Nations such as Indonesia have major issues related to disparities across geographical regions as well as gender and income.[43] A somewhat similar problem faces the Lao PDR with 18 provinces, 141 districts, and over 12,000 villages all displaying geographical inaccessibility and an uneven spread of the 5.5 million population.[44] Malaysia's problems are of a different order, as policymakers seek to close achievement gaps as well as bridge gaps between the rural and urban sectors and between major ethnic groups.

One of the most dynamic emerging nations in the region is Vietnam. Although still a poor country, Vietnam has experienced high annual rates of growth and low rates of inflation. They have achieved high rates of primary and secondary enrollments as well as literacy. At the precollegiate level, gender imbalances are a priority as are imbalances between minority groups. It is in the area of higher education that innovative plans have been proposed to bring Vietnam into a competitive position in the region by the year 2020. The higher education system has been transformed from small, specialized institutes into large composite institutions. Following the China model, fourteen institutions have been identified as key (out of about 200 total). Educational policymakers envision an expanded system including nongovernmental (similar to the *minban* institutions in China) or private institutions. Policymakers have proposed conferring legal autonomy on higher education institutions, deregulating the rigid control of the Ministry of Education, launching a quality assurance and accreditation program, and developing a more fully articulated "Higher Education Law."[45] These are bold new initiatives that will face many difficulties, principally those associated with prioritization and governance. They also face the problem of the "international education business," as foreign institutions (some of questionable quality) seek to profit from the Vietnamese higher education market.[46]

And in the Philippines, poverty in general is the dominating factor, as children are needed to provide labor to take care of the family's day-to-day needs. The Philippines, which has long had a very well developed educational system (with significant private school development) has been hampered in its development efforts by political instability, corruption, lack of differentiation, mismatch between school and workplace, and brain drain.[47]

Even in the higher income nations such as Singapore and Thailand, there are equity issues that are also present in the region as a whole related to facilities, shortage of qualified teachers, lack of good textbooks, student and parent attitudes regarding the value of education, and budget cutbacks from the government due to neoliberal policies that are shaping the region. For example, in Thailand, social targeting of student loans for needy students has been challenged and replaced to some degree by a cost-sharing approach, further evidence of the decline of social support for education.[48] All of these factors impact the availability of education and affect the access and equity of the system to the population as a whole.

SOUTH ASIA

The region, consisting of Bangladesh, Pakistan, India, Bhutan, Nepal, and Sri Lanka, has faced several major regional challenges since 2005. Political turmoil and instability have marked the past few years, which in turn have affected social services such as education.

Continued strife in Sri Lanka and Nepal has made it difficult for the governments to follow through on development plans and educational reform. A similar situation developed in Bangladesh when the security climate deteriorated in August of 2005, as government institutions were attacked by *Jama'atul Mujahideen Bangladesh* (JMB), an Islamic organization with ties to Al Queda. The Indian Ocean tsunami disaster displaced thousands of people, resulting in refugee camps and presenting major educational challenges to the governments of Sri Lanka and India.

Poverty has long characterized the region, which is home to 40 percent of the world's poor living on less than U.S.$1 a day. Nevertheless, since 1990, rapid GDP growth has helped reduce the consumption poverty (a measure that utilizes a subset of a family's total expenditures) rate substantially. India particularly has reduced its poverty rate substantially and with the exception of Pakistan, which has stagnated at around 33 percent, the rest of the region has made improvements as well, including Bangladesh, which the United Nations has recently ranked in the middle levels of development. Other indicators of social progress have been more positive, including lower mortality in children, school enrollments at primary and secondary levels (averaging about 80 percent at the primary level, and varying widely at the secondary level from a high of 86 percent in Sri Lanka to 23 percent in Pakistan), and the ratio of girls to boys in primary and secondary education. Progress still remains to be made in key areas, such as child malnutrition, primary and secondary completion rates, maternal mortality, and general health outcomes. Adult literacy is high in Sri Lanka at 90 percent, 61 percent in India, and then it falls into the 40 percent range for the remaining countries. Tertiary gross enrollment rates are rising in India to around 12 percent but below 10 percent in the rest of the region.[49]

Of course the giant of the region is India with over one billion people and set to surpass China in total population in the near future. And in education, India already outproduces most countries in terms of STEM graduates (science, technology, engineering, and mathematics). Like China, India seeks to build world-class universities but has struggled with several challenges. First and foremost, India does not spend much on higher education (about 0.37 percent of gross domestic product, compared to the United States at 1.41 and the United Kingdom at 1.07).[50] China is investing more in higher education than India at present. As in most nations, higher education drives much of the rest of the system and as Indian higher education struggles with quality, so does the precollegiate level. At the collegiate level, India has one of the world's largest higher education systems (259 institutions, 10,750 colleges, 8 million students).[51] As the system expanded, the University Grants Commission realized the need for a more appropriate accreditation system and established the National Assessment and Accreditation Council (NAAC) in

Table 13.3   **South Asia: Primary and secondary attendance, and literacy, 2004**

	Primary %	*Secondary %*	*Literacy %*
India	100	54	61
Pakistan	82	27	50
Sri Lanka	98	83	90
Nepal	100	42	48
Bangladesh	100	52	NA

Source: UNESCO Institute for Statistics, at www.uis.unesco.org/profiles/selectCountry_en.aspx.
Note: NA = not available.

1994. Inasmuch as India represents an attractive market for developed countries anxious to export their education, accreditation is even more important. The NAAC has struggled in this respect and, as is the case with accreditation in the rest of Asia, India faces a number of challenges.[52]

In general, it has been argued that education as a public good has suffered in India and that privatization is proceeding apace with public higher education sector funds being reduced. A for profit sector is emerging but many institutions are of questionable quality.[53] Neoliberal policies and globalization have increasingly taken hold in India since the 1990s, leading to a doubling of the higher education sector, a rapid increase in private institutions, and a number of problems related to access, quality, and equity; in general, an overall erosion of the public good nature of higher education. As one author argues:

> globalization has generated a new dilemma. . . . the country must choose between two options. It can promote advanced technical and professional education and research to be self-sufficient and to remain in the forefront of knowledge. Alternately, it can concentrate on providing a variety of vocational and technical courses to equip the population to take advantage of the employment opportunities that are generated as multinationals locate labor-intensive production processes in India.[54]

There will be much for India's educational policymakers to think about, as rivals like China appear to be trying to do both. The one bright spot in Indian higher education is the Indian Institutes of Technology, which continue to play a significant role in India's forward march into the twenty-first century.

India's rival in the region, Pakistan, has also sought to dramatically reform its educational system, especially higher education. In 2001, encouraged by the World Bank-UNESCO report *Higher Education in Developing Countries: Peril and Promise*, Pakistan launched major reforms led by a special task force for improving higher education. A central reform was to transform the governance and management of Pakistan's universities, introducing more autonomy and transparency into the system. While there were many good intentions, it was quickly revealed that resistance to change was paramount. A "leadership deficit" quickly became visible and the reforms stalled. As one Pakistani scholar notes:

> First, the overall mode of state functioning, policymaking, and governance is top-down, nontransparent, and rigidly hierarchical. . . . Second, at the micro level, the leadership of institutions of higher learning is extremely weak. . . . the leaders remain largely opposed to reform.[55]

The challenges for Pakistan appear to be in the area of leadership, not just within the educational sector but also systemically including the top political positions. Pakistan's current conflicted involvement with U.S. policy in the region does not make it any easier to concentrate on social issues such as education.

While some nations have been previously stigmatized as being the least developed in the region, Bangladesh, as a case in point, has made significant progress in the past ten years. Literacy, primary and secondary levels of education, as well as women's education have all made gains during this period.[56] In the area of higher education, however, much remains to be done. Access to higher education has been quite limited, with less than 10 percent of the Higher Secondary Certificate cohort being admitted to the university sector. The bulk of those who have not been admitted are from the lower socioeconomic sectors of society.[57] As is the case in much of Asia, the private sector in higher education has been booming, but characterized by the usual problems of poor quality, unmotivated faculty, low quality of teaching, and limited financial benefits. One unfortunate result of this expansion of the private sector is that as they compete with the government universities, both suffer a lowering of quality standards.[58]

One of the more interesting reforms in South Asia is the effort to decentralize primary school management in Nepal. Nepal has been wracked with internal strife, a Maoist rebellion, and the massacre of the royal family. In 2001, King Gyanendra declared a state of emergency and called up the Royal Nepal Army to fight the insurgency. By the spring of 2006, massive protests were launched, demanding that the king reinstate the Parliament. Nevertheless, the educational context is not unimpressive, with 100 percent reported enrollment at the primary level, 43 percent at the lower secondary level, and 30 percent at the upper secondary level (more boys than girls are enrolled at all levels).[59] Around the time of the Ninth Year Plan (1997–2002), the government initiated a policy of decentralization of educational management utilizing School Management Committees (SMCs). In general the SMCs were designed to prepare school improvement plans, mobilize community participation, recruit temporary teachers to deal with the teacher shortage, evaluate and monitor teachers, control school finances, and foster resources for school development.[60] It is unclear as of this writing how successful this effort will be, but it represents an interesting case of decentralization as this aspect of globalization begins to penetrate Asian education at all levels.

FUTURE PROSPECTS

The region as a whole is advancing into the twenty-first century both boldly and with some trepidation. Boldly because economic indicators are positive even for the poorest regions; and for the more prosperous, they are reaching developed world standards. Educational indicators, too, are in the positive range as the demand for schooling has risen and nations in the region are struggling to supply the capacity. The populations view education positively in general, and test scores in the region are more than competitive with world standards. Social indicators such as food supply and health are also enviable. The Internet has had a positive impact on public political participation and has been a factor in challenging one-party rule in the region; thus, the region exhibits increased diversity and sharing in the economic successes. There is much to be enthusiastic about for the future of Asia.

This does not mean that the region is without challenges. The historic role of the state in providing both basic and higher education as a public good is undergoing change, and raises numerous questions about the state's "proper" role in providing and assuring the production of public goods. At the core of the issue is the extent to which education, basic and higher, will be viewed as a public good to be provided largely by the state on behalf of the production of "the public good," or whether higher education is produced as a commodity to be acquired through market-based transactions. Issues of equity are central to these distinctions, especially in terms of how the state perceives and accepts its responsibility for both basic and higher education provision. The forces of neoliberalism that have buttressed this shift away from education as a public good are strong, yet there is also resistance. There is increasing pressure for more participation and access to education and a lagging capacity. The issue of quality is also significant, as the new privatization thrust has produced educational institutions of varying worth. For large nations such as China and India, there are great challenges for the many who have been left out of the prosperity that has characterized recent economic growth in these nations. For the smaller nations, the competitiveness they face for continued growth in the region will be important. Progress still needs to be made in the areas of access and equity, gender, minority education, appropriateness of training for future development, and the effects of globalization (both negative and positive).

There are important demographic issues for both China and Japan as school-age populations are in the decline. The situation is most acute in Japan, where private universities and colleges are faced with economic ruin as they compete with the public sectors for new students. In China, the timeline is further down the road, but a similar tension between public and *minban* (or nongovernmental) schools is already beginning to develop.

Strategically, there remain a number of hot spots in Asia, the most notable being North Korea, but also looming are the issues of relations between Taiwan and China, a more confident Japan possibly looking to increase its military stance, historical conflicts between India and Pakistan (made more dangerous due the introduction of nuclear weapons by both nations), and other regional political problems. Yet, the international bilateral and multilateral agencies seem to be doing a good job of mediating regional stability.

The dynamism of the region is unmistakable, however, and morale is high among the leaders and general populations. The educational challenges the region faces are significant as leaders face a number of daunting issues ranging from simple demographics (both increasing and decreasing school age cohorts depending on the country) to complex bilateral and multilateral relations and the overall climate of globalization. A relatively new development worth watching is an increasing sense of an "Asian/Pacific Community" that cuts across previously well-defined subregional boundaries. The degree to which that can be further promoted and developed will go a long way toward addressing the challenges facing education and globalization in Asia.

NOTES

* Throughout this chapter a number of statistics will be provided principally to indicate trends in education throughout the Asia region. Most of these numbers are self-reported by the nations concerned and often are out of date or unreliable and thus they are provided only to indicate some comparative trends between nations in the region.

1. J. F. Williams, "Asia," in *Compton Interactive Encyclopedia*, ed. D. Good et al. (Cambridge, Mass.: Softkey Multimedia, 1996); J. N. Hawkins, "Education in Asia," in *Encyclopedia of Educational Research*, ed. M. Alkin (New York: MacMillan, 1991); G. A. Postiglione and G. C. L. Mak, eds., *Asian Higher Education* (Westport, Conn.: Greenwood, 1997).

2. D. Neubauer and J. Hawkins, eds., *Education Transformation in Asia: Public Good or Private Commodity*, unpublished manuscript, available at East West Center, Honolulu, Hawaii (Forthcoming, 2007).

3. U.S. Central Intelligence Agency, *World Fact Book*, at www.cia.gov/cia/publications/factbook/index.html.

4. L. Q. Li, *Education for 1.3 Billion* (Beijing: Foreign Language Teaching and Research Press, 2006).

5. K. H. Mok, *Education Reform and Education Policy in East Asia* (London: Routledge, 2006).

6. D. Aston, F. Green, D. James, and J. Sung, "The Development State and the Education Training System," in *Education for Training and Development in East Asia* (London: Routledge, 1999); see also their chapter "Is there a 'Four Tigers' Model of Skill Formation."

7. J. Xiao, "Education Expansion in Shenzhen China: Its Interface with Economic Development," *International Journal of Educational Development* 11, no. 1 (1998).

8. H. Choi, "Shifting Human Resources in South Korean Science and Technology," *Comparative Education Review* 43, no. 2 (1999): 212–32; W. W. Law, "The Accommodation and Resistance to the Decolonisation, Neocolonisation and Recolonisation of Higher Education in Hong Kong," *Comparative Education* 33, no. 2 (1997): 187–209; N. Warwick, "Restructuring Tertiary Education in Malaysia: The Nature and Implications of Policy Changes," *Higher Education Policy* 11, no. 4 (1998): 257–79.

9. G. R. Teasdale, "Local and Global Knowledge in Higher Education: A Search for Complementarity in the Asia-Pacific Region," *International Journal of Educational Development* 18, no. 6 (1998): 501–11.

10. G. A. Postiglione, "Maintaining Global Engagement in the Face of National Integration in Hong Kong," *Comparative Education Review* 42, no. 1 (1998).

11. C. M. Broaded, "The Limits and Possibilities of Tracking: Some Evidence from Taiwan," *Sociology of Education* 70, no. 1 (1997): 36–53.

12. G. W. Jones, "The Expansion of High School Education in Poor Regions: the Case of East Nusa Tenggara Indonesia," *Bulletin of Indonesian Economic Studies* 34, no. 3 (1998): 59–84.

13. Z. Deng and D. Treiman, "The Impact of the Cultural Revolution on Trends in Educational Attainment in the People's Republic of China," *American Journal of Sociology* 103, no. 2 (1997): 391–428; E. Hannum, "Political Change and the Urban-Rural Gap in Basic Education in China: 1949–1990," *Comparative Education Review* 43, no. 2 (1999): 193–211.

14. W. K. Cummings, M. T. Tatto, and J. N. Hawkins, *Values Education for Dynamic Societies: Individualism or Collectivism?* (Hong Kong: Comparative Education Research Centre, 2001).

15. F. K. S. Leung, "The Implications of Confucianism for Education Today," *Journal of Thought* 33, no. 2 (Summer 1998): 25–36.

16. K. Zeng and G. LeTendre, "Adolescent Suicide and Academic Competition in East Asia," 42, no. 4 (1998): 513–28.

17. D. Gladney, "Making Muslims in China: Education, Islamicization, and Representation," in *China's National Minority Education, Culture, Schooling*, ed. G. Postiglione (New York: Falmer, 1999).

18. D. Adamson and W. A. Lai, "Language and Curriculum in Hong Kong: Dilemmas of Triglossia," *Comparative Education* 33, no. 2 (1997): 233–46; J. J. Smolicz and I. Nical, "Exporting the European Idea of a National Language: Some Implications of the Use of English and Indigenous Languages in the Philippines," *International Review of Education* 43 (1997): 1–21.

19. W. Jayaweera, "Women, Education, and Empowerment in Asia," *Gender and Education* 9, no. 4 (1997): 411–24; I. Patel, "The Contemporary Women's Movement and Women's Education in India," *International Review of Education* 45, nos. 5–6 (1999): 155–75.

20. U.S. Agency for International Development, *Global Education Data Base*, at qesdb.cdie.org/ged/index.html.

21. U.S. Agency for International Development, *Global Education Data Base*.

22. K. H. Mok, *Education Reform and Education Policy in East Asia* (London: Routledge, 2006).

23. The World Bank, *Topic Brief: Education in the East Asia and Pacific Region*, at go.worldbank.org/JJI1B58WE0.

24. C. J. Bjork, ed., *Educational Decentralization: Asian Experiences and Conceptual Contributions* (New York: Kluwer Press, 2006).

25. The World Bank, *Topic Brief*, 5.

26. Y. Tsuruta, "On-going Changes in Higher Education in Japan and Some Key Issues," in *Inside the Higher Education Institution in Japan: Responding to Change and Reforms* (Tokyo: Daiwa Anglo Japanese Foundation, 2003).

27. Tsuruta, "On-going Changes in Higher Education in Japan."

28. S. Hatakenaka, "The Incorporation of National Universities: The Role of Missing Hybrids," in *The Big Bang in Japanese Higher Education*, ed. J. S. Eades et al. (Melbourne, Australia: TransPacific, 2005).

29. H. Akabayashi, "Private Higher Education and Government in Japan," *International Higher Education* no. 42 (Winter 2006).

30. J. N. Hawkins, "Walking on Three Legs: Centralization, Decentralization, and Recentralization in Chinese Education," in *Education Decentralization*, ed. C. Bjork (New York: Kluwer Press, 2006).

31. J. N. Hawkins, "Deschooling Society Chinese Style: Alternative Forms of Non-Formal Education," *Educational Studies* Vol. 1 (Fall 1973): 113–23.

32. Z. Xin, "Tax Reform not to Affect Education," *China Daily*, March 7, 2001.

33. *Reform of China's Educational Structure—Decision of the CPC Central Committee* (Beijing: Foreign Languages Press, 1985), 9.

34. *Reform of China's Educational Structure*, 20.

35. Hawkins, "Walking on Three Legs"; K. Mohrman, "Higher Education Reform in Mainland Chinese Universities," *Fulbright Report* (Hong Kong: Fulbright, 2003).

36. U.S. Agency for International Development, *Global Education Data Base*.

37. U.S. Agency for International Development, *Global Education Data Base*.

38. Ministry of Education, *Building a Modern Nation through Education* (Government of the Union of Myanmar, 2003); Ministry of Education, *Education in Malaysia: A Journey to Excellence* (Kuala Lumpur: Author, 2001).

39. R. Hamid, "Education in Brunei Darussalam," *Journal of SEA Education* 1, no. 1 (2000): 21–51.

40. Southeast Asian Ministers of Education Organization (SEAMEO). *Workshop on SEAMEO's Role in the 21st Century* (Mallaca: SEAMEO Secretariat, 2001).

41. U.S. Central Intelligence Agency, *The World Fact Book*.

42. U.S. Central Intelligence Agency, *The World Fact Book*.

43. Nizam, "Indonesia," *Higher Education in South-East Asia* (Bangkok: UNESCO, 2006).

44. S. Mitaray, "Education in the Lao People's Democratic Republic: Challenges in the New Millennium," *Journal of Southeast Asian Education* 1, no. 1 (2000): 103–12.

45. M. Hayden and L. Q. Thiep, "A 2020 Vision for Vietnam," *International Higher Education*, no. 44 (Summer 2006): 11–13.

46. M. A. Ashwill, "Caveat Emptor! US Institutions in the Vietnam Market," *International Higher Education*, no. 44 (Summer 2006).

47. A. Gonzalez, "The Philippines," *Higher Education in South-East Asia* (Bangkok: UNESCO, 2006).

48. A. Ziderman, "Student Loans in Thailand," *International Higher Education*, no. 42 (Winter 2006).

49. U.S. Agency for International Development, *Global Education Database*.

50. P. Altbach, "The Achilles Heel of India Higher Education," *International Higher Education*, no. 44 (Summer 2006).

51. A. Stella, "Institutional Accreditation in India," *International Higher Education*, no. 27 (Spring 2002).

52. A. Stella, "Institutional Accreditation in India."

53. J. B. G. Tilak, "Transition from Higher Education as a Public Good to Higher Education as a Private Good: The Saga of India," in *Education Transformation in Asia: Public Good or Private Commodity*, ed. D. Neubauer and J. N. Hawkins. Unpublished manuscript, available at the East West Center, Honolulu, Hawaii.

54. S. Chitnis, "Higher Education in India—Seriously Challenged," *International Higher Education*, no. 27 (Spring 2002), 20.

55. S. Z. Gilani, "Problems of Leadership and Reform in Pakistan," *International Higher Education*, no. 42 (Winter 2006), 23.

56. U.S. Agency for International Development, *Global Education Database*.

57. Y. Kitamura, "Expansion and Quality in Bangladesh," *International Higher Education*, no. 44 (Summer 2006).

58. Y. Kitamura, "Expansion and Quality in Bangladesh."

59. R. Edwards, "Impacts of Decentralization in Nepal: An Assessment of a New School Management Scheme" (unpublished manuscript, 2006).

60. R. Edwards, "Impacts of Decentralization in Nepal."

14

Education in the Middle East: Challenges and Opportunities

Rachel Christina with Golnar Mehran and Shabana Mir

Education has long been a source of both power and promise in the Middle East. Flows of knowledge in the region's pre-Islamic civilizations shaped the economic and social development of both western and eastern civilizations. Pharaonic, Phoenician, Persian, Greek, Roman, and Byzantine cultures around the Mediterranean dominated, in turn, the intellectual, social, and economic worlds of their times. The advent of Islam brought the Qur'anic injunction "Read, in the name of your Lord!" (Surat Al-'Alaq) and the vision of the pursuit of knowledge as an obligation "of every Muslim" (Sunan Ibn Majah), and the underlying power of Islam's regard for learning remains an integral component of the educational culture of the countries in which the faith has taken root.

The blossoming of Middle Eastern education and scholarship under the Muslim caliphates and the concurrent role of regional institutions in preserving the legacy of Western classical knowledge are well documented in the history of education. Unfortunately, this period was followed by a six-century decline, and most Middle Eastern education systems have entered the twenty-first century in disarray. However, while the present moment is one of uncertainty and conflict, it is also one of potential. The region's rich and varied history and cultures offer it the means to engage with the global as more than a simple marketplace or a labor provider, but mobilizing the creativity and the commitment necessary to rejuvenate ailing school systems and mechanisms of nonformal learning will have much to do with its ability to reassert political, cultural, and economic power on the international stage.

This chapter examines the current status of Middle Eastern education as the product of repeated and dramatic changes in the region during the twentieth and early twenty-first centuries: in particular, the establishment of independent nation-states; the boom and decline (and now partial resurgence) of Arab oil wealth; and a series of wars, internal conflicts, and revolutions—all of which have redefined the dynamics of power within the region and between the region and the rest of the world. The modern history of the Middle East is complex, and the interaction of its social, economic, and political changes with education is equally so. The legacy of colonialism and dependency on Western aid for development have colored Middle Eastern education, but they are not the only factors to be considered: nationalism, pan-Arabism, and waves of Islamic renewal have all left their stamp on the educational systems of the various countries in the region. Middle Eastern education is now in a period of transition and transformation, characterized by a reevaluation of its form, content, and function, and our analysis explores some of the complex tensions that are currently influencing change across this diverse and dynamic region. Essentially, we view the current debate over education as a reevaluation of the equation of development with modernization and a critical assessment of the primacy of economic as opposed to social welfare foci in development efforts. An infusion of moral and social concerns, both those specific to local cultures and those more generally defined, is as current in education as in other debates about development in the region. Such a reframing of discourse is particularly significant in a period where the political, social, and economic costs of educational choices appear higher than ever before.

In our analysis, we present an overview of historical trends in Middle Eastern educational development and then examine the current status of schooling across the region. To highlight challenges facing Middle Eastern educators and policymakers, we examine three areas in which the tension between traditional and innovative forces is promoting a rethinking of structure and content in the interest of more equitable and empowering development: early childhood education, the education of girls and women, and higher education. Early childhood education is increasingly seen as a significant point of leverage for breaking the cycle of poverty in the region and is therefore being targeted for expansion and reform, with a redirection of services in the interest of the most disadvantaged of children as at least the rhetorical goal. Girls' education has been shown to be a key factor in successful development efforts, and it is a focus for the promotion of gender equity and the reduction of discrimination against women. Higher education in the Middle East has been a contributor to indigenous national and regional development and has served to promote the autonomy and identity of states within the region. Preserving its role as a democratizing and empowering institution in a period of financial crisis and declining quality is a key challenge for Middle Eastern educational policymakers. How these various and competing agendas will be addressed in the future is uncertain, but our discussion highlights some of the possibilities inherent in current reforms, and the effects those reforms may have on the region as a whole.

In this discussion we use the terms Middle East and MENA to refer to the twenty-one members of the League of Arab States (Algeria, Bahrain, Djibouti, Egypt, Iraq, Jordan, Kuwait, Lebanon, Libya, Mauritania, Morocco, Oman, Palestine [West Bank and Gaza Strip], Qatar, Saudi Arabia, Somalia, Sudan, Syria, Tunisia, United Arab Emirates [UAE], and Yemen), and to the non-Arab countries of Iran and Turkey. This approach is consistent with UNESCO, UNICEF, and World Bank designations for the region and allows for relative comparability in analysis. Nevertheless, the region itself is notably diverse in terms of income, culture, and status of development, and any exploration of Middle Eastern education must take this diversity into account.

Countries of the Middle East may be grouped in various ways. Cultural designations often divide the area into the Eastern Mediterranean, North Africa, and the Arabian Peninsula. The first and second groups have relatively higher levels of contact with other cultures and as a result greater internal diversity; the peninsular countries, by virtue of their relative isolation, have been more homogeneous and consistent over time.[1] Economic designations evaluating wealth, sources of income, and development status generally group the region's countries into categories such as least developed states (low income, poor in natural resources and manpower—e.g., Sudan and Yemen), middle-income non-oil states (human resource based, with large populations and few natural resources—e.g., Egypt, Jordan, and Tunisia), and oil/gas-rich states with small populations and high surplus that often finance development in other parts of the Middle East (e.g., Kuwait, Saudi Arabia, Qatar, and UAE).[2] Indeed, although the region as a whole is considered to be part of the developing world, it contains some of the world's wealthiest states, whose per capita income is as much as seventy-five times that of the poorest in the region.[3] The resultant differences in local capacity and priorities are important. Our discussion of Middle Eastern education, although general, should be read in the context of these cultural and developmental differences among the states in the region.

With the establishment of independent nation-states across what had previously been the Ottoman Empire, "development" of the Middle East took on new energy. Commitments to welfare state models, supported both by the influence of Western state theories and the social welfare ethos within Islam, were common across the emerging political systems in the area, and the provision of free public education was quickly established as a responsibility of the state and a right of the citizenry. Education was seen by all emerging governments as one of the keys to modernization and economic growth, and the resultant expansion of the region's school systems was dramatic. Between 1955 and 1984, double- and triple-digit increases in enrollment across the region were the norm. The oil producers demonstrated the greatest gains (Saudi Arabia's 58.1 percent per year average increase is staggering), but even in non-oil countries, the gains were significant (Syria averaged a 15.6 percent per year increase over the same period).[4]

It was the oil boom of the 1970s, however, that had the greatest effect on the development of education in the Middle East. As Adnan Badran notes, "the great regional inflow of oil revenues in the 1970s, both directly to the Arab oil producing countries as well as indirectly through grants and the transfer of workers' salaries to non-producers, fueled a tremendous investment increase in education."[5] Between 1970 and 1985, eighty thousand new primary schools, ten thousand new secondary schools, and thirty-two new universities (or major extensions of existing facilities) were built in the Arab states alone, and enrollment rates nearly doubled.[6]

A significant characteristic of this period was the massive transfer of educational labor within the region, as well as a sharp increase in migration of students and faculty. The education boom that occurred across the region was most noticeable in the newly rich oil-producing states, and the resultant demand for educational personnel in countries with insufficient numbers of qualified local educators resulted in a dramatic increase in migration from the human resource–rich states (e.g., Egypt, Lebanon, and Palestine) to the human resource–poor oil states. At its height, such migration was incredibly lucrative for those who moved. Hussein El-Din notes that "an Egyptian professor [migrating to the oil states] would earn in only four years twice as much as would be earned in 30 years of a professional career in Egypt."[7] The prospects for primary and secondary school teachers were equally bright.

By the 1980s, however, the fortunes of states in the region had taken a turn for the worse. Decreased demand for oil and a decline in prices led to a "'loss' to those countries by 1985 of over half their earnings as they stood in 1980,"[8] and the late 1980s witnessed the emergence of the Arab states as a "major indebted group of countries in the Third World."[9] Patterns of high consumption of imported goods and staples, combined with high levels of military spending (as of 2004, MENA still had the highest level of military expenditure in the world, at 4 percent of gross domestic product)[10] and a lack of reinvestment into local systems, left governments scrambling to cover their expenditures, and social services, including education, suffered as a result. This pattern of consumption and spending overreaching resources also had negative outcomes in Turkey, and the 1979 Iranian revolution was largely a reaction to poverty and inequity that resulted from the extravagance of the shah's regime.[11]

With the decline of the oil market, many Middle Eastern states found themselves dependent on external aid for the maintenance and support of their social networks. Consistent with the principles of donor assistance in the 1980s, recipient states embarked on programs of structural adjustment and fiscal austerity designed to bring national economies more in line with those of the developed world and stimulate sustained economic growth. At the same time, Middle Eastern countries were encouraged to continue to expand their primary education systems toward a goal of universal primary education and to redesign their secondary and tertiary systems to address more effectively the manpower needs of the region. The long-term outcomes of these policies in the region are still unclear, but it may be argued that although a reassessment of the form and content of Middle Eastern education was necessary, the particular responses (primarily privatization and decentralization) advocated by international donors have reinforced existing inequities in the system and in many cases have limited the access of the poor to the education that is intended to serve as their ladder out of poverty.[12]

What is certain is that in spite of the region's impressive gains in educational provision over the twentieth century, quantitative expansion has come largely at the expense of educational quality, and the prevailing conditions of education leave much to be desired.[13] This is true whether one examines educational provision from a social justice or an economic growth standpoint. In the first case, women, rural populations, and the poor are not well served; in the second, the models in place do not meet the human resource needs of the region. Expenditure on education in the Middle East, although higher than in any other developing region (an average of 5.3 percent of gross domestic product across the Arab States, for example), has simply failed to produce systems that are effective contributors to national and human development. Although enrollment continues to increase, the region's school systems have not kept pace with population growth, and demand still outreaches supply. Although the 2001 gross primary enrollment ratios in Arab countries averaged 90 percent and in Turkey and Iran stood at 95 percent and 96 percent, respectively, net ratios are much lower (with the Arab states at 81 percent, Turkey at 88 percent, and Iran at 87 percent). Class sizes in most countries continue to grow, dropout rates are climbing, and the number of out-of-school children continues to increase. The region's dependency ratio is 0.8, well above the world average, and youth dependency is particularly high. Indeed, with an average of 34 percent of the population under the age of fourteen and highs above 50 percent in areas as diverse as Yemen and Palestine, quantitative pressure on educational systems in MENA is strong, and the goal of universal primary education is unlikely to be reached by 2015.[14] Adult illiteracy is also a problem, as educational development efforts have tended to focus on educating children in the formal system, and adults have received little attention. Exceptions to this policy include a generally unsuccessful literacy campaign in Iran prior to the 1979 revolution,[15] and more successful programs in Iraq (prior to the Gulf War of 1990–1991), Egypt, and Sudan.[16] Currently, however, only South Asia has a poorer standard of literacy than

MENA, which even with its high-income areas registers well below figures for developing countries as a group. In the Arab states, for example, 2000 to 2004 literacy figures indicate that nearly 38 percent of the adult population is illiterate, including 50 percent of women.[17] Although literacy efforts are increasing in many Middle Eastern countries, emphasis by national governments and donor institutions on expanding primary education continues to divert funding and attention away from the needs of the illiterate in most cases. For women, the situation is actually growing worse: while the female illiteracy rate has dropped from the 1980s' 60 percent, all indications are that it is again on the rise.

Funding and administration are also areas in which Middle Eastern education is weak. Although many governments cite poverty as a major factor in the failings of their schools, Richards and Waterbury argue that "lack of spending is not the major problem with most educational systems in the region. . . . The real difficulty is in how the money is spent."[18] Middle Eastern education systems are, as a rule, heavily centralized and bureaucratic, and appointments are often based on connections and influence. As a result, administration is unidirectional (top-down), there is a physical and conceptual separation between administration and instruction, instructional supervision is limited and ineffective, and the administrative cadre is often unqualified and untrained.[19] Planning is unorganized and incoherent, and funds are ineffectively allocated, with rural and poor populations continuing to receive less priority than urban and wealthy groups, and funding across the system skewed in favor of higher education.[20]

Finally, instruction and curricula are broadly unsuited to either economic or social justice models of education for development. Rote learning and lecturing are the norms in Middle Eastern classrooms, and the authoritarian structure of the system as a whole is devolved to the level of student-teacher interaction—democratic interaction and critical inquiry are not fostered by instructional methods or by school culture. Many teachers are poorly trained, and teaching as a rule is a low-status, low-pay occupation. Resources and materials are costly and limited in availability, and an examination focus works against creativity and innovation in the classroom.[21]

Faced with these weaknesses in their education systems, governments in the Middle East are in the process of reexamining the nature and extent of their commitment to education as a vehicle for national development. Economic growth and modernization models continue to remain powerful in terms of policy and planning, but there is also a growing consensus that such models need to be more carefully integrated with the cultural norms of the region. The resurgence and politicization of Islam that began in the 1980s has been a significant factor in this reassessment of educational policies and practices, as have secular calls for movement away from dependency on the West and Western-dictated development agendas. A general feeling of "disenchantment with the west [and] disillusionment over pervasive social and political decline" has generated a "quest for identity and authenticity—new indigenously-rooted answers for pressing problems."[22] These solutions range from extreme rejectionism to democratic and cooperative efforts across the region to devise development solutions that promote human development in addition to economic growth.

As Badran notes, "there is great concern about the appropriateness of western education in a region with a predominantly Muslim population who have been raised in religious traditions that cannot immediately be reconciled with the western culture inevitably introduced along with western educational methods."[23] A perceived moral and spiritual vacuum in education and a desire to have educational systems reflect local identity are salient issues for the Middle Eastern states. Iran's Islamic revolution attempted to "correct" for the negative influences of the West by radically transforming the philosophy and organization of the country's education system.[24] Turkey's long tradition of forced secularization and westernization in education has also given way in recent years to efforts at reintegrating its Islamic heritage with modernization[25] (efforts that are a source of contention within Turkish society), and in some Arab states, Islamism has been seen as "a factor of modernization permitting local cultures to equilibrate their own heritage with new social and political evolutions."[26] Following the events of September 11, 2001, many international and some domestic critics of Middle Eastern education have implicated the Islamic content and orientation of schooling as factors supporting violence. Such accusations fail to take into account the diversity of "Islamic education" and are largely a diversion from the social, political, and economic issues that have eroded educational quality and undermined development in MENA more broadly. However, they place even greater pressure on regional educators to balance cultural and religious values with international norms in ways that place the Middle East in a position of strength and not one of defense or reaction to external pressures.

Suggestions for ways in which the traditional institutions and cultural norms of the region may be used to support education have included a revitalization of religious schools to serve as nonformal extensions of the formal education system, an exploration of the humanistic and critical tradition of early Islamic education, and the revitalizing of cultural-historical structures that support holistic and socially engaged educational practice.[27] Many regional educators argue that tensions between religion and secularism, autocracy and democracy, and authority and liberty, as identified by critics of educational development in the Middle East, are not as explicit as is claimed and that integration of regional with certain international norms is not only possible but also imperative.

How this integration will occur, however, remains to be seen. While the MENA states subscribe to the Jomtien Declaration on Education for All, the Declaration on the Rights of the Child, and other international agreements on human rights and education, policy and practice in this region (no less than elsewhere) remain largely nonsynchronous. In addition, application of new or "renewed" philosophies is inconsistent across sectors and may have very different effects, depending on the target group. The rest of this chapter will explore in greater detail the context for reforms and their potential effects on three segments of the region's population: young children, women, and university faculty and students. The first two groups are traditionally disempowered and underserved populations, while the latter are the traditional educational elite. Examination of how each is affected by current policy and practice highlights the variety of ways in which John Badeau's question "How shall we, the ancient peoples yet new nations, of this area, modernize ourselves and our society?"[28] is being answered across the Middle East.

EARLY CHILDHOOD CARE AND EDUCATION

Early childhood care and education (ECCE) in the Middle East have traditionally been privileges of the elite. Nevertheless, recent conclusions by donor agencies and promoters of early childhood education worldwide that "investment in [early childhood] education . . . yields a far higher rate of return than does equal investment in secondary or higher education," and that "integrated early childhood development programs may be the single most effective intervention for helping poor children, families, and communities break the intergenerational cycle of poverty,"[29] are beginning to turn the tide of early education program development in the direction of those who need it most. All MENA governments have expressed a desire to expand and equalize access to their limited early childhood programs, yet as in other areas, financial and human resource constraints may limit the extent to which rhetoric will be accompanied by practice.

The adoption by MENA member states of the U.N. Convention on the Rights of the Child in 1989 and the Jomtien Declaration on Education for All in 1990 have provided conceptual underpinnings for recent early childhood reforms. The Jomtien Declaration's Article 5 statement that "learning begins at birth" and the Convention on the Rights of the Child's Article 18 provisions for the development of institutions and services for the care and development of children are rallying cries for early childhood educators in the region. Bolstered by a growing body of evidence that early childhood programming is a key to long-term school success and community development, these advocates continue to argue that the years prior to a child's entry into the formal school system are of signal importance and should be given appropriate consideration within the educational policymaking arena.[30] Nevertheless, emphasis by local governments and international funding agencies on basic education[31] and a persistent perception of early childhood issues as falling outside the purview of the government have created an imbalance between policy discourse and practical developments through which the early childhood sector continues to lag behind other sectors in growth, suffer from sharp inequities along lines of gender, income, and location, and remain primarily the product of nongovernmental initiatives.

At the state level, support for early childhood programming is increasing. The majority of Arab governments have adopted social and educational policies that are favorable to early childhood initiatives,[32] and the 2000 regional conference on education for all recommendations included an emphasis on "expanded and improved early childhood care and development, which includes, besides providing health care, nutrition and other basic social services to young children, providing them opportunities for learning and development at educational institutions with a view to fully developing their capacities including their physical, cognitive, creative and psycho-social abilities."[33] Turkey has implemented a strongly supportive framework for early childhood that incorporates optional public preschool, community education, and the provision of child care. Morocco and Mauritania fund traditional Islamic *kuttabs* as early education institutions. Iran provides limited state subsidies for early care and education programs, both through the Ministry of Education's public early childhood institutions and through support for workplace child care. Egypt and Jordan are making strides toward including early childhood in integrated education system planning.[34] Nevertheless, policy is still generally based on what Mohammed Khattab calls a principle of "noninterference" by government, resulting in an inconsistent vision of early childhood care and education across the region, and strongly varied and conflicting approaches to practice in a broad constellation of private and civil-sector service providers.[35]

A UNESCO survey of early childhood care and education organizations in the Arab states illustrated this diversity, noting that programs clustered around three primary foci—the child, the family, and the community—and that activities within these arenas varied from a strong emphasis on care to a strictly academic conception of early childhood education. Child-centered programs were the most narrowly focused, addressing in relative isolation issues of children's health and development or academic preparation for children over three. Family-centered programs incorporated children's issues, addressing family health care and welfare, parent education and awareness about issues of child development and socialization, the needs of families at risk, and general advocacy supporting the rights and priorities of families. Community-centered programs were the most broad-based, integrating education and health services, women's income-generating projects and environmental protection campaigns, and community advocacy in favor of the protection and rights of children as the basis for the community's future.[36]

These differing orientations and programs reflect the diversity of resources and priorities within the region. They also reflect the significant influence of trends in international development assistance. The early childhood care and education sector in the Middle East is heavily dependent on the financial and moral support of international actors in the field of ECCE, including UNICEF, UNESCO, Save the Children, the Bernard van Leer Foundation, the High/Scope Foundation, and the World Bank. Programming in the region has developed in layers that largely reflect the priorities of these various agencies.

Until the 1980s, many international early childhood care and education agendas were centered around child survival, viewing survival and development as separate and sequential processes, and care and education as distinct issues.[37] The MENA states have embraced maternal and child health and nutrition initiatives wholeheartedly and with great success, reducing child mortality there faster than any other region of the world (from an under-five mortality rate of 25 percent regionally in 1960 to one of 5.6 percent in 2004).[38] Philosophical and conceptual changes in the early childhood arena, which include emotional and social dimensions along with the physical and extended concepts of learning and cognitive development from birth to age eight, however, have been less uniformly embraced,[39] and transition to integrated care and education programming is uneven across the region. Separation between care-based (mainly for the under-four age group) and academic preschool preparation (for four- to six-year-olds) programs continues, and early childhood programs and the first years of primary school remain vastly different in conceptual terms. The overall level of service to children in the preprimary years is very low. Nineteen percent of three- to five-year-olds were enrolled in preschools regionally in 2001, but only 4 percent of MENA children were served from birth to school entry, with a high of 35 percent in the UAE and a low of 0.3 percent in Djibouti. Absolute enrollment in preschool education programs has doubled since 1980, but the rapid population growth has meant an actual decline in representation from that year's 4.8 percent, and services remain biased toward the wealthy.[40] Calls at the global level to increase provision internationally with preference for the least advantaged of children, however, have been echoed by early childhood advocates in the Middle East as well,[41] and growth in programs integrating community development, caregiver education, and multifaceted service delivery may serve to address some of the inequities that currently characterize the ECE system in the region.[42]

As discussed elsewhere in this chapter, processes of modernization and democratization and the rise and decline of the regional economy have altered family structures within Middle Eastern societies; transformed the position of women within the economic, political, and social spheres; and challenged "traditional" understandings of child rearing and education.[43] The extended family, the dominant model in much of the region, has begun to give way to smaller family units, with the nuclear family an increasingly common structure, particularly in urban areas. Migration and the inability of infrastructure and social service development to keep pace with changes in demographics have contributed to a widening gap between the rich and poor, and have lessened the ability of traditional social networks to meet social needs. More and more Middle Eastern women have moved into the formal labor market and into positions of prominence in political and civil circles, and the traditional understanding of a woman's primary role as "housewife/lactating mother"[44] has been dramatically challenged. Ultimately, as UNESCO notes, these "changes in family structures and socio-economic levels in the region have led to changes in values, attitudes and child-rearing habits [and] families have had to look for alternative ways of taking care of their children."[45] Early childhood providers have responded to the challenge, but the solutions they have generated are as yet unequally distributed across the population.

In addition to being mainly an urban phenomenon, early childhood programs are also largely biased in favor of middle-class and upper-middle-class populations. Their primarily urban location and primarily fee-based admission structure make access for these groups easy, while raising both the real and opportunity costs of enrollment for others. Programs also tend to serve a higher proportion of male than female children, although increases in female participation have been significant over the last twenty years.[47] While UNESCO statistics for 2001 showed near-parity in gross preprimary enrollment by gender for children aged three to five, there is a gender imbalance of 70 percent in favor of males when the age range receiving services is expanded to birth to six years of age.[48] In a sector with already-limited gross provision, the minority status of females is significant. If early childhood programs do indeed lay a foundation for success in future schooling, selection against long-term female success may well begin here.

A turn toward a community focus in expansion of ECCE programs is characteristic of many current reform initiatives in the Middle East.[49] In addition to considerably diversifying the populations served, these programs, it is hoped, will also improve the "fit" between programs and the local context. A concern for modernization and development's effect on "the erosion of culture . . . with the influence of outside cultures replacing existing beliefs, attitudes, and practices with modern ideas [and] disorienting the community,"[50] has led to initiatives intended to rejuvenate and incorporate traditional institutions into the ECCE framework. These include programs that attempt to strengthen community and family support for children, drawing on extended family/community patterns of child care and working away from center-based methodology to develop more flexible and accessible programs (particularly for rural populations). Qur'anic schools, which have provided religiously based early education for generations of Middle Eastern children, are also being explored as a potential low-cost, value-centered venue for ECCE programs.[51] These schools can be modernized, it is argued, "without detracting from their spiritual standing or their original educational role," and they are particularly well suited to "reaching children at risk in rural and remote areas."[52] Whatever the direction and success of reforms at the community level, however, their going to scale will depend largely on the mobilization of political will and support within governments to act in conjunction with nongovernmental agents who are designing and providing early childhood services. The policy-practice dialectic, in this arena no less than in formal education, remains the key to change.

WOMEN'S EDUCATION

Any analysis of women's education in the Middle East must include a discussion of the role and status of Muslim women in that region. Although not all Middle Eastern women are Muslim and not all Muslim women in the Middle East are treated alike or behave in a similar fashion, any discourse about female education in MENA must acknowledge that the teachings of Islam, combined with indigenous customs and traditions, play a crucial role in determining the status of women and their education in the region.

As previously noted, Middle Eastern countries are dissimilar in their levels of political development, economic prosperity, and educational achievement, and these dissimilarities contribute to marked differences in the roles and status of women in each country. The experience of women in countries with a long history of educational provision for them, such as Egypt and Lebanon, is different from that of women in countries in which female schooling is a relatively recent phenomenon, such as Kuwait and Oman. There are also marked differences between rich oil-producing states and poor countries such as Djibouti.[53] The colonial experience in Morocco, Algeria, and Tunisia and the revolutionary ideology in Libya have left their imprint on female education, as has the push toward modernization and secularization in countries such as Turkey and Iran before the 1979 revolution.[54] Islamic revival, the battle against westernization in postrevolutionary Iran, and the struggle for national liberation in Palestine have also contributed to the diversity of women's education in the region.[55]

Middle Eastern Muslim women do, however, share the experience of a basic "moral order"[56] that has significantly influenced the quantity and quality of service they receive relative to men. We deliberately use moral as opposed to religious order to differentiate between Islamic teachings, which do not discriminate against women in the realm of education, and the prevailing moral code, which mingles interpretations of religious law with traditional practices and attitudes regarding the appropriate amount and kind of schooling for women. In principle, no restrictions are imposed on Muslim women in the area of education, and, contrary to widespread belief, Islam has never prevented women from pursuing learning. None of the reasons given by parents in Middle Eastern societies for not sending their daughters to school—including the charges that girls may learn new and challenging ideas in school and that it is better to invest in education for boys rather than for girls because girls enrich only their husbands' households, whereas boys provide returns to their immediate family—are based on Islamic law. Rather, such statements reflect the persistence in Muslim societies (as elsewhere) of traditional beliefs about women's economic value and social roles.

Islamic faith has not prevented women from receiving education in traditional *kuttabs* or *maktabs*, or from private tutors in the home. Women have attended *madrasas* and Islamic colleges. Muslim girls were not prevented from entering the Christian missionary schools established in the region in the late nineteenth and early twentieth centuries, and they were even sent abroad to study when no indigenous options were available.[57] The introduction of modern public schools along with nondiscriminatory compulsory education laws in the twentieth century further facilitated the education of girls. Traditional customs and beliefs particular to populations within the region have, however, limited women's enrollment at various levels and have restricted and/or redirected their fields of study. This is where the moral order is in command.

In general, recent expansion of women's involvement in education in the Middle

East has been favorable when compared to the rest of the developing world. The average increase in female enrollment in the Arab states between 1990 and 2001, for example, was 7 percent, as compared to 3 percent in developing countries as a group.[58] Increases in the number of female teaching staff have also been higher than the developing country average: 4.7 percent (2.4 percent for the developing countries) at the primary level and 5.2 percent (as compared to 3 percent) at the secondary level from 1990 to 1994.[59] In 1998, women accounted for 51 percent of primary teachers and 42 percent of secondary teachers in MENA states.[60] However, a significant gender gap in education still persists in the region, and female gross enrollment rates are higher only than those of South Asia and sub-Saharan Africa at both the first and second levels of education,[61] with a gender parity index of 0.89 at primary and 0.90 at the secondary level.[62]

Indeed, despite significant quantitative expansion in recent years, there is still room for improvement in female education in the region. Many girls are still left out of the school system, and many girls repeat grades. At the primary school level, the female repetition rate varied from 1 percent in Palestine to 14 percent in Mauritania in 2000.[63] Finally, many girls (up to 21 percent per year by grade five in Mauritania)[64] drop out of the formal system, particularly at the primary level and among nomadic and rural populations. These figures are alarming not only because they indicate serious educational inefficiencies and high rates of wastage but also because fourth-grade dropouts in the region are unlikely to have acquired sufficient competencies to remain literate.[65]

Many female primary school graduates in the Middle East fail to enter secondary school. Even when the transition to education at the secondary level is made, a significant number of girls choose traditionally "female" fields of study. The reason is not simply because they are uninterested in "male-oriented" specializations or are unqualified to enter them, but rather because doing so is not deemed appropriate within the social norms of the region. According to Nagat El-Sanabary, curriculum bias is mild in academic secondary programs, yet "females are more likely than males to choose the humanities and social sciences track."[66] Gender bias is more pronounced in the technical and vocational schools because gender role traditions have limited women's access to "male programs" and have restricted them to "female crafts" such as home economics, nursing, typing, shorthand, and simple bookkeeping.[67] Nevertheless, once girls are allowed access to male-dominated fields, they have an equal and at times higher rate of success than boys. Girls have, for example, achieved higher scores than boys on secondary examinations in selected Arab countries and have performed better than boys in all science subjects in traditional societies such as Kuwait.[68]

Middle Eastern women have had access to modern higher education since the 1920s. Such a long tradition may account for the fact that the percentage of MENA women studying at institutions of higher learning (12.4 percent in 2002) is considerably higher than the rate for developing countries in general, although still less than the world average (16.7 percent for that year).[69] Yet available statistics on female participation in tertiary education reveals significant diversity in terms of gender inequity in the region. Yemen's gender parity index for tertiary education stood at 0.28 in 2001, while the gender index for Qatar in the same period was 3.9. Indeed, societies such as Qatar and Kuwait, which are known for their traditional attitudes toward women, are among those with the most significant levels of female enrollment at the tertiary level (with 46 and 32 percent, respectively).[70] It should, however, be noted that the high rate of female enrollment in the Gulf states may result from the fact that male students are often sent abroad for study or drop out of school early to enter the labor force.

As in secondary education, gender disparity in higher education is also reflected in the fields of study chosen by students.[71] The fields of the humanities, education, and medicine were long deemed "appropriate" for women in the region since they led to respectable, sex-segregated employment for them in the future.[72] Thus, societal norms and limited job opportunities determined not only the specializations offered to women but also the ones chosen by them as a result of a realistic assessment of sociocultural taboos and labor market conditions.[73] Recent studies, however, are pointing to a shift in women's emphasis toward science and technology, including such male-dominated fields as engineering and agriculture. A combination of increased employment opportunities and an increase in female role models in science-related professions has led to a higher proportion of Middle Eastern secondary and tertiary-level females choosing science and mathematics—higher, even, than their Western counterparts.[74]

Increasing attention is being devoted in policy circles to improving quality and opportunity for female students. But the barriers to increased participation and equity remain strong. The available literature on female education in the region points to a number of obstacles to greater integration of women into the educational system, including the absence of political commitment to implementing gender equity in education and in society;[75] the type of schooling, curricula, and teaching methods common to systems in the region;[76] and economic constraints faced by poor and working-class families.[77] Ultimately, Middle Eastern female students are subject to three sets of hindering forces: school-centered push-out factors that act to push girls out of the educational system, family-centered factors that pull girls out of the system for socioeconomic reasons or as a result of cultural beliefs, and child-centered reasons that eventually lead girls to drop out of the system in a final surrender to push-and-pull factors.[78]

Various approaches to the redesign of women's education have been proposed for the region. Legal recommendations include legal reforms that facilitate women's access to education, based on research findings indicating a strong correlation between restrictive legal systems and limited female school enrollment in Muslim countries.[79] International donor agencies are also recommending remedial measures that make schools more "girl-friendly,"[80] such as "providing schools within walking distance, boarding facilities or school busing, relevant curricula, school-lunch programs, adequate sanitation, and expanded teacher training."[81] Those who view the existence of discrimination in teaching and gender bias in the curriculum as the causes of persistent problems in female education recommend gender-sensitive teacher training and the elimination of sex stereotypes in textbooks.[82]

It is worth noting that the academic success of girls in the Middle East, especially at the secondary level (where single-sex education prevails), has led to critical reflection on and reappraisal of the "separate is rarely equal" principle of the UN/UNESCO Committee on the Elimination of Discrimination against Women. The principle that "cultural, family, or religious pressure for separate forms of education should not be tolerated"[83] is not necessarily valid in countries in which single-sex education is the only alternative open to girls. The ideal of an environment in which "girls and boys, men and women . . . interact in the freedom of the academy," must bow to the reality that in many cases the school doors are open to women only if the schools are segregated.

The challenge is to ensure that such environments contribute to women's empowerment as well as to their struggle for equal opportunity. We contend that a major cause of limited female participation in education is a moral order that bestows second-class status on women and leads them to believe in their "inferiority." Thus, solutions cannot be limited to restructuring institutional arrangements or changing public attitudes toward women, although these are essential steps.[84] Equally important is the assertion of the dignity of Middle Eastern women, and an affirmation of their pride in themselves and their abilities. While schooling has often acted as an agent of stability, preserving the nonthreatening roles of women as wives, mothers, sisters, and daughters rather than as independent individuals in their own right, the educational system can also have an empowering effect by stimulating the intellectual growth of women in the region, raising their consciousness, and enabling them to reflect on and determine their status in society.[85]

HIGHER EDUCATION

Higher education in the Middle East is beset by a dilemma of dramatic growth and poor quality. Increasing access to higher education has facilitated relative equity, but economic pressures and declining quality have led to a reexamination of the feasibility of public higher education in many of the region's states. Exclusive state provision has also resulted in tightly centralized control and a concomitant restriction of academic freedom. Democratization of higher education therefore stands in a problematic relationship with educational quality.

In the past several decades, higher education in the Middle East has expanded phenomenally. In the 1940s, there were eight universities. In 1985, the number of institutions offering some form of postsecondary education in the Arab world was estimated at about four to five hundred.[86] Although the general rate of growth has been considerable (total enrollment grew by 6.3 percent between 1980 and 1985 and by 3.5 percent between 1990 and 1994), the actual numbers (16 percent of the population of MENA was enrolled in tertiary programming in 1997) are still far behind those of developed countries.[87] Moreover, even the spectacular expansion of higher education facilities may not be able to meet the demand for higher education, as it increases with demographic change. An estimate of the MENA population in 1980 was roughly 168 million; this jumped to 300 million in 2004.[88] Clearly this increasing demand confronts countries in the region with questions regarding means of provision.

Most higher education in the Middle East (in 2002, 128 out of 175 universities in the Arab world, and almost all in Iran and Turkey) is controlled and financed by the government. Lebanon is the only Arab country in which most higher education is private, although Palestine (with a mixed public-private structure for tertiary education) and Jordan (where ten of seventeen universities are private) are also moving in that direction, and Qatar and the United Arab Emirates have begun to experiment with privatization.[89] In general, the central role of the state in planning, financing, and administering educational programs is common across political systems, including traditional Saudi Arabia, socialist Libya, secularist Turkey, and the Islamic state of Iran,[90] reflecting the expectation that education is a basic service that the state should provide. The concerned ministry generally ensures that the university system operates according to state policy, and there is strong state involvement in the appointment of heads of universities, with more or less interference depending on the context.

Such trends toward centralization and bureaucratization work against university autonomy. Despite historical Arab traditions of higher learning, modern Arab universities have been strongly influenced by the colonial model based on centralized administration. As Massialas notes, this model led to "conflict . . . between governments that wanted universities to adhere strictly to civil service rules and policies and universities striving for academic freedom and autonomy." Consequently, affairs that could lie within the jurisdiction of a university council or senate tend to become a state concern. With some exceptions, there is little statutory basis for faculty participation in decision making through a university body.[91]

Political centralization and the growth of the bureaucracy have also seriously affected academic freedom in the Middle East, hampering the development of a robust and innovative tertiary education sector. According to Parisima Shamsavary, for example, "Iran's higher education has seriously suffered from lack of academic freedom in both pre- and post-revolutionary Iran." Under the shah, policies of academic repression and secularization were followed. After the Islamic revolution (for about fifteen months before the Cultural Revolution), Iranian higher education "enjoyed an autonomy not previously seen in the history of these universities." Later, however, faculty supportive of the shah were purged, and a Cultural Revolution staff was appointed to supervise higher education. Considerable centralization of authority resulted, which nevertheless permitted a level of local autonomy that did not threaten the central authority.[92] Similar restraints on faculty activity (in some cases, without the features of local autonomy) in the Arab states limit the production of original research and the participation of university employees in the negotiation of civil, political, and social developments.[93]

The state's role in Middle Eastern higher education has also expanded under the influence of common perceptions of state responsibility and the effect of education on the economic welfare of the masses. It has been argued that the university model is based on the need for governments to "enhance the welfare of their people by creating an environment of equal opportunity" to "provide avenues for people to improve their standard of living."[94] Government investment in education, according to this model, would help create the infrastructure for more equitable income and wealth distribution and would help generate more wealth in the future. The population explosion in MENA and the consequent increase in demand for higher education over recent decades did lead to democratization of the system, and open admissions in the 1950s and early 1960s led to mass higher education in, for example, Egypt, Syria, Iraq, Algeria, and Morocco. The mainly academic secondary education in the Arab world, however, led to severe pressures on universities, and the association of a university degree with upward social mobility no longer remains universally valid.[95]

High faculty-student ratios, economic pressure, low salaries, the lack of academic freedom, and poor infrastructure and research facilities are strong disincentives for faculty to work toward high professional standards.[96] Overcrowding at most Middle Eastern higher education institutions has affected their ability to provide adequate classroom space, science laboratories, libraries, and other facilities. A different state of affairs prevails in the oil-rich Gulf states, but there the scale of educational provision relative to the size of national populations is too large, giving rise to "an education system top-heavy with misdirected, poor quality students, despite high drop-out rates from the bottom, primary levels of the system." Maintaining these lavish education systems may not be feasible, particularly when oil revenues begin to diminish.[97]

Lecture-centered modes of teaching, inadequate facilities, and centralized educational administration have narrowed the tertiary experience for the average Middle Eastern student, and limited employment prospects for graduates. Many, especially in theoretical disciplines, cannot be easily absorbed in the workplace. National needs for trained technicians and management to assist development remain unfulfilled. Across the Middle East, as elsewhere, "socio-economic pressures of society have led to the creation of 'degree mills' rather than universities, which flood the market with incompetent degree holders."[98] However, "flooded markets" are relative. In spite of sustained efforts to open enrollments, participation in higher education remains relatively difficult for people of lower socioeconomic status, people from rural areas (because most universities were established in metropolitan centers), and women (with the exceptions noted above). Although tuition is free at many state universities, students from poorer or rural backgrounds generally cannot afford housing, even if subsidized. Gaps between traditional elites and non-elites, ostensibly the target of increased public provision of higher education, remain and, in some cases, appear again to be increasing.

The crisis of higher education has drawn two main responses: blaming the use of Western institutional models in non-Western societies (a common indigenous response) or blaming state inefficiencies (the usual response by donors and international critics). Over the past three decades, government subsidization of higher education has generated fiscally unsustainable enrollment growth and declining quality. To the World Bank, this indicates the need for private educational provision.[99] Badran agrees, citing large public debts and growing demand to show that the public sector will not be able to assimilate the same proportion of students as it has in the past. However, he emphasizes the state's crucial role in providing guidelines for and monitoring higher education to ensure quality and equity as private institutions expand. While the standard of emerging private institutions in the Middle East is often superior to their public counterparts, many educationalists contend that privatization and decreased state investment in tertiary education may aggravate inequalities that already exist, and it would be wiser for governments to follow policies of protection, or even expansion, of investment in postprimary education through a combination of state and private enterprises.[100]

Although most Middle Eastern countries "seek to meet the rising demand for higher education by going down the well-trodden path of creating universities," demographic change, improved economic feasibility, and socioeconomic and political pressures have increased awareness of the need to create or improve such alternative formal institutions as community colleges, teacher-training institutes, and vocational schools. Nearly one-third of the region's tertiary students are currently enrolled in technical institutes,[101] and careful attention to the enhancement of those institutions and to the continued creative development of other alternatives is essential if the gap between university elites and other groups is not to be exacerbated.[102] Innovative use of the mass media is another cost-effective way to increase access to higher education. Turkey is making productive use of television in its Open University program. The Arab world, with a common language, can use it with even more utility and cost-effectiveness (as in Palestine, where Al-Quds Open University enrolls more students than any single university campus).[103]

Large sections of Middle Eastern populations have been unable to benefit from higher education; benefits have flowed mainly toward the upper classes and the urbanized middle class. Problems related to the unplanned growth of higher education will not be solved simply by restricting higher education.[104] Nor will open admissions and state-sponsored education suffice by themselves. A "diversified system that reaches all strata of society, providing relevant education that will produce productive members in their own communities" is the need of the hour.[105]

CONCLUSION

The variety of political, social, economic, and cultural realities in countries of the Middle East make it necessary to guard against a monolithic view of educational conditions in that region. Complex and multifaceted realities in the various levels and fields of education have created a moment of educational promise as well as decline, and warrant a thorough review of the direction that education has been taking in the region. The drive to expand educational provision, which needed no justification some decades ago, has not as dramatically reduced inequities by gender, class, rural-urban distribution, and region as had been hoped. Indeed, while system expansion has benefited many of the traditionally disadvantaged—notably women—legal, structural, and attitudinal change to render it effective are still in many cases lacking, and rapid population growth undermines quantitative gains. Impressive and beneficial in many ways though it has been, the continued expansion of public education may not even be economically feasible for some countries in the region over time. Though poor quality increases the difficulty of keeping education on the list of public priorities, it is the area in which reforms should be most strongly focused. Finally, in the current environment of financial and political strain, the need for socioeconomic and cultural relevance in Middle Eastern education has become more pressing than ever. Ensuring that such relevant education is also made available to the sections of Middle Eastern populations hitherto deprived of it must become more of a priority in the countries of the region, if human and national development goals are to be met and stability and security attained.

NOTES

1. Nicholas Kittrie, "Responsibility for Education: A Social, Religious, and Economic Partnership," in *At the Crossroads: Education in the Middle East*, ed. Adnan Badran (New York: Paragon, 1989); Byron Massialas and S. A. Jarrar, *Arab Education in Transition* (New York: Garland, 1991); Saad Eddin Ibrahim, *The New Arab Social Order: A Study of the Social Impact of Oil Wealth* (Boulder, Colo.: Westview, 1982).

2. Kunibert Raffer and M. A. Mohamed Salih, "Rich Arabs and Poor Arabs," in *The Least Developed and the Oil-Rich Arab Countries*, ed. Kunibert Raffer and M. A. Mohamed Salih (New York: St. Martin's, 1992); Stephen Heyneman, "Human Development in the Middle East and North Africa Region," in *Economic Development of the Arab Countries*, ed. Samih El-Naggar (Washington, D.C.: International Monetary Fund, 1993); A. Richards and J. Waterbury, *A Political Economy of the Middle East* (Boulder, Colo.: Westview, 1996).

3. International Monetary Fund, 1996, cited in Patricia Alonso-Gamo and Mohammed El-Erian, "Economic Reforms, Growth, Employment, and the Social Sectors in the Arab Economies," in *The Social Effects of Economic Adjustments on Arab Countries*, ed. Taher Kanaan (Washington, D.C.: International Monetary Fund, 1997), 15.

4. Nathir Sara, "Administrative Aspects of Education in the Arab Countries," in *At the Cross-roads*, ed. Badran (New York: Paragon, 1989).

5. Adnan Badran, in *At the Crossroads*, ed. Badran (New York: Paragon, 1989), 159.

6. Abdulaziz Saqqaf, "Educational Expenditure Patterns in Arab Countries," in *At the Cross-roads*, ed. Badran (New York: Paragon, 1989), 170.

7. El-Din, cited in Ibrahim, *New Arab Social Order*, 69.

8. Yusif Sayigh, *Elusive Development: From Dependence to Self-Reliance in the Arab Region* (London: Routledge, 1991), xi.

9. Abbas Alnasrawi, *Arab Nationalism, Oil, and the Political Economy of Dependency* (New York: Greenwood, 1991), 175.

10. World Bank, *World Development Indicators* (Washington, D.C.: Author, 2004).

11. Robert Looney, *Economic Origins of the Iranian Revolution* (New York: Pergamon, 1982), 12–25.

12. Abdelatif Benachenhou, comment in *The Social Effects of Economic Adjustments*, ed. Kanaan (Washington, D.C.: International Monetary Fund, 1997), 184.

13. Stephen Heyneman, "The Quality of Education in the Middle East and North Africa," *International Journal of Educational Development* 17, no. 4 (1997): 449–66; World Bank, *Education in MENA* (Washington, D.C.: Author, 2002); United Nations Development Programme (UNDP), *Arab Human Development Report* (New York: Author, 2002).

14. UNDP, *Arab Human Development Report*, 36; UNESCO, *EFA Global Monitoring Report*, Statistical Annex, table 5 (Paris: Author, 2005); UNFPA, *Country Profiles for Population and Reproductive Health, Policy Developments and Indicators, Arab States* (New York: Author, 2005).

15. Naz Rassool, "Theorizing Literacy, Politics, and Social Process: Revising Maktab Literacy in Iran in Search of a Critical Paradigm," *Comparative Education Review* 15, no. 4 (1995): 423–35.

16. Byron Massialas, "Arab Countries: Adult Education," in *International Encyclopedia of Education*, 2nd ed., vol. 1, ed. Torsten Husen and T. Neville Postlethwaite (London: Pergamon, 1994), 324–26.

17. UNESCO, *EFA Global Monitoring Report*, table 2.

18. Richards and Waterbury, *Political Economy*, 117.

19. Sara, "Administrative Aspects," 253–55.

20. Heyneman, "Quality of Education," 457–59.

21. Massialas and Jarrar, *Arab Education*, 32–49, Salem Al-Qahtani, "Teaching Thinking Skills in the Social Studies Curriculum of the Saudi Arabian Secondary Schools," *International Journal of Educational Development* 15, no. 2 (1995): 155–63; UNDP, *Arab Human Development Report*, 54.

22. Esposito, cited in Massialas and Jarrar, *Arab Education*, 16.

23. Badran, *At the Crossroads*, ed. Badran (New York: Paragon, 1989), 1.

24. Bahram Mohsenpur, "Philosophy of Education in Post-Revolutionary Iran," *Comparative Education Review* 32, no. 1 (1988): 76–86; Jan Derry, "Iran," in *Education in Times of Transition*, ed. D. Colby, R. Cowen, and C. Jones (London: Kogan Page, 2000).

25. Sabahaddin Zaim, "The Impact of Westernization on the Educational System in Turkey," in *At the Crossroads*, ed. Badran (New York: Paragon, 1989), 18–42.

26. Burgat, cited in Tuomo Melasuo, "Maghreb Conflicts, Socioeconomic Crisis, and Unity," in *The Least Developed and the Oil-Rich Arab Countries*, ed. Raffer and Salih, 52; see also S. A. Ashraf, "Can University Education be Anything but Liberal?" *Muslim Education Quarterly* 11, no. 1 (1993); Y. Mohamed, "Islamization: A Revivalist Response to Modernity," *Muslim Education Quarterly* 10, no. 2 (1993): 17; K. E. Shaw, "Higher Education and Development in the Lower Gulf States," *Higher Education Review* 25, no. 3 (1993): 36–47.

27. Helen N. Boyle, *Qur'anic Schools* (New York: Routledge-Falmer, 2004); Rachel Christina, *Tend the Olive, Water the Vine: Globalization and the Negotiation of Early Childhood in Palestine*

(Greenwich, Conn.: IAP, 2006); Bradley J. Cook, "Islamic versus Western Concepts of Education: Reflections on Egypt," *International Review of Education* 45, nos. 3–4 (1999): 339–57.

28. Cited in Sami Hajjar, ed., *The Middle East: From Transition to Development* (Leiden: Brill, 1985), 3.

29. Mary Eming Young, *Early Childhood Development: Investing in the Future* (Washington, D.C.: World Bank, 1996), 12.

30. UNDP, *Arab Human Development Report*, 60; UNESCO, *EFA 2000 Review*.

31. World Bank, *Priorities and Strategies in Education* (Washington, D.C.: Author, 1995); International Consultative Forum on EFA, *Regional Policy Review*; Ministries of Education, MENA Member States, "Country Reports: Middle East and North Africa," in *Proceedings of the International Conference on Education* (Paris: IBE, 1994 and 2000); World Bank, *Education in MENA*.

32. UNESCO, "Early Childhood in the Arab States: Challenges and Opportunities," in *Directory of Early Childhood Care and Education Organizations in the Arab States* (Paris: UNESCO, 1995); Ministries of Education, MENA, "Country Reports."

33. Regional Conference on Education for All in the Arab States, *The Arab Framework for Action to Ensure Basic Learning Needs in the Arab States in the Years 2000–2010* (Cairo, Egypt: Author, 2000).

34. Tanju Gurkan, "Early Childhood Education in Turkey," in *International Handbook of Early Childhood Education*, ed. Gary Woodhill, Judith Bernard, and Lawrence Prochner (New York: Garland, 1992); M. Sorkhabi, "Preacademic and Academic Education in Iran," in *International Handbook*, ed. Woodhill, Bernard, and Prochner (New York: Garland, 1992); Z. Sabbaghian, "Kindergarten and Primary Education in Iran," in *International Handbook*, ed. Woodhill, Bernard, and Prochner (New York: Garland, 1992); Ministries of Education, MENA, "Country Reports: Turkey and Iran."

35. Mohammed Khattab, *A Comprehensive Survey of the Status of Early Childhood Care and Education in the Middle East and North Africa* (Amman, Jordan: UNESCO, 1995).

36. UNESCO, "Early Childhood Care and Education in the Arab States: Survey Findings," in *Directory of Early Childhood Care and Education Organizations in the Arab States* (Paris: UNESCO, 1995).

37. Robert Myers, *The Twelve Who Survive* (London: Routledge, 1992).

38. UNICEF, *State of the World's Children* (New York: Author, 2006).

39. Khattab, *Comprehensive Survey*.

40. Mohammed Khattab, "Early Childhood Education in Eighteen Countries in the Middle East and North Africa," *Child Study Journal* 26, no. 2 (1996): 149–59; UNESCO, *Early Childhood Care and Education: Basic Indicators on Young Children—Arab States* (Paris: Author, 1995); UNESCO, *EFA Monitoring Report 2005*, table 3; UNDP, *Arab Development Report*, 52.

41. Indu Balagopal, *Report on Dialogue '95: First Annual Consultative Days of the Arab Resource Collective Regional Consultative Resource Group on Early Childhood Care and Development* (New York: Consultative Group on Early Childhood Development, 1996); UNESCO/International Consultative Forum on EFA, *Regional Policy Review* (Paris: UNICEF, 1996).

42. UNESCO, "ECE Challenges and Opportunities."

43. Richards and Waterbury, *Political Economy*; Samih Farsoun and Christina Zacharia, "Class, Economic Change, and Political Liberalization in the Arab World," in *Political Liberalization and Democratization in the Arab World*, ed. R. Brynen, B. Korany, and P. Noble (Boulder, Colo.: Lynne Rienner, 1995); Elizabeth Warnock Fernea, "Childhood in the Muslim Middle East," in *Children in the Muslim Middle East*, ed. Elizabeth Warnock Fernea (Austin: University of Texas Press, 1995); Ibrahim, *New Arab Social Order*, 92–93.

44. Ghanem Bibi, cited in UNESCO, "ECE Challenges and Opportunities," 29.

45. UNESCO, "ECE Challenges and Opportunities," 29.

46. Khattab, "Early Childhood Education in Eighteen Countries," 157.

47. UNESCO, *Statistical Yearbook* (Paris: Author, 1996), table 2.3.

48. Khattab, "Early Childhood Education in Eighteen Countries," 156; UNDP, *Arab Development Report*, UNESCO *EFA Monitoring Report, 2005*, table 3.

49. Cikzem Kagitcibasi, *The Early Enrichment Program in Turkey* (Paris: UNESCO-UNICEF-WFP, 1991); Early Childhood Resource Center, *Towards the Year 2000* (Jerusalem: Author, 1995); Myers, *Twelve Who Survive*; Rachel Christina, "Contingency, Complexity, Possibility: NGOs and the Negotiation of Local Control in Palestinian Early Childhood Programming," in *Civil Society or Shadow State? State/NGO Relations in Education*, ed. Margaret Sutton and Robert F. Arnove (Greenwich, Conn.: IAP, 2004).

50. Balagopal, *Report on Dialogue '95*, 2.

51. Khattab, *Comprehensive Survey*; Myers, *Twelve Who Survive*; Boyle, *Qur'anic Schools*.

52. Khattab, *Comprehensive Survey*, 96.

53. Edith A. S. Hanania, "Access of Arab Women to Higher Education," in *Arab Women and Education*, Monograph Series of the Institute for Women's Studies in the Arab World, no. 2 (Beirut: Beirut University College, 1980), 24–28; Nagat El-Sanabary, "Women's Education: History of Islamic Countries," in *International Encyclopedia of Education*, 2nd ed., ed. Husen and Postlethwaite, 6753–61; H. A. S. Khattab, "Female Education in Egypt: Changing Attitudes over 100 Years," in *Muslim Women*, ed. F. Hussain (New York: St. Martin's, 1984); Jonathan P. Berkey, "Women and Islamic Education in the Mamluk Period," in *Women in Middle Eastern History: Shifting Boundaries in Sex and Gender*, ed. Beth Baron and Nikki R. Keddie (New Haven, Conn.: Yale University Press, 1991); May Rihani, *Learning for the 21st Century: Strategies for Female Education in the Middle East and North Africa* (Amman, Jordan: UNICEF, 1993); Sheikha Al-Misnad, *The Development of Modern Education in the Gulf* (London: Ithaca, 1985), 172–88; UNICEF Sudan and the Ministry of Education, the Republic of Sudan, *Report on the Study of Girls' Education in Sudan* (Khartoum: Undersecretariat for Educational Planning, Ministry of Education, 1993); Fathi Salem Abdou, *La Scolarisation des Enfants dans la Republique de Djibouti* (Djibouti: UNICEF, 1994).

54. Marie Thourson Jones, "Educating Girls in Tunisia: Issues Generated by the Drive for Universal Enrollment," in *Women's Education in the Third World: Comparative Perspectives*, ed. Gail P. Kelly and Carolyn M. Elliot (Albany: State University of New York Press, 1982); Massialas and Jarrar, *Education in the Arab World*, 252–58; F. Ozbay, "The Impact of Education on Women in Rural and Urban Turkey," in *Women in Turkish Society*, ed. N. Abadan-Unat (Leiden: Brill, 1981); Handan Kepir, "Turkish Women in an Era of Transition," in *At the Crossroads*, ed. Badran (New York: Paragon, 1989); Joseph S. Szyliowicz, *Education and Modernization in the Middle East* (Ithaca, N.Y.: Cornell University Press, 1973); David Menashri, *Education and the Making of Modern Iran* (Ithaca, N.Y.: Cornell University Press, 1992).

55. Nagat El-Sanabary, *The Saudi Arabian Model of Female Education and the Reproduction of Gender Divisions*, Center for Near Eastern Studies Working Paper, no. 16 (Los Angeles: UCLA Press, 1992); Jacquiline Rudolph Touba, "Cultural Effects on Sex Role Images in Elementary School Books in Iran: A Content Analysis After the Revolution," *International Journal of Sociology of the Family* 17 (1987): 143–58; Golnar Mehran, "The Creation of a New Muslim Woman: Female Education in the Islamic Republic of Iran," *Convergence* 24 (1991); Nesta Ramazani, "Women in Iran: The Revolutionary Ebb and Flow," *Middle East Journal* 47 (1993): 412–13; Agustin Velloso, "Women, Society, and Education in Palestine," *International Review of Education* 42 (1996): 524–30.

56. Afsaneh Najmabadi, "Iran's Turn to Islam: From Modernism to Moral Order," *Middle East Journal* 41 (1987): 202–17.

57. Hanania, "Access of Arab Women," in *Arab Women and Education* (Beirut: Beirut University College, 1980), 16–19, 29–31.

58. UNESCO, *EFA Monitoring Report*, table 16.

59. UNESCO, *Statistical Yearbook*, table 7.

60. UNESCO, *2000 Education Statistics*.

61. UNESCO, *EFA Monitoring Report*, table 16.

62. UNESCO, *EFA Monitoring Report*, table 16.

63. UNESCO, *EFA Monitoring Report*, table 6.

64. Golnar Mehran, *Girls' Drop-Out from Primary Schooling in the Middle East and North Africa: Challenges and Alternatives* (Amman, Jordan: UNICEF, 1995), 13.

65. UNESCO, *Development of Education in the Arab States: A Statistical Review and Projection* (Paris: Author, 1994).

66. El-Sanabary, "Women's Education," 6758.

67. Massialas and Jarrar, *Education in the Arab World*, 239.

68. A. E. Al-Methun and W. J. Wilkenson, "In Support of a Sociological Explanation of Sex Differences in Science and Mathematics Achievement: Evidence from a Kuwaiti Study of Secondary School Certificate Examinations," *Research in Science and Technological Education* 6 (1988): 91–101.

69. UNESCO Regional Office for Education in the Arab States, *Higher Education in the Arab States* (Beirut: UNESCO, 2002), 5–6.

70. UNESCO, *Statistical Yearbook 1996*, table 10; UNESCO Regional Office for Education in the Arab States, *Higher Education in the Arab States*.

71. UNESCO, *EFA Monitoring Report 2005*, table 9.

72. Audrey C. Smock and Nadia H. Youssef, "Egypt: From Seclusion to Limited Participation," in *Women: Roles and Status in Eight Countries*, ed. Janet Z. Giele and Audrey Smock (New York: Wiley, 1977), 59.

73. Massialas and Jarrar, *Education in the Arab World*, 242.

74. Gawdat Bahgat, "Education in the Gulf Monarchies: Retrospect and Prospect," *International Review of Education* 45, no. 2 (1999): 127–36; El-Sanabary, "Women's Education," 6758.

75. El-Sanabary, "Women's Education," 6756.

76. Massialas and Jarrar, *Education in the Arab World*, 233–45.

77. Nagat El-Sanabary, "Middle East and North Africa," in *Women's Education in Developing Countries: Barriers, Benefits, and Policies*, ed. Elizabeth M. King and M. Anne Hill (Baltimore: Johns Hopkins University Press, 1993), 153–54.

78. Mehran, *Girls' Drop-Out from Primary Schooling*, xi.

79. Elizabeth H. White, "Legal Reform as an Indicator of Women's Status in Muslim Nations," in *Women in the Muslim World*, ed. Lois Beck and Nikki Keddie (Cambridge, Mass.: Harvard University Press, 1978), 63–67.

80. UNICEF, *Strategies to Promote Girls' Education* (New York: Author, 1992); Karen Tietjen, *Educating Girls: Strategies to Increase Access, Persistence, and Achievement* (Washington, D.C.: Creative Associates International, 1991); Rihani, *Learning for the 21st Century*; Rosemary T. Bellew and Elizabeth M. King, "Educating Women: Lessons from Experience," in *Women's Education in Developing Countries*, ed. King and Hill, 285–326.

81. El-Sanabary, "Women's Education," 6757.

82. J. Abu Nasr et al., *Identification and Elimination of Sex Stereotypes in and from School Textbooks: Some Suggestions for Action in the Arab World* (Paris: UNESCO, 1983).

83. United Nations Committee on the Elimination of Discrimination against Women in Cooperation with the United Nations Educational, Scientific, and Cultural Organization, *Towards a Gender-Inclusive Culture through Education: Principles for Action* (Paris: UNESCO, 1995).

84. Munir Bashshur, "Arab Women and Education," in *Arab Women and Education* (Beirut: Beirut University College, 1980), 70.

85. UNDP, *Arab Human Development Report*, 28; World Bank, *Gender and Development in the Middle East and North Africa* (Washington, D.C.: Author: 2004).

86. George E. Za'rour, *Universities in Arab Countries* (Washington, D.C.: International Bank for Reconstruction and Development/World Bank, 1988), 3, 80; Munir Bashshur, "Similarities

and Constraints in Patterns of Higher Education in the Arab World" (paper delivered at the Nordic Conference on Higher Education in the Arab World and the Middle East at Lund University, Sweden, 28 March 1985), 1.

87. Massialas and Jarrar, *Arab Education*, 49; Byron G. Massialas, "The Arab World," in *International Higher Education: An Encyclopedia*, vol. 2, ed. Philip G. Altbach (London: Garland, 1991), 981; Mohamed I. Kazem, "Higher Education and Development in the Arab States," *International Journal of Educational Development* 12, no. 2 (1992): 116; UNESCO Regional Office for Education in the Arab States, *Higher Education*, 6; UNESCO, *EFA Monitoring Report 2005*, table 9.

88. World Bank, *World Development Indicators*, 2006.

89. Heyneman, *Quality of Education*; William Rugh, "Arab Education: Tradition, Growth and Reform," *Middle East Journal* 56, no. 3 (2002): 410–11; UNDP, *Arab Human Development Report*; World Bank, *Education in MENA*.

90. Massialas and Jarrar, *Arab Education*, 193; Massialas, "The Arab World," in *International Higher Education*, ed. Altbach (London: Garland, 1991), 987; Taylan and Taylan, "Turkey," and Shamsavary, "Iran," in *Encyclopedia of Higher Education*, Vol. 1, ed. Clarke and Neave (Oxford: Pergamon, 1992), 745 and 327; H. M. Al-Baadi, "Planning Education: Arab World," in *International Encyclopedia of Education*, 2nd ed., ed. Husen and Postlethwaite (London: Pergamon, 1994), 4484.

91. Massialas and Jarrar, *Education in the Arab World*, 193, 196.

92. Shamsavary, "Iran," 332; Asghar Rastegar, "Health Policy and Medical Education," in *Iran after the Revolution: Crisis of an Islamic State*, ed. Saeed Rahnema and Sohrab Behdad (London: Tauris, 1995), 220; Nancy W. Jabbra and Joseph G. Jabbra, "Education and Political Development in the Middle East," in *The Middle East: From Transition to Development*, ed. Hajjar (Leiden: Brill, 1985), 87; Rastegar, "Health Policy," in *Iran after the Revolution*, ed. Rahnema and Behdad (London: Tauris, 1995), 221.

93. Badran, "Meeting the Demand," in *At the Crossroads*, ed. Badran (New York: Paragon, 1989), 244–45.

94. Massialas and Jarrar, *Education in the Arab World*, 203–4; Rugh, "Arab Education," 409.

95. Massialas and Jarrar, *Education in the Arab World*, 214–20; Massialas, "The Arab World," in *International Higher Education*, ed. Altbach (London: Garland, 1991), 990; Za'rour, *Universities in Arab Countries*, 8; Massialas and Jarrar, *Education in the Arab World*, 219.

96. Massialas, "The Arab World," in *International Higher Education*, ed. Altbach (London: Garland, 1991), 990.

97. H. M. Al-Baadi, "Planning Education," in *International Encyclopedia of Education*, ed. Husen and Postlethwaite (London: Pergamon, 1994), 4484; Massialas, "The Arab World," in *International Higher Education*, ed. Altbach (London: Garland, 1991), 985–86; Badran, "Meeting the Demand," 250; World Bank, *Education in MENA*; UNDP, *Arab Human Development Report*.

98. Massialas, "The Arab World," in *International Higher Education*, ed. Altbach (London: Garland, 1991), 984; Massialas and Jarrar, *Education in the Arab World*, 217.

99. S. Schwartzman, "Non-Western Societies and Education," in *Encyclopedia of Higher Education*, vol. 2, ed. Burton R. Clark and Guy Neave (Oxford: Pergamon, 1992), 974; World Bank, *Higher Education: The Lessons of Experience* (Washington, D.C.: Author, 1994), 2–3; World Bank, *Education in MENA*, 27–28.

100. Rugh, "Arab Education," 401; Jacques Van der Gaag, "Social Development during Adjustment in the MENA Region: Contradiction or Opportunity," in *The Social Effects of Economic Adjustments on Arab Countries*, ed. Taher Kanaan (Washington, D.C.: International Monetary Fund, 1997), 147.

101. Abdul Ghafour al Heeti and Colin Brock, "Vocational Education and Development: Key Issues, with Special Reference to the Arab World," *International Journal of Educational Development* 17, no. 4 (1997): 373–89.

102. Badran, "Conclusion: Considerations for the Future," in *At the Crossroads*, ed. Badran (New York: Paragon, 1989), 316.

103. Massialas and Jarrar, *Education in the Arab World*, 217; Schwartzman, "Non-Western Societies," in *Encyclopedia of Higher Education*, ed. Clark and Neave (Oxford: Pergamon, 1992), 973–74.

104. Sofronis Sofroniou, statements in discussion in *At the Crossroads*, ed. Badran (New York: Paragon, 1989), 306.

105. Shamsavary, "Iran," 330–31; Massialas and Jarrar, *Education in the Arab World*, 217.

15

Russia and Eastern Europe

Maria Bucur and Ben Eklof

With the demise of the Soviet empire, the vast social and political landscape of Eurasia has been fundamentally altered. The political monopoly exerted by the Communist Party has been eliminated and state monopolies on the economy and the press have been challenged; even the political map of the region has been redrawn as new (or newly reconstituted) states have emerged. The enormous energies released in this process have undoubtedly benefited some regions or countries as a whole. But uncertainty, impoverishment, and marginalization have also been the lot of many millions. In the former Soviet Union, for example, some eighty million blue-collar workers have seen their living standards plummet as their factories have closed or have failed to pay wages for months on end. Disproportionately, women have found themselves out of work. And perhaps twenty-five million Russians living in the non-Russian republics of the former Soviet Union have suddenly discovered they were foreigners or minorities in countries now detached from their Russian homeland. Border disputes proliferate, and a plutocracy built out of the Soviet Union's old informal networks linking the criminal underworld and the party bureaucracy has emerged to feed on the carcass of the Soviet economy. Whether this plutocracy is actually generating new wealth or simply reaping windfalls from the virtually untaxed export of extracted natural resources and sweetheart privatization deals is unclear. Elsewhere, the Czech Republic, Hungary, Poland, Slovenia, and Slovakia have fared relatively well after the first decade of postcommunism, having joined the European Union (EU) in 2004.

Since 1989, educational reform has also swept across Eastern Europe and the former Soviet Union. Attempts have been launched to dismantle the Soviet legacy and to bring schools in line with European and American practices. At the same time, reformers have turned to older national and imperial legacies from the Ottoman, Austro-Hungarian, and Russian empires for inspiration and emulation. Broadly speaking, reformers have pushed for democratization of governance and classroom practices, for diversification and choice, and for decentralization (or even privatization) of education. This ambitious agenda has achieved notable success in some areas. But elsewhere drastic reductions in education budgets undercut many programs. Precipitous decentralization led to chaos and undermined efforts to coordinate reform. As if these problems weren't enough, growing ethnic

and economic polarization has been reflected in tensions over school admissions and curriculum policy. In general, schools now seem to be exacerbating instead of mitigating
society's inequities. At the same time, the prestige of a diploma has rapidly fallen, especially in the former Soviet Union. Some economists have argued that this generational
loss of human capital, in combination with the emigration of close to one hundred thousand highly trained scientists will, in the long term, inflict a greater body blow to the
postsocialist economy than even the virtual collapse of the manufacturing sector. Finally,
as a reaction to the inequities, to the friction and chaos that reform introduces, many
voices, including that of Vladimir Putin, have been raised for preserving those elements
of the Soviet-type system of education worth saving.

This chapter surveys educational change since 1989 in Russia and Eastern Europe,
with only brief mention of the newly independent states of the former Soviet Union. The
discussion highlights general trends and acknowledges differences observed from region
to region and from country to country. But the reader should recognize the shortcomings
of this approach. First, a common nineteenth-century European educational tradition
shaped pedagogy throughout the area covered in this chapter and provided a commonality of school practices and discourse. Second, the Soviet-type schools and administrative
practice introduced in Eastern Europe after World War II imposed a new and different
layer of uniformity across state borders. Finally, the underlying cultural diversity of the
region was never fully eradicated in the schools. The cultural mosaic of Eastern Europe
is no secret to the educated reader; fewer readers may be aware that Russian traditions
vied with Baltic, Muslim, Turkic, and other legacies beneath a sometimes weighty, sometimes superficial veneer of communist beliefs and practices. Thus, separating the educational narrative into Russian and Eastern Europe educational histories both exaggerates
and understates differences. Moreover, although school reform accelerated after Gorbachev came to power in 1985, much discussion and experimentation had taken place
before that date. So we must begin with legacies and vastly simplify our presentation to
preserve even a semblance of cohesion.

The political rhetoric of transition in Russia and Eastern Europe has detached terms
such as *liberal* and *conservative*, *progressive* and *democratic* from their traditional moorings.
Russians talk of an "ideology" of reform, but to them this means an explicit conceptualization, not a political agenda, as we think when we hear that word. Yet when they talk
of "depoliticizing" the school curriculum, many Western observers see such talk as naive,
for all educational reform involves political choices, however explicit. Thus, our task of
description is complicated by lexical as well as boundary confusion.

OLD REGIME SCHOOLS

It is not possible to speak of a single precommunist legacy in Eastern Europe with regard
to education. Before 1918, this area was divided among three empires with very different
outlooks on education—the Hapsburg, Ottoman, and Russian empires. Since the middle
of the eighteenth century, the rulers of the Hapsburg empire had become interested in
providing basic education for all subjects as a means of creating a cohesive empire. Primary education served to imbue pupils with feelings of loyalty toward the crown and the
values for which it stood. Catholicism was an important element of this education, serving thus as an important counterforce against the threat of nationalism and ethnic chal-

lenges. Over the nineteenth century, the Hapsburgs offered ambitious students of all nationalities the opportunity to study in its reputable schools (e.g., the Theresianum) or to become part of the officer corps, another important education institution in the empire. At the same time, authorities made it increasingly difficult for students who wanted to study in their own local language—be it Slovene, Croat, or Romanian—limiting their subventions only to schools that used German or (after 1867, especially) Hungarian as their primary language. Be that as it may, the empire offered many people (not just its German- and Hungarian-speaking populations) an opportunity to study in reputable Viennese universities and other schools abroad. The level of literacy and general education were higher here than elsewhere in Eastern Europe.

No such cohesive policy developed in the Ottoman Empire. The authorities were uninterested in the local administration and education of the non-Muslim populations. Instead, through the millet system each religion recognized under Islam—Orthodox Christian, Catholic, Protestant denominations, and Judaism—ruled over their respective flocks with little interference from the outside. The Orthodox Church, which came to dominate the lives of most Balkan Christians, had few education goals beyond the training of parish priests. As the empire waned in the face of challenges from the growing nationalist movements, the various ethnic groups in the Balkans began building education institutions that would ensure the creation of autonomous educated elites. Education reform proceeded from the top down, starting with the creation of elite schools and academies and only slowly spreading throughout the rest of the population. In addition, a small number of schools for vocational training appeared. The legacy of Ottoman rule for the development of education in the Balkans was meager, in part because the Orthodox Church lacked interest in education that was not strictly canonical. The various newly independent states tried to make up for these inadequacies but had a hard time catching up with the institutions, personnel, and other resources available in the Hapsburg lands. After 1918, the newly independent Balkan countries succeeded in passing legislation that made education compulsory to the fourth grade, although its implementation was rather haphazard. The illiteracy rate remained very high in this part of the world.

In the Russian empire, which at its zenith encompassed roughly one-sixth of the Earth's land surface, eighteenth-century rulers made education a state concern by establishing universities, an academy of science, and then secondary schools. The Orthodox Church also founded seminaries, many of whose graduates later became prominent civil servants or revolutionaries. The Ministry of Education was created in 1802, and the Great Reforms of the 1860s included legislation encouraging state schooling for the newly liberated serfs and expanding opportunities for women at the secondary level. Trying to finance an army to support Russia's imperial and great power ambitions on the basis of a backward economy, the state had little left to spend on basic education. However, in the quarter century before World War I, a combination of societal and state initiative gave an enormous boost to public schooling for the lower classes, and educators hoped to achieve universal literacy in the empire by 1922.

Russian pedagogy and classroom practices were derivative of European, especially Prussian, approaches. Universities, though plagued by issues of autonomy and political freedom, made substantial contributions to world science; at the secondary level, the atmosphere was formal, discipline often harsh, and the curriculum rigorous. At the primary level, however, Tolstoyan child-centered practices were influential, and after the turn of the century, progressivism made deep inroads into educational practice. Dewey's democratic classroom became part of a powerful radical democratic and socialist movement against autocracy, in which redistributive justice was combined with decentralization and political freedom; indeed, self-government, or *samoupravlenie*, came to be seen as a panacea in education: if only the oppressive weight of the central state could be removed, popular initiative would be unleashed and Russia catapulted into a better world.

Religion and language were problems for educators, whether oppositionist or autocratic. Most progressives insisted on the right to use local languages in the schools, yet most also believed in the civilizing mission of empire and argued that Russian should also be taught. Reformers were overwhelmingly secular in orientation and believed that the Orthodox Church had no place in the schools. Yet many, believing in cultural autonomy, argued that local populations should be allowed to establish private confessional schools, whether Catholic, Muslim, or (Orthodox) Old Belief. The practical problems involved in implementing such policies (e.g., teachers facing a classroom with children from a half dozen minority groups) were never confronted, and tensions over ethnic and linguistic issues mounted in Russia's borderlands after 1900.

SOCIALISM AND THE STALINIST SCHOOL

World War I led to the collapse of the Ottoman, Austro-Hungarian, and Russian empires and the emergence of numerous new states, many having ethnically and religiously diverse populations and sharply contrasting rural and urban cultures.

After 1918, all Eastern European countries focused on building a strong educational infrastructure. Education policies had been important in the nationalist debates in the nineteenth century, and political leaders recognized the power that such institutions had to create a loyal, mobilized community of citizens. Furthermore, as these states had significant minority populations, education institutions and curriculum development became one of the main venues for constructing a homogeneous national identity. Policymakers favored highly centralized models over regional administrative and curricular autonomy, since they appeared to be destabilizing centripetal forces.

The practical challenges faced by all Eastern European countries had to do primarily with financial resources. Ambitions for creating a comprehensive primary education system and a secondary system with possibilities for vocational and theoretical education were high among most policymakers. They also encouraged the growth of higher education institutions, with growing diversification among the liberal professions from engineering to law and social sciences. Demography, anthropology, and sociology came to displace the central position held by philosophy and history among the humanities. These multiple agendas for developing various levels of education suffered especially after the Great Depression. Unfortunately for the bulk of the population, compulsory primary education suffered most. In Romania, for instance, the shrinking education budget prompted the minister of education to reduce the number of state-paid teachers by two thousand in 1934, whereas university research institutes retained most of their state funding. This abatement of primary education was not as marked in places in which higher education was not as significant to the policymakers, such as Bulgaria. Finally, Czechoslovakia was able to weather the 1930s better, since it already had a well-developed primary and higher education infrastructure, inherited from the Hapsburgs, and an economy less vulnerable to a depression than that of other Eastern European countries.

By the end of the 1930s, all Eastern European countries except Albania had an integrated education system that included university and other higher education institutions. Czechoslovakia led the rest of the region in both extent of institutional development and diversity. It also had the highest rate of literacy. Throughout the area, the state had become the most important agent for the dissemination of knowledge through schools at the expense of the Catholic and Orthodox Churches especially. Independent education institutions did survive, especially those funded by religious denominations—Christian and Jewish. Efforts were also made by different nongovernmental organizations to develop vocational schools and schools for women. Access to education, especially at the postprimary levels, was still very difficult for women, and none of the Eastern European states made a very sustained effort to eliminate the institutional, economic, and cultural obstacles faced by women who wished to engage in education.

Meanwhile, the Russian Revolution of 1917 had swept away the old czarist order, and the new Bolshevik leaders, borrowing heavily from Dewey, set about creating a new, secular, democratic, and progressive school system without uniforms, grades, textbooks, or conventional disciplinary boundaries. Open access to all levels of the school "ladder" was guaranteed for workers and peasants, and the walls separating school, work, and community were to be broken down. A genuine effort was launched to promote local languages and foster indigenous elites on the borderlands, though Enlightenment presumptions of Europe's civilizing mission remained deeply entrenched in the mind of Russian leaders. In 1921, as part of the introduction of a mixed economy in Russia, school financing was made the responsibility of local government. The result was chaos, since four years of revolution and civil war had destroyed the Russian economy, and its people were cold, hungry, and diseased. By the end of the first decade of Soviet rule, when the economy had rebounded to its prewar level, the democratic and decentralized school had been thoroughly discredited.

In 1929, Stalin swept away the mixed economy; he also inaugurated a new era in the schools. The Stalinist school system created after 1931 imposed a breathtaking uniformity and hierarchy on education across the vast territories and ethnically diversified populations of the Soviet Union (by now approximating the boundaries of the old czarist empire). Stalinist education was nominally egalitarian and "polytechnical," as well as strongly "collectivist" in that it discouraged individual initiative or choice. Textbooks were restored to their traditional place, the authority of the teacher was reinforced, uniforms were reintroduced, and rote learning once again reigned supreme. Rapid expansion of education did provide opportunity for millions of peasants and workers, many of whom gained a secondary technical education and rose to positions of power and status. But the genuinely emancipatory and redistributive aspects of socialism, not to mention the learner-based tenets of democratic education, were scarcely evident in this system. All were cogs in a wheel, some were more equal than others, and everyone—teacher, student, administrator—knew his or her place in a "command system." After graduating, students were assigned jobs by the state. In reality, the system was not foolproof, and millions of enterprising individuals managed to beat the rules to get the education and career they wanted, regardless of the state's plans for them; but individual choice was not prominent. Stalinism also meant the ruthless suppression of local languages (and often those who spoke them) in an attempt to establish a "New Soviet Person" implicitly dominated by

Russian culture. By 1953, whether in Ukraine, Russia, Central Asia, or Moldova, all schools looked alike, all textbooks were the same, and all teachers followed the same lesson plans. In this system, an insidious ideology of bombast, distortion, and untruth corrupted the teaching of history and literature, and it profoundly compromised the singular achievement of unprecedented educational expansion, the other hallmark of Stalinism.

In Eastern Europe, the communist regimes established after World War II did not completely do away with existing education legacies and institutions. Many qualified educators were purged between 1948 and 1956. Faculty in higher education institutions suffered the most. Taking their cue from the Soviet Union, the East European communists used education as a tool for legitimizing their control on ideological grounds. Studying Russian became compulsory for all students, and dialectical materialism became the basis for all social sciences. The applied sciences became a priority, and many of the new specialists from these countries received their training in the Soviet Union.

In their efforts to modernize and remain ideologically untainted, policymakers had to choose between replacing certain structures, institutions, and programs for the sake of ideological purification or preserving them, if in an ideologized fashion, for the sake of economic progress. In Czechoslovakia, Hungary, and especially East Germany (where the existing institutions for technical education were already well developed, especially at the higher levels), the communists used these assets in their plans for modernization. It was different in Bulgaria and, to a great extent, in Yugoslavia and Romania, where it was the communists who created many of the technical education schools.

ACHIEVEMENTS AND PROBLEMS OF THE SOVIET SCHOOL

The achievements of the Soviet-type school were considerable. First, it was effective in delivering full literacy under Stalin and, under his successors, a complete secondary education to the population of a far-flung and linguistically diverse country. By the 1980s, access to higher education lagged only behind that of the United States: vocational and technical schools, one network of special schools for the gifted and another for children with special needs, boarding schools, a vast network of preschool and extramural institutions—all enhanced opportunity and recruited talent. The communist regimes also opened up greater access to all levels of education for women. Illiteracy was greatly reduced, save in Albania. The state also provided some education for minority groups in their maternal language.

As for the quality of this education, there is no simple formulation. Graduates of Soviet schools who have emigrated to the West often praise the education they received and speak of caring and highly competent teachers; émigré children who enroll in American schools tend to be two to four years ahead of their cohorts in science and math, and they are far better read. Many Soviet and East European schools developed innovative art and music programs in the 1970s and 1980s. According to a World Bank study, students in Soviet-type schools, although excelling at the awareness of facts, fared less well in their application, and did poorly at using knowledge in unanticipated settings. (This assessment has been largely confirmed by the 2002 Organisation for Economic Co-operation and Development/Programme of International Student Assessment investigation of attainment in reading, math, and science in twenty-eight countries, including the Russian

Federation; see www.pisa.oecd.org.) Preschool institutions were woefully overcrowded, vocational schools had severe discipline problems, and 70 percent of all university graduates earned engineering degrees of questionable worth. Children with special needs were isolated, gender stereotyping was ubiquitous in textbooks, and minority cultures were paid only lip service.

Fitting the curriculum of the humanities and social sciences into the straitjacket of Marxism-Leninism had a stupefying effect. Even in the better schools a "conceptually overtaxing" curriculum (stemming, ironically, from the so-called Zankov reforms initiated in the 1960s, which sought to modernize instruction and enhance independent thinking) resulted in first-grade children having up to three hours of homework daily, widespread falsification of records, and social promotion (*protsentomania*). Bribes flourished as competition for places at universities intensified.

By the end of the Brezhnev era (1966–1982), planners in the Soviet Union and Eastern Europe were aware that their schools were in trouble. Seemingly intractable social and pedagogical issues were exacerbated by chronic underfunding. As a proportion of national income, investments in education lagged and schools declined. Rural schools lacked all amenities; overcrowded and crumbling urban schools met in two and sometimes three shifts daily; science laboratories were antiquated; underpaid and overworked teachers left in large numbers. Structural rigidities made it difficult to adapt schools to the changing needs of the economy, and the area's primitive communications infrastructure created daunting obstacles to participation in the information revolution by Soviet schools. Finally, an expensive network of research institutions under the various academies of science made only a limited contribution to economic growth; in Eastern Europe, a growing brain drain stunted any significant contributions to research and development.

In Russia and Eastern Europe, women were relegated to secondary positions in all branches of the economy and administration, in spite of academic performance equaling that of men. Schools for minorities were supported in an inconsistent manner. In Romania, for instance, support for such schools rose and then fell with the waves of defensive nationalism among the Romanian leadership. In most cases, special education remained limited to providing spaces for isolating individuals with physical and mental handicaps from the "normal" population. In Czechoslovakia, traditions in developing special education programs that focused on integrating these individuals in society as full participants were replaced by a policy of isolating individuals with mental disabilities and ignoring the needs of individuals with physical disabilities. This attitude was typical of all Soviet bloc countries.

In the Eastern European bloc, one of the most important weaknesses of the communist education policy was the centralized nature of its allocative distribution powers. This system fostered the continuous dependency of local educators in budgetary and curriculum matters on the local representatives of the party and, in turn, on the higher chain of command that led to the top of the party hierarchy. During the 1980s, the quality of basic education, research, and development, as well as the training of technical and humanities elites, steadily declined, not only in comparison with Western Europe but also in the context of the goals and expectations of the education policymakers in each individual country. The intellectual brain drain that started in the 1970s and intensified in the 1980s due to waves of emigration among the educated strata also deprived Eastern Europe of some of its best and most educated minds. Although this phenomenon has been present in other developing countries with noncommunist regimes, such as India,

Eastern Europe's patterns of emigration are particular in their one-way direction. The intelligentsia that has left Eastern Europe since the 1970s has not in most cases returned and has not maintained close professional relations with colleagues there, at least before 1989.

The same strict, top-down control that fostered emigration also led to pedagogical restraints against creative and critical thinking among those who remained. By the early 1980s, the economic and administrative infrastructure in Eastern Europe had reached a level of modernization, yet was incapable of generating the type of creative, dynamic change needed to compete in international markets. The more advanced countries— Hungary, Czechoslovakia, and Poland—attempted to address these problems as early as the 1970s, with reforms similar to the Zankov initiative in Russia. The Gierek regime attempted to reduce the ideological content in all disciplines in Polish education. The Hungarian leadership also attempted such a change after Janos Kadar came to power, but it took another thirteen years from the initial resolution in 1972 before any substantial change occurred. In 1985, the Education Act was passed, which finally decentralized administrative, budgetary, and, to some extent, curriculum matters. With this legislation, which transferred some responsibilities from the ministerial level to local administrators and teachers, Hungary became the first East European country to understand and grapple with the educational inadequacies of the communist regime. Another remarkable development occurred in Poland starting in 1980, when the Polish church, in collaboration with Solidarity, established alternative education institutions, such as primary and secondary schools under the administrative control of the Catholic Church. This development was essential to fostering values, goals, and attitudes divorced from the communist order.

REFORM AND THE COLLAPSE OF THE SOVIET EMPIRE

In the Soviet Union in 1986, a year after Mikhail Gorbachev came to power, a powerful reform movement emerged in education, with roots in Estonia, Georgia, and Russia. So-called Eureka initiative groups of parents and teachers, supported by the country's leading educational newspaper, *Teachers' Gazette*, as well as innovators in the Academy of Pedagogical Science, promoted a "pedagogy of cooperation." For a brief period, education was a topic of genuine public interest, and in the rhetoric of reformers the belief grew that new schools could transform society. Through learner-based instruction, children would grow into critically thinking, self-aware, and democratically inclined citizens to replace the "cogs" and "drones" of the totalitarian system. Between 1988 and 1990, the reformist platform of decentralization, differentiation, democratization, and enhancement of the humanities in a humanized school won official endorsement. Radical reformer Edward Dneprov was catapulted into national office as minister of education (1990–1992) in a highly centralized state.

With the dissolution of the Soviet Union in 1991, Dneprov found himself in charge of Russia's newly independent schools, and Boris Yeltsin's Decree 1 proclaimed education a top priority of the state. Yet Dneprov confronted a dilemma. He believed profoundly in decentralization as the key to unleashing public initiative, but he also saw that the only way to overcome the stifling inertia of a monolithic bureaucracy was to use his "fists" as minister to achieve a "breakthrough" and make reform irreversible. To his dismay, he learned that only a minority of teachers and parents actively supported the reformist agenda. Worse yet, he presided over school reforms as Russia spiraled into an economic collapse that dwarfed America's Great Depression in scale. As in the aftermath of the Russian Revolution, energetic, progressive reformers found empty coffers.

In a situation of growing disarray and disillusionment, Dneprov's reformers pursued a three-stage agenda of reform: conceptualization, legislation, and implementation. They believed that the conceptualization stage had been completed by 1990; their chief mission now was to promote a foundational law on education, which was promulgated to great fanfare in 1992. Reformers did not expect every article of the law to be implemented immediately, but they hoped that in the long run it would serve as a cornerstone for a profound transformation of attitudes and practices in education.

Dneprov promoted privatization, which won him many enemies; he also insisted on keeping the church out of state schools and fought against military training in the schools, which won him other enemies. He was replaced in 1992, but by then he had launched a major shake up of the Russian school system, including curriculum, structure, and governance. But when he left office, the Ministry of Education had significantly diminished in power and influence. A policy of decentralization as well as a sharply reduced Kremlin budget for education contributed to a historic shift in control over schooling to Russia's regions, as part of an even larger transformation of Russian politics, from a highly centralized to a federal system.

The fall of the communist regimes in Eastern Europe since 1989 has had a tremendous impact on education institutions in these countries, especially in regard to their role in society in the post–Cold War era. Change in this sector of public life has varied, as countries of the former bloc have adopted their own particular strategies. The success of these policies in meeting the current economic and political challenges has been uneven in this region as well. They have hinged to a great extent on the desire to "rejoin" Europe in a broad cultural sense and also in terms of institutional requirements made by the European Parliament and education commissions as a precursor to joining the EU.

CHANGES IN STRUCTURE AND GOVERNANCE

In the Soviet-type school, legislation was a fig leaf hiding administrative chains of command through which directives were issued to run the system. Directors and inspectors were charged with ensuring compliance; professional unions were also controlled by the party-state, though they occasionally defended teachers. Forums to bring teachers and parents together often turned into shaming sessions for parents who were not bringing up their children properly. Budgets for individual schools were controlled in the smallest detail by the central authorities. And the "central authorities" were overwhelmingly male. Although women made up a majority of state employees in the education system, men dominated the middle and upper levels of the administrative hierarchy. Corruption and inefficiency, and perhaps the more decent side of human nature, made the running of these schools far less rigid and monolithic than is sometimes claimed. Still, this was what local reformers would call an *administrative-command* system rather than a *law-governed* system. *Structural rigidities* were a reality as ugly as the term itself.

Attempts to turn to a law-governed system, practice negotiation and adjudication, and develop transparent procedures and budgets have had to come to grips with the lingering command culture and its remaining personnel. In Russia, programs have been set up with Western aid to teach more flexible management approaches. Gradually, agreements are being reached among Moscow, the regions, and municipalities to share authority in decision making, and various collegial bodies have been established for resolving issues among the various authorities.

At the international level, some success has been achieved in re-creating a "common educational space," or agreements among the states of the former Soviet Union to promote cooperation and to establish equivalencies. At the local level, the school boards created in the early stages of reform have not proven their viability, but school principals undoubtedly enjoy more autonomy than before. As for alternative education, private schools, gymnasia, and the like have clearly established a foothold in Russian education but still account only for 1–2 percent of all schools. The 1992 law endorsed a limited privatization of education facilities and provided for setting up state-subsidized experimental schools. Reformers also flirted with the notion of vouchers. But in 1995, a Duma hostile to privatization forced revisions to the law prohibiting privatization of state school property. And there is widespread hostility among teachers to breaking up the state's monopoly over schooling.

In Eastern Europe, policymakers began to explore institutional reform at an early stage, but change has been uneven for a variety of reasons. Initially, discussion centered around issues of decentralization and local autonomy in a visceral reaction to the centralist setup under communism. Decentralizing was identified with rejecting communism. Decentralization became an important tool for asserting more autonomy in curricular and governance matters, especially at the university level. More recently, in their desire to reach a level of compatibility with their counterparts in the EU, Ministries of Education are pushing for greater standardization of the curriculum offerings, in both content and format, as well as a different system of offering courses, closer to that in the EU. The Bologna Process has created pressure in terms of curriculum reform and standardization among countries like Romania and Bulgaria, which have seen their chances of joining the EU measured against their reform programs, including those in education. The incentive is also a positive one, as curricular reform would enhance the competitiveness of these countries' labor forces in the larger European market, especially among higher levels of white-collar jobs.

When policymakers began to discuss the effects of decentralizing the administration and budgets of education institutions more systematically, it became apparent that the quality of education might suffer from such changes. How could they monitor the quality of instruction without retaining control over the purse? The debate concerning local institutional autonomy vis-à-vis ministerial control has not yet been resolved, and it has not helped that a tug-of-war has ensued among bureaucrats at the center fearful of losing their positions and bureaucrats on the periphery hoping to increase their paltry salaries. Over the last decade, government spending for education has gone up in some countries, such as Latvia, Lithuania, Poland, the Czech Republic, and Romania, but it has decreased in all other former Soviet bloc countries. Yet by comparison with the Organisation for Economic Co-operation and Development (OECD) average, the levels of government spending in this area remain relatively comparable, with the exception of Russia, Romania, and Albania. In some countries, such as Latvia, Lithuania, Poland, and Hungary, government spending on education surpasses the OECD average. Clearly, the gap among the postcommunist European countries has widened, with those aspiring for EU membership focusing more efforts and resources in the direction of education development.

In some cases, the debate over decentralization has had a political and especially nationalist side. In Romania, for instance, leaders of the Hungarian minority have relentlessly called for a comprehensive reevaluation of minority education, with the hope of reinstating locally administered Hungarian-language primary and secondary schools wherever Hungarians are the majority. Many Romanians are still skeptical of the loyalty of the Hungarian minority, so Bucharest has been reluctant to agree to such demands. Similarly, in now-separated Czechoslovakia, debates between the Czechs and Slovaks about ending Prague's control over Slovak schools played an important role in the partition (2003). Since the separation, nationalist trends have only grown in Slovakia, and the government has subsidized the attempts by a nationalist organization, *Matica Slovenska*, to prepare textbooks in history, language, and literature. Nationalists have also used the trump card of accession to the EU as a way to suppress some efforts to support primary and secondary education in languages of various minorities. This has been the case especially with Hungarians in Romania and Roma populations everywhere in the region. However, given the particular interest of the EU with regard to minority rights, the efforts to improve the education of ethnic minorities in their languages have continued with some success. For instance, Bulgaria created a somewhat successful program of increasing school attendance among the Romas through bus services. In Romania, Hungarian communities have secured the creation of a private, state approved university that offers courses taught exclusively in Hungarian.

Independent schools have added a new dimension to the debate over authority by introducing a market component of choice for the consumer. Since 1990, the Catholic Church has provided the most sustained challenge, creating a number of schools in Poland and Hungary at both primary and secondary levels. These schools are now recognized as equal competitors with the state schools. Nonreligious private establishments such as Montessori schools have opened as well, but the general public's unfamiliarity with them, as well as high tuition rates, have limited their growth.

Marketization of schooling has met a mixed reception in Eastern Europe. In Poland, nongovernmental education institutions can benefit from state subsidies of up to 50 percent of their operating costs. This has encouraged a proliferation of such schools and has enhanced their credibility among parents. In Hungary, by contrast, the state is still reluctant to subsidize independent schools; in Bulgaria and Romania, the state cannot find enough money to meet its commitments to state schools, much less consider financing independent institutions. Moreover, commissions set up in the early 1990s in Eastern Europe to monitor the quality of private schools often abused their power for the sake of personal interest by practicing favoritism. As a result, the integrity of private schools as institutions of learning was called into question during the first decade of postcommunism. The uncertainty is even greater in that parents cannot be sure their child's degree will be recognized upon graduation.

More recently, the pressure of EU accession has led to stricter guidelines and enforcement of the regulations that govern the accreditation of private institutions. Generally speaking, government institutions have been more successful than private ones in moving toward compliance with EU accreditation, and they have thus situated themselves at a clear advantage vis-à-vis private institutions. Yet these private institutions continue to grow, especially in the tertiary or higher education sector, where there has been a boost in enrollments over the past decade. In Russia, fee-paying students and private institutions now make up a sizeable minority in this sector. On the other hand, a law promulgated in 2001 subjects all state institutions engaging in for-profit activities to heavy taxation. And in Eastern Europe, the process of accreditation for private institutions has fallen in line with the Bologna Process. Accordingly, their credibility has grown both in the eyes of the tuition-paying parents and of prospective employees.

CURRICULUM REFORM

After 1989, educators in Russia and Eastern Europe sought to "de-ideologize" the curriculum by allowing a choice of textbooks and free discussion of long forbidden topics in history, eliminating *scientific communism*, and *scientific atheism*, and introducing sociology, civics, global education, and even religion. In Eastern Europe, the dismantling of old curricula took place almost spontaneously, before the formulation of any projects for legislative reform. Hungary and Poland began the process before the rest of the bloc countries, and by 1990, reformers had removed many of the humanities textbooks of the old regime, as well as mandatory courses such as political economy. Czechoslovakia soon followed, with Romania, Bulgaria, and Albania lagging behind. Another symbolically powerful change was eliminating Russian language study from most of the other countries' curricula. Central authorities have allowed the regions and municipalities to choose what they will teach and how they will teach it, and many schools in Russia and the Commonwealth of Independent States now offer students a range of electives. As Steve Heyneman has emphasized, in theory at least, a major paradigm shift from teacher-based to learner-based approaches has occurred everywhere, and the promotion of academic freedom and choice has been a genuine achievement of the past decade. In Romania, Bulgaria, and Albania, by contrast, discussions about fostering a pluralist political culture have led to more limited change. Only in the last few years, with incentives from the European Union and various PHARE (Poland and Hungary: Assistance for Restructuring their Economies) programs have these governments encouraged the founding of alternative institutions at the level of secondary education. These countries have only recently begun their own active campaign to produce reforms in teachers' understanding of pluralist values and their ability to foster such a spirit in the classroom.

At the same time, these advances have been limited if not crippled by economic constraints, the inertia of tradition, and outright resistance. They have proceeded unevenly in different regions and at different levels. Even where academic freedom has struck deep roots, it has often been with deleterious consequences.

Economic constraints, palpable in all areas of schooling, have wreaked the most damage. Despite generous funding by George Soros, producing adequate numbers of new textbooks (often in several languages) has proven a daunting task, and in Russia many schools still use Soviet-era books. To make matters worse, in a sharp break from the Soviet era, since 1996 the state now requires parents and local school districts to pay for textbooks. In Eastern Europe, the textbook situation is brighter. Change occurred first in Hungary and Poland, which eliminated old textbooks by 1990. Most of the other countries in the former Soviet bloc had introduced new textbooks by 1997. Yet the burden of paying for textbooks has also reverted primarily to local school administrations and parents.

Retraining teachers is an expensive and lengthy process that involves in-service release time and support, as well as an overhaul of pedagogical institutions, which, generally speaking, were the poor stepchildren of the Soviet-era and had even fewer resources than "classical" universities or institutes to bring about change. Learner-based and problem-solving instruction also call for smaller classes, but low salaries (often months in arrears) caused widespread flight from the teaching profession in the 1990s. Many empty slots were filled by retired teachers unable to live on their meager pensions, but these pensioners tended to be conservative and wedded to the old ways of rote instruction. Teachers who did not leave and were not ill-disposed to innovation often were simply too overworked and exhausted from the daily stresses of an impoverished existence to make major changes in their routines. By all accounts, rote learning in large classrooms continues to prevail in many schools and institutions throughout Eastern Europe. One positive development has been the reduction of student-teacher ratios across the area. But the impact of this change on the quality of teaching is still not clear. More recently, teacher salaries in Eastern Europe have been raised to more decent standards, though they lag behind the economic power commanded by employees in any other public service job requiring a college education.

Even with European markets pressuring Eastern Europe in regard to the need for better training in managerial, business, and high-tech skills, curriculum reformers are driven by the desire to offer more humanities courses and fewer science courses in primary and secondary schools. Because Soviet-era educators had packed the curriculum with up to sixteen different disciplines for each academic year, the initial reaction against this overburdening of students was to eliminate disciplines "tainted" by ideology. More high schools have begun to focus on applied disciplines—computer science, business, accounting—at the expense of theoretically-oriented offerings. In the mid-1990s in Poland and the Czech Republic, there was an effort to return to a focus on individual development, on humanizing students instead of accumulating technical knowledge. More recently, studies have shown that the Eastern European countries fare well in mathematics and science education at the secondary level in comparison to the OECD average.

One important element of this new emphasis on personal rather than professional growth has been the inclusion of religion in the compulsory curriculum, starting with primary education. Outside the former Soviet Union, all Eastern European countries, save Albania, teach religious studies from the primary level onward in both state and private schools. Countries with a predominantly Catholic population (Poland, Slovakia, and Hungary) have offered a more ecumenical version of religious studies, but Orthodox countries (Romania in particular) offer students little unbiased information about other religions.

The resurgence of nationalism in all humanities disciplines was a prominent feature of curriculum reform in the area in the 1990s. Focusing on national traditions at the expense of a comparative international framing of knowledge has been especially popular among the older generation of policymakers and teachers. In Hungary, for instance, a large contingent of specialists voiced their criticism against a 1991 reform project because it seemed too immersed in the challenges of the globalized economic market and not mindful enough of national values. Romanians embraced this nationalist outlook even more fervently. Since 1989, Romania has pursued reforms regarding education opportunities for its ethnic minorities in their own language more because of international pressures than because of an earnest desire to deal with these issues. With increased pressure for greater awareness of European-wide developments and criteria for accession to the EU, more effort has been made to dilute the nationalist content of some of the curriculum. Since 2004, in particular, the ethnonationalist component in education has been in retreat. It remains to be seen whether euro-skepticism will bring back a new wave of nationalism in the humanities after 2007.

Language, religion, and history everywhere present especially thorny problems for educators. Decentralization and pluralism allow local minorities to teach more fully and truthfully their own languages, history, and culture. In language instruction, however, this often disenfranchises other resident minorities. Russians have a notoriously poor record of learning local languages, whether they live in Riga or Bishkek. Being forced to learn (or even study) a local language, as students now are in Tallin, is perhaps long overdue, and young citizens of Russian ethnic origins now seem to be doing so with alacrity. Finding a realistic way to encourage a flowering of tongues as well as a common language (not to mention training teachers and generating textbooks for schools balancing these needs) will be no easy task, even with the best of intentions.

In history, narratives of conquest, expropriation, deportation, exploitation, and even genocide were long banished from school textbooks, and the creation of empires was described in fairy-tale terms. But the Bashkirs and Tatars and dozens of other ethnicities in Russia, the banished populations of the Crimea, Caucasus, the Roma, and others now want their stories told in the schools, and they want the creation of empire presented as an unqualified evil. Religious conflict is also part of the narrative, not only the suppression of religion as such but also the collaboration of a dominant church (often Orthodoxy) in the persecution of "sects" (Protestantism) or non-Christian faiths, whether Judaism, Islam, or Buddhism. Yet instruction in religion, especially in Eastern Europe after 1989, has often been treated as an integral part of national and spiritual rebirth in the aftermath of communism. In some areas (a prominent example is Bosnia and Herzegovina), new textbooks have "increased ethnic divisions, exacerbated differences, and prevented social cohesion." An October 2002 decree of the Russian Ministry of Education recommending instruction in the rudiments of Orthodox faith according to a curriculum drawn up by the church ran into heavy opposition, even within the ministry itself. As one commentator queries: would such an innovation set a precedent allowing the authorities in Tatarstan to mandate courses in Islam for the local population, including the 40 percent who are Russian?

Thus decentralization and emancipation have created thorny issues in some communities. Educators as well as international organizations are concerned that schools are now being used to sustain ethnic grievances rather than promote citizenship tenets, reconciliation, and development of the "social capital" societies need to prosper in a global market environment. History's didactic function of building consensus around common myths, which sometimes conflicts with seeking the truth, is at issue. Civic education courses, energetically promoted by various international organizations, may play a significant role in resolving conflicts now evident in the teaching of history, language, and religion. But these subjects will be a source of contention for some time to come.

Not all the news is bad. Many individuals and organizations in the Baltics, Russia, and Eastern Europe are working actively to promote social reconciliation. In one notable case, Central Asia, the ministers of education from neighboring countries signed an agreement (in 1992) to create schools for the large mix of ethnic groups from surrounding states and to allow textbooks to be imported across borders for local minorities; thus, Uzbeks in Kazakhstan can use textbooks imported from Uzbekistan. The ministers also agreed to meet annually, recognizing that tolerance and mutual understanding are crucial for the survival and stability of the entire region. Yet in Russia, no less prominent a figure than Prime Minister Kasianov has also spoken out in the Duma, in 2001, to lambaste textbook authors for insufficient patriotism.

International pressures have become important factors in the debate over curriculum reform everywhere in Eastern Europe, but perhaps less so in Russia. The prospect of becoming part of the European Union has become a prominent factor in the education policies of these countries since the early 1990s. In Hungary, for instance, as early as in 1991, one criterion for education reform was to "link up to the European education standards," with the hope of having degrees conferred in Hungary recognized everywhere in Europe. Similar ambitions have dominated discussions about reform after the initial period of transition in Poland, Slovenia, and more recently Romania and Bulgaria. As these countries prepare to become members of the EU, curriculum reformers have paid increasing attention to the structure and content of curriculum in EU schools, especially from the secondary level up. Even in Russia, the need to update curriculum has been acknowledged, and information sciences as well as foreign languages will soon be taught at the level of the elementary school.

One of the consequences of these international pressures for reaching EU standards has been the greater inequality in the quality of education within each country. Given their limited economic resources and availability of good personnel, Eastern European governments have focused their energies on elite, well-established schools, usually those located in their capitals, often at the expense of more generalized, but not so spectacular developments throughout the country. Thus, primary and secondary education institutions in rural areas or small cities may use the same textbooks and standardized tests for evaluation, but the quality of education available there is usually greatly inferior to the quality of teaching in the elite schools at the center. According to the results of the OECD's Programme for International Student Assessment study released in 2002, international comparisons suggest that as these school systems differentiate, it will be hard to maintain high levels of achievement in ordinary schools.

Other curriculum issues have been created by decentralization and pluralism. How, given the primitive state of licensing and certification, can quality be measured? How can the rights of students to receive a decent education and to transfer from school to school or region to region be protected? The Russian Ministry of Education has worked hard to develop a choice of syllabi for schools, in the hope that schools will avail themselves of one of these choices. In addition, the ministry has issued "minimal competencies" and has propagated the notion of standardized testing. A lot of creative thinking has gone into developing a three-tiered core curriculum with national, regional, and local school components. Progress has been made, but there is widespread suspicion that Moscow wants to use standards to reimpose central control. Nevertheless, dozens of regions have worked out agreements with Moscow on this issue.

ECONOMIC ISSUES

Economic pressures have deeply compromised reform efforts in every area of education. Even before the economies in this region began their sharp decline, education was underfunded in per capita terms, and it made up a declining proportion of gross domestic product (GDP). For example, the Soviet Union spent 7 percent of its GDP on education in the 1970s, but this declined to less than 4 percent by the late 1980s. According to official data, in 1988, 21 percent of all Soviet schoolchildren attended schools in buildings without central heating, 30 percent were in schools lacking indoor plumbing, and 40 percent studied in schools with no access to sports facilities. By 1996, education funding in Russia and Ukraine had dropped to 3 percent of GDP. Slovakia, Bulgaria, and Albania have suffered from similar declines. Yet over the last decade, government spending for education has gone up in some countries, such as Latvia, Lithuania, Poland, the Czech Republic, and Romania. The levels of government spending in this area remain relatively comparable to the OECD average, with the exception of Russia, Romania, and Albania. In some countries, such as Latvia, Lithuania, Poland, and Hungary, government spending on education surpasses the OECD average. Clearly, the gap among the post-communist European countries has widened, with those joining the EU focusing more efforts and resources in the direction of education development. By contrast, education officials in Russia estimate that the schools currently receive less than half the sum needed for a minimally adequate schooling.

All sectors of education have suffered, but preschool programs have suffered most. This is particularly unfortunate, since unemployment and impoverishment have severely strained family life, and the need for intervention programs has only grown. The decline in health and nutrition programs, as well as in support for children with special needs, is an especially bitter pill to swallow. In the Soviet era, more than a quarter of all public expenditures on education went to preschool programs, compared to 4 percent in Japan, 6 percent in the United States, and 5 percent in the United Kingdom. The only areas where support for and enrollment in preschools has remained high are Hungary, Poland, the Czech Republic, and Slovakia, where by 1999 the rate recovered to its 1989 level, 75 percent. The Baltics have also seen a strong recovery to over 60 percent by 1999, while the rest of the area has seen a relative decline. One should add, however, that state spending for these programs has gone down, so that the low level of enrollment reflects both the total decline in number of children of preschool age, as well as a shift in the finance burden toward parents and private resources.

During the Soviet era, family income and occupation affected children's opportunities to gain admission to prestigious schools; bribes, personal connections, and private tutors hired to prepare students for entrance examinations were all widespread. Nevertheless, children from less fortunate families could take advantage of special schools for the gifted and a well-developed network of free extramural enrichment programs. Those who won admission to an accelerated school, professional and technical institute, or university paid no tuition fees and received free housing as well as small stipends for living expenses. But now access to education has narrowed. The sharply curtailed availability of inexpensive child care has reduced women's opportunities to study or take part in professional retraining programs. Tuition has been introduced in elite secondary schools and all of tertiary education (roughly one-half of all students are *biudzhetniki*—i.e., funded by the state); even where schooling is nominally free, parents have been dragooned into paying large sums for "optional courses," "special services," or capital improvements. Despite efforts to introduce standardized exams, bribery persists in admissions to higher education, and private tutoring continues to privilege children of wealthier families, especially when tutors also sit on admissions committees. In 1998, Alexander Tikhonov, minister of education, openly admitted to the editor of *Teachers' Gazette* that bribes prevail in competition for admission, and not only to the most prestigious institutions. The same problems persist throughout Eastern Europe.

Special education has been the Cinderella of education reform in Eastern Europe. In the early stages of reform, much attention was devoted to improving the quality of special education, and in 1991 Poland passed a comprehensive law making special education an integral part of the school system. But elsewhere financial constraints have generally led to a decline in the quality of special education programs. Credit belongs to the many international organizations that have worked to educate policymakers, train families of children with handicaps, and provide direct aid for such children. Equipment such as wheelchairs, virtually unavailable a decade ago, has now appeared, again partly thanks to international efforts.

The market has also created obstacles for reformers devoted to humanizing the curriculum and helping children to become well-rounded adults with a pronounced civic ethos. Instead, parents and children want training that leads directly to lucrative jobs. In their eyes, the liberal arts and humanities, except for foreign languages, are an unaffordable luxury. By contrast, programs in law, economics, business administration, and computer technology have become growth industries. Yet the same market forces have made it very hard to retain teachers of foreign languages in the schools. Vocational education has suffered greatly in the past decade, especially in southeastern Europe, since most of its programs prepared students for jobs that are no longer available in the manufacturing sector. To survive, vocational schools must undergo expensive reforms. But how can programs in banking, marketing, commerce, or computer training be established just as funding from the state and bankrupt enterprises is drying up? Remarkably, enrollments at vocational schools remained steady during the past decade of upheaval in Russia, but this was largely because the state feared the societal consequences of releasing thousands of largely unemployable youth onto the streets and continued their stipends. In this period, vocational schools performed a largely social rather than economic service, and their future is now imperiled.

Finally, other areas of education have been especially hard hit by marketization. Research has proven to be very expensive and very difficult to sustain. Russia's central education bureaucracy has only a handful of statisticians collecting and analyzing data, so the ministry must often make crucial decisions without adequate information. The tradition of promoting research in specialized academies is withering away for lack of funding, but only a handful of universities (twelve in Russia, according to one estimate) are capable of supporting basic research. A decade ago, laboratory equipment in Soviet-style institutions lagged far behind the West. Accelerated technological change and collapsing budgets have made that gap even greater, and more than one hundred thousand scholars and scientists, both junior and senior, have left, compounding the decline by removing human capital. In Russia, the situation has deteriorated so far that one Western observer, writing in the *Chronicle of Education*, warned of a system-wide collapse of higher education and scientific research. Reportedly, the country's venerated musical academies have fared little better. Virtually everywhere libraries are in woeful shape. In Eastern Europe, a valiant effort has been made to address these problems by creating access to information resources through the Internet.

UNIVERSITIES

Universities share, as well as inherit, the problems confronting lower-level schools, but the post-Soviet period has been especially turbulent for higher education. Of the more than five hundred state higher education institutions functioning in Russia today, under a dozen can properly be called research oriented, and the academies of science traditionally responsible for the production of knowledge are crumbling. Enrollments in higher education institutions were expected to plummet after 1991, as the value of a college degree declined. Instead, enrollments have surged, but largely in new, market-oriented fields of study. Everywhere fee-paying students have replaced those enrolled with merit-based stipends. At the university level, living stipends have dwindled to the point that most high school graduates now apply only to institutions that allow them to continue to live at home. This has had the paradoxical effect of reducing applications to more prestigious institutions located in the expensive large cities and boosting enrollments in run-of-the-mill VUZY (higher education institutions). Once the state covered all tuition fees, but now fewer than half of all students receive scholarships, and "tuition has become an essential part of public institutions." Yet tuition fees exceed annual average income by almost 200 percent. To meet this changed environment, the concept of student loans was introduced in the 1992 Law on Education, but no practical loan schemes have yet been proposed (much less funded) in Russia. A plethora of private universities now exist, but many are phantom institutions, existing in a parasitic relationship with state facilities; endowments, critical to long-term stability and autonomy, are virtually unknown. In Russia's regions, local VUZY are often consolidating, since agricultural, pedagogical, and humanities-oriented institutions see their survival in reorganizing as comprehensive universities.

In terms of governance, the post-Soviet transition brought autonomy from the state to universities. Academic freedom has been achieved across the East European plain, and in a handful of locations changes have created vibrant institutions of higher learning. In Eastern Europe, university professors have seen a remarkable increase in their paltry salaries, enabling them to pursue a research agenda, something that was a luxury in the 1990s. But in most Russian universities, demoralization prevails. Generous amounts of Western aid have been funneled into a select number of programs (assuming a long-term trickle-down effect), and some rectors are paid thousands of dollars monthly. Although salaries of professors have improved in recent years in Eastern Europe, in Russia, most faculty, like teachers in schools, are paid a starvation wage and must teach a double or triple load (sometimes moonlighting at "private" institutions using the very same classrooms). Merit-based competition for research money and peer reviews are virtually unknown, and accounting procedures are laughable; instead, patronage and clientelism prevail as most institutions are ruled by the heavy hand of Soviet-style bosses and fixers. Teachers show little interest in university affairs outside the classroom, and faculty governance bodies now exert little influence. Inside the classroom, a culture of rote instruction to bored students survives from the Soviet era. According to OECD/World Bank specialists, little change has taken place in the humanities curricula, though new programs in business, marketing, and law are springing up like mushrooms. Facilities are in shocking disrepair, and university communities must often cope without heat, light, or running water.

In Eastern Europe, however, a more diverse picture has emerged. As mentioned earlier, pressures for EU integration have weighed particularly heavily on the shoulders of the tertiary education institutions. Resources have been concentrated in the oldest and most reputable institutions, as well as those who were enterprising enough in the early 1990s to create academic exchanges and other intuitional bridges with their counterparts in the EU. Thus, Charles University in Prague, Babes-Bolyai University in Cluj, Romania, and Jagellonian University in Krakow are well situated to receive accreditation in the EU. But this is not the case for less prestigious institutions of higher learning in other regions of these countries

CONCLUSION

A decade after revolutionary change in Eastern Europe shook the world, schools remain in an unsettled state. Change has occurred much more rapidly and profoundly in some areas than in others. Internationalization has left a mark, but much less so in, say, Kazan, than in Prague. Freedom and opportunity beckon, but equity has declined. Corruption, bribery, incompetence, and lip service to reform can all be found, but so can remarkable dedication and a capacity for innovation even in very difficult circumstances. A revival of national and imperial traditions proceeds, but a fascination with Western approaches also persists; textbooks fomenting xenophobia and ethnic animosities can be found along with others promoting reconciliation and tolerance.

Russia has been on a wobbly path. The economy virtually collapsed in 1998, and in many areas schools were forced to relinquish much of their pedagogical mission in favor of social welfare functions, due to pervasive impoverishment, family breakdown, and the spread of epidemic disease as well as drug use. In Stephen Kerr's words, "social surroundings offer young people less a supportive environment than a virulent set of pathologies." According to Kerr, the percentage of children unable to progress in school because of debilitating mental or physical conditions, estimated to be between 5 and 20 percent in the United States, may be as high as 50 to 70 percent in Russia today. Consequently, Kerr concludes, the school is still in a "downward spiral" and "a distinctive culture of learning, developed under the Soviet regime and preserved in remarkably good shape until recently" is seriously endangered.

But since the crash of 1998, Russia has enjoyed four years of modest economic growth. The Duma and the state have demonstrated renewed interest in education by pursuing measures of amelioration and reform. Notably, this has been evident in the sustained effort to establish first a "doctrine" of education and then, late in 2001, the passage of a "modernization" decree, unifying and integrating several major policy initiatives and seemingly restoring the role of the central state as a major player in school affairs.

The proclaimed goals of the modernization program are to enhance "quality, access, and effectiveness" throughout the school system. The components are many, including the re-channeling of monies out of the "shadow" economy into public (state) channels. Vladimir Putin's chief economic adviser has argued that fully one-half of all money spent on education in Russia went to bribes, tutoring, and other "private" ends (sometimes these categories overlap: of 350,000 new matriculants at VUZY this year, 300,000 had taken "preparatory courses" with professors at the university they later won admission to). Now the state is rapidly introducing standardized exams that will serve both as high school graduation and university entrance exams; a related component of modernization is GIFO (*Gosudarstvennye imenne finansovye obiazatelstva*, meaning "money chasing students"), a new approach to financing higher education, which will peg the size of the state subsidy to VUZY for each enrolled student to grades on the standardized exams. Furthermore, to bring the school curriculum in line with university entrance requirements (the existing gap has made it almost impossible to gain admission without special preparatory classes), the government has been moving forward with a revised curriculum based on set standards for each course, an additional (twelfth) year of secondary education, and "profiling" or accelerated courses in the last two years of study. After some initial bumps, the standardized exams are rapidly being implemented; and with the government decree issued in the summer of 2006 it was finally decided that 2009 will become a year of the comprehensive implementation of the EGE (Russian abbreviation for the Unified State Examination). However, an important disclaimer here is that the most prestigious VUZYs of the country (among which are Moscow State University and Saint Petersburg State University) are still negotiating with the government the possibility of introducing additional tests for admission to these elite institutions along with taking the unified exam. Thus, even if the EGE becomes compulsory it will unfortunately not be universally so. The transition to a twelve-year curriculum is under way in some areas; GIFO is still in preparation (and meeting resistance from the powerful Union of Rectors). Drawing up standards has been very controversial; a commission of two hundred experts headed by former minister Dneprov had its recommendations torn apart by the president of the Russian Academy of Education at a conference in the summer of 2002, and in a review of developments at the close of the year, a top official reported that the educational world remained polarized on standards.

A new state-directed modernization program has been launched at the initiative of President Putin—a National Project on Education. This priority project will have at its disposal thirty billion rubles (approximately one billion dollars) to be expended between 2006 and 2008. Supervision of the project's money has been given to a special Presidential Council established in October of 2005, headed by First Deputy Prime Minister Dmitrii Medvedev. Other members include Vice Prime Minister Alexander Zhukov, several presidential aides and ministers, regional leaders as well as federal district leaders (there are seven recently created federal districts, each of which bring together several of the country's eighty-nine regions), and prominent business executives—all told fifty members. The project is one of four priority projects: the others are healthcare, affordable housing, and commercial agriculture. According to Putin in his May 2006 state of the nation address, priority project expenditures will amount to 5 to 7 percent of total state outlays in each designated area. The Ministry of Education, in turn, views the basic goals of the Project as the following: (1) support and development of the "best practices" of the Russian educational system; (2) development of IT in education; (3) creation of national mega universities and world-class business schools (MBA programs); (4) increasing the role of civic/character education in schools; and (5) expanding educational and training opportunities within the armed forces.

As far as the first goal (best practices) is concerned, the main measures being taken are to provide governmental support, on a competitive basis, to the following institutions and programs: (1) 30 universities (totaling 20 billion rubles, equivalent to approximately U.S.$950,000) and 6,000 schools that are actively implementing innovational educational programs; (2) 2,500 annual grants to talented youth; and (3) an annual bonus of

100,000 rubles (equivalent to approximately U.S.$4,000) to the 10,000 best teachers, which will allow for the support of the best in the profession and thus raise the prestige of teaching. To address these needs, the federal budget made appropriations of 9.2 billion rubles for FY 2006 and 19.2 billion rubles in FY 2007.

With regard to the second goal of IT development in education, the government is providing 20,000 schools (10,000 schools annually) with Internet access and 2,500 with computers to facilitate implementation of modern educational technologies. For those purposes the federal budget allocated 1.5 billion rubles for 2006 and 2007. They are supplying no fewer than eight thousand schools annually with instructional aids and other technical equipment totaling 2.3 billion rubles for the year 2006.

With regard to the third goal, the key goals involve creating, by the year 2008, the following: (1) two mega university centers for thirty thousand students each, one in the Southern and one in the Siberian Federal Districts respectively; (2) two business schools with MBA programs for five hundred students each in Moscow and Saint-Petersburg. For these purposes the federal budget allocated three billion rubles in 2006 and six billion rubles in 2007 in addition to monies to be provided by the targeted regions and by private investors.

With regard to the fourth goal (civic/character education), the implementation is to be guaranteed by a monetary supplement for primary and secondary education teachers. These additional fiscal supplements will be paid one thousand rubles (approximately U.S.$35) a month for each full class (defined here as twenty-five city pupils and fourteen rural pupils). If the class is not full, the money will be reduced proportionately. For these purposes, in 2006, the federal budget allocated 7.7 billion rubles. (The pedagogical press and mass media immediately ridiculed this initiative, pointing out that the sum could hardly stimulate teachers to undertake new initiatives. Yet, the sum does seem to be meaningful for some.) President Putin gave a public reprimand to Minister Fursenko for initially not including homeroom teachers of military academies, boarding schools, and evening schools for returning students (all told, an additional fifty-nine thousand teachers) in this scheme. Needless to say, the oversight was promptly corrected.

With regard to the fifth goal (armed forces education), these initiatives have been taken: (1) broadening opportunities for recruits to receive basic vocational and professional training while serving; (2) providing preferential entry to higher education institutions for those having served no fewer than three years in the Russian Federation army forces; (3) creating one hundred educational centers of basic vocational training in territories with military detachments; (4) establishing special preparatory classes for entry into institutions of higher education; and (5) providing special stipends to those enrollees. For these purposes the federal budget allocated 0.3 billion rubles in 2006 and 0.6 billion rubles in 2007.

Modernization components also underway include a campaign to computerize all schools and major efforts to upgrade rural education. Moreover, a recent Rural School Bus project appropriates 2.08 billion rubles (to be matched by regional funds) to purchase 3,500 buses to facilitate rural children getting to school. Village schools in Russia have chronically been in distress; because of population decline, many have ten pupils or fewer, and efforts to upgrade cost twice as much per capita as do improvements in municipal areas. Yet attempts to consolidate or close down village schools have met with fierce local resistance, since the schools remain the cultural hearth and key social welfare institutions in remote areas. Regrettably, a final component of the original modernization draft law, to peg the minimum wage for teachers to the average wage prevailing in the economy by 2006, was dropped from the final version. Thus, the "center" (the presidential office, the ministries, and the Duma) has recently reemerged as a major player in Russian education and produced a comprehensive set of measures to reshape Russian education. Although officials have repeatedly intoned that "nothing is yet set in stone," that "fine-tuning" is still called for, and that several key components are still "experimental," there is undoubtedly more momentum to these recent state initiatives than to any federal program since the collapse of the Soviet Union. We will see a new look to Russian education in the next decade.

Looking ahead, Eastern Europe is in a more advantageous position, with the countries of this region continuing the catch-up game with the European Union. There is greater diversity among these countries in 2007, with countries slated for EU membership generally in better shape in terms of curriculum reform, standardization of education, and government spending on education. But there is also much greater diversity within each country between elite central schools and regional or rural institutions. Some problems remain, however, across the board. The quality of teacher training and standard of living still poses questions about long-term trends regarding the classroom experience and education quality. This problem is, however, related more to opportunities and problems in the global economy.

* The authors of this chapter chose to include a bibliography because the information included in the text is broad, generally available, and best evaluated by reading the sources listed in full. We also avoided direct quotations. The articles and books are chosen from a much larger list of work on education in Central and Eastern Europe to serve also as a recommended list of English language sources. A scholarly bibliography would be comprised of works largely in languages inaccessible to the general reader. The authors also would like to thank Olga Shonia and Simona Popa for their assistance in preparing this chapter.

Bain, Olga. "The Costs of Higher Education to Students and Parents in Russia: Tuition Policy Issues." *International Higher Education* 11 (Spring 1998): 6–8.

Bartz, Brunon, and Zbigniew Kullas. "The Essential Aspects of Education Reform in Poland." *European Education* 25, no. 2 (Summer 1993): 15–26.

Baskerville, Stephen. "East Central Europe: The Future of American Higher Education?" *Academe* (November–December 1997): 22–26.

Bollag, Burton. "Nationalist Group Gains Power over Slovakian Education." *Chronicle of Higher Education* 28 (February 1997): 49.

Bolotov, Victor, et al., eds. "The Reform of Education in New Russia: A Background Report for the OECD Review of Russian Education." *ISRE Newsletter on East European, Eurasian, and Russian Education* 6, no. 1 (1997): 4–21, and no. 2 (1997): 9–62.

Communication from the Commission to the Education Council, *European Benchmarks in Education and Training: Follow-up to the Lisbon European Council.* COM (2002) 629 F (Brussels, 20 November 2002), at europa.eu.int/comm/education/policies/2010/doc/bench_ed_trai _en.pdf.

Eklof, Ben, and Edward Dneprov, eds. *Democracy in the Russian School.* Boulder, Colo.: Westview, 1993.

European Commission. *Maastricht Communiqué "on the future priorities of enhanced European cooperation in vocational education and training (VET)."* (review of the Copenhagen declaration of 30 November 2002). (Maastricht, 14 December 2004), at europa.eu.int/comm/education/news/ip/docsmaastricht_com_en.pdf.

European Commission, Eurostat: *Education across Europe 2003* (Office for official publications of European Communities: Luxembourg, 2003). ISBN 92-894-5783-X. European Commission, DG Research: *Key Figures 2003-2004. Towards a European Research Area: Science, Technology and Innovation* (Brussels, 2003). Also available at europa.eu.int/comm./research/era/pdf/indicators/benchmarking2003_en.pdf.

Eurydice, Eurostat. *Key Data on Education in Europe 2002.* (Luxembourg: Office for Official Publications of the European Communities, 2002.

Gutsche, Marta. "The Hungarian Education System in the Throes of Change." *European Education* 25, no. 2 (Summer 1993): 5–11.

Heyneman, Stephen P. "From the Party/State to Multi-Ethnic Democracy: Education and Its Influence on Social Cohesion in the Europe and Central Asia Region." *International Journal of Educational Development* (forthcoming).

———. "Education and Economic Transformation." Papers presented to the National Academy of Sciences, Washington, D.C., September 1996.

———. *Russia: Education in the Transition.* Washington, D.C.: World Bank, 1995.

Holmes, Brian, Gerald H. Read, and Natalya Voskresenskaya. *Russian Education: Traditions and Transition.* New York: Garland, 1996.

Joint Interim Report of the Council and of the Commission. *"Education and Training 2010:" The Success of the Lisbon Strategy Hinges on Urgent Reforms.* Outcome of the proceedings of the European Council on 26 February 2004. 6905/04 EDUC 43. COM (2003) 685 F (Brussels, 3 March 2004), at europa.eu/int/comm/education/policies/2010/doc/jircouncilfinal.pdf.

Jones, Anthony, ed. *Education and Society in the New Russia.* New York: Sharpe, 1994.

Kerr, Stephen T. "Demographic Change and the Fate of Russian Schools." *REECAS Newsletter* (Summer 2001): 10–14.

Kirk, Mary, and Aaron Rhodes. "Continental Responsibility." In *European and International Support for Higher Education and Research in East Central Europe.* Vienna: Institut für die Wissenschaften von Menschen, 1994.

Kodin, Evgenii. "Problems of Private Higher Education in Russia." *International Higher Education* 6 (December 1996): 11–13.

Mitter, Wolfgang, et al., eds. *Recent Trends in Eastern European Education.* Frankfurt: German Institute for International Educational Research, 1992.

Muckle, James. *Education in Russia: Past and Present: An Introductory Study Guide and Select Bibliography.* Nottingham: Bramcote, 1993.

———. *Portrait of a Soviet School under Glasnost.* New York: St. Martin's, 1990.

Organization for Economic Cooperation and Development. *Secondary Education Systems in PHARE Countries: Survey and Project Proposals.* Paris: Author, 1996.

———. *Reviews of National Policies for Education: Russian Federation.* Author: OECD, 1998.

———. *Review of National Policies for Education: Tertiary Education and Research in the Russian Federation.* Paris: Author, 1999.

Prucha, Ian, and Eliska Walcherova. "Czechoslovak Education within the Broader Social Framework." *European Education* 25, no. 2 (Summer 1993): 27–35.

Sutherland, Jeanne. *Schooling in the New Russia: Innovation and Change, 1984–1995.* New York: St. Martin's, 1999.

Tjeldvoll, Arild, ed. "Education in East/Central Europe: Report of the Oslo Seminar." *Special Studies in Comparative Education* 30 (1992). Oslo and Buffalo: University of Oslo Institute for Educational Research and State University of New York at Buffalo.

UNICEF, comp. "A Decade of Transition." *Regional Monitor Report* 8 (2001).

Valery, Soyfer. "Who Offers a Better Education—The USA or Russia?" *Izvestiia*, 15 November 1995. In Russian.

Verdery, Katherine. *National Ideology under Socialism: Identity and Cultural Politics in Ceausescu's Romania.* Berkeley: University of California, 1989.

Wanner, Cathy. "Educational Practices and the Making of National Identity in Post-Soviet Ukraine." *Anthropology of East Europe Review* 13, no. 2 (Autumn 1995).

Watson, Peggy. "Gender Relations, Education, and Social Change in Poland." *Gender and Education* 4, no. 2 (1992): 127–47.

Webber, Stephen L. *School, Reform and Society in the New Russia.* New York: St. Martin's, 2000.

Weselowsky, Tony. "Russia: Costs Render Educational Reforms Almost Prohibitive." Radio Free Europe/Radio Liberty, Prague, February 12, 1998.

16

Education for All in Africa: Still a Distant Dream

Joel Samoff with Bidemi Carrol

Education held extraordinary promise at Africa's independence. Nearly unbounded aspirations. More schools. More teachers. More learners. Imaginative innovations. Yet that rapid progress was not sustained. By the late twentieth century, crisis had become the norm. Schools in many countries had no teachers' guides, no textbooks, not even chairs. The new century has seen reflection and rejuvenation, often accompanied by significantly increased dependence on external resources. While some of its excitement has reappeared, education in Africa—widely understood as critical to national development and the focus of a major share of national budgets—remains troubled. Education for all in Africa remains a distant dream:

> This Report re-confirms the diagnosis of the World Education Forum that almost one-third of the world's population live in countries where achieving the EFA [Education for All] goals remains a dream rather than a realistic proposition. . . . By the end of the decade, countries with [Gross Enrollment Ratios] below 70 percent were concentrated in sub-Saharan Africa.[1]

Yet Africa has also been the site of imaginative experiments, innovations in the content and forms of education, and critical reflections on the role of education in society. Long before Europeans arrived, and to this day, Africa's intellectual contributions have had global influence.

How, then, to make sense of this transition from expansive expectations to pervasive degeneration to renewed growth, from promise to progress to crisis to new hope? While we must not underestimate the achievements or lose hope, moving beyond crisis requires careful analysis of its origins and persistence. That analysis requires attention to both content and forms, and especially process. In the remainder of this brief overview, I explore major issues and themes in education in contemporary Africa,[2] considering both outcomes and analytic frameworks.

"Education in Africa," like "African education," is of course a simplification fraught with risk. For most purposes, neither exists. With care, it is possible to study education in Guinée and to explore the unique characteristics of, say, Ugandan education. But since the diversity within countries is vast and most countries are themselves of recent origin, it is foolhardy to speak in general terms about a continent comprising more than fifty countries. Still, the craft of comparative education requires just that. Identifying and understanding similarities and commonalities sometimes requires deferring attention to individual variations. Our continuing challenge and responsibility is to use each sort of analysis—detailed examination of what is unique at the small scale and synthetic overview of what is common at the larger scale—to illuminate and strengthen the other. Hence, as we consider shared patterns across Africa, we must at the same time constantly recall and respect Africa's rich diversity.

EDUCATION IN AFRICA: FROM CRISIS TO RENEWED HOPE

The turn of the century marked a period of reflection and reevaluation for African development. The optimism that accompanied the decolonization of the late 1950s and early 1960s has been displaced by a deep dismay at persisting poverty and a profound pessimism about the viability of any strategy of social transformation. For many, the objective was no longer broad improvement in the standard of living or self-reliance but simply survival.

Education experienced a similar transition.[3] Earlier, education (formal and nonformal) was expected to be the principal vehicle for social change, both helping to define the new society and enabling its citizens to function effectively within it. Not only were the illiterate to learn reading and writing, but they and other newly educated were also to foster innovation, accelerate the generation and diffusion of ideas and technologies, and monitor and manage a responsive political system. Education was to be the vehicle for redressing discrimination and inequality, both in daily practice and in popular understanding.

There was progress and, in some countries, very substantial achievements. Still, by the end of the twentieth century in much of Africa, many children received little or no schooling, illiteracy rates remained high, school libraries had few books, laboratories had outdated or malfunctioning equipment and insufficient supplies, and learners lacked chairs, exercise books, even pencils. The common term was crisis. Many, both inside and outside Africa, were pessimistic about the ability of national authorities to address the crisis effectively.

In this setting, recourse to foreign aid, always important for education in Africa, became a way of life. Almost without exception, education reform proposals were presumed to require external funding. Increasingly, even the day-to-day operation of the education system depended on overseas support.

As the general crisis unfolded, external aid agencies proffered development advice as well as finance. Notwithstanding its critical role, generally their funding remained a very modest portion of total education expenditures. Consequently, their influence was far greater than the absolute value of their aid suggests. Indeed, some agencies, and especially the World Bank, insist that their development expertise is even more important than their funds. "[The World Bank's] . . . main contribution must be advice, designed to help governments develop education policies suitable for the circumstances of their countries."[4]

The increased reliance on foreign aid to support education innovation and reform has been accompanied by another transition, from understanding education as a human right and general good to viewing it primarily in terms of its contribution to national growth and well-being through the development of the knowledge and skills societies are deemed to need. Occasional voices continue to insist that education is liberating, that learning is inherently developmental, and that therefore education is a public responsibility. Notwithstanding the rhetoric of the rights approach, however, most often education is regarded as distinctly instrumental, an investment in a country's future, a production system that (more or less successfully) turns out people with particular competencies and attitudes, and a delivery system that transfers wisdom, expectations, ways of thinking, and discipline to the next generation.[5] As we shall see, these two currents—on the one hand the expanded role for foreign aid and its providers and with it the tendency to address education through the prism and with the tools of finance and, on the other, the understanding of education primarily as preparation for the world of work—reinforce each other with enduring consequences for education in Africa.

PROMISE, DECAY, AND REJUVENATION

Nearly all African countries became independent with an inherited education system that excluded most of the population. In Tanzania (then Tanganyika), for example, both Christian missionaries and the British government operated schools. But at independence in 1961 those schools accommodated fewer than half the country's children. For most of them, the course of study was four (or fewer) years. As former Tanzanian president Julius Nyerere noted, at independence "85 percent of [Tanzania's] adults were illiterate in any language. The country had only two African Engineers, 12 Doctors, and perhaps 30 Arts graduates."[6] Although the schooled population was larger in a few African countries, many faced the new era with as few educated citizens as Tanzania.

If education were to transform society, access to it had to be extended massively and rapidly. Indeed, expanded access had become both a popular demand of the anticolonial nationalist movement and a promise of the newly installed postcolonial leadership. The premise was personal as well as political. Access to education was the primary route by which nearly all of Africa's initial leaders escaped (or rather mitigated) the discrimination and domination of European rule. Wherever there was a clear effort to reject race and other ascriptive criteria for employment and promotion, education's selection role became even more important. And opening schools in urban neighborhoods and rural villages was the most readily achievable and visible manifestation of the new government's accomplishments. Progress in this regard was indeed remarkable.

Let us consider the record. Doing so requires recognizing that the apparent precision provided by numbers is often fundamentally misleading. Put sharply, the margin of error on reported African education data is often far larger than the observed variation. Hence, an apparent change over time, say, in enrollment or public spending, may not be a change at all. Unfortunately, while the quality of data collection and analysis have continued to improve, problems of accuracy and comparability, and thus inference, persist.

The problems are several. Available figures are often inaccurate, inconsistent, and not readily comparable. Schools, districts, and other sources provide incomplete and inaccurate information. Sources differ on periodization and on the specification of expenditure categories. Especially common are the confusion of budget and actual expenditure data and the comparison of budget figures in one year with expenditure reports in another. Recurrent and development (capital) expenditures are treated inconsistently. Often the available data do not include individual, family, local government, and direct foreign spending. Discussions of the cost of education in fact generally refer to government expenditures on education and sometimes only to education ministry spending. Inflation, deflation, and exchange rates are treated inconsistently. Data series are frequently too short to be sure that observed variation reflects significant change.

One example of this problem must suffice as the caveat for the data that follow.[7] How many children are in school? Or, more important, compared with the relevant age group, how many children are actually[8] in school? Table 16.1 lists the primary gross enrollment ratio for sub-Saharan Africa in 1970, 1980, and 1990, as reported in several widely used sources. Notice that the reported figures for 1970 from different editions of the World Bank's own annual publications vary from 46 percent to 50 percent. Similarly, in this very limited sample, the reported figures for 1990 vary from 66 percent to 76 percent. What happened over those two decades? Did primary enrollment increase by two-thirds (from 46 percent to 76 percent) or by half that (a 32 percent increase, from 50 percent to 66 percent), or something in between? From the available data, we cannot be sure. What we can probably say with some confidence is that (1) fewer than half of school-aged children were in school in 1970, (2) by 1980 progress had been substantial, with some three-fourths in school, and (3) there seems to have been a decline by 1990.

The implications seem clear. First, it is essential to take the margin of error seriously, that is, to treat most national education statistics as rough approximations. Second, even relatively large observed changes may reflect nothing more significant than random fluctuations, annual variations, and flawed statistics. Consequently, apparent changes of that magnitude are a weak foundation for broad inferences and public policy. Third, both researchers and policymakers must reject statistics whose underlying assumptions require a level of precision, linearity, or continuity that the data do not reliably support. Finally,

Table 16.1   African education statistics: an example of data problems

Source	Primary Gross Enrollment Ratio (%)[a] Sub-Saharan Africa		
	1970	1980	1990
UNESCO, *World Education Report 1991*	46.3		76.2
UNESCO, *World Education Report 1993*		77.5	68.3
World Bank, *Education in Sub-Saharan Africa*[b]	48.0	76.0	
World Bank, *African Development Indicators 1994–1995*		77.0	66.0
World Bank, *World Development Report 1993*[b]	46.0		68.0
World Bank, *World Development Report 1995*[b]	50.0		
World Bank, *World Development Report 1996*[c]		80.0	
World Bank, *World Development Report 1997*[c]		79.0	

[a] School enrollment as a percentage of the relevant age group.
[b] Weighted average.
[c] Weighted average; male and female combined.

effective use of available data requires seeing through the facade of precision and demystifying the use of statistics. Although number-density is the order of the day in international education policy and planning, pages bristling with numbers may obscure far more than they reveal.

Duly cautious, let us consider the accomplishments. Primary school enrollments increased nearly ninefold from 1960 to 2004 (table 16.2). In the same period, secondary enrollments were thirty-nine times larger, and tertiary enrollments grew even faster. In societies in which less than a tenth of the population was deemed literate at the end of colonial rule, illiteracy steadily declined (table 16.3). Comparable figures for the number of schools opened, postsecondary institutions created, and new teachers recruited show similar substantial growth. Clearly, access to education expanded dramatically and rapidly.

But those growth rates were not sustained. Although the literacy rate increased, so did the absolute number of illiterates. For many countries, the primary enrollment ratio stagnated or even declined in the 1980s and 1990s, one indication of the deterioration of public services and of the inability of governments to meet their commitment to move toward schooling for all their citizens (table 16.4). At the same time, the supporting infrastructure for expansion was sorely stretched. In many countries, buildings were not maintained, crash teacher recruitment programs were not accompanied by in-service professional development, low salaries forced teachers to look outside their classrooms to supplement their incomes, curriculum revision and textbook preparation proceeded slowly if at all, and morale plummeted. By the late 1980s African education was in crisis:

It is not uncommon to find a teacher standing in front of 80–100 pupils who are sitting on a dirt floor in a room without a roof, trying to convey orally the limited knowledge

Table 16.2   Enrollment growth in sub-Saharan Africa, 1960–2004 (in thousands)

	1960	1970	1980	1990	2000	2004
Primary	11,853	20,971	47,068	64,400	84,443	103,897
Secondary	793	2,597	8,146	17,700	23,431	31,170
Tertiary	21	116	337	1,400	2,298	3,303

Sources:
1960–1980: World Bank, *Education in Sub-Saharan Africa*, tables A-1, A-2, and A-4.
1990–1997: UNESCO, *World Education Report 2000*, regional tables 6, 7, and 8.
2000–2004: UNESCO Institute of Statistics at www.uis.uneco.org, January 14, 2007.

Table 16.3   Estimated adult literacy rates, sub-Saharan Africa, 1960–2000 (Percentage)

	1960	1970	1980	1990	2000	2004
Adult Literacy	9.0	22.6	40.2	47.3	60.3	61.1

Sources:
1960: World Bank, *Education in Sub-Saharan Africa*, table C-4.
1970: UNESCO, *World Education Report 1991*, table R8.
1980: UNESCO, *World Education Report 1995*, table 3. (UNESCO, *World Education Report 1993*, gives 32.5 percent for 1980.)
1990: UNESCO, *World Education Report 1993*, table 3. (UNESCO, *World Education Report 2000*, gives 50.3 percent for 1990.)
2000: UNESCO, *Education for All Global Monitoring Report 2002*, table 2.
2004: UNESCO Institute of Statistics, at www.uis.unesco.org, January 14, 2007.

Table 16.4   Primary gross enrollment ratio, sub-Saharan Africa, 1970–1990, as a percentage

1970	*1980*	*1985*	*1990*	*2000*	*2004*
46.3	77.5	76.1	68.3	83.0	93.2

Sources:
1970: UNESCO, *World Education Report 1991*, table R4.
1980: UNESCO, *World Education Report 1993*, table 6.
1985: UNESCO, *World Education Report 1998*, table 6.
1990: UNESCO, *World Education Report 1993*, table 6.
2000–2004: UNESCO Institute of Statistics, at www.uis.unesco.org, January 14, 2007.

he has, and the pupils trying to take notes on a piece of wrinkled paper using as a writing board the back of the pupil in front of him. There is no teacher guide for the teacher and no textbooks for the children.[9]

Decay was also apparent in higher education, especially as the emphasis on basic education was accompanied by efforts to shift resources from postprimary to primary schooling. Indeed, the rhetoric became shrill and accusatory, insisting that universities had become unaffordable and therefore exploitive luxuries that benefited only a small elite.[10]

By the end of the century, education growth in most countries resumed and higher education received renewed recognition and additional funding. Several countries have had many years of relatively high-volume external funding, both targeted at specific programs and more recently, provided as budget support. Schooling in those countries, however, continues to confront very large classes, teachers with little preparation and limited instructional materials, and periodic promising reforms that rarely progress beyond the pilot stage or receive too little funding or political support to flourish. As well, the primary indicator of progress toward global goals, substantially increased enrollment in the first year of school, often has not been sustained. Throughout the region it is not uncommon to find that many of the new students do not return for their second year and that most do not reach the end of the primary school cycle. For example, in Rwanda, Malawi, and Uganda, where enrollment growth has been rapid, the primary completion rates in 2004 were 37 percent, 58 percent, and 57 percent, respectively. In Mozambique, fewer than 30 percent of those who start primary school will complete that level.[11] The very rapid expansion that followed the abolition of primary school fees in several countries has been followed not only by high attrition but also by very large classes for those who remain in school. Even where it was achieved, expanded access to school was not readily translated into learning for all.

Nongovernmental organizations (NGOs) of various sorts, international, national, and local, have played an increasing education role in Africa, often as the implementing agency for externally funded programs. In some countries, mosques have joined churches as prominent education providers. While in principle NGOs can be especially responsive to unique local needs and conditions, their activities can also undermine national responsibility for education and disempower communities. Periodically, where NGOs have asserted their autonomy and developed a critical role, governments have sought to constrain and control them.

In 1990, governments and international and nongovernmental organizations enthusiastically committed themselves to Education For All.[12] Small meetings, big conferences, national plans, and many reports followed. Meeting in Dakar a decade later, the world's education community considered a sobering assessment.[13] Notwithstanding the reaffirmation of the goals, education for all in Africa remained a long way off. As they renewed the commitment, educators and policymakers deferred the targets, strengthened the infrastructure, and maintained optimistic expectations.[14] While an extended analysis of the Education For All campaign and the Jomtien (1990) and Dakar (2000) meetings is not possible here,[15] three observations are important. First, since in some countries there has been little or very slow progress toward education for all over four decades of independence, it is reasonable to conclude that despite the rhetoric and formal pronouncements, education goals and priorities lie elsewhere. Second, it is far from clear that massive international conferences, an international secretariat, and insistence on national plans and reports are an effective or cost-efficient strategy for transforming and shaping education policy and practice in Africa.

Third, the progress noted here is confronted by a persisting pessimism about achieving global education goals. By early 2007, the group responsible for monitoring progress toward those goals had issued five reports.[16] All incorporated specially commissioned studies, careful data collection, and systematic analysis. Although their primary emphasis varies, and although they chronicle progress in several domains, their refrain for Africa is common: the Education For All targets have not been met (for example, gender parity in 2005) and are unlikely to be met by the new deadlines. With a few exceptions, sub-Saharan African countries remain very distant from the agreed targets. Many other reports reach similar conclusions. Even those that remain upbeat highlight the slow progress in Africa.

> Achieving [Millennial Development Goal 2: universal enrollment in primary education] will require dramatically scaled-up efforts in sub-Saharan Africa. . . . Sub-Saharan Africa has made progress, but still has over a third of its children out of school. In five African countries, less than half the children of primary school age are enrolled.[17]

Large Commitments, Little Wealth

What explains the slow growth, spurts and reverses, and difficulty in sustaining progress? In Africa as elsewhere it is common to blame governments for education problems. Particularly striking, however, is the extent to which African governments maintained their commitment to education even in periods of dire economic distress. Many African countries adopted structural adjustment programs, commonly termed *liberalization*, that generally emphasized substantial devaluation, decreased direct government role in the economy (especially in productive activities), reductions in the size of the civil service, encouragement of foreign investment, and support for privatization of many activities, including public services. Nearly everywhere, the implementation of these policies meant increased prices for consumer goods and new or increased fees for social services, including education. Notwithstanding pressures to constrain or reduce education spending, for example by employing paraprofessional or other lower-paid instructional personnel, many African governments maintained their basic commitment to funding education. Expressed as a percentage of the national budget, spending on education has not declined (table 16.5). Indeed, in terms of the overall economy, the level of spending on education

Table 16.5   Public expenditure on education as a percentage of total government expenditure in sub-Saharan Africa, 1970–2004, as a percentage

1970	1975	1980	1985	1990	1995	2004
16.7	16.6	16.2	15.0	16.7	17.6	18.0

Sources:
1960–1980: World Bank, *Education in Sub-Saharan Africa*, table A-14 (weighted mean).
1985: UNESCO, *World Education Report 1998*, table 10.
1990: Association for the Development of African Education, *A Statistical Profile of Education in Sub-Saharan Africa, 1990–1993*, table A-14.
1995: UNESCO, *World Education Report 1998*, table 10.
2004: UNESCO Institute of Statistics at www.uis.unesco.org, January 14, 2007.
Note: In view of my earlier comments about unreliable data and in view of the multiple sources of error in these derived figures, I present them reluctantly. Since the margin of error is likely to be large, the most reliable interpretation is that these data suggest that there has not been significant change in the proportion of sub-Saharan Africa's national budgets allocated to education over this long period.

in much of Africa has been comparable to or greater than that in the world's most affluent countries (table 16.6).

Even a large part of a small budget, however, is still small. Although Africa's relative spending on education was high, the actual amounts spent were very small. By 1995, sub-Saharan Africa was spending U.S.$87 per pupil, North America was spending U.S.$5,150, Europe, U.S.$4,552, and Latin America and the Caribbean, U.S.$444 (table 16.7). Equally dramatic, while per capita education spending increased 66 percent in North America between 1985 and 1995, 152 percent in Europe, and 110 percent in

Table 16.6   Estimated public expenditure on education, 1980–1995, as percentage of gross national product

	1980	1985	1990	1995
Sub-Saharan Africa	5.1	4.8	5.1	5.6
World total	4.9	4.9	4.9	4.9
North America	1.2	5.1	5.4	5.5
Europe	5.2	5.2	5.1	5.4
Latin America and Caribbean	3.8	3.9	4.1	4.5
Eastern Asia (including China)	2.8	3.1	3.0	3.0
Southern Asia (including India)	4.1	3.3	3.9	4.3

Source: UNESCO, *World Education Report 1998*, table 12.

Table 16.7   Estimated public current expenditure on education, 1985, 1995—per pupil and as a percentage of GNP per capita (U.S.$ and percentage)

	1985		1995	
	US$	% of GNP	US$	% of GNP
Sub-Saharan Africa	92	29.0	87	30.4
World total	683	22.4	1,273	22.0
North America	3,107	19.0	5,150	22.0
Europe	1,803	22.1	4,552	22.7
Latin America and Caribbean	211	11.7	444	12.9

Source: UNESCO, *World Education Report 1998*, table 13.

Latin America and the Caribbean, in sub-Saharan Africa during the same period, the per capita spending declined 5 percent. That African countries came to independence with few educated people and a very small education infrastructure and have a larger school-aged population makes the comparison even more stark. Thus a major constraint has been total government revenue, not a lack of commitment or a failure of leadership or inefficiency, although there has clearly been ineffective and inefficient education (and national) management. Increasing indebtedness, another consequence of aid dependence, consumes an increasing portion of the available revenue. Even with great sacrifices, in absolute terms there was little money for education.

Education was to be the developmental engine, the principal strategy for eliminating poverty and closing the gap between the most and least affluent countries. In order to play that role, however, education required resources that were simply not available. A consequence of this dilemma is that for poor countries (most of the world's poorest countries are in Africa), the development gap is likely to continue to expand.

It is useful to note here that within countries, differences in communities' and individuals' ability to invest in education are reduced by redistributive education financing. Though the specific mechanisms vary, the common general principle is that the most affluent segments of the population bear the largest share of supporting the education system, including the education of the poorest children. The contemporary fascination with globalization notwithstanding, there has yet to emerge a serious proposal for establishing that pattern globally, that is, for internationally redistributive education funding. Notwithstanding the broad commitment to education for all, external support to education declined sharply in the 1990s.[18] With a few exceptions, foreign aid provides a very small percentage of Africa's total spending on education,[19] and whatever its magnitude, much of that support is spent on personnel, services, products, and scholarships in the aid-providing country. Hence, in at least some settings, far from redistribution toward Africa, foreign aid may in fact function to generate a net outflow from Africa of both capital and skills.

THE FAST TRACK TO PLANNED DEPENDENCE

As I have noted, modern education in Africa has both local and foreign roots. For most African countries, the continuing external role looms large. Government education spending pays teachers' salaries. It also builds and maintains schools, purchases textbooks, and often supports students' accommodation and board. Very little of it buys chalk or wall maps or copying machines or other supplies and equipment. Hardly any is available for innovation, experimentation, and reform. There lies foreign aid's powerful roar. Its leverage has not been its total volume but rather that educators with exhausted budgets can use it to expand, to alter priorities, to modify practices, and more generally to respond to their own and others' sense of what needs to be done. Across Africa, foreign aid has become the center of gravity for education and development initiatives. Beyond the need for additional resources, over time it has come to seem not only obvious but also unexceptional that new initiatives and reform programs require external support, and therefore responsiveness to the agenda and preferences of the funding agencies: aid dependence.

Thus, aid dependence refers not to the volume of aid or to education systems whose principal funding comes from abroad. Rather, aid dependence is the internalization within those education systems of the notion that improvement and change require external support, advice, and often personnel. Aid dependence is also the adoption and institutionalization of constructs, analytic frameworks, and assessment strategies developed elsewhere. That internalization and institutionalization, supplemented by the elaborate reporting routines now required by funding agencies, make the policies and preferences of the foreign funders far more consequential than could be explained by the volume of their assistance.

That orientation is even more dramatic in several African countries, especially in East and Southern Africa. Foreign aid now pays the teachers. Not only education development efforts but also recurrent expenditures are significantly dependent on external funding. While that seems unsustainable, there is little discussion of how African countries will wean themselves from that support. Indeed, the effort to increase and accelerate aid has become a fast track to planned dependence. Even more important than the unsustainability of that reliance on foreign aid is the tension between intensified and entrenched dependence and a country's ability to orient and manage its education system—a vital set of activities that are central to development efforts and that shape the national character.

At the same time, the major international conferences have been accompanied by an ever-increasing collection of indicators, country reports, and reviews. As the education goals were incorporated into still broader poverty reduction goals, governments of the affluent countries launched major commissions to study poverty and foreign aid, generally with a strong focus on education and often followed by promises of substantially increased funding. In 2005, the major affluent countries agreed to double foreign aid to Africa and to forgive at least part of Africa's encumbering aid debt. Rock, cinema, and television personalities joined in to call for a massive expansion of foreign aid. That reliance on foreign support carries both the promise of immediate benefits and the risk of undermining education's developmental role.

While the international conferences and the parallel efforts to modify the aid process, especially to shift from supporting individual projects to subsidizing the national budget, are not specific to Africa, their consequences weigh heavily on Africa. Several are worth noting here. First, the global conferences established international reporting machinery. In principle, in addition to other reporting obligations, all affected countries must provide periodic reports on their current situation and their progress toward global goals. Effectively, that establishes external accountability well before accountability within the country has been developed and institutionalized. The advantage: greater clarity on what is (and is not) being done and by whom. The disadvantage: strengthened accountability to outsiders undermines efforts to create direct accountability of leaders to communities and organizations within the country. The eligibility rules of debt relief (HIPC) and related accelerated aid (FTI) programs become in practice an externally set policy agenda for African education, at least as powerful as explicit conditions set by aid providers.[20] Third, the associated planning and reporting requirements further constrain national education policy even as they proclaim their commitment to nationally led development.[21] Fourth, although intended to reduce the duplications and distractions of reporting to multiple foreign agencies, the required reports remain a significant administrative burden and, more important, reinforce an imposed orthodoxy in the constructs and analytic frameworks used to review the education system, indicate and measure progress, analyze problems, and suggest remedies. Like the aid relationship, the international conferences and the global goals promote progress along specific paths (say, expanded schooling for girls) at the cost of further entrenching external direction and accountability.

Let us continue this overview of education in Africa by exploring briefly several major initiatives and contested policies.

DESEGREGATION WITHOUT INTEGRATION

Along with expanded access, the second major commitment of Africa's postcolonial leadership was desegregated schools and curriculum. Progress has been substantial. Formal racial restrictions were eliminated immediately. Informal barriers weakened as senior civil servants and other more affluent Africans moved into formerly white neighborhoods and sent their children to elite schools. Although the most egregious elements were addressed immediately—for example, teaching the history of Europeans in Africa as the history of Africa itself—revising the general curriculum has taken longer and has proved more difficult.

Postcolonial education systems had few African staff with relevant expertise and experience, and in any case revising instructional materials and teacher guides is a time-consuming and often expensive process. Equally important, since curriculum revision revolves around issues of quality and standards, proposed replacements for the inherited materials were often sharply debated. The persisting powerful role of national examinations, widely accepted as the official and formal measure of the quality of education and revised much more slowly and less radically than instructional materials, continues to be a brake on curriculum revision.

At the same time, there are clear indications of continuing racial differentiation in at least some African countries. Deteriorating school quality and financial crisis have led to efforts to transfer a larger share of the cost of schooling to students and their families, generally through school fees and, in some countries, an expanded role for private schools. High-fee schools, whether public or private, can offer better prepared and better paid teachers, well-equipped and adequately staffed libraries, laboratories, and computer centers, and, frequently, increased likelihood of success at the next selection point. Where that occurs, schools become stratified. Commitments to equal opportunity notwithstanding, in practice, access to elite schools is a function of disposable resources. The differentiator is money rather than race, but the two are related, and thus racial distinctions have reemerged, in some countries even within government schools. Ironically, where the (formerly) white schools are perceived to provide the highest-quality education, the newly admitted African elite often becomes their staunchest defenders. This problem has proved to be particularly daunting for South Africa, where decentralized authority provides some protection for white parents who seek to preserve their better-funded, better-staffed, and better-equipped schools.

EQUALITY AND EQUITY

A third commitment of the postcolonial leadership was to use the education system to address the inequalities and injustices of the larger society. Expanded access was an important but insufficient step in that direction.

Historically, schools had been primary agents in reproducing a sharply unequal social order. Limited recruitment and severely constrained academic pathways restricted most Africans to less-skilled and lower-paid jobs and to their social status. There were important exceptions. A few Africans did reach the highest levels of the education system, surpassing many of their European peers. A few poets, novelists, and playwrights found ways to publish their work. A few West Africans were elected to the French Parliament and served in the cabinet. Especially in places that had a longer history of missionary education, a few families could point to several generations of university graduates. Still, most Africans simply never had a chance to go to school. Of those who did, few advanced far. Hence, converting schools from institutions for creating and maintaining inequality into vehicles for achieving equality requires a fundamental transformation. What in fact has occurred in this regard? To address this question, we must first consider several issues of terminology and public policy.

First, common to much of the analysis of education is a confusion of equity and equality. This confusion is potentially quite problematic for public policy. Although equity generally requires equal treatment, in some circumstances achieving equity may require differentiation. Equality has to do with sameness, or, in public policy, with non-discrimination. Equality has to do with making sure that some learners are not assigned to smaller classes, do not receive more or better textbooks, or are not preferentially promoted because of their race, gender, regional origin, or family wealth. Although there may be valid educational grounds for differentiating among students, equal access requires that status differences not function to limit or guide admission, promotion, and selection.

Equity, however, has to do with fairness and justice. And there is the problem. Sometimes the two do not go together, at least in the short term. A history of discrimination (at the core of the colonial experience) may mean that justice requires providing special encouragement and support for those who were disadvantaged. For example, given its history, what is equitable education in post-apartheid South Africa? Clearly, repealing discriminatory laws cannot in itself quickly achieve equality of access. Nor do the discriminatory elements embedded in curriculum, pedagogy, and examinations disappear of their own accord. Wherever it is deemed reasonable, affirmative action to redress injustice may involve pursuing policies that treat different groups of people in somewhat different ways. Achieving equity—justice—may thus require structured inequalities, at least temporarily. Assuring equal access, itself a very difficult challenge, is a first step toward achieving equity. But conflating equity and equality diverts attention from addressing the links between discrimination and injustice and sets nondiscrimination, rather than justice, as the major objective.

One manifestation of equating the two terms occurs in the World Bank's 1995 review of education policies, which assigns equity a high priority and defines it in terms of access to school.[22] Basic education should be universal, and "qualified potential students [should not be] denied access to institutions because they are poor or female, are from ethnic minorities, live in geographically remote regions, or have special education needs." That is, equity is taken to mean equal treatment.

Even when equity is specified as equality, what is generally envisioned is equality of opportunity. But how is it possible to know whether or not opportunities have been equal without considering outcomes? A careful study might, for example, find no visible gender discrimination in selection to primary school or in the primary school pedagogy.

But if that study also finds that attrition and failure rates are much higher among girls, it seems likely that opportunities were not equal after all. Similarly, if examination results are differentiated by regional origin, race, or ethnicity, notwithstanding the lack of explicit discrimination, opportunities were not equal. That is, measures of access are insufficient for assessing equality of opportunity. Discovering and redressing inequalities of opportunity require considering outcomes as well as starting points. (See chapter 6 in this volume.)

Second, discussions of equality and equity commonly assume a fundamental tension between those goals and growth. African countries must choose, commentators often assert, between allocating resources to promote growth or using them to achieve equality. African governments must of course make development choices. Yet it is far from clear that growth and equality are alternatives, especially in education. Reducing inequality by expanding access to education, for example, may fuel growth as increased consumer demand stimulates the expansion of production and productive capacity. Similarly, broader diffusion of competencies and understandings may reduce the reliance on much more expensive imported labor and facilitate reorienting the workforce as forms and circumstances of production change. As well, persisting inequality is both a barrier to broad participation in democratic governance and a breeding ground for socially disruptive discontent. There are thus strong grounds for rejecting the assumption that there is a necessary tradeoff between growth and equality and concluding instead that growth and equality are mutually dependent, each requiring and advancing the other.

Third, as access has expanded, in part because of the massive resources required to transform primary education for a selected elite into basic education for all, while the base of the education pyramid has broadened, its top remains very narrow in most of Africa. The exclusion point has moved farther along in the school cycle. Still, as table 16.8 shows, in all of sub-Saharan Africa, fewer than one-third of those who start school proceed beyond the basic level and scarcely 3.2 percent reach tertiary education. While these continental figures obscure significant variations among African countries, they show clearly that for most Africans, schooling is a process of ever narrowing selection, with only a few learners proceeding to the advanced levels.

Fourth, although earlier discussions of (in)equality and (in)equity in education were generally concerned with region (a surrogate for ethnicity and, more commonly, tribe), in recent years the principal focus has shifted to gender. Explaining that dramatic transition in focus and exploring its consequences is beyond the scope of this chapter. It is useful to consider briefly, however, both the persistence within education of other societal cleavages and the efforts to reduce gender inequality.

Substantial and reliable evidence indicates that access to and success in school contin-

Table 16.8 Education enrollment and selection in sub-Saharan Africa, 2004

Level	Enrollment (millions)	Enrollment as % of preceding level	Enrollment as % of primary
Primary	104.0	—	—
Secondary	31.2	30.0	30.0
Tertiary	3.3	10.6	3.2

Source: UNESCO Institute of Statistics, at www.uis.unesco.org, January 20, 2007.

ues in many countries to be sharply differentiated by region, religion, race or national origin, and class. Available data indicate that Christian communities, for example, generally have more schools, more children in school, and more graduates than Muslim communities. Within Africa, Qur'anic and other Muslim schools have generally not been a serious academic alternative to secular (i.e., Western and at least unofficially Christian) education. When relevant data are collected, the systematic finding is that children from more affluent and higher status families are more likely to find places in school and to proceed to higher levels. The ample evidence of these inequalities notwithstanding, they are far less often the focus of discussion and systematic research than gender differentiation. Several countries have implemented gender affirmative action programs. But there seem to be no comparable initiatives to assist prospective learners who are discouraged or disadvantaged by region, ethnicity, race, national origin, religion, or socioeconomic status. Earlier age-related affirmative action, for example, mature-aged entry schemes for higher education with reserved places for older applicants, seems to have been de-emphasized or discarded.

Efforts to encourage and support girls to enter and succeed in school have been extensive but only partially successful. Table 16.9 shows that the percentage of literate adult females in sub-Saharan Africa has quadrupled over the past three decades. Nevertheless, nearly half remain illiterate, whereas more than two-thirds of adult males are literate. Although progress has clearly been made toward equal gender access to primary school, in the countries of sub-Saharan Africa as a group, females do not yet constitute half of the enrollment (table 16.10). From lower starting points (one-fourth of the secondary school population and one-tenth of tertiary enrollment in 1960), there has been similar progress at secondary and tertiary levels. Still, by the early twentieth century, females constituted less than 40 percent of total tertiary enrollment. The variation among African countries is substantial. At the primary level, for example, the female gross enrollment ratio in 2004 varied from 22 percent (Niger) to 132 percent (Sao Tome and Principe).[23] In the same year, female gross enrollment ratio at the secondary level varied from

Table 16.9   Estimated adult literacy rates in sub-Saharan Africa, 1970–2004

Year	Total %	Female %	Male %
1970	22.6	13.2	32.5
1980[a]	32.5	22.3	43.2
1980[b]	40.2	29.2	51.8
1985	45.6	34.9	56.7
1990	47.3	35.6	59.5
1995	56.8	47.3	66.6
2000	60.3	52.0	68.9
2004	61.2	53.3	69.5

Percentage of literate adults in the population aged 15 years and older.
Sources:
1970: UNESCO, *World Education Report*, 1991, table R8.
1980[a]: UNESCO, *World Education Report*, 1993, table 3.
1980[b]: UNESCO, *World Education Report*, 1995, table 3.
1985: UNESCO, *World Education Report*, 1998, table 3.
1990: UNESCO, *World Education Report*, 1993, table 3.
1995: UNESCO, *World Education Report*, 1998, table 3.
2000: UNESCO, *Education for All Global Monitoring Report 2002*, table 2.
2004: UNESCO Institute of Statistics, at www.uis.unesco.org, January 20, 2007.

Table 16.10   Female enrollment as a percentage of total enrollment in sub-Saharan Africa, 1960–2004

Year	Primary %	Secondary %	Tertiary %
1960	34	25	10
1970	39	31	16
1980	43	34	21
1985	45	41	25
1990	45	40	26
1995	45	44	35
2000	46	44	38
2004	46	43	38

Sources:
1960: World Bank, *Education in Sub-Saharan Africa*, tables A-1, A-2, and A-4 (weighted average).
1970: World Bank, *Education in Sub-Saharan Africa*, tables A-1, A-2, and A-4 (weighted average).
1980: UNESCO, *World Education Report*, 1993, regional tables 6, 7, and 8.
1985: UNESCO, *World Education Report*, 1995, regional tables 6, 7, and 8.
1990: UNESCO, *World Education Report*, 1993, regional tables 6, 7, and 8.
1995: UNESCO, *World Education Report*, 1998, regional tables 6, 7, and 8.
2000–2004: UNESCO Institute of Statistics, at www.uis.unesco.org, January 21, 2007.

6 percent (Niger) to 106.1 percent (Seychelles), and at the tertiary level from 0.3 percent (Chad, Eritrea, and Malawi) to 20 percent (Mauritius).[24]

A research overview concludes that although tremendous gains have been made since the 1960s in most places, participation levels of girls still remain lower than those of boys:

> Repetition, drop-out and failure is very high among girls, beginning at the primary level and continuing throughout the system. . . . The small number of girls who remain in the system tend to be directed away from science, mathematics and technical subjects. . . . Consequently, female participation in the [formal] labour market is limited. . . . Female illiteracy remains high.[25]

It is striking that in a very short period, women's experiences in education have become a central focus of education analysis and, in at least some countries, of education policy and planning.[26] A review of nearly 150 broad studies of African education undertaken during the late 1980s found little explicit attention to girls' education. A review of some 240 studies completed in the early 1990s found that essentially all addressed that topic.[27] That increased attention has been accompanied by the development of organizations, institutions, and networks concerned with girls' education at the continental, national, and local levels. Several external funding agencies provide significant support for efforts to increase girls' recruitment and school success.

Some dissonant voices, however, believe that the differential experiences of males and females simply reflect deep characteristics of human society and therefore cannot be modified dramatically. Others see concern with gender as yet one more value and priority imported to Africa and imposed by outsiders, often as a condition for foreign aid. Still others accord gender no special prominence, insisting instead on addressing gender as part of a broader focus on equality and equity. (For further discussion, see chapter 7 in this volume.)

The increased attention to gender in education highlights important issues of approach and method in comparative education and in the links between research and policy. The prevailing research orientation in this arena clearly reflects both the dominance and the limitations of what has come to be the standard model for social science research. Generally, the starting point is a set of instrumental assumptions about the value and importance of educating females, especially expanding and strengthening workforce skills, increasing employability, improving family health, and reducing fertility. Yet, if educating females produces clear social and individual benefits, why do they not constitute half the school population? To address this question, researchers seek to identify factors that explain lower enrollment or higher attrition. The candidate causes are by now well-known: parental attitudes, gender-differentiated expectations for future income, the labor and household responsibilities of women, the absence of role models at home and in school, explicit and implicit discouragement for pursuing particular courses of study, parents' educational achievement, family religious and moral precepts, sexual harassment and early pregnancy, and more.

Some analysts, however, insist that the problem is power and authority relations, not exclusion. From this perspective, schools reflect the social order in which they function, and thus it is not surprising that societal gender distinctions infiltrate and orient the schools. That is, to confront gender inequality in education requires not so much identifying individual causative factors but modifying social, and therefore economic and political, relations. In this approach, schools must become locations and agents of social transformation rather than trying to incorporate females more efficiently into a nonegalitarian society. This understanding of the problem, though forcefully presented in the general literature on African development, is with few exceptions little evident in studies of African education, which for the most part continue to list variables and attempt to test their relative importance.

DECENTRALIZATION

The widespread sense of crisis in education in Africa, combined with the perceived failure of central institutions, has fueled a fascination with decentralization. A late 1980s World Bank report on education exemplifies the widespread optimism by declaring "decentralization . . . the key that unlocks the potential of schools to improve the quality of education."[28] The rationales for decentralization are multiple. Some are explicitly philosophical and ideological. Greater local autonomy is deemed inherently desirable on human, societal, and intellectual grounds: the development of human potential, the intrinsic—as contrasted with instrumental—value of democracy and thus citizen participation in governance, and the inescapable limits on the ability of any individual or agency to command and manipulate the necessary information. A second set of rationales for decentralization is political. The devolution of authority is deemed essential to maintaining and expanding political power or control, or, from the opposite perspective, for challenging and reforming the political system. As previously excluded groups develop a stake in the political system and thus a rationale for working within and maintaining it, they are less likely to seek to overthrow or destroy it. A third set of rationales, the most commonly asserted in the education literature, focuses on organization and administration. Assigning decision-making authority to local officials is expected to shift responsibility to those likely to be better informed and more sensitive to the local setting, reduce bureaucratic delays, improve local government capacity, facilitate national integration, increase efficiency by reducing reliance on distant central government and reducing diseconomies of scale inherent in the (over)centralization of decision making, foster greater central-local coordination, encourage more flexible, creative, and innovative administration, stimulate small-scale experimentation, and enable more effective monitoring and evaluation.

Experiences with decentralization in education have been mixed, often disappointing. Expected benefits have proved illusory. In part, the rhetoric of decentralization has not been accompanied by real transfer of authority. Recall that the inherited model of government was highly centralized and authoritarian. Emphasizing the importance of concentrating skills and resources and avoiding regional particularisms and divisiveness, national leaders, sometimes with local support, have been reluctant to devolve responsibility and have generally opposed enabling local authorities to generate and manage their own income.

In part, regarding decentralization primarily as a strategy for improving administration and implementation has itself been self-limiting. Decentralization is inherently a political process concerned with specifying who rules in particular settings.[29] Indeed, there is no absolute value in either central direction or local autonomy. Both are more or less important at different moments. (See, for example, chapter 8 in this volume.) They must coexist. While the common claim is that decentralization empowers citizens, neither centralization nor decentralization necessarily benefits the disadvantaged. Where privilege is maintained by strong central authority, increased local autonomy may help to challenge it. But where inequality is maintained by local authorities, disadvantaged groups may prefer greater, not less, central authority. The appropriate mix of central authority and local autonomy is always situationally specific and always responsive to some interests more than others.

Within education, to the extent that decentralization strengthens local interests and their institutions, it obstructs redistribution. Parents may be willing to pay more for their children's education. But except in unusual circumstances they are generally reluctant to see their increased school fees used to improve the schooling of other children elsewhere. As experiences in South Africa have shown, local control permits advantaged communities to entrench their privilege and resist change.

SOUTH AFRICA

Education in South Africa warrants brief attention here. Though extreme, South Africa was perhaps never as unique as is commonly thought. As elsewhere, education was used to structure economic, political, and social roles, in South Africa to segregate and subordinate. Central to maintaining minority rule and to organizing and managing a sharply differentiated society, education was at the same time an escape valve for a selected elite. Education has also been a sharply contested terrain, manifested repeatedly in South Africa, including student uprisings in Soweto in 1976. Indeed, the major themes addressed in this chapter and in other chapters in this volume are as relevant to South Africa as they are to other African settings. The delayed and very dramatic transition to majority rule in South Africa combines with its more developed productive capacity and infrastructure, and therefore available national and individual wealth, to extend and entrench South Africa's influence across the continent.

Like colonial education elsewhere in Africa, education in apartheid South Africa sought explicitly to structure roles and relationships in society. Especially as apartheid education philosophy was elaborated by the National Party government that came to power in 1948, most Africans were to receive little education, if any at all, focused on the basic literacy, numeracy, and other skills deemed necessary in the country's industrializing economy. Educators were cautioned to avoid raising expectations that education would lead to "greener pastures." At the same time, a small segment of each subordinate group was to have access to more advanced education, to provide the administrative staff, the teachers, the nurses, even a few doctors and lawyers, that the system required. As elsewhere in Africa, then, from that elite came both the lower-level officials and administrators of minority rule and the activist leaders who militantly opposed it.

When education is primarily concerned with structuring roles, it is the experience of schooling that matters, not learning. As the critics of apartheid education highlighted its shortcomings, they sought also to shift its emphasis from schooling to learning.[30] As the anti-apartheid struggle intensified, education became a mobilization strategy as well, concerned with raising political consciousness and enabling disadvantaged groups to seize the initiative. In this domain too, South African experiences paralleled those in other countries. During their struggles, for example, liberation movements in Zimbabwe, Mozambique, and Namibia recognized the importance of education as mobilization and politicization. Schools in war zones were mobile community centers concerned with confronting not only the military power of their opponents but also the internalization of subordination within the African population. In the initial years of South Africa's majority rule, however, the emphasis has perceptibly shifted from learning and mobilization to schooling.[31] Schools are the markers of modernity, the entry gates to desired futures, the fruits of the defeat of the old order. With a long history of attention to examinations and certification, the education system and its officials are more comfortable dealing with schooling than with learning. The widely heralded efforts to restore the culture of learning have in practice had more to do with reestablishing the discipline of schooling than with nurturing and harnessing curiosity and the intrinsic rewards of the learning process. Like other African countries in an earlier era, South Africa has apparently moved from education as politics to education as administration.

Following the 1994 majority rule election, the new education leadership did not assume the mantle of radical and militant educators. Entering an education department still staffed largely by the creators and maintainers of apartheid education, the new leadership moved cautiously. Whereas the period before the majority rule election was marked by the energy, dynamism, populism, and urgency of the education democratic movement, the immediate postelection period was remarkable for its uncertainty and for the absence of a visible, energetic, and purposive leadership. That became even more consequential as South Africa struggled to provincialize responsibility for education, a constitutional compromise forged to secure broad participation in the majority rule election. The initial consequence of this extensive decentralization was to blunt still further the radical education initiative. Decentralization permitted desegregation without integration and offered to advantaged communities a new framework for preserving privilege. More recently, consolidation in higher education may similarly retard rather than accelerate institutional change and social transformation more broadly.

South Africa's inherited inequalities combined with its commitment to national reconciliation to generate a financial crisis for education in a relatively affluent country. The general agreement was to expand access without reducing quality, understood to mean maintaining spending in elite schools and affluent communities. A redistribution strategy was slow to emerge, difficult to implement, and resisted by the teachers who had been the strong allies of education reform. As well, potentially radical curriculum reform initiatives were increasingly swamped by the burdens of implementation and by public pressure to improve results on largely unchanged national examinations.

Education had been at the center of the anti-apartheid struggle. Its task, everyone agreed, was social transformation. As the new government assumed power, responding to both general and specific pressures, it moved from mobilization to planning to implementation. As elsewhere in Africa, its principal concerns were expanded access, desegregation, and redressing inequality. In the context of a constitutionally required decentralization, education debates focused less on learning and liberation and more on schooling and examinations, and more generally on education as preparation for the world of work. With surprising speed, education's conservative charter once again became paramount.

EDUCATION AND DEVELOPMENT

Understandings of the role of education in African development (broadly, improved standard of living and the economic changes required to achieve that) diverge sharply, with important educational and political consequences. Efforts to expand access, desegregate schools and curriculum, and promote equity reflect the premise and promise of decolonization. Viewed from that perspective, education has a broad and transformative mission. Parallel to that orientation and often in tension with it is a narrower view of the relationship between education and development. Often mechanically economic, this view assigns primary importance to the instrumental role of education in expanding production and productive capacity and generally considers other education objectives to be societal luxuries that must be deferred as currently unaffordable. However desirable, the humanist aspirations of liberal education, the moral obligation to redress inequalities, the expected social benefits of promoting equity, and the potential power of political mobilization and expanded democratic participation all must wait or, alternatively, must be achieved as by-products of insisting that schools focus on preparing the next generation for its expected role in the national and global economies. These are indeed difficult choices, its advocates insist, but unavoidable for poor countries.

That orientation is reinforced by widespread concern with what is generally termed *educated unemployment*. This terminology is itself revealing. What is the problem here? What distinguishes the unemployment of the more educated from the joblessness of those with little or no schooling? Surely neither the society at large nor the young people who cannot find jobs would be better off if they were illiterate as well as unemployed.

That young people who finish school are frustrated in not finding jobs (or not finding the jobs they think they should have) is primarily a function of job creation, not schooling. That those in power feel threatened by rising levels of education among the unemployed is primarily a problem of politics, not education.

Modifying the content and practice of education is expected to increase employability, alter expectations, or both. But even with better trained and better paid teachers, less crowded classrooms, and sufficient instructional materials, the education system cannot single-handedly overcome the consequences of a stagnant economy. If job seekers outnumber job openings, modifying school curriculum and pedagogy may affect which students find employment but not how many. Life experiences, far more than school lessons, shape expectations. In the absence of economic growth, neither the subject content taught in schools nor the political education they provide will do much to reduce frustration or relieve the anxiety of the political elite.

Together, the instrumental view of education's role in development and the concern with educated unemployment have generated efforts to link education closely with perceived skills needs. Over time, strategies for forging that link have evolved. An earlier notion was *manpower planning*, which relied on projected labor needs to guide education programs and allocations. Widely criticized, that approach is still used. Yet projecting needed skills far into the future is difficult, perhaps impossible, especially in economies experiencing rapid industrial and technical change. Just a few years ago, human resources planners in Africa had no entries in their job lists for computer programmer, microelectronics technician, or education technology instructor. Yet today every African economy needs those skills. This approach commonly underestimates the extent and rapidity of career changes. As well, it tends to disregard intellectual growth, the development of critical and problem-solving ability, the encouragement of creativity and expression, and many other dimensions of education that have no immediate or direct vocational outcome.

Several alternative approaches have emerged. One emphasizes society's broad interest in access to education and uses social demands to shape education programs. Focusing on demand enables education institutions to be sensitive to changing perspectives and preferences. But this approach is also subject to misunderstandings, fashions, and special circumstances that make it difficult to develop a coherent and integrated national education agenda. A different response to humanpower planning is to locate principal programmatic decision making within education and training institutions. If institutions are especially sensitive to their economic, political, and social context, that institutional autonomy may be very desirable. Yet this approach is not readily compatible with efforts to set national policies and priorities. Nor does it facilitate coordinating the activities of different institutions. And when institutions are primarily responsive to their own internal pressures for new and enlarged programs, the risk of a mismatch between labor market demand and graduates' specializations is very high.

The effort to link curriculum and the education system more generally to the labor market has also led to the regularly reiterated complaint that schooling is too academic and too humanist. Education must be, the constant refrain goes, relevant to national needs. In this view, national needs, relevance, and their curriculum implications tend to be construed very narrowly. Beyond a rate and pattern of economic growth that enable people to improve their standard of living and develop spiritually as well as materially, what exactly are national needs?[32] Steel mills and a microelectronics industry? More village boreholes and grain mills? Do national needs include reliable, high-quality public services or the demand—often termed *need*—for more video recorders and other consumer goods? Should moral and ethical behavior, nonviolent conflict resolution, and the equitable treatment of all citizens also be considered national needs? Where to rank cultural, aesthetic, and literary needs? Everywhere, needs and priorities are regularly debated and redefined. In all societies, some groups assert that their particular demands are national needs. Education surely has a role in both shaping and addressing national needs, but equally surely has no linear paths to be followed.

Relevance makes sense only in terms of context and process. Often, for example, the observation that most people in Africa are rural agriculturalists leads to the assertion that education should focus on the tools and skills of farming. Unemployment is attributed to miseducation, this is, to studying history and language rather than chemistry and accounting. From that perspective, schools that teach languages to introduce young people to other cultures or assign books intended to expose learners to new ideas and different ways of thinking or insist that students use microscopes to understand and master systematic observation and comparison are wasting time with irrelevant programs. If so, how will Africa ever escape its dependence on the ideas and technologies of others? How will Africa move beyond exploiting nonrenewable resources to creating and developing new resources? If no Africans experiment with subnuclear particles, write new computer programs, or devise new approaches to dysentery, malaria, and AIDS, how can Africans assume responsibility for their own direction? If education is to expand rather than limit horizons, determining what is relevant requires not a simple statement of the obvious but an ongoing engagement with values, expectations, and constraints. Relevant programs emerge not from an authoritative decision but from collaboration and negotiation.

In summary, two sharply divergent perspectives on education and development have emerged in Africa. In one, education's role is transformative, liberating, and synthetic. Education must enable people to understand their society in order to change it. Education must be as much concerned with human relations as with skills, and equally concerned with eliminating inequality and practicing democracy. Education must focus on learning how to learn and on examining critically accepted knowledge and ways of doing things. Favoring innovation and experimentation, that sort of education is potentially liberating, empowering, and, as such, threatening to established power structures, both within and outside the schools. This orientation has remained the minority view.

Occasional initiatives to redefine the core and practice of education notwithstanding (e.g., education for self-reliance in Tanzania and production brigades in Botswana), the dominant perspective understands education primarily as skills development and preparation for the world of work. The emphasis on relevance assigns low priority to educating historians, philosophers, poets, and social critics, and thereby to cultivating the historian, philosopher, poet, and critic in all learners. Fearing unemployed graduates, leaders expect schools to limit learners' aspirations. Shaped by national examinations, curriculum revolves much more around information to be acquired than around developing strategies and tools for acquiring that information, generating ideas, or crafting critiques.

EXPERIMENTATION AND INNOVATION

Like much of education, experimentation and innovation are contested terrain.[33] As I have noted, Africa has witnessed important experiments and innovations in education at larger and smaller scales. In the late 1960s, Tanzania rejected manpower planning in favor of education for self-reliance. At independence the priority was developing higher-level skills. Projected skills needs guided allocations. As the 1960s proceeded, Tanzania's leaders became increasingly critical of that approach, primarily because it constrained the expansion of primary education, a benefit of independence and a requisite for democratic development. Major resources were focused on a small part of the population, Tanzanian president Julius Nyerere noted, creating an arrogant elite detached from their social roots.

The priority for scarce resources should be those with little or no education rather than those with the most (and the most alienating) education. Reversing the earlier orientation, Nyerere's widely read and cited *Education for Self-Reliance* shifted the emphasis to primary and adult education.[34] Schools were to become community institutions, intimately connected with the patterns and rhythms of the local setting. Schools were also to have farms and workshops, both to value directly productive activities and to generate supplementary income. In Botswana, production brigades sought to integrate learning and the local setting by creating community schools in which learners and teachers were also producers.[35] To expand access rapidly, several African countries experimented with preservice and in-service teacher education. Others—Zimbabwe's efforts stand out—explored how to draw effectively on the local setting to develop lessons and materials for teaching science despite nonexistent or poorly equipped laboratories. Several countries have explored the uses of radio, television, and computers to extend the reach of a limited pool of experienced educators and to extend learners' access to resources unavailable at local schools. Dispersed and locally managed resource centers for teachers have proved effective in providing continuing support to instructional staff. Imaginative and energetic literacy campaigns have brought rapid progress in several countries. Innovative community-based nonschool education programs have emerged across Africa, often with the support of a local or international nongovernmental organization.

Though materially poor, several of Africa's higher education institutions are intellectually rich, exploring ideas and constructs with contacts and influences around the world. Ghana, for example, nurtured the rejuvenation of studies and debates about pan-Africanism. Through seminars, research, and major student holiday research projects, scholars at the University of Dar es Salaam explored the claims and problems and refined the methods of oral history, thereby joining and advancing an international debate among professional historians.

Recognizing the importance of interchanges across Africa, especially since it has often been easier for African scholars to communicate with colleagues in Europe than with colleagues in a neighboring country, researchers have established several continent-wide organizations. A few examples must suffice. Founded in Dar es Salaam in 1973, the African Association of Political Science has regularly brought scholars together, published a journal, supported participation in international meetings, and generally challenged Africa's political scientists to be critical and to cooperate. Two parallel networks link education researchers in West and Central Africa and in Eastern and Southern Africa, concerned especially with the role of research in making public policy. Several research institutes and centers have sought to provide a venue for critical research and debate and to support both established and younger scholars. Especially active has been the Council for the Development of Economic and Social Research in Africa (Dakar).

Thus, despite a parched and bleak landscape, education innovation and experimentation have periodically flourished in Africa. While some initiatives have won wide recognition and influence, most have struggled to survive after the founders departed or initial funding was exhausted.[36] Although foreign funds have periodically supported reforms and experiments, overall, aid dependence has generally discouraged experimentation, especially activities that are oriented toward broad national political and social goals rather than more narrowly defined instructional tasks.

SETTING EDUCATION POLICY

Education policy and agenda setting in Africa have taken many forms, from broadly inclusive to narrowly authoritarian.[37] The inherited model was distinctly bureaucratic, oriented more toward control and management than innovation and development, a pattern that has been widely retained and reinforced. In some countries, key individuals (often the education minister but occasionally the head of state) have played the central role in defining problems and charting directions. In other countries, select commissions have gathered evidence, sponsored studies, and recommended new policies. In still other settings, a major national conference (in francophone Africa, états-généraux) provided opportunities for the diverse interests of the education community to present their views and construct coalitions to support particular policies. Some countries have employed several different approaches.

Tanzania's experience is instructive.[38] Both the policies and the policymaking process reflected the changing times, influences, and balance of forces. With a very small pool of educated officials at its independence in 1961, Tanzania, like many other African countries, sought external advice and assistance in setting priorities and developing concrete plans. Guided by consultants recruited by the World Bank, Tanzania decided initially to emphasize postprimary education and a manpower planning approach. With the publication of *Education for Self-Reliance*, the priority shifted to primary and adult education. Earlier, the principal education policy advisers had been external experts. By the end of the 1960s, the influential voices were those of the president and Tanzania's single political party.

As primary education expanded, public discontent and especially middle-class protest focused on limited access to secondary school. President Nyerere appointed a national commission to review education policy in the early 1980s. The commission toured the country, heard testimony, commissioned studies, and offered analyses, projections, and recommendations. Publicly released and then abruptly withdrawn, its report initiated a national debate, including contentious exchanges on the introduction of secondary school fees. Thus the education policymaking process had again been modified. Whereas in the preceding decade the president and the party had initiated the new policies, by the 1980s the circle of participants in policymaking had widened.

By the early 1990s, the situation had again changed. A new national review of education policy was launched. This time the initiative lay with the Ministry of Education and Culture, and the principal participants were not politicians but rather academics, who relied heavily on external funding.[39] Here, then, is another approach to formulating education policy, directed by the education bureaucracy with education experts in the central roles. This orientation was quite consistent with the general 1990s trend of seeking to depoliticize the public policy process. That orientation, in turn, coincided with the vastly increased role of the World Bank in Third World education research and policymaking, a role that was particularly evident in Tanzania in the early 1990s.

In short, over the years, Tanzania experimented with several different policymaking models: reliance on externally recruited experts, initiative by the president and the party, consultation managed by an inclusive and distinctly political national commission, and renewed recourse to education experts, this time Tanzanian, though heavily dependent on external funding.

Note that often studies of education policy are frustratingly narrowly gauged. Most of the writing on public policy focuses on formal pronouncements by authoritative institutions. Since making policy is assumed to be the prerogative of those in power, policy researchers study elites and formal documents. Most often, this perspective understands policymaking as a sequence of activities and feedback loops, moving from vision to formulation to negotiation to policy specification and announcement to implementation to evaluation. This understanding of policy is widespread and regularly asserted in Africa.

Yet policy is made as much (or often a good deal more) in practice as by pronouncement. Indeed, it is essential not to equate policy with official statements that may have little or no influence on what actually occurs. Consider, for example, policy on language of instruction. The education ministry may have formal rules, officially recorded and publicly announced, specifying that instructors are to use a particular language to teach certain subjects. Suppose, however, that an on-site study shows that 90 percent of the instructors use other languages to teach those subjects. When asked, a school principal might say that "our policy in this school is to use the language that our students understand. To do otherwise will make their examination marks even worse." What, then, is the policy? From one perspective, the policy is what the ministry has promulgated, and what the teachers do is a deviation from official policy. From the other perspective, the actual policy (i.e., the working rules that guide behavior) is what the teachers are doing. In this view, the ministry documents are just that: official statements that may or may not be implemented and certainly not guides to what people actually do.

Recognizing that policy results from practice as well as from official pronouncements helps identify other major influences on education policy in Africa. Increased reliance on foreign funding has expanded the direct role of both the finance ministry, which generally manages all external aid, and the funding and technical assistance agencies, whose own agendas have come to guide and constrain education initiatives and reforms in Africa. Explicit conditions attached to foreign aid may require particular policies or priorities. Even if there are no explicit conditions of that sort and foreign aid is a very small portion of total national spending on education, external influence can still be decisive. Consciously or unconsciously, African policy and decision makers shape their programs and projects, and thus policies and priorities, to fit what seems most likely to secure foreign funding. As the director of planning in Tanzania's education ministry explained, planning had in fact become marketing.[40] His task was less a process of exploring needs and developing strategies to address them than an effort to study the market of prospective funders. He then identified its priorities and value points, using that market knowledge to craft, advertise, and sell projects and programs. That strategy was perhaps effective for coping in difficult circumstances. Nevertheless, it entrenched the role of the funding agencies in setting national education policies and priorities. It also reinforced the status and influence of a particular set of actors within the country, not those with the clearest or most dynamic education vision or those with the most solid national political base but rather those who proved to be most effective in securing foreign funding. In these ways, too, aid dependence becomes a vehicle for internalizing within African education establishments externally set policies, priorities, and understandings.

EDUCATION AND THE STATE

In Africa as elsewhere, education and the state are intimately interconnected. The state in Africa has come to play a major role in the processes of accumulation and legitimacy.[41]

Sometimes on behalf of an emerging indigenous bourgeoisie and often in a context where foreign capital dominates in the absence of local capitalists capable of controlling the national political economy, the state in Africa assumes responsibility for fostering and managing the accumulation and reinvestment of capital that are essential both for economic growth and development and for the security of the tenure of the national leadership. In practice, that often requires the African state to manage conditions for accumulation that are largely specified externally (structural adjustment programs are one example). As it does so, the African state must at the same time maintain its own legitimacy. As students of industrialized capitalist states have stressed, there is a necessary tension between legitimacy and accumulation. (For further discussion, see chapter 3 in this volume.)

Within a peripheral capitalist economy with fragile political authority, accumulation requires a relatively weak, poorly integrated, and politically disorganized labor force. A liberal democratic capitalist system requires even more: a state that can successfully present itself as a representative of the popular will and not an agent of the dominant class(es). The policies the state pursues to maintain its universalist image, however, threaten its ability to manage, or even assist, accumulation. Each arena in which citizen participation is encouraged and democratic choice is permitted becomes a point of potential vulnerability for the state itself, and for the capitalist order. Promoting legitimacy through controlled democratic practice—which surely has been occurring in Africa—risks threatening the accumulation process. Empowered peasants may organize and demand greater control over both the organization of production and the distribution of wealth. At the same time, facilitating accumulation by constraining participation—which has also occurred in Africa—undermines legitimacy. The tension between these two is also reflected in the demands of external actors. To maximize extraction from the periphery, the earlier preference was for strong leaders who could control labor and dissent. But as authoritarian rule was challenged within Africa, leaders required popular legitimacy to implement harsh structural adjustment measures. Increasingly, aid providers insisted on democratization.

Accumulation is particularly problematic for the leadership of peripheral conditioned capitalist states.[42] As Frantz Fanon foresaw, the structural interests of Africa's postcolonial leadership maintained and reinforced their dependence.[43] The rhetoric of decolonization notwithstanding, the agenda of most who assumed office after the European rulers left was neither radical transformation of the peripheral economy nor the risk-taking required for capitalist innovation. Fragile states with insecure elites were unable or disinclined to take a long-term view of what national development would require and reluctant to make a continuing investment in a skilled, disciplined, and accountable public service.[44] One consequence has been a constellation of interests and power that found it difficult to create conditions conducive to accumulation and sustained investment in the development of new production and productive capacity. Another consequence has been a generally inefficient and not infrequently corrupt administration. For education, this situation has been manifested in the ineffective use of limited resources. Funds are poorly managed, both nationally and locally, with little accountability and reliable oversight. Inefficiency becomes normal, both expected and tolerated.

This tension between accumulation and legitimacy is regularly reflected in education policy, perhaps the most contested of public policies. Establishing and managing the conditions for accumulation favor regarding education instrumentally, primarily as a set of institutional arrangements concerned with preparing the future labor force, which includes developing both skills and work discipline. That orientation reinforces the inclination to link schooling with projected labor needs, to emphasize acquiring information, to regard teachers as transmitters and students as receivers of knowledge, and to rely heavily on examinations and other selection and exclusion mechanisms. The commonly asserted view that young Africans must be prepared for their role in the global economy (i.e., that their jobs and the skills those jobs require are likely to be defined not within the country but at distant centers of economic and political power) bolsters the external orientation of this instrumental view of education. Schools, it is argued, need to prepare workers who will, say, assemble automobiles more efficiently than automobile workers elsewhere.

Legitimacy, however, is rooted in popular participation and consent. Beyond opening new schools,[45] maintaining the legitimacy not only of particular officeholders but also of governing arrangements more generally, requires the active involvement of an informed public that is aware of the power that it wields and is willing to use it. From this perspective, education must be concerned with, and must be seen to be concerned with, encouraging participation, redressing inequality, promoting social mobility, and fostering cooperation and nonviolent conflict resolution. This orientation reinforces the inclination to regard learners as active initiators, not passive recipients.

In short, as it struggles with its own fragility, the state adopts two different, and at times incompatible, postures toward the education system. Most often its orientation is functional and technical. Periodically, however, its expectations for schools are more liberal and transformative. The appropriate institutional configurations, even spatial arrangements, for these two orientations also differ. The school-as-factory architecture so common throughout the world—classrooms with the teacher-authority at the front, separated by a buffering space from students in orderly rows, and hierarchical administrations within schools and school systems—reflects the instrumental role of schooling. Open classrooms, activity-group seating patterns, and shared leadership responsibilities generally reflect a preference for the liberal and transformative perspective.

At work here are two related but distinct tensions. One is confronted in the political system as the state works to promote both accumulation and economic growth and at the same time to establish and reinforce its legitimacy. The second is confronted in the education system, which is charged both with preparing students for the world of work and at the same time with nurturing the development of individual potential, intellectual critique, and societal well-being. These two tensions, each with its own characteristics, participants, institutional configurations, and consequences, are interdependent but not identical. Although they intersect frequently and are often mutually reinforcing, neither fully determines the other.

Understood somewhat more broadly, education in Africa has a dual charter. Its major task is to reproduce the economic, political, and social order.[46] Schools assume responsibility for developing requisite skills (training), generally by assigning students to ability groups (tracking). Schools then become the mechanism by which society selects young people who will proceed far in their education and certifies their accomplishments. The internalization of the reasonableness of that certification is crucial. For schools to serve their reproductive role, students who fail must attribute their problems to their own lack of skill or application, to circumstances beyond their control, or perhaps to bad luck. What the schools must avoid is the understanding that tracking, achievement, and certification, and their consequences for subsequent life chances, are planned and controllable outcomes of schools and schooling. (Consider for a moment teachers whose students all receive high marks. The immediate assumption is that the teacher must be doing something wrong, since the classes of teachers who behave appropriately have both successes and failures.) Schools must legitimize as well as track, select, and certify. Their assessments must be accepted as just and appropriate and internalized. When students do not secure the jobs they seek, the emphasis on schooling as job preparation functions to direct their frustrations toward the apparent deficiencies of their education rather than toward the economic and political system that has not created sufficient jobs.

Reproducing the social order, however, also requires critique and innovation. To survive in capitalism's fiercely competitive environment, national economies must have some people who reject the old ways of doing things, insist on looking for better alternatives, and are willing to run the risks associated with criticism and innovation. Hence, schools have a radical as well as a conservative role. They must enable and encourage at least some students to ask difficult questions, to be impatient with the answers they receive, to trust their own judgment at least as much as their teachers' opinions.

The education system is thus charged with contradictory tasks in reproducing society: preserving and protecting the major features of the social order and at the same time challenging and changing them.[47] Commonly, education systems try to manage that combination by separation—emphasizing the conservative role in most schools for most students and encouraging critique in a few schools, generally for elite students. In practice, that separation is difficult to establish and maintain. Each orientation is corrosive of the other. Critique and innovation have a momentum of their own. Schools become sites for rebellion, indirect (withdrawal, rejection) and direct (militant organization).

During the nationalist and liberation struggles, education emphasized its critical role. After minority rule was dismantled and the new order emerged, education in Africa turned back to its conservative charter, more concerned with preserving order than with challenging common understandings and forging new paths. In the circumstances of the peripheral conditioned state and dependent legitimation, accumulation is deemed more important than redistribution.

FROM EDUCATION AS SOCIAL TRANSFORMATION TO EDUCATION AS (AND FOR) PRODUCTION

African countries came to independence with high aspirations and expectations. For capitalists and socialists alike, education held the promise of national development, community improvement, and individual social mobility. Nearly everywhere, schools mushroomed and enrollments increased. Community centers, radio, television, and village newspapers were employed in efforts to enable older learners to participate in the march toward education for all.

Yet in much of Africa, the rate of education expansion could not be sustained. Facilities deteriorated, worn-out textbooks were not replaced, libraries and laboratories were empty, gross enrollment ratios stagnated or declined, and universities could support neither library nor laboratory research. Measures of education quality, school efficiency, and teacher and learner satisfaction showed similar distress. Far from being an engine for social transformation, Africa's education systems found it increasingly difficult to provide even basic schooling. Some imaginative experiments continued, but in general promising innovations were localized and rarely sustained.

As they confronted this education crisis, whose roots lay in poverty, the international division of labor, fragile dependent states, deteriorating public service, and a leadership more concerned with schooling for skills than with learning for development, African countries turned increasingly to foreign funding. Innovation and reform, and in some countries even textbooks and desks, were assumed to require external support. With the foreign funding came ideas and values, advice and directives on how education systems ought to be managed and targeted. Although external resources are often a very small portion of total education spending, their direct and indirect influence on policy and programs is substantial. A wide range of approaches to setting education policy notwithstanding, their imprint on education agendas and priorities is clearly visible across the continent. Education in some countries has become even more directly dependent on external resources, increasing that influence. As external agencies undertake research, as well as providing funding and development advice, their perspectives on scholarship and science shape approaches, methodologies, and the definition of universities' missions and more generally the scientific enterprise. Throughout Africa, unable to find local support, education researchers became contracted consultants. As they did so, those imported understandings of research, from framing questions to gathering data to interpretive strategies, were internalized and institutionalized, no longer foreign imports but now the apparently unexceptional everyday routines of universities, research institutes, and indeed informed discourse.

We see here international convergence at several levels. Increasingly, the specification of education quality is presumed to be universal rather than nationally, culturally, or situationally specific. Similarly, notions of effective schools, good school management, and community participation are also treated as universals.

Far from the globalization of the knowledge era that is expected to be developmental and democratizing, this globalization is one form of the integration of African political economies into a world system on terms largely set outside Africa. Clearly the international integration of goods, technology, labor, and capital has a long and energetic history. Throughout that period controllers of capital have been powerful decision makers, not infrequently determining state behavior. New technology permits instantaneous transmission from one end of the world to the other and enables researchers in Africa to consult the same electronic databases as researchers in, say, Sweden, Japan, or the United States.[48] Yet the movement of labor remains sharply controlled and restricted by nationally set rules. Colonial rule was, among other things, a general strategy for integrating Africa into the global political economy on terms set largely in Europe. Formally managed by the World Bank and the International Monetary Fund, structural adjustment and the poverty reduction strategy process play similar roles. Strategies for reducing debt have become the fast track to planned dependence.

In a context of persisting poverty, aid dependence, increasing debt, and powerful pressures from within and without to adopt a particular understanding of development, African governments have been inclined to emphasize accumulation over legitimating. Similarly, though pockets of innovation and radical reform persist, the trajectory of education policy and practice in Africa has generally been to discard or devalue education's role in economic and social transformation in favor of education's role in maintaining particular patterns of economic, social, and political organization. In practice, the productivist and conservative charter for education contributes to entrenching still further the conditioned state and Africa's dependence. Within Africa, the consequence is to acquiesce in (even see as necessary) fundamental societal inequalities and the politics they breed.

Consistent with that conservative role for education, attention has increasingly focused on efficiency, quality, and school improvement, often modeled on approaches and experiences elsewhere. Ironically, many of the strategies intended to achieve education for all in practice, render it a distant dream. The rhetoric of liberation and empowerment notwithstanding, the commonly held view is that education must enable Africa to run faster as it tries to catch up with those who are ahead rather than forge new paths or transform the international economy and Africa's role in it. Scrambling to catch up always leaves those presumed to be in front to determine where they, and thus everyone else, are going.

NOTES

1. UNESCO, *Education for All: Is the World on Track?* (Paris: UNESCO, 2002), 15–16.

2. As we shall see, beyond the mystification and exoticism associated with the *dark continent*, the terminology commonly employed regularly structures the discussion in ways that are not immediately apparent, even to careful readers and active participants in policy debates. The specification of what is *Africa* is an instructive case in point. Nearly all World Bank documents on Africa, as well as many others, include a note that indicates "Most of the discussion and all of the statistics about Africa in this study refer to just thirty-nine countries south of the Sahara, for which the terms Africa and Sub-Saharan Africa are used interchangeably." This example is from World Bank, *Education in Sub-Saharan Africa: Policies for Adjustment, Revitalization, and Expansion* (Washington, D.C.: Author, 1988), viii; emphasis added. That is, "Africa" is not the Africa specified either by geography—countries on the African continent and its adjacent islands—or by African states themselves—membership in the African Union—but rather a subset of those states grouped to reflect the foreign policy interests and categories of the World Bank, the United States, and other countries of the North Atlantic. Unfortunately, there is currently no straightforward resolution to this dilemma. Much of the most readily available data on education in Africa come from publications of those organizations, and to date no one has systematically revised those data to include North Africa or reorganized other data that do include North Africa to make them directly comparable. In this discussion, other than explicitly noted exceptions, my comments generally refer to the entire continent.

3. I am concerned here primarily with formal education through secondary school. Higher education, including colleges, universities, and other postsecondary programs, distance education, and vocational education are indeed important but unfortunately beyond the scope of this discussion. It is useful to note that after a period of severely reduced support, higher education is receiving renewed attention and funding. In some countries, privatization is progressing rapidly at that level.

4. World Bank, *Priorities and Strategies for Education* (Washington, D.C.: Author, 1995), 14.

5. For a fuller discussion of these understandings of education, see Joel Samoff, "Institutionalizing International Influence," chapter 2 in this volume.

6. Julius K. Nyerere, "Africa: The Current Situation," *African Philosophy* 11, no. 1 (June 1998): 8.

7. I addressed this problem in more detail in "The Facade of Precision in Education Data and Statistics: A Troubling Example from Tanzania," *Journal of Modern African Studies* 29, no. 4 (December 1991): 669–89.

8. Since late entry and repetition increase the gross enrollment ratio (primary pupils may be 7–20 years old, rather than 7–14), the gross enrollment ratio somewhat overstates the actual enrollment percentage.

9. The country is Tanzania. UNESCO, *United Republic of Tanzania: Education in Tanzania, vol. 1, Overview* (Paris: Author, 1989), 15.

10. Among the funding agencies, the World Bank was often sharply critical of allocations to higher education. For an exploration of the World Bank's role in this arena, see Joel Samoff and Bidemi Carrol, *From Manpower Planning to the Knowledge Era: World Bank Policies on Higher Education in Africa* (Paris: UNESCO Forum on Higher Education, Research and Knowledge, 2004).

11. UNESCO Institute of Statistics (EdStats), www1.worldbank.org/edstats.

12. Inter-Agency Commission, World Conference on Education for All (UNDP, UNESCO, UNICEF, World Bank), *Final Report, World Conference on Education for All: Meeting Basic Learning Needs* (New York: UNICEF, 1990).

13. As coordinating agency, UNESCO published the major preparatory and follow-up documents, including UNESCO, *Education for All 2000 Assessment: Global Synthesis* (Paris: UNESCO, 2000), UNESCO, *Education for All 2000 Assessment: Statistical Document* (Paris: UNESCO, 2000), and UNESCO, *Education for All 2000 Assessment: Thematic Studies—Executive Summaries* (Paris: UNESCO, 2000). Since 2002 Education for All global monitoring reports have highlighted progress and problems: for basic documents, country reports, monitoring procedures, meetings, and more, see the World Education Forum website: www.unesco.org/education/efa/index.shtml.

14. World Education Forum, *The Dakar Framework for Action* (Paris: UNESCO, 2000).

15. Rosa Maria Torres provides an insightful and critical perspective on the 1990 and 2000 conferences: *One Decade of Education for All: The Challenge Ahead* (Buenos Aires: IIEP/UNESCO, 2000), and "What Happened at the World Education Forum?" available at http://www.fronesis.org/documentos/whathappenedatdakar.pdf.

16. Available at www.efareport.unesco.org/.

17. United Nations, *Millennium Development Goals Report 2005* (New York: United Nations, 2005), 10.

18. UNESCO, *Education for All: Is the World on Track?*, 23 and chapter 5.

19. Unfortunately, there have been few systematic studies of aid to education in Africa and especially of its volume and its impact on the direction of capital flows. For South Africa in 1993, foreign aid was estimated to account for less than 1.5 percent of total spending on education. See Baudouin Duvieusart and Joel Samoff, *Donor Cooperation and Coordination in Education in South Africa* (Paris: UNESCO, Division for Policy and Sector Analysis, 1994). In some countries the situation seems to have changed dramatically, with foreign aid supporting a major portion of education expenditures, especially as the funding agencies have provided direct budget subsidies.

20. For details: www.worldbank.org/hipc/ and www.imf.org/external/np/exr/facts/hipc.htm (HIPC); www1.worldbank.org/education/efafti/ (FTI).

21. Overview, guidelines, papers, and progress reports are at www.worldbank.org/prsp.

22. World Bank, *Priorities and Strategies for Education*, 113.

23. UNESCO Institute of Statistics, "Online Database," www.uis.unesco.org. The broad age range of enrolled students permits figures greater than 100 percent.

24. UNESCO Institute of Statistics, "Online Database," www.uis.unesco.org.

25. Adhiambo Odaga and Ward Heneveld, *Girls and Schools in Sub-Saharan Africa: From Analysis to Action* (Washington, D.C.: World Bank, 1995), 14.

26. Marianne Bloch, Josephine A. Beoku-Betts, and B. Robert Tabachnick, *Women and Education in Sub-Saharan Africa: Power, Opportunities, and Constraints* (Boulder, Colo.: Lynne Rienner, 1998); Nelly P. Stromquist, "Gender Sensitive Educational Strategies and Their Implementation," *International Journal of Educational Development* 17, no. 2 (1997): 205–14.

27. See Joel Samoff, with N'Dri Thérèse Assié-Lumumba, *Analyses, Agendas, and Priorities in*

African Education: A Review of Externally Initiated, Commissioned, and Supported Studies of Education in Africa, 1990–1994 (Paris: UNESCO, 1996).

28. Marlaine Lockheed et al., *The Quality of Primary Education in Developing Countries* (Washington, D.C.: World Bank, 1989), 1.

29. Joel Samoff, "Decentralization: The Politics of Interventionism," *Development and Change* 21, no. 3 (July 1990): 513–30.

30. Peter Kallaway, ed., *Apartheid and Education: The Education of Black South Africans* (Johannesburg: Ravan Press, 1984); Mokubung Nkomo, ed., *Pedagogy of Domination: Toward a Democratic Education in South Africa* (Trenton: Africa World Press, 1990).

31. Peter Kallaway, Glenda Kruss, Aslam Fataar, and Gari Donn, eds., *Education After Apartheid: South African Education in Transition* (Cape Town: UCT Press, 1997); Jonathan Jansen and Pam Christie, eds., *Changing Curriculum: Studies on Outcomes-Based Education in South Africa* (Cape Town: Juta, 1999); Yusuf Sayed and Jonathan D. Jansen, eds., *Implementing Education Policies: The South African Experience* (Cape Town: University of Cape Town Press, 2001).

32. I draw here on critical discussions of education and relevance in two major Namibian policy statements, *Toward Education for All* (Windhoek: Ministry of Education and Culture, 1993), and *Investing in People, Developing a Country: Higher Education for Development in Namibia* (Windhoek: Ministry of Higher Education, Vocational Training, Science, and Technology, 1998).

33. For an overview of recent education innovations and reforms, see Association for the Development of Education in Africa, *What Works and What's New in Education: Africa Speaks! Report from a Prospective, Stocktaking Review of Education in Africa* (Paris: Association for the Development of Education in Africa, 2001).

34. Julius K. Nyerere, *Education for Self-Reliance* (Dar es Salaam: TAN, 1967); reprinted in Julius K. Nyerere, *Freedom and Socialism/Uhuru na Ujamaa* (Dar es Salaam: Oxford University Press, 1968), 267–90.

35. Ingemar Gustafsson, *Integration between Education and Work at Primary and Post-Primary Level—the Case of Botswana* (Stockholm: University of Stockholm, Institute of International Education, 1985). For a parallel effort in Zimbabwe, see Ingemar Gustafsson, Zimbabwe Foundation for Education with Production, *ZIMFEP. A Follow-Up Study* (Stockholm: Swedish International Development Authority, 1985).

36. Joel Samoff and E. Molapi Sebatane, with Martial Dembélé, *Scaling Up by Focusing Down: Creating Space to Expand Education Reform* (Arusha, Tanzania: Biennial Meeting of the Association for the Development of Education in Africa, 2001).

37. For case studies of education policymaking in Africa, see David R. Evans, ed., *Education Policy Formation in Africa: A Comparative Study of Five Countries* (Washington, D.C.: USAID, 1994), and Association for the Development of African Education, *Formulating Education Policy: Lessons and Experiences from sub-Saharan Africa* (Paris: Association for the Development of African Education, 1996).

38. I draw here on Joel Samoff, "Education Policy Formation in Tanzania: Self-Reliance and Dependence," in *Education Policy Formation in Africa: A Comparative Study of Five Countries*, ed. David R. Evans (Washington, D.C.: USAID, 1994), 85–126.

39. Note that *politicians* here is not a pejorative term but simply refers to individuals who hold political office or whose concerns and activities revolve around the expression, confrontation, integration, and mediation of political interests. Nor do I assume that education policy ought to be set by professional educators or that decisions guided primarily by the findings of education researchers will necessarily produce better policy.

40. Joel Samoff, with Suleman Sumra, "From Planning to Marketing: Making Education and Training Policy in Tanzania," in *Coping with Crisis: Austerity, Adjustment, and Human Resources*, ed. Joel Samoff (London: Cassell, 1994).

41. Since an extended discussion of the state in Africa is far beyond the scope of this chapter, I limit my attention here to the tension between accumulation and legitimation and its implica-

tions for education. For a more extended development of these and related themes, see Martin Carnoy and Joel Samoff, *Education and Social Transition in the Third World* (Princeton: Princeton University Press, 1990), especially part 1, and Martin Carnoy, "Education and the State: From Adam Smith to Perestroika," in *Emergent Issues in Education: Comparative Perspectives,* ed. Robert F. Arnove, Philip G. Altbach, and Gail P. Kelly (Albany: State University of New York Press, 1992).

42. Martin Carnoy, "Education and the Transition State," in *Education and Social Transition,* ed. Carnoy and Samoff (Princeton: Princeton University Press, 1990).

43. Frantz Fanon, "The Pitfalls of National Consciousness," in *The Wretched of the Earth* (New York: Grove, 1963).

44. The World Bank and other external agencies have increasingly focused major attention on problems of governance and administration, though generally without addressing the structural roots of managerial inefficiency and the lack of transparency and accountability. "The World Bank views good governance and anti-corruption as central to its poverty alleviation mission." (World Bank governance and anti-corruption website, www.worldbank.org/wbi/governance.)

45. Hans Weiler explores what he terms *compensatory legitimation* in "Education and Power: The Politics of Educational Decentralization in Comparative Perspective," *Educational Policy* 3, no. 1 (1989): 31–43.

46. Samuel Bowles and Herbert Gintis have developed and refined the notion of the correspondence between school and society. See "Education as a Site of Contradictions in the Reproduction of the Capital-Labor Relationship: Second Thoughts on the 'Correspondence Principle,'" *Economic and Industrial Democracy* 2 (1981): 223–42.

47. Carnoy and Levin characterize this tension as between education as a democratizing force (social mobility, public education as an equalizing experience, instruction on the democratic ideal) and education as a mechanism for reproducing capitalist inequalities (class, race, or gender division of labor, unequal access to knowledge): Martin Carnoy and Henry M. Levin, *Schooling and Work in the Democratic State* (Stanford, Calif.: Stanford University Press, 1985).

48. Joel Samoff and Nelly P. Stromquist, "Managing Knowledge and Storing Wisdom? New Forms of Foreign Aid?" *Development and Change* 32, no. 4 (September 2001): 631–56.

17

Comparative Education: The Dialectics of Globalization and Its Discontents

Carlos Alberto Torres

> It takes more time and effort and delicacy to learn the silence of people than to learn its sounds. . . . The learning of the grammar of silence is an art much more difficult to learn than the grammar of sounds.
>
> —Ivan Illich, *Celebration of Awareness*, 1969.[1]

It is relevant to ask what changes have taken place in the world since the publication of *Comparative Education* more than three years ago. What has changed in the global economy, in the global culture, in the global political systems, and how might those changes affect education? What follows is a description of some of the most important changes that we have witnessed in the world since the first edition.[2]

The most obvious change is the terrorist attack of September 11, 2001, which undermined the invincibility of the United States, never before attacked in its continental territories, and the implications of this attack for the global economy, politics, culture, and education. There is a heightened feeling that most salient among these transformations are the changes in the definition, enjoyment, and administration of freedom worldwide. The challenges to the liberal notion of freedom add to the growing fear of apocalypse resulting from an eventual world confrontation in an increasingly volatile world. After the demise of the former Soviet Union, there are journalistic reports of enriched uranium and even nuclear bombs unaccounted for, and a growing threat of biological and chemical weapons of mass destruction.

An ongoing debate centers on how the terrorist attacks have played into the hands of a Republican administration in the United States that has displayed a narrow view of international politics, a complete sense of political intransigence and disrespect for human rights,[3] and a determined interest in enforcing narrow U.S. interests on a global scale, including the ignoring of Mexico's request for an immigration agreement.[4] Many observers, including Nobel Peace laureate Jimmy Carter, have warned of the potential dangers of U.S. unilateralism in international affairs. The U.S. refusal to participate in the Kyoto Accords is symptomatic of the way in which energy security increasingly drives

U.S. policy. Energy politics is seen as the key reason why the Bush administration—an administration closely connected with U.S. energy corporations like Enron—went to war against Iraq, the fourth largest oil producer in the world, holding the second largest crude oil reserves.[5] Allegations of the existence of weapons of mass destruction were the putative reason given by the Bush administration for the U. S. invasion of Iraq in March of 2003. These allegations have yet to be substantiated.

A preliminary analysis of the political-educational implications of the terrorist attacks of September 11 has been done elsewhere and need not be repeated here.[6] Nevertheless, we have not yet seen in the United States or elsewhere how these changes are provoking a new understanding of patriotism in the schools. In concluding his assessment of his personal feelings and his professional responsibility as a teacher in dealing with the attacks, cultural critic Michael Apple warns us of unintended, and perhaps still unobservable, consequences of the events:

> In any real situation there are multiple relations of power. Any serious understanding of the actual results of September 11 on education needs to widen its gaze beyond what we usually look for. As I have shown, in the aftermath of 9/11 the politicization of local school governance occurred in ways that were quite powerful. Yet, without an understanding of "other" kinds of politics, in this case race, we would miss one of the most important results of the struggle over the meaning of "freedom" in this site. September 11 has had even broader effects than we recognize.[7]

The war in Afghanistan, the immediate U.S. and allied response to the September 11 attack, showed the difficulties of combating global terrorism. Despite the massive bombardment and deployment of personnel, and after heralding the war as one low in allied casualties and high in military results, the majority of the objectives have not been fully achieved. Sheikh Osama bin Laden and the leader of the Students of Islamic Knowledge Movement (Taliban), Mullah Mohammad Omar, have not been found. The majority of their lieutenants and hundreds of war-hardened al Qaeda fighters are still at large. The government of Afghanistan remains shaky, plagued by political assassinations of its leadership, and under considerable pressure from the different ethnic tribal groups and warlords reasserting their independence from the central government and even protecting representatives of the old deposed regime.

Terror has a logic of its own. Common citizens discover the dimensions of this logic only when a particularly spectacular attack is orchestrated, or when new developments prompt attention in terms of personal security. In the United States, the creation of the Homeland Security Office, including twenty-two government agencies, the most important reorganization of the federal government since the New Deal, is an indication of the realignment of priorities in the United States. And these administrative changes take place in an administration that inherited a fiscal surplus and in less than two years in office has managed to reach U.S.$600 billion in fiscal deficit. With the tax cuts enacted in 2003, the deficit of the federal government may continue to grow substantially. The tax cuts and fiscal deficit may also deeply affect the budgets of the states, which are nearly bankrupt given the transfer of responsibilities since the Reagan administration and simultaneous diminishing revenues.

In regional terms, Latin America is changing in ways that were virtually unimaginable just a few years ago. The formidable economic failure of Argentina, the model country for the application to the letter of the law of neoliberal prescriptions of the International Monetary Fund (IMF) and the World Bank in the region, calls the neoliberal development model seriously into question. Yet, at the level of human tragedy, Argentina offers an even more somber note, enduring high levels of poverty and the tragic documented death of starving children in a country historically known as a producer of food staples. The Nobel laureate economist George Stiglitz has written provocative ideas about these questions,[9] and a debate has been initiated with powerful effects on different fronts, including renewed severe criticism of neoliberal bilateral organizations and their implications in development, particularly in education.[10] Responses to neoliberalism have also reached other fronts, with a new interest for democratic socialism in the region. The rise to power of Hugo Chavez in Venezuela is one such antineoliberal response. Under the combined mantle of populism and nationalism, the attempt of former paratrooper and elected President Hugo Chavez to dismantle the old democratic system, and his erratic policies and behavior, have generated a great deal of resistance from many different quarters, and have destabilized one of the world's largest oil exporting countries.

There is no question that the arrival of Ignacio "Lula" da Silva, a metallurgical union leader and founder of the Workers' Party, or PT, to the presidency of Brazil is an unexpected political novelty in Latin America. The importance of education in Lula's success is highlighted in the remarks of his spiritual adviser, Frei Betto: "Lula arrives to the presidency of Brazil thanks to a social movement articulated in the past forty years, in which the pedagogy of Paulo Freire carried more weight than the theories of Marx."[11]

The truth is that the PT has won the presidency twice with the support of a great majority of Brazilians and on the shoulders of the political activism of many social movements in the country, most prominently the agrarian reform movement, *Sem Terra*, so well portrayed in the photography of Sebastian Salgado.[12]

The Asian economies, not long ago considered a central engine of economic development in the world system, continue to revolve and struggle around the continuing economic stagnation of Japan.[13] Yet the growing economic and political power of China, which continues to show surprising rates of economic growth, solidifies its position as a major regional and world player. China's power is also evident in the recent confrontation over North Korea's nuclear program technology transfer.

The ongoing confrontation between India and Pakistan, two countries with atomic bombs, is perhaps one of the most destabilizing conflicts in the world. In addition to the religious hate between Muslim and Hindu activists, there is the thorny issue of India's administration of Kashmir and growing militaristic and religious movements on both sides of the border that contributed to the development of the atomic bomb. The fact that both countries possess nuclear weapons and that they have already waged a bloody war (in December of 1971) adds to the danger. The triumph of India in the 1971 war led to the separation of East Pakistan from West Pakistan and the creation of Bangladesh, one of the poorest countries on Earth. Unfortunately, as some scientists claim, the Indian subcontinent is the most likely place on the planet for a nuclear war.[14]

Despite all sorts of political gestures from the United States and European governments, sub-Saharan Africa continues its downward spiral, and growing political unrest in several nations (Zimbabwe, Ivory Coast, Nigeria) indicate that political instability and economic crises continue to go hand in hand in the region. The hoped-for ends of the Angola and Sierra Leone wars offer a window of hope, yet the same hope for democratization and economic development represented by postapartheid South Africa will be crushed by its population's AIDS epidemic.

The success that the antiglobalization movement has had since 1999 in Seattle in constructing a more proactive alternative globalization agenda has already—though not well represented in the hegemonic mass media—impacted economic summit meetings. Even the deliberations of the multilateral and bilateral economic organizations have lost the "privacy" of their discussions of how to prime the economic engines of the world and/or how to salvage the countries in economic distress.

In the last few years, the creation of the European Community and the euro seems to be the success story of globalization, with the entry of new members and the rise of the euro as the strongest exchange currency in the world. The resulting harmonization of European higher education in this process will have a long-term impact in the region, a model that is being contemplated in several other common markets.[15]

HOW MIGHT THESE CHANGES AFFECT EDUCATIONAL PRIORITIES?

"To those of you who received honors, awards and distinctions, I say, well done. And to the C students, I say, you, too, can be president of the United States."[16]

The epigraph from George W. Bush that opens this section may sound shocking to educators who believe in meritocracy and the selection role of education. It bespeaks opportunity and chance beyond tenacity and study. The unspoken truth of this statement by President Bush is that education not only reproduces inequality, as theories of social reproduction have amply demonstrated, but it also legitimizes privilege.[17] That education could indeed foster social mobility within certain limits is a subject that has been well documented in the economics of education. Yet the implication in this apparent joke by the president of the United States is the subtle indication that race, class, and gender matter in achieving the highest echelons of the political system in a bureaucratic rational society like that of the United States.

As the epigraph indicates, the holder of the highest political office in the United States is proud to underscore how political and business success is often more related to whom you know, and what kind of network you are a member of, than of academic achievement. The statement is even more telling because it was made at the commencement of one of the most distinguished private universities in the United States, justifying Vilfredo Paretos's view of reproduction and the circulation of elites.[18]

In George W. Bush's views, politics has nothing to do with education. This seems perhaps reasonable, coming from somebody of patrician origins who attended a fine private university, obviously receiving what Ronald Reagan, referring to his own educational experience, called "Gentleman's Cs."[19] Though Bush's comments are telling, they should not be considered an *aphorismus*. He replaced President Bill Clinton, who, though from humble origins, managed to be a Rhodes Scholar, the governor of Arkansas, and president of the United States.

In the realm of education, the United States is often cited as a model for private higher education. Yet, per-student expenditures in four-year public colleges and universities in the United States have increased by roughly 20 percent over the past decade or so, whereas in Canada and other countries they have decreased by about the same amount.

So it is strange that neoliberal policy advisers, many of them trained in U.S. universities, suggest decreasing support of public universities elsewhere, even though the great success of the United States in R&D is based on the public system, as is indicated by the growing number of Nobel Prize recipients teaching in U.S. public universities.

The continuing expansion of the use of the Internet for the globalization of higher education is prompting several studies to focus on the transformation of the university systems given the political economy of globalization and the new role of languages.[20] By *globalization* here, I refer to the "increasing interdependent and sophisticated relationships between economies, cultures, institutions, and nation states. . . . Such relations challenge higher education leaders and policy makers in ways heretofore difficult to imagine as the autonomy of the nation-state becomes compromised and the role of the university is increasingly aligned with market-driven interests."[21]

A casualty of September 11 in the United States, and a factor that presumably could affect other industrialized countries given changes in visa requirements and process, is the availability of international education for foreign students—not a minor source of income for the countries involved. The United States is the biggest exporter of international education, which had

547,867 "foreign students" studying in American institutions in 2000/2001. This represents earnings of U.S.$11 billion to its national economy. . . . After the United States, the largest producer of international education is the United Kingdom. In 1999/2000, the U.K. enrolled 277,000 international students of which 129,180 were university students. Earnings from the international education exports and consumption of goods and services by students was estimated then at 8 billion British pounds.[22]

What is happening in the world, as de Souza Santos has indicated, is a paradigmatic transition.[23] Hence, it is important to explore the connections between social changes and theoretical analysis. When we ask what, if anything, may result from the impacts of September 11 in educational settings, Michael Apple's remarks discussing the question of schooling and patriotism are a fitting conclusion for this section:

No analysis of the effects of 9/11 on schools can go on without an understanding of the ways in which the global is dynamically linked to the local. Such an analysis must more fully understand the larger ideological work and history of the neo-liberal and neo-conservative project and its effects on the discourses that circulate and become common sense in our society. And no analysis can afford to ignore the contradictory needs and contradictory outcomes that this project has created at multiple levels and along multiple axes of power. Thus, I argue that educators—whether teaching a university class or participating in local school board decision making—must first recognize our own contradictory responses to the events of September 11. We must also understand that these responses, although partly understandable in the context of tragic events, may create dynamics that have long-lasting consequences. And many of these consequences may themselves undercut the very democracy we believe that we are upholding and defending. This more complicated political understanding may well be a first step in finding appropriate and socially critical pedagogic strategies to work within our classes and communities to interrupt the larger hegemonic projects—including the redefinition of democracy as "patriotic fervor"—that we will continue to face in the future.[24]

THE OUTSTANDING DEBTS
OF COMPARATIVE EDUCATION

"I am the wound and yet the knife . . . The torturer and yet he who is flayed."

—From Baudelaire's poem *Héautontimoroumenos*[25]

By looking ahead, it is perhaps wise to outline some of the still "outstanding theoretical debts" of comparative education. What are some of the enigmatic theoretical relationships still unsolved? What elusive analytical dimensions still lack understanding? What theoretical connections have been missed? Unquestionably, from the pragmatic perspective I have chosen to outline changes and challenges, limited space mandates that my analysis of the outstanding debts be subjectively selective and purposeful.

The connections between politics and education remain an unresolved theoretical enigma in comparative education. In this debate, the analytical and normative positions of the establishment (liberals, conservative, neoconservative, and neoliberals) remain comfortably close but in startling contrast to the New Left positions.

The view of the establishment is that politics and education are clearly two separate sets of practices, which do not, and should not, interconnect. Education remains *objective*, in theoretical terms (because the truth could be told objectively); *neutral*, in political terms (because educators don't take sides); and above all, *apolitical*, considering normative and political choices (politics usually embodies the praxis of fighting for ideological positions defending social and/or particular interests, while education is a noble practice that seeks the public good for everyone involved).

The establishment view sees scholars, practitioners, and policymakers leaving their political clothes—be they a political affiliation, doctrine, or ideology—outside the classroom, or some distance from their research or policy cabinets. Otherwise, the merging of politics and education necessarily results in the manipulation and ideologization of the subject matter. Good, decent educators practice a value-neutral education in their teaching, policymaking, and research. Education is thus a practice that should be devoid of ideology and political interests. Though the establishment's normative view recognizes that there are inequities and disparities in the world, the differences in this assessment, in the naming of the victims as well as in assessing the magnitude of the problem, depend on the ideology of the analyst. Moreover, the view of the establishment is that in many instances, even in rational-legal societies, processes of discrimination are taking place, processes that need to be prevented through social engineering and the application of the law.

Therefore, a quality education (one documented through testing and accountability), when it is understood and practiced scientifically, as well as informed by rigorous empirical research, will be the most important asset in the social engineering of a more efficient and equitable society.

For the New Left, there is a very different and much more complex story. Politics is intimately linked to power and is concerned with the control of means of producing, distributing, consuming, reproducing, and accumulating material and symbolic resources. Politics and the political should not be restricted to political parties, the activities of the governments and its critics, or voting. Political activities take place in private and public spheres, and they are related to all aspects of human experience that involve power. It is from this vantage point, of politics as a set of relations of force in a given society, that the relationships between education and politics need to be examined.[26]

Freire developed a *Pedagogy of the Oppressed*.[27] His analysis of the relationships between politics and education,[28] speaking in the code of class analysis, indicates that politics, power, and education are indissolubly united. His analysis deserves to be quoted at length:

> The comprehension of the limits of educational practice requires political clarity on the part of educators in relation to their project. It demands that the educator assume the political nature of her practice. It is not enough to say that education is a political act, just as it is not enough to say that political acts are also educative. It is necessary to truly assume the political nature of education. I cannot consider myself progressive if I understand school space as something neutral, with limited or no relations to class struggle, where students are seen only as learners of limited domains of knowledge which I will imbue with magic power. I cannot recognize the limits of the political-educative practice in which I am involved if I don't know, if I am not clear about, on whose behalf I work. Clarifying the question of in whose favor I practice puts me in a position, which is related to class, in which I see against whom I practice and, necessarily, for what reason I practice.[29]

This book, the first one published by Freire after leaving his post of secretary of public education of the city of São Paulo, is exemplary of the position of the New Left regarding politics and education.[30]

Despite Freire's immensely rich analyses and insights, coined in the phrase "the politicity of education," a neologism that he popularized in English, the nature of the relationship between politics and education is far from being clearly understood. Freire's positions have been the subject of important debates also in his native Brazil and elsewhere.[31]

If one considers Freire's analysis, many questions remain regarding the connection between politics and education at a theoretical level. Besides the criticism to grand narratives, or the charge of idealism in Freire's views of oppression, or the question of how can we empirically construct indicators of oppression, other pressing questions need to be addressed. If there is a relative autonomy of education and a relative autonomy of politics in the context of the dialectics of agency and structure, are these two independent domains that intersect only at some point? Or, as Freire seems to indicate, do they overlap completely? As Illich's dictum on the atmosphere of "monastic" studies seems to indicate, is there any autonomy of knowledge production independent of politics?

The question of dependence/independence between politics and education begs the question of the real nature of both human domains, their goals and purposes, and their similarities and differences in practice—in short, a whole gamut of questions that may require, following the insightful analysis of Freire, a much more developed, refined, and completed theoretical solution.

In searching for a more complete theoretical answer, we cannot forget that as sites of confrontations of public and private interests, politics and education are also mediated by state actions, tools, regulations, codes, controls, and resources.

Another key unresolved theoretical challenge is the postmortem analysis of postmodernism in education. In theoretical terms, the extreme forms of postmodernism have lost their momentum, and the shift of some postmodernists to Marxist revolutionary perspectives and other forms of structuralist traditions is perhaps symptomatic. These changes deserve to be discussed in light of the utility of postmodernism for educational studies.

In one of the most recent attempts to unthink postmodernism while rethinking modernism from a critical perspective, Greg Dimitriadis and Dennis Carlson offer an excellent summary of the new cultural terrain of the postmodern age:

> Inequalities are increasing between the haves and the have-nots within the United States, and between economically elite nations and the "developing" world. It is an age of hyperconsumerism in which one's sense of self and identity is defined by what one consumes in popular culture icons and styles marketed in the new shopping mall public. It is an age of backlash and resentment against the gains made by people of color, women, gays and lesbians, and other marginalized identity groups, and a time of the rise of religious fundamentalism in both America and around the world. And it is an age in which conservatives use the democratic language of equity to oppose affirmative action and "special rights" for gay people. In public education, it is an age of a corporate state discourse of high-stakes testing, "accountability," "standards," and "efficiency," an age of preparing America's young people to be more competitive and productive in the new global labor market. Meanwhile, commercialized popular culture is busy blurring the lines between "reality" and "hyperreality," the material world and the virtual world. It is an age in which identity is constructed around performance, style, and image, and hybrid, border-crossing identities subvert the naturalness of race, gender, and sexual identity categories. . . . The aim of postmodernism is thus to push modernism to supercede itself and become something new. Postmodernism is not, in itself, a sufficient basis for forging a new progressivism in American education and public life. But it does play an important role in establishing the conditions for the emergence of a new progressivism, for allowing us to unthink modernism and rethink it in new ways.[32]

In the same vein, Foucault's acknowledgment of his myopic analysis having missed the connection to the established tradition of critical theory (in itself tributary of Marxist theory) stands out as a sobering reminder of the honesty of one of the most important theoreticians of the last century, so influential in the development of critical pedagogy.[33] Foucault muses, in celebrating Kant's essay "What Is Enlightenment":

> Now, obviously, if I had been familiar with the Frankfurt School, if I had been aware of it at the same time, I would not have said a number of stupid things that I did say, and I would have avoided many of the detours I made while trying to pursue my own humble path—when, meanwhile, avenues had been opened up by the Frankfurt School. It is a strange case of nonpenetration between two very similar types of thinking which is explained, perhaps, by that very similarity. Nothing hides the fact of a problem in common better than two similar ways of approaching it.[34]

While these theoretical challenges should be at the top of our theoretical agendas, inspiring our empirical research, since the publication of the first edition of this book, we have seen the death of three giants in the study of education who deserve to be mentioned here: Bernard Basil Bernstein, Pierre Bourdieu, and Illich. Counting the death of Freire in 1997, or, a bit more removed from the field of comparative education, the death of political philosopher John Rawls (1921–2002), we have witnessed the passing of some of the most important theorists in education, a generation that will be very difficult to replace. Standing on the shoulders of giants is certainly easier than filling their shoes.

Bernard Basil Bernstein (1924–2000) passed away after a long illness. From 1979 until his retirement in 1991, he was the holder of the most prestigious chair in sociology of education in the world, the Karl Mannheim Professor in the Sociology of Education at the University of London Institute of Education.

Bernstein leaves behind a legacy of more than forty years of rigorous research and a new understanding of the connections between class, codes, and control. His published works, in particular the five-volume series on *Class, Codes and Control,* have become classics in the field. Bernstein's theory has shown how people use language in everyday conversation, reflecting but at the same time shaping assumptions of certain social groups; hence, private and public codes matter, and play an enormous role in the curriculum of public education.[35]

With the death of the multifaceted and prolific Pierre Bourdieu (1930–2002), professor of sociology at the Collège de France and also director of studies at the École des Hautes Études en Sciences Sociales in Paris, we have lost, without any question, one of the most important sociologists in the history of the discipline. Jointly with Basil Bernstein one of the founders and past president of the Research Committee of Sociology of Education of the International Sociological Association, Bourdieu inspired our studies in education (where *Reproduction* stands out as a landmark which impacted a whole generation of intellectuals), aesthetics, in social theory, popular culture, mass media, French intellectual thought, and literature.[36]

In the last years of his life, Bourdieu single-handedly constituted himself in one of the most severe and intransigent European critics of globalization and one of the most uncompromising critics of the Americanization of the global world. His criticism of globalization in the intellectual and cultural spheres is coupled with his questions about the depoliticization of the academic world and the role of intellectuals. One of his last books, *Counterfire: Against the Tyranny of the Market,* is an eloquent testament to his analytical abilities and to his personal and political commitments.[37]

Ivan Illich (1926–2002)—characterized by Eric Fromm in his famous preface to *Celebration of Awareness* as a radical humanist—was also an emblematic thinker of possibilities. Illich leaves behind a legacy of a genial man, as Freire described him, but one who, being ahead of his time, described himself as an "Errant Pilgrim," as "one that was caught between the contesting powers of Byzantium and Venice."[38]

Perhaps there is no better tribute to the geniality of Illich than to remember that he considered himself a disciple of a twelfth-century monk, Hugh of St. Victor. This association with the monastic life explains why he always considered the hospitality of monastic asceticism, coupled with rigorous disciplinary training and jovial friendship, indispensable conditions for nurturing an environment where meaningful scholarship could flourish:

> Learned and leisurely hospitality is the only antidote to the stance of deadly cleverness that is acquired in the professional pursuit of objectively secured knowledge. I remain certain that the quest for truth cannot thrive outside the nourishment of mutual trust flowering into a commitment to friendship. Therefore I have tried to identify the climate that fosters and the "conditioned air" that hinders the growth of friendship. Of course I can remember the taste of strong atmospheres from other epochs in my life: I have never doubted that—today, more than ever—a "monastic" ambience is the prerequisite to the independence needed for a historically based indictment of society.[39]

The deaths of Freire, Bernstein, Bourdieu, and Illich have deprived comparative education of powerful intellectual voices in the midst of a very perilous epoch in human history. Though their deaths will not help in settling the many theoretical debts of comparative education, the theoretical paths they have opened remain an invitation to continue the journey.

The pedagogical challenges for comparative education are enormous. There is a profound crisis in the understanding of who is to be educated. What could be considered an endemic crisis of the educational systems is reflected in the real and symbolic dislocation between the discourses of the teachers and the students, which is reflected also in the dislocation, also marked, between the discourses of the new generation (which has been denominated the Nintendo generation) and adult generations. This cultural dislocation in school settings adds to the proverbial issues of equality and relevance of education, equity, equality, and social mobility as well as discrimination in the school curriculum. In addition, we confront now a crisis of legitimacy in the educational systems in terms of their effectiveness—that is, the effectiveness of the educational agents per se, including the teachers, parents, and private and public educational institutions. However, with the rupture of the public link between generations, this perhaps may give rise to a crisis that supersedes the secular deficiencies of the system. The presence of massive systems of communication and new technologies creates new combinations between popular traditional cultures, a popular transnational culture, and the political cultures developed by the state institutions, occasionally drastically confronted by the institutions of civil society, social movements, and unions.

In short, obsolete school rituals, opposing discourses, problems in the definition of the cultural capital of the schools and the incorporation of diverse populations, crisis in the concepts of citizenship and democracy, growing disparity between the educational models and the job market, now accentuated with the impact of neoliberalism, provide all sorts of challenges to comparative education. Not surprisingly, many of these challenges need to be addressed, in understanding the connection between education, power, politics, and the culture of modernity.[40]

In solving this enigmatic connection between politics and education, analyzing the crisis of legitimacy of public education, or assessing the role of postmodernism in comparative education, there is no question that the years ahead will demand a clearer and more compelling theorizing in the field. Comparative education is still in debt for having failed to produce a definitive understanding of the role and theories of area studies and ethnic studies in the development of the discipline. Similarly, discussions about minority education with respect to issues of multiculturalism in the United States, or interculturalism in Europe, will continue to besiege the field many years from now, igniting the theoretical imagination of scholars. I hope that the second edition of this book will contribute to this rethinking of the field and to the profession in solving the dilemmas of contemporary education and, in the words of Freire, "in the creation of a world in which it will be easier to love."[41]

AFTERTHOUGHTS FOR THE THIRD EDITION

In the second edition I queried what had changed in the world since the first edition of *Comparative Education*.[41] In working toward the third edition of this book, a number of questions about the future of comparative education remain. Perhaps they should be nested in the context of a highly aggregated and succinct description of the historical process of comparative education since its establishment as a discipline.

First stage: From my perspective, the first generation of comparative educators came to the fore approximately ninety years ago as an intellectual exploration with a strong positivistic overtone of the possibilities of educational development outside the confines of national or domestic processes. Indeed a valuable tool, but simply complementary to discussions in educational foundations (for example, John Dewey, without having had a title, spent significant time studying education and revolutionary change in Mexico, the Soviet Union, and China).

Second stage: Fifty to sixty years ago, comparative education began to ride the wave of educational expansion in the world (fueled by theories such as human capital theory), becoming increasingly important to the growing network and communities of the nascent international system. This is the second generation of comparativists whose writing must be set against the context of the Cold War, the struggle between Western and Eastern bloc countries over whether capitalism or communism would triumph in the newly independent nations of Africa, Asia, and Oceania. While there were strong international influences on the goals, forms, and contents of education in the so-called "Third World," national educational systems also displayed a substantial degree of autonomy. This autonomy fueled the growth of national educational systems to unprecedented levels—sometimes to that extent there may have been overbuilding of schools in some societies, and generating an abundance of teachers. During this period, comparativists not only promoted school expansion, but they also identified and promoted the importance of teacher unions in collective bargaining while laying the foundations of systematic policy planning and educational budgeting.

Third stage: Thirty-five to forty years ago, the next generation of comparative scholars, in the spirit of the 1960s, attempted to create alternative visions of education. The contributions of Illich and Freire were central to this rethinking. A new school of scholars considered comparative education as the key to understand not only development but also liberation. They pushed the envelope by critiquing dominant paradigms, such as rate-of-return analyses of education (the obsession of the previous generation), while advocating nonformal education, revolutionary education, incipient multiculturalist policies, and the like. As such, this generation may be responsible for the most "social democratic" development in the field.

By the first decade of the twenty-first century, this generation is beginning to retire. Their vision and ideas must face the challenge of the economic crisis of the eighties, and the consolidation of the neoliberal state as the model guiding educational reform worldwide, as detailed in various chapters in this book. This generation has coexisted with several streams of scholars, including socialists, libertarians, business-minded people (e.g., the World Bank experts), and social democrats. The Comparative and International Education Society, as the premier society of its kind in the world, reflects with rare clarity this cohabitation.

Fourth stage: The current generation of scholars, which entered the field approximately twenty-five years ago, is well established within the academy today. In attempting to preserve the achievements of previous generations in contributing to progressive educational policy and practice, they necessarily must take corrective action against strong negative policy trends. To mention just two: diminished support for social science research and social welfare programs as unlimited funds go to support military operations; in the academy, erosion of tenure and replacement of full-time faculty with part-time and contractual labor. To counter these trends, as Raymond Morrow and Carlos AlbertoTorres have argued in this book, activists in our field need to link up with social movements that are directed at achieving more democratic and just societies.

I would argue that more than ever, we are needed and can contribute to better-informed and more enlightened educational policy—linking theory with action, the type of praxis that Freire called for. As comparativists are hired in educational policy, teacher education, and foundation fields we can impact the future generation of teachers and policymakers; and, given the increasing importance of nongovernmental organizations, many of our graduates will work with them and are likely to have a significant positive impact on the lives of the people with whom they work at the grassroots.

Perhaps, in a Socratic way, it is useful to end these reflections with some questions: How relevant are comparative education theories to a dialogue across fields and cultures? How different is European education, with new models of educational and scholarly exchange and standardized educational programs across borders, from the rest of the world? What can be learned from the Middle East, with the crisis of "radical Islam" and the rejection of the modernizing West? What can be learned from Africa, with the failure of development, the growing AIDS crisis, and the power of self-enriching elites, many of them duly educated in Europe or the United States? What role does comparative education in play in the academies of the emerging twenty-first century powers of China and India?

We obviously need statistical data, historical analysis, and a political economy discussion of the new trends in academia and societies, not vignettes, human stories, or simply hunches. Here is where comparative theories, scholarly analyses, systematic research and insights can contribute to improved understanding of the workings of education systems and their evolving national and transnational contexts. Here is where our field can contribute to unmasking failed policies while contributing to progressive social and educational change.[42]

NOTES

1. Ivan Illich, *Celebration of Awareness: A Call for Institutional Revolution*, introduction by Erich Fromm (Garden City, N.Y.: Doubleday, 1969), 46.

2. How to interpret those changes may deserve a different type of theoretical scrutiny and empirical analysis than the one permitted by the tenor of this chapter.

3. According to Human Rights Watch, "The U.S. government's willingness to compromise on human rights to fight terrorism sets a dangerous precedent and drives some nations away from joining that war. . . . Washington has so much power that when it flouts human rights standards, it damages the human right causes worldwide." From Associated Press, "Group Says Bending on Rights Risky," *Los Angeles Times*, January 15, 2003, A20.

4. Which many analysts consider is partly the reason why Jorge G. Castañeda resigned as Mexico's foreign minister at the beginning of 2003. For a detailed analysis of the implications of September 11, see Douglas Kellner, *From 9/11 to Terror War: The Dangers of the Bush Legacy* (Lanham, Md.: Rowman & Littlefield, in press).

5. Iraq is the second largest OPEC country in terms of proven crude oil reserves (112,500 millions of barrels) after Saudi Arabia (262,697 millions of barrels). Another country that Presi-

dent Bush named as part of the triple evil axis, Iran, is the third largest country in terms of proven crude oil reserves (99,080 millions of barrels), followed by the United Arab Emirates (97,800) and Venezuela (77,685 millions of barrels). In terms of crude output exports, Iraq, even under severe restrictions after the Gulf War, is the fourth largest producer of crude (2,593.7 millions of oil barrels), with Saudi Arabia as the first (7,888.9 millions of oil barrels), and Iran ranks third in volume (3,572 millions of oil barrels). This combination of oil reserves with crude oil output make Iran and Iraq targets for the U.S. policy in the Middle East. Energy policy concerns are shown also in the uneasiness of the United States in dealing with the conflicts with the government of Hugo Chavez, since Venezuela possess the fifth largest crude oil reserves in the world and ranks third in terms of crude oil output (2,791.9 millions of oil barrels). See the OPEC website at www.opec.org/.

6. Carlos Alberto Torres, "Requiem for Liberalism? Editorial," *Comparative Education Review* 46, no. 4 (November 2002).

7. Michael Apple, "Patriotism, Pedagogy, and Freedom: On the Educational Meanings of September 11th," *Teachers College Record* 104, no. 8 (December 2002): 1770. This entire issue of *Teachers College Record* is devoted to the discussion of the events of September 11 and its impact on the life of the schools, teachers, and students. At a more theoretical level, many articles tackle the meaning of September 11 for the discussion of patriotism versus cosmopolitanism in the constitution of democratic life.

8. "In May [2002], a Russian-built SA-7 missile was fired at a U.S. military jet taking off from Prince Sultan Air Base in Saudi Arabia but missed its target. On Nov. 28, two missiles of the same brand and factory batch as the one used in Saudi Arabia were fired at an Israeli jetliner seconds after it took off from Mombasa, Kenya." From the Washington Post News Service, "U.S. Working to Avert Portable-Missile Attacks on Airplanes," *Los Angeles Times*, January 15, 2003, A21.

9. Nobel laureate economist Joseph E. Stiglitz spent seven years in Washington as chair of President Clinton's Council of Economic Advisors and Chief Economist of the World Bank. His views have been popularized in his best-seller, entitled—as an economic paraphrasing Sigmund Freud's book about Western civilization—*Globalization and Its Discontents* (New York: Norton, 2002).

10. The World Bank has the rare privilege of being criticized by representatives of the right, of liberalism, and the left. Hence, there is an abundant critical bibliography that could be used to illustrate the critique of the implications of the World Bank's neoliberal expert knowledge and policy orientations. See, for instance, from a conservative perspective, similar to the one underscoring a viewpoint of important conservative sectors in the U.S. Republican Party, Doug Bandow and Ian Vásquez, eds., *Perpetuating Poverty: The World Bank, the IMF, and the Developing World* (Washington, D.C.: CATO Institute, 1994). From a different critical perspective, see Carlos Alberto Torres, "The State, Privatization and Educational Policy: A Critique of Neo-Liberalism in Latin America and Some Ethical and Political Implications," *Comparative Education* 38, no. 4, (1994): 365–85. See also John Harriss, *Depoliticizing Development: The World Bank and Social Capital* (London: Anthem-Wimbledom, 2002).

11. Frei Betto, "El amigo de Lula," *La Jornada*, November 2, 2002, my translation. I would like to thank Raymond Allen Morrow for bringing this statement to my attention and for his careful reading and critical commentary on this chapter.

12. It is also known that most of the organizational meetings of the *Sem Terra* movement start with an invocation to Paulo Freire's name and his role in community organization and popular education. For a graphic description of the movement see Sebastião Salgado, *Terra: Struggle of the Landless* (New York: Phaidon, 1997).

13. The paradoxical situation of economic stagnation and deflation in Japan has reached a certain surrealism when the *Financial Times* of London reports that "Japan's Interest rates fall below zero." This, in fact, means a negative rate of 0.01. "The negative rate means that Société Générale and BNP are, in effect, being paid to borrow funds as they find themselves in the fortu-

nate situation of having to pay back less than they were lent." *Financial Times*, January 25–26, 2003, 3. The same article concludes that the policy of the Bank of Japan in keeping rates "virtually zero and flooding the money market with liquidity has largely been ineffective in stimulating the economy, which is set to contract in the fourth quarter."

14. M. V. Ramana and A. H. Nayyar, "India, Pakistan and the Bomb: The Indian Subconti-nent Is the Most Likely Place in the World for a Nuclear War," *Scientific American* (December 2001): 72–83; available at www.scientificamerican.com.

15. There is a growing interest in the NAFTA countries to reach similar agreements across the board for accreditation models, as described in the document produced by the American Council on Education, with the support of a grant from the Fund for the USA Department of Education— Improvement of Post-Secondary Education, "Where CREDIT Is Due: Approaches to Course and Credit Recognition across Borders in U.S. Higher Education Institutions," available at www.a cenet.edu/bookstore/pdf/2003_where_credit_due.pdf.

16. U.S. President George W. Bush, addressing the graduates at his alma mater, Yale Univer-sity, at its 2001 commencement. Cited in James Gerstenzang, "That Retro Feel to Bush's Style: It's Reaganesque," *Los Angeles Times*, January 12, 2003, A18.

17. For a discussion of theories of social and cultural reproduction, see Raymond Allen Mor-row and Carlos Alberto Torres, *Social Theory and Education: A Critique of Theories of Social and Cultural Reproduction* (New York: State University of New York Press, 1995).

18. Vilfredo Pareto, *The Mind and Society*, ed. Arthur Livingstone, 4 vols. (New York: Har-court, Brace, 1935).

19. Cited in Gerstenzang, "That Retro Feel to Bush's Style," A18.

20. The decision of literary publisher Alfred A. Knopf to publish in the United States the first book of Colombian Nobel laureate Gabriel Garcia Marquez's memoirs in Spanish, *Vivir para con-tarla*, has been heralded as a sea change in the U.S. publication markets, with its first printing of fifty thousand copies sold out in a matter of weeks and a second printing of five thousand ordered immediately. See Tim Rutten, "Nobel Laureate's Memoir Is a Success in Any Language," *Los Angeles Times*, January 15, 2003, 1, 16.

21. Robert A. Rhoads and Carlos Alberto Torres, "The Political Economy of Globalization: The University, the State, and the Market in the Americas," (unpublished manuscript, University of California, Los Angeles, Graduate School of Education and Information Studies, January 2003), 1.

22. Ravinder Sidhu, "Selling Futures to Foreign Students: Global Education Markets," (unpublished manuscript, University of Queensland, Australia), 12.

23. For a broad and insightful perspective on globalization, see Boaventura de Sousa Santos, *Toward a New Common Sense: Law, Science and Politics in the Paradigmatic Transition* (New York: Routledge, 1995); de Sousa Santos presents a distinctive perspective, based on his Portuguese ori-gins, his studies in the United States, and research in Brazil.

24. Michael Apple, "Patriotism, Pedagogy, and Freedom: On the Educational Meanings of September 11th," *Teachers College Record* 104, no. 8 (December 2002): 1770–71.

25. Charles Boudelaire:

> Je suis la plaie et le couteau!
> [Je suis le soufflet et la joue!
> Je suis les membres et la roue,]
> Et la victime et le bourreau!

LXXXIII, "L'héautontimorouménos," in *Les Fleurs du Mal* (1861), available at www.poetes.com/ baud/.

26. See Mark Ginsburg, "A Personal Introduction to the Politics of Educators' Work and Lives," in *The Politics of Educators' Work and Lives*, ed. Mark Ginsburg (New York: Garland, 1995). For an analysis playing with the limits between fiction and reality in the politics of educa-

tion, see Carlos Alberto Torres, "Fictional Dialogues on Teachers, Politics, and Power in Latin America," in *The Politics of Educators' Work and Lives*, ed. Ginsburg (New York: Garland, 1995).

27. Paulo Freire, *Pedagogy of the Oppressed* (New York: Continuum, 1970), several reprints.

28. Paulo Freire, *Politics and Education*, trans. Pia Wong (Los Angeles: UCLA Latin American Center Publications, 1998), with an introduction by Carlos Alberto Torres, "The Political Pedagogy of Paulo Freire."

29. Paulo Freire, *Politics and Education*, 46. See also Paulo Freire, with S. Aronowitz and T. Clarke, *Pedagogy of Freedom: Ethics, Democracy and Civic Courage* (Lanham, Md.: Rowman & Littlefield, 2000).

30. Pilar O'Cadiz, Pia Linquist Wong, and Carlos Alberto Torres, *Education and Democracy: Paulo Freire, Educational Reform and Social Movements in São Paulo* (Boulder, Colo.: Westview, 1998); Carlos Alberto Torres, *Education, Power and Personal Biography* (New York: Routledge, 1998).

31. Dervemal Saviani, *Escola e Democracia* (São Paulo: Cortez-Autores, 1982); Giomar de Mello, *Social democracia e educação: Teses para discussão* (São Paulo: Cortez-Autores, 1990).

32. Greg Dimitriadis and Dennis Carlson, "Introduction," in *Promises to Keep: Cultural Studies, Democratic Education, and Public Life*, ed. Greg Dimitriadis and Dennis Carlson (New York: Routledge Falmer, 2003), 16–17.

33. Raymond Morrow and Carlos Alberto Torres, *Reading Freire and Habermas: Critical Pedagogy and Transformative Social Change* (New York: Teachers' College Press, 2002).

34. See Michel Foucault, *Essential Works of Foucault 1954–1984: Vol. 2. Aesthetics, Method, and Epistemology* (New York: New Press, 1998), 440–41.

35. For a complete reference to Bernstein's work, particularly his research articles, see the OCLC Online Union Catalog, available at www.firstsearch.oclc.org. A recent issue of the *British Journal of Sociology of Education* 23, no. 4 (December 2002), is entirely devoted to the influence of Bernstein—exemplary of the extent and nature of his contributions to the disciplines.

36. Just to give an idea of how prolific Bourdieu was, a search at the World Cat database (www.firstsearch.oclc.org) turned out 36 books in English, out of a total of 346 references in several languages.

37. Pierre Bourdieu, *Counterfire: Against the Tyranny of the Market* (London: Verso, 2002).

38. Ivan Illich, "The Cultivation of Conspiracy," a translated, edited, and expanded version of an address given by Ivan Illich at the Villa Inchon, in Bremen, Germany, on the occasion of receiving the Culture and Peace Prize of Bremen, March 14, 1998, p. 3, available at www.paulo freireinstitute.com.

39. Illich, "The Cultivation of Conspiracy," 4. See also the tribute to Illich with the participation of Peter McLaren, Douglas Kellner, and Carlos Alberto Torres, "Deconstructing Schooling: Revisiting the Legacy of Ivan Illich," Graduate School of Education and Information Studies and Paulo Freire Institute, available at www.paulofreireinstitute.com.

40. Carlos Alberto Torres, "Education, Power and the State: Successes and Failures of Latin American Education in the Twentieth Century," in *The International Handbook on the Sociology of Education: An International Assessment of New Research and Theory*, ed. Carlos Alberto Torres and Ari Antikainen (Lanham, Md.: Rowman & Littlefield, 2003), 256–84.

41. Paulo Freire, *Pedagogy of the Oppressed*, rev. ed. (New York: Continuum, 1997), 22.

42. Bob Arnove read in great detail and commented critically to this afterthought. I am deeply grateful to him for his contributions to this book, for his many contributions to my academic work, and particularly for his emblematic work in comparative education, from which so many of us have benefited over the years.

Index

About the Contributors

Robert F. Arnove is Chancellor's Professor Emeritus of Educational Leadership and Policy Studies, Indiana University, Bloomington. He is an Honorary Fellow and past president of the Comparative and International Education Society.

Edward H. Berman is a retired professor of education, University of Louisville.

Mark Bray is the director of UNESCO's International Institute for Educational Planning in Paris, to which he moved in 2006 after twenty years at the University of Hong Kong. He is a past president of the Comparative Education Society of Hong Kong, and from 2004 to 2007 was president of the World Council of Comparative Education Societies.

Maria Bucur is a professor of history and the John W. Hill Chair of East European History and acting director of the Russian and East European Institute at Indiana University, Bloomington.

Bidemi Carrol is an education policy analyst at the Education Policy and Data Center. She received her doctorate in international comparative education in 2005 from Stanford University.

Rachel Christina is senior project director in the Middle East and Francophone Africa Regional Center at Education Development Center, Inc.

Ben Eklof is a professor of Russian history and the director of the Institute for the Study of Russian Education, Indiana University, Bloomington.

Joseph P. Farrell is a professor emeritus in the Comparative, International, and Development Education Centre of the Ontario Institute for Studies, University of Toronto. He is a past president of the Comparative and International Education Society.

Christine Fox is a senior academic at the Faculty of Education, University of Wollongong, Australia. She is a past president of the Australian and New Zealand Comparative and International Education Society and is currently the secretary-general of the World Council of Comparative Education Societies.

Stephen Franz has a doctorate in education policy studies and is working as a researcher and analyst for the Columbus-Area Economic Growth Council and Su Casa in Columbus, Indiana.

John N. Hawkins is a professor of social sciences and comparative education and the director of the Center for International and Development Education, the University of California, Los Angeles. He is a past president of the Comparative and International Education Society, and the immediate past editor of the *Comparative Education Review.*

Anne Hickling-Hudson is a senior lecturer in international and intercultural education in the Faculty of Education, Queensland University of Technology, Australia. She is a past president of the World Council of Comparative Education Societies, and a past president of the Australian and New Zealand Comparative and International Education Society.

Simon Marginson is a professor of higher education in the Centre for the Study of Higher Education at the University of Melbourne. Together with Marcela Mollis, he was the 2002 winner of the Comparative and International Education Society's George Z. F. Bereday award for contributions to scholarship.

Vandra Lea Masemann is an adjunct associate professor in the Comparative and International Development Education Program at the Ontario Institute for Studies in Education at the University of Toronto. She is a past president of the World Council of Comparative Education Societies, the Comparative and International Education Society, and the Comparative and International Education Society of Canada.

Golnar Mehran is associate professor in the School of Education, Al-Zahra University, Iran.

Shabana Mir has a doctorate in education policy studies at Indiana University, Bloomington. She won the Outstanding Dissertation Award (Council on Anthropology and Education, American Anthropological Association) in 2006.

Raymond A. Morrow is a professor of sociology at the University of Alberta, Edmonton.

Rosemary Preston was director of the International Centre for Education in Development at the University of Warwick. She is past chair of the British Association of International and Comparative Education, the U.K. Forum for International Education and Training, and the Congress Standing Committee of the World Council of Comparative Education Societies. She is also past editor of *Gender and Education* and *Compare.*

Joel Samoff is a consulting professor at the Center for African Studies, Stanford University.

Daniel Schugurensky is an associate professor at the Ontario Institute for Adult Education, and associate director of the Centre for Urban and Community Studies at the University of Toronto.

Nelly P. Stromquist is a professor of comparative and international education in the Rossier School of Education at the University of Southern California. She is a former president of the Comparative and International Education Society and a 2005–2006 Fulbright New Century Scholar.

Carlos Alberto Torres is a professor of social sciences and comparative education at the University of California, Los Angeles, and director of the Paulo Freire Institute. He is a past president of the Comparative and International Education Society and past president of the Research Committee of Sociology of Education, International Sociological Association.

Anthony Welch is a professor in the faculty of education and social work at the University of Sydney, Australia. He is a past president of the Australian and New Zealand Comparative and International Education Society, and a past vice president of the World Council of Comparative Education Societies.